# GENEALOGICAL NOTES

—OF—

# BARNSTABLE FAMILIES,

BEING A REPRINT OF THE

# AMOS OTIS PAPERS,

ORIGINALLY. PUBLISHED IN

# THE BARNSTABLE PATRIOT.

*REVISED BY C. F. SWIFT,*

*Largely from Notes Made by the Author.*

## VOLUME I.

CLEARFIELD

Reprinted by Genealogical Publishing Company
with an Index by
Charles A. Holbrook, Jr.

Volume I
Originally published by
F. B. & F. P. Goss, Publishers and Printers [The "Patriot" Press]
Barnstable Massachusetts
1888

Reprinted, two volumes in one, by
Genealogical Publishing Company
Baltimore, Maryland
1979, 1991

Library of Congress Catalogue Card Number 79-52085

Reprinted, two volumes in one,
for Clearfield Company by
Genealogical Publishing Company
Baltimore, Maryland
2007

Reprinted, in its original two-volume format,
for Clearfield Company by
Genealogical Publishing Company
Baltimore, Maryland
2010

ISBN, Volume I: 978-0-8063-5472-9
Set ISBN: 978-0-8063-0844-9

*Made in the United States of America*

# EDITOR'S NOTE.

When Mr. Goss, some months ago, informed me of his intention to reproduce the papers of Mr. Amos Otis relating to the early families of Barnstable, and asked me to assist in preparing them for the press, I felt that the undertaking was one which merited the commendation and encouragement of all who revere the memory of our ancestors. Having in my possession Mr. Otis's extensive revision of those papers, together with some notes of my own bearing upon the subjects, I consented to assist in this work. The volumes, thus presented, will be as near as possible as Mr. Otis himself would have presented them in his latter years, and will constitute an enduring monument to his memory. I may, I trust, be permitted to say, that I have endeavored to perform my duty in an unobtrusive and friendly way, erasing some passages of temporary importance reflecting upon contemporaries; correcting a few verbal slips of style and expression; and adding an occasional explanatory note, sometimes with, but generally without, my initial. It will thus be apparent that I should not be held responsible for judgments or conclusions in the text which may be a subject of controversy, for which, of course, Mr. Otis is alone answerable. Neither would I undertake to vouch for the entire accuracy of all these papers. I can only say that thus far, by Mr. Otis's own efforts mainly, the series is much more perfect than when the papers first issued from the press.

CHARLES F. SWIFT.

# INTRODUCTION.

For several years past, I have spent much of my leisure time in examining records and collecting materials for a history of my native town. Old age is "creeping on" and I find I have done little towards arranging the materials I have collected. There are more difficulties to be surmounted than the casual observer dreams of. Records have been destroyed, lost, mutilated,—tradition is not to be relied on and the truth can only be arrived at by diligent inquiry and comparison of various records and memorials of the past. The fact is, the writer of a local history finds himself environed with difficulties at every step in his progress, and is compelled to use such words as perhaps and probably, much oftener than good taste would seem to require. If the reader would be satisfied with facts chronologically arranged, the task would not be so difficult, diligence and industry would soon accomplish it. But something more is required. A dull monotonous array of facts and figures would soon tire and disgust all, excepting perhaps a few plodding antiquarians who are never happier than when poring over a black letter manuscript. The page to be made readable must be enlivened with descriptions, narratives and personal anecdotes. When writing history, I often feel that I am in the condition of the children of Israel, when they were required by their Egyptian taskmasters to make bricks without straw. Three times I have written the first chapter of a history of the town of Barnstable, and three times have thrown the manuscript into the fire. Progressing at such a rate my head will be whiter than it now is, before the last chapter is written.

My friends are constantly urging me to do something and not let the materials I have collected be lost, and I have decided to write a series of "Family Sketches," like those of Mr. Deane in his history of Scituate. These sketches, though far from being accurate, are the most interesting portion of his work. As a general rule, I do not intend that each number shall occupy more than a column and a half. To give a full history of some of the families, namely, that of Hinckley, Crocker, Otis, Lothrop, Bacon, and a few others would require a volume. These will necessarily be longer; but a sketch of some of the families need occupy only a few paragraphs.

I shall write them in an alphabetical series, beginning with the Allyn family. That there will not be a thousand mistakes, and omissions in each, I would not dare to affirm; but there is one thing I will venture to assert, I can point out more deficiences in them than any other living man. I desire, however, that persons having additional information, or the means of correcting any error into which I may have fallen would communicate the same. I presume there are many documents preserved in family archives which would afford me valuable aid, in the work I have undertaken, and it would give me much satisfaction, if the owners would loan me the same or furnish copies.

In giving a genealogical account of the families, nearly all the facts in relation to the history of the town will have to be given. In the Allyn family, I give some account of the original laying out of the town; in the Lothrop family a history of the first church, and in other families where the ancestor was the leading man in any enterprise, the history of that work cannot well be omitted. In this manner nearly all the principal events in the history of the town will pass in review, and such consideration be given to them as time, space or opportunity will admit.

I make no promises—I claim no immunity from criticism. I may get tired, before writing one-half of the proposed sixty columns, and it may be that the publisher will get sick of his bargain even before that time. To those who take no interest in genealogy, I have only one remark to make. My ancient friend and schoolmaster, Dea. Joseph Hawes, would often say he was a skiptic, that is, if he met with an article in a book or newspaper that did not please him he "skipt over it."

I have one more suggestion to make. I would recommend

to those who do take an interest in these articles to cut them out and paste them into a scrap book leaving on each page a wide margin for corrections, additions and notes. To those who take less interest in the matter, I would suggest that they cut out the article in relation to their own families and paste at least the genealogical portion, on the fly leaf of their family bibles :—their grand-children may take an interest in the subject if they do not.

AMOS OTIS.

Yarmouth, Nov. 15, 1861.

# INDEX TO FAMILIES.

———

# ALLYN.

---

This name is variously written on the records, Allyn;
Allyne, Allin and Allen ; but the descendants of Mr. Thomas Allyn, one of the first settlers in Barnstable, usually write
their name Allyn. He owned a large estate, and was probably the most wealthy among the first settlers. The date
when he first came over is not ascertained. It appears, by
an affidavit made by him March, 1654, on the Plymouth
Colony records, that his ancestors resided not far from Taunton, in England. His business is not stated ; but he was
probably engaged in trade. It appears by the document
above referred to, that he was in England in 1649, on business of his own, and as the agent of "divers friends." This
visit he speaks of as "att my last being in Ould England,"
implying that he had "returned home" more than once after
he first came over.

The records of the laying out of the lands in Barnstable
in 1639 are lost.* The entries made of the lands of Mr.
Allyn furnish the best information we have on the subject.
The house lots contained from six to twelve acres, and were
all laid out on the north side of the highway west of Rendezvous Lane. In 1654, Mr. Allen owned six of the original
house lots, namely :

No. 1. Originally Isaac Robinson's contained eight

---

*NOTE.—In respect to these records, I have the following information: My Great-Grandfather, Solomon Otis, was many years Register
of Deeds. My father informed me that he had heard many inquire for
them, and that his grandfather's uniform answer was, that they were
in early times carried to Plymouth, and were there lost by fire. This
is tradition; but considering the directness of the testimony, I think it
reliable.

acres of upland, and the salt marsh, at the north end. It was bounded westerly by Calves Pasture Lane, northerly partly by the creek and partly by the land of Tristram Hull, easterly by the lot formerly Samuel Jackson's, and southerly by the highway. In 1654 the highway was a few rods farther south, at this place, than at the present time. Mr. Charles Hinckley is the present owner of this lot.

No. 2. Was laid out to Samuel Jackson, who returned to Scituate in 1647. He sold it to Samuel Mayo, who sold the same to Mr. Allyn. This lot contained eight acres of upland, and the marsh at the north end. It was bounded westerly by Lot No. 1, north by the harbor, easterly by the highway (now discontinued) leading to Allyn's Creek, and southerly by the highway. This lot is now owned by descendants of Mr. Allyn.

No. 3. Was laid out to Mr. Allyn, and contained ten acres of upland, with the marsh adjoining, and was bounded west by Allyn's Lane or highway to the creek, north by the harbor, east by the house lot of Rev. Joseph Hull, and southerly by the present highway. This land is owned by Capt. Matthias Hinckley.

No. 4. Contained twelve acres of upland and the marsh adjoining, bounded on the west by Lot No. 3, north by the harbor, easterly by the lot of the Rev. John Mayo, and southerly by the present highway. On this lot Rev. Mr. Hull built his house in 1639, afterwards occupied by his son-in-law, Mr. John Bursley, and sold to Mr. Allyn about the year 1650. The first Meeting House stood in the ancient grave yard on the opposite side of the road. This land is now owned by Capt. Matthias Hinckley. Capt. Thomas Harris perhaps owns a small portion of it.

No. 5, containing twelve acres of upland, more or less, with the meadow adjoining, was the Rev. John Mayo's before his removal in 1646 to Eastham. It was bounded westerly by Lot No. 4, north by the harbor, easterly by the lot that was John Casly's, and southerly by the highway. The lot is now owned by Capt. Thomas Harris.

No. 6, contained ten acres of upland and the meadow adjoining. It was laid out to John Casly and by him sold to Samuel Mayo and by the latter to Mr. Allyn. It was bounded westerly by Lot 5, north by the harbor, east by a lot owned in 1654 by Tristram Hull,* and south by the highway.

Beside his house lots, he owned meadow at Sandy Neck, and in 1647 owned the land on the north of the Hallett Farm, adjoining the bounds of Yarmouth. Besides the above he had rights in the common lands, and other large tracts. He sold at one time 100 acres to Roger Goodspeed.

Mr. Allyn's house lots, with the lots named in the note, constituted the central portion of the village as originally laid out. On the west probably in the order named, were the lots of Gov. Hinckley, Samuel Hinckley, Gen. Cudworth, James Hamblen, Lawrence Litchfield, Henry Goggin, (on the west of Goggin's Pond) Henry Bourne, William Crocker, Austin Bearse, John Cooper, Thomas Hatch, Robert Sheley, William Betts, Henry Coxwell, Dollar Davis, John Crocker, Thomas Shaw, Abraham Blish, and Anthony Annable. The farm of the latter is now owned by Nathan Jenkins.

On the east of Rendezvous Lane, Mr. John Lothrop, John Hall, Henry Rowley, Isaac Wells, John Smith, Geo. Lewis, Edward Fittsrandle, (Lot on west side of the road to Hyannis) Bernard Lumbard, Roger Goodspeed, (Henry Cobb, Thomas Huckins, John Scudder, Samuel Mayo,) Nathaniel Bacon, Richard Foxwell, Thomas Dimmock. Isaac Davis' house stands near where the Old Dimmock house stood. The Agricultural Hall stands on Foxwell's land.

Mr. Allyn was not much in public life. March 1, 1641-2 he was propounded to be a freeman of the Plymouth Colony, admitted 1652; in 1644, 1651 and 1658 he was

———

*NOTE.—In 1647 the highway run on a straight line from Mr. John Burseley's corner to the head of Rendezvous Lane. In 1686 when the present road was laid out, the ancient road was followed as far as Jail Hill when it was turned to the northeast through the lands of Capt. Joseph Lothrop. I am inclined to the opinion that the ancient road was on the south of the swamp and joined the present road where the first court house stood, on the east of the Sturgis tavern. Joseph Hull, son of Tristram, sold Lot No 7 in 1678 to John Lothrop. Thomas Annable, Doctor Abner Hersey, Isaiah Hinckley, and Elijah Crocker have since owned it. No. 8, 6 acres, was Wm. Casly's lot, afterwards Hon. Barnabas Lothrop's; No. 9, 10 acres, was Robert Lynnell's. No. 10, 12 acres, Thomas Lombard's lot, sold to Thomas Lewis; No. 11. 12 acres, Thomas Lothrop's Land. bounded easterly by Rendezvous Lane. These Lots embraced the central position of the village as it was originally laid out.

Surveyor of highways; in 1648, 1658 and 1670 constable, and in 1653 a juryman, offices of not much profit or honor. The Court in passing up and down the County often stopped at his house, a fact which indicates that he set a good table, and was well supplied with provender for man and beast.

He married for his first wife Winnifred ———. His second wife was Wid. ———. He named in his will, dated Feb. 28, 1675, proved 5th of March, 1679-80, his daughters-in-law     Sarah, wife of William Clark,

        Martha, wife of Benjamin ———

        Rebecca, wife of Samuel Sprague.

He names his sons Samuel and John, his daughter Mehitable Annable, and Samuel's oldest son, Thomas. After disposing of a part of his estate by legacies he ordered the rest to be equally divided between his three children. He died in 1679, and was buried in the ancient burying ground,

"Where the forefathers of the hamlet sleep."

*Children of Thomas Allyn born in Barnstable:*

I.   Samuel, born 10 Feb., 1643-4, bap'd 18 Feb., 1643-4.

II.   John, born 1646, bap'd 27 Sep., 1646.

III.   Mehitable, born 1648, bap'd 28 Aug., 1648. She married Samuel Annable June 1, 1667, and had a family of four children. She married second May 6, 1683, Cornelius Briggs of Scituate. She inherited one-third of her father's estate, Mr. Allyn in his will giving her an equal portion with her brothers, an unusual circumstance in those days.

Mr. Samuel Allyn, son of Thomas, was a freeman in 1670, constable 1671, called Lieutenant in 1678. He was many years Town Clerk, and held other responsible offices. He resided at West Barnstable. In 1686, his house is described as on the south side of the highway about half of a mile east of Hinckley's Bridge. He married May 10, 1664, Hannah, daughter of Rev. Thomas Walley. She died, Tuesday, Oct. 23, 1711, at 10 o'clock, A. M. Her age is not stated. She was born in England and came over with her father in the ship Society, Capt. John Pierce, and arrived here May 24, 1662. Mr. Samuel Allyn died Friday, 25th November, 1726, aged 82 years. Mr. Samuel Allyn's will is dated Nov. 12, 1726, and proved on the 30th of Nov. following. He gives to his daughter-in-law Sarah, then wife of Deacon

Samuel Bacon, 40 shillings; to his grandsons Thomas Allyn and John Jacobs, and his daughter Hannah Lincoln, 20 shillings each; to his grandson Samuel Allyn, son of his son Joseph "only one shilling"; and to his great-grandson Thomas, son to his grandson James, 40 shillings. All his other estate, both real and personal, he devised to his son Joseph Allyn, to grandson James of Barnstable, to daughter Hannah Jacob, and his grandson Samuel Allyn of Barnstable, to be divided equally. His son Joseph and grandson James executors. The inventory of the estate is dated January 4, 1726-7, but the oath of Allyn was refused by the Judge of Probate "because I thought he could not do it with a safe conscience." Joseph swore to it Feb. 18, 1726-7.

*Children of Mr. Samuel Allyn born in Barnstable:*

I.   Thomas, born 22 March, 1654-5, married Elizabeth, daughter of Hon. John Otis, 9 Oct., 1688, and had three children, James, Thomas and Hannah. He died 25th Nov., 1696, aged 31. His widow married 20 January, 1699, David Loring of Hingham. She died in Barnstable, June 17, 1748, aged 79.

II.  Samuel, born 19 January, 1666, married Sarah, daughter of Edward Taylor, 20 Dec., 1705, and had Samuel, 26 Nov., 1706. The father died Dec., 1706, in the 39th year of his age. His widow married 26 January, 1708, Dea. Samuel Bacon. She died Sept. 24, 1753, aged 73.

III. Joseph, born 7 April, 1671. He removed from Barnstable about the year 1700. He was one of the executors of the will of his father 1726. He then had a son Samuel, showing he was married and had a family.

IV.  Hannah, born 4 March, 1672-3, married 7 Dec., 1693, Peter Jacob of Hingham, and had twelve children.

V.   Elizabeth, born 26 Nov., 1681, died 23 Dec., 1698, aged 17.

John Allyn, son of Thomas, married 1673 Mary, daughter of John Howland.

*Children born in Barnstable:*

I.   John, born 3 April, 1674.
II.  Mary, born 5 Aug., 1675; died 7 July, 1677.
III. Martha, born 6 Aug., 1677; died Oct., 1680.
IV.  Isaac, born 8 Nov., 1679.

The family of John Allyn was not of Barnstable January, 1683-4. He had probably removed. There were at that time so many John Allyns in New England, that in the absence of records it is difficult to fix the place of his after residence.

In January, 1693-4, there were in Barnstable and entitled to a share in the common lands, being either 24 years of age, or married, Lieut. Samuel Allyn, eldest son of Thomas, Sen'r, and Samuel and Thomas, sons of Lieut. Samuel. January, 1697, Thomas was dead, and Joseph, youngest son of Lieut. Samuel, was added to the list, he being then 25 years of age, but in 1703 his name is omitted.

The present Allyn families in Barnstable, are nearly all descendants of James, son of Thomas, and grandson of Lieut. Samuel. His house was very ancient, the east part two stories, and the west one story. It stood on Lot No. 1, where Charles Hinckley's house now is, and it was taken down about 50 years ago. He married July 24, 1712, Susannah Lewis, daughter of Ebenezer. He was 21 and she 18 at the time of their marriage.

No family in Barnstable could claim to be more respectably connected than this. Their eldest daughter, Elizabeth, born in 1713, married 1732, Col. John Gorham, and removed to Portland. He was a man of note in his day. Susannah, born 1715, married 1735, Capt. Jonathan Davis, Jr., a shipmaster. Anna, born 1718, married in 1736, John Davis, Jr. Thomas, born 1719, married Elizabeth Sturgis 1752; Hannah, born 1721, married 1743, Doctor Abner Hersey, an eminent physician, but most eccentric man; Rebecca, born 1723, married 1742 Rev. Josiah Crocker of Taunton; Abigail, born 1725, (an Abia Allin married Seth Cushman of Dartmouth;) Mary, born 1727, married 1751, Nymphas Marston, Esq.; James, born 1729, married 1752, Lydia Marston; Sarah, born 1730, married 1755, Mr. Justin Hubbard, of Hingham; Martha, born 1733, died 1740; Olive, born 1735, married 1754, Capt. Samuel Sturgis, Jr.

At a family meeting almost every profession in life would have been honorably represented. Mr. Allyn himself had a suit of armor, and two of his sons-in-law had done good service for their country on the field of battle, so that the military element would have been strongly represented; the legal profession by two; divinity by one, and medicine by that strange compound, Doctor Hersey, perhaps in his usual winter dress—cowhide boots, baize shirt, red cap and leather great coat.

Mr. James Allyn died Oct. 8, 1741, (his grave stones say 1742,) aged 50 years, and his widow Susannah Oct. 4, 1753, aged 59. In his will, proved Nov. 11, 1741, he provides liberally for the support of his wife and younger children. To his daughters, who had not already had their portion, £30 each, and to his son James £150. To his son Thomas he gave his cane, marked with his grandfather's name, his armor, valued at £16.10., and all his warlike weapons and appurtenances, his books, excepting his Great Bible, his "dwelling house from top to bottom," tools and stock belonging to a saddler's trade, &c., &c. His estate was appraised at £3.091. 19. 4, a large estate in those times.

Thomas was a saddler by trade. His house stood where Mr. Charles Hinckley's now does. His children were Polly, Hannah, Susan and Samuel.

James* was a cabinet maker. He resided in the old Allyn house now standing. His children were James, Benjamin, two named Marston, who died young, Thomas, Nymphas, who died young, and John, who was educated at Harvard College, graduated in 1775, and was afterwards pastor of the church at Duxbury.

Mr. Thomas Allyn has very few descendants in the male line now living in Barnstable. Whether or not his son John and grandson Joseph, who removed early from Barnstable, were the ancestors of more prolific races I cannot say.

The first inhabitants selected the beautiful sweep of high land between Rendezvous Creek and Coggen's Pond as the seat of their town, the principal men built houses there, but

---

*Mrs. Chloe Blish, now aged 95, relates the following witch story in relation to James Allyn. She lived at the time in Gov. Hinckley's house, on the opposite side of the road:

Lydia Ellis, a daughter of Lizzy Towerhill, (a reputed witch, of whom I have given an account,) resided in the family of Mr. Allyn as a servant. Lizzy took offence at the treatment of her daughter, and threatened vengeance. A night or two after, a strange cat appeared in Mr. Allyn's house, mewing and caterwauling—unseen hands upset or turned bottom upwards every thing in the house. Six new chairs, brought in the day before, were broke to pieces and destroyed. The inmates were kept awake all night, and for a long time after, strange noises were heard, at times, in the house, and the peace of the family greatly disturbed.

in less than fifteen years half the lots belonged to Mr. Allyn and the houses had been abandoned or removed. In selecting that location for the centre of the town, one fact was overlooked: no water could be procured without sinking wells to a great depth. They soon were compelled to remove to situations near to ponds or springs of water.

----

### JOHN ALLEN.

Mr. Baylies in his history states that John Allen removed from Scituate to Barnstable in 1649, and Mr. Deane in his history of Scituate, says he probably removed from Barnstable to Scituate in 1645. He appears to have been of Plymouth in 1633 and of Scituate in 1646, where he died in 1662. His widow was named Ann and he had a son John.

John Allen of Barnstable was another man. Perhaps he was the John who was taxed at Springfield in 1639, removed soon after perhaps to Rehoboth 1645, and to Newport 1650 and thence to Swansey in 1669. He married Oct. 10, 1650, Elizabeth Bacon of Barnstable, probable a sister of Samuel. Allen and his wife were both ana-baptists, yet no objection was made to their marriage, Gov. Hinckley officiating at the nuptials. To this fact I shall have occasion hereafter to refer. From Barnstable they went to Newport, R. I., and there had Elizabeth, born July, 1651; Mary, Feb. 4, 1653; John, Nov., 1654; Mercey, Dec., 1656; Priscilla, Dec., 1659, and Samuel, April, 1661.

# ANNABLE

ANTHONY ANNABLE,

One of the forefathers, came over in the Ann in 1623, bringing with him his wife, Jane, and his daughter Sarah. He remained in Plymouth till 1634 when he removed to Scituate, and was one of the founders of that town and of the church there. In 1640 he removed to Barnstable. With the exception of Gov. Thomas Hinckley, no Barnstable man was oftener employed in the transaction of public business. He joined Mr. Lothrop's church at its organization, January 8, 1634-5, was always an exemplary member, yet he was never dignified with the title of "Mr." and was all his life called "Goodman Annable." That a man who was "most useful in church and state," thirteen years a deputy to the Colony Court, on a committee to revise the laws, frequently employed in most important and difficult negotiations, and one of the 58 purchasers, was not thought worthy of that dignity may seem strange to modern readers. In the Plymouth Colony, the governor, deputy governor, and magistrates and assistants; the ministers of the gospel and elders of the church, school-masters, commissioned officers in the militia, men of great wealth, or men connected with the families of the gentry of nobility, alone were entitled to be called *mister* and their wives *mistress*. This rule was rigidly enforced in early colonial times, and in all lists of names, it was almost the invariable custom, to commence with those who stood highest in rank and follow that order to the end.

Goodman Annable had four acres of land alloted to him in the division of lands in 1623, to those who "came over in the shipe called the Anne." At the division of the cattle in 1627, there had been no increase in the number of his family, it then consisted of four, namely, himself, his wife

Jane and daughters Sarah and Hannah.   His name appears in the earliest list of freemen, made in 1633, and in that year he was taxed £0. 18., and in the following year 9 shillings.   Comparing these figures with the other taxes, it appears that he was then a man to whom the petition in Agur's prayer, "give me neither poverty nor riches," might well apply.   Oct. 1, 1634, he was elected a member to treat with the partners for the colony trade, and the next January he was chosen constable of Scituate.   Oct. 4, 1636, Goodman Annable and James Cudworth were a committee from the town of Scituate to assist in the revision of the laws of the colony.   He was a juryman that year and in 1638. March 6, 1637-8 he was again chosen constable of Scituate. In January of that year the Rev. John Lothrop, Mr. Timothy Hatherly, Goodman Annable and others of Scituate, represented to the Court that they had small portions of land, and petitioned to have the lands set off to them, between the North and South rivers, which was granted.

In 1638 and 9 many meetings were held in Scituate to adopt measures respecting a removal to another plantation. Five days were set apart for humiliation, fasting and prayer for success in their removal.   The first fast was kept Feb. 22, 1637-8, and the last June 26, 1639.   Several letters signed by Mr. Lothrop, Goodman Annable and others in behalf of themselves and other members of the church, addressed to the governor, stating the grievances under which they were suffering, and asking to be better accommodated in some other part of the colony.   At first they proposed to remove to Sippican, now Rochester, and at the January Court the lands at that place were granted to them.   But many were opposed to going to Sippican, preferring a residence at Mattakeese, now a part of Barnstable.   But the lands at the latter place had previously been granted to Mr. Richard Collicut and others of Dorchester; but in June, 1639, this grant was revoked and an opening was made for Mr. Lothrop and his church.   In the previous May Rev. Joseph Hull of Weymouth, and Mr. Thomas Dimmock and others removed to Mattakeese, and commenced the settlement of the town.   After the revocation of the grant to Mr. Collicut, the Court, June 4, 1639,* O. S., corresponding to

*The centennial celebration of the 200th anniversary of the town was held September 3, 1839, why and wherefore I cannot explain.

June 14, new style, granted the lands at Mattakeese to Messrs. Hull and Dimmock as a committee for themselves and their associates, and incorporated the town, naming it Barnstable. June 13, 1639, O. S., a fast was kept by Mr. Lothrop's church to implore "God's directing and providing for us in the place of removal," and on the 26th of the same month another fast was kept "For the presence of God in mercey to goe with us to Mattakeese."

Mr. Lothrop and a majority of his church removed from Scituate to Barnstable Oct. 11, 1639, O. S. (Oct. 21, N. S.). On their arrival, the first settlers had built themselves houses, any many of Mr. Lothrop's church found dwellings provided for them on their arrival. Goodman Annable did not remove with the first company, but some few months after.

He was a member of the first General Court held in 1639, also in 1640, '41, '42, '43, '44, '45, '47, '50, '51, '53, '56 and '57. He was not a member when the obnoxious laws against Quakers were enacted.

In 1643 he was appointed by the Court a member of a committee to provide places of defence against any hostile attack of the Indians, and in 1645 "to propose laws to redress present abuses, and to prevent future."

In 1646 he was on a committee of one from each town in the colony, "to consider a wav of defraying the charges of the magistrate's tables by way of excise on wine and other things." In 1661 he is named as one of the grantees of the lands in Suckanesset, now Falmouth, and in 1662 land was granted to his daughter Hannah, one of the first born children in the colony, and in 1669 a tract of land was granted to him on Taunton River, near Titicut.

I do not find that Goodman Annable had a houselot assigned to him in the village. He settled at West Barnstable on the farm now owned by Nathan Jenkins, Esq. It is thus described on the record:

1. Forty acres of upland, be it more or less, butting northerly by the marsh, southerly by ye commons, bounded easterly by Goodman Blush, westerly by Goodman Blush.

2. Twenty-two acres of marsh butting southerly, partly upon his own and partly upon Gdd. Blush's upland, bounded easterly partly upon ye creek between Goodman Wells

and him, and partly by ye commons, westerly by Gdd. Blush, northerly by ye commons.

3.   Fifteen acres more or less of swamp bounded easterly by Gdd. Blush, westerly by Gdd. Bowmans, southerly by ye commons, northerly partly by Gdd. Blush and partly by Gdd. Bowmans.

This is one of the best farms in Barnstable.   His land was principally on the north side of the present County road.   Fifty-four acres were afterwards added to this farm, extending to Annable's Pond on the south.

Goodman Annable died in 1674, and his widow Ann administered on his estate.   His age is not recorded, he was probably 75 years old.   His widow Ann was living in 1677 when she was fined £1 for selling beer without a license.   In 1686 she is spoken of as recently deceased.   She is called "the aged widow Annible" in 1678, and was probably nearly 80 years of age at the time of her death.

Gdd. Annable resided in the Colony fifty and one years.   He was a puritan of the school of blessed John Robinson, neither bigoted nor intolerant.   Sympathizing in feeling with Cudworth, Hatherly and other leading men of the tolerant party—an opponent of the harsh measures, and bloody laws enacted and enforced against Quakers and anabaptists in the Massachusetts Colony, and adopted in the Plymouth Colony in 1653, but never enforced in Barnstable.   His moral character was unimpeachable.   He was never a party to a law suit, and only in one instance engaged in any controversy with his neighbors.   In 1664, he was presented for removing a land-mark.   The Court after a full investigation of the charge, decided that he was blameable for removing the boundary; but being convinced that he did not willfully intend to do wrong, the complaint was dismissed.

Intellectually Goodman Annable had many superiors in the Colony.   He was a man of sound judgment, discreet, cautious,—never acting hastily or unadvisedly, a good neighbor, a useful man, and one who exhibited in his daily walk, his Christian character.

His descendants for several generations inherited from him, to some extent, the same excellent traits of character. None of them were brilliant men; but I have never heard of an Annable who was convicted of crime or who was a bad neighbor. There were not many of this name who came over. There was a John at Ipswich in 1642, a tailor, and a Matthew at Newbury aged 18, 1672. Goodman Annable uniformly wrote his name as it is now written ; but it occurs also on the records written Annible, Anible, Anniball and Anable.

The following account of his family differs from that given either by Mr. Deane or by Mr. Savage. The latter in attempting to correct the errors of the former, made greater mistakes himself. I have carefully examined all accessible records, and have not varied from these gentlemen only on evidence which appears entirely conclusive. I am aware that my account is defective, all I claim is that it is fuller and has a less number of mistakes in it than those which have been published :

Anthony Annable came over in the Ann in 1623, bringing with him his wife Jane and his daughter Sarah. Mr. Savage says daughters Sarah and Hannah. On the list of the first born in Plymouth is Hannah, daughter of Anthony Annable. A grant of land was afterwards made to her in virtue of her right as one of the first-born. No stronger evidence of a fact can be adduced. The members of the Court knew that Hannah Annable was born in Plymouth, otherwise they would not have made the grant.

Mr. Savage says Susannah was probably born in Barnstable. If so she was very young when she married on the 13th of May, 1652, William Hatch, Jr., of Scituate. .

His first wife, Jane, died in Barnstable, and was buried Dec. 13, 1643, on the lower side of the Calves Pasture. The exact locality of her grave is not known ; but is probably at a place called Hemp Bottom. He married, March 3, 1644-5, his second wife, Ann Clark. There are three several entries of this marriage, two on the Plymouth and one on the Barnstable town records. The entry in the "Court Orders" (vol. 2, page 80, of the printed volumes) is the only one that can be called an original record, the other two are copies, and the transcriber evidently made a mistake of one year in the date. The chirography of the entry on the "Court Orders" is very obscure. The late Judge Mitchell, who was familiar with the records, having spent his leisure time for several years in their examination, copied the name "Ann Clark." Mr. Pulsifer and Doctor Shurtleff, gentlemen equally distinguished for their skill in deciphering ancient manuscripts, read the name Ann Elocke. I prefer the reading of Judge Mitchell.

Mr. Savage adds "The second wife was buried 16th of May, 1651, and he married soon third wife, Ann Barker, by whom he had Desire, 11th Oct., 1653, and the wife was buried about 16th March, 1658." Mr. Savage or his amanuensis has strangely mixed up in the passage quoted, facts in relation to the families of Anthony Annable and Abraham Blish. They were both good neighbors, very kind and accommodating to each other, but I doubt whether they ever swapped wives,* as the passage quoted indicates.

*Family of Anthony Annable, by his wife Jane—born in England:*

I.   Sarah, born about 1622, married Nov. 22, 1638, by Mr. Winslow, at Green's Harbor, to Henry Ewell of Scituate. She died in 1687, leaving a family.

*Born in Plymouth:*

II.   Hannah, born about 1625, being his first born child, after his arrival. She married, March 10, 1644-5, Thomas Bowman of Barnstable.

III.   Susannah, born about 1630, married 13th May, 1652, Wm. Hatch, Jr., of Scituate.

*Born in Scituate:*

IV.   A daughter stillborn, buried 8th April, 1635.
V.   Deborah, baptized May 7, 1637.

*By his second wife, Ann Clark, born in Barnstable:*

VI.   Samuel, born January 22, bap'd Feb. 8, 1645-6, married, June 1, 1667, Mehitable Allyn, died 1678, aged 32.

VII.   Esek, (or Ezekiel) bap'd 29th April, 1649, probably died young.

VIII.   Desire, bap'd 16th Oct., 1653, married January 18, 1676-7, John Barker, Esq., died at Scituate July 24, 1706.

Samuel Annable married June 1, 1667, Mehitable,

---

*NOTE.—Mr. Savage will put this matter right in his fourth volume, soon to be published. That he has made so few mistakes is wonderful. The late Capt. Isaac Bacon, Sen., said he wished it was the fashion to swap wives, as it was old horses—he would cheat somebody most d——nably.

daughter of Mr. Thomas Allyn of Barnstable.   He resided at West Barnstable, and inherited a large portion of the estate of his father, whom he survived only four years, dying in the year 1678, aged 32.   His widow married, May 6, 1683, Cornelius Briggs of Scituate.

### Family of Samuel Annable:

I.   Samuel, born 14th July, 1669, married Patience Dogget, April 11, 1695, and had Desire, 3d Jan'y, 1695; Anna, 27th Sept., 1697, married, Aug. 19th, 1720, Nathaniel Bacon; Jane, 24th Dec., 1699, married Oct. 8th, 1719, Dea. Robert Davis; Samuel, 14th January, 1702; Patience, 15th May, 1705, married Joseph Bacon, 1722; Thomas, 21st June, 1708, married Ann Gorham Aug. 7th, 1740.   The father died June 21st, 1744, and his widow Patience, Oct. 11th, 1760, aged 90 years.

II.   Hannah, born March, 1672, died August following.

III.   John, born 19th July, 1673, married June 16th, 1692, Experience, daughter of Edward Taylor, and had Samuel, born 3d Sept., 1693; Mehitable, 28th Sept., 1695, married, July 23d, 1713, Andrew Hallet, died Oct. 23d, 1767; John, born April, 1697, died May following; John, born 3d May, 1698, removed to Rochester; Mary, born Dec., 1701, married David Hallet Aug. 19th, 1720; Cornelius, born 3d November, 1704, and Abigail, born 30th April, 1710, married Oct. 22d, 1730, Wally Crocker.

IV.   Anna, born 4th March, 1675-6, married Oct. 14th, 1696, Dea. John Barker.   She died March 21st, 1732-3, "aged near 57 years," and is buried at West Barnstable.

The estate of Samuel Annable, deceased, included the farm of his father, then in possession of his mother, and the fifty-four acres on the south side of the highway which he held in his own right by a grant from the town, and the estate which his wife held in her right, by gift from her father, was settled, by order of the Court, Oct. 30, 1678, as follows:

"The seate of land which was formerly Mr. Thomas Allyn's" at Barnstable, was settled upon Samuel, the eldest son, he paying to his sister Anna £25, one-half in current silver money of New England, and the other half in "current pay att prise current" within two years after he become of age.

To John Annable, the youngest son, the farm that the "aged widow Annible hath her life in, and now liveth on; which was pte of the lands which formerly Anthony Annible lived on," he to pay his sister £25, one-half in current silver money of New England, and one-half in current pay, within two years after he becomes of age.

To the widow Mehitable Annable was assigned all the moveables and all the stock, "to be att her own dispose for and towards the bringing up of the children, hopeing that shee will have a care to bringe them up in a way of education as the estate will beare, and to have all the proffitts of all the lands untill the said Samuel Annible and John Annible comes to be of age, and then the third in the proffitts of the lands during her natural life."

In 1703 there were only two of the family, Samuel and John, in Barnstable entitled to a share in the common lands. The West Barnstable family disappeared many years ago, some removed to Rochester and some to other places, and the ancient farm is now owned by strangers. The Barnstable family eighty years ago was numerous, wealthy and influential,—now there is not a solitary voter of the name in the town. The family has dwindled down, and almost become extinct. There are a few of the descendants of Anthony Annable in Boston, and in other places. The last parcel of the Annable farm (formerly Mr. Thomas Allyn) was sold out of the family the present year (1861), and there is no memorial of the family, now remaining in Barnstable, save the monuments in the grave yards which mark the places of their sepulchres.

# BACON.

To write a genealogical memoir of Nathaniel Bacon and his descendants would require a volume. I shall not attempt it. Among the many of the name who came over early, were Nathaniel and Samuel, supposed to be brothers, and Elizabeth, probably a sister, all of whom settled in Barnstable.* Michael of Dedham, who has numerous descendants probably came from Ireland. William of Salem, who married Rebecca, daughter of Thomas Potter, mayor of Coventry, had resided in Dublin. On the outbreak of the Irish rebellion, she was sent over to this country, and her husband followed soon after. Andrew who was early of Cambridge, and one of the magistrates at Hartford, 1637, and died at Hadley 1669, probably came from Rutlandshire, England. He has no descendants in the male line, his son Isaac having died young. Nathaniel Bacon of Middletown, was a nephew of Andrew and a son of William of Stretton, Rutland County, England. The Bacons of Connecticut were prominent men, and the prevalence of the same names in the Connecticut and Barnstable indicates a community of origin.

Mr. Nathaniel Bacon was one of the first settlers, and the house lot assigned to him, is now owned by his descendants. Without a plan, it will be difficult to state intelligibly, the manner in which the lots in the vicinity of the Meeting House in the East Parish were laid out. The locations of

*Mr. Savage in commenting on the evidence given in 1661 by Dea John Fletcher of Milford, Conn., relative to the ancestry of Nathaniel Bacon, of Middletown, remarks that it "might without violence be construed to refer equally to the Barnstable family, though it is less probable." It it very much "less probable." The affidavits of Dea. Fletcher and some others were taken at New Haven, before Nathaniel Bacon, Esq , and they state distinctly that "Nathaniel Bacon then present, was the oldest son of William Bacon,"&c. The abstracts of these affidavits given by Hinman, are wanting in clearness, and justify the caustic remarks of Mr. Savage.

all the roads, excepting that to Hyannis, anciently Baker's Lane, have been changed, and the ancient boundaries on the dividing lines between the lots have mostly been removed. As early as 1653, nearly all the land in this neighborhood had changed ownership. The present county road, probably passed on the south of Mr. James Lewis' house, now owned by Frederick W. Crocker, Esq. When the town was settled, the present county road, from the Meeting House to Baker's Lane, was a deep gully, impassable for teams. When the present road was laid out in 1686 it was located "up Cobb's Hill" through this gully. The "Old Mill Way" joined the county road on the east of the Meeting House, the gate at the entrance standing north of the town pound. From this point the "Old Mill Way" extended north to the Mill Pond, and thence across the ancient causeway sometimes called Blushe's bridge, to the Common Field. The ends of the house lots butted on Mill Way not on the county road. Beginning at the south the first lot on west side was Roger Goodspeed's. His house stood on this lot in 1649, but in 1653, he had surrendered it to the town and taken other lands in exchange. The Meeting House on Cobb's Hill and the lands now occupied for burying grounds were included in this lot.

The second lot on the north of Goodspeed's contained seven acres, and was set off to Elder Henry Cobb.

The third lot containing six acres was laid out to Thomas Huckins by an order of the town dated 14th Sep. 1640.

The fourth lot, where the late Dea. Joseph Chipman resided, was Dolar and Nicholas Davis.

On the east of the "Mill Way" the first lot was Mr. Nathaniel Bacon's, bounded south by the county road, west by Roger Goodspeed and the Mill Way, north (in 1654) by Goodman Cobb, and east partly by Goodman Cobb, and partly by Goodman Foxwell's land. At the settlement of the town the land on the north of the Bacon house lot was a dense swamp, unfit for cultivation, or building purposes. It contained some valuable timber and was reserved as town commons. It was subsequently granted in small lots to Goodman Cobb, John Davis and others, and subsequently bought by the Bacon family. The land between the swamp and mill pond, on the east of the Way was mostly owned by

Dolar Davis who sold it to Abraham Blish in 1657, who afterwards sold it to the Bacons.

Mr. Bacon owned sixteen acres of land in the old Common Field, a name still retained and eleven acres in the new Common Field.* He also owned the house lot and land now owned by Frederick Cobb, containing twelve acres, "bounded northerly by the highway, westerly by the road running into ye woods, 80 rods, easterly by Goodman Foxwell." Also four acres bought of Henry Taylor, "bounded southerly by ye highway, northerly by Mr. Dimmock's marsh, easterly partly by Mr. Dimmock and partly by John Scudder's upland, westerly by Nicolas Davis."

In addition to these lots he owned thirty-two acres of land and meadow at Cotuit, meadows in the mill pond and at Sandy Neck, and other tracts of land and rights in the commons.

Mr. Bacon was a tanner and currier. He had vats in the low grounds near his house. As there were other tanneries in town, it is probable that he worked at his trade in the winter and was employed in the cultivation of his lands the remainder of the year. During the latter part of his life, his public duties absorbed a large part of his time.

He built his house in the year 1642. It was taken down about thirty-five years ago and the old oak timber was as sound and as hard as when cut from the forest. It was two stories high, and built in the style then common. It was about 22 feet in the front and 26 feet in the rear. The lower story was divided into three rooms. The front room was 16 feet square, low in the walls with a large summer beam across the centre overhead. The bedroom floor was elevated two feet above the other floors to give more height to the cellar under it. The kitchen was very small. The second story, which was very low in the wall, was divided into three rooms corresponding in size with those in the lower story. The chimney was of stone, few if any bricks had then been made in the Colony. The fire place in the

*The Old Common Field extended from Blushes Point to the west Watering place, bounded north by the harbor, and south by the mill pond. The name is a free translation of the Indian name Mattakeese which means "old" or "worn out planting lands." The new Common Field extended from the West Watering place to the bounds of Yarmouth, bounded north by the harbor, and south by the County Road, and included the Indian reservation.

front room was eight feet wide, four feet deep, and the mantle laid high, so that a tall person could walk under it by
stooping a little.   The oven was often built on the outside
of the house with the mouth opening in one corner on the
back side of the fire place.   The fire was built in the centre,
and on a cold winter evening a seat in the chimney corner was
a luxury unknown in modern times.   The fire place in the
kitchen was necessarily smaller, in a house of this construction, especially when the oven opened into it.   There was
usually a fire place in the front chamber.   The windows
were small and oiled paper was used instead of glass in many
houses.   The successive occupants of this house, altered
and enlarged it so many times, that in 1825 it was entirely
unlike the original.   The height of the rooms had been increased, by lengthening the posts three feet,—a large addition had been put on the west, and several on the rear.
So that it covered more than four times as much ground as
at first.

Mr. Bacon was proposed as a freeman in June 1645 and
admitted June 1646.   In 1650 he was constable of the town
of Barnstable, and a deputy to the Colony Court thirteen
years from 1652 to 1665.   In 1657 he was chosen an assistant and was re-elected annually till his death in 1673.   In
1658 and 1667 he was a member of the council of war.   He
frequently served on committees appointed by the Court,
and was a prominent and influential man in the Colony.

It would be instructive and interesting to trace step by
step the progress of Mr. Bacon through life.   He came to
Barnstable a young man, comparatively poor, without
friends to assist him, and without the advantages of a good
education ; but a good moral character, good business habits,
energy and industry more than compensated for the want of
these advantages.   He died Oct. 1673, probably not 60
years of age.   His widow survived him many years.   She
was living in 1691.

I do not find his will on record ; he probably made none.
The inventory of his estate, appraised at £632, 10. 2, is
dated Oct 29, 1673, sworn to by his widow Mistress Han-
nah Bacon, and letters of administration granted to her.—
On the 4th of March following "Mr. Thomas Hinckley, Mr.
Thomas Walley, William Crocker, John Thompson, and

Thomas Huckins were appointed by the Court to settle the estate of Mr. Nathaniel Bacon deceased, among Mrs. Hannah Bacon and her children, which settlement under their hands, or any three of their hands, shall be accompted against all claims, or contentions at any time arising about the aforesaid estate or any part thereof."

Nathaniel Bacon married Dec. 4, 1642, Miss Hannah, daughter of the Rev. John Mayo,then teacher of the church in Barnstable,

### Children Born in Barnstable.

I.   Hannah, born Sept. 4, 1643, bap'd 8th Dec. 1644. She married Mr. Thomas Walley, Jr., son of Rev. Thomas Walley of Barnstable, and had one son Thomas, who died leaving no issue; and daughters, Hannah, who m. first, Wm Stone, and had two dau's; second, James Leonard, by whom she had Lydia who m. Thomas Cobb; and Elizabeth, who m. Edward Adams. Hannah m. Feb.16,1675, her second husband Rev.George Shove of Taunton, and had Mary Aug 11, 1676, Johanna Sept. 28, 1678; Edward Oct. 3, 1680, and Mercy May 1682. She is named as one of the "remote members" of the Barnstable church in 1683. She died in Taunton Sept. 1685, aged 42 years.

II.   Nathaniel, bap'd 15th Feb. 1645-6.

III.   Mary, born Aug. 12.1648, bap'd 20 Aug. 1648.

IV.   Samuel, born Feb. 25, 1650-1.

V.   Elizabeth, born Jan'y 28, 1653-4.    She died unmarried in 1676, according to the Plymouth records "in the 28th year of her age." She was only 21, or at most, 22 years of age. Her estate was settled by agreement on record.

VI.   Jeremiah, born May 8, 1657.

VII.   Mercy, born Feb. 28, 1659-60, married Hon. John Otis, the third of the name, July 18, 1683. She died

NOTE.—In the account of the Allyn family I inadvertantly stated that Capt. Samuel Mayo bought his house lot of John Casely. This is a mistake. John Casely's house lot was on the South side of the road. It contained four acres, the south-west corner being near the Jail lands An investigation of this matter, seems to confirm the tradition that the present road between Jail Hill and the old Sturges tavern was a private way belonging to the Lothrops, before the year 1686, when it was laid out as a public highway. In 1654 there was a highway from near the Savings Bank Building to the wharf now owned by Josiah Hinckley, and the house lots were bounded by that road.

Dec. 10, 1737 aged 77 years.  She was buried at West Barnstable, where a monument is erected to her memory.—[See Otis Family.]

VIII.  John, born June, 1651 the record says, but according to his grave stones in the burying ground near the Meeting House in the East Parish, he was born in June 1665.  He "died Aug. 20, 1731, in the 67th year of his age."

Nathaniel Bacon, 2d, bought a part of the house lot of Elder Henry Cobb, including the stone or fortification house thereon, afterwards owned by the third Nathaniel Bacon, who kept a public house.  He also inherited the mansion house of his father; but his mother having a life estate therein, it did not come into his possession.

He married March 27, 1673, Sarah, daughter of Gov. Thomas Hinckley.  She died February 16, 1686-7, aged 40.  He married for his second wife Hannah [Lumbert?] a young woman.  He died Dec., 1691, aged 46.  In his will dated Aug. 6, 1691, proved May 9, 1692, he does not provide liberally for his wife Hannah*, and contrary to the usual custom, did not name her executrix of his will.

He also names his son Nathaniel and Samuel, his daughter Mary and Elizabeth, by his second wife, and his "honored mother Bacon."  He had two dwelling houses, to Nathaniel he gave "one house which he will," and the other to his younger son Samuel.  He appointed as executors of his will, "My loving brethen Jeremiah Bacon and John Otis, and my trusty and well beloved friends Jonathan Russel and Lieut. James Lewis, all of this town of Barnstable."

*Children of Nath'l Bacon 2d, and his wife Sarah Hinckley, born in Barnstable.*

I.  Nathaniel, born Sept. 9, 1674.  He was married by Maj. Mayhew, Nov. 11, 1696, to Ruth Doggett, at Martha's Vineyard.  His children were Thomas, born Sept. 30, 1697; removed to Eastham; David born Dec. 11, 1700; Jonathan, born March 11, 1703; Hannah, born Jan'y 15, 1704-5, and Sarah, born Jan'y 6, 1707-8.  He

*In 1698 she married John Davis, Jr., his third wife, and had Nicholas, Jedediah, Desire, Noah and perhaps other children   In 1705 she *is* called of Falmouth.  She had one daughter, Elizabeth, by her second husband.

died in Barnstable Jan'y 1737-8 aged 63, and his widow died Aug 6, 1756, aged 80.    He was a deacon of the church, a blacksmith by trade, and kept a public house.

II.    Mary, born Oct. 9, 1677, married Nov. 5, 1702, John Crocker, of Barnstable.    She died March 1711, aged 33.

III.    Elizabeth, born April 11, 1680, married Aug. 31, 1704 Israel Tupper, of Sandwich.

IV.    Samuel, born Jan'y 20, 1682, married March 30, 1704 Mary, daughter of Thomas Huckins.    His second wife was Sarah, daughter of Edward Taylor, and widow of Samuel Allyn, Jr., whom he married 26th Jan'y 1708.— His children were Ebenezer, born March 16, 1705, died July 17, 1706; Ebenezer, Dec. 4, 1708; Mercy, born May 22, 1710; and Edward, Jan'y 23, 1714-15.

Deacon Samuel Bacon, resided in the ancient family mansion which he transmitted to his son Edward.    Dea. Bacon died April 29, 1728, aged 46, and his widow Sarah, Sept. 24, 1753, aged 73.    Ebenezer of this family married Jan'y 17, 1734, Lydia Lothrop, and he removed with his wife and five children in 1745, to Lebanon, Conn.    His house, a one story, gambrel roofed, double house, stood on the easterly part of the land, which was the great lot of Rev. Mr. Lothrop, where Daniel Downes now lives.    He sold his house and land to Capt. John Cullio, a Scotchman.    Mercy, daughter of Deacon Samuel, married Aug. 5, 1744, Jonathan Hallett, of Hyannis, a son of David Hallett.    The late Benjamin Hallett, Esq., was a son, and the present Hon. Benjamin F. Hallett, of Boston, a grandson, and of the sixth generation from Nathaniel Bacon, the first settler.    He has numerous descendants.

Hon. Edward Bacon, youngest son of Dea. Samuel, was a distinguished man in his time.    He held many important offices.    He took an active part during the Revolution, and in the stirring times immediately preceding it.    His patriotism was at one time doubted : but the resolutions passed by the town and recorded, vindicate his character as patriot and a man.    He inherited the ancient mansion house of the Bacons, afterwards owned by his youngest son Ebenezer. He married Sept. 7, 1744, Patience daughter of Benjamin Marston ; she died Oct. 21, 1764, and he married Dec. 21, 1765, Rachel Doane, of Wellfleet.    He died March 16,

1783, aged 68, and is buried near the church in the East Parish. His widow Rachael m. Dr. Thomas Smith, Woods Holl. He had nine children, five of whom died in infancy, namely : 1. Edward, born Oct. 19, 1742, who married Lydia Gorham, and died in 1811. 2. Lydia, born February 3, 1744-5, died April 28, 1745. 3. Nymphas, June 2, 1746, died Dec. 1, 1746. 4. Samuel, Oct. 17, 1747, died Nov. 7. 1747. 5. James, Oct. 30, 1748, who married Johanna Hamblen, and removed to Freeport Maine. 6. Susannah, Dec. 13, 1750, died March 24, 1753. 7. Sarah, born Dec. 25, 1752, died April 11, 1776. 8. Susannah, Feb. 14, 1755 ; and Ebenezer, Aug. 30, 1756, a distinguished man. He held many important offices was a correct business man, of sound judgment, intelligent, a good neighbor and citizen, and hospitable to a fault. Whatever Squire Bacon said was regarded as law by his neighbors, a fact which shows that he was a man of worth and influence. He died of consumption, in 1811. aged 55 years, leaving a numerous family, who were "trained up in the way they should go," and now that "they are old they do not depart from it."

Samuel Bacon, son of Nathaniel, removed to Hingham, and married 17th Dec., 1675, Mary, daughter of John Jacob. He died in Hingham, Feb. 18, 1680-1, aged 29 years, 11 mos., 23 days. In his will dated Jan'y 13, 1680-1 he names his honored mother. Hannah Bacon, widow ; his two daughters, Hannah and Mary, and his wife, Mary. whom he appoints sole executrix ; and for overseers, his father-in-law, John Jacob, of Hingham, his brother-in-law George Shove, of Taunton, Shubael Dimmock, of Barnstable, and his brother Jeremiah Bacon. He had property in Hingham and Barnstable, all of which was apprized at £334,8,2. His children born in Hingham were Hannah, born Oct. 1676. died aged two months. Hannah, again. born Feb. 16, 1678 and Mary, born Feb. 1680. Respecting these daughters I have no certain information. Tradition says they removed to Barnstable, never married, and built the large two story gambrel roofed house occupied by John Bacon, Jr., and afterwards by his son, the late Capt. Isaac Bacon.

Jeremiah Bacon, son of Nathaniel, was a tanner. His house which was a two story building with a Leantoo on the west end, stood a little distance north-east from William Cobb's house. His tannery was in the low ground on the north-east his house. He married Dec. 1686, Elizabeth Howes of Yarmouth. He died in 1706, aged 49, leaving a good estate, which was settled Feb. 15, 1712-13. His house lot, a part of the Dimmock farm, contained nine acres and he had thirty acres in the Common Field, adjoining the house lot on the north, lands at Stony Cove, and at Middleboro, meadows and wood land. Of the homestead two and three fourths acres were set off to Job, bounded south by the highway, west by land of Mr. John Otis, (now Lot N. Otis,) and the meadow of Samuel Dimmock, north by the Creek. This land is now owned by William Cobb. To Samuel, his eldest son, and his mother, three acres, bounded south by the highway, west by Job Bacon, and north by the creek, with the barn and other buildings thereon. This land is now owned by Solomon Hinckley. To Jeremiah, second son, 3 and 1-2 acres, bounded south by the highway, west by Samuel Bacon's land, (now by the town road to the Common Field,) north by the creek, and east by Shubael Dimmock's land. This lot was afterwards owned by James Delap, and is now owned by the widow Anna Otis. Samuel had 10, Jeremiah 9 1-2 and Job 9 acres in the Common Field. Joseph had land at Stony Cove, and 1-3 of land at Middleboro, &c. Ebenezer one third of land at Middleboro, &c. Nathaniel had one third of land at Middleboro, &c.; in his portion were 1 silver spoon, 1 silver porringer, &c.— His Wid. Elizabeth, and daughters Anna and Mary had portions set to them in severalty. Sarah and Elizabeth are not named, and were probably dead.

Children of Jeremiah Bacon and his wife Elizabeth Howes born in Barnstable.

I.   Sarah, born Oct. 16, 1687, probably died young.

II.   Anna, born Mar. 16, 1688-9.

III. Mercy, born Jan'y 30, 1689-90, married Mar. 19, 1719, Thomas Joyce of Yarmouth, had a large family of girls noted for their beauty, which however did not prevent the father from committing suicide.

IV.   Samuel, born Aug. 15, 1692. He married three wives. 1st, Deborah daughter of Nathaniel Otis, who came from Nantucket and settled in Barnstable. She

died May 29th, 1721. 2d, he married Jan'y 7, 1724-5
Wid. Hannah Russell, a daughter of Joseph Paine, Esq.,
of Harwich. She had previously married on the 20th of
Jan'y 1715-16, Philip Russell. She died May 8, 1753
aged 58, (the church records say "about 50.") 3d Mary
Howland, Feb. 21, 1754. He was a captain, a man of
some property, and had the bump of self esteem largely
developed. Notwithstanding his official standing and his
being junior to Dea. Samuel, he was always known as
Scussion Sam, a nickname exceedingly mortifying to his
dignity. He believed that his family was entitled to more
respect than the other Bacon families and was often vexed
because his neighbors thought otherwise. He had a habit
of saying, "we will discuss that matter," hence his nick-
name. He resided in the house which was his father's
and died Jan'y 29, 1770 aged 77. His children born in
Barnstable were Sarah, Feb. 24, 1713-14, who married
Jabez Linnell, Nov. 11, 1736; Oris, May 7, 1715, married Hannah Lewis Nov. 23, 1738, and died July 11,
1773, without issue, and bequeathed his estate to his
nephew, the late Mr. Oris Bacon; Thomas, Oct. 23, 1716,
married Desire Hallett Feb. 1, 1745; Susannah, Dec. 24,
1718, married Nath'l Cobb Dec. 14, 1738; Deborah, Dec.
4, 1720, married Peter Pierce Nov. 12, 1741; Hannah,
baptized Feb. 13, 1725-6, and Mary baptized July 26,
1730. There are no descendants in the male line of Capt.
Samuel Bacon now living in Barnstable. A great-grandson
residing in Wisconsin has many. Oris Bacon, son of Oris
died at Lima Centre, Wisconsin, Nov. 21, 1862, aged 85
years, 7 months, 5 days.

V.   Jeremiah, born Oct. 2, 1694, married Abigail Parker
(she married 2d, Nov. 10, 1732, Mr. Eliphalet Carpenter
of Woodstock,) and had Prince June 15, 1720, and Jeremiah, Jan'y 14, 1723-4. The latter married Hannah
Taylor April 23, 1750.

VI.   Joseph, born June 15, 1695, married Patience Annable
1722, and had seven children. 1. Joseph born April 11,
1723, married Mirian Coleman Dec. 13, 1750; 2. Desire,
born Dec. 3, 1724, married Joseph Davis, Jr., Sept. 24,
1745. 3. Jane, born Feb. 28 1727-8 married James
Davis, Jr., Sept. 24, 1745. 4. Samuel, father of Robert

Bacon of Boston, born March 26, 1731. He died on board the Jersey prison ship. One account says: "Samuel Bacon of Barnstable, died on board the prison ship at St. Lucia 1781." 5. Patience, born June 29, 1734, married May 19, 1747, Ben. Davis. 6. Annah, born July 29, 1737, died June 20, 1761. 7. Mercy, born April 17, 1740, married Sept. 4, 1760, Ben. Lumbert.

VII. Ebenezer, born March 11, 1698.

VIII. Nathaniel, born Sept. 11, 1700, married June 11, 1726, Sarah Cobb. He lived in the Otis Loring house and removed to New Jersey about 1750. He had born in Barnstable, Rebecca, Dec. 17, 1726; Jeremiah, born June 25, 1732; Elizabeth, born May 1, 1734; Sarah, born May 9, 1736; (she said her sister Elizabeth walked from New Jersey, barefooted;) died unmarried in 1815; Nathaniel born March 3, 1737-8.

IX. Job, born March 23, 1703, married Elizabeth Mills, March 10, 1725.

X. Elizabeth, born Aug. 6, 1705.

John Bacon, Esq., youngest son of Nathaniel, was eight years of age when his father died in 1673. Beside his share in his father's estate, his brothers Nathaniel and Samuel bought for him Nov. 25, 1676, twelve acres of land of Major John Walley, administrator on the estate of Nicholas Davis, deceased. The eastern half, however, seems to have been transferred to his sister Mercy, afterwards wife of Hon. John Otis.

Extracts* from ancient deeds, and other records, enable me to state in an intelligible form the original laying out of the lands east of Cobb's, or Meeting House Hill. The house lot of Roger Goodspeed as already stated was bounded west by the present Mill Lane and the Hyannis road. On the north side of the highway the next lot on the east was laid out to Nathaniel Bacon, this extended to the top of the Hill a little east of the spot where the late Capt. Isaac Bacon's house stood. On the south side of the road, the lot next east of Goodspeed's was owned in 1654 by the Wid. Mary Hallett, and is now owned by S. B. Phinney and the heirs of Timothy Reed, deceased. The next lot was laid out to

---

*The extracts referred to are omitted.

Lieutenant James Lewis and is now owned by F. W. Crocker.   The next lot now owned by Frederick Cobb, on the
east of the Lane (called Cobb's lane) was laid out to Nath'l
Bacon.   The eastern boundary of this lot corresponding
with the eastern boundary of his house lot on the north side
of the highway.   Richard Foxwell's lots were next east,
four acres lying on each side of the road.   The Bacons
bought this land early.   A part of that bought of Foxwell
on the north side is yet owned by them, and a part by the
Agricultural society.   The Foxwell land on the south of the
road is now owned by Joseph H. Hallet and James Otis.
Next east of the Foxwell land on the south of the road, was
the great lot of Elder Henry Cobb containing sixty acres.—
It extended to the range of fence a little west of the present
dwelling house of Joseph Cobb.   Henry Taylor owned two
acres at the north east corner of this lot.   Next east of Elder
Cobb's great lot was the farm of Joshua Lumbard extending
to the range on the east of the house of Amos Otis, deceased,
and bounded east by the great lot of Rev. John Lothrop.
Joshua Lumbert, when he removed to South Sea, sold this
lot.   The front was owned by Schoolmaster Lewis, and the
rear by Robert Shelly, who sold to Samuel Norman.   Mr.
Lothrop's great lot contained 45 acres, and extended to the
range of fence between the houses of Daniel Downes and
Joshua Thayer.   This lot was sold by the heirs of Mr.
Lothrop to John Scudder, and he sold his house and six
acres of land to Stephen Davis, and the remainder of the
land to the Bacons.   On the north side of the road the lot
next east of Foxwell's was Nicholas Davis'; this land extended to the eastern boundary of the Dimmock farm, which
is the range of fence between the houses of Charles Sturgis
and Solomon Hinckley.   From this point, the Dimmock
land was bounded 115 rods on the south by the highway to
the turn in the road east of the house of William W. Sturgis.   The Dimmocks sold some of their land very early.
Nicholas Davis bought six acres at the west end and which
was a part of the tracts which his administrator sold to John
Bacon, but was afterwards transferred to his sister Mercy,
and is now owned by her descendants Solomon Hinckley
and Lot N. Otis.   Four acres on the east of the last named
lot were bought by Henry Taylor, and by him sold in 1659
to Nath'l Bacon.   John Scudder bought six acres of the

Dimmock land which he sold to the Bacons.    The two last lots were afterwards the property of Jeremiah Bacon, and divided in 1712 as above stated.

The Bacons owned extensive tracts of land.  John Bacon, Esq., owned on the road the lots which belonged to Foxwell, and the lot of Nicholas Davis.   He owned a house and farm at Strawberry Hill at South Sea, and extensive tracts of wood land and meadows.

He was bred a lawyer, and had an extensive practice. He was a Judge of the Court of Common Please, and held other offices.   He wrote the worst hand, for a man of business, that I have ever met with ; his lines were crooked in every direction ; his letters cramped and awkwardly formed, and difficult to decipher ; the execution shabby and miserable.   It has been remarked that a man's character is developed in his hand-writing.    If John Bacon, Esq., is to be judged by that rule, a high estimate cannot be placed on his orderly habits or intellectual endowments.   He was much employed in public business, was a church member in good standing, and his moral character was unblemished.

John Bacon, Esq., youngest son of Nathaniel, married June 17, 1686, Mary, daughter of Capt. John Hawes of Yarmouth.   She died March 5, 1725–6, aged 61 years. He married for his second wife, Sept. 9, 1726, Madame Sarah Warren of Plymouth, a widow-woman having children and grand-children of her own.   He died "Aug. 20, 1731, in the 67th year of his age," and is buried in the grave yard near the Meeting House in the East Parish.

In his Will, a most elaborate document, occupying four and one-half large and closely written pages on the records, he provides that in certain contingencies, his negro slave Dinah shall be sold by his executors, "and all she is sold for shall be improved by my executors in buying of Bibles, and they shall give them equally alike unto each of my said wife's and my grand-children."    Whether this pious act was performed by his executors, I am not informed.

He left a large estate, which he divided nearly in equal proportions to his children then living.   His wife was provided for in a marriage contract dated 27th of May, 1729. He owned his homestead on the north side of the road, containing about thirty acres, bought of Foxwell, Nicholas Davis and Abraham Blish ; this he divided into five lots, giving to Nathaniel the eastern, containing six acres, on which his son had built a two-story single house. This lot is now owned by Charles Sturgis, S. B. Phinney and Joseph Basset. The next lot on the west, to his daughter Desire Green, on which there had also been built a two-story single house, afterward owned by Lot Thacher. The next lot containing five acres, he gave by deed to his son Solomon, who sold it to John Sturgis, jr. These two lots are now owned by Joseph Basset. The fourth lot with the mansion house thereon, he gave to his son Judah, and the west lot to his son John by deed. These, excepting about an acre at the southwest, are now owned by the Barnstable County Agricultural Society. The Foxwell land on the south side of the road he gave to Judah with the barn, orchard, &c.

His farm and dwelling-house at Strawberry Hill, South Sea, he gave 1-8 to Hannah, 1-8 to Solomon, 1-4 to Nathaniel, 1-4 to John, and 1-4 to Judah. Solomon to have the improvement of the house till he had one of his own.

His woodland he gave in equal shares to Desire, Nathaniel, John, Solomon and Judah.

His meadows he divided to his sons, and daughter Desire.

His clothing he divided to Nathaniel 1-4, and his best hat and wig, John 1-2 and his cane, Solomon 1-4 and law books, and to Judah 1-4 and his horse furniture.

His "household wares," 1-3 to Desire, and 1-3 to Hannah and I presume the other 3d to his wife. His one-sixth of the mill at Blushe's Bridge he gave to Solomon; and his great Bible to Hannah. He gave to all his sons and grandsons, liberty to use his two landing-places, one at the mill and the other at Blushe's Point. To his grand-daughter Mary, daughter of his son Isaac, then deceased, 20 shillings, and if Isaac's widow had another child, then £40, provided either lived to be 21 years of age.

His orchard he gave to Judah, but his children, notwithstanding, were to have the fruit of five trees each for seven years.

Judah had the largest share in the estate, but he had duties to perform that the others had not. He had to provide among other things "a good gentle beast to go in my wife's calache to any part of Barnstable, and once a year to Plymouth."

*Children of John Bacon, Esq., and his wife Mary Hawes.*

I.      Hannah, born June 7, 1687, married March 25, 1709,
        Ebenezer Morton, of Plymouth, and had a family.

II.     Desire, born March 15, 1688-9, married March 25,
        1709, (at the same time with her sister Hannah)
        William Green, and had six children.   She died
        Dec. 29, 1730, aged 41.   He died Jan'y 28, 1756,
        "aged above 70."

III.    Nathaniel, born Jan'y 16, 1691-2, married Aug. 19,
        1720, Anna Annable, who died soon, leaving no issue.
        He married in 1730, Thankful Lumbert, by whom he
        had Lemuel, Benjamin, Jabez, Hannah and Jane, bap-
        tized April 26, 1741.   She had afterwards Lurania,
        illegitimate, baptized Aug. 28, 1743.   She married
        Sept. 7, 1744, Augustine Bearse, and had other chil-
        dren.   She died Nov., 1774, aged "about 70."   Jabez
        died 1757, leaving his estate to his brothers and
        sisters.

IV.     Patience, born June 15, 1694 ; died young.

V.      John, born March 24, 1697, married Elizabeth Free-
        man, May 3, 1726.   The record says he died "abroad
        May 24, 1745."   He fell overboard at sea and was
        drowned*   He owned and occupied the large two-
        story gambrel-roofed dwelling, on the rising ground
        east of the ancient mansion-house of the Bacons.
        He was called a saddler in 1729 ; but I have
        understood he was a sea captain at the time of
        his death.   He had ten children, Mary, born
        March 24, 1725-6, died in infancy ; John, born
        April 29, 1728 ; he died a young man leaving no
        issue ; Barnabas, born April 17, 1729, died in
        infancy ; a daughter, Jan'y 3, 1730-1, died "in half
        an hour"; Elizabeth, born May 8, 1731, married
        Oct. 6, 1755, Thomas Dimmock ; Isaac, born Dec.
        25, 1732, married Oct. 29, 1762, Alice Talor.   He
        died June 26, 1819, aged 87 years.   He resided in
        the house which was his father's.   He had a small

---

*The circumstances are thus told: When he fell overboard there was
only one other man on deck—a man who stammered, but a good sin-
ger.   When Capt. Bacon fell overboard he attempted to call the crew,
but could not articulate a word.   One said to him  "sing it," and  he
commenced and sung "John Bacon's overboard."

farm which he cultivated, raising a large quantity of onions for market. He was master of a packet running between Boston and Barnstable many years, and in the fall carried a large quantity of onions to the Boston market. He was tall, over six feet, and well proportioned—a man that was never vexed at anything. If a man assailed him, he would always have a witty reply, and thus turn the tables on his opponent. Many anecdotes are related of him. In the article on the Annable family a characteristic story is told of him. His packet was called "the Somerset," not her real name—a small craft—the remains of which lie in the raft dock at Blushe's Point. One time he sailed from Barnstable with a southwest wind. After crossing the bar his vessel began to leak. Unable to keep her free by pumping; he hove about to return, and continuing to pump she was soon free. It did not take Capt. Isaac long to find the trouble. A wicked rat had gnawed a hole through the planking on the starboard side, which was under water when on the other tack. He made a plug, let himself down on the side of the vessel, and drove it into the rat-hole, hove about and went to Boston.

One year straw to bunch early ripe onions could not be procured, and the farmers cut green bullrushes for the purpose. Purchasers who wanted onions for the West India market, objected to them. In reply, Capt. Bacon said: "Gentlemen, these are what are called 'tarnity onions'; they'll keep to all eternity." He sold his onions, but the purchasers had to throw them overboard in a week after.

Capt. Samuel Hutchins, no relation of Capt. Bacon's, also run a packet to Boston and carried onions. At one time he sold a load to be delivered in Salem. Capt. Bacon heard of it, and having his vessel loaded, sailed for Salem, and called on the merchant to buy. The merchant said he had engaged a load of Capt. Huckins. Capt. Bacon replied: "He is my son-in-law and these are the very onions."

The town records say the 7th child of John Bacon, jr., was named Mark, the church records say

Mercy, born Jan'y 27, 1734-5, baptized Feb. 2, 1734-5. She died unmarried March 29, 1765; Simeon, born July 26, 1736, died March 21, 1740; Desire, born May 20, 1738; she was never married, lived in the house with her brother Isaac, in which she had a life estate. She died March 2, 1811; Mary, born Aug. 23, 1740. married Joseph Davis.

VI.    Isaac, born March 29, 1699, married Hannah Stevens. He removed to Provincetown where he died in 1730, leaving a daughter Mary, and a posthumous child, born after the death of the father.

VII.    Solomon, born April 3, 1701, married July 16, 1726, Hannah Capron, a Rehobeth name. He was a physician and resided some time in Barnstable. Whether he removed or died young, I am unable to say. I have a memorandum that he had a daughter Sarah, who died April 11, 1775, aged 20.

VIII.    Judah, born Dec. 9, 1703. I do not find that he left issue.

Nathaniel Bacon, including the male and female lines, is the ancestor of a very large proportion of the eminent men of Cape Cod. The sketch which I have given, is only an outline. There are an abundance of materials for an interesting, useful and popular work, and I hope the author of the Sears' Memorial will deem it a subject worthy of his eloquent pen.

The descendants of Jeremiah Bacon did not inherit the business talents for which the other branches of the Bacon family were distinguished. Some of them were noted for their pleasant humor and ready wit. The saying of Nathaniel, brother of the second Oris, are often repeated in the neighborhood where he resided. He married a granddaughter of William Blatchford, and his wife Elizabeth, the reputed witch. He was a poor man, had a large family, and died at the Almshouse in Barnstable. At first he resided near the late Mr. Ebenezer Sturgis, afterwards in a small house, at a distance from neighbors. On a cold, stormy winter's day, when the roads were blocked by drifts of snow, he sat in his comfortable room, while Mr. Sturgis and his sons were out watering and taking care of their large stock of cattle. Nathaniel remarked: "I am thankful that I do not own that stock of cattle; Sally and I have been sitting at ease by a cheerful, blazing fire, they have been toiling all day, exposed to the cold, driving storm.

When in the eastern country he boastingly said, 'Squire Bacon and I keep more cows than any other two men in Barnstable"; Nathaniel had one; 'Squire Bacon twenty.

He took up a bar of iron in a blacksmith's shop and said, "I can bite an inch off of this bar," at the same time showing a good set of teeth. A bet on the performance of the feat was accepted. Putting the iron near his open mouth, he brought his teeth quickly together. "There, gentlemen," said he, "I have bitten more than an inch off."

Of his wife he related the following anecdote: One stormy winter morning, when he had no wood to kindle a fire, no provisions in his house, and six small children clamoring for breakfast, his wife got up, scraped a little frost from a window, and looking out exclaimed in piteous tones, "Oh, what would I give for one pipe of tobacco."

Samuel Bacon, of Barnstable, took the oath of fidelity in 1657. How long he had then been of Barnstable does not appear. In 1662, he had a grant of "six acres of land more or less, sixty poles north and south, and 18 poles wide," (less than 5 acres) at the head of Richard Foxwell's land, bounded northerly thereby, east by the land of James Cobb, south by the commons, and west by Nathaniel Bacon. He married 9th of May, 1669, Martha Foxwell, and had

I.   Samuel, born March 9, 1669-70.
II.  Martha, born Jan'y, 1671.

This family disappeared early. Samuel is supposed to have been a brother of Nathaniel and Elizabeth, but I find no positive evidence that such was the fact.

# BACHILER.

This eccentric and learned divine has the honor of being the first white man who settled within the present limits of the town of Barnstable. He lived a hundred years, and his long life was checkered with exciting incidents on which the imaginative pen of the novelist would delight to dwell. He was born in England in 1561, received orders in the established church, was settled in the ministry, and ejected by the bishops for non-conformity, at whose hands Gov. Winthrop says he had suffered much. He married early in life, and four of his sons and three daughters are named : John Wing, afterwards of Sandwich, married his daughter Deborah, probably before his removal to Holland, where he resided several years. During his residence in that country, Christopher Hussey, the ancestor of the Nantucket family of that name, became enamored with his daughter Theodate, and sought her hand in marriage ; but Mr. Bachiler refused assent, without the bridegroom would agree to remove to New England. Hussey assented to the condition imposed, and took, probably in 1629, Theodate to wife. Mr. Bachiler, intending to emigrate to New England, soon after returned to London. Mr. Lewis states that his church in Holland consisted of six members beside himself, and that these returned with him to London. No names are given ; but it is uniformly stated that they were his friends, or members of his own family. If so, the seven probably were Mr. Bachiler and his wife, John Wing and his wife Deborah, John Sanborn and his wife, a daughter of Mr. Bachiler, and Theodate Hussey. Sanborn's wife died in England, and it does not appear that he came over. His sons John, William and Stephen came over with their grandfather and settled in Hampton. Christopher Hussey and his mother, the widow Mary Hussey, were afterwards members of his church, and followed their pastor in all his wanderings. Mr. Savage, whose authority is not to be rejected on light or inconclusive testimony, thinks the Husseys came over in the same ship with Mr. Bachiler. The court records, and the decisions of the ecclesiastical councils favor his supposition, and it will be hard to show how the ubiquitous number of six members is made up, if he is not right.

On the 9th of March, 1632, Mr. Bachiler and his company embarked at London in the ship William and Francis, Capt. Thomas, and arrived in Boston Thursday, June 5, 1632, after a tedious passage of 88 days, and on the day next after his arrival went to Lynn.

Mr. Lewis* states that "In Mr. Bachiler's church were six persons who had belonged to a church with him in England; and of these he constituted a church at Lynn, to which he admitted such as desired to become members, and commenced the exercise of his public ministrations on Sunday, the 8th of June, without installation." Four months after a complaint was made of some irregularities in his conduct. He was arraigned before the court at Boston, Oct. 3, when the following order was passed: "Mr. Bachiler is required to forbeare exercising his gifts as a pastor or teacher publiqely in our Pattent, unlesse it be to those he brought with him, for his contempt of authority, and until some scandles be removed." Mr. Bachiler, however, succeeded in regaining the esteem of the people, and the court on the 4th of March, 1633, removed their injunction against him. In 1635, some of the members became dissatisfied with the conduct of their pastor, "and doubting whether they were regularly organized as a church," withdrew from the communion. A council of ministers was held on the 15th of March, and after deliberating three days, decided "that although the church had not been properly instituted, yet after-consent and practice of a church-state had supplied that defect. So all were reconciled," says the record. Mr. Bachiler, however, perceiving no prospect of terminating the difficulties, requested a dismission for himself and the six who had accompanied him from England, which was granted, on the supposition that he intended to remove from

---

*The dates given by the author of the history of Lynn are not always reliable. He states that Hussey settled in Lynn in 1630. The evidence favors the supposition that he did not come over till 1632.

Lynn. Instead of this, he remained and formed another church of his friends, that is of those who came over with him.

This conduct gave great offence to "the most and chief of the town" of Lynn, and they entered a complaint against Mr. Bachiler to the assistants who forbade him to proceed in the organization of his church until the subject was considered by other ministers. Still he goes on. The magistrates require his attendance before them. He refuses to obey; they send the marshall who brought him into their presence. He submits and agrees to leave the town in three months.

Mr. Bachiler was admitted a freeman May 6, 1635, and removed from Lynn to Ipswich in Feb. 1636, where he received a grant of fifty acres of land, and had the prospect of a settlement; but some difficulty arose and he left the place.

Gov. Withrop in the first volume of his history, under the date of March 30, 1638, has the following passage :

"Another plantation was now in hand at Mattakeese ["now Yarmouth," is written on the margin] six miles beyond Sandwich. The undertaker of this was one Mr. Batcheller, late pastor at Saugus, (since called Lynn) being about 76 years of age ; yet he walked thither on foot in a very hard season."

"He and his company, being all poor men, finding the difficulty, gave it over and others undertook it."

Mr. Bachiler settled in the easterly part of Mattakeese, at a place which is known to this day as "Old Town." The names of his associates are not given ; probably the company consisted of persons who belonged to, or were connected by marriage, with the family of Mr. Bachiler, namely, sons, sons-in-law and grand-sons, with their families.*

Mr. Bachiler probably obtained the consent of Mr. Collicut, to whom the lands at Mattakeese had been granted, before he undertook to establish a plantation ; for without

---

*There is a remarkable parallelism between the character of Mr. Bachiler and that of Mr. Wm. Nickerson, the ancestor of the family of that name. Both were, or assumed to be, religious men; both were stiff-necked and wayward; both were often involved in difficulties; both were undertakers of new plantations, and in both their families, the same clannish feeling prevailed. Bachiler had more wives and Nickerson more law suits; the former "undertook" several plantations; the latter only one; otherwise their histories were parallel.

such consent he would have been a trespasser and liable to ejectment. The terms of the grant cannot be quoted; but it does not thence follow that no permit was given or grant made. We know by the Old Colony records that in 1637 or 1638, certain lands in Barnstable were run out into house and other lots; that these lands were laid out by or under the authority of Mr. Richard Collicut of Dorchester. He was a surveyor, but there is no evidence that he was ever in Barnstable. The Plymouth records tell us the thing was done; but they do not tell us who did it. The passage quoted from Gov. Winthrop clearly and distinctly states that at, or about the time, the Plymouth records say the lands were run out, Mr. Bachiler and his company undertook to form a plantation at Mattakeese. The very first thing that he and his company did, undoubtedly, was to do what all such companies did in those times first do; that is run out house lots for each of their party, and farming lands and meadows to be held by each in severalty. Not to presume this, is to presume that Mr. Bachiler and his company were not only wanting in common prudence, but wanting in common sense. The first settlers in new countries never failed to appropriate a sufficiency of land to themselves, and in order to make such appropriation, they must first run them out and put up boundaries.

That there were some among his company that could survey lands, scarce admits of doubt. Mr. Bachiler, as Mr. Prince informs us, was a "man of learning and ingenuity, and wrote a fine and curious hand," and he could undoubtedly run lines and draw plans. His son John Wing, one of the company, was a man of skill and energy—and he probably had with him his sons Daniel, Stephen and John, three stout youths, if not all men grown—one of whom in aftertimes was a surveyor of lands.

That Mr. Bachiler's party were capable of doing all that the Colony records say was done, does not admit of doubt, and in the absence of all proof to the contrary, it is to be presumed that they did do it.

Sandwich was settled in 1637, mostly by people from Lynn—old neighbors and acquaintances of Mr. Bachiler's company—and it is probable, that being the nearest settlement to Mattakeese, that they left their women and little ones there till shelter could be procured for them in the new settlement.

The first house built within the present bounds of Yarmouth (of which there is a record), is that of Mr. Stephen Hopkins, afterwards owned by his son Gyles, and by him sold to Andrew Hallet, jr. This was in the summer of 1638, and was built as a temporary residence for his servants who had the care of cattle sent from Plymouth to be wintered at Mattakeese. Whether or not cattle had been sent from Plymouth in previous years does not appear; if so, then Mr. Bachiler found whites within a mile of the place he selected for settlement. It was also in the immediate vicinity of "Iyanough's town," a place not inhabited by the Indians in the winter, and their deserted wigwams perhaps afforded them a temporary shelter.

Mr. Bachiler and his company were all poor men, illy provided with the means of establishing a plantation, even in the mild season of the year, and it is hardly possible that they could have sustained themselves during the intensely cold winter of 1637, without some kindly herdsmen, or some friendly Indians gave them shelter while they were preparing their rude habitations.

Early in the spring of 1638, Mr. Bachiler, "finding the difficulties great," abandoned his plantation at Mattakeese. John Wing and his family stopped in Sandwich. Mr. Bachiler and Christopher Hussey went to Newbury, and on the 6th of September the Massachusetts Legislature gave them and others leave to begin a plantation at Hampton, of which he became the minister. The next year, according to Mr. Felt, he was excommunicated for unchastity, though Gov. Winthrop says he was then "about eighty years of age, and had a lusty, comely woman to wife." In November, 1641, he was restored to the church, but not to his office. About this time his house in Hampton took fire and was consumed with nearly all his property.

In 1644, the people of Exeter invited him to settle there; but the court forbid his settlement. In 1647, he was at Portsmouth, now Portland, where in 1650, he being then 89 years old, his second wife Helena being dead, he married his third wife Mary, without publishing his intention of marriage according to law, for which he was fined ten pounds, half of which was afterwards remitted.

With his third wife he lived only a few months. She went to Kittery, and, according to the York records, on the 15th of October, 1651, was presented for committing adultery with George Rogers, and sentenced "to receive forty stripes save one, at the first town meeting held at Kittery six weeks after her delivery, and be branded with the letter A." In October, 1656, she petitioned for a divorce from Mr. Bachiler, because he had five years before "transported himself to Ould England, and betaken himself to another wife," and because she desired "disposing herselfe in the way of marriage." Whether or not she obtained a divorce does not appear on record.

Mr. Bachiler, after his return to England, married a fourth wife, his third being then living. At last he died in the year 1660, at Hackney, near London, in the one hundreth year of his age.*

No record of his family is preserved. Four sons and three daughters are named. Henry, settled at Reading; Nathaniel, born about 1611, "a chip of the old block," settled at Hampton, and Francis and Stephen, both remained in London, the latter said to have been living in 1685. Of his daughters, one as before stated, married John Sanborn, and died before 1632. Theodate, married Christopher Hussey, and died in Hampton in 1649. Deborah married John Wing of Sandwich. On the Yarmouth town records I find the following entry: "Old Goody Wing desesed the last of January, '91 and '92," that is Jan'y 31, 1692, N. S. This record probably refers to Deborah, widow of the first John Wing. Her son John resided at Sawtucket (now Brewster), then within the corporate jurisdiction of Yarmouth, and his aged mother probably resided with him. There is no one beside to whom the record will apply. Her age is not given. but an approximation to it may be made. Her son Daniel of Sandwich, if he had then been living, would have been 70 years of age, consequently the mother must have been about 90 years of age at her death

---

* In preparing this article, I have consulted Gov. Winthrop's History, the Plymouth and Massachuetts Records, Felt's Ecclesiastical History, Savage's Genealogical Dictionary, and Lewis's History of Lynn; the latter gives the fullest sketch of the life of Mr. Bachiler yet published. The reading of the extracts from the records, given by Mr. Lewis, leave the impression on the mind that Mr. Bachiler was not such a man as a minister of the gospel should be. A literary friend, who for several years has been collecting materials for a memoir of Mr. Bachiler, says he is not deserving of the odium which has been heaped on his character.

# BASSET.

William Basset, one of the forefathers, came over in the ship Fortune in 1621; settled first in Plymouth, then in Duxbury, and finally in Bridgewater—of which town he was an original proprietor. He died there in 1667. He was comparatively wealthy, being a large land-holder, only four in Plymouth paying a higher tax in the year 1633. He had a large library, from which it is to be inferred that he was an educated man. In 1648, he was fined five shillings for neglecting "to mend guns in seasonable times"—an offence of not a very heinious character—but it shows that he was a mechanic as well as a planter. Many of his descendants have been large land-holders, and even to this day a Basset who has not a good landed estate, thinks that he is miserably poor.

His name is on the earliest list of freemen, made in 1633; he was a volunteer in the company raised in 1637, to assist Massachusetts and Connecticut in the Pequod war; a member of the committee of the town of Duxbury to lay out bounds, and to decide on the fitness of persons applying to become residents, and was representative to the Old Colony Court six years. His son William settled in Sandwich; was there in 1651, and is the ancestor of the families of that name in that town, and of some of the families in Barnstable and Dennis. His son, Col. William Basset, was marshall of Plymouth Colony at the time of the union with Massachusetts, and in 1710, one of the Judges of the Inferior Court, and afterwards Register of Probate. He was an excellent penman, and wrote a very small, yet distinct and beautiful hand, easily read. The records show that he was a careful and correct man. He was the most distinguished of any of the name in Massachusetts. He died in Sandwich, Sept. 29, 1721, in the 65th year of his age.

Elisha Basset, a grandson of Col. Basset, removed to Dennis, then a part of Yarmouth. He was a captain in the Provincial militia ; had three commissions, each signed by a different Royal Governor. At the commencement of the Revolution he was a zealous whig and surrendered his commission, and was offered a captain's commission in the Continental Army ; but the circumstances of his family obliged him to decline accepting it. He was the representative from Yarmouth at the Provincial Congress, as it was called, which assembled at Cambridge and Watertown in the years 1774 and '75.

Nathaniel Basset, son of the first William, is the ancestor of the Yarmouth, Chatham and Hyannis, and some of the West Barnstable families of the name. On the 2d of March, 1651-2, "Nathaniell Basset and Joseph Prior, for disturbing the church of 'Duxburrou,' on the Lord's day, were sentenced each of them to pay twenty shillings fine, or the next towne meeting or training day both of them to bee bound unto a post for the space of two hours, in some public place, with a paper on their heads on which theire capital crime shall be written perspecusly, soe as may bee read." Whether they paid the fines imposed, or suffered the novel mode of punishment to which they were sentenced, does not appear.

Nathaniel settled first in Marshfield, but removed to Yarmouth where he was an inhabitant in 1664, and perhaps earlier. He resided near the first meeting-house, and his descendants still enjoy his lands. Notwithstanding the trifling irregularity in his conduct when a young man at Duxbury, he was a very worthy and respectable citizen, had a large family—ten of whom lived to mature age. He died January 16, 1709-10, aged 82.

No record of the family of the first William Basset has been preserved. It appears that he was married but had no children at the division of the land in 1623 ; but at the division of the cattle in 1627, he had two, William and Elizabeth. His wife was named Elizabeth, and it is stated by Judge Mitchell that she was probably a Tilden.* His children,

---

*His wife Mary presented the inventory of his estate, May 12, 1667, and took the oath required. The names of Mary and Elizabeth were formerly considered synonymous, and it may be that Mary was not his second wife.

born in Plymouth and Duxbury, were

I.   William, born 1624, removed to Sandwich, was called
     Mr., married Mary, daughter of Hugh Burt of Lynn,
     and died in 1670, leaving a large estate.  Had daughter
     Mary born 21st November, 1654 ; William, 2d, 1656, and
     probably others.  Col. William, 3d, married Rachel, had
     Mary, Oct. 20, 1676 ; Nathan, 1677 ; Rachel, Oct. 25,
     1679 ; William, Jonathan, and another daughter.  Wil-
     liam married Abigail, daughter of Elisha Bourne, and
     had Elisha, who removed to Yarmouth, and other chil-
     dren.  Nathan married Mary Huckins, 1690, removed to
     Chilmark and had eleven children.  His son Nathan
     graduated at Harvard in 1719, and was afterwards set-
     tled in Charleston, S. C.   An interesting account of the
     Bassets of Martha's Vineyard has recently been pub-
     lished by R. L. Pease, Esq.  Mary, the wife of Nathan,
     was a daughter of John Huckins of Barnstable, and
     was brought up in the family of her grandfather, Elder
     John Chipman.  The account of her religious expe-
     rience, written by herself, is a narrative of thrilling in-
     terest.   Jonathan married Mary ———, and died Dec.
     13, 1683, leaving, I think, one son, Jonathan, who is
     named in his grandfather's will.

II.  Elizabeth, born about 1626, married Thomas Burgess,
     jr., of Sandwich, 8th Nov. 1648, was divorced June
     10, 1661.   He removed to Rhode Island, and was a
     resident at Newport in 1671, having a wife Lydia.

III. Nathaniel, born 1628, married for his first wife a
     daughter of John Joyce [Mary or Dorcas] of Yar-
     mouth.  His wife Hannah, who died in 1709, was prob-
     ably a second wife.  The record of his family is lost.
     His will, dated Jan'ry 10, 1709-10, six days before his
     death, is a carefully drawn instrument, witnessed by
     Rev. Daniel Greenleaf, Experience Rider, and his
     nephew Col. William Basset, and furnishes much gen-
     ealogical information.  He names his nine children then
     living, says he is "aged and under much decay of
     body," being then 82 years of age.  To his son Wil-
     liam he gave meadow and upland, which was John
     Joyce's drying ground, bought of Mr. Thomas Wally,
     and meadow bought of Mr. Thornton.  He names the
     eldest son of Thomas Mulford of Truro, who married
     his daughter Mary ; the eldest son of his son Nathan-

iel ; the eldest son of his son Joseph ; to Nathaniel he gave property that was his Grandmother Joyce's, and his lands in Middleboro'. He names his daughter-in-law Joannah, perhaps wife of Nathaniel, who removed to Windham, Conn., and his daughter Ruth Basset. He gives certain property unto six of his children, Mary Mulford, Samuel Basset, Hannah Covell, Joseph Basset, Sarah Nickerson and Nathan Basset, Mr. Thomas Mulford of Truro, and his son Joseph of Yarmouth, Executors. Estate appraised at £228,11. One of the oldest monuments in the Yarmouth grave-yard is that of Dorcas Basset, who died June 9, 1707, aged 31. She was probably a daughter of Nathaniel. Though William is first named in the will, he was probably the youngest son.

IV.  Sarah, born about 1630, married in 1648, Peregrine White of Marshfield, the first born of the English at Cape Cod Harbor, Nov. 1620. Her third son Jonathan, born June 4, 1658, is the ancestor of the White families in Yarmouth.

His other children named are Ruth, who married John Sprague, 1655 ; Jane ; Joseph, who settled with his father in Bridgewater, married Martha Hobart, 1677, and died 1712. He had Joseph, William, Elnathan, Jeremiah, Lydia, Ruth and Elizabeth. The posterity of Joseph are numerous.

William, son of Nathaniel, married Feb. 23, 1710, Martha Godfrey, and had Isaac, July 17, 1711 ; Moses, Nov. 4, 1713 ; Fear, April 12, 1716, who married Joseph Rogers of Harwich, Oct. 19, 1737. His second wife was Sarah Jenkins of Barnstable, to whom he was married Jan'y 30, 1722-3. He and his wife Sarah were dismissed from the Yarmouth to the Barnstable Church, Aug. 1727. His children recorded as born in Barnstable are Samuel, Aug. 21, 1724 ; Experience, May 5, 1727 ; Mary, May 18, 1729, and Nathaniel, Sept. 4, 1732. Only the two last were baptized in Barnstable. He had probably another son, William, born in Yarmouth, who married May 8, 1741, Margaret Merryfield. The Bassets of West Barnstable are descendants of William, son of Nathaniel, and of Samuel of Yarmouth, a great-grandson of Col. William of Sandwich. This Samuel married June 15, 1743, Susannah Lumbard of

Truro, and had born in Barnstable, Nehemiah, Sept. 22, 1743; Ebenezer, Dec. 27, 1744, and probably others. There was also a Nathan Basset, jr., called of Middleboro', who settled at West Barnstable and married Oct. 25, 1739, Thankful Fuller, and had born in Barnstable, Nathan, Dec. 30, 1750, and Cornelius, Jan'y 20, 1753, and perhaps others.

Joseph, son of Nathaniel, is the ancestor of the Yarmouth and Hyannis families. He married Feb. 27, 1706-7, Susannah Howes, she died Feb. 27, 1718-19, and he married for his second wife Thankful Hallet, Dec. 3, 1719. His children were Sarah, born Dec. 10, 1707, died July 3, 1736; Joseph, June 15, 1709; Daniel, Nov. 17, 1710; Joshua, Sept. 13, 1712; Susannah, Jan. 22, 1714-15, married John Hawes, Jan'y 2, 1732; Samuel, Oct. 23, 1716, a whaleman died unmarried, 1740; John, Dec. 14, 1720; Ebenezer, July 9, 1722, died Aug. 16, 1723; Thankful, married 1750, Joshua Brimhall of Hingham, and Nathan, Oct. 17, 1725.

Mrs. Thankful Basset died Aug. 12, 1736, and Mr. Joseph Basset, Jan'y 6, 1749-50.

Joseph Basset, son of Joseph, married Feb. 25, 1737, Mary Whelden. He died Sept. 5, 1833, aged 94. He had 1st, Joseph, Dec. 23, 1738, who inherited the paternal estate; married three times. One of his wives was a daughter of Capt. John Bearse, who came over as a revenue officer before the Revolution. He bought the Rev. Mr. Smith's house, in Yarmouth, where Joseph Basset and Elisha Doane afterwards kept a public house. He had two children who lived to mature age, Susannah, who married the late Elisha Doane, Esq., and Joseph, now living, unmarried, on the Basset farm. 2d, Mary, Oct. 20, 1744, married Edward Sturgis, jr., Jan'y 28, 1767. 3d, Jonathan, Nov. 10, 1746, and Samuel, Dec. 4, 1748, both of whom removed to Hallowell, Maine.

Daniel Basset, son of Joseph, married July 1, 1735, Elizabeth, daughter of Seth Crowell, and had one son, Daniel, born Aug. 7, 1736. The father died soon after and his widow married in 1742, Hezekiah Marchant, and removed to Hyannis. Daniel, the grandfather of the present Hon. Zenas D. Basset, resided at Hyannis, and is the ancestor of the Bassets in that vicinity. He married a daugh-

ter of Jabez Bearse, and had sons Joseph, Daniel and Seth.
He was a Lieutenant in the Continental Army.  Joseph, his
son who enlisted as a soldier, but served in the capacity of
waiter to his father, was one of the last surviving revolutionary pensioners of the town of Barnstable.   He died July
7, 1855, aged 93.  He married two wives and was the father
of twenty-four children, of whom the Hon. Zenas D. is the
oldest.   One of his wives had four children by a former husband, so that in fact there were twenty-eight in his family
who called him father.

Joshua, son of Joseph, was an ensign in Col. Gorham's
Regiment in the expedition to Louisburg, in 1745.   He
married in 1738, Hannah Brimhall of Hingham, and had
Sarah, Oct. 28, 1739; Susannah, May 16, 1741; Anna,
March 3, 1742-3, and Joshua, Nov. 18, 1744.   The latter
probably died young.

Nathan Basset, son of Joseph, lived in the ancient
Hallet house, situated nearly opposite the Barnstable Bank.
He married first, Hannah Hallet, 1751, by whom he had
seven children, and second, Desire, widow of Prince Crowell.   He had 1st, John, Nov. 4, 1753, who has no descendants now living; 2d, Thankful, Nov. 3, 1756, who died
young; 3d, Joseph, Feb. 13, 1759; 4th, Ebenezer, May
24, 1761; 5th, Thankful, Sept. 19, 1763, married Ebenezer
Taylor; 6th, Francis, Jan'y 14, 1766; 7th, Joshua, Aug. 7,
1768, father of the present Capt. Joshua Basset.

Nathan Basset, son of Nathaniel, is the ancestor of the
Chatham and Harwich families.  He married March 7, 1709,
Mary, daughter of Thomas Crowell of Yarmouth.   He died
in 1728, leaving seven children.   She died in 1742, and
names in her will sons Nathan, Thomas, Nathaniel, who
married Sarah Chase of Yarmouth, Aug. 23, 1729, Samuel,
and daughters Mary Basset, Dorcas Nickerson and Hannah
Covell.

Capt. Elisha Basset of Sandwich, grandson of Col.
William, married Ruhama, daughter of Samuel Jennings of
Sandwich, and removed to Dennis, then Yarmouth.   His
children, born in Yarmouth, were, 1st, Lydia, Aug. 14,
1740, married Abraham Howes, 1761; 2d, Abigail, Jan'y
30, 1742; 3d, Elisha, March 14, 1744-5, who removed with
his family to Ashfield in 1797, where he has descendants;
4th, Samuel, April 17, 1747, who went to Barnstable; 5th,
William, June 22, 1750, married Betty Howes, and had one

son, the Hon. Francis Basset, whose parent died when he was a child ; 6th, Deborah, Oct. 30, 1752 ; 7th, Lot, Jan'y 22, 1755.

---

NOTE.—I intended in this series of articles to write sketches of the families of the first comers, and of no other. I have been induced to depart from that rule in this instance. Nearly all of the materials used in preparing this article I collected fifteen years ago, and I am aware that it is not so full or so accurate as it might be made. Hon. Francis Basset has an extended memoir of his family, which he has spent much time in preparing, and I presume will publish it at some future time.

# BEARSE.

## AUSTIN OR AUGUSTINE BEARSE.

Austin or Augustine Bearse, the ancestor of this family, came over in the ship Confidence of London, from Southampton, 24th April, 1738, and was then twenty years of age. He came to Barnstable with the first company in 1639. His house lot, containing twelve acres of very rocky land, was in the westerly part of the East Parish, and was bounded westerly by John Crocker's land, now owned by his heirs, northerly by the meadow, easterly by Goodman Isaac Robinson's land, and "southerly into ye woods." He owned six acres of meadow adjoining his upland on the north, and two thatch islands, still known as Bearse's islands. He had also six acres of land in the Calves Pasture, esteemed to be the best soil in the town, eight acres of planting land on the north side of Shoal pond, and bounded by Goodman Cooper's, now called Huckins' Neck, and thirty acres at the Indian pond, bounded easterly by the Herring River. The Indian pond lot he sold to Thomas Allyn, who sold the same in 1665 to Roger Goodspeed.

He was proposed to be admitted a freeman June 3, 1652, and admitted May 3, following. His name rarely occurs in the records. He was a grand juror in 1653 and 1662, and a surveyor of highways in 1674.

He became a member of Mr. Lothrop's church, April 29, 1643. His name stands at the head of the list, he being the first named who joined after its removal to Barnstable.* He appears to have been very exact in the performance of his religious duties, causing his children to be baptized on the Sabbath next following the day of their birth. His son

---

*Since writing this passage I have become satisfied that there is an omission in the Cape Church records preserved 1642, of members admitted in 1640 and 1641.

Joseph was born on Sunday, Jan'y 25, 1651, O. S., and was carried two miles to the church and baptized the same day. Many believed in those times that children dying unbaptized were lost, and it was consequently the duty of the parent to present his child early for baptism. Goodman Bearse was influenced by this feeling; he did not wish, by a week's delay, to peril the eternal salvation of his child. Now such an act would be pronounced unnecessary and cruel.

The subject of baptism had disturbed Mr. Lothrop's church from its organization. In London the Baptists quietly separated themselves and formed the first Baptist Church in England. In Scituate the same question arose, disturbing the harmony of the church, and to avoid these troubles, Mr. Lothrop and a majority of his church came to Barnstable. His book on the subject of baptism, printed in London, was written and prepared for the press while he was in Barnstable. I have not met with a copy, but incidentally from his records, I infer that he considered baptism an ordinance of primary importance, and that the parent, being a church member, who unnecessarily delayed the performance, thereby periled the salvation of the child. Some of the old divines taught this doctrine, and at the present day it is not entirely obsolete.

Goodman Bearse was brought up under such teachings, and however differently the present generation may view such questions, he did what he honestly believed to be his duty, and he that does that is to be justified.

He was one of the very few against whom no complaint was ever made; a fact which speaks well for his character as a man and a citizen. He was a farmer, lived on the produce of his land, and brought up his large family to be like himself, useful members of society. His house stood on the north side of the road, and his cellar and some remains of his orchard, existed at the commencement of the present century. I find no record of his death, or settlement of his estate on the Probate records. He was living in 1686; but died before the year 1697. A road from his house to Hyannis is still known as Bearse's Way. His grandsons settled early at Hyannis. John Jenkins and John Dexter afterwards owned the ancient homestead. The planting lands at Shoal Pond were occupied by his descendants till recently.

The marriage of Goodman Austin Bearse is not on record.    His children, born in Barnstable, were

I.      Mary, born 1640, bap'd May 6, 1643.

II.     Martha, born 1642, bap'd May 6, 1643.

III.    Priscilla, born March 10, 1643-4, bap'd March 11, 1643-4, married Dea. John Hall, jr., of Yarmouth, 1660.

IV.     Sarah, born March 28, 1646, bap'd March 29, married John Hamblin of Barnstable, Aug. 1667, and had twelve children.

V.      Abigail, born Dec. 18, 1647, bap'd Dec. 19, married April 12, 1670, Allen Nichols of Barnstable, and had nine children.

VI.     Hannah, born Nov. 16, 1649, bap'd Nov. 18.

VII.    Joseph, born Jan'y 25, 1651-2, bap'd same day, married Dec. 3, 1676. Martha Taylor.

VIII.   Hester, born Oct. 2, 1653, bap'd same day.

IX.     Lydia, born end of Sept. 1655.

X.      Rebecca, born Sept. 1657, married Feb. 1670-1, William Hunter.    Additional investigation will probably show the above to be an error of the record. William Hunter of Sandwich, married Rebecca, daughter of Wid. Jane Besse, who married second, the notorious Marshall George Barlow.    If the record is correct, she was only 13 years, 5 months old when married.

XI.     James, born end of July, 1660.    He was admitted a townsman in 1683, being then only 23 years of age. In the division of the meadows in 1694, he had four acres, and in the final division in 1697, the same number was confirmed to him.    In the division of the common lands in 1703, his name does not appear according to the rules adopted for the admission of townsmen, and the division of common land; the above facts indicate that James Bearse was married in 1683, as no unmarried men were admitted townsmen till 24 years of age; that he was a man who had good property, (2 1-2 or 3 being the average), this proportion indicates, and his name not appearing on the list in 1703, shows that he was then dead or had removed from town.    There was a Bearse family early in Halifax, Plymouth county.    An Austin Bearse is named who removed to Cornwall, Nova Scotia.    Andrew Bearse of Halifax, Plymouth county, married Margaret Dawes of East Bridewater, 1736. There were others of the name in Halifax. It is probable that James, son of Austin, removed to that town.

Joseph Bearse, son of Austin, probably was a soldier in King Philip's war, his sons having rights in the town of Gorham, granted to the heirs of the soldiers who served with Capt. Gorham. He married Dec. 3, 1676, Martha Taylor, daughter of Richard of Yarmouth, a "tailor" by trade, and so called to distinguish him from another of the same name called "Rock." He died about the year 1695. She died January 27, 1727-8, aged 77 years.

*Children born in Barnstable:*

I. Mary, born Aug. 16, 1677. She did not marry— was admitted to the East Church, 1742, and died Jan'y 19, 1760, aged 84 years.
II. Joseph, born Feb. 21, 1679. He was one of the Grantees of Gorham, and his name is on the list of the first settlers in that town, dated 1733. He resided at Hyannis before his removal to Maine.
III. Benjamin, born June 21, 1682, married, Feb. 4, 1701-2, Sarah Cobb, second, Anna Nickerson of Chatham.
IV. Priscilla, born Dec. 31, 1683, died March 31, 1684.
V. Ebenezer, born Jan'y 20, 1687, married Nov. 25, 1708, Elizabeth Cobb, and second Joanna Lumbert, Sept. 4, 1712.
VI. John, born May 8, 1687, married Nov. 15, 1711, Elinor Lewis.
VII. Josiah, born March 10, 1690, married first, Nov. 2, 1716, Zeurich Newcomb of Edgartown, and second Mary. Removed to Greenwich, Conn., 1734.
VIII. James, born Oct. 3, 1692, married Mary Fuller, March 17, 1719-20.

Benjamin Bearse, son of Joseph, was one of the early settlers at Hyannis. His homestead was bounded east by David Hallet's land, the corner being two rods from Hallet's house, and is now owned by his descendants. In his will dated March 26, 1748, proved on the 7th of July following, he named his sons Augustine, Benjamin, Joseph, Samuel, Peter and Stephen; his daughters Martha Lewis, Priscilla Lewis, Sarah Nickerson and Thankful Nickerson, and his wife Anna, to whom he gave all the household goods she brought with her, and the improvement of one-third of all his real and personal estate. To Augustine he gave land bounded S. E. and N. by the heirs of Jonathan Lewis, deceased; to Joseph and Samuel his house and orchard; to Peter a house and one acre of land on the north side of the road; to Stephen and Benjamin all his lands in Gorham town; to Joseph, Peter and Samuel all the rest of his real and personal estate, they paying debts, legacies, and allowing Augustine a convenient way to the landing "where I make oysters," and a place to land and dry fish; to Benjamin, Martha and Priscilla £12 old tenor each ($5.33), and to Sarah and Thankful £2 each, a bed and other articles to be divided equally. His personal estate was appraised at £431, 16 s., 6 p., and his real estate at £910, and his mulatto boy Tom at £60—all I presume in old tenor currency, corn being appraised at £1 per bushel—that is 50 coppers equal to 44 cents.

He was engaged in the fisheries, and the success of himself and sons was sung by some contemporary troubadour, whose verses are remembered though the name of the poet is forgotten. He married first, Sarah, daughter of Samuel Cobb, Feb, 4, 1701-2, she died January 14, 1742, and he married in 1747 his second wife, Anna Nickerson of Chatham. He died May 15, 1748, aged 66, and is buried with his first wife in the old grave-yard in Hyannis, where their son Samuel caused grave stones to be erected to their memory.

*Children of Benjamin Bearse born in Barnstable:*

I.      Martha, born 9th Nov., 1702, married Antipas Lewis, Oct. 15, 1730.

II.     Augustine, born 3d June, 1704, married June 3, 1728, Bethia, daughter of John Linnell, she died 7th Oct., 1743, aged 39, and he married Sept. 7, 1744, for his second wife, Thankful, widow of Nathaniel Bacon. He died June 2, 1751, aged 47, and his widow, Nov. 1774, aged 70. He resided at first at Hyannis, perhaps after his second marriage, with his wife at Barnstable. He was engaged in the whale fishery and owned try-works which were sold after his death. He had seven children, all of whom are named in his will. 1. Prince, born 12th March

1730-1, married Desire Downs, 1754; 2d, Temperance, 17th March, 1732-3, married Lemuel Lewis, March 7, 1750; 3d, Mercy, 9th March, 1734-5, married Feb. 20, 1752, Thomas Buck; 4th, Lydia, 25th Dec., 1736; 5th, Simeon, 27th June, 1739; 6th, Sarah bap'd March 9th, 1745-6, married Samuel Bearse Nov. 15, 1764; Levi, bap'd Oct. 25, 1747.

III. Elizabeth, 3d May, 1706, probably died young.

IV. Joseph, 30th Oct. 1708, married Lydia Deane Oct. 12, 1749, died in 1751, leaving a son Joseph, bap'd Apl. 14, 1754. She married Feb. 17, 1756, Thomas Annis.

V. Benjamin, 26th March, 1710. He was a blacksmith, and married Jean or Jane, daughter of Moses Godfrey of Chatham, to which town he removed, and is the ancestor of the Bearse families in that town. He died in 1753, leaving widow Jean, sons Jonathan, George, Benjamin, David and Moses, and daughters Elizabeth, wife of Thomas Eldridge, Hannah, Sarah and Martha. His real estate was appraised at £399, 11s., and his personal estate at £204, 2s., 3d., probably in lawful money.

VI. Jesse, 22d Oct., 1712, probably died young.

VII. Priscilla, 5th June, 1713, married Oct. 16, 1735, Elnathan Lewis.

VIII. David, 27th March, 1716, probably died young.

IX. Peter, 25th Oct., 1718, married Nov. 12, 1741, Deborah, daughter of Capt. Samuel Bacon, and had 1st, Samuel, 10th Sept., 1742, who married Nov. 15, 1764, Sarah Bearse; 2d, Jesse, 2d Nov. 1743; 3d, David, 20th Nov., 1745; 4th, Edward, 12th June, 1750.

X. Samuel, 9th Dec., 1720, died Oct. 30, 1751, aged 30 years. He resided in Yarmouth at the time of his death, and in his will dated 15th Oct., 1751, he orders tomb-stones to be placed at the graves of his father Benjamin and mother Sarah. He devises his estate to his brothers, sisters and cousins [nephews]. To his cousin [nephew] Samuel, son of his brother Peter, his gold buttons.

XI. Sarah, 5th July, 1722, married Ebenezer Nickerson of Yarmouth, Feb. 17, 1744.

XII. Thankful, Feb. 4, 1724, married Shobael Nickerson, March 6, 1746.

XIII. Stephen, named in his father's will, but I find nothing farther respecting him.

Ebenezer Bearse, son of Joseph, married 25th Nov., 1708, Elizabeth, daughter of Samuel Cobb. She died 15th July, 1711, and he married Joanna Lumbert, Sept. 4, 1712. He died Feb. 1759, and his widow being "non compus," had a guardian appointed May 9, 1759. In his will he names his grandsons Daniel and Solomon, children of his son Stephen, deceased, his son Ebenezer, and daughters Bethiah Lovell, Abigail Lewis, Elizabeth Basset and Ruth Pitcher.

*Children born in Barnstable.*

I. Bethiah. born 6th Aug., 1709, married John Lovell Nov. 14, 1732.

II. Samuel, 26th Feb., 1711. His grandfather Cobb gave him a legacy in his will, and his father was appointed his guardian March 27, 1728. He probably died unmarried.

III. Elizabeth, 22d March, 1714, died young.

IV: Abigail, 22d Nov., 1715, married Melatiah Lewis, Oct. I, 1742.

V. Ebenezer, 1st March, 1717, married Mary Berry of Yarmouth, 1754.

VI. Daniel, 17th July, 1720. Probably died young.

VII. Stephen, born 1st Oct., 1721, married Hannah Coleman, June 9, 1748, and had sons Daniel and Solomon, named in their grandfather's will.

VIII. Rebecca, born 3d June, 1725. Probably died young.

IX. Patience, bap'd 6th April, 1729. Probably died young.

X. Elizabeth, bap'd 19th Oct., 1729, married Nathaniel Basset of Rochester, 1752.

XI. Ruth, bap'd 2d June, 1734, married Jonathan Pitcher, Feb. 9, 1758.

John Bearse, son of Joseph, married Eleanor Lewis 15th Nov., 1711. He died May 3, 1760, aged 72. His children were Lydia, born 28th July, 1712, who married Capt. John Cullio, a Scotchman, Jan'y 1, 1735; John, who married Lydia Lumbert, Feb. 12, 1746; Hannah, who married Jabez Bearse, March 26, 1761, second wife; Eleanor, who married John Loggee, Jan'y 13, 1753; Martha, who married Isaac Lewis, Feb. 10, 1748; Mary and Dinah.

Josiah Bearse, son of Joseph, married Zerviah Newcomb, by whom he had no children, and second Mary. He was dismissed from the East Barnstable Church to the Church in Greenwich, Conn., Dec. 29, 1734, and afterwards to New Fairfield, in the same State. His children born in Barnstable were Anna, 11th July, 1719; Josiah, 3d Feb., 1720-1; Eunice, 2d Jan'ry, 1722-3, died April 6, 1727; Jonathan, born 22d Nov., 1724, died Dec. 2, 1731; Lois, born 17th July, 1726; Thomas, 10th March, 1728-9, and Eunice, 13th Feb., 1731-2; Martha, June 26, 1738; Mary, May 8, 1741.

James Bearse, son of Joseph, married March 19, 1719-20, Mary Fuller, and second, Thankful Linnell in 1726. He died Oct. 11, 1758, aged 66. In his will dated 13th Sept., 1758, he gives to his wife Thankful, his Indian maid servant Thankful Pees, and other property in lieu of dower. To his son Jabez, the estate that was Augustine Bearse's, and one-half of the cedar swamp near his house; to his daughter Thankful Lumbert, £20 lawful money, and one-fourth of his in-door moveables; and to Lemuel all the rest of his estate. His children born in Barnstable were

I. Jabez, 20th Feb., 1720-1, married Nov. 26, 1747, Elizabeth Hallet, and second, March 26, 1761, Hannah Bearse.

II. James, 3d Feb., 1728-9, died Sept. 29, 1729.

III. Lemuel, 3d May, 1731, married Patience Phinney, April 30, 1761.

IV. Thankful, 1st Aug., 1736, married Lemuel Lumbert, Sept. 20, 1753.

# BAKER.

The Baker families in Barnstable and West Barnstable, are descendants of Rev. Nicholas Baker of Scituate; the Hyannis families from Francis, who settled in Yarmouth.

Rev. Nicholas Baker was a graduate of St. John's College, Cambridge, England, had his Batchelor's degree in 1631-2, and Master of Arts, 1635. His brother Nathaniel came over with him and both settled at Hingham in 1635. He received a share in the first division of house lots in that town. He afterwards became a large landholder in Hull. He was ordained in Scituate in 1660, where he was instrumental in effecting a reconciliation of the two churches which had held no communication with each other for twenty-five years. Cotton Mather says: "Honest Nicholas Baker of Scituate, was so good a logician that he could offer up to God a reasonable service, so good an arithmetician that he could wisely number his days, and so good an orator that he persuaded himself to be a Christian." He died Aug. 22, 1678, aged 67, of "that horror of mankind, and reproach of medicine, the stone," a memorable example of patience under suffering.

He was twice married. His first wife died at Scituate in 1661, and he married the following year his second wife Grace, who died in Barnstable, January 22, 1696-7. In his will dated 1678, he names his wife Grace, whom he appointed executrix, his brother Nathaniel Baker, his sons Samuel and Nicholas, and four daughters, namely, Mary, who married Stephen Vinal, 26th Feb., 1662; Elizabeth, married 1664, John Vinal; Sarah, married Josiah Litchfield, and Deborah married 1678, Israel Chittenden.

Samuel, to whom his father gave an estate in Hull, was a freeman of that town in 1677. He married Fear, daughter of Isaac Robinson, and had a family. May 12, 1687, he was admitted an inhabitant of Barnstable, and the same year he and his wife were admitted to the Barnstable Church by dismission from the Church at Hull. The venerable Isaac Robinson resided a year or two at the close of his life with his daughter Fear, and the fact that the widow Grace Baker had also resided in this family, probably gave rise to the tradition that Isaac Robinson's mother came over with him, and died in Barnstable.

I find no record of the children of Samuel and Fear Baker. Deacon John and Nathaniel were their sons, and Mary, who married Oct. 26, 1699, Adam Jones, and Grace, who married Dec. 16, 1701, Israel Luce, were probably their daughters.

Deacon John Baker married 14th Oct. 1696, Anna, daughter of Samuel Annable. She died March 21, 1732-3, "aged near 57 years," and was buried in the ancient graveyard at West Barnstable. After the death of his wife he removed to Windham, Conn.

*Children born in Barnstable.*

I.      Annah, 8th Sept., 1697, married Oct. 17, 1717, Capt. Samuel Lombard.  She died May 19, 1747.
II.     Mary, 18th Aug., 1699, married April 20, 1720, Benjamin Lothrop, and afterwards removed to Connecticut.
III.    John, 14th June, 1701.  Died young.
IV.     Rebecca, 8th Sept . 1704.
V.      Samuel, 7th Sept., 1706, married May 30, 1732, Prudence Jenkins; had 1st, Martha, 24th Jan'y, 1732-3; 2d, Anna, 12th May, 1735; 3d, Bethia, 12th June, 1737; 4th, Samuel, 30th Sept., 1740; 5th, Mercy, 30th May, 1743.   This family removed to Windham, Conn.
VI.     Mary, 25th March, 1710, married Lemuel Hedge of Yarmouth, 1733.
VII.    Mehitabel, 7th May 1712, married Eben'r Crosby of Yarmouth, Jan'y 10, 1734.
VIII.   Abigail, 1st Feb., 1713-4, married Ichabod Lathrop of Tolland, Conn., Nov. 9, 1732.
IX.     John, 1st Dec., 1716, married Mercy Cary of Windham, Conn., Dec. 7, 1744.
X.      Hannah, 24th March, 1718.

Nathaniel Baker resided in the East Parish, his house, yet remaining, is on Baker's Lane.  His first wife, the mother of all his children, is not named on the record.  He married 5th Jan'y, 1718-19, Wid. Mercy Lewis.  He died in 1750, and his widow, Dec. 7, 1768, aged 80, according to the Church records; but according to the town records, she was older.

### Children born in Barnstable.

I.    Benney, born 15th Aug., 1705, died June, 1706.

II.    Mercy, born 4th Feb., 1706, married Nov. 7, 1728, Sylvanus Cobb, and had eight children.

III.    Sarah, born 4th Oct., 1708, died Nov. 19, 1708.

IV.    Nathaniel, born 15th Dec., 1709, married 1732, Ann Lumbard of Newtown, and had 1st, Isaac, born 2d April, 1734; 2d, Mercy, 6th May, 1738; 3d, Benne, 2d Oct., 1751; 4th, Anna, 18th Jan'y, 1754. Isaac of this family married Rebecca Lewis, Oct. 6, 1754, and had Rebecca, James, Lewis, Ezekiel, Nathaniel, John, who removed to Brewster, and Isaac who died in Barnstable, unmarried, about 20 years ago.

V.    Nicholas, born 6th Nov., 1711, married Dorcas Backus of Sandwich, was of Dighton, removed to Barnstable in 1635. He was a mariner, and died Jan'y 31, 1739-40. He had 1st, Nath'l who died young; 2d, Ebenezer, and 3d, David.

VI.    Sarah, 2d Nov., 1713, married Oct. 26, 1732, Jona. Sturgis.

VII.    Thankful, 28th March, 1715, married Jan'y 1, 1734, Jesse Cobb.

VIII.    Benne, 28th Sept., 1716, married Patience Lumbard, Nov. 19, 1741. He died 29th Dec., 1747, and she died 28th Dec., 1748, leaving two orphan children, John, born 3d Jan'y, 1743, and Thankful, born 29th June, 1745—both of whom married and had families.

IX.    Elizabeth, born 9th March, 1718, married Benjamin Nye, Jr., of Falmouth, Sept. 28, 1738.

There are very few descendants of Honest Nicholas Baker, now remaining in Barnstable. Dea. John, who removed to Windham, Conn., was a prominent man; but the other members of the family have not been distinguished.

The Baker families at Hyannis are descendants of Francis, who settled in Yarmouth. Their pedigree is as follows: Francis Baker, from Great St. Albans, Hertfordshire, England, came over in the Planter, 1635, aged 24, married in 1641, Isabel Twining, and had six sons and two daughters. Nathaniel, his eldest son, born March 27, 1642, had three sons; Samuel, the eldest, born Oct. 29, 1670, married July

30, 1702, Elizabeth Berry, and had three sons and five daughters; the eldest son, Judah, born Aug. 19, 1705, married Feb. 15, 1728-9, Mercy Burgess, and had three sons and five daughters; the oldest son, Timothy, born Ap. 21, 1732, married ———, 1753, Kezia, and had six sons (one of whom was the father of the present Capt. Timothy Baker), and three daughters.

The descendants of Francis Baker of Yarmouth, may be numbered by tens of thousands. None have been very much distinguished; but among them will be found very many able seamen, and good business men.

# BARKER AND BORDEN.

John Barker, Sen., of Duxbury, married in 1632, Ann, daughter of John Williams, Sen., of Scituate. He removed to Marshfield, then called Rexame, in 1638, and was drowned in 1652. He had children Deborah, John, Williams, and perhaps others. His widow Ann married Abraham Blush of Barnstable, and died Feb. 16, 1657-8. Deborah came to Barnstable with her mother and probably her son John. At fourteen John chose his uncle, Capt. John Williams of Scituate, his guardian, with the understanding that he should be brought up to some trade or profitable employment. After he became of age, John sued his uncle, who was a man of great wealth, for wages during his minority, averring that his uncle had violated his contract; that he had not brought him up to a trade that would be of use to him, and that his uncle had kept him employed in menial duties, and therefore he was entitled to wages. He also brought an action for rents collected from his estate in Marshfield, during his minority, and his uncle brought an action against him for slander. The details of these actions occupy much space on the records. They were finally settled by the good offices of mutual friends. Afterwards he had another lawsuit with his uncle, making it evident that they did not live together on terms of amity or friendship.

He was a sergeant in Philip's war, probably in the company of which his uncle was captain, and was severely wounded in an engagement with the Indians, from the effects of which it seems he never entirely recovered, for in 1680 he was freed from serving in the train bands on account of the injury received. He removed from Scituate in 1676 or 7, and resided in Barnstable till 1683, and perhaps later, when he removed to Marshfield, of which town he was the deputy in 1689, and soon after returned to Scituate, where he died Dec. 1729, aged nearly 30 years.

John Barker, Esq., was a prominent man in the Colony. He was often engaged as an attorney for parties in the transaction of legal and other business; was a referee in many important cases. Though a resident of Barnstable, only when young, and for about ten years after the time of his marriage, he was not entirely disconnected with the business of the town and county, after his removal. He was one of the referees in the important case between the Winslows and Clarks, which alienated those families and made their descendants bitter enemies for more than a century.

The account which Mr. Deane gives of this family will not bear the test of criticism. He says that Williams Barker was a son of John Barker, Esq., second of the name, and that Capt. John Williams gave his farm in Scituate to Williams Barker. The latter was a brother, not a son of John Barker, 2d. Capt. Williams in his will, gives to "Nephew Williams Barker, son of John Barker of Marshfield, the 200 acre farm formerly purchased of Mr. Hatherly." He also gives legacies to nephews John Barker of Marshfield and Abraham Blush of Boston.

It can be shown by the Barnstable town records that if John Barker, 2d., had a son Williams, he could not have been over six years of age at the date of Capt. John Williams' will in 1691; yet Mr. Deane assures us that Samuel Barker, Esq., only son of Williams Barker, was born in the year 1684; that is, that Samuel was only one year younger than his father Williams. If this is true, the Barkers of early times were a more prolific race than the present John Barker ——— of Barnstable.

The following account of his family is principally obtained from the Barnstable town records. He married Jan. 18, 1676-7, Desire, youngest daughter of Anthony Annable of Barnstable. She died, according to the inscription on her grave-stones, at Scituate, July 24, 1706, in the 53d year of her age. He married the same year for his second wife Hannah, daughter of Thomas Loring of Hingham, and widow of Rev. Jeremiah Cushing of Scituate. She died May 30, 1710, aged 46, and he took for his third wife Sarah ———, who died Sept. 7, 1730.

### Children born in Barnstable.

I.  John, born 4th May, 1678. He married in 1706, Hannah, daughter of Rev. Jeremiah Cushing, whose widow

had married, as above stated, his father.   This is the
statement of Mr. Savage, and I think reliable, though
in direct conflict with the account given by Mr. Deane.
II.   Desire, born 22d Sept., 1680.
III.  Anne, 26th Aug., 1682, died 22d Nov., 1682.
IV.   Anne, born 1st Nov., 1683.

He probably had other children after his removal from
Barnstable.   His sister Deborah married William Barden,
Burden or Borden.   He was, perhaps, one of the youths of
fourteen years of age, of good habits, sent over to be bound
out as apprentices.   He came over probably in 1638, and
was bound to Thomas Boardman of Plymouth, to learn the
trade of a carpenter, Jan'y 10, 1638-9; six and one-half
years of the term of his apprenticeship being unexpired,
Boardman released him, and he was bound to John Barker
of Marshfield, to learn the trade of a bricklayer.   After the
expiration of his apprenticeship, he went to Concord, then
a mere settlement, and after his marriage he resided a short
time in Duxbury.   From Barnstable he removed to Middleborough, his wife being dismissed from the Barnstable
Church to Middleborough in 1683.   31st Oct., 1666, John
Bates and William Burden were fined 3 shillings, 4 pence
each for "breaking the King's peace by striking each other.
Burden was drunk at the time, and was fined 5 shillings beside, and Bates was ordered by the Court to pay Burden 20
shillings for abusing him."

He married Feb., 1660, Deborah Barker, and had
children born in Barnstable, namely:
I.    Mercy, born 1st Nov., 1662.
II.   Deborah, 28th June, 1665.
III.  John, 17th March, 1667-8.
IV.   Stephen, 15th April, 1669.
V.    Abraham, 14th May, 1674.
VI.   Joseph, Sept., 1675.
VII.  Anna, 26th Aug., 1677.

John "Bardon," son of William, had John, born May
1, 1704, in Middleborough, Ichabod, Dec. 18, 1705.

Stephen "Borden," son of William of Middleborough,
had Sarah, Apl. 30, 1695; William, Mar. 2, 1697; Abigail,
Mar. 3, 1698-9; Stephen, May, 1701; Timothy, Jan'y 3,
1703-4; Mary, Oct. 27, 1705, and Hannah, March 13,
1707-8.

Abraham, son of William, married Mary Booth, 1697.

Perhaps the reader may think I am severe in my criticisms on the Rev. Mr. Deane. All I do is to take his own statements and place them in a position where their absurdity will be seen. No one has a higher respect for Mr. Deane than the writer. He was a pioneer in the work, and the wonder is that he has made so few, rather than so many mistakes.

In his article on the Cushing family, he says that Samuel Barker, Esq., was a son of John Barker, Esq., and that he married in 1706, Hannah Cushing. This is much more probable than his other statement that Samuel was the son of Williams.

The children of this Samuel were, Samuel, Ignatius, Ezekiel, Hannah and Deborah. Samuel married Deborah Gorham of Barnstable. The Crockers at West Barnstable are also connected by marriage with the Barkers.

The Bordens of Fall River probably descend from Stephen, son of William of Barnstable, and not from the Rhode Island families of the name.

# BODFISH.

The ancestor of this family wrote his name "Robert Botfish," yet on the records it is written Botfish, Botfish, Bodfish, Badfish, Bootfish and Boatfish. He was early at Lynn, a freeman May 5th, 1635, and of Sandwich in 1637, of which town he was one of the original proprietors. The Indian title to the lands in Sandwich was purchased by William Bradford and his partners of the old Plymouth Company in 1637, for £16, 19 shillings, payable "in comodities," and Jan'y 24, 1647-8, they assigned their rights to Edmund Freeman, and on the 26th of February following, he assigned the same to George Allen, John Vincent, William Newland, Robert Botfish, Anthony Wright and Richard Bourne, a committee of the proprietors of the town of Sandwich. In 1640, the meadow lands were divided, giving to each in proportion to his "quality and condition." Robert Bodfish had five acres assigned to him, a little less than an average amount.

Jan'y 1, 1638-9, Robert Bodfish "desired to become a freeman of the Plymouth Colony; in 1641 he was a surveyor of highways; in 1644 on the grand jury, and the same year licensed "to draw wine in Sandwich." He died in 1651, leaving a wife Bridget, who became Dec. 15, 1657, the second wife of Samuel Hinckley (the father of Governor Thomas.) He had a son Joseph, born in Sandwich April 3, 1651, a daughter Mary, who married Nov., 1659, John Crocker, and Sarah, who married June 21, 1663, Peter Blossom, and a son Robert, who did not become an inhabitant of Barnstable. The family removed to Barnstable in 1657.

Joseph, the ancestor of all of the name in Barnstable,

married Elizabeth Besse, daughter of Anthony Besse,* of
Sandwich. He resided at West Barnstable; his house was
on Bursley's Lane, (Proprietor's Records), on the farm
owned by the late Lemuel Bursley, and died Dec. 2, 1744,
in the 94th year of his age.

When he was eighteen, Plymouth had been settled fifty
years, and though liberal bounties had been paid to English
and Indians for wolves' heads, yet these ravenous animals
abounded in the Colony. In 1654, the whole number killed
was nineteen—of which three were killed in Barnstable, and
in 1655, thirty-one—nine in Barnstable. In 1690, the
number killed was thirteen, and in 1691, nineteen. Jonathan Bodfish said his grandfather could set a trap as cun-
ningly as the oldest Indians, and that the duck or the goose
that ventured to come within gunshot of him, rarely escaped
being shot. Wolf Neck, so named because it was the resort
of these animals, was about half a mile from Joseph Bodfish's house, and there he set his traps. Once he narrowly
escaped losing his own life. Seeing a large wolf in his trap,
he incautiously approached with a rotten pine pole in his
hand. He struck—the pole broke in his hand, and the en-
raged beast sprang at him with the trap and broken chain
attached to his leg. Mr. Bodfish stepped suddenly one side,
and the wolf passed by him. Before the wolf could recover,
Mr. Bodfish was beyond his reach. This trap is preserved
in his family as an heir-loom.

----

*Anthony Besse, born in 1609. Came over in the James, 1636, from
London, settled in Lynn and removed to Sandwich in 1637, and was
many years a preacher to the Indians. He died in 1657, leaving wife
Jane, and children Nehemiah: David, born May 23, 1649, killed in the
Rehobeth battle March 26, 1676; Ann, who was the wife of Andrew
Hallet, Jr., of Yarmouth; Mary; and Elizabeth who married Joseph
Bodfish.

His widow married, second, George Barlow, and had by him John,
who has descendants, and Rebecca who married William Hunter. The
widow Barlow died in 1693. Her last marriage was an unhappy connection. Barlow was appointed June 1, 1658, Marshal of Sandwich,
Barnstable and Yarmouth. His name adds no honor to the annals of
the Old Colony—a hard-hearted, intolerant, tyrannical man, abusing the
power entrusted to him, and seemingly taking delight in confiscating the
property of innocent men and women, or in dragging them to prison, to
the stocks, or the whipping post.

In his family he exercised the same tyrannical spirit, and it is not surprising that the aid of the magistrate was frequently called into requi-
sition to settle the difficulties that arose. The reader of the Colony records may think the Besses were not the most amiable of women—perhaps they were not; but in these family quarrels Barlow was in fault,
and deserving of the infamy which will forever attach to his name.

Some years after a wolf was followed by hunters from Wareham to Barnstable, and they wished Mr. Bodfish to join them, but he declined. Having studied the habits of the animal, he felt certain it would return on the same track. Taking his gun he went into the woods, concealed himself within gunshot on the leeward side of the track, and waited for the return of the wolf. He was not disappointed, the wolf at last appeared and was shot. He returned to his house, and soon after the Wareham hunters came in and reported that they had followed the wolf to the lower part of Yarmouth, and the dogs had there lost the track, and they gave up the pursuit. They felt a little chagrined when the dead body of the wolf was shown to them.

All his sons, excepting Benjamin, were good gunners. Wolf hunting, however, was not a sport in which they engaged. It is said that the last wolf killed in Barnstable was shot by Joseph Bodfish; but this story requires confirmation.

Joseph Bodfish* joined the Church in Barnstable, Feb. 12, 1689, N. S., and his wife Elizabeth on the 16th July following. His seven children, Benjamin, Ebenezer, Nathan, Robert, Elizabeth and Melatiah, were baptized March 26, 1699, and his daughter Sarah, April 6, 1700.

### Children born in Barnstable.

I.    John, born Dec. 2, 1675. Removed to Sandwich, where he has descendants. He married Sarah Nye, May 24, 1704, and had Mary, March 9, 1705-6; John, Feb. 5  1708-9; Hannah, Sept. 23, 1711; Joanna, Oct. 22, 1714; Sarah, March 21, 1717; Elizabeth, March 30, 1720; Joseph, Sept. 20, 1725.

II.   Joseph, born Oct. 1677, married Oct. 11, 1712, Thankful Blush, daughter of Joseph. He was not living in 1735.

III.  Mary, born March 1, 1679-80, married Josiah Swift, of S., April 19, 1706.

IV.   Hannah, born May, 1681, married Richard Thomas. He had baptized Dec. 4, 1715, Peleg, Ebenezer and Ann. The children of Richard and Hannah recorded,

---

*Erroneously printed "Bradford" in the Genealogical Register for 1856, page 350. Elizabeth, his wife, was baptized on the day she was admitted to the Church—a fact perhaps not without significance in the history of the Besses.

are Anne, born June 15, 1715, and Joseph, born Aug. 24, 1721. His son Ebenezer and grandson Nathan, had families resident in Barnstable. Joseph Bodfish, Sen., calls Ebenezer Thomas his grandson.

V.   Benjamin, born July 20, 1683, married Nov. 10, 1709, Lydia Crocker, daughter of Jonathan. He died in 1760, aged 77. He was an active man, and may be called the founder of the Bodfish family of recent times. He bought for £100, by a deed from his father-in-law, Jonathan Crocker, dated Oct. 20, 1713, one-half of the twenty-acre lot and meadow which the latter bought of his father, John Crocker, including the dwelling-house then standing thereon. This tract of land is situated on the east of Scorton Hill, and is bounded southerly by the County road. It was a part of the great lot of Abraham Blush, containing fifty acres, and sold by him Feb. 10, 1668, to John Crocker, Sen., and by him given in his will to children of his brother, Dea. William Crocker, of whom the John Crocker, first named, was one. The house above mentioned, a high, single house, with a leantoo, was occupied by Benjamin Bodfish and his son Jonathan till 1809, when it was taken down, and the present Bodfish house built on the same spot.

VI.   Nathan, born Dec. 27, 1685. He married Abigail Bursley, daughter of John. She died March 31, 1739, in the 49th year of her age, and is called on her grave-stones at West Barnstable, the wife of Nathaniel. I find no record of his family, and tradition says he had no children. A Nathan Bodfish married Patience Hathaway, and had Abigail, July 10, 1756, and Patience, Dec. 10, 1761. But this man was perhaps a son of Robert, by his first wife.

VII.   Ebenezer, born March 10, 1687-8, removed to Woodbridge, N. J., where he died unmarried in 1739, and bequeathed his estate by will to his brother Benjamin, who was executor, and to his sisters Hannah Thomas and Mary Swift.

VIII. Elizabeth, born Aug. 27, 1690, married and had a family—not living in 1735.

IX.   Rebecca, born Feb. 22, 1692-3, married Benjamin Fuller, March 25, 1714. She died March 10, 1727-8, leaving a family.

X.    Melatiah, born April 17, 1669, married Samuel Ful-
      ler, June 20, 1725-6.
XI.   Robert, born Oct. 10, 1698. He was published in
      1729, to Jemima Nye of Sandwich. He afterwards
      married Dec. 10, 1739, Elizabeth Hadaway, and had
      Elizabeth, Sept. 11, 1741, and Ebenezer, Feb. 15,
      1743-4.
XII.  Sarah, born Feb. 20, 1700, married March 8, 1726-7,
      Joseph Smith, Jr., his second wife, by whom she had
      Sarah, born Jan'y 22, 1727-8.
      Joseph Bodfish, son of Joseph, born Oct. 1677, mar-
ried 11th Oct. 1712, Thankful, daughter of Joseph Blush of
West Barnstable.

### Children born in Barnstable.

I.    Elizabeth, 6th Sept., 1713, married Eben Goodspeed,
      3d, Sept. 29, 1736.
II.   Hannah, 18th July, 1716, married Samuel Blossom,
      Oct. 28, 1744.
III.  Mary, 17th June, 1719, married Joseph Nye of Sand-
      wich, Dec. 10, 1741.
IV.   Joseph, 8th March, 1722, married Mehetabel Good-
      speed, 1749. He resided at West Barnstable, and
      had Mary, Hannah, Thankful, Lydia and Ruth, twins,
      Thankful again, Elizabeth and Joseph.
V.    Thankful, 6th June, 1724, married Peter Conant,
      May 4, 1741.
      Benjamin Bodfish, son of Joseph, born 20th July, 1683,
married Lydia Crocker, 10th Nov. 1709.

### Children born in Barnstable.

I.    Sylvanus, 2d Sept., 1710, married Mary Smith, Dec.
      20, 1738.
II.   Hannah, 12th Feb., 1712, married Caleb Nye of
      Sandwich.
III.  Thankful, 19th Feb., 1714, married Joseph Shelly of
      Raynham.
IV.   Solomon, 20th March, 1716, married Hannah Burs-
      ley, Jr.
V.    Joseph, 16th April, 1718, married and had a family.
VI.   Benjamin, 18th March, 1720.
VII.  Lydia, baptized 9th June, 1723.
VIII. Rachel, baptized Jan'ry, 1725-6.

IX.　Jonathan, born 10th Aug., 1727, married Desire Howland, May 3,·1753. He died Jan'y 1818, aged 91, and his wife April 1813, aged 81. The farm of Mr. Jonathan Bodfish and his sons, at the time of his death, consisted of six hundred acres of tillage, meadow and woodland. They had all their property in common, and at the end of each year invested their surplus earnings in real estate. They were farmers, raising large crops—often 400 bushels of Indian corn in a season—and of other agricultural products, a proportional amount. They usually kept 50 head of cattle and 120 sheep. Benjamin was a carpenter and mason, and a very skillful workman. Isaac lived thirteen years with Edward Wing, receiving from $10 to $13 per month as wages. It is said of him, that during all this time, his idle expenses amounted to only 20 cents. The earnings of both were put into the common stock. For more than seventy years the property of Jonathan Bodfish was owned in common, and during the whole time nothing occurred to disturb the harmony and good feeling which subsisted between the different members of the family. They were hard-working, prudent and industrious; and in all their dealings were honest and honorable. Jonathan, the father, was treasurer, and all deeds, excepting enough to make his sons voters and qualify them for holding civil offices, were taken in his name. Jonathan Bodfish, the father of this remarkable family, was a venerable old man—the patriarch of his family. In person he was nearly six feet tall, large and well proportioned, weighing ordinarily 230 pounds. His sons, excepting Josiah, were over six feet, large boned, spare men, and in personal appearance, would hardly be recognized as belonging to the same family with Jonathan.

The children of Jonathan Bodfish born in Barnstable were

I.　Sylvanus, born Nov. 15, 1754; died in 1801, aged 47. He did not marry, and his estate was a part of the common stock.

II.　Benjamin, born April 14, 1756, died Jan'y 14, 1827, aged 70. He was a carpenter, mason and farmer; did not marry, and his estate was also a part of the common stock.

III.    John, born March 16, 1761, married Mary, daughter
        of Joseph Smith, and had a family. He was for
        many years one of the selectmen of Barnstable. He
        died Aug. 1847, aged 86, and his wife in 1849.
IV.     Isaac, born July 22, 1763, married Elizabeth Bod-
        fish, and had a family. He died Aug. 30, 1837,
        aged 74.
V.      Josiah, born Nov. 8, 1765; died Oct. 8, 1845, aged
        80. He did not marry.
VI.     Deborah, born June 11, 1768, married Benjamin
        Goodspeed.
VII.    Simeon, born Feb. 10, 1771; died young.
VIII.   Alice, born about 1773; did not marry, and died
        April 21, 1854, aged 81.

    Some members of the Bodfish family removed to New
York, New Jersey and other places, and their connection
with the Barnstable stock can be easily traced.

# BLOSSOM.

Deacon Thomas Blossom, one of the Pilgrims, and the ancestor of the Blossom family of Barnstable, came from Leyden to Plymouth, England; but being on board the Speedwell, did not obtain a passage in the Mayflower from England in 1620. He returned to Leyden to encourage the emigration of the residue of Mr. Robinson's Church. He came over in 1629, with Mr. Higginson and others, who were bound to Salem. Judge Mitchell says he was first deacon of the Church in Plymouth, and his letter to Gov. Bradford gives evidence that he was a well educated and a pious man. He died in Plymouth in the year 1632.* Of his family no record has been preserved. He had a son in 1620, who went to England with him and returned to Leyden; but was not living Dec. 1625. At the latter date he had two other children, but their names are not recorded. Circumstantial evidence proves, beyond a reasonable doubt, that he had two sons who survived him; Thomas, who was sixteen or over in 1643, and Peter who was younger.

Anna, the widow of Dea. Thomas Blossom, married Henry Rowley, Oct. 17, 1633. They were members of Mr. Lothrop's Church at its organization, Jan'ry 8, 1634-5, and removed with him to Barnstable in 1639. Thomas and Peter came to Barnstable with their mother, and were probably members of the family of their father-in-law. Thomas

---

*The date of the death of Deacon Blossom is uncertain. Gov. Bradford, who was his contemporary. says he died of the malignant fever which pervaded in the summer of 1633. The accurate Prince copies Gov. Bradford's statement, and the careful Mr. Savage refers to Prince as his authority. Judge Mitchel says "about 1633." Notwithstanding this array of authorities it can perhaps be demonstrated that Dea. Blossom died in 1632. In the tax lists for the town of Plymouth, dated Jan'y 12, 1633, N. S., (1632 O. S.), Dea. Thomas Blossom is not taxed; but the Wid. Blossom is. The record now existing was made in March 1632-3, and proves conclusively that Dea. Blossom was dead when that record was made.

was a landholder in 1647, and he and his brother Peter had a lot granted to them in partnership at Cotuit. Thomas does not appear to have been a householder. He resided in the easterly part of the town, and after his marriage, probably at the house of Thomas Lothrop, who was father-in-law to his wife. He was a mariner, and at the time of his death, April 22, 1650, was on a fishing voyage.

Peter removed with his father-in-law to West Barnstable about the year 1650. His farm, containing forty acres of upland, was on the east of the Bursley farm, and separated from it by Boat Cove and the stream of fresh water emptying into it. On the northeast it was bounded by Thomas Sharv's marsh and the land of Henry Rowley, and on the southeast by the farm of Mr. Thomas Dexter, Sen'r. He owned twelve acres of meadow. A part of his land is now owned by his descendants.

### Children of Deacon Thomas Blossom born in Leyden.

I.     A son, who died before Dec. 1625.
II.    Thomas, born about the year 1620, married June 18, 1645, by Major John Freeman, to Sarah Ewer, at the house of Thomas Lothrop in Barnstable. She was a daughter of Thomas Ewer, deceased, of Charlestown, and was then residing with her mother. He and another Barnstable man, Samuel Hallet, were drowned at Nauset, April 22, 1650. He left one child, a daughter named "Sara," and had, perhaps, a posthumous son named Peter.
III.   Peter, born after the year 1627, married Sarah Bodfish, June 21, 1663. He resided at West Barnstable, was a farmer, and died about 1700, intestate. His estate was settled Oct. 5, 1706, by mutual agreement between his widow Sarah and sons Thomas, Joseph and Jabez, and daughters Thankful Fuller and Mercy Howland. His children born in Barnstable were :

I.     Mercy, born 9th April, 1664; died in 1670.
II.    Thomas, born 20th Dec., 1667, married Dec. 1695, Fear Robinson. He resided at West Barnstable.
III.   Sarah, born 1669; died 1671.
IV.    Joseph, born 10th Dec. 1673, married Mary Pinchon, 17th June, 1696.
V.     Thankful, born 1675, married Joseph Fuller, 1700.

VI.   Mary, born Aug. 1678, married Shubael Howland, Dec. 13, 1700.

VII.  Jabez, born 16th Feb., 1680, married Mary Goodspeed, 9th Sept. 1710.

Thomas Blossom, son of Peter, married Dec. 1695, Fear, daughter of John Robinson of Falmouth, and a great-grand-daughter of Rev. John Robinson of Leyden. His children born in Barnstable were :

I.    Peter, born 28th Aug. 1698, married Hannah Isum, June 9, 1720. According to the town record he had an only son, Seth, born 15th March, 1721-2. Seth married Jan'ry 8, 1746-7, Sarah Churchill of Sandwich, and second Abigail Crocker of Barnstable, Jan'ry 10, 1754. Children—Churchill, 15th Oct. 1749 ; David, 12th Jan'ry, 1755 ; Peter, 4th Dec. 1756 ; Abigail, 10th May, 1760 ; Seth, 4th Dec. 1763 ; Hannah, 15th Aug. 1766 ; Levi, 15th April, 1772, who removed to Bridgewater.

II.   John, born 17th April, 1699, married April 6, 1726, Thankful Burgess of Yarmouth, and had two children born in Yarmouth. Fear, Feb. 3d, 1730-1, and Thankful, March 5th, 1732-3.

III.  Sarah, born 16th Dec. 1703 ; died young.

IV.   Elizabeth, born Oct. 1705, married July 1, 1725, Israel Butler.

V.    Sarah, 30th July, 1709, married James Case of Lebanon, Sept. 23, 1736.

Joseph Blossom, son of Peter, married 17th June, 1696, Mary Pinchon. She died April 6, 1706, and he married second, Mary ———.

*Children born in Barnstable.*

I.    A child, born 14th March, 1696-7 ; died March, 1696-7.

II.   A son, born May, 1702 ; died May, 1702.

III.  Joseph, born 14th March, 1703-4, married Temperance Fuller, March 30, 1727. Children born in Barnstable : Lydia, 19th March, 1729, married Matthias Fuller, 1765 ; James, born 9th Feb. 1731, married Jan'ry 19, 1758, Bethia Smith ; Sarah, 14th Oct. 1734, and Mary, 14th Sept. 1736.

IV.   A son, May 1705 ; died June, 1705.

V.    Mary, 11th Dec. 1709, married Joseph Bates of Middleborough. 1743.

VI. Thankful, 25th March, 1711; married Eben'r Thomas, Dec. 8, 1736.

Jabez Blossom, son of Peter, married 9th of Sept. 1710, Mercy Goodspeed.

### Children born in Barnstable.

I. Sylvanus, born 20th Jan'ry, 1713, married Charity Snell, 1738, and settled in South Bridgewater. His grandson Alden went to Turner, Maine, where he was a general and high-sheriff.

Sylvanus is the only child of Jabez recorded; but there was a Jabez Blossom, Jr., who married May 17, 1739, Hannah Backhouse of Sandwich; also, a Ruth, who married June 8, 1738, Sylvanus Barrows.

In addition to the above, there was a Peter Blossom, born as early as 1680, who was entitled to a share in the division of lands in 1703. If he was a son of Peter, son of Dea. Thomas, it is difficult to account for the omission of his name on the town and probate records. Perhaps he was a son of Thomas, Jr. None of the Blossoms, excepting the deacon, appear to have been church members, consequently their children's names do not appear on the church records.

There was a Samuel Blossom of Barnstable, who married Hannah Bodfish, Oct. 28, 1744, and had Thankful, 5th Sept. 1745; Joseph, 28th Oct. 1747; Samuel and Hannah, twins, 24th Jan'ry, 1752, and Mehitable, 23d June, 1753. The mother of this family was a church member.

There was also a Benjamin Blossom of Sandwich, published Dec. 22d, 1750, to Elizabeth Linnell, and married Oct. 31,1751, Bathsheba Percival, and had one son born in Barnstable, Benjamin, 18th Aug. 1753.

James Blossom, son of Joseph, married Jan'ry 19th, 1758, Bethia Smith, and had children born in Barnstable: James, Feb. 3, 1760; Temperance, Oct. 1761; Matthias, Sept. 12, 1765; Lucretia, Oct. 8, 1768, and Asenath, Aug. 30, 1770.

There was also a Thomas Blossom of Yarmouth, who married Thankful Paddock, 1749, and had five children born in Yarmouth, namely: Enos, Aug. 18, 1750; Thomas, March 11, 1753; Thankful, Jan'y 6, 1756; Sarah, July 13th, 1758, and Ezra, May 10, 1761.

Benjamin Blossom, of Sandwich, by his wife Elizabeth, had Sarah, Oct. 23, 1752; Mary, Nov. 27, 1757; Meribah,

Jan'y 27, 1760.

Mehitable, wife of Joseph Blossom, of Cushnet, died March 16, 1771, aged 80 years, 6 mos., and 10 days.

Benjamin, of Acushnet, died Oct. 25th, 1797, aged 76, who had by his wife Rebecca, Levi, who died May 8th, 1785, aged 8 1-2 months.

---

NOTE.—Some of the Blossoms lived in Sandwich, a fact that I was not aware of when I commenced writing this article. A consultation of the records of that town, will, I presume, enable those interested to fill up the gaps in this genealogy.

# THOMAS BOURMAN.

This name is written on the records Bourman, Burman and Boreman. Some of his descendants write it Bowman, others Bowerman. Thomas Boardman's name is written Boardman and Boreman. In some cases it is difficult to decide which man is intended. Thomas Boreman was taxed in Plymouth in 1633, and in the following year contracted to repair the fort on the hill which was a wooden structure, and Thomas Boardman being a carpenter, I infer that he was the man intended. A Thomas Boreman was a freeman of Massachusetts, March 4, 1634, and a representative from Ipswich, 1636. It has been supposed that he removed to Barnstable, but I think it very doubtful. Thomas Bourman of Barnstable could not write, and though one of the first settlers, he was not admitted to be a townsman for some reason; perhaps he favored the Quakers. It is not probable that the inhabitants of Ipswich would have selected such a man for their representative. Again, Bourman was in aftertimes a common name in that town, and there is no evidence whatever that Thomas of Ipswich removed.

Thomas Bourman was of Barnstable in 1643. He resided at West Barnstable, on a farm on the South side of the cove of meadow, at the head of Bridge Creek. It is thus described on the town records :

1. Twenty-five acres of upland, be it more or less, butting northerly upon ye marsh, easterly upon a brook, and westerly upon a brook, and so running eighty rods southerly into ye woods.

2. Sixteen acres of marsh, more or less, bounded westerly partly by John Jenkins, and partly by a ditch cast up between Abraham Blush and him ; northerly, partly by ye highway, and partly by Gdd. Blush, easterly, partly by ye great swamp and partly by Gdd. Blush's, his marsh.

3. Five acres of upland, more or less, butting north-

erly upon ye marsh, southerly upon a foot-path, easterly upon a flashy swamp, westerly upon his own land.

The above described land and meadow with his dwelling house thereon, he sold 28th Oct. 1662, to Robert Parker for £78. Bourman signed this deed with his mark; his will is signed in the same manner; but the latter would not be evidence that the testator was never able to write.

He was a surveyor of highways in 1648, and a grand juror in 1650, and was a proprietor of the lands in Sucka-nesset, now Falmouth. He died in 1663, and is called of Barnstable at the time of his death.

### Children born in Barnstable.

He married 10th of March, 1644-5, Hannah, daughter of Anthony Annable, and his children born in Barnstable were

I.    Hannah, May 1646.
II.   Thomas, Sept. 1648, married Mary Harper, April 9, 1678.
III.  Samuel, July, 1651, slain at Rehobeth, March 26, 1676.
IV.  Desire, May 1654.
V.   Mary, March 1656.
VI.  Mehitable, Sept. 1658.
VII. Tristram, Aug. 1661.

This family removed to Falmouth. They early joined the Friends. Thomas, 22d April, 1690, bought of Jonathan Hatch, Senior, and Robert Harper, agents of the inhabitants of Suckanesset, one hundred acres of land formerly John Robinson's, described as situate on the easterly side of the "Five Mile River," bounded from the head of the river on a straight line to the pond, northerly by the pond and southerly by the river. One acre to be on the' south easterly side of the road that leads from the river to Sandwich.

Samuel Bourman was a soldier in King Philip's war from Barnstable, and was slain at Rehobeth March 26, 1676. In the same battle Lieut. Samuel Fuller, John Lewis, Eleazer Clapp, Samuel Linnet and Samuel Childs of Barnstable were also killed.

Thomas Bourman was town clerk of Falmouth 1702, 1704 and 1705. March 26, 1691, Thomas Bourman and

William Wyatt, a committee to lay out lands at Woods Hole.

The following account of the family after the removal to Falmouth, collected by Mr. Newell Hoxie of Sandwich, from ancient papers, is the best I have been able to obtain. The illumination of dates would made it more intelligible :

Thomas Bourman, though belonging to the Society of Friends, was taxed for the support of the ministry in the town of Falmouth. All non-conformists were then required to pay a double tax, one to their own society and one to the settled minister of the town. Many resisted this law as tyrannical and oppressive, and of this number was Thomas Bourman. In the winter of 1705-6, he was committed to Barnstable Jail for non-payment of a ministerial tax. On the 4th of the 11th mo., 1705-6, the Friends monthly meeting, held at the house of William Allen in Sandwich, ordered "A bed and bedding to be sent to Thomas Bourman, he being in prison for the priest's rate." The following distraints was subsequently made of his property to pay his taxes to Rev. Joseph Metcalf, of Falmouth, one whose ministry neither himself nor his family attended :

19th, 3d mo. 1709—2 cows, worth £5, for £3, 12s. 2d. tax.

13th, 3d mo.—1 cow and calf, worth £2, 2s. tax.

22d, 3d mo.—1 cow worth £3, 10s. for £1, 13s. tax.

24th, 1st mo. 1710—1 cow worth £2, 14s. for £1, 17s. tax.

17th, 1st mo. 1715—1 cow worth £3, 10s. for £1, 3s. 1d. tax.

9th, 1715—1 fat swine worth £3, 00, for £1 tax.

21st, 11th mo. 1716—2 calves worth £2, 10s. for £1, 2s. 9d.

10th, 3d mo. 1728—5 sheep worth £2, 10s. for £0, 16s. tax.

30th, 3d mo. 1728—12 lbs. wool worth £1, 10s. for £0, 16s. 10d.

As these distraints were made by different constables, the presumption is that the three first named were for taxes of former years.

His son, Thomas Bowman, also, refused to pay his ministerial tax, and in 1727 the constable seized three bushels of Malt, worth 16s. 6d. to pay the same. On the 2d of the 3d mo. 1728, the constable seized one Linen Wheel and one Bason, worth 20 shillings.

These exactions were very moderate in comparison with those made by Constable Barlow half a century earlier.

Thomas Bourman, born in Barnstable, Sept. 1648, married Mary Harper, April 9, 1678. Their children were Samuel; Thomas, who married Jane Harby; Stephen, who did not marry; Benjamin, who married Hannah——; Hannah, who married Nathan Barlow 1719, and Wait, who married Benjamin Allen, 1720.

Thomas Bourman, son of the second Thomas, resided at West Falmouth on the estate now owned by Capt. Nathaniel Eldred. He married Jane Harby, and had children: Ichabod; Judah, who married Mary Dillingham 1758; David, married Ruth Dillingham 1751, and Hannah Wing 1770; Silas, married second, Lydia Gifford; Joseph, married Rest Swift, Sept. 17, 1766; Sarah, married Melatiah Gifford 1743; Jane, married Joseph Bowman; Elizabeth; Peace, who did not marry, and Deborah.

Benjamin Bourman, son of Thomas 2d, married Hannah——. He resided at Teeticket, Falmouth, was a man of enterprise and wealth, and died in the year 1743, leaving sons Daniel, Samuel and Stephen, and a daughter "Rest," all of whom belonged to the Friends' Meeting. He wrote his name Bowerman, as many of the family now do. In the inventory of his estate, one-half of the sloop Falmouth and one-eighth of the sloop Woods Hole, are appraised. His son Stephen, married 1756, Hannah, daughter of Caleb and Reliance Allen; Samuel married three wives; first, 1743, Rose Landers; second, 1746, Jemimah Wing; third, Oct. 10, 1785, Grace Hoxie. Daniel married Joanna, daughter of Simeon Hathaway, and had Barnabas, grandfather of the present Barnabas, and a daughter "Rest," who rested in single life.

Beside those mentioned in the will of Benjamin Bourman, Mr. Hoxie says he had a son Enos, who married in 1764, Elizabeth, daughter of Recompence and Lydia Landers; Joseph, who died young; Wait, who married 1741, Benjamin Swift, and a son Benjamin, who married in 1755, Elizabeth, daughter of William and Mary Gifford. This Benjamin lived at Teeticket. His children, Elihu, married Sept. 23, 1779, Anny Allen; Harper, who married, first,

Elizabeth Shepherd, and second, Meribah Jones; Hannah, who married Eben Allen; Zacheus, married Sept. 26, 1810, Elizabeth Wing; Benjamin, married 1796, Phebe Shepherd; Elizabeth; Anna, married Abel Hoxie; Samuel, and Rest who married Francis Allen. Several of this family lived to a great age.

# BUMPAS.

Edward Bompasse came over in the Fortune, and arrived at Plymouth Nov. 10, 1621. The name is probably the French Bon pas—a similar name to the English Goodspeed. At the division of the land in 1623, and of the cattle in 1627, he was unmarried. He sold land in Plymouth in 1628, and removed to Duxbury and there bought land of William Palmer, on which he built a house and "palisado," which he sold to John Washburn in 1634. In 1640 he was of Marshfield, and was living at Duck Hill in that town in 1684.

It appears that he married about the time he removed to Duxbury, and according to the Marshfield records his wife was named Hannah. The record says "Hannah, widow of old Edward Bumpas, died 12th Feb. 1693," and that Edward Bumpas died nine days before. Mr. Savage supposes that the latter record refers to Edward Bumpas, Jr.

This Barnstable family descend from Thomas, probably the youngest son of Edward, the pilgrim. He was not a proprietor, and I do not find that he was admitted an inhabitant of Barnstable. He and his son Thomas claimed to be proprietors, but the lands laid out to them in 1716, were in consideration of fifteen shares purchased by them of Lieut. John Howland, and in settlement of "their whole right or pretence to any claim in the division of the common land in Barnstable." Thomas Bumpas' house was on "Lovell's Way," in Cokachoiset, now Osterville.

Samuel Bumpas' house was at Skonkonet, now called Bump's river, and on the road south of Thompson's bridge. His house stood near the cedar swamp. His house lot and other lands in the vicinity of Thompson's bridge, laid out to him in 1716, was for one share he bought of his brother-in-law Samuel Parker, and one of John Howland.

The family in Barnstable is extinct, but the descendants of Edward in other parts of the country are very numerous.

No record has been preserved of the family of the first Edward. His children as well as can now be ascertained were :

I.    Faith, born 1631.

II.    Sarah, married March, 1659, Thomas Durham.

III.    John, born 1636, probably the oldest son, had at Middleborough, Mary, born 1671; John, 1673, Samuel, 1676; James, 1678; at Rochester, Sarah, 16th Sept. 1685; Edward, 16th Sept. 1688, and Jeremiah, 24th Aug. 1692. The latter married Nov. 15, 1712, Jane Lovell of Barnstable. The family was afterwards in Wareham.

IV.    Edward, born 1638. Mr. Savage supposes he died in Marshfield in 1693.

V.    Joseph, born 1639, first of Plymouth, and afterwards of Middleborough. Mr. Winsor in his history of Duxbury doubts whether Joseph was a son of Edward, though he puts his name among his children. A deed of land recently found settles this question. He was a son of Edward, and had Lydia, born 2d Aug. 1669; Wybra, 15th May, 1672; Joseph, 25th Aug. 1674; Rebecca, 17th Dec. 1677; James, 25th Dec. 1679; Penelope, 21st Dec. 1681; Mary, 12th Aug. 1684, and Mehitable, 21st Jan'y, 1692.

VI.    Jacob, born 1644. Mr. Deane says he was of Scituate in 1676, where he married in 1677, Elizabeth, widow of William Blackmore, and had Benjamin, 1678, and Jacob, 1680. Benjamin had nine children, and has numerous descendants.

VII.    Hannah, born 1646.

VIII.  Philip. Winsor says Philip was the son of Edward, and he was living in 1677; but gives no additional information.

IX.    Thomas, born about the year 1660, married Nov. 1679, Phebe, eldest daughter of John Lovell of Barnstable. His children born in Barnstable were :

### Children born in Barnstable.

I.    Hannah, born 28th July, 1680, married Samuel Parker, Dec. 12, 1695. The bride was 15, and the bridegroom 35.

II. Jean, born Dec. 1681.
III. Mary, born April, 1683.
IV. Samuel, born Janr'y 1685, married Joanna Warren, Aug. 1, 1717, and had Sarah, April 5, 1718, married Samuel Lothrop, July 17, 1740; Joanna, May 15, 1719, married Samuel Hamblin, Jr., Nov. 16, 1749; Jabez, June 25, 1721; Thomas, March 20, 1722-3; John, May 17, 1725; Warren, June 28, 1727; Bethia, Aug. 23, 1729, married Seth Phinney, Oct. 26, 1748; Mary, Jan'y 1, 1731-2, and Phebe, April 21, 1734.
V. Thomas, born May, 1687.
Vl. Sarah, born Jan'ry 1688.
VII. Elizabeth, born Jan'y 1690.
VIII. Abigail, born Oct. 1693.
IX. John, baptized June 21, 1696.
X. Benjamin, born 27th, March 1703.

Phebe, wife of Thomas Bumpas, became a member of the Barnstable Church, May 24, 1696, and on the 21st of June following, his children Samuel, Thomas, John, Mary, Sarah, Abigail and Elizabeth were baptized. Hannah, his eldest child, was then married, and respecting Jane under the date of July 5, 1696, is the following entry: "Jane of Phebe, wife of Thomas Bump, ye girl being about 14 or 15 years old, was examined, and being one of ye family and looked upon in her minority, was baptized." The baptism of Benjamin does not appear on the church records. Phebe Bumpas of Barnstable, married Nov. 11, 1724, John Fish. She was probably daughter of Thomas, Sen'r, The Thankful Bumbas, who married Dec. 12, 1744, Jonathan Hamblin, was perhaps another daughter. There was also a Samuel Bumpus, Jr., of Barnstable, who married in 1733, Sarah Rogers of Plymouth. She died April 10, 1736, leaving a son Levi, born March 17, 1734-5.

# BETTS.

WILLIAM BETTS,

Aged twenty years, came over in the Thomas and John, Richard Lombard, master, from Gravesend, 6th Jan'y 1635. He joined Mr. Lothrop's church Oct. 25, 1635, married Alice, Goodman Ensign's maid in the Bay (Massachusetts), Nov. 23, 1638, removed with the church to Barnstable in 1639. Mr. Savage says he was a tanner by trade, and that he was afterwards of Dorchester. In the list of those who were able to bear arms in 1643, his name is written Beetts. Perhaps the name is Bills. There was a family of that name early in Barnstable. The children of William Betts, born in Barnstable, were:

*Children born in Barnstable.*

I.   Hannah, bap'd Jan'y 26, 1639-40.
II.  Samuel, bap'd Feb. 5, 1642-3.
III. Hope, a son, bap'd Mar. 16, 1644-5.

After the date of the birth of his son Hope, his name disappears on the Barnstable records. His lands are not recorded; probably they were transferred to another without a formal deed, as was the custom at the first settlement. He, perhaps, settled in the westerly part of the plantation, near John Crocker.

# BLUSH.

## ABRAHAM BLUSH.

This name is uniformly written on the Colony and early Barnstable records Blush. Many of his descendants now spell their name Blish, though the popular pronunciation of the name continues to be Blush.

He was an early settler at Duxbury. Nov. 1, 1637, he bought of Richard Moore, for twenty-one pounds sterling, (payable in money or beaver,) a dwelling-house and twenty acres of land at Eagle's Nest in Duxbury. On the 26th of Nov. 1638, he sold the easterly half of the land to John Willis for £8, 10s. sterling.

He was of Barnstable in 1641, and was probably one of the first settlers; was propounded to be admitted a freeman June 1, 1641; again in 1651, and 1652. The date of his admission is not given; his name is on the list of freemen in 1670. He was a grand-juror in 1642, 1658, and 1663; surveyor of highways 1645, 1650 and 1652; constable, 1656, 1660 and 1667. He is styled a planter, and was a large landholder, owning at West Barnstable eight acres of land on the east side of Bridge Creek or Cove, and seventeen acres of meadow adjoining. Fourteen acres of upland, eight on the south, and six on the north side of the road and bounded easterly by the Annable land, and three acres of meadow adjoining. His great lot containing forty acres was on the east of Scorton Hill, and bounded southerly by the highway. This he sold Feb. 10, 1668, to John Crocker, Sen'r, for £5, 10s.

In 1662, he owned another strip of land on the east of the Annable Farm, containing eight acres, extending from the marsh across the highway to Annable's pond.

The above lands were his West Barnstable farm, on which it appears that he resided in 1643, being one of the

earliest settlers in that part of the town.  His old homestead on the west of the Annable land was owned by him
and his descendants about two centuries.

July 17, 1658, he bought for £75, the Dolar Davis
farm, in the easterly part of the town containing fifty acres
of upland and ten of meadow.  Twelve acres of this land
was at Stony Cove, and was sold by him in 1680 to Nathaniel and Jeremiah Bacon ; twenty-two acres in the Old Common Field, and sixteen acres (his house lot), on the south
of the Mill Pond.  His dwelling-house stood a short distance south-easterly from the present water-mill.  The
causeway which forms the Mill Dam was called in early
times Blushe's Bridge, and the point of land at the western
extremity of the Old Common Field is now known as
Blushe's Point.

The first wife of Abraham Blush was named Anne,
perhaps Anne Pratt.  She was buried in Barnstable, according to the Town and Colony records, May 16, 1651 ;
but according to the Church records, which are more reliable, on the 26th of May, 1653.  His second wife was Hannah, daughter of John Williams of Scituate, and widow of
John Barker of Marshfield.  She was buried in Barnstable,
March 16, 1658, according to the Colony records ; but the
Barnstable record probably gives the true date, Feb. 16,
1657-8.  He married for his third wife, January 4, 1658-9,
Alice, widow of John Derby of Yarmouth.  He died Sept.
7, 1683 ; his age is not stated.  His children born in Barnstable were

*Children born in Barnstable.*

I.    Sarah, born 2d Dec. 1641, bap'd 5th Dec. 1641.
II.   Joseph, born 1st April, 1648, bap'd 9th April, 1648 ;
      married Hannah Hull, 15th Sept. 1674 ; died June 14,
      1730, aged 82 years.
III.  Abraham, born 16th Oct. 1654.  In the will of his
      uncle, Capt. John Williams of Scituate, he is called of
      Boston in 1691.  In 1698, Thomas Brattle of Boston,
      conveyed to Abraham Blush and twenty others, land
      called Brattle Close.  He was one of the founders of
      the church in Brattle street in 1698.  Mr. Savage does
      not find that he had a family.

Joseph Blush, son of Abraham, married Sept. 15, 1674,

Hannah, daughter of Tristram Hull.  He resided at West Barnstable.  He died June 14, 1730, aged 82, and his widow died Nov. 15, 1733, aged 75 years.  His will is dated June 25, 1722, and was proved Aug. 30, 1731.  He names his wife Hannah, and sons Tristam sole executor, Benjamin, Abraham and Joseph; and daughters Annah, Thankful and Mary.  He gives his cane to his son Joseph, and remembers all his grand-children then four years of age.

## Children born in Barnstable.

I.      Joseph, born 13th Sept. 1675, married Hannah Child, 30th July, 1702.
II.     John, born 17th Feb. 1676-7; died young.
III.    Annah, born Feb. 1678-9.
IV.     Abraham, born 27th Feb. 1680-1, married Temperance Fuller, Nov. Nov. 12, 1736.
V.      Reuben, born 14th Aug. 1683, married two wives.
VI.     Sarah, born Aug. 1685, died 3d Jan'y 1686.
VII.    Sarah, born Sept. 1687, died 1705.
VIII.   Thankful, born Sept. 1689, married Joseph Bodfish, Oct. 11, 1712.
IX.     John, born 1st Jan'y 1691; died Oct. 14, 1711.
X.      Tristram, born April, 1694.
XI.     Mary, born April 1696, married Samuel Jones 26th June, 1718.
XII.    Benjamin, born April, 1699.

Joseph Blush, Jr., son of Joseph, resided at West Barnstable.  He married 30th July, 1702, Hannah, daughter of Richard Child.  She died 11th Nov. 1732, aged 58 years, and he married in 1733 his second wife, Remember Backus of Sandwich.  He died March 4, 1754, aged 79 years.

## Children born in Barnstable.

I.      Joseph, born 2d Feb. 1704, married Oct. 28, 1730, Mercy Crocker, and had Joseph, born July 20, 1731, who married Sarah Crocker, May 19, 1757.  During the Revolution he was an active and energetic Whig. Hannah, born Oct. 28, 1732, married Zachariah Perry of Sandwich, Feb. 7, 1744-5; William, Dec. 22, 1733; Samuel, bap'd March 16, 1734-5; Seth, bap'd March

25, 1739; Mercy, born Oct. 24, 1740; Benjamin, bap'd July 18, 1742; Ebenezer, born April 1, 1744, and Timothy, Feb. 16, 1745-6.

II. Abigail, born 29th Nov. 1705, married Seth Crocker.
III. Sarah, born 1st Oct. 1707, married Seth Hamblin, Oct. 9, 1735.
IV. Mehitable, 14th June, 1711, married Ben. Jenkins, Oct. 29, 1730.
V. Abraham, born 29th Sept. 1712; died Feb. 8, 1723-4.
VI. Hannah, 14th June, 1715.

Abraham Blush, son of Joseph, married Nov. 12, 1736, Temperance Fuller. He was fifty-five and she was only twenty at their marriage. Joseph Blush, Jr., had a son Abraham born in 1712, who died in 1724, and as there was no other Abraham in Barnstable, it is to be presumed that the match was made notwithstanding the disparity in the ages of the bride and bridegroom.

### Children born in Barnstable.

1. Abraham, 20th Oct. 1737.
II. Elijah, 5th March, 1738-9, married Sarah Stewart, Jan'y 25, 1761.
III. Rebecca, 14th Nov. 1740.
IV. Benjamin, 9th May, 1743.
V. Elisha, 23d April, 1745; died 17th Nov. 1645.
VI. Elisha, 1st March, 1746-7.
VII. Martha, 14th July, 1749.
VIII. Temperance, 21st Nov. 1751.
IX. Timothy, 3d Aug. 1756, probably died young.

Reuben Blush, son of Joseph, is not named, if my abstract is reliable, in his father's will, and though he married twice and had a family, the births of his children are not on the Barnstable records. By his first wife Elizabeth, he had six children baptized Dec. 20, 1730, namely: John, Silas, Reuben, Elizabeth, Hannah and Thankful.

He married for his second wife, Mary Thomas, Oct. 25, 1735. In his will dated July 3d, 1738, proved on the 20th Oct. following, he names his wife Mary, and sons John, Reuben and Silas. His widow, who is styled Mrs., married March 5, 1745, Lieut. John Annable.

Tristram Blush, son of Joseph, married Oct. 17, 1717, Anne Fuller, and had children born in Barnstable, namely:

I. Benjamin, June 16, 1718.
II. Anna, Nov. 19, 1719.
III. Sylvanus, Oct. 13, 1721.
IV. Thankful, bap'd Nov. 1725. A Thankful Blush married Caleb Perry of Sandwich, Oct. 1758.

John Blush, son of Reuben, married Nov. 15, 1739, Mary, daughter of Ebenezer Goodspeed, Jr., and had John, Nov. 14, 1745; Mary, Feb. 17, 1748, (who had Mary Crocker by Enoch Crocker, Aug. 20, 1765;) Stacy, March 26, 1751, and Rebecca, Oct. 14, 1756.

Reuben Blush, son of Reuben, married May 11, 1747, Ruth Childs, and had Reuben, 20th Oct. 1747; David, 11th May, 1749; Thomas, 21st July, 1751, and Elizabeth, 19th Oct. 1755.

Silas Blush, son of Reuben, married Nancy Tobey of Falmouth in 1747, and had Rebecca bap'd Jan'y 25, 1748-9; Abigail, June 2, 1751; Mercy, Sept. 30, 1752; Silas, Aug. 1, 1756; Elisha, Jan'y 15, 1759, and Mercy, April 18, 1762.

Silas of this family married Chloe, daughter of Nicholas Cobb. His widow is now living at the advanced age of ninety-six.

His brother Elisha was a very worthy man; but he made one sad mistake, he married for his first wife a woman because she had lands and money.

ELISHA BLUSH—AUNT "BECK" AND HER MUSEUM.

Elisha Blush married for his first wife June 2, 1790, Rebecca Linnell—familiarly known as "Aunt Beck,"—the third wife and widow of John Linnell, deceased. The first wife of the latter was Mercy Sturgis, his second, Ruth, a sister of Rebecca, and both daughters of James Linnell. By Mercy and Ruth he had no issue, by Rebecca a daughter Abigail. By the ecclesiastical law of England it was then illegal for a man to marry his deceased wife's sister, and the issue of such marriages was declared illegitimate. Under this law the other heirs of John Linnell claimed his large estate to the exclusion of his widow and daughter. Before any settlement was made, the daughter died, the widow married, and the law was changed.   The matter was finally settled by compromise, and Rebecca Blush came into possession of nearly all her first husband's estate.

Elisha Blush was a shoemaker by trade, a very honest and worthy man, and an exemplary member of the Methodist Church.   At the time of his first marriage he was thirty-one and his wife forty-six years of age.   She died Nov. 7, 1830, aged 86 years, and six weeks and three days after he married Rebecca Linnell. a grand niece of his first wife, a young woman aged 29.   Elisha Blush died May 1836, aged 77, and his widow is the present wife of the Rev. Scolly G. Usher, now a practicing physician at the West.

When young I had often heard of Aunt Beck's Museum, and there are very few in Barnstable who have not.   In the winter of 1825, I resided in her neighborhood, and made several calls to examine her curiosities.   Her house, yet remaining, is an old-fashioned, low double-house, facing due South, with two front-rooms, a kitchen, bedroom and pantry on the lower floor.   The east front-room, which was her sitting-room, is about fourteen feet square.   The west room is smaller.   Around the house and out-buildings every thing was remarkably neat.   The wood and fencing stuff was carefully piled, the chips at the wood-pile were raked up, and there was no straw or litter to be seen about the barn or fences.   It was an estate that the stranger would notice for its neat and tidy appearance.

In my visits to her house the east front-room was the only portion I was permitted to see, though I occasionally caught a glimpse of the curiosities in the adjoining rooms through the half-opened doors.   I was accompanied in my visits by a young lady who was a neighbor, and on excellent terms with Aunt Beck.   She charged me not to look around the room when I entered, but keep my eye on the lady of the house, or on the fire-place.   To observe such precautions was absolutely necessary, for the stranger who, on entering, should stare around the room, would soon feel the weight of Aunt Beck's ire, or her broom-stick.   I followed my instructions, and was invited to take one of the two chairs in the room.   It was a cool evening, and all being seated close to the fire, we were soon engaged in a friendly chat, and I soon had an opportunity to examine the curiosities.   In the northeast corner of the room stood a bedstead with a few ragged, dirty bed-clothes spread thereon. The space under the bed was occupied partly as a pantry. Several pans of milk were set there for cream to rise, (for Aunt Beck made her own butter) ; but when she made more than she used in her family, she would complain of the dullness of the market.   In front of the bed and near the centre of the room stood a common table about three feet square. Respecting this table a neighbor, Captain Elisha Hall, assured me that to his certain knowledge it had stood in the same place twenty years, how much longer he could not say. On this table, for very many successive years, she had laid whatever she thought curious or worth preserving.   When an article was laid thereon it was rarely removed, for no one would dare meddle with Aunt Beck's curiosities.   Feathers were her delight ; but many were perishable articles, and in the process of time had rotted and changed into a black mould, covering the table with a stratum of about an inch in thickness.

In front of the larger table stood a smaller one near the fire-place, from which the family partook of their meals. This table was permanently located, and I was informed by the neighbors that no perceptible change had been made in the ORDER, or more properly DISORDERLY, arrangements of the furniture and curiosities for the ten years next preceding my visit.   The evening was cool, and though my hostess was the owner of extensive tracts of woodland, covered with a heavy growth, she could not afford herself a comfortable fire.   A few brands and two or three dead sticks, added after we came in, cast a flickering light over the room ; but, fortunately for our olfactories, did not increase its temperature.

The floor, excepting narrow paths between the doors, fire-place and bed, was entirely covered with broken crockery, old pots, kettles, pails, tubs, &c., &c., and the walls were completely festooned with old clothing, useless articles of furniture, bunches of dried herbs, &c., &c., in fact every article named in the humorous will of Father Abby, excepting a "tub of soap."   The other articles named in the same stanza were conspicuous :

> "A long cart rope,
> A frying-pan and kettle,
> An old sword blade, a garden spade,
> A pruning-hook and sickle."

But in justice to Aunt Beck, I should state that she did for many long years contemplate making "a tub of soap." For thirty years she saved all her beef-bones for that purpose, depositing the same in her large kitchen fire-place and in other places about the room. During the warm summer of 1820, these bones became so offensive that Aunt Beck reluctantly consented to have them removed, and Captain Elisha Hall, who saw them carted away, says there was more than an ox-cart load.

Of the other rooms in the house I cannot speak from personal knowledge; but the lady who went with me and who is now living, informed me that in the west room there was a bed, a shoemaker's bench, flour barrels, chests containing valuable bedding, too good to use, and a nameless variety of other articles scattered over the bed and chairs; from the walls were suspended a saddle and pillion, and many other things preserved as rare curiosities. In time the room became so completely filled that it was difficult to enter it. The kitchen, bedroom, pantry and chambers were filled with vile trash and trumpery, covered with dirt and litter.

This description may seem imaginary or improbable to the stranger; but there are hundreds now living in Barnstable who can testify that the picture is not drawn in too strong colors. Truth is sometimes stranger than fiction, and this maxim applies in all its force to Rebecca Blush. That she was a monomaniac is true; but that she was insane on all subjects is not true. Early in life she was neat, industrious and very economical, but her prudent habits soon degenerated into parsimony. Economy is a virtue to be inculcated, but when the love of money becomes the ruling passion, and a man saves that he may hoard and accumulate, he becomes a miser, and as such, is despised. The miser accumulates money, or that which can be converted into money. Aunt Beck saved not only money, but useless articles that others threw away. These she would pick up in the fields, and by the roadside, and store away in her house. During the latter part of her life she seldom went from home. During more than twenty years she thus gathered up useless trash, and as she did not allow any thing (except the bones) to be carried out for more than forty years, it requires no great stretch of the imagination to form a correct picture of the condition and appearance of the place, she called her home.

Her estate, if she had allowed her husband to have managed it, would have been much larger at her death. Her wood she would not be allowed to be cut and sold, and the proceeds invested. She lost by investing her money in mortgages on old houses and worn-out lands, and loaning to persons who never paid their notes. She also had a habit of hiding parcels of coin among the rubbish in her house, and sometimes she would forget not only where she had placed the treasure, but how many such deposits she had made. It is said that some of her visitors, who were not over-much honest, often carried away these deposits, unknown and unsuspected by her.

On one subject, saving, Rebecca Blush was not of sound mind. She was, however, a woman naturally of strong mind—no one could be captain over her. She knew more or less of almost every family in town, and was always very particular in her inquiries respecting the health of the families of her visitors. She delighted in repeating ancient ballads and nursery tales. In her religious opinions she was Orthodox; and she hated the Methodists, not because they were innovators, but because the preachers called at her house, and because her husband contributed something to their support.

Not a dollar of the money saved and accumulated by her, during a long life of toil and self-denial, now remains. In a few short years it took to itself wings and flew away. Her curiosities, which she had spent so many years in collecting and preserving, were ruthlessly destroyed before her remains were deposited in the grave. She died on Sunday. On the Thursday preceding, her attendants commenced removing. She overheard them, and asked if it thundered. They satisfied the dying woman with an evasive answer. Before her burial, all her curiosities were either burnt, or scattered to the four winds of heaven.

The old house soon lost all its charms, and its doors ceased to attract visitors. Its interior was cleansed and painted; paper-hangings adorned the walls, and handsome furniture the rooms. Forty-five days after her death there was a wedding-party at the house. Mr. Blush endeavored to correct the sad mistake which he made when a young man, by taking in his old age a young woman for his second wife, forty-three years younger than himself, and fifty-seven years younger than his first wife.

During the closing period of his life, a term of nearly six years, Elisha Blush enjoyed all those comforts and conveniences of life of which he had been deprived for forty years, and to which a man having a competent estate is entitled. This great change in his mode of living did not, however, afford him unalloyed happiness. One remark which he made at this period is worth preserving; it shows the effect which habits of forty years growth have on the human mind. Some one congratulated him on the happy change which had taken place. "Yes," said he, "I live more comfortably than I did," but he added with a sigh, "my present wife is not so economical as my first."

NOTE.—I read the manuscript of this article to the only persons now living whom I presumed would have any feeling in regard to its publication. They are relatives of Aunt Beck, and when young were frequent visitors at her house. I altered whatever they said was not literally true, excepting things of which I was myself an eye witness. They requested me to say nothing of her eccentricities. I replied that Aunt Beck and her museum, like Sarcho and Dappie, were born for each other, and if the account of the museum was omitted, Aunt Beck sunk into insignificance.

# BLACHFORD.

### WILLIAM BLACHFORD.

According to tradition William Blachford, the ancestor of this family, came from London. His wife, Elizabeth Lewis, was a daughter of Benjamin Lewis, who had a house at Crooked, now called Lampson's Pond. She was popularly known, not by her true name, but as Liza Towerhill, because the family of her husband is said to have resided in that part of London. She was reputed to be a witch. Some of the marvels which are related of her I have published. It is unnecessary now to re-produce them, or other equally improbable relations since collected. That Elizabeth Blachford was a witch, and transformed herself into a black cat at pleasure, and performed most wonderful feats, all her neighbors three-fourths of a century ago believed, or at least pretended to believe. Even at this day, there are persons who firmly believe that Liza Tower Hill was a witch, and did all the wonderful things that they have heard ancient people relate.

She was a daughter of Benjamin Lewis by his second wife, Hannah Hinckley. Her father was a grand-son of the first George Lewis, and her mother was a grand-daughter of the first Samuel, and own cousin to Gov. Thomas Hinckley. Her family and connections were among the most respectable and influential in Barnstable. She was born Jan'y 17, 1711-12, married William Blachford, Nov. 12, 1728, admitted to the East Church, in full communion, Jan'y 9, 1736-7, of which she was an exemplary member until her death in July, 1790. She was honest, industrious, energetic and shrewd in making a bargain. The records of Rev. Mr. Green furnish evidence that she was an exemplary and pious woman, fifty-three years of her life—a period covering the whole time in which, according to popular belief, she was in league with the Evil One.

Her husband was a very worthy man, admitted to the church at his own house on the day preceding his death; died June 15, 1755, leaving a small estate and seven children, four under seventeen, to be provided for by their mother. She spun and wove for those who were able to pay for her services, managed her small farm, working thereon with her own hands,* kept several cows, and thus was able to bring up her children respectably.

A question here arises which covers the whole ground respecting the popular belief in witchcraft. It is difficult perhaps satisfactorily to explain this phase in the popular mind. Fifty years before the time of Liza Towerhill, the intelligent and the ignorant alike believed in the existence of witches. The Bible taught that there witches in olden times; and the laws of Old and New England recognized witchcraft as an existing evil, the practice whereof was criminal and punishable with death. Respecting the meaning of the words "being possessed with devils," and "witches" in the Scriptures, our ancestors had vague and uncertain notions. The imaginations of the ignorant and the superstitious, perhaps aided by the malice of the wicked, gave form and substance to those vague notions, and they became visible forms to their eyes, more frequently in that of a cat than any other animal. That such transformations actually occurred was believed by very many; and not a few held that the hanging of witches was a religious duty. We may regret that such was the popular delusion, or we may laugh at the simplicity of those who believed in such vageries; yet five generations have since passed, and time has not entirely eradicated from the popular mind a belief in the existence of apparitions and witches.

---

*A man now living informs me that when a small boy, he went with his father to assist Liza in breaking up a piece of new ground. At that time she must have been over seventy-five years of age, yet she performed the most laborious part of the operation—holding down the plough. During the operation the plough was suddenly brought up against a stump, and the concussion threw her over it. She suffered no inconvenience by the accident, and continued to work till the job was completed. All admit that she was not a weak-minded woman, aud this anecdote shows that she was also physically strong.

Phenomena which Science now enables us to explain in accordance with the laws which govern the Universe, were inexplicable to them, and without imputing to them wrong notions, or being influenced by a superstitious fear, we may safely admit that their conclusions were honest. All diseases which affected both the mind and the body, including diseases of the nervous system, epilepsy, monomania, &c., were classed in ancient times under the general head of being "possessed of an evil spirit." Without entering upon this inquiry, it is sufficient to say that our fathers believed that the devil had something to do with persons thus afflicted. I am, however, satisfied that nineteen-twentieths of the witch stories told, originated in dream-land. All that are told of Liza Towerhill are of this class. Some were proved to be so during the life-time of the parties. The case of Mr. Wood of West Barnstable is an illustration. He charged Liza with putting a bridle and saddle on him and riding him many times to Plum Pudding Pond in Plymouth, where the witches held their nightly orgies. Though Mr. Wood had palpable evidence of the falsity of the charge, yet for many years he continued to relate the story, and evidently believed he was telling the truth. This case, if it proves anything, proves that Mr. Wood was a monomaniac.

Another question arises, how it happened that a woman who sustained the good character of Elizabeth Blachford, should be made the scape-goat of the flock, and be charged with being in league with the devil, and as a witch, persecuted for more than half a century. Some of the reasons may be found that induced the belief; but none that will justify her persecution. Her father's house was in the forest, two miles from a neighbor. At that time wolves and other wild animals abounded ; Indians were constantly scouring the forests for game, and their great "trail" from Yarmouth to Hyannis, now visible, passed near Mr. Lewis' house. The solitariness of the residence, and the associations of ravenous beasts, and of more cruel Indians therewith, inspired awe, and led the popular mind into the belief that the family must be connected with evil spirits, or they could not live in such a wild place in safety. Elizabeth's husband built a house a mile west of her father's, on the borders of Half-Way Pond. She was only sixteen and one-half years old, and that a young woman should have the courage to live alone in the woods, seemed in that superstitious age to carry with it the evidence that she was in league with the devil. It is unnecessary to add that such reasoning is unconclusive ; the superstitious never examine facts, or inquire respecting the soundness of the opinions they adopt.

When Mrs. Blachford was charged with being a witch, she always took offence, and resented the charge as false and malicious. Her children would not allow any one with impunity to tell them that their mother was a witch. Even her grandson Uriah, who died about fifteen years ago, aged over eighty, was very sensitive on the subject, and the man who dared to tell him his grandmother was a witch, he would never forget or forgive.

The days of witchcraft are now numbered and past,— the few who still believe in it cautiously conceal their opinions. It is fortunate for the reputation of the Plymouth Colony that no one therein was ever convicted, condemned, or punished for that crime. Our rulers had the good sense to punish the complainant in the first case that arose, instead of the person complained of. If a different decision had then been made, a thousand complaints would have arisen and similar acts to those which disgrace the annals of Salem and Massachusetts, would now disgrace the history of Plymouth and Barnstable.

The ashes of Elizabeth Blachford rest quietly in the grave-yard near the East Church. No phœnix spirit has arose therefrom to disturb the equanimity of the living, or disturb the repose of the dead. Neither ghosts nor hobgoblins are seen to dance over her grave, or sigh because the manes of the last witch have fled.

The family of William Blachford and his wife Elizabeth Lewis, born in Barnstable :

I.    Peter, born May 10, 1729.
II.   Lydia, April 5, 1734; died young.
III.  Benjamin, June 11, 1738, married 1761, Sarah Godfrey of Yarmouth, and had a family.
IV.   Remember, March 3, 1739-40, married Luke Butler of Nantucket, Oct. 9, 1760.
V.    Mercy, April 13, 1742.
VI.   David, June 17, 1744, married Elizabeth Ellis of Provincetown, 1765. He died Nov. 16, 1822, aged 78.

VII.  Lydia, May 22, 1746, married ——— Ellis.

VIII.  William, June 25, 1750.  He married Monica ———.
I believe she was an Eldridge from Harwich.  She
lived at one time in a house built over a large, flat
rock, on the west side of Monica's Swamp in Barnstable.  After their marriage they lived in the house
which was his mother's at Half-Way Pond.  He was
a soldier in the Revolutionary Army.  He deserted;
but being an invalid and unable to stand up straight
no effort was made to secure his return to the army.
Col. Otis was instructed to have him arrested as a
deserter as an example to others.  Bill, however, on
his way home, passed the house of Col. Otis.  At the
time, he and some of his neighbors were standing in
his yard.  One of them said "There comes Bill Blachford."  The Colonel turned quickly around, and looking in an opposite direction, exclaimed, "Where is
the rascal?"  Without turning, the Colonel went into
his house and Bill escaped.  A little further on Bill
met with others who knew him, and they inquired
where he was from.  Bill replied, "STRAIGHT from
the camp."  "Then," replied the first speaker, "you
have got most d——y WARPED by the way."  He died
Aug. 30, 1816, aged 66, leaving no children.

# BOURNE.

___

### RICHARD BOURNE.

In the biographical dictionaries and in many historical works, there are short sketches of the life and character of Richard Bourne. No biography of this distinguished man has been written. I shall not attempt it. My purpose is to elucidate one point in his character, namely : the political influence of his labors as a missionary,—a point not entirely overlooked by early writers,—but historians have failed to give to it that prominence it deserves. The facts bearing on this point will be stated in a condensed form.

Aside from his labors as a missionary, Richard Bourne was a man of note. He was often a representative to the General Court ; held many town offices ; often served on committees, and as a referee in important cases. He was a well-informed man ; discreet, cautious, of sound judgment, and of good common sense. There is reason to doubt whether he brought to New England so large an estate as has been represented. The division of the meadows at Sandwich does not indicate that he was a man of wealth. He was a good business man, and while he carefully guarded the interests of the Indians, he did not forget to lay up treasures for himself.

John Eliot, Thomas Mayhew, father and son, Richard Bourne, John Cotton, Daniel Gookin, and Thomas Tupper consecrated their lives to the philanthropic purpose of meliorating the condition of the Indians. They instructed them in the arts of civilized life ; they established schools, and they founded churches. Many of the Indians were converted to Christianity, and lived pious and holy lives ; very many of them were taught to read and write their native language, and a few were good English scholars.

Mr. Bourne was the pastor of the Indian Church at Marshpee,* gathered in 1670. The apostles Eliot and Cotton assisted at his ordination. His parish extended from Provincetown to Middleboro'—one hundred miles. He commenced his labors as a missionary about the year 1658, and in his return to Major Gookin, dated Sandwich, Sept. 1, 1674, he says he is the only Englishman employed in this extensive region, and the results of his labors are stated in his return, of which the following is a condensed abstract :

"Praying Indians that do frequently meet together on the Lord's Day to worship God." He names twenty-two places where meetings were held. The number of men and women that attended these meetings was three hundred and nine. Young men and maids, one hundred and eighty-eight. Whole number of praying Indians, four hundred and ninety-seven. Of these one hundred and forty-two could read the Indian language, seventy-two could write, and nine could read English.

The labors of Mr. Bourne and his associates have not been sufficiently appreciated by historians. In 1675, the far-seeing Philip, Sachem of Mount Hope, had succeeded in uniting the Western Indians in a league, the avowed object whereof was the extermination of the white inhabitants of New England. His emissaries in vain attempted to induce the Christianized Indians to join that league. They remained faithful. Richard Bourne, aided by Thomas Tupper of Sandwich, Mr. Thornton of Yarmouth and Mr. Treat of Eastham had a controlling influence over the numerous bands of Indians then resident in the County of Barnstable, in Wareham, Rochester and Middleboro'. Mr. Mayhew exerted a like controlling influence over the natives of Martha's Vineyard and the adjacent islands.

In 1674, the year preceding King Philip's war, the returns made to Major Gookin, show that the aggregate number of Christianized or praying Indians

---

*MARSHPEE.—Mr. Hawley. who understood the Indian language, says it should be written MASSAPE. This word is from the same root as MISSISSIPPI, and literally means Great River. The principal stream in the plantation is called Marshpee or Great River.

| | |
|---|---:|
| In Massachusetts, was - - - - - | 1100 |
| In Plymouth, Mr. Bourne's return, - - - | 497 |
| In      "      Mr. Cotton's partial, - - - | 40 |
| Estimated number not enumerated, - - - | 170 |
| On Martha's Vineyard and Chappaquidock, - | 1500 |
| On Nantucket, - - | 300 |
| | 3607 |

It is not to be presumed that, at that time, more than one-half of the Indians had been converted, or were nominally Christians. Perhaps a fair estimate of the Indian population in 1675, in the territory comprised in the eastern part of the present State of Massachusetts, would be 7000; one-fifth, or 1400 of whom were warriors.

On account of the jealousies and suspicions entertained by the English in Massachusetts, the Indians rendered little service to the whites. Mr. Eliot and Major Gookin suffered reproaches and insults for endeavoring to repress the popular rage against their pupils. Some of the praying Indians of Natick, and from other places in Massachusetts, were transported to Deer Island in Boston harbor. Some of the Indians in Plymouth Colony, particularly those at Pembroke, were conveyed to Clarke's Island, Plymouth.

On Martha's Vineyard and on the Cape, the Indians were friendly to the English. Many enlisted and fought bravely against the forces of Philip. Capt. Daniel of Satucket, (Brewster), and Capt. Amos distinguished themselves in the war and are honorably mentioned. In the course of the war, the number of prisoners became embarrassing, and they were sent to the Cape and Martha's Vineyard, and were safely kept by the friendly Indians.

Major Walley says that the English were rarely successful when they were not aided by Indian auxiliaries, and urges this as a reason for treating them kindly. The reader of the "History of the Indian Wars" will find many facts to corroborate the opinion of Major Walley.

In the spring of 1676 the armies of Philip were victorious, and the inhabitants of Plymouth Colony were panic stricken and despondent. If at that time the one thousand Indian warriors, who were influenced and controlled by Bourne and Mayhew had become enemies, the contest in Plymouth Colony would not have been doubtful, the other towns would have been destroyed and met the fate of Dartmouth, Middleboro' and Swanzey.   At this time three hundred men could not be raised to march for the defence of Rehobeth.   All the towns, excepting Sandwich and Scituate, raised their quotas; but many of the soldiers that went forth, returned to their homes without marching to the defence of their frontier towns.

In 1675, Gov. Hinckley enumerated the Christianized Indians embraced in the region of country which had been under the superintendence of Mr. Bourne.   The number had increased from four hundred and ninety-seven in 1674, to ten hundred and fourteen in 1685.   Showing that in a period of eleven years the number had more than doubled.

In 1676, no enumeration of the Indians was made; but it is within the bounds of probability to assume that in the district of country under the supervision and care of Mr. Bourne there were at least six hundred Indian warriors. Had these at this particular conjuncture turned rebels, the whites could not have defended their towns and villages against the savages, and Plymouth Colony would have become extinct.

It may be urged that Mr. Bourne could not have done this unaided and alone; or, if he had not, God in his providence would have raised up some other instruments to have effected this great purpose.   The fact is Richard Bourne by his unremitted labors for seventeen years made friends of a sufficient number of Indians, naturally hostile to the English, to turn the scale in Plymouth Colony and give the preponderence to the whites.   He did this, and it is to him who does, that we are to award honor.   Bourne did more by the moral power which he exerted to defend the Old Colony than Bradford did at the head of the army.   Laurel wreaths shade the brows of military heroes—their names are enshrined in a bright halo of glory—while the man who has done as good service for his country by moral means, sinks into comparative insignificance, and is too often forgotten.

The Apostle Eliot, Mr. Mayhew, and other missionaries, performed like meritorious services.   The people of Massachusetts were more suspicious of the good faith of the converted Indians, than the residents in the Plymouth Colony.   These Indians were treated unkindly by the English, yet a company from Natick proved faithful, and did good service in the war.

Of the early history of Mr. Richard Bourne little is known. It is said he came from Devonshire, England. He was a householder in Plymouth in 1636, and his name appears on the list of freemen of the Colony, dated March 7, 1636-7. On the 2d of January preceding, seven acres of land were granted to him to belong to his dwelling-house. At the same court seven acres of land were granted to John Bourne, in behalf of his father, Mr. Thomas Bourne.

May 2, 1637, he was on a jury to lay out the highways about Plymouth, Duxbury and Eel River. June 5, 1638, he was a grand juror, and also a member of a coroner's inquest. On the 4th of September following, he was an inhabitant of Sandwich, and fined 18 pence for having three pigs unringed. He was a deputy to the first general court in 1639, and excepting 1643, represented the town of Sandwich till 1645; again in 1652, 1664, '65, '66, '67 and '70.

In the division of the meadows in Sandwich in 1640, he had seven acres assigned to him.

In 1645 he was on the committee elected to draft laws for the Colony; in 1652 agent of the Colony to receive oil in Sandwich. In 1655, Sarah, daughter of Richard Kerby, was sentenced to be punished severely by whipping, for uttering divers suspicious speeches against Mr. Bourne and Mr. Freeman, but the execution was respited till she should again be guilty of a like offence. In 1659 he and Mr. Thomas Hinckley were authorized to purchase lands of the Indians at Suckinesset,* and the same year he and Mr. Freeman were ordered to view some land at Manomet, and confirm the same to Thomas Burgis.

In 1658 he was one of four referees to settle a disputed boundary between Yarmouth and Barnstable. The boundary established by them is the present bounds, but the grant of the township to which they refer in their report is lost.

In 1661, he and Nathaniel Bacon and Mr. Thomas Hinckley were authorized to purchase all lands then unpurchased at Suckinesset and places adjacent.

---

*SUCKINESSETT the Indian name of the town of Falmouth is variously spelled on the records. It means "the place where black wampum (Indian money) is made." I prefer the orthography here given, because the roots of the words from which the name is compounded can be more easily traced. SUCKI means black; the terminal syllable is applied to places on the sea-shore, or by water. The other syllables I cannot explain.

In 1650, he and others of Sandwich petitioned to have lands granted to them at the following places : Marshpee pond, Cotuit river, and meadow at Mannamuch bay.    In 1655, he and others had meadows granted them at Manomet, and the use of some upland meadow at the end of Marshpee pond was granted to him, if the Indians consented.    In 1660, he had authority to locate land at South Sea, above Sandwich, and in 1661 Mr. Alden and Mr. Hinckley laid out to him "a competency of meadow" there.

At a General Court held at Plymouth June 4, 1661, the Court granted unto Richard Bourne of Sandwich, and to his heirs forever, a long strip of land on the west side of Pampaspised river, where Sandwich men take alewives—in breadth from the river to the hill or ridge that runs along the length of it, from a point of rocky land by a swamp called Pametoopauksett, unto a place called by the English Muddy Hole, by the Indians Wapoompauksett.    "The meadow is that which was called Mr. Leverich's ; " also, the other strips that are above, along the river side, unto a point bounded with two great stones or rocks ; also all the meadow lying on the easterly side of the said river unto Thomas Burgess, Senior's farm.*    Also, "yearly liberty to take twelve thousand alewives at the river where Sandwich men usually take alewives, him and his heirs forever."    Likewise a parcel of meadow at Marshpee—one-half to belong to him and the other half to be improved by him.    Also, a neck of meadow between two brooks with a little upland adjoining, at Mannamuchcoy, called by the Indians Auntaanta.

Feb. 7, 1664-5, "Whereas, a motion was made to this Court by Richard Bourne in the behalf of those Indians under his instruction, as to their desire of living in some orderly way of government, for the better preventing and redressing of things amiss amongst them by meet and just means, this Court doth therefore in testimony of their countenancing and encouraging to such a work, doe approve of

---

* The farm of Thomas Burgess was at West Sandwich, and is now owned by his descendant, Benjamin Burgess, Esq.    He had also another farm at Manomet, which adjoined Mr. Bourne's land.    Mr. Leverich's meadow was granted in 1660, but fraudulent means having been used to obtain it, the grant was revoked and the meadow granted to Mr. Bourne in 1661.    The long track of land above described is near the Monument station on the Cape Cod Railroad, the railway passing through its whole length.

these Indians proposed, viz: Paupmunnacke,* Keecomsett, Watanamatucke and Nanquidnumacke, Kanoonus and Mocrust, to have the chief inspection and management thereof, with the help and advice of the said Richard Bourne, as the matter may require; and that one of the aforesaid Indians be by the rest instated to act as a constable amongst them, it being always provided, notwithstanding, that what homage accustomed legally due to any superior Sachem be not hereby infringed.—[Colony Records, Vol. 4, page 80.]

April 2, 1667, Mr. Richard Bourne, William Bassett and James Skiffe, Senior, with the commissioned officers of Sandwich, were appointed on the Council of War. He was also on the Council in 1676. June 24, 1670, he and seven others agreed to purchase all the tar made within the Colony for the two years next ensuing at 8 shillings per small barrel, and 12 shillings per large barrel, the same to be delivered at the water-side in each town.

Nearly all the purchases of land of the Indians made in Sandwich or vicinity during the life-time of Mr. Bourne, were referred to him, a fact which shows that the English and the Indians had confidence in him as a man of integrity.

At the solicitation of Mr. Bourne, the tract of land at South Sea, containing about 10,500 acres, and known as the plantation of Marshpee, was reserved by grant from the Colony to the South Sea Indians. The late Rev. Mr. Hawly of Marshpee, says, "Mr. Bourne was a man of that discernment that he considered it as vain to propagate Christian knowledge among any people without a territory where they might remain in peace, from generation to generation, and not be ousted." The first deed of the Marshpee lands is dated Dec. 11, 1665, signed by Tookenchosen and Weepquish, and confirmed unto them by Quachateset, Sachem of Manomett. In 1685, the lands conveyed by said deed were by the Old Colony Court "confirmed to them and secured to said South Sea Indians and their children forever, so as

---

* Paupmunnacke was the sachem of the Indians in the westerly part of Barnstable, at Scorton, and perhaps of Marshpee. Keencumsett was sachem of the Mattakesits. His house stood a little distance north of the present Capt. Thomas Percival's. He was constable. The residences of the other sachems named I cannot define. These facts show that as early as 1665 an orderly form of government was established among the Indians. They held courts of their own, tried criminals, passed judgments, etc. Mr. Bourne and Gov. Hinckley frequently attended these Indian courts and aided the Indian magistrates in difficult cases.

never to be given, sold or alienated from them without all their consents."

The first marriage of Mr. Richard Bourne is not on the Colony Records. As he was a householder in Plymouth in 1636, it may safely be inferred that he was then a married man. His first wife, and the mother of all his children, was probably Bathsheba, a daughter of Mr. Andrew Hallet, Senior. He married 2d July, 1677, Ruth, widow of Jonathan Winslow, and daughter of Mr. William Sargeant of Barnstable. Mr. Bourne died in 1682, and his widow married Elder John Chipman. She died in 1713, aged 71 years.

No record of the births of the children of Richard Bourne has been preserved. His eldest son was probably born in Plymouth ; the others in Sandwich.

I.   Job married Dec. 14, 1664, Ruhama Hallet.
II.  Elisha, born 1641, married Oct. 26, 1675, Patience Skiff.
III. Shearjashub, born 1644, married Bathshea Skiff, 1673.
IV.  Ezra, born May 12, 1648. He was living in 1676, when he was fined £2 as a delinquent soldier.

Job Bourne, son of Richard, married Dec. 14, 1664, his cousin, Ruhama, daughter of Andrew Hallet of Yarmouth. He resided in Sandwich, where he was find in 1672 for not serving as constable. He died in 1676, leaving a large landed estate, which was settled March 6, 1676-7. His widow afterwards married ——— Hersey.

In the record, which is very full, it is stated that the deceased left five children, but the names of John and Hannah are omitted, probably by mistake. On the Barnstable Probate records is an instrument bearing date of 13th Sept. 1714, signed by Jonathan Mory and his wife Hannah, called a settlement of Job Bourne's estate. In this paper all the children are named excepting John. Jonathan's mother-in-law, Ruhama Hersey, is named. Children cɔ Job Bourne, born in Sandwich :

I.   Timothy, born 18th April, 1666, married Temperance Swift.
II.  Hannah, born 18th Nov. 1667, married Jonathan Mory, Esq., of Plymouth.
III. Eleazer, born 20th July, 1670.

IV. John, born 2d Nov. 1672. He resided with his grandmother Hallet, at Yarmouth.

V. Hezekiah, born 25th Sept. 1675.

Timothy, son of Job, married Temperance Swift of Sandwich, and had Job, Benjamin, Timothy, Joanna and Mehitable. His will is dated in 1729, and proved in 1744. His son Timothy married Elizabeth Bourne, and had sons Benjamin and Shearjashub, H. C., 1764. Benjamin, son of Benjamin, married —— Bodfish, and had Benjamin, Timothy, Sally, Martha, Temperance, Elizabeth and Hannah. Shearjashub married —— Doane, and had John, Shearjashub, Elisha, Abigail, Nancy and Elizabeth.

Eleazer, son of Job, married —— Hatch, and had Isaac, Job and Mercy. Job, son of Eleazer, married —— Swift, and had Thomas, Thankful, Maria, Deborah and Lydia.

Thomas, son of Job, married —— Bourne, and had Alvan, Job, John, Mary, Deborah, Lydia, Hannah and Abigail.

John, son of Job, married and had a daughter Amia, who married a Sturtevant.

Hezekiah, youngest son of Job, married Eliza Trowbridge, and had a son Ebenezer, who married Annah Bumpas, 1746, and had Ebenezer, John, Benjamin, Mehitable and Mary. Ebenezer, Jr., married three wives, and had four sons, John, Josiah, Ebenezer and Leonard C. Benjamin, son of Ebenezer, Senior, married Hannah Perry, and had Alexander, Ebenezer, Elisha, Sylvanus, Abigail and Bathsheba.

The Sylvanus last named, is the late Sylvanus Bourne, Esq., of Wareham, widely known as the late Superintendent of the Cape Cod Railroad.*

Elisha Bourne, son of Richard, born in Sandwich in 1641, resided at Manomet, near the present location of the Monument Depot, on the Cape Cod Railroad. He was constable of Sandwich in 1683, and a deputy from that town to the last General Court held at Plymouth in 1691. His will

---

* I have a genealogy of the Bournes prepared by Sylvanus Bourne; but it gives no dates, and does not give the Christian name of the wife. It is of little service. The portions of this genealogy where dates and the Christian names of the wives are omitted, is copied from that genealogy, and I cannot vouch for its accuracy.

is dated June 9, 1698, proved March 3, 1706-7.   He names his wife Patience, his sons John and Elisha (the latter it appears was not in good health), and his five daughters, Abigail, Hannah, Elizabeth, Mary and Bathsheba.   The estate was finally settled by agreement, dated April 8, 1718, at which time Mrs. Bourne and her son Elisha were dead.   The agreement is signed by Nathan, "only son," and all the daughters and their husbands.

Elisha Bourne married 26th Oct. 1675, Patience, daughter of James Skiff, Esq., of Sandwich.   She was born 25th March, 1652, and died in 1718, aged 66.   He died in 1706.

*Children born in Sandwich.*

I.   Nathan, born Aug. 31, 1676, married Mary Basset.
II.   Elizabeth, born June 26, 1679, married John Pope.
III.   Mary, born Feb. 4, 1681-2, married John Percival.
IV.   Abigail, born July 22, 1684, married William Basset, Jr.
V.   Bathsheba, born Dec. 13, 1686, married Micah Blackwell.
VI.   Hannah, born May 4, 1689, married Seth Pope.
VII.   Elisha, born July 27, 1692; died young.

Nathan, only surviving son of Elisha, was a shipwright. He died in 1789, in Hanover.   His estate in that town was appraised at £727.17.2, and in Sandwich at £898.18.10; a large estate in those times.   He married ——— Basset, had Jonathan, John, Nathan, Elisha, Thomas, Maria, Elizabeth and Mary.   Jonathan married Dec. 22, 1748, Susannah Mendal, and had John, Elisha, Nathan, Maria and Abigail. John, son of Nathan, married ——— Dillingham, and had Edward, Mary, Abigail and Hannah.   Nathan, Jr., married ——— ———, and had Samuel and Remembrance.   Elisha, son of Nathan, Senior, married ——— ———, and had Stephen and Eunice.   Thomas, son of Nathan, Senior, married ——— Randall, and had Nathan, Lemuel, William, Anselm, Samuel, Asa, Bethuel, Thomas, Lucy, Elizabeth and Mary.   Of the sixth generation of this branch of the family, Elisha, son of Jonathan, married ——— Nye, and had Jonathan, Charles, Hannah, Mehitable, Abigail and Joanna.   Stephen, son of Elisha, married ———Pope, and had Elisha and Richard.

Shearjashub Bourne, Esq., son of Richard, resided on the Marshpee Plantation until his death, living in reputation and presiding over the Indians, with whom he carried on a lucrative trade. I cannot find, says Mr. Hawley, that he made any trespasses on their lands, or was instrumental in bringing about an alienation of any part thereof. He was much employed in public business, was often a representative to the General Court at Plymouth and in Boston. He married in 1673, Bathsheba, daughter of James Skiff, Esq., of Sandwich. She was born 20th April, 1648, and was not living at the decease of her husband. He died March 7, 1718-19, aged 75. In his will, dated on the day next preceding his death, he names all his children, except Sarah, who probably died young. To his eldest son Melatiah, he gave all his lands in the town of Falmouth; to his son Ezra all his lands in Marshpee; to his grandson Shearjashub, £100; to his grandson Joseph, £100; to his daughter Mary, £200; to his daughter Remember, £200; to his daughter Patience, £200; and to the Church in Sandwich £8. His estate was appraised at £943.16.

He took a deep interest in the well-being of the Indians and was their constant friend, and adopted measures to secure to them and their heirs forever their lands.

The children of Shearjashub Bourne, born in Sandwich, were:

1. Melatiah, born 12th Jan'y, 1673-4, married Feb. 23, 1695-6, Desire Chipman.
II. Ezra, born 6th Aug. 1676, married Martha Prince.
III. Mary, born 21st Oct. 1678, married ——— Allen.
IV. Sarah, born 6th Feb. 1680-1.
V. Remember, born 6th Feb. 1683-4, married ——— Mayhew.
VI. Patience, born 20th April, 1686, married ——— Allen.

Ezra, the youngest son of Shearjashub, inherited the Marshpee estate on which he lived, and presided over the Indians, over whom to the day of his death, he maintained a great ascendency. He was one of the most distinguished and influential men of his time. He was Chief Justice of the Court of Sessions, and Court of Common Pleas. He died Sept. 1764, in the 88th year of his age. The late Rev. Gideon Hawley of Marshpee, says of him, "In him I lost a good friend."

Hon. Ezra Bourne married Martha, daughter of Samuel Prince, and had

I.   Joseph, who was liberally educated, and ordained as the pastor of the Marshpee Church in 1729. He resigned the mission in 1742. He married July 25, 1743, Hannah Fuller of Barnstable, and died in 1767, leaving no issue.

II.  Samuel, son of Ezra, married ―――― L'Hommedieu, and had Benjamin, Samuel, Nathaniel, Nathan, Timothy, Sarah and Elizabeth, all of whom married.

III. Ezra, son of Ezra.

IV.  Searjashub, married ―――― Bosworth, and had Shearjashub, Benjamin and Martha, all of whom married— the eldest having a family of thirteen. Benjamin was Judge of the District Court of Rhode Island.

V.   Martha, daughter of Ezra, married a Mr. L'Hommedieu.

VI.  Mary, daughter of Ezra, married 1733, John Angier, first minister of East Bridgewater.

VII. Elizabeth, daughter of Ezra, married Timothy Bourne.

The descendants of Ezra Bourne, Esq., as they are not of Barnstable, I shall not trace farther. In 1794, three of his grandsons were members of Congress; one from Massachusetts, one from Rhode Island and another from New-York.

Hon. Melatiah Bourne,* oldest son of Shearjashub Bourne, Esq., inherited his father's lands in Falmouth, but he settled in Sandwich. He was a distinguished man, held many responsible offices, and during the last years of his life was Judge of Probate for the County of Barnstable. He married Feb. 23, 1692-3, Desire, youngest daughter of Elder John Chipman. She died March 28, 1705, and he married second, Abigail, widow of Thomas Smith. In his will, dated 24th Sept. 1742, proved Feb. 15th following, he gives to the Sandwich Church £10, old tenor, or 50 shillings lawful money. He names his wife Abigail, her sons Samuel and John Smith, her daughter Rebecca, Mary and Isaac, children of her son Shubael, deceased, and her grandson, Doctor Thomas Smith, to all of whom he gave

---

* His house is yet remaining in Sandwich; it was most substantially built. The clapboards on the walls were shaved from cedar about an inch in thickness, and nailed with wrought nails. They are now tight and as good as new.

legacies.  He gave his cane to his eldest grandson, Melatiah,
and his clock to his son Silas.  Names his son Sylvanus;
gave to his son John and grandson Joseph, his lands in
Falmouth.  He gave legacies to his daughter Bathsheba
Ruggles and to each of the children she had by her late
husband, William Newcomb.  He orders his negro man Nero
to be manumitted.  Children of Hon. Melatiah Bourne:

I.      Sylvanus, Sept. 10, 1694, married Mercy Gorham,
        March 20, 1718.
II.     Richard, Aug. 13, 1695; died in Falmouth, 1738.
III.    Samuel, Feb. 7, 1697; died young.
IV.     Sarah, Feb. 7, 1697; died young.
V.      John, March 10, 1698, married March 16, 1772,
        Mary Hinckley.
VI.     Shearjashub, Dec. 21, 1699, married four wives.
VII.    Silas, Dec. 10, 1701, married ——— Allen.
VIII.   Bathsheba, Nov. 11, 1703, married William New-
        comb; second, Timothy Ruggles, 1736.

    Hon. Sylvanus Bourne, son of Melatiah, of Sandwich,
born Sept. 10, 1694, married in 1717, Mercy, daughter of
Col. John Gorham of Barnstable.  In 1720, he was an inhabitant of Falmouth, but soon after removed to Barnstable,
where he resided till his death.  He bought the estate which
was Mr. James Whippo's, who removed to Boston in 1708.
Mr. Thomas Sturgis, who died that year, bought this estate
for his son Edward; but it passed not many years after into
the possession of the Bourne family, in which it continued
about a century.

    He inherited a good estate from his father, and his wife
belonged to one of the most wealthy families in Barnstable.
In early life he was a merchant, and engaged in commercial business, in which he was successful, and became
wealthy.  He was a Colonel of the militia, many years one
of the Governor's Council, Register of Probate, and after
the death of his father in 1742, was appointed Judge of
Probate.

    He died in 1764.  In his will, dated May 20, 1763, he
names his sons Melatiah, to whom he gives £66.13; William, £133.6.8; and Richard, £133.6.8.  To each of his
five daughters, namely, Desire Clap, Mary Stone, Hannah
Hinckley, Mercy Jordan and Eunice Gallison, £66.13.4
each.  He also gives legacies to his grand-children Reuben,

Joseph and Abigail Winslow, children of his deceased daughter Abigail. He appoints his wife Mercy sole executrix, and gives her the residue of his large estate.

The will of Mrs. Mercy Bourne, widow of Hon. Sylvanus, is dated July 10, 1781, and was proved May 28, 1782. She gives to her son Richard, all her real estate—lands, buildings, woodlands and meadows, a silver hilted sword that was his father's, a large silver tankard that was his grandfather's, her best great Bible, two pair of oxen, one cow, half her sheep, all her husbandry tools, &c.

To her three daughters Desire Clap, Mary Stone and Hannah Hinckley, she gave all her plate (except tankard to Richard, and silver porringer to Mercy), all her wearing apparel and household furniture, excepting what she had given Richard, and £30 each.

To her granddaughter Abigail Gallison, her mother's work, called a chimney-piece. Also, two mourning rings, her grandfather Bourne's and her mother's.

She gave to her daughter Mercy Jordan, a work called the Coat of Arms, one silver porringer and £6, over and above what she had already had of her.

She also gave the following legacies :

To the children of her son Melatiah, deceased, £30.
To the children of her daughter Abigail, deceased, £20.
To the children of her daughter Eunice, deceased, £20.
To the children of her son William, £20.
To son-in-law John Gallison, Esq., £10.
To daughter-in-law Hannah Bourne, £3.

She gave her negro boy Cato to her son Richard, on the following conditions, that is, as soon as the said Cato shall arrive to the age of 35 years, her said son Richard shall manumit him. Her negro girl Chloe she gave "to such daughter as Chloe should prefer to live with, the daughter receiving her to pay such sum as said girl shall be apprized at."

She appointed her son Richard sole executor and residuary legatee, and ordered him to pay all the legacies in silver dollars at six shillings each.

The portrait of Mrs. Bourne, painted by Copley in 1766, has been preserved, and some of the worsted work named in her will. The old family portraits were stowed away in the garret of the late Sylvanus Bourne, and finally removed to his barn, where they were destroyed by fire. One of them was saved; and after having been used as a target, is now in the possession of Major S. B. Phinney, who has had it restored. He also has a view of Boston Common taken more than a century ago, wrought in worsted, which formerly belonged to his ancestor, Colonel Sylvanus Bourne. N. S. Simpkins, Esq., who is also a descendant, has a specimen of worsted work that belonged to the Bourne family.

The facts which have been stated show that Colonel Sylvanus Bourne was a man of wealth; and that he lived in the style of an English country gentleman. Facts are perhaps not wanting to show that he had little respect for the simplicity of his puritan ancestry. Some of the family joined the Episcopal Church, and the fact that Mrs. Bourne in her portrait is represented as holding in her hand a copy of the English prayer book, shows that she had a predilection for the Episcopacy.

Mrs. Bourne joined the Barnstable Church Sept. 20, 1724, and on the Fourth of July, 1729, was admitted to the Church in the East Parish, being dismissed with many others at that time from the West Parish. All her children were baptized at the Barnstable Church. She died according to the inscription on her grave stones, April 11, 1782, in the 87th year of her age.

The children of Colonel Sylvanus Bourne and his wife Mercy Gorham, were all born in Barnstable, except Mary, who was born in Falmouth.

### Children born in Barnstable.

I.    Desire, born Jan'y 19, 1718; bap'd Oct. 4, 1724, married Nathaniel Clap, Esq., of Scituate, Dec. 22, 1737. He was a son of Deacon Stephen, and a brother of Thomas, President of Yale College—one of the most distinguished men of learning of his time.

II.   Mary, born April 22, 1720, bap'd Oct. 4, 1724, married 1742, Nathaniel Stone, Jr., of Harwich.

III.  Melatiah, born Nov. 14, 1722, bap'd Oct. 4, 1724, married Mary Bayard, niece of Gov. Bowdoin. His son, Capt. Sylvanus, was Consul many years at Amsterdam. Portraits of his children taken at Amsterdam, are in the possession of Major S. B. Phinney. His son Melatiah, married Olive Gorham, and had Melatiah, Sylvanus and Olive—the latter the mother of Major S. B. Phinney of Barnstable, and George Phinney, Esq., of North Bridgewater. The other children of Melatiah were Sarah and Mary.

Melatiah Bourne, Esq., died Sept. 1778, after a long and painful illness, aged 56. His monument in the grave-yard, near the Church, in the East Parish in Barnstable, says:

"He was a gentleman who, in public employ, conducted with great reputation to himself, and honor to his country. And in the more private walks of sociable life exhibited those virtues which have raised in the bosoms of those who knew him, a monument that shall exist when this stone shall be mouldered to its native dust. In him the Christian graces shone with peculiar lustre, and the plaudit of an approving conscience was the summit of his ambition."

> "Surely when men like these depart,
> The cause of virtue deeply feels the wound."

IV. William, born Feb. 27, 1723-4, bap'd Oct. 4, 1724. Tradition saith, and its accuracy is vouched for by Col. Swett, that when a child he was prostrated by an appalling disease, pronounced by the medical faculty incurable. The Indians, who remembered all the members of the Bourne family with affection, did not despair, and came with the medicine men of their tribe to try the effect of their simple remedies and incantations. The tender mother did not hesitate to submit her beloved son to savage rites and Indian remedies; and from that hour, says Col. Swett, the child was made whole.

He served in Gorham's Rangers at the taking of Louisburg in 1757. He settled in Marblehead, and was a wealthy merchant. He was a Justice of one of the Courts. He exerted his influence in procuring a charter and raising funds to build the bridge at Newbury, and for his services he had the honor to be the first to pass over it. He was a Colonel of the militia, and died in 1770.

He married for his first wife a daughter of Lieut. Gov. Hazard, and for his second a daughter of Judge Tasker, and widow of James Fessenden of Marblehead.

He had three daughters : Clarissa, Charlotte and Fanny. One married Col. Orne of Marblehead, another Dr. Swett of Newburyport, and the third Judge Peabody of Exeter, N. H., the father of the authors of that name.

[From the Boston Weekly News Letter of 30th August, 1770.]

"On Wednesday were interred the Remains of the Hon. William Bourn, Esq., Son of the Hon. Sylvanus Bourn, Esq. ; late of Barnstable :—A Gentleman blessed with good natural Abilities, which were improved by a liberal Education and an extensive acquaintance with the world.

In early Life he was engaged in the military Service, and has since been constantly honored with public Employments, which he filled with dignity, and discharged with uprightness.

In the vale of private life, where merit is impartially examined, his worth was conspicuous : His vivacity, frankness, and delicacy of sentiment, endeared him to every acquaintance, and to his honor, his free, social hours will long be remembered by them with delight.

The goodness of his heart and the integrity of his life corresponded to the clearness of his head ; so that he beheld with philosophic firmness and Christian resignation his approaching dissolution ; and, a few days before his death, discovered an uncommon vigor and serenity of mind in the orderly disposition of his affairs.

Quis desiderio sit pudor aut modus Tam cari capitis ? &c., to Quando ullum inveniet parem."

V.    Hannah, born Dec. 8, 1725, bap'd Jan'y 9, 1726, married Isaac Hinckley, Jr., Dec. 18, 1748, of Barnstable.    She had eight children.

VI.    Mercy, born Monday, Aug. 22, 1727, says the record, and bap'd Aug. 27, following.    She married Samuel Jordan, Esq., of Biddeford, Maine, April 10, 1751.

VII.    Abigail, born Saturday, June 21, 1729, bap'd next day according to Puritan custom.    She married March 14, 1754, Kenelm Winslow, Jr., of Marshfield.    She died before her father, leaving three children as above stated.

VIII. Sylvanus, born (says the town record, and his grave-
stones), Nov. 21, 1731, and bap'd, according to the
church records, on the 14th of the same month.   He
married Feb. 3, 1757, Hannah Sturgis.   He had no
children.   Before leaving for Cape Breton he made
his will, dated May 24, 1758; but it was not proved
till July 16, 1761.   He styles himself a merchant, and
says he is bound on a dangerous enterprise.   He gave
his whole estate to his wife.   He died suddenly at
Martha's Vineyard, May 22, 1761.   He was then a
captain in the provincial army, and was recruiting men
for the service, in which he had been employed several
years.   He was 29 years of age.   The inventory of
his estate amounted to £122.9, including a small stock
of merchandize.   His widow died June 13, 1798,
aged 62.

IX. Eunice, born Feb. 16, 1732-3, bap'd on the 25th of the
same month; married June 19, 1754, Capt. John Gallison of Marblehead.   Her grandson, John, was a dis-
tinguised Counsellor at Law.

X. Richard, born Nov. 1, 1739, bap'd 18th of same month.
He was a physician, and though he usually laid his saddle bags and spurs on his table every night, so that he
could promptly respond to a call, he rarely had a patient.
He was a very different man from his brothers.   He inherited none of the energy of character and good business habits of his ancestors.   He was a man of feeble intellectual power,—simple-minded and incapable of making much exertion.   He was a well educated man, and it
has been remarked of him by persons well qualified to
judge, that he had a good knowledge of the theory and
practice of medicine; but being wanting in judgment,
his learning was of no practical advantage to him.   He
was very courteous and gentlemanly in his habits, and
one of the most accommodating and obliging of men.
He was the first Postmaster in Barnstable, an office which
he held many years, and the Barnstable Social Library
was kept at his house.   For many years he was the only
Postmaster, and his house was a place of frequent resort.
At first, there was only a weekly mail; afterwards a
semi-weekly, and in 1812 a tri-weekly—only two however were paid for by the Post Office Department; the

third was paid by private subscriptions. The mail left Boston about four o'clock in the morning, and was due in Barnstable at eight in the evening. During the war the people were anxious to obtain the news, and the men of the neighborhood, and messengers from distant parts of the town, assembled at the post-office on the evening of the days when a mail was due. It was also a favorite resort for boys who were very troublesome to the doctor. On winter evenings when the mail was delayed by the bad condition of the roads, or a storm, a large company assembled in the doctor's parlor. The men were usually seated in a semi-circle around the fire, and the boys were seated on the floor with their feet pushed between the rundles of the chairs to obtain some warmth from the fire. The doctor had a few stereotype stories which he repeated every evening, the scenes whereof were laid in Maine, where he resided some time when a young man.

His wife was a very intelligent woman, and their only child, Abigail, was a kind-hearted and accomplished lady, extremely courteous and obliging to all who called at the office, or to obtain books from the Social Library, of which she took the charge. After the death of her parents she married her relative, Nathan Stone, Esq., of Dennis.

Doctor Bourne was temperate in his habits; that is he never was intoxicated at his own expense. During his time, there were few who could say as much in their own vindication. It was fashionable at that time for the men to assemble frequently at the taverns, where they often remained till late, drinking, carousing, and sometimes to gamble. The doctor was sometimes invited to these parties. He sung the same song "Old King Cole," on all festive occasions. After two or three drams, he would sing his song, which would cause infinite diversion to the company. Liquor deprived the doctor of the little wit he ordinarily had, and his grotesque acts and uncouth expressions rendered him a boon companion. The story of one of these adventures was often told by the late Abner Davis, Esq., who probably added some embellishments of his own, for there were few men who could tell a story better than he.

About the year 1810, Doctor Bourne was invited to

attend a Christmas party at Hyannis.   He rode his gray
mare, which did him excellent service for twenty years,
and arrived at the place appointed soon after sunset.
There was an abundance of liquor on the table, and the
doctor was frequently pressed to partake thereof.   The
company had a jolly time, the doctor repeatedly sung
his favorite song, and told the story of his adventures in
Maine.   It was twelve o'clock when the party separated,
and the doctor had to be helped on to his horse.   It was
a clear, moonlight evening, the ground was covered with
snow and a north-west wind rendered the air cold and
piercing.   He had to pass four miles through woods,
and along a narrow road on which no inhabitants resided.
The horse knew the way better than the master, and if
the animal could have had its own way the rider would
have escaped the perils he soon after encountered.   Riding about a mile he left the direct road and turned into
the way that leads to Half-Way Pond.   He had not
travelled far before he caught sight of a rotten stump
which reflected a phosphorescent light.   The doctor
imagined it was a fire, and as his feet were very cold, he
dismounted, pulled off his boots and placed his feet on
the stump.   When sufficiently warm, he remounted;
but unfortunately omitted to put on his boots.   He wan-
dered about the woods till morning, when he found his
way out.   On arriving at the main road, instead of turning westerly towards his own house, he turned in an
opposite direction, and urged his beast into a gallop.   He
had not rode far, when he met Abner Davis, Esq., and
several gentlemen of his acquaintance.   He suddenly
reined up his horse, and accosted them thus : "Gentlemen," said he, "can you tell me whether I am in this
town or the next?"   Mr. Davis replied, "You are in
this town now, but if you drive on you will soon be in
the next."   The company perceiving that he had no
boots, and that he was wild and excited, invited him to
a house where he was furnished with a warm breakfast
and a pair of boots.   After resting a few hours he rode
home ; but it was several days before he entirely recovered from the excitement and fatigue of his Christmas
frolic.

Often when waiting for the mails in the doctor's parlor

there would be a knock at the door of the office.   The
doctor would  open the door, and  with his usual suavity
of manner, would say, "Good evening, sir."   The reply
would sometimes be, "Doctor, I just called to inquire
whether or  not you have found your boots?"   At other
times the inquiry would be, "Am I in this town or the
next?"   These inquiries irritated the doctor, and he
would grasp his whip, which he kept hanging by the
door, and make a dash at the boys, who always took the
precaution to be beyond the reach of the lash.

## AN ERROR CORRECTED.

"A few years before his death, Matthew Cobb, Esq.,
succeeded him in the office of Postmaster.   This was a great
grief to him, and was regretted by many.   However simple
or foolish the doctor may have been, he was a very accommodating officer, and took much pains to ascertain the residences
of parties, and forward them their letters or papers.
On the settlement of his accounts, he was found to be a
defaulter for nearly a thousand dollars, which was levied on
his estate, and rendered him poor at the close of his life.
His accounts were not carefully kept, and several who examined them were of the opinion that he was not a defaulter ;
that he had neglected to take vouchers for several sums
of money he paid over, and he was therefore unable to
prove that he had faithfully accounted for the receipts of his
office."

When writing the above paragraph, I had the impression in my mind that subsequently it was ascertained that
the errors were committed at the Post Office Department,
and not by the doctor ; but those of whom I inquired had a
different impression.   No one of whom I inquired seemed to
know certainly.   I am now happy in being able to state that
Doctor Bourne was not a defaulter.   Asa Young, Esq., who
was his agent, informs me that Doctor Bourne's property had
been set off by execution, sold, and the proceeds paid over
to the Department, when it was ascertained that the error
occurred at the Post Office Department.   The money was refunded, and the draft for the same was received by Miss
Abigail Bourne, the sole heir, on the very day she was married to Nathan Stone, Esq.—a most happy coincidence.
According to the doctor's accounts, kept by  his daugh-

ter Abigail, he owed the Department thirty dollars when his successor was appointed. This sum was laid aside to be paid over when called for. Subsequent investigation proved that Doctor Bourne's accounts were right. His property was wrongfully taken from him, and he did not live till it was rectified.

Justice to Doctor Richard Bourne as an honest and honorable man, requires this correction to be made, and those who preserve files of my papers are requested to note this fact in the margin of No. 28, *that the money was subsequently refunded by the Post Office Department.*

He died in Barnstable April 25, 1826, aged 86 years. His wife died in Barnstable March 5, 1826, aged 85 years.

I. Capt. Richard Bourne, a son of Melatiah, born Aug. 13, 1695, was an officer in the army, and distinguished himself at Norridgwalk. He settled in Falmouth, where he died in 1738, leaving no issue.

II. John Bourne, son of Melatiah, born March 10, 1698, married March 16, 1722, Mercy, daughter of Joseph Hinckley of Barnstable. He removed to Falmouth and had Joseph, John, David, Thomas, Sarah, Mary, Elizabeth and Mary. All the sons, excepting Thomas, married and had families. Mr. John Bourne, the father of this family, died early in life, leaving a good estate.

III. Shearjashub, son of Melatiah, born Dec. 21, 1699. He received his degrees at Harvard College in 1720, and was ordained pastor of the First Church in Scituate, Dec. 3, 1724. He married 1725, Abigail, daughter of Rev. Roland Cotten of Sandwich, and had Elizabeth, 1726; Abigail, 1727; Desire, 1728; Bathsheba, 1730; Shearjashub in 1732, who died young. His first wife died in 1732, and he married in 1738, Sarah Brooks of Medford, by whom he had one son, Shearjashub, born in 1739. His second wife died in 1742, and he married in 1750, Deborah Barker, by whom he had one son, Roland, born the same year. His third wife died in 1750, and he married in 1757, Joanna Stevens of Roxbury.

He was a man of feeble constitution, and depressed and melancholy spirits. In 1755, his health was impaired by a paralytic affection. He tendered his resignation of the pastoral office, and Aug. 6, 1761, was dismissed; his society generously presenting him with £100, and the use of the parsonage for a year and a half. From Scituate he removed to Roxbury, the native place of his wife, where he died Aug 14, 1768, in the 69th year of his age.—[See Deane's Scituate, pages 186 and 187.]

# BURSLEY.

Mr. John Bursley, the ancestor of the families of this name, came over very early, probably before Gov. Endicot. From what part of England he came, I have not ascertained. There is a parish in England called "Burslem," and as surnames often originated in the names of places or trades, it is probable that some of his ancestors resided in that parish.* The name is variously written on the old records,—Burslem, Burslin, Burslyn, Burseley, Bursly. When first named, he is styled Mr.—a title of respect in early times. He appears to have been an active business man, engaged in the fisheries, and in trade with the Indians, and a planter.

He may have been a member of the Dorchester Company, that settled at Cape Ann in 1624. In 1629, he was at Wessaguscus, now Weymouth, where he was an associate of Mr. William Jeffrey. The following assessment levied to defray the expenses of the arrest and sending of Merton to England in 1628, proves that he was a resident in the country prior to 1629. This is the oldest tax bill on record, and shows the comparative wealth or ability of the different settlements in 1629 :

---

* Sur-names were often suggested by the appearance, character or history of the individual. Burse is a purse; hence the name of Bursely may have originated thus—"John the Burser," or treasurer, and in course of time contracted to "John Bursley." The importance of signing all legal and other instruments with the Christian name written at full length is not well understood. The "Christian" name is the "signature." It is not, however, so important now as formerly, that it should be written at full length. Legally, the man who writes only the initial letter of his Christian name, only "makes his mark;" he does not "sign" the document.

| | |
|---|---|
| Plymouth, | £2.10 |
| Naumkeak, (Salem,) | 1.10 |
| Piscataquack, (Portsmouth,) | 2.10 |
| Mr. Jeffrey and Mr. Burslem, Wessaguscus, (Weymouth,) | 2.00 |
| Nantascot, (Hull,) | 1.10 |
| Mrs. Thompson, (Squantum Neck,) | 15 |
| Mr. Blackstone, (Boston,) | 12 |
| Edward Hilton, (Dover,) | 1.00 |
| | £12.7 |

Mr. Savage says that Mr. Bursley was an early settler at Weymouth; reckoned some three or four years among "old planters." That he was early of Weymouth, is evident from the record of the proceedings May 14, 1634, in relation to his servant Thomas Lane. Lane "having fallen lame and impotent, became chargeable to the town of Dorchester, his then place of residence. The General Court investigated the questions at issue, and ordered that the inhabitants of Wessaguscus should pay all the charges of his support." From this it appears that Lane had previously to 1634, resided a sufficient length of time at Wessaguscus, as the servant of Mr. John Bursley, to make the inhabitants of that place legally chargeable for his support.

Mr. Palfrey, in his history of New England, says the cottages of Mr. Jeffrey and Mr. Burslem probably stood at Winnisimmet, now Chelsea. The foregoing abstracts from the records show that he was mistaken in his supposition. It also appears that John Bursley was one of the assessors of Dorchester, June 2, 1634.

From 1630 to 1635, Wessaguscus appears to have been included within the corporate limits of Dorchester. Oct. 19, 1630, Mr. Bursley and Mr. Jeffrey requested to be admitted freemen of Massachusetts, and were sworn in the 18th of May following. They were then called Dorchester men, though residents at Wessaguscus, which was incorporated in 1635, and named Weymouth.

Mr. Bursley was deputy from Weymouth to the Massachusetts General Court, May, 1636, and was appointed a member of the Committee to take the valuation of the estates in the Colony. He and two others were elected to the September term of the Court; but it was decided that

Weymouth, being a small town, was not entitled to send three deputies, and he and John Upham were dismissed. In Nov. 1637, he was appointed by the Court a member of a committee to measure and run out a three mile boundary line. In May, 1639, he removed to Barnstable, in company with Mr. Thomas Dimmock of Scituate, and Mr. Joseph Hull of Weymouth, to whom the lands in Barnstable had been granted by the Plymouth Colony Court. In 1643 and 1645 he was at Exeter; in 1647 at Hampton and Kittery; Sept. 9, 1650, at Neweechwannook; and at Kittery from 1650 to Nov. 1652. Excepting at Kittery, he did not reside long at either of these places,—he visited them and the Isles of Shoals, when his father-in-law was settled in the ministry, and other places on the coast, for the purposes of trade, his family residing at Barnstable. In 1645, he is called of Exeter, yet he was that year chosen constable of Barnstable, sworn at the June Court, and served in that office. In 1647, he is called of Kittery, yet he was that year one of the grand jurors from the town of Barnstable. These facts show that his residence in the eastern country was not permanent.

In 1652, the General Court of Massachusetts appointed a commission to assume jurisdiction over the township of Kittery, and require the inhabitants to submit to the government of that Colony. A meeting of the inhabitants was called on the 15th of Nov:, and while the matter was under consideration, "complaints were made against one Jno. Bursly* for uttering threatening words against the Commissioners, and such as should submit to the government of Massachusetts." "The said Bursly upon his examination at length in open Court, did confess the words, and uppon

* "One Jno. Bursly." Mr. Bursley was well-known to the Commissioners, for some of them had been his associates in the General Court of Massachusetts. The right of that Colony to assume the jurisdiction claimed, to say the least of the matter, was doubtful. The Bursleys of the present day are firm and unwavering in the support of their opinions and never yield a point that is just and for their interest to maintain.— Their ancestor it is to be presumed was as firm and unyielding as any of his descendants, and would not be overawed by the Commissioners.— They say in their return—"Bursly submitted." He resisted their authority and refused to sign the articles of submission which were signed by forty-one of the inhabitants. Their own record shows that he fearlessly exercised his right as a freeman, and the Commissioners vented their spleen by contemptuously calling him "one Jno. Bursly."

his submission was discharged." After much debate forty-
one of the inhabitants submitted; but Mr. Bursly was not
of the number. He returned to Barnstable, and it does not
appear that he afterwards visited the eastern country.

Mr. John Bursley married Nov. 28, 1639, Joanna,
daughter of Rev. Joseph Hull of Barnstable. The marriage
was solemnized in Sandwich, no one in Barnstable being
then authorized to officiate. He resided in the house of his
father-in-law, which stood near where Capt. Thomas Harris'
now stands, till about the year 1650, when he removed to
the Bursley farm at West Barnstable. His first house was
built on the north side of the County Road across the little
run of water, and about one hundred yards north easterly
from the barn of the present Mr. Charles H. Bursley. The
remains of the old chimney and the ancient hearthstone were
removed not many years ago. An incident in his personal
history which occurred during his residence at the old house
has been preserved by tradition. The low land in front or
south of the house was then a quag-mire. One day when
he was confined to the house with a broken leg, and when
all the male members of the family were absent, a calf sunk
in the quag-mire, and would have been lost without assistance. The women were alarmed, being unable to extricate
the calf. Mr. Bursley directed them to fasten a rope around
it, and pass the end into the house. They did so, and with
his aid, the calf was drawn out and saved.

The ancient Bursley mansion was taken down in 1827.
The John Bursley, then living, born in 1741, said it was
one hundred and thirty years old, according to the best information he could obtain. This would give the year 1697,
as the date at which it was built. He had no record of the
time; he knew its age only from tradition, and was mistaken. A house was standing on the same spot in 1686,
when the County Road was laid out, and was then occupied
by the Wid. Joanna Davis, who had previously been the
wife of the first John Bursley. The description given of
the house at the time of the death of the second John Bursley in 1726, corresponds very nearly with its appearance in
1827, showing that few alterations had been made. The
style was that of the wealthy among the first settlers. The
Bacon house, which has been described, was built in 1642.
The style of the Bursley house was the same, only it was

originally a larger and better building. As late as 1690, dwelling houses were built in a very similar style, and there was a general resemblance. Both had heavy cornices, the front roof was shorter and sharper than the rear. The more ancient houses were lower in the walls, especially the chambers, and the sleepers of the lower floors were laid on the ground, leaving the large sills used in those days, projecting into the rooms.

The style of the old Bursley house indicated its early origin, and there seems to be no good reason to doubt that it was built by the first John Bursley, before the year 1660. If it was a matter of any importance, it could be shown by other facts that the house was built before 1660. I have pursued the inquiry thus far mainly to show how uncertain and unreliable is tradition, especially in regard to time.

The Bursley farm at West Barnstable is thus described on the town records :

Forty-five acres of upland, more or less, bounded partly by two rivers that run into Boat Cove, and partly by the Commons, as it is marked out.

Feb. 1655. Eighty acres of upland, more or less, bounded easterly by Boat Cove, westerly by a runlet, adjoining Goodman Fitz Randle's, southerly partly by Mr. Linnell's and partly by ye Commons, northerly to the marsh.

Fifteen acres of marsh, more or less, bounded easterly by Boat Cove, westerly by Goodman Fitz Randle's, northerly to a creek, southerly to his upland.

The eighty acres on the north side of the road, is bounded on three sides by water ; a very desirable location because the water courses saved much labor and expense in building fences. The soil is generally a strong loam, free of rocks, and good grass land. From the first it has been carefully cultivated, and is now one of the most fertile and productive farms in Barnstable. Forty acres of the upland on the north side of the road are now owned by a lineal descendant, Mr. Charles H. Bursley, and thirty by Frederick Parker, Esq.

The first John Bursley died in 1660. The inventory of his estate, taken Aug. 21, of that year by John Smith and John Chipman, amounted to only £115.5. I do not know whether this sum covered both the real and personal estate, but presume it did. I copy from the Genealogical Register, in which only the gross is given. The same estate was appraised at £137.13.10 in 1726. I have called Mr. Bursley wealthy. Wealth is a comparative term, and when a man is called rich, a great variety of circumstances are taken into account. What was the cash value of Mr. Bursley's farm at the time of his death, has little to do with the question. Eight years after, the Blush farm, now Bodfish's, the next west, excepting one, sold for £5.10. This was worth about one-third of the Bursley farm, exclusive of buildings. A common one-story house at that time cost only about £5. That was the price paid William Chase for building the first Hallett house in Yarmouth. Very little glass, lime, iron or brick, was used in those days, and the expense of lumber was the cost of cutting and sawing it. They were very rudely constructed, and as late as 1700, it was not common for the walls of a house to be plastered. The joints between the boards were filled with clay or mortar. The meeting house built in 1725, in the East Parish, was constructed in that manner. A house like the ancient Bursley mansion would not, when that was built, have cost more than £50 sterling. Very little money was in circulation in those times, and as a consequence prices ruled very low. It is said on good authority, and there can be no doubt of its truth, that in the year 1675, five hundred pounds in money could not be raised in Plymouth Colony; and, for a good reason, there was not so much money in the Colony.

In 1669, the Otis farm, about half a mile east of the Bursley, was bought for £150. The latter was then much more valuable. It was easier land to till, and was in a better state of cultivation. The Bourman farm, not so valuable as the Bursley farm, sold in 1662 for £78. There is apparently a wide difference in these prices of property of the same description, in the same neighborhood at about the same time. But it must be remembered that the value of landed estate depended then very much on the value of the improvements thereon, and on the kind of pay for which the property was sold. The usual consideration being provisions at "prices current with the merchants." Very few contracts were made payable in silver money.

The names of the children of the first John Bursley are not entered on the town or probate records. At the time of his marriage, Nov. 28, 1639, he was probably forty years of age, and the bride, Miss Joanna Hull, a blushing maid not out of her teens. Their children, as entered on the church records, are as follows :

I. A child—name not recorded—died suddenly in the night, and was buried Jan'y 25, 1640-1, at the lower side of the Calves Pasture.

II. Mary, bap'd July 29, 1643, married April 25, 1663, John Crocker. She was his second wife, and was the mother of ten children.

III. John, bap'd Sept. 22, 1644, buried Sept. 27, 1644.

IV. Joanna, bap'd March 1, 1645-6, married Dea. Shubael Dimmock, April, 1662 ; had a family of nine children born in Barnstable. She died in Mansfield, Conn., May 8, 1727, aged 83 years.

V. Elizabeth, bap'd March 25, 1649, married, first, Nathaniel Goodspeed, Nov. 1666, by whom she had a daughter Mary, who married Ensign John Hinckley. She married, second, Increase Clap, Oct. 1675, and by him had four children born in Barnstable.

VI. John, bap'd April 11, 1652, married, first, Elizabeth Howland, Dec. 1673, and second, Elizabeth ————.

VII. Temperance, who married Joseph Crocker, Dec. 1677, and had seven children born in Barnstable, and was living in 1741.

Mr. John Bursley died in 1660, and his widow married Dolar Davis, who died in 1673. The widow Joanna Davis was living in 1686. The date of her death I am unable to ascertain.

John Bursley, 2d, only son of John, was eight years of age when his father died. He inherited the mansion house taken down in 1827, and two-sixths of his father's estate. The right of his sisters it appears that he bought, for at his death in 1726, he owned all the lands that were his father's. He married twice ; first, Elizabeth, daughter of Lieutenant John Howland, Dec. 1673, who was the mother of his ten children. His second wife was also named Elizabeth ; but her maiden name does not appear on record.

He was a farmer, industrious and enterprising, and died leaving a large estate. The old mansion house he bequeathed to his son Joseph.

Children of John Bursley, 2d, born in Barnstable:

I.    Elizabeth, born Oct. 1674; died Oct. 1675.

II.   Mercy, born Oct. 1675; died April 1676.

III.  John, born March, 1677-8. He married Mary Crocker, daughter of John, and was living in the year 1741, Feb. 11, 1702, and had three children. Two died in infancy, and the other, Experience, married Benjamin Lothrop. He inherited the southwesterly part of the old farm on which he resided. He was captain of a vessel employed in the whale fishery, and died in Barnstable, 1748.

IV.   Mary, born, 23d May, 1679, married Joseph Smith, after the year 1722.

V.    Jabez, born 21st Aug. 1681. His father in his will gave him the northwest quarter of his farm, since known as Doctor Whitman's farm, and now owned by Frederick Parker, Esq. He married Hannah ———, 1705, and had Benjamin, 21st July, 1706, married Joanna Cannons, July 7, 1735; second, Mary Goodspeed, Feb. 2, 1744, and had Jabez, 26th July, 1745; Martha, 25th Aug. 1740; Elizabeth, 23d Dec. 1744; Sarah, 3d Feb. 1748; Benjamin, 27th March, 1752, and Lemuel, 17th June, 1755; John, born 1st Sept. 1708, married Eliz. Saunders, 1743; Elizabeth, born 1st Feb. 1710-11; Abigail, 25th Feb. 1714, married Benoni Crocker, Feb. 19, 1736; Hannah, Nov. 1715, married Solomon Bodfish, Dec. 17, 1741; Joanna born June, 1719, married Charles Connett, 1733; Mary, Aug. 1723, and Barnabas, 16th Jan'y 1725, married Thankful Smith, May 16, 1754, and had Hannah, Feb. 3, 1756; Thankful, March 29, 1759, and Barnabas, April 24, 1761. Jabez Bursley died in 1732, and names in his will all his eight children. Estate, £1.281.12.6.

VI.   Joanna, born 29th Nov. 1684, married March, 1708-9, Nathan Crocker of Barnstable.

VII.  Joseph, born 29th Jan'y 1686-7, married Sarah Crocker, Nov. 7, 1712, and had Joseph, who married Dec. 20, 1739, Bethia Fuller, and had John, Nov. 1, 1741, grandfather of the present Mr. Charles H. Bursley; Bethia, born March 2, 1743; Lemuel, March 2, 1745, father of the present Mr. Joseph

Bursley of Barnstable; Sarah, born Oct. 24, 1748; Abigail, Oct. 23, 1750, and Joseph, 27th March, 1757.

Joseph Bursley, Sen'r., also had Lemuel, 8th Sept. 1718, and Mercy, 10th July, 1721, married May 22, 1757, John Goodspeed.

VIII.   Abigail, born 27th Aug. 1690, married Nath'l Bodfish, March 10, 1713.

IX.   Elizabeth, born 5th Aug. 1692, married Nov. 28, 1723, Jon. Crocker.

X.   Temperance, born 3d Jan'y 1695.   She was of feeble health, and died unmarried Sept. 20, 1734.

John Bursley, 2d, bequeathed to his son Joseph the ancient house then appraised, with the house lot, at £240, and all the easterly half of the estate.   John Bursley, 2d, owned at his death in 1726, the same real estate that his father did in 1660, with the addition of shares in the commons, to which his father was also entitled.   The estate was appraised at £115.5 in 1660, and in 1727, £3.137.13.10. Presuming that each had the same proportional amount of personal estate, these appraisals show a rapid appreciation of value during the 68 years.   After allowing for the depreciation of the currency, £115.5 in 1660, if the appraisal was in sterling money, would be about 520 ounces of silver, and if in lawful money 384 ounces.   In 1727, an ounce of silver was worth 17 shillings, and £3.137.13.10, was equal to 3.486 ounces of silver.

# BERRY.

In the list of those who were able to bear arms in Barnstable, in 1643, is the name of Richard Berry. It is not slanderous to say the son is a better man than the father, or that the daughter is a better woman than the mother. This remark applies to Richard Berry and his wife Alice. They did not sustain good characters, but their children followed not in their footsteps. He did not reside long in Barnstable. He probably removed to Boston in 1647, and thence to Yarmouth where his large family of children were born.

Oct. 29, 1649, Berry accused Teague Jones of Yarmouth, of the crime of sodomy, and Jones was put under heavy bonds for his appearance at the March term of the Court to answer. At that Court Berry confessed that he had borne false witness against Jones, and for his perjury was whipped at the post in Plymouth.

His wife Alice was a thievish woman, and husband and wife were well matched. May 3, 1653, she was presented for stealing a neckcloth from the wife of William Pierce of Yarmouth; at the June Court for stealing bacon and eggs from Mr. Samuel Arnold; at the March Court, 1654-5, for stealing from the house of Benjamin Hammond a woman's shift and a piece of pork, and at the following Court in

June for thievishly milking the cow of Thomas Phelps* of Yarmouth. For the latter offence she was fined ten shillings, "or, refusing to pay, then to sit in the stocks at Yarmouth an hour the next training day." This is a sufficient specimen of her character, and it is unnecessary to trace it farther.

It would, however, be unjust to the wife to say nothing more respecting the husband. Richard, notwithstanding his humiliating confession that he had sworn falsely, and his visit to the whipping-post, continued to live on excellent terms with his friend Teague at Doctor's Weir, near the mouth of Bass River. The Court, however, thought differently, and caused them "to part their uncivil living together." In March, 1663, he was fined forty shillings for playing cards; but at the March Court following, the fine was remitted. In 1668, Zachary Rider, the first born of the English in Yarmouth, complained that Berry had stolen his axe, and the matter was referred "to Mr. Hinckley and Mr. Bacon to end it at home." Richard, notwithstanding his vicious propensities, went to meeting on the Sabbath days carrying with him his pipe and tinder-horn. One Sabbath, during "the time of exercise," he and others, instead of listening to the exhortations of the preacher, seated themselves "at the end of Yarmouth Meeting House," and indulged in smoking tobacco. For this offence he and his companions were each mulcted in a fine of five shillings, at the March Court in 1669.

Richard Berry died Sept. 7, 1681, having at the time of his death a house therein, though he had in early times been forbidden to erect a cottage in Yarmouth. In his old age he lived a better life, was admitted a townsman of Yarmouth, and his wife became respectable. They were very poor, and having a large family, it was very difficult for them to provide the necessaries of life. They thought it less criminal to steal than to starve. Necessity may palliate dis-

---

* This name should perhaps be Thomas Philips, who was an early settler in Yarmouth. He is not named by Mr. Savage, and I have been unable to find much respecting him. His wife's name was Agnesse or Annis. In 1665, he was find ten shillings for lying. A woman supposed to be his daughter, was found dead in the wreck of a boat at Duxbury, Dec. 6, 1673. He died in 1674, leaving an estate appraised at £61.0.3, a widow and eight children then surviving. In 1678, Hugh Stewart, the administrator, had liberty to sell the house and land belonging to the estate of Thomas Philips, deceased, and it would appear from the mode of expression employed, that the family had then removed.

honest acts, but it cannot justify. Another consideration
may be named ; as soon as their children were able to contribute something by their labors for the support of the
family, no more is heard of the thievish propensities of husband or wife.

He had eleven children born in Yarmouth, but the
record is imperfect, most of the names being torn off and
lost. The dates remain. John, born 29th March, 1652 ;
one, 11th July, 1654 ; Elizabeth, 5th March, 1656 ; one,
12th May, 1659 ; one, 23d Aug. 1662 ; one, 16th Oct.
1663 ; one, 5th Oct. 1668 ; one, 1st June, 1670 ; one, 31st
Oct. 1673, one, 12th Dec. 1677, and one other. It is probable that five of the above died before July, 1676. I judge
so from a mutilated record under the entry of the births.
He certainly had sons John, Richard, Samuel, Nathaniel,
who died Feb. 7, 1793-4, and Joseph, who died in 1686,
and a daughter Elizabeth, who married Josiah Jones, 28th
Nov. 1677.

John Berry was a resident of Yarmouth; he was a
soldier in King Philip's war, and died in 1745, aged 93.
In his will he names his children Judah, Ebenezer,
Elizabeth, who married Samuel Baker, July 30, 1702 ;
Experience, who married —— Bangs, and Mary, who
married Isaac Chase, July 23, 1706.

Samuel Berry, son of Richard, married Elizabeth,
daughter of John Bell, and had six children born in Yarmouth, viz : A daughter, born Jan'y 19, 1682 ; Elizabeth,
Dec. 21, 1684 ; Patience, June 22, 1687 ; John, July 9,
1689 ; Samuel, Nov. 1691, and Desire, June 29, 1694.
The father died Feb. 21, 1703-4.

---

NOTE.—A friend for whose opinion I have a high respect, reproves me
for speaking so plainly of the faults of those whose biography I write.
In the common intercourse of life, I admit that it is a good rule to say
nothing, when you cannot speak well of a man. Such a rule does not
apply to the writer of history. Shall all that is said in the Bible respecting Judas Iscariot and other vile persons be stricken out? Shall the
name of Nero and of Benedict Arnold cease to appear in history? Shall
the name of Judge Jeffries be hereafter chronicled among the saints?—
What if a man's blood "has crept through scoundrels ever since the
flood," is he to blame? Is it not meritorious in him to have controlled a
constitutional predisposition to do wrong? I know prudes will condemn,
and the very discreet object, yet their objecting or condemning does not
relieve the writer of history from telling the whole truth.

From these two sons of Richard, John and Samuel, both of whom sustained good characters and were useful citizens, the numerous families of the name of Berry on the Cape appear to descend. As it is not a Barnstable name I shall not trace the family farther. Among the descendants of Richard, are many active and successful business men, and shipmasters, and they probably would not have succeeded any better in the world if their ancestor had been one of the most pious and distinguished among the Pilgrim fathers.

# BOURNE.

### HENRY BOURNE.

Jan'y 25th, 1634-5, Henry Bourne joined the church of Mr. Lothrop at Scituate. The suppositions of Rev. Mr. Deane, respecting his family and relatives, appear to be mistakes. He says, Richard of Sandwich, was his brother; but I find no evidence that he was a relative of the pastor of the church at Marshpee. He supposes John of Marshfield, to be his son. John was a son of Thomas, and it does not appear that he was connected with Henry.

He settled at first in Scituate. His wife Sarah was dismissed from the church in Hingham to that of Scituate, Nov. 11, 1638, and it is probable that he was married about that time. He bought in 1637 or 8, the dwelling-house of Richard Foxwell, the eleventh built in that town.

He was admitted a freeman of Plymouth Colony, Jan'y 2, 1637-8; on the grand jury in 1638, '41, '42, '46, '56, '58 and '61; deputy to the Colony Court from Barnstable in 1643 and '44, and surveyor of highways in 1655. At the March Court, 1641, he was a witness against John Bryant and Daniel Pryor of Barnstable, on a complaint for "drinking tobacco on the highway."

He removed with Mr. Lothrop's Church to Barnstable in 1639. His house lot was the second west from Coggin's Pond, now called Great Pond.* His house stood on the

---

* Coggin's Pond was afterwards called Hinckley's Pond, now Great Pond—a very indefinite name. Cooper's or Nine Mile Pond is also called Great Pond. I would suggest that the old name be revived. No objection can be urged against it; it is definite, and is the name by which it was known by our ancestors.

north side of the road.   The ancient house known as "Brick John Hinckley's," taken down a few years since, stood near the location of Bourne's house.

Henry Bourne was a large land holder.   In 1654, he owned eight acres on the north of Coggin's Pond, bounded westerly by the marsh, northerly by the Calves Pasture and easterly by the land of Thomas Hinckley; and five acres of salt meadow adjoining the same.   His house lot on which he built his house contained eight acres of upland, with three acres of marsh adjoining; bounded on the east by the land of the heirs of Henry Coggin, southerly by the commons, west by the land of James Hamblin, and north by the Main Creek or Harbor.   The house lot extended across the highway.   The three acres was called "Bourne's Hill," and as it was bounded westerly by his house lot, must have been the hill west of the house of the late Robinson Hinckley.   He also owned two acres in the Calves pasture adjoining his lot at Coggin's Pond, bounded northeasterly by the highway, called Calves Pasture Lane; three acres on the south side of the road, near the present railroad crossing; ten acres of upland in the woods on the west of Pine Hill, and six acres of marsh at Scorton.

In May, 1659, his great lot was assigned to him, and is thus described on the records : "Forty acres of upland more or less, bounded northerly by ye lands of Henry Coggin's heirs; southerly by Dolar Davis, butting easterly by ye Indian Pond, westerly by ye commons, with an acre of marsh more or less adjoyning to it."

"One acre of upland at Scorton, bounded southerly by his own marsh, westerly by John Chipman, easterly by John Coggin's upland."

I do not find the record of the death of Henry Bourne, or his will.   He was living in 1661, but at the time of the settlement of Mr. Jonathan Russell in Sept. 1683, he had deceased.   An entry on the Church records, Jan'y 28, 1684-5, refers to him as "late deceased."   I am, however, inclined to the opinion that he had then been dead several years.   His widow Sarah was living in Sept. 1683; but died soon after that date.

Henry Bourne had a still-born daughter born 7th May, 1641, and a daughter Dorcas, bap'd 26th Aug. 1649, but the latter does not appear to have survived long.

It seems by an entry in the Church records, that he made a will, and gave a legacy to the Barnstable Church. £6.13. was paid to Mrs. Bourne before her death, and the balance, which was to be paid by Thos. Huckins, Jr., and John Phinney, was remitted to Thomas Huckins, excepting £5, which was paid to the deacons of the church.

# BENJAMIN.

Joseph Benjamin, son of John, of Watertown, married 10th June, 1661, Jemimah, daughter of Thomas Lumbert of Barnstable. He settled in Yarmouth before 1670, on a farm near the meadows, on the north of the Miller farm.— He owned an estate in Cambridge, which he sold 30th Oct. 1686. In 1680, he exchanged his farm in Yarmouth for that of Joseph Gorham in Barnstable, now owned by Nathan Edson. He removed to New London, Conn., where he died in 1704, leaving a widow, Sarah, and seven children. The births of his children were recorded in Yarmouth, but the record is torn and imperfect. He had Abigail; Joseph, 1666; Hannah, Feb. 1668, not living in 1704; Mary, born April, 1670, married John Clark, 16th Nov. 1697, who was a schoolmaster; Mercy, born March 12th, 1674; Elizabeth, born Jan'y 14th, 1679-80, not living in 1704; John, born 1682, and Jemimah, Sarah and Kezia named in the settlement of his estate.

"The admirable, accurate and precise," record of the settlement of his estate, dated in 1704, says his son Joseph was aged 30; John, 22; and Abigail, Jemima, Sarah, Kezia, Mary and Mercy *were all aged twenty years.* Six at one birth if the New London record is deserving of credit.

# BUTLER.

---

Respecting the ancestors of Israel Butler, I have no information. He married July 1, 1725, Elizabeth, daughter of Thomas Blossom; she died Jan'y 7, 1734-5, aged 29, and he married for his second wife, Oct. 29, 1735, Mary, daughter of Daniel Parker, Esq. She died in 1745, aged 35.— Children of Israel Butler born in Barnstable.

*Children born in Barnstable.*

I. Nathaniel, born April 11, 1726, 9 o'clock, P. M.
II. Benjamin, Dec. 18, 1727, sunset.
III. Elizabeth, June 6, 1720, 12 at noon.
IV. Sarah, Oct. 31, 1732, P. M.
V. James, Dec. 15, 1736, 6 at night.
VI. Hannah, May 11, 1738.
VII. Mary, Sept. 26, 1739.
VIII. Daniel, Feb. 23, 1740-1.

This was a Sandwich and Falmouth name. There was a family of the name in Harwich. It is said that General Butler is a descendant of the Cape family.

# BATES.

There was a John Bates in Barnstable in 1666; perhaps only a temporary resident. He had a fight with William Borden, the latter being drunk at the time, came off second best. Bates was condemned to pay Borden twenty shillings for abuse, and three shillings and four pence to the Court for breach of the peace. Borden was fined five shillings for being drunk, and three shillings and four pence for the breach of the peace.

The present family in Barnstable are descendants of another John Bates, who, by his wife Abigail, had eight children born in Barnstable, viz.: Susannah, born July 15, 1739; Samuel, March 7, 1741-2—died twenty-one days after; John, Jan'y 10, 1742-3; Job, Feb. 3, 1745-6; Mehitable, Feb. 19, 1748-9; Thomas, March 17, 1750-1; Samuel, Sept. 27, 1754, and Seth, March 7, 1758-9.

# BRYANT.

---

### JOHN BRYANT.

John Bryant, house carpenter, was of Barnstable in 1640. He married in 1643, Mary, daughter of George Lewis, for his first wife. He returned to Scituate and was an active and useful man, much employed in the division of lands, and other public business. In 1657, he married his second wife, Elizabeth, daughter of Rev. William Witherell, and in 1664, Mary, daughter of Thomas Hiland. By his first wife he had seven, and by his third, ten children.

# CARSELY.

Two of this name were of the first settlers. William, admitted a freeman of the Massachusetts Colony, Nov. 2, 1637, and of new Plymouth, Dec. 3, 1639. He came from Scituate to Barnstable. He was the first constable, having been appointed June 4, 1639, O. S., the day the town was incorporated. He married Nov. 28, 1639, at Sandwich, a sister of the Rev. Marmaduke Matthews of Yarmouth. It does not appear by the record that he had any family. A still-born child of his was buried May 7, 1641.

His 'house lot, containing six acres of upland more or less, was bounded easterly by Mr. Linnell's, westerly by Tristram Hull's, southerly by the highway, and northerly by the marsh. He had one acre of meadow at the north end, butting northeasterly on the harbor. He sold a part of his house lot to Hon. Barnabas Lothrop about the year 1658.

William Casely was a man who had received a good education,—had some knowledge of Latin, had perhaps studied law, and was employed by the first settlers to draw legal instruments. He was a member of Mr. Lothrop's Church, but the date of his admission does not appear. Thus far he has a clean record. He was a vain, self-conceited, vulgar fellow. Common decency forbids stating particulars. He was excommunicated from the Church, Sept. 5, 1641, and among other reasons which I omit, he is charged with being "much given to Idleness, and too much to jearing"—"observed alsoe by some to bee somewhat proud." The sentence of excommunication was pronounced by Rev. Mr. Mayo. The record adds: "William Carsely took it patiently."

John Carsely was also one of the first settlers, and it has been supposed that he was a brother of William. I find no evidence that such was the fact. He came from Scituate. He was unlearned, not a church member, and his record is not creditable to him. March 1, 1661-2, he and his wife Alice were presented "for fornication in unlawfully companying before their marriage." John was condemned to be whipped, and Alice to set in the stocks while the punishment was inflicted; all of which was duly performed June 7, 1642. He was fined three shillings and four pence, March 6, 1665-6, for a breach of the public peace.

His house lot contained four acres. The southwest corner of his lot was near "the prison," there being a narrow strip of common land between it and the road now known as Jail Lane. The northwest corner of Carsely's lot was at the southwest corner of Mr. John Lothrop's orchard in 1703. On the north it was bounded partly by the hill "against the highway," and partly by the swamp, the northeast corner stake standing south of James Paine's shop. On the east it was bounded partly by Mr. Linnell's land and partly by Richard Child's land, the eastern boundary being in 1708 in the range of Wid. Abigail Sturgis' barn. On the south it was bounded by common land, afterwards granted partly to Mr. Linnell, and three-fourths of an acre near the Jail to John Otis. In 1661, four acres in addition were granted to him, bounded north by Mr. Linnell, east by Joseph Lothrop,* south and west by the commons.

---

* It it erroneously stated in the account of the lots purchased by Mr. Thomas Allyn, that Capt. Samuel Mayo bought the lot between Rev. Mr. Mayo's and Tristram Hull's lot, of John Casely. When I wrote that article, I had not read the proprietor's records. The descriptions are very indefinite, but a comparison of the records of lots in the vicinity of John Casely's house lot has been made, and the description above given I think is reliable. This tract of land containing eight acres was above the "poly pod swamp," and extended forty rods east and west and thirty-two rods north and south, and was bounded west by John Casely, and east by James Naybor's land. The latter was bounded east by the highway,—probably the road into the woods east of the old Sturgis tavern. It would seem from this investigation that the ancient road followed the present road from the Jail to Capt. Wilson's house, then turning to the south to the head of Capt. Joseph Lothrop's land, then followed the south edge of the swamp and joined the present road, near the house of the late Capt. Joshua Loring. This view of the matter makes the record of the laying out of the road in 1686 intelligible. On reaching Capt. Lothrop's land, instead of turning to the southeast they turned to the north, through his land over a private causeway across the swamp which was narrow at that place.

Twenty acres were also granted to him on the west of the land of James Claghorn, which he sold 20th April, 1675, to Joshua Lumbert for £7.

He married twice; first, in 1642, to Alice ———, and second, Sarah ———. He died in 1693, and his widow married Samuel Norman. There is no record of his family. In the settlement of his estate on the probate records, his children John, Benjamin, Sarah, who married Elisha Smith, April 20, 1719, are named; John, Jr., removed to Yarmouth where he died Jan'y 13, 1705-6.

Benjamin Casely married March 4, 1713-14, Mary Godfrey of Yarmouth.

John Casely married May 17, 1739, Dorcas Hamblin, and had children born in Barnstable, namely :

*Children born in Barnstable.*

I.    John, born Feb. 14, 1740.
II.   Ebenezer, born Aug. 12, 1744.
III.  Mary, born May 23, 1749.
IV.   Seth, born Feb. 21, 1751.
V.    Isaac, born July 10, 1753.
VI.   Dorcas, born July 8, 1755.
VII.  Eunice, born Sept. 19, 1759.

Benjamin Casely, Jr., married Nov. 29, 1739, Huldah Hinckley, and had children, namely :

I.     Ambrose, June 19, 1741.
II.    Benjamin, March 9, 1743.
III.   Thomas, Feb. 14, 1745 ; lost with Capt. Magee, Dec. 27, 1778.
IV.    Lemuel, Nov. 17, 1747.
V.     Samuel, Dec. 3, 1749.
VI.    Hannah, Dec. 2, 1750.
VII.   Mehitabel, Jan'y 8, 1758.
VIII.  David, March 15.

Lemuel, son of Benjamin, Jr., had a family, the last of the name in Barnstable.

It is a fact worthy of note that of the forty-five first comers to Barnstable, who were heads of families, proprietors, and regularly admitted townsmen, prior to January 5, 1643-4, there were only four who did not sustain good moral characters, and whose lives were not in accordance with the religion which they professed. These four were John Crocker,

William and John Casely, and Thomas Shaw, neither of whom have any male descendants in the town or county of Barnstable. John Crocker's crime was committed before he came to Barnstable, and strictly cannot be charged as the act of a Barnstable man. The charges against William Casely were not criminal, and did not subject him to any legal punishment. Though educated, he was a vulgar man, and though a professor of religion, he did not live a Christian life. He was weak-minded, vain, frivolous, and committed acts that gentlemen are ashamed to have laid to their charge. The sentence of ex-communication pronounced against him was a righteous one; and though he continued to reside in Barnstable, he sunk into merited ignominy.— The crime for which John Casely was punished is not stated, and as the laws are now administered he would not be held liable in the manner he was two centuries ago.

The complaint against Thomas Shaw was that he went into the house of his neighbor, John Crocker, on the Sabbath, and helped himself to something to eat. It was not a justifiable act, neither was it very criminal. (See Matthew, Chap. xii : 1 to 6.)

In these three short paragraphs I have given an abstract of the criminal calender of a generation of men, the first settlers, the ancestors of nineteen-twentieths of the present inhabitants of Barnstable. If a parallel can be found in the annals of any of our towns, I am not aware of it.

# CHAPMAN.

Ralph Chapman came in the Elizabeth from London in 1635. His age is stated in the Custom House return to be 20. He was a ship carpenter of Southwalk, in Surry, near London. He settled first in Duxbury, and there married 23d Nov. 1642, Lydia Wells, a daughter of Isaac, afterwards of Barnstable.* His children were Mary, born 31st Oct. 1643; Sarah, 15th May, 1645: Isaac, Aug. 4, 1647; Lydia, born and died 26th Nov. 1649; Ralph, 20th June, 1653, died next month, and Ralph again. His daughter Mary married 14th May, 1666, William Troop of Barnstable, and Sarah married William Norcut of Yarmouth, afterwards of Eastham. His son Ralph of Marshfield, had a son John reputed to be 104 years of age at his death. The elder Ralph died at Marshfield in 1671, aged 56.

Isaac Chapman, son of Ralph, settled in Barnstable. He married Sept. 2, 1678, Rebecca, daughter of James Leonard. His house and shop stood on the south side of the County road on the lot formerly owned by Isaac Wells, a short distance west of the Court House. Children born in Barnstable.

## Children born in Barnstable.

I.   Lydia, 15th Dec. 1679.
II.  John, 12th May, 1638.
III. Hannah, 26th Dec. 1682, died July 6, 1689.

---

* Mr. Savage says Lydia Wills or Willis. I read the record Wells; but cannot at this moment give the authority for saying she was a daughter of Isaac Wells of Barnstable. Isaac Chapman and John Miller of Yarmouth, were heirs to the estate of Margaret, widow of Isaac Wells. It may be that Ralph Chapman's wife was not a daughter, but it is probable.

IV.    James, 5th August, 1685, married Aug. 14, 1723,
        Mehitabel Sharp.
V.      Abigail, 11th July, 1687.
VI.     Hannah, 10th April, 1690.
VII.    Isaac, 29th Dec. 1692.
VIII.   Ralph, 19th Jan'y, 1695.
IX.     Rebecca, 1st June, 1697.

Isaac Chapman removed to Yarmouth, now Dennis,
with his family where he has descendants.   His son Isaac,
by his wife Elizabeth, had Isaac, 7th April, 1711; Mary,
6th June, 1713; Rebecca, 14th Nov. 1725, died Dec. 30,
1726; Samuel, 14th Nov. 1727; Rebecca, 25th June, 1730;
Ruth, 13th April, 1733; Micah, 18th July, 1735.

Ralph Chapman, son of Isaac, by his wife Elizabeth,
had John, born 22d ——, 1728-9; Betty, 15th Oct. 1736,
and David, 15th Nov. 1739.

---

NOTE.—As this is not a Barnstable family, I have not carefully examined the Yarmouth or the Probate Records.   Persons interested can
find materials for a full geneaology of the family.

# CHIPMAN.

Elder John Chipman is probably the ancestor of all of the name of Chipman in the United States and British Provinces. The following statement, drawn up by himself, is printed from an ancient copy of the original in the possession of the family of the late Mr. Samuel Chipman of Sandwich. An incorrect copy was published in the Genealogical Register of 1850. The following has been carefully collated with the manuscript, and is a true transcript thereof, excepting four words, which are repetitions and erased in the manuscript. Interlineations are printed in italics.

*A Brief Declaration in Behalf of Jno. Chipman of Barnstable.*

A Brief Declaration with humble Request (to whom these Presents shall come) for further Inquiry & Advice in ye behalf of John Chipman, now of Barnstable in the Government of New Plimouth in New England In America, being ye only Son & Heir of Mr. Thomas Chipman Late Deceased at Brinspittell 1 about five miles from Dorchester in Dorsetshire in England concerning *some certain* Tenement or Tenements with a Mill & other Edifice thereunto belonging Lying & being in Whitchurch of Marhwood vale near Burfort alias Breadport, in Dorsetshire aforsd hertofore worth 40 or 50 Pounds pr Annum which were ye Lands of ye sd Thomas Chipman being entailed to him & his Heirs for Ever but hath for Sundry years Detained from ye sd John Chipman the right & only Proper Heir thereunto, By reason of Some kinde of Sale made of Inconsiderable value by the sd Thomas (In the time of his Single Estate not then minding marriage) unto his kinsman Mr. Christopher Derbe Living Sometime in Sturtle near Burfort aforsd being as the Said John hath been Informed, but for 40 lb And to be maintained Like a man with Diet Apparel &c by the sd Christopher as Long as the sd Thomas Should Live whereat ye Lawyer wc. made the Evidences being troubled at his Weakness in taking Such an Inconsiderable Price tendered him to Lend him money or to give to him ye sd Thomas Seven Hundred Pounds for ye sd Lands. But yet the matter Issuing as Aforsd The Vote of the Country who had knowledge of it was that the sd Thomas had

much wrong in it Especially After it pleased God to change his
condition, and to give him Children, being turned off by the sd
Christopher only with a poor Cottage and Garden Spott instead of
his forsd Maintainance to the great wrong of his Children Especially of his Son John Aforsd to whom ye Sd Lands by right of En-
tailment did belong Insomuch that mr William Derbe who had the
sd Lands in his Possession then from his father Christopher Derbe
told the sd John Chipman (being then a youth) that his father
Christopher had done him wrong, but if ye sd Lands prospered
with him that he would then consider the sd John to do for him in
way of recompence for the Same when he should be of capacity in
years to make use thereof.    The sd John further declareth that
one mr Derbe A Lawyer of Dorchester (he supposes ye father of
that mr Derbe now Living in Dorchester) being a friend to the
mother of the sd John told her being Acquainted with ye Business
and sorry for the Injury to her Heir, that if it pleased God he
Liv'd to be of Age he would himself upon his own charge make a
tryal for the recovery of it, and in case he recovere it Shee Should
give him 10 lb Else he would have nothing for his trouble and
charge.    Furthermore John Derbe late deceased of Yarmouth in
New Plimouth Government Aforsd hath acknowledged here to
the sd John Chipman that his father Christopher had done him
much wrong in the forsd Lands but ye sd John Chipman being but
in a poor and mean outward condition, hath hitherto been Afraid
to stir in it as thinking he should *never* get *it* from ye rich and
mighty, but being now Stirred up by some friends as Judging it
his Duty to make more Effectual Inquiry after *it* for his own comfort his wife and childrens which God hath been pleased to bestow
on him if any thing may be done therein, & in what way it may be
attained, whether without his coming over which is mostly Desired
if it may bee.    Because of exposing his wife & children to Some
Straits in his Absence from them, he hath therefore, Desired these
as aforsd Desiring also Some Search may be made for farther
Light in ye case into the Records the conveyance of the Said
Lands being made as he Judgeth about threescore years Since as
Also that Enquiry be made of his Sisters which he supposeth
*lived* about those parts & of whom else it may be thought meet,
and Advice sent over as Aforsd, not Else at present But hoping
that there be Some Left yet in England alike Spirited with him in
29 Job whom the Ear that heareth of may bless God for Deliver-
ing ye poor that crieth and him that hath no helper Bein Eyes to
the blind feet to the Lame A father to the Poor Searching out ye
cause which he knoweth not, &c.    Barnstable as Aforsd this 8th
of Feb. (57.)    John Chipman Desires his Love be presented to
his Sisters Hannor and Tamson and to hear particularly from them
if Living and doth further request that Enquiry be made of mr
Oliver Lawrence of Arpittle who was an intimate friend of his

fathers. He desires also Enquiry be made of his Sisters what those parchment writeings concerned in the custody of his mother when he was there.

The sd John Chipman Supposeth his age to be About thirty seven years ; it being next may Twenty & one year Since he come out of England.

On the 2d of March, 1641-2, Ann Hinde, the wife of William Hoskins, deposed before Gov. Edward Winslow, relative to a matter in controversy between John Derbey and John Chipman. She stated that she was then about 25 years of age, that she lived with Mr. Christopher Derbey at the time when John Chipman came to New England to serve Mr. Richard Derbey a son of Christopher, and a brother of John, that she afterwards came over to serve the said Richard, and that when she left, old Mr. Derbey requested her "to commend him to his cozen (nephew) Chipman, and tell him if he were a good boy, he would send him over the money that was due to him, when he saw good." She also testified that she had heard John Derbey affirm that the money had been paid to John Chipman's mother, who died about three months before her old master sent this message by her to his nephew Chipman. The object of this deposition was to establish the fact that John Derbey did not pay the money to Chipmans's mother, because she died three months before Mr. Christopher Derbey made the promise to send it.

John Chipman, only son of Mr. Thomas Chipman, was born in or near Dorchester in Dorcetshire, England, about the year

---

1. Brinspittell or Brinspudel, Dorsetshire, is between Affpudel and the river Piddle. Dorsetshire, from the mildness of the air and the beauties of its situation has been termed the garden of England.

2. Whitchurch, west of Bridport, a seaport town, is one of the largest parishes in the county. It has a large and ancient church in which are some antique ornaments.

3. Marshwood, with its vale and park, four miles N. W. of Whitchurch, was formerly a barony of great honor.

4. Burtport, or rather Britport, called also Bridport and Britport, Dorsetshire. A seaport borough and market town in the hundred of Sturminster.

5. Sturhill, Bridport Division, Godbertorne Hundred, Dorcetshire.

6. Athpuddel in Dorcetshire.

All the places named are in Dorcet County or shire England, as stated in an article in the Genealogical Register communicated by Rev. Richard M. Chipman. In the same article Mr. Chipman presumes that "Hannor" and "Tamson," the sisters of Elder John. are the names of their husbands. He reads the name of Tamson, Jamson ; and supposes Thompson was intended. This reading probably led to the error. Hannah and Tamson or Thomasine, are common names, and there seems to be no good reason to doubt that they were the Christian names of his sisters. The Declaration is dated Feb. 8, 1657. O. S., which is Feb. 18, 1658, N. S. Deduct 21 years, and it gives May, 1637, as the date of his leaving England. The date of his birth by the same rule is 1621.

1621.   He had two sisters Hannah and Tamson, who married and remained in England.   His father died early, and he resided with his uncle, Mr. Christopher Derbey.   In May, 1637, Mr. Richard Derbey, a son of Christopher, came to New England, bringing with him his cousin John, then sixteen years of age, and others, in the capacity of servants.   It was then customary to send over orphan youths of good habits, to be bound for a term of years, to the planters and other early settlers.   Mr. Richard Derbey settled at Plymouth, where he remained several years; but no mention is made of his cousin John till the spring of 1642, when he had arrived at legal age, and when he brought an action against his cousin, Mr. John Derbey, for a sum of money sent to him by his uncle Christopher, and not paid over by said John Derbey. It is probable that during the four years that had intervened, he had served an apprenticeship with a carpenter.   This is not certain; but it appears by his will that he was a carpenter, though in deeds he is styled a yeoman.

In Aug. 1643, he was absent from the colony, or was sick and unable to bear arms; but it appears that he was afterwards a resident of Plymouth.   In 1646, he married Hope, second daughter of Mr. John Howland.   In 1649, he was of Barnstable, and that year bought the homestead of Edward Fitzrandolphe, the original deed whereof is in my possession.   The land has since been sub-divided many times, and is now owned by several individuals.   It was bounded on the north by the County road, east by the Hyannis road, extending across the present line of the railroad, and was bounded south by the commons, and on the west by the homestead of George Lewis, Senr., and contained eight acres.   The deed also conveyed a garden spot and orchard on the north side of the County road, now owned by Capt. Heman Foster. The ancient house on this estate stood between the present dwellings of the heirs of Anna Childs, deceased, and the house formerly owned by Isaiah L. Greene, Esq.   How long he resided on this estate is not known.   In 1659, it was owned and occupied by John Davis, Senr.   Probably about this time he removed to Great Marshes.   No lands are recorded as belonging to him in 1654,* when all were required to have their possessions entered and described on the town books.   He may have resided about that time in another town, though he was of Barnstable in 1659.   He bought of his brother-in-law, Lieut. John Howland, one half of his farm

---

* Perhaps he did own lands; but neglected to have them recorded. That he was not careful in regard to his title deeds there is evidence. His deed from Fitzrandolphe was not executed till 1669, twenty years after the purchase, and the consideration in his deed from Howland indicates that the purchase was made many years before the date of the deed.   Farms no better in the same vicinity were sold about that time for four times £16.

which is now owned by his descendants.   The deed is dated Dec.
10, 1672, and for the consideration of £16 Mr. Howland conveys
to him one-half of his lands in Barnstable, containing forty-five
acres of upland.   The deed is in the hand writing of Gov. Thomas Hinckley, is on parchment, and is now in the possession of the
family of Mr. Samuel Chipman of Sandwich.   The lands sold
were bounded, easterly, partly by the land of John Otis and partly
by the land of William Crocker, northerly by the marsh, westerly
by the other half of the lands not sold.   The boundaries are particularly described, and the range between Howland and Chipman
ran over a well or spring, giving each a privilege thereto.   Mr.
Howland names his northern orchard, showing that at that early
date he had set out two.   Elder Chipman owned lands at West
Barnstable before 1672, for in the same deed he makes an exchange of meadow with his brother-in-law.   After his second marriage in 1684 he removed to Sandwich.   He was admitted an
inhabitant of that town in 1679, but appears to have been in Barnstable in 1682.   His removal was deeply regretted by the people,
and many efforts were unsuccessfully made to induce him to return
to Barnstable.   The church, though dissatisfied at his removal
without their consent, agreed to pay him five or six pounds annually, if he would resume his office of Elder, and the town voted
to make him a liberal grant of meadow lands if he would return.
These votes show that his services were appreciated by the members of the church, with which he had held communion nearly
forty years, and that he was highly esteemed as a man and a
christian by his fellow townsmen and neighbors.

His connection with the Barnstable church was most happy.
His wife Hope joined the church Aug. 7, 1650, and he joined
Jan'y 30, 1652-3.   "Henry Cobb and John Chipman were chosen
and ordained to be ruling Elders of this same church, and they
were solemnly invested with office upon ye 14th day of April Anno
Dom : 1670." [Church Records.

It is probable that he was a deacon of the church before he
was elected Elder.   He survived Mr. Cobb many years, and was
the last Ruling Elder of the church.   Subsequently, attempts were
made to revive the office.   The question was frequently discussed
at church meetings ; but a majority opposed another election.

His talents and services in civil life were duly appreciated.
In June, 1659, he and Isaac Robinson and John Smith of Barnstable, and John Cook of Plymouth, were appointed by the Plymouth Colony Court to attend the meetings of the Quakers "to en-
deavour to reduce them from the errors of their wayes."—The result was that Robinson, whose name appears most prominent in
these proceedings, recommended the repeal of the severe laws that
had been enacted against that sect.   Smith and Chipman did not
incur the censure of the Court, though there is no reason to doubt

that they sympathized with Robinson in his views respecting the impolicy of those laws.

In 1649 he was a freeman, and in 1652 he was a grand juror, and appointed by the Treasurer of the Colony, a committee for the Town of Barnstable to receive the proportion of oil taken which belonged to the Colony; in 1663, '4, '5, '8 and '9 he was representative from Barnstable to the Colony Court; in 1665, '6, '7, and '8 he was one of the selectmen of Barnstable, who at that time exercised, in addition to other duties, the functions since pertaining to justices of the peace; and in 1667 he was one of the council of war. For his public services the court in 1669 granted him one hundred acres of land, between Taunton and Titicut, which was afterwards confirmed to him.

His will is dated at Sandwich, Nov. 12, 1702, and was proved May 17, 1708. In it he says: "I will and bequeath to Ruth, my dear and loving wife, all whatsoever is left of her estate, which I had with her when I married her. I also give her one half part of my whole personal estate which shall be found in Sandwich at my decease. Besides and moreover, all the carts plows and husbandry implements, as also all the corn meat, flax wool, yarn and cloth that is in the house at my decease, and I do give her twenty pounds in money which is due to her by ye compact made between us at our inter-marriage; she according to sd compact, upon payment of this twenty pounds to quitt claim to all right and title and interest in my housing and lands att Barnstable, and this twenty pounds shall be paid her out of that money of mine in ye hand of my friend Mr. Jonathan Russell of Barnstable."

He bequeathes to his sons Samuel and John his whole real estate in Barnstable, Samuel two parts and John one part, unless my son Samuel pay his brother John £70 in lieu of his third part. He gives his son Samuel his carpenters tools, then in his possession. To his two grand children Mary Gale and Jabez Dimmock £5 apiece. He names his daughters, Elizabeth, Hope, Lydia, Hannah, Ruth, Bethia, Mercy and Desire. He appoints his sons Samuel and John executors, and Mr. Jonathan Russell and Mr. Rowland Cotton overseers. Witnesses, Rowland Cotton, Samuel Prince and Nathan Bassett. In the inventory of his estate, taken by Wm. Bassett and Shubael Smith, it stated that he died 7 April, 1708. His real estate is not apprised.—Among the articles apprised is plate at 8 sh per ounce, £8.2.; Cash, at 8 sh per ounce, £51.5.3.; Bills of Credit, £6.6.; Cash in Mr. Jonathan Russell's hands £20. 18 books, small and great, £1.

The will of his widow Ruth is dated Dec. 7, 1710, proved Oct. 8, 1713. As she had no children living, she gave her estate to her relatives and friends. Of the Chipman family she names only Bathsheba, a daughter of Mr. Melatiah Bourne, and Jabez

Dimmock, both grand children of Elder Chipman. Family of Elder John Chipman :

The births of twelve children of Elder Chipman are recorded ; one at Plymouth and eleven in Barnstable, Elizabeth is the only child named, older than Hope. In his will dated at Sandwich, Nov. 12, 1702, and proved May 17, 1708, he names sons Samuel and John, and daughters Elizabeth, Hope, Lydia, Hannah, Ruth, Mercy, Bethia and Desire.

To his daughters, he gave half his moveable estate in Sandwich and Barnstable, excepting the articles given to Samuel, and he adds the following proviso : "And in case any of my said daughters be dead before their receiving this my bequest, my will is that their part be given and distributed equally to their surviving children." Two of the daughters, Hannah and Ruth, were then dead, and it is probable that Bethia had also deceased.

His first wife was Hope, second daughter of John Howland and Elizabeth Tiley. Until the discovery of Bradford's History in 1855, in the Library of the Bishop of London, it had been supposed that his first wife was a daughter of Gov. Carver.—She died in Barnstable and was buried in the ancient burying ground on Lothrop's Hill. Her monument is in good preservation, and the following is a copy of the inscription :

HERE LYETH
INTERRED YE BODY OF
M R S.   H O P E   C H I P M A N
WIFE OF ELDER JOHN CHIPMAN
A G E D   54   Y E A R S
WHO CHANGED THIS LIFE
FOR A BETTER
YE 8TH OF JANUARY
1 6 8 3 .

He married for his second wife the Wid. Ruth Bourne. She was a daughter of Mr. William Sargeant, born in Charlestown 25 Oct. 1642, married first, Jonathan, son of Josiah Winslow of Marshfield, second, Mr. Richard Bourne of Sandwich. She died in Sandwich in 1713, aged 71, leaving no issue. Elder John Chipman died in Sandwich 7 April, 1708, aged 87 years. Children of Elder John Chipman :

I.     Elizabeth, born 24 June, 1647 at Plymouth, baptized in Barnstable, Aug. 18, 1650. Mrs. Hope Chipman was admitted to the church on the 7th of Aug. 1650, and Elder John Chipman Jan'y 30, 1652-3. Hope was baptized, according to Puritan usage, on the Sabbath next succeeding her birth, namely on the 5th of Sept. 1652, having been born on the 31st of the preceeding August.—Elizabeth was the second wife of Hosea Joyce of Yarmouth. He married first Martha, and had John and Dorcas. His wife Martha died April 3, 1670, and he married Elizabeth Chipman before 1676, and had Samuel, June 1, 1676; Thomas, June 3, 1678, and Mary, Sept. 19, 1680. The above is all that can now be obtained from the Yarmouth record, which is mutilated and a part of the leaf gone. By his will it is ascertained that he had ten children, two by his first wife Martha, and eight by his second wife Elizabeth Chipman. 1, John, married first, Margaret, daughter of John Miller, Feb. 5, 1701-2, and second, Esther, daughter of Jonathan White, Nov. 7, 1707. He died in 1714, leaving two daughters, Desire and Fear. His widow married John Drake of Yarmouth, and removed to East Greenwich, R. I., about the year 1726 ; 2, Dorcas, married Aug. 8, 1695, Prince Howes of Yarmouth ; 3, Samuel, died unmarried in 1741, aged 65 ; 4, Thomas, married March 19, 1719, Mary, daughter of Jeremiah Bacon of Barnstable. He had one son Jeremiah a cripple, died unmarried in 1755, and five daughters noted for their beauty. He was a man of wealth, became melancholy, and from fear of starvation committed suicide 20 April, 1743 ; 5, Mary, married James Gorham Sept. 29, 1707, and had five children. · The other children of Hosea Joyce were Hosea, whom his father cut off in his will by giving him his "small gun"; Lydia who married Nov. 20, 1706, Ebenezer Howes ; Martha, who married——Godfrey ; Mehitable ; and Dorothy who married Dec. 12, 1717, John Oats, an Englishman. His descendants write their name Otis, and reside principally in Maine. Hosea Joyce died in Feb. 1712, and his widow Elizabeth survived him. He had a large landed estate, and in his will calls his wife "well beloved," though he appears to have loved his money better, for he gave her but a small portion of his estate. "The stille-borne maide childe of John Chipman buryed Sept. 9, 1650."—[Church Records.

II.    Hope, born August 31, 1652, in Barnstable, married Aug. 10, 1670, John, son of Mr. Thomas Huckins of Barnstable, and had Elizabeth, 1 Oct. 1671 ; Mary, 3 April, 1673 ; Experience, 4 June, 1675, and Hope, 10 May, 1677. John Huckins died 10 Nov. 1678, aged 28, and she married March 1, 1682-3, Jonathon, son of Elder Henry Cobb of Barnstable, born 10 April, 1660. He was twenty-two and his wife thirty at the time of their marriage. By him she had five children born in Barnstable. June 3, 1703, she was dismissed from the Church in Barnstable, to the Church in Middleboro'. From that town the family removed to Portland, Maine. (See Cobb.)

III. Lydia, born Dec. 25, 1654. She was the third wife of John, son of Mr. William Sargeant of Barnstable, removed to Malden, where she died March 2, 1730, aged 76, leaving no issue.

IV. John, born 2d March, 1656-7, died 29th May, 1657.

V. Hannah, born 14th Jan'y, 1658-9, married Thomas Huckins, May 1, 1680. She died in Barnstable, 4th Nov. 1696, aged 37, leaving eight children. (See Huckins.)

VI. Samuel, born 15th April, 1661.—He had ten children. Many of his sons were distinguished men. (See an account of his family below.)

VII. Ruth, born 31st Dec. 1663, married 7th April, 1682, Eleazer Crocker of Barnstable. She died 8th April, 1698, aged 34, leaving ten children. (See Crocker.)

VIII. Bethia, born 1st July, 1666, married, as I have noted, Shubael Dimmock. The Jabez Dimmock and Mary Gale named in the will of Elder Chipman were probably children of Bethia. She died early. Shubael Dimmock married 4th May, 1699, Tabitha Lothropf or his second wife.

IX. Mercy, born 6th Feb., 1668, married Dea. Nathaniel Skiff, removed to Chilmark where she died.

X. John, born 3d March, 1670-1. (See account of him below.)

XI. Desire, born 26th Feb., 1673-4, married Hon. Melatiah Bourne of Sandwich, Feb. 23, 1695-6. She died March 28, 1705, aged 31. (See Bourne, where her name in one place is erroneously printed Bethia, and in the same paragraph "Rev." before the name of Thomas Smith should be erased.)

Dea. Samuel Chipman, son of Elder John Chipman, born in Barnstable, 15th April, 1661, inherited the homestead of his father. He was a carpenter ; but farming was his principal business. He kept a public house, and was a retailer of spirituous liquors, a business not then held to be incompatible with the office of Deacon of the church. He was a man of good business habits, often employed as a town officer, and there were few in town who stood higher than he in public estimation. He was ordained a deacon of the church in Barnstable, Sept. 1, 1706.* He married Dec. 27, 1686, Sarah, daughter of Elder Henry Cobb. He died in 1723, aged 63, and his widow Sarah Jan'y 8, 1742-3, aged 79 years.

Children of Dea. Samuel Chipman born in Barnstable.

I. Thomas, born, 17th Nov., 1687. He removed to Groton,

---

*After this date the custom of ordaining deacons appears to have been discontinued. The subject was discussed at several meetings of the Church, but a majority was not in favor of reviving the custom. The deacons of the East Church, organized in 1725, were not ordained. Aug. 6, 1732, a church meeting was held to consider the propriety of reviving the office of Ruling Elder and ordaining deacons. Aug. 21, 1734, another meeting was held, which was not harmonious.

Conn., where he remained several years, and from that town removed to Salisbury, Conn., where he held high rank in the town and county. He was appointed a judge in 1751 ; but died before he held a court. His son, Samuel, who removed to Tinmouth, Vt., was the father of Chief Justice Nathaniel Chipman, L. L. D., and of the late Hon. Daniel Chipman of Vermont. (See Hinman, page 576.)

II.    Samuel, born Aug. 6, 1689. He was a deacon of the Barnstable Church, and kept the "Chipman tavern," noted in former times. He married Dec. 8, 1715, Abiah, (bap'd Abigail) daughter of John Hinckley, Jr., (son of Gov. Thomas.) She died July 15, 1736, and he married second, Mrs. Mary Green of Boston, 1739. His children were, 1, a son born Aug. 1717, died 25th Aug. following ; 2, Hannah, born 1st July, 1719 ; 3, Samuel, born 21st November, 1721, removed to Groton, Conn., and had descendants in that vicinity ; 4, Dea. Timothy, born 30th April, 1723, married Elizabeth Bassett of Sandwich, Jan'y 23, 1752. He was a deacon of the church in West Barnstable, and died Aug. 24, 1770. His children were Abigail, Dec. 9. 1752, died young ; Samuel, May 8, 1754 ; Mary, Nov. 1, 1755 ; Abigail, again Jan'y 31, 1758, died young ; William, Feb. 4, 1760 ; John, June 24, 1762 ; Timothy, May 6, 1764 ; and Elizabeth, Jan'y 27, 1767, who died young. Ebenezer, 5th child of Dea. Samuel, born 9th of Sept., 1726, removed to Middletown, Conn., where he has descendants. John, sixth child of Dea. Samuel, born June 30, 1728, removed to Stratford, Conn., and thence to Middletown. Hinman says he has descendants residing at New Haven, Waterbury, &c. ; 7, Mary, daughter of Dea. Samuel, born 2d May, 1731, married March 11, 1750, Samuel Jenkins of Barnstable, and removed to Gorham, Maine. Mr. Charles H. Bursley has two interesting letters from her, and one from her husband after their removal. Her children born in Barnstable were, Josiah, Sept. 30, 1750 ; Deborah, Feb. 2, 1752 ; Abiah, Jan'y, 27, 1754 ; Samuel, Nov. 23, 1755 ; Mary, Jan'y 16, 1758, and Joseph, June 6, 1760. The three sons were soldiers in the Revolutionary army. Joseph died April 20, 1783, near West·Point, of consumption. He had been in the army two years. The other members of the family married and had families. Mr. Jenkins writing respecting his grand children, says "It seems to me they are the prettiest children that I see anywhere." Nathaniel, eighth child of Dea. Samuel was born 31st January, 1732-3 ; Joseph, ninth child, born 26th May, 1740, died July 4, 1740.

III.    John, born 16th Feb., 1691, graduated at Harvard College, 1771, and ordained over the second church at Beverly, Dec.

28, 1715. He married Feb. 12, 1718, Rebecca, daughter of Dr. Robert Hale. He died March 23, 1775. His son John, born Oct. 23, 1722, graduated at Harvard College 1738. He was a lawyer and resided at Marblehead. His son Ward, a graduate of Harvard College, 1770, was a Judge of the Supreme Court of New Brunswick, and died president of that province. He left an only child, the late Chief Justice Ward Chipman, L. L. D.

IV.  Abigail, born 15th Sept., 1692, she was baptised Oct. 30, 1692, by the name of Mercy. Probably her name was changed to Abigail after her baptism. She married March 14, 1713, Nath'l Jackson.

V.  Joseph, born 10th January, 1694, according to the town record. He was baptized March 4, 1692-3, so that both records cannot be accurate.

VI.  Jacob, born 30th Aug., 1695, married 25th Oct., 1721, Abigail Fuller, she died Oct. 5, 1724, and he married for his second wife in 1725, Bethia Thomas. He had children, Sarah, born Nov. 23, 1722, and Elizabeth, June 16, 1724, afterwards changed to Abigail. The latter married July 8, 1742, Stephen Cobb.

VII.  Seth, born 24th Feb. 1697. In 1723 he was of Plymouth and called a cooper. He was afterwards of Kingston, and is the ancestor of most of the name in Maine.

VIII.  Hannah, born 24th Sept., 1699, married Dec. 25, 1713, Barnabas Lothrop, Jr., his second wife, she died, June 11, 1763.

IX.  Sarah, born 1st November, 1701. She died July 1, 1715, aged 14 years and 8 months, and is buried near her grandmother in the ancient burying ground.

X.  Barnabas, born 24th March, 1702. He was a deacon of the West Church, and was an influential citizen. He has descendants in Vermont, Michigan and Iowa. He married 20th Feb., 1727-8, Elizabeth Hamblen and had 1, Barnabas, 28th Dec., 1748, who married Mary Blackwell of Sandwich, in 1721, and had Martha, Sept. 4, 1752 ; Elizabeth, Feb. 8, 1755 ; Joseph, May 14, 1758, deacon of the East Church ; Hannah, June 6, 1760 ; and Barnabas, Nov. 20, 1763 ; 2, Joseph, born 22d Dec. 1731 ; 3, Elizabeth, 12th May, 1734, she married Nov. 23, 1758, Nath'l Hinckley, 2d. ; 4, Thomas, born 5th March, 1735-6, married Bethia Fuller of Colchester in 1760, and had Timothy Fuller, Feb. 1, 1761 ; Isaac, Sept. 12, 1762, and Rebecca, Jan'y 26, 1764 ; Hannah, 20th Feb. 1737-8.

John Chipman, son of Elder John, born in Barnstable, March 3, 1670, was a cordwainer, or shoemaker. He removed early to Sandwich, and from thence to Chilmark, Martha's Vineyard, and afterwards to Newport, R. I. During his residence at Martha's Vineyard he was one of the Justices of the Court, and after his removal to Newport, he was an assistant to the governor. Respecting him I have little information ; but it is just to infer that if a poor mechanic rises to places of honor and trust, he must be a man of some talent and of sound judgement. He was thrice married. First, in 1691, to Mary Skeffe, a daughter of Capt. Stephen. She died in 1711, aged 40. Second, in 1716, to Widow Elizabeth Russell, her third marriage. She was a daughter of Capt. Thomas Handley, and married first,——Pope. Third in 1725, to (Hannah?) Hookey of R. I. His thirteen children were probably all born in Sandwich.

I.  John, died young.
II.  James, born 18th Dec., 1694.
III.  John, born 18th Sept. 1697, married Hannah Fessenden of Cambridge, Sept. 26, 1726.
IV.  Mary, born Dec. 11, 1699.
V.  Bethia, twin sister of Mary, married Samuel Smith, Oct. 6, 1717.
VI.  Perez, 28th Sept., 1702, is the ancestor of the Delaware, Carolina and Mississippi families of the name.
VII.  Deborah, 6th Dec., 1704.
VIII.  Stephen, 9th June, 1708.
IX.  Lydia, twin sister of Stephen.
X.  Ebenezer, 13th Nov., 1709. He married Mary —— , resided at Falmouth where his son John was born April 10, 1733, afterwards of Barnstable, where he had Ebenezer.
XI.  Handley, 31st Aug., 1717. He removed with his father to Chilmark, thence to Providence, R. I., and in 1761 to Cornwallis, N. S. He was a distinguished man, and his descendants are numerous and respectable.
XII.  Rebecca, 10th Nov. 1719.
XIII.  Benjamin.

Few families are more widely disseminate than this. Elder Chipman had eleven children and eighty-two grand-children, nearly all of whom married and had families. The Rev. K. M. Chipman has for several years been employed in compiling a genealogy of the family, extending to the ninth generation.—Want of funds has prevented him from publishing. No harm will result from the delay. It will give him an opportunity to correct some important mistakes into which he has fallen, and from which no genealogist can claim exemption.

The manuscript of the "Declaration" of John Chipman, from which we copy is not, as has been supposed, an original document in the handwriting of the Elder. It is in the handwriting of John Otis, Esq., an elder brother of Col. James, born thirty years after the date of the Declaration. Notwithstanding it is reliable, for the principal facts are corroborated by the deposition of Ann Hinde and by records in Dorcetshire, England. I cannot learn that his descendants ever obtained anything from the estate, which was illegally conveyed by Thomas Chipman to Christopher Derby.

Mr. Hinman says there is no evidence that John Chipman received any benefit from the grants made to him by the Plymouth Colony. The presumption is that he did. The others to whom grants were made at the same time, and at the same place, received theirs, and no legal or other difficulty prevented Mr. Chipman from obtaining his right.

Chipman is an ancient name and occurs as early as A. D. 1070, on the Doomsday Survey Book. Originally the name was written De Chippenham, or by the armorial bearings Chippenham. There are three places in England of this name, and whether these places derived their names from the family, or the family from the places is a matter of no importance. The meaning of of the name is Chapman's town or home.

# COBB.

Elder Henry Cobb the ancestor of the Cobb Family of Barnstable, was of Plymouth in 1632, of Scituate in 1633, and of Barnstable in 1639. According to the Rev. Mr. Lothrop's records, Goodman Cobb's dwelling house in Scituate, was constructed before September 1634, and was the seventh built in that town by the English. He afterwards sold this house to Henry Rowley, and built on his lot in Kent Street, house numbered thirty-two on Mr. Lothrop's list. Mr. Deane in his history of Scituate says he was one of the "men of Kent," and that in addition to his house lot, he owned eighty acres on North River, which was afterwards the farm of Ephraim Kempton, and then of John James.

On the 23d of November, 1634, Goodman Cobb and other members of the church at Plymouth "were dismissed from their membershipp in case they joyned in a body att Scituate." On the 8th of January following, Mr. Lothrop makes the following entry in his records: "Wee had a day of humiliation and then att night joyned in covenannt togeather, so many of us as had beene in Covenannt before; to witt, Mr. Gilson and his wife, Goodman Anniball and his wife, Goodman Rowley and his wife, Goodman Cob and his wife, Goodman Turner, Edward Foster, myselfe, Goodman Foxwell and Samuel House." The two last named may have been a part of the company who arrived in the Griffin with Mr. Lothrop; but the others had been in the Colony several years. It is probable that many of them had been members of the Congregational Church in London, and that this meeting was a reunion under their old Pastor of those who had before been "in convenannt togeather." Goodman Cobb was a leading and influential member, and for forty-four years was either the senior deacon, or a ruling elder of the church.

When it was proposed that the church remove to Sippican,

now Rochester, Dea. Cobb was one of the committee to whom the Colony Court in 1638 granted the lands for a township; and when it was afterwards decided to remove to Mattakeese, now Barnstable, he was a member of the committee having charge of the selecting of a suitable location for the settlement.

Deacon Cobb's house lot in Barnstable containing seven acres, was situate at a little distance north from the present Unitarian Meeting House, between the lots of Thomas Huckins on the north and Roger Goodspeed on the south, extending from George Lewis' meadow on the west to the "Old Mill Way" on the east. This tract of land is uneven and a large portion was originally a swamp. It was not one of the most desirable lots in the settlement.

His other lands were the neck of land and the meadows adjoining, where Cobb & Smith's wharf and stores are now situate, bounded southerly by Lewis Hill and John Davis' marsh and on the other sides by the surrounding creeks.

His Great Lot, containing three score acres, was situate on the south side of the County road, between the present dwelling houses of Joseph Cobb and James Otis. It was bounded in 1654, easterly by the lands of Henry Taylor and Joshua Lumbard, southerly by the commons, westerly partly by the commons and partly by Goodman Foxwell's land, and northerly by the highway and Henry Taylor's land.

Two lots of six acres each in the new Common Field.

One acre of Goodspeed's lot, (the deep bottom on the north of the Meeting House) then town's commons was granted to him in 1665, in payment for land damages "by ye highway running over or between his land from ye gate to Thomas Huckins." This acre was situated between "The Gate" at the entrance to the old mill way and the present Pound. He was also one of the proprietors of the common lands in the town of Barnstable, and owned lands in Suckinneset, now Falmouth.

Deacon Cobb's house lot was rough and uneven, and not desirable land for cultivation. His great lot had some good soil. It was a good grazing farm, and as the raising of cattle was the principle business of the first settlers, his lands were probably selected with reference to that object. His two lots in the new Common Field had a rich soil, and was occupied as planting lands.

He appears to have built two houses on his home lot. The first was probably a temporary one to shelter his family till he had time and means to build a better. It is a curious fact that the three deacons of the church lived in stone or fortification houses. It was required that such houses should be built in every plantation as a place of refuge for the inhabitants, should the Indians prove treacherous or hostile. It seems that the deacons then provided for the personal safety, as well as the spiritual wants of the people. Deacon Cobb built his house on his lot, where the house formerly occupied by Josiah Lewis stands—a spot well selected for defence against Indian hostilities. Dea. Dimmock's stood a little east from the dwelling house of Isaac Davis, and Dea. Crocker's at West Barnstable. The two latter were remaining within the memory of persons now living. They were about twenty-five feet square on the ground; the lower story was of stone, the upper of wood.

Elder Cobb died in 1679, having lived to a good old age, and was buried in the grave yard on Lothrop's Hill. No monument marks the spot where rest his mortal remains—no *epitaph* records his virtues. Deane says "he was a useful and valuable man," and there is beauty and truth in the words. He lived to be useful not to amass wealth or acquire political distinction.

When a young man, he separated himself from the Church of England and joined the Puritans, then few in numbers, without influence, poor, despised and persecuted by the civil and ecclesiastical powers. It appears that he joined Mr. Lothrop's church in London, the members whereof were tolerant in their views, independent and fearless in advocating the cause of religious liberty and the rights of conscience, and bold in their denunciations of all human creeds. He did not escape persecution, but he fortunately escaped being confined for two long years with Mr. Lothrop and twenty-four members of his church in the foul and loathsome prisons of London.

He came to this country to secure religious liberty and the freedom of conscience—utterly detesting all human creeds, and firmly believing that the life is the best evidence of christian faith. He remained in Plymouth a few years, joined in church fellowship with the followers of Robinson, and listened to the teaching of the mild and venerable Brewster.

In 1633, he went to Scituate, then a new settlement, and assisted in clearing the forests and building up a town. The next year his pastor Mr. Lothrop came over and settled in that town, and soon after, many of his ancient friends and brethren were his townsmen. After the organization of the church, they invested him with the office of senior deacon, a mark of their confidence in his ability and of their esteem for him as a man and a christian.

In Barnstable he was active and useful in promoting the temporal, and in ministering to the spiritual wants of the first settlers. He was a town officer, a member of the most important town committees, and in 1645, 1647, 1652, 1659, 1660 and 1661, a deputy to the Colony Court. On the 14th of April, 1670, he was chosen and ordained a ruling elder of the Barnstable church, an office which he held till his death in 1679.

Elder Cobb was not a man of brilliant talents. He was a

useful man, and an exemplary Christian. With perhaps one exception his life was a living illustration of his political and religious opinions. When in 1657, mainly through the influence of men in the Massachusetts Colony, a spirit of intolerance spread through the Plymouth Colony, and laws were enacted that an enlightened common sense condemns, and which were in violation of the principles of religious liberty which the fathers had held sacred. Elder Cobb was one of the deputies to the General Court, and there is no evidence to show that he did not approve of their enactment. In so doing he violated principles which he had long cherished and held sacred. It would have been better for his reputation had he like his friends Smith, Cudworth and Robinson and nearly all of the "first comers" then living, protested against these intolerant measures, and like them retired to private life with clear consciences and an unspotted reputation.

Four years were sufficient to sweep away every vestige of the fanatical and intolerant spirit which had spread over the Old Colony. How could it be otherwise? How could men who had themselves suffered persecution, imprisonment and stripes for conscience sake, and who had through life stoutly maintained that God alone was the judge of men's consciences, how could they, when the excitement had passed away, believe it right to persecute Baptists and Quakers and wrong to persecute Puritans. The absurdity of such a course forced itself upon the minds of such men as Elder Cobb, and soon wrought a complete change in public opinion.

Three of the name of Cobb came to New England, and if John of Plymouth and John of Taunton are not the same, four. The Cobbs of Georgia are a different family, though perhaps remotely related. Thomas R. R. Cobb a brother of the rebel general Howell Cobb in a letter dated at Athens, Geo., April 7, 1857, says, "I have but little information as to my remote ancestry. The tradition as I have received it from my father, is that seven brothers originally emigrated from England. Four settled in Virginia, three went to Massachusetts. Their names or subsequent history I never learned. I have heard my father say that his grandfather would frequently relate that the brother from whom he was descended, bought his wife from an emigrant ship for 700 lbs. of tobacco. My father, grandfather and great-grandfather were all named John."

Traditions are usually worthless. Three of the name came to Massachusetts, as stated in the letter; but there is no evidence that they were brothers. The presumption is they were not. Mr. Pratt in his history of Eastham, page 27, gives an account of the origin of the Cobb families founded on a tratition which is wholly unreliable. He says four of the name, sons of Sylvanus, came over, namely, Jonathan from Harwich, England, settled in

Eastham; Eleazer in Hingham; Sylvanus north of Boston; and
Benjamin, whose son Isaac was Port Admiral of Yarmouth, Eng-
land.   Jonathan was a descendant of Henry and born in Barn-
stable.   Respecting Benjamin, the document quoted by Mr.
Pratt, says he settled near Rhode Island, which is very doubtful.
Descendants of Augustine were in that vicinity.   The Eleazer and
Sylvanus he named were probably both descendants of Henry.
No Eleazer settled in Hingham.   The earliest of the name in that
town was Richard who is called of Boston.   He had a son
Thomas born 28th March, 1693, probably the one of that name
who settled in Eastham, and married Mary Freeman, before 1719.
A Thomas Cobb, Sen'r, died in Hingham Jan'y 4, 1707-8.

Edward Cobb was of Taunton in 1657, married at Plymouth,
28th Nov. 1660, Mary Haskins, and died 1675, leaving a son
Edward.   His widow married Samuel Philips.

Augustine Cobb was of Taunton in 1670, and had Elizabeth,
born 10th Feb. 1771; Morgan, 29th Dec. 1673; Samuel, 9th Nov.
1675; Bethia, 5th April, 1678; Mercy, 12th Aug. 1680; and
Abigail, 1684.   Gen. David Cobb, one of the aids of Washington
in the army of the Revolution is a descendant from Augustine.

John Cobb of Taunton from 1653 to 1677, Mr. Boylies says,
came from Plymouth, if so, he was a son of Henry of Barnstable.
A John Cobb who appears to have been a resident in Taunton,
administered on the estate of his brother Gershom who was killed
at Swanzey by the Indians, June 24, 1675.   Mr. Savage thinks
there were two John Cobbs; but I prefer the authority of Mr.
Baylies.   There is only one entry on the records, that favors the
supposition that there were two John Cobbs, and that after careful
examination, I think is an error of the town clerk of Taunton.

Elder Henry Cobb married in 1631, Patience, daughter of
Dea. James Hurst, of Plymouth.   She was "buryed May 4, 1648,
the first that was buryed in our new burying place by our meeting
house."   (Lothrop's Church Rec.)   He was married to his second
wife, Sarah, daughter of Samuel Hinckley by Mr. Prince, Dec. 12,
1649.   He died in 1679, and his wife Sarah survived him.

In his will dated April 4, 1678, proved June 3, 1679, and in
the codicil thereto dated Feb. 28, 1678, he gives his great lot of
land in Barnstable to his son James, the latter paying Elder Cobb's
John £5 for his interest therein.   Names his sons John, James,
Gershom and Eleazer, to whom he had theretofore given half his
lands at Suckinesset,—gave his "new dwelling house"* and all

---

* "His new dwelling house." I am inclined to the opinion that Elder Cobb sold his
stone house to Nathaniel Bacon, in his life time and that the house to which he refers was
on his "great lot," and that it was afterwards owned by son James and grandson Gershom.
In 1823, Mr. Josiah Childs a descendent in the female line pointed out a post to me in his
fence, and said fifty years ago I mortised that post from a timber taken from the house of the
first Gershom Cobb, and said that from information he had obtained from his ancestors, the
house was over one hundred years old when consequently was built in the life time of the
Elder. That house stood on his "great lot," near the ancient pear tree now standing.
(See account of 3d Gershom Hall.)

the rest of his uplands and meadows to his wife Sarah.   In his will he gave his dwelling house after the decease of his wife to his son Samuel; but in the codicil to his son Henry.   He also named his son Jonathan, and daughters Mary, Hannah, Patience and Sarah.

### Children born in Plymouth.

I.    John, born 7th June, 1632.   Removed from Barnstable to Plymouth and from thence, according to Mr. Baylies, to Taunton, and returned again to Plymouth about the year 1678.   He married twice, first 28th Aug. 1658, Martha Nelson of P.   Second, June 13, 1676, Jane Woodward of Taunton.   His children were John, born 24th June, 1662, in P., died young.   Samuel, Israel and Elizabeth, the dates of whose births are not given, probably born in Taunton.   John, born in Taunton 31st March 1678, according to the return, probably 1677; Elisha, in Plymouth, 3d, April, 1678, and James, 20th July, 1682.   Elisha of this family probably settled in Wellfleet, and had Col. Elisha and Thomas.   Col. Elisha had five sons, and has descendants in the lower towns of this County.   A Thomas Cobb married Mary Freeman of Eastham, before 1719, and probably was not the Thomas above named.

II.   James, born 14th Jan'y, 1634.   (See account of him and his family below.)

### Children born in Scituate.

III.   Mary, 24th March, 1637.   She married 15th Oct. 1657, Jonathan Dunham then of Barnstable and his second wife. His first wife was Mary, daughter of Phillip Delano, whom he married 29th Nov. 1655.   He removed to Middleboro', was sometime minister to the Indians at the islands; but was in 1694 ordained at Edgartown.

IV.   Hannah, 5th Oct. 1639, married 9th May, 1661, Edward Lewis.   She died Jan'y 17, 1729-30, aged 90 years, 3 months, 12 days.

### Children born in Barnstable.

V.    Patience, bap'd 13th March 1641-2, married Robert Parker Aug. 1667, his second wife.   After his death in 1684, she probably married Dea. William Crocker.

VI.   Gershom, born 10, bap'd 12th Jan'y, 1644-5.   He removed to Middleboro', where he was constable in 1671 and on the grand jury in 1674.   He was buried at Swanzey 24th June, 1675, having, with eight others, been killed that day by the forces of Philip.   His brother John administered on his estate, which was divided in equal proportions to the children of Mr. Henry Cobb of Barnstable, only John, the older son, to have a double portion.

VII.   Eleazer, born 30th March, 1648.   He was admitted a
       townsman Dec. 1678, when he was 24, indicating that he
       was then unmarried.   He was of Barnstable in 1703, and
       as he had only 12 1-2 shares in the common lands, the
       presumption is that he was not then a householder.   It does
       not appear that he had a family.   His death is not re-
       corded, and the settlement of his estate is not entered on
       the probate records.   It may be, but is not probable, that
       he was the Eleazer whom Mr. Pratt says settled in Hing-
       ham.

VIII.  Mehitabel, born 1st Sept. 1751, died 8th March, 1652.

IX.    Samuel, born Oct. 12, 1654.   (See account below.)

X.     Sarah, born 15 Jan'y, 1658, died Jan'y 25, 1658.

XI.    Jonathan, born 10th April, 1660.   (See account below.)

XII.   Sarah, born 10th March, 1662-3, married 27th Dec. 1686,
       Dea. Samuel Chipman of Barnstable.   She had ten chil-
       dren.   Her sons Thomas, Samuel, John, Seth and Barna-
       bas, were men who held a high rank in society.   The late
       Chief Justice Nathaniel Chipman, L. L. D., was her grand-
       son.   She died Jan'y 8, 1742-3, aged nearly 80.

XIII.  Henry, born 3d Sept. 1665, inherited the paternal mansion.
       He was married by Justice Thacher, 10th April 1690 to
       Lois Hallet.   Oct. 9, 1715, he was dismissed from the
       Barnstable, to the church in Stonington, Conn.   His chil-
       dren born in Barnstable were, Gideon, 11th April, 1691 ;
       Eunice, 18th Sept. 1693 ; Lois, 2d March, 1696 ; and
       Nathan, bap'd June 1, 1700.   Margaret the wife of Gideon
       of this family was admitted July 31, 1726, to the church
       in Hampton, Conn.   He afterwards removed from H.

XIV.   Mehetabel, born 15th Feb. 1667.

XV.    Experience, born 11th Sept. 1671.

Neither of these two daughters being mentioned in the will of
their father, the presumption is they died young.

Sergeant James Cobb, son of Elder Henry Cobb, born in
Plymouth, January 14, 1634, resided in Barnstable.   He married
26th Dec. 1663, Sarah, daughter of George Lewis, Sen'r.   He
died in 1695, aged 61.   He left no will.   His estate was settled
Feb. 1, 1695-6, and all his eleven children are named.   His
widow Sarah married 23d Nov. 1698, Jonathan Sparrow of Eastham.   She died Feb. 11, 1735, in the 92d year of her age, and
was buried in the grave-yard near the East Church, Barnstable.

*Children born in Barnstable.*

I.     Mary, 24th Nov. 1664, married May 31, 1687, Capt. Caleb
       Williamson of Barnstable.   The family removed to Hart-
       ford after 1700, where she died in 1737, aged 73.

II.    Sarah, 26th Jan'y 1666, married 27th Dec. 1686, Benjamin
       Hinckley of Barnstable.   She had ten children, the. five

first born all dying young.

III.    Patience, 12th Jan'y, 1668, married 1694, James Coleman, and had eight children.   She married 10th Sept. 1715, Thomas Lombard of Barnstable.   She died March 30, 1747, aged 79 years.   Her second husband was 95 at his death May 30, 1761.

IV.    Hannah, 28th March 1671, married Joseph Davis March 1695, and died May 3, 1739, aged 68.   She left a family of eight children.

V.    James, 8th July, 1673.   (See account below.)

VI.    Gershom, 4th August, 1675.   (See account below.)

VII.    John, 20th Dec. 1677, Mr. John Cobb as he is called on the records, married 25th Dec. 1707, Hannah Lothrop. He owned the house now the residence of Mr. David Bursley, and his son Ephraim resided there within the memory of persons now living.   His children were Ephraim, born 5th Dec. 1708.   He married Margaret Gardner of Yarmouth, Jan'y 7, 1729-30.   He had also John born 1st July, 1711, died March 1, 1713, and John again born Oct. 2, 1719, who died May 25, 1736.   Mr. John Cobb died Aug. 24, 1754, aged 77 years, and his wife Hannah April 3, 1747, aged 66 years.

VIII.    Elizabeth, 6th Oct. 1680.

IX.    Martha 6th Feb. 1682.

X.    Mercy, 9th April, 1685.

XI.    Thankful, 10th June, 1687.

The four daughters last named had shares in the estate of their father at the settlement made in 1696.   Their mother married in 1698, Jonathan Sparrow, Esq., of Eastham, and these daughters probably removed to that town with her.   Mercy was May 24, 1701, a witness to the will of Miriam Wing of Harwich.   At the proof of the will Jan'y 8, 1702-3, she is called "now Mercy Sparrow."

Samuel Cobb, son of Elder Henry Cobb, born in Barnstable 12th Oct. 1654, was a farmer and resided in the lower part of the town, and built a house on the six acre lot that was his father's in the new commonfield.   His first house stood on the south-east corner of the land, on the west side of the lane leading to Indian lands.   He soon after built a two story house, a little farther west on the same spot where the late farmer Joseph Cobb's house stood. It was two stories and constructed in the style common in those days.   It was taken down about the year 1805.   He married Dec. 20, 1680 Elizabeth, daughter of Richard Taylor, called "tailor" to distinguish him from another of the same name.   He died Dec. 27, 1727 aged 73, and his wife May 4, 1721 aged 66.

*Children born in Barnstable.*

I.    Sarah, 20th Aug. 1681.   She married Feb. 4, 1701-2

Benjamin Bearse, and resided at Hyannis where she died Jan. 14, 1742, and is buried in the old grave yard there.

II.    Thomas, born 1st June 1683, married Rachel Stone of Sudbury, Jan. 1, 1710, and had eleven children born in Barnstable, namely: 1, Abigail 29th March 1711, married Nathaniel Sturgis Feb. 20, 1734-5; 2, Nathaniel, 15th Oct. 1713, married Susannah Bacon Dec. 14, 1738. He died Feb. 14, 1763, aged 50. His children were Thomas Dec. 1, 1739; Oris Nov. 9, 1741, father of the present Lewis; Samuel Nov. 30, 1744; Susannah Jan. 1, 1746-7; Nathaniel March 19, 1748-9, died Sept. 26, 1839 aged 90; Sarah March 31, 1751. 3, Elizabeth 14th Feb. 1715, married Jonathan Lewis, Jr., Oct. 13, 1737; 4, Samuel 20th March 1717; 5, Matthew 15th April 1719, married Mary Garret January 24, 1750-1, and had Matthew, a merchant at Portland and a man of wealth and considerable distinction; Daniel engaged in trade many years in Barnstable, and the father of the present Matthew Cobb, Esq., and others; 6, David 28th Feb. 1721, married Thankful Hinckley Aug. 12, 1745, and had four children, died May 23, 1757; 7, Henry 16th April 1724, married Bethiah Hinckley Jan. 31, 1753-4; 8, Thomas 30th April 1726, died Aug. 1726; 9, Ebenezer, twin brother of Thomas, died January 5, 1856, married Mary Smith, had 5 daughters; 10, Eunice, bap't 23d Feb. 1728-9; and 11, Mary, bap'd Nov. 7, 1731. Thomas Cobb was taxed in 1737 for £1000, and was a man of wealth for the times.

III.    Elizabeth, born Nov. 1685, married 25th Nov. 1708 Ebenezer Bearse. She died 15th July 1711.

IV.    Henry, born 1687.

V.    Samuel, 10th Sept. 1691, married first Sarah Chase of Tisbury, Jan. 25, 1716, and in 1725 Hannah Cole.

VI.    Mehitable, 10th Sept. 1691, twin sister of Samuel, married 30th June 1715, Nathan Taylor.

VII.    Experience, 8th June 1692, married 18th Feb. 1713-4 Jasher Taylor of Yarmouth.

VIII.    Jonathan, 25th Dec. 1694, married Oct. 20, 1715, Sarah Hopkins of Harwich. The records of his family are incomplete. He had Benjamin, born June 25, 1726, married Bethia Homer of Yarmouth, and was afterwards a merchant of Boston; Samuel, born May 21, 1728; Elkanah, born Aug. 9, 1731; Eleazer born Dec. 28, 1734, married Kesiah, daughter of Eleazer Crosby; and Elizabeth born April 30, 1738, married ——— Crosby. Beside the above he had a son Jonathan, who married Mary Clark, born about 1716, who was the father of Elijah,—Scotto, 1741, Isaac 1745, John, Seth, Mary, Sally, Hannah, Betsey and

Elkanah. Scotto above named, was the father of the late Gen. Elijah Cobb,* whose son Elijah, a merchant of Boston, died Aug. 1861.

IX. Eleazer, born 14th Jan. 1696, married Reliance Paine Oct. 18, 1724. He occupied the house built by his father. He died Sept. 21, 1731 aged 35, and his widow married John Coleman Aug. 5, 1736. She continued to reside on the Cobb farm till her death, June 11, 1742. The children of Eleazer Cobb born in Barnstable were, Benjamin Nov. 20, 1725 ; Joseph 28th March, 1727, died 11th Oct. 1737 ; and Reliance, 30th Sept. 1728, married 1747 Paul Crowell, Jr., of Chatham ; and Patience, bap't 15th Aug. 1731, married Nathaniel Allen of Barnstable. Benjamin, the son of Eleazer, married May 29, 1749, Anna Davis, and had Reliance May 9, 1750 ; Eleazer, Aug. 7, 1752 ; Benjamin, Jan. 28, 1759, married Persis Taylor of Barnstable, Nov. 13, 1783, the second marriage recorded by Rev. Mr. Mellen. He had one son, the present Enoch T. Cobb, and a daughter Hannah ; Joseph, February 19, 1763, known as farmer Joseph, married June 19, 1785, Elizabeth Adams ; and Samuel April 23, 1765, the latter a tanner and shoe maker.

X. Lydia, born Dec. 1699, married Ebenezer Scudder, 1725, and is the ancestor of nearly if not all of the name in Barnstable.

Jonathan Cobb, son of Elder Henry Cobb, born in Barnstable 10th April 1660, married March 1, 1682-3, Hope, widow of John Huckings, and daughter of Elder John Chipman. He resided in Barnstable till 1703, when he removed to Middleborough, and from thence to Falmouth, now Portland, Me. His children were, 1, Samuel, born 23d Feb. 1683-4 ; Jonathan 26th April, 1686 ; Ebenezer 10th April 1688 ; Joseph 24th Aug. 1690 ; Lydia 17th Jan. 1692-3 ; Gershom bap't 7th July, 1695. That this Jonathan was not the one who removed to Harwich, the following facts show. His son Samuel married Abigail and had at Middleboro, Chipman born 5th March 1708-9, and probably others ; at Portland, Peter, Feb. 1720, and at Manchester, James, born July 7, 723. Jonathan, son of Jonathan, had by his wife Betty at Portland Lydia, Aug. 9, 1720 ; Ebenezer, Feb. 19, 1722 ; Mary, Nov. 8, 1723 ; Deborah, Aug. 14, 1725. Ebenezer, son of Jonathan, married Mary. He died at Portland Oct. 29, 1721, aged

---

* I have a genealogy of the Cobb family based on the recollections of Gen. Cobb. It seems to be the same on which Mr. Pratt relied, and which has always been noticed. Gen. Cobb's information respecting his great grandfather is very imperfect, and of the preceeding generations mostly if not entirely suppositions. It is certain that Gen. Cobb was a descendent of Henry of Barnstable. The Truro and Wellfleet families probably descend some from Elisha of Plymouth and some from James Cobb born Sept. 13, 1698, who removed to Truro. Elisha Cobb, born 24th Dec. 1702, married Mary Harding, and probably removed to Wellfleet, and Thomas, son of Richard of Hingham to Eastham.

33. Chipman, son of Samuel, married Elizabeth and had, at Portland, Nathan, January 7, 1732; and Andrew, March 27, 1734.

James Cobb, son of James and grandson of Elder Henry Cobb, born 8th July, 1673, resided on his grandfather's "great lot." He married 18th Sept. 1695, Elizabeth Hallett. She died April 1, 1759, aged 80. Their children born in Barnstable were:

I.     James, born 13th Sept. 1698, he married Hannah Rich of Truro, May 14, 1724, and had 1, James, June 16, 1725, died Oct. following; 2, Elizabeth, Saturday Oct. 29, 1726; 3, Lois, Friday June 27, 1729; 4, Isaac, Tuesday Dec. 21, 1731; 5, Ezekiel, Saturday Aug. 31, 1734; 6, Hannah, Wednesday, April 20, 1737; 7, Dinah, bap'd June 1, 1740; 8, Deliverance, bap'd Sept. 19, 1742. Hannah, wife of James Cobb, Jr., was dismissed from the church in Barnstable to the church in Truro, Jan'y 15, 1663-4, and probably the family removed to that town.

II.    Sylvanus, born 25th Nov. 1700, married Mercy Baker, Nov. 7, 1728. He died Sept. 30, 1756, aged 55. His children born in Barnstable were, 1, Mercy, Oct. 13, 1729, married James Churchill, Jan'y 10, 1751, died Sept. 25, 1756; 2, Ebenezer, Aug. 13, 1731, married 1754 Lydia Churchill of Middleboro', and had James and Ebenezer; 3, Sylvanus, Feb. 18, 1734-5, died May 10, 1737; 4, Bennie, Jan'y 23, 1736-7; 5, Rebecca, April 2, 1739, died Aug. 17, 1756, aged 17; 6, Sylvanus, July 21, 1741; 7, Thankful, bap't Sept. 25, 1743; 8, Lydia, bap'd Jan'y 5, 1745-6. From this family I am informed that Rev. Sylvanus Cobb is descended.

III.   Elisha, born 24th Dec. 1702, married Mary Harding, of Truro, Feb. 25, 1724-5.

IV.   Jesse, born 15th April, 1704, married Thankful Baker, Jan'y 1, 1733-4. She died May 6, 1742, and he died Dec. 1777, aged 72. His children born in Barnstable were Joseph, born 22d Sept. 1734, who married Desire Lumbard and had Thankful Nov. 14, 1757; Remember-Mercy, Jan'y 13, 1760, and Joseph, Aug. 18, 1762, (the father of the present Mr. James Cobb). The daughters Thankful and Mercy it is said were bewitched when young, and marvelous stories are related of them. Jesse Cobb had also Seth, bap'd Sept. 4, 1737, removed to Sandwich; Rowland, bap'd Oct. 15, 1738, married Thankful Garret of S.; Nicholas, bap'd Feb. 10, 1739-40, married Ann Perry had Chloe Blush now living, aged 96, and others; Nathan bap'd Jan's 18, 1740-41. Jesse Cobb was an illiterate man. He could neither read or write; but he considered himself a great poet and employed an amanuensis. His two nearest neighbors, John Lewis, many years town school master, and Solomon Otis, Esq., were graduates of Harvard College. John Bacon, Esq., and Capt. Samuel Bacon, "gentlemen," were also his neighbors, and he thus had the advantage of daily intercourse with literary men. Jesse's poetry has not been preserved. Some verses are however repeated by his descendants. The extravagance of the times, the fashions, and the ladies, whom he did not treat with much courtesy, where his favorite themes. The dogerel rhymes in the note* are extracts from his *poem* addressed to James Paine, Esq., who kept a school several years in Barnstable, and who, during his leisure hours, courted the muses.

V.     Seth, born 15th April, 1707.
VI.    Ebenezer, born 7th March, 1709, died Sept. 1710.
VII.   Jude (or Judah), born 24th June, 1711.·
VIII.  Nathan, born, 15th June, 1713, married Bethia Harding of Eastham, 1735.
IX.    Stephen, born 27th Jan'y 1716, married July 8, 1742, Abigail Chipman, and had Mary, Judah, James, Abigail, Stephen, Chipman and Jacob.
X.     Elizabeth, born 18th April, 1718, married March 10, 1736-7, David Hawes of Yarmouth.

Gershom Cobb, son of James and grand son of Elder Henry Cobb, born Aug. 4, 1675, married Hannah Davis, 24th Feb. 1702-3

His house stood near the centre of Elder Cobb's great lot. Some ancient pear trees now mark the spot. Elder Cobb probably built a house there, afterwards owned by his son James. His children born in Barnstable were:

I.     John, 22d May, 1704, died April 1706.
II.    Sarah, 27th Oct. 1705, married Nath'l Bacon, 1726.
III.   Gershom, 15th Nov. 1707, married April 20, 1732, Miss Sarah Baxter of Yarmouth, and died the same year leaving a son Gershom, who married Feb. 6, 1751-2, Mehitebel, daughter of Job Davis. He died in 1758 leaving three

---

* "Christ, he was a carpenter by trade,
And he the doors of Heaven made,
And he did swear
That high crowned caps and plaited hair
Should never have admittance there."

A fashion prevailed among the ladies in Jesse's time of wearing the hair combed and plaited over a cushion resting on the top of the head· This was surmounted with a high crowned cap.

The following is the closing stanza and is particularly addressed to Mr. Paine who was the champion of the ladies:

"He who for a pis'treen twice told,
Will labor for a week in school,
Can offer nothing very great,
So here is all I shall relate."

In another stanza Jesse commends to Mr. Paine the perusal of the third chapter of Isaiah.

sons, bap'd Nov. 25, 1759, named Edward, (born Nov. 6, 1752) Gershom and Josiah. Gershom the father was a very honest, upright man, a weaver. In the summer months he was employed in the fishing business, and the remainder of the year in weaving, &c. His widow in 1776 married Nathaniel Lothrop, his second wife, and she had by him a daughter Susan, who married Eleazer Cobb, Jr. She died in 1812 or 13, aged about 80. Her son Edward was a carpenter, married Jan'y 29, 1778, Hannah Hallett of Yarmouth, removed in 1782 to Westborough, where he died Oct. 27, 1819. He had ten children. Gershom was a mariner and taken a prisoner by the English during the Revolution. He returned to Barnstable about the year 1793, and it is said that he returned to England married and had two children there. Josiah went to Boston to learn a shoemaker's trade, but disliking the trade left. It is supposed that he was lost at sea.*

IV.  John, born 17th Nov. 1709.  Removed to Plymouth.
V.   Hannah, 29th Aug. 1711, married Jan'y 29, 1734, David Childs of Barnstable.
VI.  Thankful, 10th July, 1714, married Oct. 14, 1746, David Dimmock.
VII. Anne, 8th Dec. 1716, died 4th Nov. 1720.
VIII. Josiah, twin brother of Anne.
IX.  Edward, 2d Nov. 1718.
X.   Mary, 14th June, 1721, married first, Isaac Gorham, Sept. 2, 1742, and second, James Churchill, Feb. 3, 1756-7.

Jesse Cobb was a loyalist or tory. He was one of the party who assembled on the evening of the night when the liberty pole in Barnstable was cut down. Jesse was called on by the company to compose a notice to be posted up, and he dictated the following, impromptu :

> Your Liberty pole,
> I dare be bold,
> Appears like Dagon bright,
> But it will fall,
> And make a scrawl,
> Before the morning light.

Jesse was seventy years of age when he dictated the above, and it indicates that he was ready, and possessed more wit than we have given him credit for. The Liberty pole stood in front of the public house of Mrs. Abiah Crocker, where the willow tree now stands. It stood on a knowl or small hill there which has

---

*The account of the family of Gershsom Cobb I obtain from the records, a manuscript of one of the descendants, and other sources. Respecting the third Gershom (son of Gershom and Sarah) I rely on the manuscript which seems to be corroborated by the Probate records. Gershom Cobb, Jr.'s inventory is dated Jan'y 23, 1733, showing that he died soon after his marriage.

since been leveled.   The pole was very tall, and surmounted with a gilt ball, to which allusion is made by Mr. Cobb.   During the night the pole was cut down and fell across the road.   Who cut it down has never been satisfactorily ascertained.   I persume it would have been difficult for Jesse Cobb, Samuel Crocker and Otis Loring, to have proved that they were not present.

# CLAGHORN.

James Claghorn was not one of the first settlers. He was of Barnstable in 1654, and took the oath of fidelity in 1657. He removed to Yarmouth about the year 1662, when his wife committed suicide Oct. 1677, by hanging herself in the chamber of her house. This is the first suicide on record in this part of the Colony.

James Claghorn married 6th January, 1654, Abigail, sometimes written Abia, probably a daughter of Barnard Lombard, though she may have been a sister. His children born in Barnstable were:

I.   James, 29th January 1654. He probably died early. Mr. Savage was led into a mistake by a typographical error in the Genealogical Register of 1856, page 348, where Jane is printed James.

II.  Mary, born 26th October, 1655, married March 28, 1682, Joseph Davis, had four children, died 1706.

III. Elizabeth, April 1658.

IV.  Sarah, 3d January, 1659.

V.   Robert, 27th Oct. 1661.

VI.  Shubael. Birth not recorded.

Robert Claghorn, son of James, married 6th November, 1701, Bethia, widow of Nathaniel Lothrop. By her first husband she had John and Hannah. She died, say the church records, 'last end of October, 1731, aged about 60.' Robert Claghorn's estate was settled 22d Aug. 1715, and his widow Bethia, sons Joseph, Nathaniel and Samuel, and only daughter Abia are named. He owned 7 1-2 acres of land in the common field, a lot in the neck below Joshua Lumbard's, and lands bought of the heirs of Joseph Davis at South Sea, shares in the common lands, and about £300 in money. No house is named in the settlement. He administered on the estate of his sister Mary, and probably resided at her house at the time of his death. In 1702 he owned a part of the Lumbert farm, and had a house at the east end of the pond and for that reason it is sometimes called in the records

Claghorn's instead of Lumbert's pond. This estate he sold to a Crocker, and it afterwards was bought by the Lothrops. Respecting Robert Claghorn I have little information. He appears to have been a very worthy man.

### Children of Robert Claghorn.

I. Abia, born Aug. 13, 1702. She did not marry, was admitted a member of the East Church Nov. 3, 1745, and died Feb. 4, 1763.

II. Joseph, born Aug. 25, 1704.

III. Nathaniel, born Nov. 10, 1707.

IV. Samuel, June 23, 1709. In the division of his father's estate, the lands bought of the heirs of Joseph Davis at Chequaquet were set off to him. He married September 11, 1742, Hannah, probably daughter of Job Hinckley, and had a son Nathaniel, April 29, 1743.

Shubael Claghorn, a son of James, married Jane, daughter of John Lovell. He died before 1729, when his widow married John Bumpas of Rochester.

### Children born in Barnstable.

I. James, August 1689. By his wife Experience he had, at Rochester, Lemual June 10, 1713, and Mary April 12, 1715. He afterwards, in 1736, married Elizabeth King of Kingston. His wife died in Barnstable, Dec. 25, 1774, aged 66.

II. Thankful, 30th January, 1660-1, died January, 1696.

III. Thomas, 20th March 1692-3. A Thomas Claghorn of Edgartown had a daughter Hannah baptized at the West Church July 17, 1756.

IV. Shubael, 20th September, 1696.

V. Robert, 18th July, 1699. He married January 16, 1722-3 Thankful Coleman. He died July 11, 1750, aged 50, and his widow April 1770, aged 70. He had : 1, James, Dec. 8, 1723, married 1747, Temperance Gorham, removed to Salisbury, returned in 1770 ; 2, Nehemiah, Jan. 30, 1725-6 ; 3, Eunice, May 4, 1728 ; 4, Benjamin, Dec. 17, 1733 ; 5, Jabez, May 9, 1736, married Nov. 10, 1780, Eunice Davis, died June 10, 1821, aged 85.

VI. Benjamin, 14th June, 1701.

VII. Reuben, baptized 28th April, 1706, married 1733, Eleanor Lovell and had :  , Jane, April 12, 1733 ; 2, Nathaniel, 22d Aug. 1735 ; 3, Seth, Nov. 1, 1737 ; 4, Joanna, January 12, 1742 ; Lois, Feb. 8, 1747. His autograph signature is affixed to a paper in the Probate Office. It is the best executed signature that I have seen in that office.*

VIII. Mary, baptized 3d Aug., 1707, married 1729, Eben Clark of Rochester.

IX. Jane, baptized 31st July 1709, married Joshua Lumbert, Jr., 1755.

X. Ebeneazer, 30th July, 1712, married Oct. 30, 1734, Sarah Lumbert. She died. He married Sept. 7, 1763, Elizabeth Hamblin—had Joseph, Oct. 9, 1743 ; Sarah, July 27, 1764 ; Jane, Oct. 1, 1765, married Job Childs, Nov. 24, 1785.

---

*Note.—Some would perhaps give precedence to the signature of Hon. Barnabas Lothrop or Col. William Bassett. Specimens of the chirogrophy of Mr. Lothrop are preserved. The form of his letters resemble the Old English black letter type. He was not a rapid writer, and evidently took much pains. Col. Bassett was a rapid penman, wrote a fine running hand, yet distinct and easily read. Of the early settlers, Rev. Joseph Lord of Chatham was the best penman. He wrote a splendid hand. I have a volume of his manuscript written as compactly as a printed page yet perfectly distinct. Joseph Lothrop, Esq., the first Register of Probate, wrote a very neat hand. Anthony Thatcher and his son, Col. John, were excellent Clerks. In the Gorham family were many who wrote good hands. There is a remarkable similarity in the signatures of the successive John Gorhams, so great that it requires a practised eye to distinguish them. William, son of Col. David Gorham, wrote a splendid hand for records.

# CHILD.

The earliest notice I find of Richard Child is in Mr. Lothrop's Church records. It is there recorded that "Richard Childe and Mary Linnett marryed the 15th day of October, 1649, by Mr. Collier at my Brother Linnett's house."

I find no record of his children; but it appears that he had a family, for March 5, 1660, he was ordered by the Court to desist from erecting a cottage within the bounds of Yarmouth, the putting up of such buildings being contrary to law.—He afterwards gave security to save harmless the town of Yarmouth from all charges on account of the children he then had, and he was thereupon permitted "to enjoy his cottage."*

It thus appears that Richard Childs had a family, Samuel and Richard Childs of Barnstable were probably his children. Samuel was killed at Rehobeth battle March 25th, 1675.—There was a Richard Child in Marshfield in 1665, perhaps the same who had been of Barnstable and Yarmouth. He there built him a house and married, and had a family. Richard Child of Watertown, born in 1631, was another man. He married March 30, 1662, Mehitable Dimmock, a daughter of Elder Thomas of Barnstable. His daughter Abigail married Joseph Lothrop of Barnstable, and Hannah, Joseph Blush.

I find no positive evidence that Dea. Richard Child, from whom all the Barnstable families of the name descend was a son of the Richard who married Mary Linnell; but there is little reason to doubt that such was the fact.

---

*In the account of Richard Berry I stated that he was forbidden to erect a cottage in Yarmouth. That was a mistake, it was Richard Child that was so forbidden. The practice which prevailed in early colonial times, of warning strangers out of town and forbidding them to build houses or settle in a town without a license was sanctioned by law. The case of Richard Child is not a solitary one. Men of good standing who were strangers were often warned out of town. The law may seem harsh and tyranical; but reasons then existed which have now passed away. If Richard Child had been allowed to build in Yarmouth without protest, he would have been entitled to a personal right in the common lands and a tenement right amounting in Yarmouth to 16 1-2 shares out of the 3,118 into which the town was divided; and if unfortunate, the town would be liable for the supplies of his family. A protest not only saved the town harmless; but prevented the person moving in from claiming the rights of a proprietor.

The name is written Childe, Child, Chiles and Childs on the records. The true orthography is Child ; but all the descendants of Richard, resident in Barnstable, write the name with a final s.

Dea. Richard Child, probably a son of the first Richard of Barnstable, resided in the westerly part of the East Parish, on the estate owned by the late Mr. John Dexter, deceased. He had a shop, which indicates that he was a mechanic. He was admitted to the church May 4, 1684, and ordained a deacon Sept. 4, 1706. He married in 1678, Elizabeth, daughter of John Crocker. She died January 15, 1696, and he married, second, Hannah ——.

*Children born in Barnstable.*

I.　Samuel, born 6th Nov. 1679.
II.　Elizabeth, born 23d Jan. 1681-2, died five weeks after,
III.　Thomas, born 10th January, 1682-3.　See account of family below.
IV.　Hannah, 22d January, 1684.　The Hannah Child who married 30th July, 1702, Joseph Blush of Barnstable, was as above stated a daughter of Richard Child of Watertown.
V.　Timothy born 22d Sept. 1686.
VI.　Dea. Ebenezer, born, says the town record, "March, latter end, 1691, as I think.".　He died January 17, 1756, N. S., in the 66th year of his age, and was buried at West Barnstable.　He married in 1719 Hope, and had, 1, Elizabeth, 18th July, 1720, died 18th Sept. 1720 ; 2, Ebenezer, 10th April, 1723 ; 3, Richard, baptized 1st Aug. 1725 ; 4, Mary, baptized 3d Sept., 1727, died June 15, 1762 aged 35 ; and Mercy, baptized 4th January, 1730.　The three last named are not on the town records.　Ebenezer Child, Jr., son of Dea. Ebenezer, married January 15, 1745, Hannah Crocker. She died Feb. 23, 1755, aged 37, and he married in 1756, Abigail Freeman.　His children were, 1, Ebenezer, born Nov. 3, 1747, baptized at the West Church, Nov. 8, 1747 ; 2, Josiah, Aug. 8, 1749 ; 3, Hannah, Sept. 10, 1751 ; 4, David, March 2, 1754 ; 5, by his second wife, Jonathan, May 13, 1757 ; 6, Abigail, Dec. 26, 1758 ; 7, Hope, January 21, 1761 ; and Mary, baptized April 10, 1763.
VII.　Elizabeth, born 6th June, 1692.
VIII.　James, born 6th November, 1694.　See account of his family below.
IX.　Mercy, born 7th May, 1697.
X.　Joseph, born 5th March, 1699-10, married April 23, 1724, Deliverance Hamblin.　He was admitted to the West Church Aug. 18, 1728, removed to Falmouth and returned to Barnstable in 1747.　The names of only two of his children were on the town records.　His children were, 1, Joseph, born 17th Aug. 1724 ; married Meribah Dexter of

Rochester ; 2, Benjamin, baptized 25th Aug. 1728, married Mehitable Hamblin, 1652, and had Lewis, Aug. 29, 1782 ; Hannah, Sept. 6, 1754 ; and Mehitable, Dec. 27, 1756. He died before June 10, 1758, when his three children were baptized at the West Church. 3, Elizabeth, daughter of Joseph, was baptized 24th August 1729 ; 4, Ruth, baptized 26th Sept. 1731, married 21st May, 1747, Reuben Blush ; 5, James, born 4th March, 1742 ; and Abigail, baptized 29th July 1750. Deliverance Childs who married March 3, 1757, Daniel Hamblin, was probably a daughter of Joseph born in Falmouth.

Thomas Childs, son of Richard, born 10th January, 1682, resided in the East Parish where he died, April 11, 1770, aged 88. He married in 1710, Mary ———. Of his family only David appears to have remained in Barnstable.

*Children of Thomas Childs born in Barnstable.*

I.   David, born July 20, 1711. See account below.
II.  Jonathan, Nov. 27, 1713.
III. Silas, March 10, 1715. Silas removed to Rhode Island, and it is said settled in Warren. He has many descendants.
IV.  Hannah, born July 29, 1720, married Prince Taylor of Lebanon, Conn., March 6, 1748.
V.   Thomas, Sept. 10, 1725.
VI.  Benjamin, Dec. 4, 1727, married Rebecca, daughter of Stephen Davis of B., removed to Portland, had Thomas Sept. 25, 1752 ; Isaac, Feb. 10, 1755 ; and Rebecca, March 9, 1759. He and his three children died early, and his widow gave her estate to her brothers and sisters in Barnstable.
VII. Mary, born April 1, 1733.

James Childs, son of Richard, born 6th Nov. 1694, married Sept. 27, 1722, Elizabeth, daughter of Samuel Crocker. He died Nov. 2, 1779, aged 85.

*Children born in Barnstable.*

I.   Samuel, July 15, 1723, married Feb. 20, 1752, Mary daughter of Thos. Hinckley, and had 1, Samuel, July 7, 1753 ; Elijah, baptized Oct. 21, 1764 ; and Ebenezer, Jan. 18, 1766 ; Elijah and Ebenezer of this family, owned the ancient house on the farm which was Dea. Cooper's at the settlement of the town. Ebenezer did not marry and his half of the house was sold to John Dexter. Elijah, married Nov. 10, 1785, Mary Gorham, and was the father of the present Dea. Samuel Childs and other children. He was many years master of the Barnstable and Boston packet sloop Romeo.

II.    James, born April 22, 1725, married June 5, 1755, Mary,
       daughter of David Parker, Esq., and had Elizabeth, born
       May 6, 1756; Daniel, baptized Aug. 10, 1760; Mary,
       baptized Feb. 15, 1761; Sarah, baptized Dec. 30, 1764,
       and James, baptized May 24, 1767.
III.   Elizabeth, born Dec. 20, 1730, married May 19, 1748,
       Daniel Crocker.
IV.    Sarah, born April 9, 1736, married May 2, 1754, Jonathan
       Crocker.
V.     Thankful, born Aug. 4, 1741, married Joseph Lawrence of
       Sandwich, March 27, 1760.
VI.    Richard, born March 22, 1743-4. He inherited the estate
       which was his father's and grandfather's. He did not
       marry. He had a large wen on one of his ankles, which in
       the latter part of his life nearly disabled him from walking.
       He gave his estate to John Dexter, on the condition that
       he should support him for life. He died suddenly in 1805,
       aged about 61.

    David Childs, a son of Thomas, born July 20, 1711, married
Jan. 29, 1734 by John Thacher, Esq., to Hannah, daughter of
Gersham Cobb. His children born in Barnstable were:
I.     David, Feb. 7, 1735-6, married April 4, 1758, Hannah,
       daughter of Job Davis, and had 1, Susannah, July 30,
       1762, married Joseph Cobb, Sept. 30, 1784; 2, Asenath,
       Sept. 22, 1765, married 1st, Josiah Clark, 2d, ———
       Wild, and lived in Boston; 3, Job, Sept. 8, 1767, married
       Jane Claghorn, 24th Nov. 1785; 4, Hannah, Nov. 17,
       1769, married 4th April, 1788, Josiah Gorham; 5, Anna,
       Nov. 1741, died unmarried, had Polly Allyn; 6, Josiah,
       Dec. 14, 1773, married and then removed to Westborough
       and thence to Boston; 7, David, July 8, 1775; 8, Shubael
       Davis, Dec. 16, 1777, married ———, died suddenly in
       Chelsea; 9, Benjamin, Aug. 11, 1779, died a young man,
       in Georgia; and 10, Edward, March 9, 1783, married
       thrice, 1, Jane Goodeno, 2, Cynthia Goodeno, 3, ———,
       died in Boston.
II.    Jonathan, Dec. 25, 1737, married Thankful Howland,
       March 19, 1787, removed to Sandwich.
III.   Anna, Aug. 18, 1742, died unmarried.
IV.    Asenath, Feb. 28, 1738-40, married ——— Linnell.
V.     Josiah, Sept. 7, 1745, married 1st, Temperance, daughter
       of George Lewis. She died soon after marriage, of con-
       sumption, and he married 2d, Abigail, daughter of Nathan-
       iel Sturgis. He was with his uncle, Capt. James Churchill,
       in the French War, and during the Revolution, was one of
       the Home Guard, detailed for the defence of the coast.
       He was entitled to a pension, but did not obtain it. He

was employed fifteen winters in trading voyages to the Carolinas'.

VI.    Edward, Sept. 13, 1749, married Mary, daughter of Seth Lothrop.  He was employed many years by the eccentric Dr. Abner Hersey, and as a reward for his faithful services, the Dr. in one of his early wills, gave him £100. The Dr. inquired of Edward what disposition he intended to make of the bequest.  "Fit out my daughters and marry them off," was the inconsiderate reply.  The Dr. could not tolerate even neatness in dress, was indignant at the reply, altered his will, and Edward lost the money.

Josiah and Edward bought the small estate of John Logge, (a part of Elder Cobb's great lot), which they divided, and each had a house thereon.  Both were coopers and small farmers, and displayed more taste for horticultural and floricultural pursuits than was common in those days.  Both, in early life, went on *feather voyages*, a term which few, at the present time, will understand.  About a century ago, vessels were fitted out for the coast of Labrador to collect feathers and eider down.  At a certain season of the year some species of wild fowl shed a part of their wing feathers, and either cannot fly, or only for a short distance. On some of the barren islands on that coast, thousands of those birds congregated.  The crews of the vessels would drive them together, kill them with a short club or a broom made of spruce branches, and strip off their feathers.  Millions of wild fowl were thus destroyed, and in a few years, their haunts were broken up by this wholesale slaughter, and their numbers so greatly diminished that feather voyages became unprofitable and were discontinued.

For fourteen years subsequent to 1800 these brothers were oftener seen together than seperate.  Every week day at 11 and 4 o'clock they visited the groceries with a degree of punctuality which all noticed.  Housewives that had no time-pieces, when they saw them, would say, Uncle Ned and Siah (as they were familiarly called) have passed, and it is time to set the table.  At the close of his life, Edward became estranged from his brother and would have no intercourse whatever with him.  This was a great affliction to Josiah, and no efforts or concessions he could make effected a reconciliation.  Edward had some eccentricities.  Perhaps his long and familiar intercourse with Dr. Hersey had infused that trait into his character.  His feelings were strong, and when he took a dislike he was not easily reconciled.  Josiah was a different man in this respect.  He harbored no prejudices against any one.  He was a kind hearted man, and a good neighbor.  When young he took an interest in the history of the early settlements, and remembered many things that his grandfather had said to him.  He stated that all the families of the name of

Childs, in Barnstable, were descendants of the first Richard, which is probably the fact.   He survived his brother, dying at an advanced age.

# COGGIN.

Four of this name came to New England. John, Sen'r, of Boston, said to have been the first who opened a store for the sale of goods in that city, was a ship-owner, and a man of wealth; he died in 1658; John Jr., of Boston, son of Humphrey, and a nephew of John, Sen'r., died in 1674; Thomas was of Taunton in 1643, died March 4, 1653; Henry Coggin was of Boston in 1634, afterwards of Scituate, and removed with the first settlers to Barnstable in 1639. July 1 1634, three cases, in one of which Henry, and in another, John Coggin was a party, were referred to Gov. Winthrop and three others for adjustment and settlement. The matters in dispute are not fully stated; but appear to have been connected with the settlement of a ship's voyage, in which Henry and John probably had an interest.

Dec. 4, 1638, William Andrews was convicted of making an assault on Mr. Henry Coggin, striking him several blows and conspiring against his life. Andrews, as a part of his punishment was committed, or sold into slavery; but on the 3d of September following, he was released, he promising to pay Mr. Henry Coggin eight pounds.

Feb. 13, 1639-40, Mr. Henry Coggin assigned for 50 shillings sterling, and 20 bushels of Indian Corn, paid by Manaseth Kempton, of Plymouth, the services of his servant James Glass,* for the term of five years, from June 14, 1640.

Oct. 14, 1643, he was one of the Committee appointed by the Court to cause a place or places in Barnstable to be fortified for the defence of the inhabitants against any sudden assault.

June 5, 1644, he was on the grand jury, and at the same court he and Mr. Thomas Hinckley took the oath of fidelity. They had previously taken the same oath at Scituate.

---

* James Glass settled in Plymouth. He married 31st Oct., 1645, Mary, daughter of William Pontus, had Hannah, 2d June, 1647; Wybra, 9th Aug. 1649; Hannah again 24th Dec. 1651; and Mary posthumous. He was a freeman 1648, and was lost in a storm, Sept. 3, 1652, near Plymouth harbor. Roger Glass, a servant of John Crocker, was probably a brother of James.

The record of his lands in Barnstable was not made till 3d Feb. 1661-2. His home lot containing ten and one-half acres, was bounded easterly by Coggins's, now called Great Pond, southerly by the highway, and John Finney's land, westerly by Henry Bourne's land, and northerly by the meadow. His house stood near the spot where Sturgis Gorham, Esq., built the house now owned by the Smiths. The lot originally contained eleven acres and a half, one acre, before the record was made, had been sold to John Finney. This acre was near the present railroad crossing, and was bounded on the south by the highway, and on other sides by the land of Henry Coggin, deceased.

He also owned four acres of marsh adjoining his home lot; four on Jewell's island; eight of marsh and one acre of upland at Scorton; fifty acres of land at the Indian pond; and two shares in the Calve's pasture.

He married, perhaps in England, Abigail Bishop. Her father, probably, never came to New England. Circumstance favors the supposition that Henry Coggin was a sea captain, and that his death, June 16, 1649, in England, occurred, not while he was on a visit to that country, as Mr. Savage supposes but while pursuing the regular course of his business as a trader between London and Boston. This is probably the fact. Nothing is positively known on the subject. The case which he had with John Tilly shows that he had some connection with ships, and the fact that he was entited to be called Mr. in Massachusetts, shows that he was a man of good standing, not a common sailor. His widow married John Finney, according to the Church Records, July 9, 1650, and according to the Colony Records, 10th June, 1650; she died 6th May, 1653.

### Children of Mr. Henry Coggin.

I.    Abigail, born probably in Scituate, about the year 1637. She married 21st June, 1659, John French, of Billerica. He was a son of William, and came over in the Defence with his parents at the age of 5 months. She died soon after her marriage leaving no issue.

II.   Thomas, baptized at the Barnstable Church March 2, 1639-40, died 26th Feb. 1658-9; but according to the Colony Records he was buried 28th Jan. 1658-9. †

III.  John, baptized Feb. 12, 1642-3. In 1654 his parents were dead, and all his brothers and sisters excepting Abigail. His father-in-law had taken a third wife who had no sympathy for these children. Mar. 1, 1658-9 Mr. Isaac Robinson and Gyles Rickard, Sen'r., of Plymouth, complained to the

---

† I usually follow the dates on the Church Records. These are noted in the order in which they occurred. The Town Records from which the Colony were copied, have been transcribed several times, and the order in which they are arranged affords no clue for detecting errors.

Court that these orphan children living with Finney, suffered wrong in several respects and their case was referred to Gov. Prence and Mr. Thomas Hinckley to examine. On the 3d of May following, John Coggin having made choice of Capt. James Cudwerth and Mr. Isaac Robinson, the Court appointed them his guardians ; but ordered that he should remain with his father-in-law till the June Court, and meantime to be kept at school all the time, excepting six days. The Court delayed giving any definite order, to give Mr. Finney time to make up the accounts of the estate, and because letters were expected from Mr. Bishop, the grandfather, who was probably in England. June 7, 1659, all the lands of Henry Goggin, deceased, were transferred to the guardians of John. In these proceedings Abigail is not named. She was then of age and married soon after, as above stated.

April 8, 1664, John Coggin executed a discharge of his loving friends and guardians, acknowledging himself to be fully satisfied with their management in relation to himself and his estate. On the 8th of the following June, the Court declared John Coggin to be "heir apparent" of Henry Goggin, deceased, and authorized him to make sale of the lands that were his father's. The houselot, meadows adjoining, and on Jewell's island, and shares in the Calve's Pasture, he sold to his father-in-law, the meadow at Scorton to Capt. Matthew Fuller, and his great lot at Indian Pond to Wm. Crocker. He married 22d Dec. 1664, Mary Long, of Charlestown, and had children, Henry and John.

IV.    Mary, baptized April 20, 1645, buried May·3, 1645.

V.    Henry, baptized Oct. 11, 1646. I find no record of his death ; he was not living in 1659.

The parties named in connection with this family, were among the most respectable in this, and in the Mass. Colony.‡ The name is written Coggin, Coggan, Cogan, Coggen, and by Mr. Lothrop, Cogain. The records of Mr. Lothrop's Church in London are lost, but circumstances make it probable that Mr. Coggin was a member in England, and was admitted to fellowship in the Scituate and Barnstable Church, without any formed proceedings on record. Circumstances indicate that such were the facts, not only in regard to Mr. Coggin ; but to other members of the London Church, who came over and finally settled in Barnstable.§

---

‡Mary Gaunt was a kinsman of Henry Coggin and probably resided in his family. She married Francis Crooker.

§I have heretofore suggested that the old name of Coggin's pond be restored. The present name is indefinite and without meaning. In spelling the name I have followed the town records. Cogain is perhaps better. Let the station on the Cape Cod Railroad be called Cogain's Pond station.

# COOPER.

Dea. John Cooper was one of the first settlers in Barnstable. He came to Plymouth about the year 1632, and there married on the 27th Nov. 1634, Priscilla, widow of William Wright and daughter of Alexander Carpenter,* of Leyden. She had no issue by either marriage that survived her. In 1683 she removed to Plymouth where she died Dec. 29, 1689, aged 91. The following is a copy of her letter of dismission from the Barnstable to the Plymouth Church:

"ffor ye Rev'd Elders of ye CCh. of Ct., at Plymouth, to bee communicated to ye CCh. there, Rev'd and beloved Brethren,
The providence of God having removed ye Widow Cooper A member of ye CCh of Ct. at Barnstable fro. us to dwell w'th you; and she desiring to partake with you of ye good things of God's house, and to be under yo'r watch and care, and in order y'r unto to bee dismissed fro. o'er CCh unto you; y'r fore if you judge meet to receive her, wee do dismiss her fro. us unto yo'r holy communion; as one yt has walked orderly while w'th us, and do commend her to you unto ye grace of God in all you'r holy Administrations.

In ye name and w'th consent of
ye CCh of Ct. at Barnstable,
Barnst:                           pr nos,
8 r : 15, 1683, *Jonath: Russel*, Pastor.
*John Chipman*, Elder.†

---

* Alexander Carpenter was one of Mr. Robininson's church at Leyden. Five of his daughters are named:
I.   Anna, also named Agnes, in the Dutch records, called a maid ot Wrentham, in England, married April 30, 1613, Samuel Fuller, afterwards the physician of the Plymouth Colony. She died early.
II.  Julian or Julia Ann, born 1584, married 23d July, 1612, at Leyden, George Morton, 2d, Manasseth Kempton, of Plymouth, died 19th Feb. 1664-5, aged 81.
III. Alice, born 1590, married first Constant Southworth, was a widow when she came over, married 2d Gov. William Bradford, 14th Aug. 1623, and died March 26, 1670, aged 80.
IV.  Priscilla, born 1598, married as above stated.
V.   Mary, according to Mr. Savage, born in 1577 and died unmarried at Plymouth, March 19, 1668, aged 90. Mr. Russell says in 1638, if so she was born in 1593, a letter of hers has recently been published, giving information respecting the family; but I cannot at this moment find it.

---

† This letter is printed to correspond as nearly with the original as the types usually found in a printing office will admit. In old manuscripts, th is made like the modern letter y. Many transcribers of old manuscripts use y instead of th. This practice is wrong, because the character was intended for th not for y.

Dea. Cooper was admitted a freeman Jan. 1, 1634-5; removed to Scituate before 1638; and was one of the grantees of the lands between North and South rivers, made that year. Sept. 3, 1638, Cooper's island containing 18 acres was granted to him, which he sold in 1639, to William Wills, and the island bears the name of the latter, to this day. He was constable of Barnstable in 1640, and a deputy to the Colony Court in 1642, and '43. March 24, 1640-1 he was "invested into the office of a Deacon Mr. Lothrop, Mr. Mayo and Dea. Cobb laying on hands."

His home lot was the fourth west from Coggin's pond. 1, Henry Coggins containing twelve acres; 2, Henry Bourne's, eight acres; 3, James Hamblin's, twenty acres, and 4, Dea. Cooper's, containing twenty-four acres. The latter was bounded northerly by the marsh, easterly by Mr. Groom,‡ westerly by Isaac Robinson, and southerly "running into ye woods." Deacon Cooper's house was on this lot, and stood near the present location of the ancient house now owned by William Hinckley and Elijah Childs. A part of that house is ancient and it is not improbable that it is the same which was owned by Deacon Cooper. He also owned the meadow on the north of his home-lot, of the same width with the upland and extending north to the great creek; a share in the Calve's Pasture containing half an acre; a little neck of land pointing southerly into the Great Pond, with eight acres of upland against it, bounded northerly by a great swamp; and a neck of land between the Great and Shoal ponds. The first named neck of land he sold May 9, 1656, to Roger Goodspeed, and the other to John Hall 14th Feb. 1660-1.

Dea. Cooper had no children. His sister Lydia married 25th Dec. 1635, Nathaniel Morton, son of George, and Secretary of the Colony from 1645, till he died June 29, 1685, and the author of that well known work, the New England's Memorial. Dea. Cooper was the brother-in-law of the Secretary, and his wife, Priscilla, was his aunt. She was also nearly related to the Bradford and Fuller families. Mr. Dean says that Dea. Cooper in his will, gave half of his estate to the Barnstable Church and half to his sister Lydia, after the decease of his wife. He was not a man of large estate and it is not probable that much remained at the death of his widow.

A small pond in the northerly part of his home-lot is still known as Cooper's pond, and a small island on the north thereof is called by his name. A marsh island at the north of Rendevous

---

‡ Who this Mr. Groom was I am unable to ascertain. It seems that in 1653, when the record of Dea. Cooper's land was made, that he owned a part of the land, recorded probably the next year 1654, as the property of James Hamblin. There was a family of that name in Middlesex County. There was a Samuel, or Salisbury, in 1850, a mariner, dignified with the prefix of Mr. who went home to London before 1658. Was he that Quaker who published in 1676 "A Glass for the people of N. E." Perhaps the name is Green. An Isaac Green, a surveyor, was early of Barnstable and removed to Falmouth at the settlement of that town and had a family there.

Creek is also called Cooper's island ; but I think the name is more modern than the time of Dea. Cooper.   Great or Nine Mile Pond is also called Cooper's Pond on the record—a good name—and if revived would help preserve the memory of one of the best men among the settlers of  Barnstable.§

§ There was another man of the name of John Cooper in the Colony—a man who did not sustain the excellent character of Dea. John of Barnstable, and the reader of the Colony records must be careful not to confound the two.

# COLEMAN.

Edward Coleman, of Boston, and Margaret, daughter of Thomas Lumbard, of Barnstable, were married at Eastham by Mr. Prence, Oct. 27, 1648. He was of Boston in 1655, and probably came to Barnstable soon after that date. He was admitted an inhabitant Oct. 3, 1662, and was living 26th March, 1690, when the town granted 25 acres of land at "Yannows" to his son Edward, "on the condition that he do his utmost for the maintainance of his father and mother and the rest of the family." This grant was at the south-east corner of the town, bounded easterly by the bounds of Yarmouth, "south by the harbor at Yannows," west by the Hallett land, and north by the commons. Margaret Coleman was living Nov. 12, 1714; but Edward Senior and Junior were then both dead.

*Children of Edward Coleman, born in Boston.*

I.  Edward. The date of his birth was probably 1649. He died in 1714, leaving no issue, and his estate was divided to his mother Margaret; his sister Widow Elizabeth Hadaway; his sister Sarah Coleman, and the children of his only brother James Coleman.

II.  Elizabeth, born 28th 11 mo. 1651, was the second wife of the first John Hadaway, whom she married in Yarmouth, May 1, 1672.

III.  Mary, born 12th Sept. 1653.

IV.  Martha, born 8th Aug. 1655.

V.  Sarah, probably born in Barnstable, unmarried in 1714.

VI.  James, probably born in Barnstable, married Patience, daughter of James Cobb. He was not living in 1714, and his widow married 10th Sept. 1715, Thomas Lumbard. She died March 30, 1747, aged 78 years.

*Children of James Coleman.*

I.  Edward, 25th Oct. 1695, married Thankful Lumbard, 16th Sept. 1715. The names of his children I do not find on the town records. His son Edward was baptized Nov. 7, 1725, and his daughter Miriam Oct. 29, 1727. The latter married Dec. 13, 1750, Joseph Bacon, Jr.

II. Martha, 4th March, 1698, married Sept. 25, 1718, Capt. John Phinney, the founder of Gorham, Maine. She had nine children, viz: 4 in Barnstable; 3 in Portland; and 2 in Gorham.

III. Thankful, 7th Feb. 1699-1700, married Jan. 16, 1722-3, Robert Claghorn, and died April 1770, aged 70 years and 2 months.

IV. A son, 26th Feb. 1702-3, died same day.

V. James, 11th April, 1704, married March 12, 1727-8 Patience, daughter of Dea. John Phinney. He married 2d Martha (Phinney.) His children were Martha, born Jan. 31, 1758-9, probably died young. By his second wife, Martha again, March 19, 1732-3. 3, James, Aug. 8, 1735, married, Sept. 24, 1761, Zerviah Thomas, and June 28, 1763, Ann Lumbard. 4, John, May 14, 1739, removed to Granville, N. S. married Feb. 19, 1764, Abigail, daughter of Capt. James Delap. He lived to be aged, and has descendants in Nova Scotia. 5, Mary, born March 27, 1739, married March 15, 1763, David Howland. Mr. James Coleman died April 16, 1781, aged 77, and his widow Feb. 29, 1784, aged 80.

VI. John, born 26th Sept. 1706, married Aug. 5, 1736, Reliance, widow of Eleazer Cobb. She died June 11, 1742, aged 36, and he married 2d, Mary Hamblin, Aug. 2, 1743. He resided in the ancient Samuel Cobb house till Nov. 20, 1746, when he removed to South Sea. His children were all baptized at the East Church, namely: Martha, June 19, 1737; John, Oct. 29, 1738; Mary, May 11, 1740; Mary again, August 5, 1744; Thomas, November 8, 1747; Nathaniel, Sept. 17, 1749; Zaccheus, Feb, 24, 1750-1; Reliance, April 26, 1752. Nathaniel of this family was insane the latter part of his life. He believed the land had everywhere become soft and miry. He carried a very long cane with a ram's horn on the upper end, and his hat was ornamented with feathers of various colors, stuck under the band. Notwithstanding his constant fear of sinking, he was good natured, cheerful, and inoffensive. As he walked thro' the streets, feeling his way, with his left foot always in advance of his right, he would sing these words, "Bacon's got home and brought me a new ram's horn, a new ram's horn, a new ram's horn."

VII. Patience, 6th May, 1709, married June 20, 1732, James Lothrop.

VIII. Ebenezer, 15th Aug. 1711.

The town records respecting this family are defective. The deficiencies, I presume, may be supplied from the Church and Probate records.

Edward Coleman built the first house at Hyannis. At that time all the southerly part of Barnstable was called "South Sea," and the Indians resident there, "South Sea Indians." The earliest settlers at South Sea were John Thompson, who sold his land to John Lovell, Roger Goodspeed, Jona Hatch, Thomas Bumpas, and Joshua Lumbert. The first building erected by the whites was a warehouse by Nicholas Davis, near where Timothy Baker's store now stands, and on land presented to him by the Sachem Hianna.

In 1697 the "South Sea" men were Thomas Macy, John, Benjamin, and Ebenezer Goodspeed, sons of Roger ; John Lovell, and his sons John, James, William, and Andrew ; John Issum, Thomas Bumpass, Dollar Davis, Thomas Lewis, Joshua Lumbert, John Linnell, John Phinney, Jr., Edward Lewis, Joseph Lothrop, Jr., John Lewis, and Edward Coleman.

Soon after this date the Hallett, Crowell, Bearse, and Claghorn families settled at South Sea. Jonathan Lewis, who, according to tradition, was the first settler in the present village of Hyannis, probably did not build his house before his marriage in 1703. The foregoing statement shows that Edward Coleman was the first settler at Hyannis. His house was at the south-east corner of the town, not far from Baxter's wharf.

The Indian villages at South Sea, beginning at the south-west corner of the town were, 1st, Cotuit or Satuite, the present name ; 2d, Mistic, now Marston's Mills ; 3, Cot-o-ches-et, now Osterville ; 4, Shon-co-net, now corrupted into Skunknet ; 5, Che-qua-quet, or Wee-qua-quet, now Centreville and Hyannis Port ; 6, Tam-a-hap-pa-see-a-kon. This was the name of the brook, now known as Baxter's Mill Pond and River. The lands in the vicinity were probably known by the same name. This was the uniform practice of the Indians, and it was not probably departed from in this case. The name being a long one, and difficult to pronounce was dropped, and the name of the Sachem adopted. As I intend devoting an article to this name, I will here make only one remark. In writing this name all the early writers, excepting Thacher, dropped the aspirate H at the beginning, and wrote the name Iyanough, Yanno, or Janno. The popular pronunciation of the name indicates that the orthography of Mr. Thacher's Hianno, is the best.

All the Indian names that I have succeeded in translating are descriptive terms, suggested by some physical peculiarity of the region to which they were applied. Cotuit or Satuit means "cold brook," and was so named because there are many springs of cool water in the vicinity of the pond and brook of that name.

There is a brook of the same name in Scituate, from which that town derives its name. Mistic is a name that is forgotten and lost, by the people who reside in that vicinity. Marston's Mills is not an improvement on the Indian name.

Cot-o-che-set. The manner in which this name is written on the town records, has probably had an influence in bringing it into disuse. For more than half a century it was the popular name of Oyster Island village. The island was so named on account of the abundance of Oysters found in its vicinity—a very appropriate name for the island ; but not applicable to the main land. When the post-office was established in the village, about thirty years ago, it was called Osterville, for what good reason is unknown. The old name Cot-o-che-set, is a better one, more expressive, and at the time of the change, was familiar to many of the aged.

Skon-ko-net, perhaps a derivative of Kong-kont, the crow, and so called because those birds frequent that region. This name is now incorrectly written and pronounced Skunknet. Only the northerly and westerly part of the tract formerly so-called is now so designated. The western branch of the Skon-ke-net river is now known as Bump's river, and the easterly as Phinney's mill brook.

The changing of a few letters in an Indian name, often makes a redical change in the meaning of the word. Che-qua-quet signifies "the edge of a forest." The large knurls on the oak were called by the same name. As these abound more on the edge than in the center of a forest, it is not surprising that in a language containing so few words as the Indian, that both should be called by the same name. The termination, "et," was applied to places near the water, so that the literal meaning of Che-qua-quet seems to be "a village situate on the edge of the forest and by the sea-shore." This is descriptive of the place, and probably the true signification of the name.

The village was by Bourne, as quoted, Gooken, called Wee-qua-keet, a different name, Wee-koh-quat, is "fair weather," and with the terminal "et," instead of "at," the meaning would be fair weather harbor or river. Mr. Bourne's authority is not to be rejected for slight reasons. In the records, where the name frequently occurs, it is uniformly written Che-qua-quet, with some unimportant variations in the orthography—never Wee-qua-keet. The popular pronunciation of the name is uniformly Che or Cha, not Wee-qua-quet. This is not conclusive ; but taken in connec-tion with the records, I think it settles the question in favor of Che-qua-quet as the best authorized spelling of the name.

When the post-office was established, the old name was dropped and the French Centreville adopted. This is not so objectionable as Osterville, yet it is no improvem t on the old. There is, however, one objection ; there are many post-offices of that name, and for that reason mail matter is now liable to be mis-sent. This objection would not be applicable to the name Che-qua-quet.*

* For the definition of Che-qua-quet and many other Indian names, I am indebted to an intelligent Indian Chief from the West. He had a perfect knowledge of his native tongue which was a dialect of the language spoken by the Massachusetts Indians. He could read without much difficulty Eliot's Indian bible, and Cotton's vocabulary. He was very cautious in giving his opinion. The names of places were often spelt so differently from the manner in which he was accustomed to write the equivalent words that he did not always recognize them. He asked me several times if the pronunciation of the first sylable of Che-qua-quet was Che or Tshe, not Wee, because the meaning of the name depended on that pronunciation. The meaning of the name of a pond in Mashpee, which he gave me, is confirmed by Mr. Marston, the Indian superintendent, as its true meaning. I have also attempted to obtain information from members of the Penobscot tribe, but with little success.

# CROCKER.

Two brothers named John and William Crocker, were among the first settlers in Barnstable, William came with Mr. Lothrop and his church Oct. 21, 1639, and John the following spring. There was also a Francis Crocker of Barnstable, able to bear arms, Aug. 1643. He was one of the soldiers in the Narraganset Expedition, sent from Barnstable Aug. 1645. He married in 1647, Mary Grant "a kinswoman of Mr. Goggain of Barnstable,"* and removed to Scituate, and from thence to Marshfield. He had a family, and his descendents now write their name Crocker.

John Crocker, the elder brother, left no family; but William's posterity are very numerous. Perhaps no one of the first comers, has more descendents now living. A large majority of all in the United States, and in the British Provinces of the name, trace their descent from Dea. William of Barnstable. The descendents of Francis are not numerous. A Thomas Crocker, born in 1633, settled in New London and had a family. Widow Anne Crocker of Scituate, had a son Moses born in 1650, but it does not appear that he has any descendents. Mr. Savage names an Edward of Boston, who was the public executioner in 1684, and a Daniel who married in 1660, but these were perhaps descendants of Francis.

It is said, on how good authority I have not ascertained, that John and William Crocker came over in 1634, either in the same ship with Rev. Mr. Lothrop, or in another that sailed about the same time, and that they stopped in Roxbury before they settled in Scituate. They did not remain long in Roxbury, for their

*The renowned Capt. John Smith, probably the first white who visited Barnstable harbor, wrote this name as here spelled. The town in England from which our town was named is now written Barnstaple. On his return from his voyage in 1614, he presented to Prince Charles a schedule of Indian names of places, and recommended new ones. For Naembeck, (probably Naumkeag, Salem) he proposed the name of Bastable, for Chaw-num (Shaume) part of Sandwich, Barrwick, (forAccomack, Plymouth, &c. A few of the new names are retained. Mr. John Buley (probably John Bursley) afterwards of Barnstable, owned one-fourth of the two ships which Capt. Smith commanded in 1614.

names do not appear on the Massachusetts Colony Records. Crocker or Croker as the name is usually written in England, is very ancient. An old proverbial distich record that,

"Crosker, Crewys, and Copplestone,
When the Conqueror came, were at home."

The family of Crocker, originally seated at Crocker's Hale, and Crokern. For, in Devonshire, became possessed of Lineham, by marriage with the heirs of Churchill. The genealogy of the Crokers of Lineham is accurately recorded and exhibits a descent of eleven John Crockers in almost uninterrupted succession. Members of the family removed to Cornwall, Waterford, and other places. (See Burke.)

### JOHN CROCKER.

It incidentally appears by Mr. Lothrop's church records, that John Crocker was an inhabitant of Scituate in 1636. Feb. 1, 1638-9, he and other inhabitants of Scituate took the oath of allegiance. March 3, 1639-40, he is called of Scituate, but he probably removed soon after this date to Barnstable. Mr. Deane says he probably did not remove till 1654; but this is a mistake, for he was certainly of Barnstable Aug. 1643. The account given by Mr. Deane of his family, is erroneous and the fault is perhaps chargeable to his printer, and not to the author, the name of John having been inadvertantly substituted by the printer for that of William. His wife's name was Joan or Jane. The date of his marriage does not appear on record, probably not till late in life. In Mr. Lothrop's list of the householders in Scituate his name does not occur, making it probable that he was not married till after 1637. If he had any children they all died young, for he had none living at his death in 1669.

The farm of John Crocker, now owned by the descendants of his brother William, is at the north-east corner of the West Parish in Barnstable, and is thus described on the town records: "Forty acres of upland, more or less, bounded easterly by Goodman Bearse, westerly by Mr. Dimmock, northerly by the marsh, and southerly into the woods." He also owned forty acres of salt marsh adjoining his farm on the north; and thirty acres of upland at the Indian pond, the later he sold 24th Feb. 1662-3, to John Thompson. Feb. 10, 1668-9, (the day on which he executed his will) Abraham Blush conveyed to him for £5,10, his great lot containing forty acres of upland and six of marsh. This lot is situated on the east side of Scorton Hill, and is now known as the Bodfish farm. By Blush's deed it appears that John Crocker had formerly owned meadow in that vicinity, then owned by Edward Fitzrandolph.

John Crocker was propounded to be a freeman June 6, 1649, and admitted on the 4th of June following. He was a juryman in 1647, '50 and '54; and surveyor of the highways in 1668.

June 6, 1649, he was licensed to keep an ordinary, the name by which taverns or public houses were then known.

March 2, 1646-7 he made a complaint against Thomas Shaw, which is entered on the Colony Records, and it incidentally furnishes some information that is of interest. This is the first criminal complaint made against a Barnstable man, and is interesting on that account. It shows that John Crocker was a good-liver, that his house was either pallisade built, or surrounded by a pallisade; and that small, as well as large offenders were promptly and severely dealt with. (See Casely No. 33.)

"At a General Court holden March 2d, in the x x i j th year of his Maj'etts now Raigne, of England, &c., 1646-7.

At this Court John Crocker compl. against Thomas Shawe for coming into his house by putting aside some loose pallizadoes on the Lords day, about the middle of the day, and tooke and carried out of his said house some venison, some beefe, some butter, cheese, bread, and tobacco, to the value of x i i d, which the said Thomas Shaw openly in publike Court confessed, submitting himself to the censure of the Court; whereupon, his sureties being released, he was committed to the Marshall's charge; and the Court censured him to make satisfaction for the goods stolen, 1 sh., being so valued, and 14 s, 4 d, a peece to the two men that attended on him to the Court, and to be publikely whipt at the post, which was accordingly don by the publike officer."

John Crocker's house stood near the ancient dwelling-house recently occupied by Joseph and Prince Crocker deceased. Perhaps that house was originally John Crocker's, enlarged by its subsequent owners. It appears by the above extract that the house was either pallisade built or was surrounded by pallisade fence. The nine houses first built in Scituate were small pallisade houses and intended only as temporary residences. They were not built as the log-houses at the West are built, by piling logs horizontally over each other; but with small poles, placed in paralled rows, and filled in with stones and clay. Some of the better kinds were plastered. The roofs were thatched with the long sedge that grows abundantly near the creeks in the salt meadows. The fire-place was built of stone, and the chimney of sticks piled like a cob-house and plastered on the inside with clay. Straw or thatch served for a floor and a carpet. The south-east slope of a hill, near water, was usually selected by the first settlers on which to place their dwellings. By digging into the hill-side a secure back to the fire-place was obtained and the labor of building one side diminished. As a substitute for glass, oiled paper was used. Such houses were called by some of the early writers booths, that is a shelter made of slight materials for temporary purposes. A few such houses were put up in Barnstable, by those who came with Mr. Lothrop in October, 1639. Many of those who came in the spring of that year had good substantial frame-houses.  A saw mill had then been erected in Scituate and lumber, for covering and finishing buildings, could be cheaply procured.  Mr. Hull, Mr. Mayo, Thos. Lumbert, Mr. Dimmock, and others had frame-houses.  According to tradition preserved in the family, the first house built by Gov. Hinckley, and that by his father Samuel, were on the east side of Goggins' pond, had thatched roofs, and were not much better than the booths above described, yet they were the only houses they had for several years.

It is doubtful whether the first comers ever built any houses of the description now known as log-houses.  Block houses of a similar construction to a log-house, were built early.  They were constructed of hewn timbers, two stories high, and adapted for defence against Indian hostilities as well as for a residence.  A block house was built in Yarmouth ; but in Barnstable, the lower stories of all the fortification houses were of stone, and have already been described.

Some of the pallisade houses built by the first settlers, were the most comfortable and durable houses built.  Elder John Chipman's, I believe, was so constructed, Mr. John Crow's, of Yarmouth, certainly was, and stood nearly two centuries, required but little repair, and, in fact, the recent owners did not know that it was so constructed till it was taken down.  This house was built by taking large sticks of timber for sills and plates, boring two paralled rows of holes in each, about six inches apart, except-ing where doors or windows were to be placed, and filling between with stones and clay.  This formed the walls of the house, which were plastered with shell mortar inside and out.  The Crowell house was afterwards clap boarded, which concealed the original construction from sight.

John Crocker's house probably was not so constructed, because it would be difficult for any one to have removed the pallisadoes and entered the house in the manner described. Many of the early settlers built a pallisade around their houses, and John Crocker probably did, as a defence against the Indians, and to keep out intruders and wild beasts.  Such pallisades were built of small logs 12 or 15 feet long, sharpened at each end and set or driven into the ground side by side, so as to form a fence ten feet high, which it would be difficult for man or beast to scale.

He died in 1669 leaving a wife Jane, but no children.  After providing for his widow he gave his estate to the sons of his brother William, and appointed his nephew Job, his executor. The latter came into possession of the old homestead, and it is now owned by his descendants.

He was a very different man from his brother Dea. William.

He was illiterate, kept a public house where it was customary in early times, for a certain class of people, found in all communities, to assemble to drink, and indulge in low and vicious conversation. Such company and such associations never improve the temper or moral character of a man, or add anything to his respectable standing in society. His treatment of his servant Roger Glass, a very worthy young man, shows that he was a man, "In whose veins the milk of human kindness did not flow." That he belonged to Mr. Lothrop's church, does not appear. He was one of the pioneer settlers in Scituate and in Barnstable. He was not a perfect man. His ashes rest in the old burying-ground beside those of the fathers where it will be well to let them rest in peace.

William Crocker, a younger brother of John, joined Mr. Lothrop's church in Scituate Dec. 25, 1636. He came to Barnstable Oct. 21, 1639, and his daughter Elizabeth, baptized Dec. 22, 1639, is the fourth on the list, showing that he was among the first who came. He built a frame house in Scituate in 1636—the forty-fourth built in that town. June 5, 1644, he was propounded a freeman, but does not appear to have been admitted till after 1652. He was constable of Barnstable in 1644; on the grand jury in 1654, '55, '57, '61, '67 and '75; selectman in 1668; deputy to the Colony Court in 1670, 71, and 74; and surveyor of highways 1673. In the year 1675 he was on the jury which condemned the murderers of John Sassamon, secretary of King Phillip. He was one of the leading men in early times and was often employed in the business of the town and in settling the estates of deceased persons.

He probably settled first in the easterly part of the town, and removed to West Barnstable about the year 1643. The loss of the early records makes it difficult to decide, but it is probable that his first house in Barnstable was on the lot next west of Henry Bourne's. He had a large landed estate, and for many years was perhaps the richest man in town. His sons were all men of wealth. In 1703 his son Joseph was the owner of the largest estate in Barnstable.

In 1655, Dea. William Crocker owned one hundred and twenty-six acres of upland, and twenty-two acres of meadow at West Barnstable, and forty acres of upland at the Indian ponds.* The West Barnstable farm was bounded easterly by the farm of John Smith, now known as the Otis farm, and by the farm of Samuel Hinckley, now owned by Levi L. Goodspeed, southerly

---

* The Indian ponds are three in number, and form the head waters of the stream now known as Marston's Mill river. Excepting where the water was very high, all these ponds did not originally connect with the mill stream. They were called the Indian Ponds because the Indian land reservation was on their borders. On the town records there is an entry of five dollars, paid for permanently closing one of the passages; and, at some former time a new outlet was excavated at a very considerable expense, probably for the purpose of admitting herring.

it extended into the woods. The southerly part of the farm, in 1654, was bounded on the west by the commons, and the northerly part by lands then owned by Governor Bodfish, and afterwards by Lieut. John Howland. He afterwards added largely to his West Barnstable farm, and to the farm at the Indian pond, the latter containing one hundred acres at his death. The West Barnstable farm was two miles in length from north to south, extending from the salt meadows on the waters at Barnstable harbor to the neighborhood of the West Barnstable meeting-house. The lands he first occupied were the south-easterly part of the farm, the old stone house which, according to tradition, was his first residence, was about a fourth of a mile easterly from the West Barnstable church. This stone or fortification house was taken down many years ago. A few aged persons remember to have seen it in a ruinous state. This part of the farm his son Josiah afterwards owned. There was another stone house on the south-westerly part of the farm owned by the descendants of Eleazer. This was taken down about the year 1815. It was called the old Stone Fort, and stood where Capt. Josiah Fish's house now stands. It was about 25 feet in front and 20 feet on the rear. The walls of the lower story were built of rough stones laid in clay mortar, and nearly three feet in thickness. The upper story was of wood and projected over the lower on the front, about three feet. In this projection were a number of loop holes about six inches square, closed by small trap doors. The windows in the lower story were high and narrow. These and the loop holes in the projection, were intended to be used as port-holes, should the building be assaulted by hostile Indians. The earliest known occupant, to any now living, was Mr. Benoni Crocker, a great-grand-son of Dea. William. He made a two story addition on the south-side, which was occupied by his son Barnabas.

Dea. William Crocker married in 1636 Alice. She was living in 1683, was the mother of all his children; but died soon after that date. He married second Patience, widow of Robert Parker and a daughter of Elder Henry Cobb. He died in the fall of 1692. His age is not stated, but he was propably about 80 years of age. His will is printed below at full length. It is a document that will be interesting to his descendants, and to the public as a specimen of the manner in which those instruments were drawn up in olden times.

The last will and testament of Deacon William Crocker of Barnstable, in New England.

The 6th day of September Anno Dom. 1692 I, William Crocker of Barnstable, being sick and weak in body but throu ye mercy of God of disposing mind and memory, and knowing ye uncertainty of this life on earth, and being desirous to settle

things in order, do make this my last will and testament in manner and forme following, viz : first and principally, I give and
committ my soul to God in Jesus Christ my Saviour and Redeemer
throw whose pretious death and merrits I hope to find ye free
pardon and remition of all my sinnes, and everlasting salvation,
and my body to ye earth from whence it was taken, to be buried
in such decent manner as to my Executor hereafter named, shall
seem meet and convenient, and as touching my wordly estate
which God hath in mercy lent unto me, my will is to bestow ye
same as hereafter is expressed, and I do hereby revoke and make
void all wills by me formerly made and declared and appoint this
to be my last will and testament.

Imprimus my will is that all those debts and duties which I
owe in right or conscience to any person or persons whatsoever,
shall be well and truly contented and paid when convenient by my
Executor.

Itt. I give and bequeath unto Patience my loving wife,
besides ye liberty to dispose of all ye estate which she brought
with her or had at ye time of our intermarriage, and besides ye
forty pounds I then promised to give her, in case she should survive me, I give unto her my best bedd and bedstead with all ye
ffurniture thereto belonging.

Itt. I give and bequeath to my eldest son John Crocker my
now dwelling house and lands both upland and ffresh meadows
adjoyning and belonging thereunto now and of late under my
occupation and improvement to have and to hold to him his heirs
and assignes forever he or they paying to ye s'd Patience my wife
twenty pounds of ye fores'd forty pounds she is to receive, and I
do also hereby confirm to him my son John his heirs and assignes
forever all those parcels of land I heretofore gave unto him and
are well known to have been in his quiet possession for sundry
years ; I further also give and bequeath to him my son John my
two oxen which he hath had in his posession some years.

Itt. I give and bequeath unto my son Job Crocker besides ye
land I heretofore gave him and known to be in his possession,
twenty acres of that fifty acres at ye ponds which I purchased of
John Coggin to have and to hold to him my son Job his heirs and
assignes forever and that he chuse it on which side of s'd land he
please.

Itt. I will and bequeath to my sons Josiah and Eliazer
Crocker besides those lands I heretofore gave to each of them
and are in their particular knowne possession, all my upland at
the marsh together with all ye marsh adjoining thereunto, (except
such particular parcel or parcels thereof as I have heretofore
given and is possest of late by any other or is in these presents
hereafter mentioned,) to be equally divided between them ye s'd
Josiah and Eliazer to have and to hold to them their heirs and

assignes forever : Each of them ye s'd Josiah and Eliazer paying seven pounds and ten shillings apiece to ye s'd Patience in paying of ye forty pounds above mentioned. And I further will and bequeath to my sons Josiah and Eliazer to each of them one cow.

Itt. I will and bequeath unto my son Joseph Crocker (besides ye two parcels of upland and one parcel of marsh which I heretofore gave him and is known to be in his possession ye house and land which he hired of me and now lives on) that is to say, so much of my s'd land as he hath now fenced in ; together with that parcel of marsh which he hath from year to year of late hired of me ; to have and to hold to him ye s'd Joseph his heirs and assignes forever : he or they paying five pounds to ye s'd Patience to make up ye full of s'd forty pounds I promised to her as above s'd.

Itt. I give and bequeath all ye rest of my lands att ye ponds to my grandsons, viz : to Nathaniel, ye son of John Crocker, Samuel, ye son of Job Crocker, and Thomas, ye son of Josiah Crocker to be equally divided between them and to their and each of their heirs and assignes forever.

Itt. my will is and I do hereby constitute and appoint my trusty and well beloved son Job Crocker to be my sole executor to see this my last will and testament to be performed, with whom I leave all ye residue of my estate in whatsoever it be, to be equally distributed amongst all my children unless I shall signifie my minde to have such part or parts thereof to be disposed to any in particular.

In witness whereof I have hereunto sett my hand and seal.

On my further consideration I signifie my mind before ye ensealing hereof and it is my will that Mr. Russell shall have my two steers which are att Isaac Howlands and that Mr. Thomas Hinckly shall have my nagro boy if he please he paying fourteen pounds to my Executor for him.

WILLIAM CROCKER.    [Seal.]

Signed Sealed and declared
    In presence of
        SAMUEL CHIPMAN,
        MERCY CHIPMAN.

Samuel Chipman and Mercy Chipman whose hands are sett as witnesses to this will made oath in Court October ye 19 : 1692, that they did see the above said William Crocker now deceased sign seal and declare this above written to be his last will and testament.

JOSEPH LOTHROP : c l.

Examined and duly compared with ye original will and entered October ye 22, 1692.

    Attest :        JOSEPH LOTHROP, Recorder.

The division which Deacon Crocker made of his estate in the foregoing will, may perhaps, be better understood by the following description of the shares of each of his five sons. Job had the estate which was his uncle John's homestead, and his father therefore gives him a larger proportion of his estate, not immediately connected with the West Barnstable farm.

John had the great lot of his uncle John, on which he had a house, and therefore, there was no immediate need that he should be provided for. For his other four sons he had provided houses, or they had built on his land.

The present road running north from the West Barnstable Meeting House, to the Cape Cod Rail Road Depot, divides Dea. Crocker's farm into two nearly equal parts. On the east of the road, Josiah had the south part, excepting the portion given to John, and Joseph the north. On the west side, John had the south part, including a strip running north to the meadows, and a strip on the east, adjoining Josiah's land, where Nathaniel Crocker afterwards lived, and Eleazer the north-westerly part. A question arises which will be hereafter considered, and that is, whether or not John's portion extended far enough west to include the old stone fort.

Dea. Crocker died in good old age. For many years he was deacon of the Barnstable Church, and living an exemplary and pious life. He has a clean record. Nothing dishonest or dishonorable was ever laid to his charge. Men who acquire great wealth, often make enemies of the envious; but Dea. Crocker appears to have been beloved and respected by all. When he removed to West Barnstable, the lands there had only a nominal value. He was industrious, economical, and a good manager. His boys were as industrious and as prudent as the father, and that was the whole secret of their becoming wealthy. In early colonial times a large family was considered a great blessing in a pecuniary point of view. The boys assisted the father on the farm, and at seventeen were able to do the work of a man. The girls were also brought up to more than earn their own living. They assisted the mother, spun and wove the flax and the wool, and made their own and their brother's garments, and in hay time and at harvest assisted their brothers. A man with a large family of healthy children was then the most independent of men. From his farm and his household he obtained an abundance of the prime necessaries of life. The surplus which he sold was more than sufficient to pay the bills of the mechanic, and to buy the few articles of foreign growth and manufacture then required. There was very little money in circulation, and very little was needed. Taxes were payable in agricultural products, at a rate fixed by law, and if lands or property were sold, without it was expressly stipulated in the contract, that payment should be made in silver money, it was a barter trade, payable in produce at the "prices current with the merchants."

Aged people often remark that their ancestors' estimated that every son born to them added to their wealth a £100, and of every daughter £50. However heterodox this theory may now appear to parents, or to political economists, it was undoubtedly true in early times. The Crocker's, with few exceptions, all married in early life, had large families, and excepting the few who tried to live by trade or speculation, acquired good estates, lived comfortably, and were respectable and honorable members of society.

[The genealogies of the Crocker, Gorham, Hallett, and several other families, I have drawn up in the manner recommended in the Genealogical Register, it is neccessary to transcribe them, because the columns of a newspaper are too narrow for such kind of composition, and because the varieties of type required are not kept in a newspaper office. As the same name so frequently occurs in the Crocker family, I shall preserve the serial number in Arabic or common figures, using the Roman numerals as heretofore, to distinguish members of the same family. John and Benjamin are names that frequently occur, and without the serial numbers it will be difficult to distinguish them. At one time there were four John Crocker's in Barnstable, all householders and heads of families. They were, from necessity, distinguished by nick-names; but the use of the serial number will render the repetition of those names unnecessary.]

### Family of Dea. William Crocker.

Dea. William Crocker married for his first wife, Alice, who was the mother of all his children. She was living in 1683, but died soon after that date. He married for his second wife, Patience, widow of Robert Parker and daughter of Elder Henry Cobb. He died Sept. 1692, aged probably 80 years. His children were :

2.  I.   John, born in Scituate May 1, 1637, baptized June 11, 1637.
3.  II.   Elizabeth, born in Scituate Sept. 22, 1639, baptized in Barnstable, Dec. 22, 1639. She was his only daughter and died in Barnstable unmarried, May 1658, in the 19th year of her age.
4.  III.   Samuel, born in Barnstable, June 3, 1642, baptized same day. He died Dec. 1681.
5.  IV.   Job, born March 9, 1644-5, baptized same day.
6.  V.   Josiah, born Sept. 19, 1647, baptized same day.

It seemed improbable that Dea. Crocker had three children born in succession on the sabbath, and that each was baptized on the day of its birth. Mr. Lothrop, the pastor of the church, so records the baptisms, and there is no reason to question his accuracy. Gov. Hinckley so makes his return to the Colony Court, and David Crocker, Esq., one of the early town clerks, so transcribes the earlier records. A single instance of this character was noticed in the family of Austin Bearse, (No. 12) and the comments made thereon are equally applicable to this case.

7.    VI.   Eleazer, born July 21, 1650.
8.    VII.  Joseph, born 1654.
    2. John Crocker, eldest son of Dea. William, resided at West Barnstable. His father, in his will, gave him the southwesterly part of his farm, and the dwelling-house in which he then lived. John Crocker had, at that time, been a married man thirty-three years, and had children and grand-children, and owned lands and a dwelling-house in his own right, independent of the property bequeathed to him by his father. He owned the Bodfish farm, set off to him as his portion of his uncle John's estate, on which there was a dwelling house. One half of that farm he conveyed by deed to his son Jonathan, through whom it came into possession of the Bodfish family.

    The lands bequeathed by Dea. William to his son Eleazer, are not clearly defined in the will. Eleazer owned the lands south of the Dexter farm, on Dexter's, now called Fish's Lane, bounded west by the land of Joseph Bodfish, Sen'r, including the land on which the Stone Fort stood. I infer from this, that the house named in the will of Dea. William, as then in the occupancy of Eleazer, was the old Stone Fort, consequently it was not the house given to his son John. Anciently there was another stone house on the Crocker farm, standing about a fourth of a mile easterly from the West Barnstable Church. This was probably built about the year 1643, and as it was on his first grant of land at West Barnstable, made to Dea. William, it is just to infer that it was his residence. His son Josiah afterwards owned it and the land on which it stood. Seth, a grandson of Josiah, built, about the year 1766, a large and convenient dwelling house near the old stone house, in which he had previously resided. Afterwards the latter was used as an out-building. Seventy-five years ago it was in a ruinous condition, and every vestage of it is now removed. It corresponded in size and construction to the fortification house already described. Previously to his death Deacon William built and resided in the large two story frame house on the Meeting House way, afterwards owned and occupied by his grand-children, Nathaniel and Experience. They came into the possession of it soon after the death of Dea. William, who devised it to their father John, after the death of his widow Patience. Neither Nathaniel nor Experience married. Each owned a large real-estate and had, at their deaths, money on hand and money loaned, on bonds payable in silver money. In 1740 the house required repairs, and Experience, before her death, provided lumber, nails, &c., to complete the same, and which she directed to be done after her death. This house was taken down about fifty years ago. The style was that of the first settlers. Two stories in front and one in the rear.

My main object in this inquirey, is to ascertain from records and other sources of information, what was the action of the townsmen of Barnstable under the order of the Colony Court dated Oct. 10, 1643, requiring them to fortify "a place or places for the defence of themselves, their wives, and children, against a suddaine assault." The committee to enforce this order, were Mr. Thomas Dimmock, Anthony Annable, Henry Cobb, Henry Coggen, Barnard Lumberd, and the constable James Hamblen. The three deacons of the church, Dimmock, Cobb and Crocker, each complied with the order of the court, built fortification houses, and were aided by their neighbors, because in case of a sudden assault by the Indians, the buildings were to be a common place for refuge for all. Who built the stone fort on Dexter's lane, I have been unable to ascertain. In 1692 it was owned and occupied by Eleazer Crocker.*

2. John Crocker, the second of the name, a son of Dea. William Crocker, was born in Scituate May 1, 1637, came to Barnstable with his father 1639. Married in 1659, Mary, daughter of Robert Bodfish. She died Dec. 1662, and he married April 25, 1663, for his second wife, Mary, daughter of John Bursley. He died May 1711, aged 74. His children born in Barnstable were :

9.   I.   Elizabeth, 7th Oct. 1660, married Dea. Richard Child 1678, died Jan. 15, 1716, aged 56. Her first house was next west of Lieut. Howland's. She afterwards resided as named in the account of her family.

10.  II.  Jonathan, 15th July, 1662, married Hannah, daughter of John Howland, 20th May, 1686. He died Aug. 24, 1746, aged 84, and is buried in the West Barnstable graveyard.

11.  III.  John, 17th Feb. 1663-4, married 5th Nov. 1702, Mary, daughter of Nathaniel Bacon. She died March 1710-11, and he married 22d June 1721, Sarah Hinckley. This John

---

*The earliest land owners in the vicinity of the old stone fort, were William Crocker, Joseph Bodfish, Peter Blossom, Mr. Thomas Dexter, Edward Fitzrandolph, and John Bursley. The old stone fort was impregnable against any force that the Indians could raise, and it is surprising that its history is buried in oblivion. Perhaps some future investigator may be more successful than I have been. In Yarmouth a fort was built near the Cong. Meeting House, on a rising ground known as "Fort Hill," and in the easterly part of the town, on land owned by the late Capt. Samuel Rogers, a block house. That house was formerly owned by Thomas Baxterr Capt. Rogers, who took it down in 1810, furnishes me with the following description. "It was about 20 feet by 28 feet square, walls of hewn timber, one story high, gambrel roof, windows small, diamond glass set in lead, chimney stone to chamber floor, brick above, all laid in clay mortar. Bricks large; partially burnt, Fireplace in front room, eight feet wide, with a stone hearth. Shingles on the walls and roof cedar, long, and an inch thick. Boards used apparently sawed by hand." Fortification houses were also built in Sandwich. See Freeman's History.

is called Jr., on the early records, and his father Sen'r. He resided on the west side of the road, a short distance north from the present meeting house.

12.  IV.  Hannah, 10th Oct. 1665, married 1st July, 1686, Samuel Lothrop, a grandson of Rev. John.

13.  V.  Joseph, 1st March, 1667-8, married 18th Sept. 1691, Ann, daughter of Lieut. John Howland.

14.  VI.  Benjamin, probably died young.  He is not named in his father's will dated 30th April, 1706, or in the division of his brother Jabez's estate, April 3, 1700.

15.  VII.  Nathaniel, born 1773.  He died Feb. 11, 1740-1, in the 69th year of his age, leaving neither wife nor children.

In 1715 his house is described as being near the head of the lane, on the east side, and north of the land on which the West Barnstable church now stands.  (Blue) John Crocker afterwards owned it, and subsequently the same estate was owned by the late Stephen C. Nye, deceased.  He owned only two fifteenths of the house, his sister Experience owning the other thirteen fifteenths.  His estate was apprized at £2,003 10 10.  Silver at that time was worth 28 shillings per ounce.  His homestead was apprized at £1,100.  He had 92 ounces of silver on hand, and £266,5 due him in silver, at his death.  He left no will, and his own brothers and sisters contended that Jonathan Crocker and Elizabeth Child's heirs, being only of the half blood, were not entitled to shares.  The Judge of Probate, Hon. Sylvanous Bourne, in a very able report on the law, decided that they were equally entitled, and ordered the estate to be divided into seven shares, and distributed to 1, Jonathan Crocker; 2, heirs of Elizabeth Childs; 3, Mrs. Mary Bursley, surviving sister; 4, Children of Capt. Joseph Crocker, deceased; 5, Children of Hannah Lothrop, deceased; 6, Children of John Crocker, deceased; and 7, to heirs of Experience Crocker deceased.

16.  VIII.  Experience, born in 1674, died single, April 17, 1740-1, in the 67th year of her age, and is buried in the West Barnstable graveyard.  She owned thirteen fifteenths, and her brother Nathaniel two fifteenths, of the ancient dwelling house of her grandfather, which has already been described.  Besides the estate bequeathed to her by her father, she accumulated a considerable amount by her own industry and prudence.  Her estate was apprized at £588 14.  Her silver plate were valued at £69 14 : 50 ounces at the current rate of silver at that time.  In her will she makes bequests to her brothers Jonathan and Joseph; to her sister Mary Bursley; to the children of her sister Elizabeth Childs, deceased; to Benjamin, son of her brother Joseph; to Benjamin and Samuel, sons of her sister Hannah Lothrop; to Moses, son of her brother John; to Mary

Davis, daughter of her sister Hannah Lothrop ; to Deborah, daughter of her brother Joseph ; to John, son of her nephew Moses ; to Elizabeth, daughter of her brother John ; to Joseph Lothrop, son of her nephew Joseph, deceased ; to the poor of the church of which she was a member ; to the church in West Barnstable ; and to John, son of the Rev. Jonathan Russell. To her brother John's son John, (called Blue John Crocker) she bequeathed the lower great room in her house, the bed room and the garret, and materials to put the house in good repair. The remainder of the house she bequeathed to her neice Hannah Lothrop, a single woman, then fifty years of age. All the rest of her estate she gave to her sister Mary Bursley, Experience Lothrop, Hannah Lothrop, Abigail Lothrop, and Prudence Gorham, wife of John Gorham, Esq., and daughter of Joseph Crocker.

Miss Experience had some of the good qualities of the Vicar of Wakefield's wife. He said all his wife's cousins even to the fortieth remove, never forget their relationship, and never passed his door without calling, and his table was always well filled with a happy company.

17.   IX.   Jabez, died in 1700, without issue, and his estate was divided among his brothers and sisters, by the same father and mother, then surviving.

18.   X.   Mary, married Feb, 11, 1702, John Bursley, Jr.

19.   XI.   Abigail. Her birth is not recorded on the town records. She died young, leaving no issue.

20.   XII.   Bathshua, also died young, leaving no issue.

Of the children of John Crocker, his son Joseph is the last whose birth is recorded on the town records. The names of the others are arranged in the order found on the Probate records.

4. Samuel Crocker, son of Dea. William Crocker, born in Barnstable July 3, 1642, died Dec. 1681, aged 39. It does not appear that he married. If he had left issue, his children would probably have been named in their grandfather's will. The cause of his death is stated in the following extract from the Plymouth Colony Records, Vol. 6, page 82.

### An Inditement.

"Indian James, thou art here indited by the name of James, for that thou, haveing not the fear of God before thyne eyes, on the one and twentyeth day of November 1681, in the town of Barnstable, didst felloniously, willfully, and of mallice forethought, with intent to murder, kick Samuel Crocker, son of William Crooker, of Barnstable, on the bottom of his belley, whereof the said Samuel Crocker three weeks after died ; which thou hast don contrary to the law of God, of England, and this collonie, and contrary to the peace of our sou.'r Lord the Kinge, his crowne, and dignity.

The jury find the prisenor nott guilty of willfull murder."

No Indians were on the jury, as was the usual practice in such cases; and the verdict of the jury shows that impartial justice was dispensed by our ancesters irrespective of caste or race. Against Indian James no further proceedings appear on the records.

5. Dea. Job. Crocker. Few men in Barnstable were held in higher esteem in his day, than Dea. Job Crocker. Like his father, he was honest and upright in his dealing, industrious and prudent in his habits, an obliging neighbor, a good citizen. Nurtured by pious parents, in early life he became a member of the church, and through life, his daily walk was in accordence with his profession. The church records say of him, "God and his people having elected and proved our Brother Job Crocker, for the office of deacon in this church, he was solomnly set a part for, and ordained unto that work and office in July 1684; to serve in the deaconship of this church, together with his father." For eight years, during the pastorate of the elder Russell, he and his venerable father were joint occupants of the deacon's seat. It is inscribed on his grave stones, that for thirty and four years he was a deacon of the Barnstable church.

Dea. Job Crocker was a man of good business capacity, was much employed in the business of the town, holding many offices which it is unnecessary here to enumerate. He inhabited the homestead of his uncle John, rocky and hard to cultivate, but an excellent grazing farm. The substantial stone walls built thereon in his day, remain as monuments of his industry and perseverance. His house, a large two story structure, built in the fashion of that day with a heavy cornice in front, and a long low or leantoo roof on the rear, yet remains.* It is situate near the meadows and in close proximity to the Cape Cod Railroad. The first location of the road was between the house and spring from which seven successive generations of Crockers had drawn water. Out of respect to the then venerable occupants, the location was changed to a point below, a concession rarely made by engineers.

Dea. Job Crocker married for his first wife, Nov. 1668, Mary, daughter of Rev. Thomas Walley, the then pastor of the Barnstable church. She was born in London and there baptized April 18, 1644. She came over with her father in the ship Society, Capt. John Pierce, and arrived in Boston 24th of the

---

*Some doubt may arise whether or not Dea. Job occupied the western or the eastern house. He occupied the most ancient, that is certain, and the decision of the question turns on this point; was the western, the one now standing, the most ancient. The first settlers, with scarce a solitary exception, planted pear trees near their houses and these old button and fall pear trees are their monuments. The trees near the western house were very ancient, while those near the eastern were smaller and not so old. The eastern house was a two story single house built in the style common about one hundred and forty years ago. It was taken down about forty years ago. It was occupied by David Crocker, Esq., son of Job, and I presume was built by him.

3d month (May) 1662.   She died about the year 1676, leaving two children.

For his second wife he married, 19th July 1680, Hannah, daughter of Richard Taylor of Yarmouth, called "tailor" to distinguish him from another of the same Christian name.   He died March 1718-19, aged 75 years, and is buried in the ancient burying ground.   His wife Hannah survived him, and died 14th May 1743, in the 85th year of her age.   In her will dated 10th of July 1739, proved 8th July 1743, she names her grandsons in law, Thomas and Walley Crocker, her daughters Mary Howland, Hannah, Elizabeth Allen, and Sarah Lumbert; her sons John Crocker, David Crocker, and Job, deceased; Mary, wife of Isaac Howland; Abigail, wife of Geo. Howland; Hannah, daughter of her son David; grand-daughter Hannah Allen; and her grand-son John Howland.

### Children of Dea. Job Crocker.

21.   I.    A son, born 18, 1769, died in infancy.
22.   II.   Samuel, 15th May, 1671, married Dec. 10, 1696, Sarah, daughter of Robert Parker, and for his second wife, April 12, 1719, Judeth Leavet, of Rochester.
23.   III.  Thomas, 19th Jan. 1674, married 23d Dec. 1701, Elizabeth, widow of "John Lothrop, the son of Esquire Barnabas Lothrop."
24.   IV.   Mary, born 29th June, 1681, married June 19, 1719, John Howland, Jr., his second wife, and had John, 13th Feb. 1720-21, graduate of Harvard College 1741, ordained at Carver, 1746, died Nov. 4, 1804, aged 84; and a son Job, June 1726.
25.   V.    John, 24th Feb. 1683, called Dea. John.
26.   VI.   Hannah, 2d Feb. 1685.   [A Hannah Crocker of Barnstable, married July 7, 1712, John Holden of Warwick.]
27.   VII.  Elizabeth, 15th May, 1688, married April 5, 1712, Rev. Benjamin Allen, a native of Tisbury, Martha's Vineyard.   He graduated at Yale College 1708, ordained July 9, 1718, as the first misister of the south parish in Bridgewater, where he remained about twelve years.   He was afterwards installed at Cape Elizabeth where he died May 6, 1754, aged 65.   He was improvident in his habits and in consequence often involved in troubles.   One of his granddaughters by the name of Jourdan, married Rev. Enos Hitchcock, D. D., of Providence.
28.   VIII. Sarah, born 19th Jan. 1690-1, married May 27, 1725, Benjamin Lumbard, Jr., died Nov. 1768, aged 76, leaving no issue.
29.   IX.   Job, 4th April 1694, died May 21, 1731, aged 37. He did not marry.

30.  X.   David, born 5th Sept. 1697, graduate of Harvard College 1716, married 12th Nov. 1724, Abigail, daughter of David Loring, and Jan. 27, 1757, Mrs. Abigail Stuart.   He died in 1764, aged 67.

31.  XI.   Thankful, born 14th June, 1700, died unmarried Oct. 1, 1735.

6. Josiah Crocker, son of Dea. William, born Sept. 19, 1647, was a substantial farmer, and resided in the old stone house built by his father.   He inherited the southeasterly part of his father's estate.   In the proprietor's records, it is stated that his heirs owned a house at Cotuit; whether or not it was ever occupied by him, I have no means of ascertaining.   At the division of the common meadows in 1697, he was one of the five to whom was awarded seven acres, showing that he was a man of wealth.   In 1690 there was laid out to him at Cotuit Neck, forty acres of land formerly the great lot of John Hall, and thirty acres formerly the lot of Thomas and Peter Blossom.   In 1698 he exchanged twenty-seven acres of his land at Cotuit Neck with the town, taking land at the same place adjoining Lewis's Pond, now called Lovell's Pond.

In 1688 the town granted him one and a half acres of upland on the south of his barn, bounded north and east by his other land, south and west by the commons.   He was not much in public life. He is named as a member of the grand inquest in 1679, and was surveyor of highways in 1682.   He married 23d Oct. 1668, Melatiah, daughter of Gov. Thomas Hinckley.   He died 2d Feb. 1698-9 aged 51 years.   In his will dated on the 28th of the preceding month, he names his wife Melatiah, sons Thomas, Josiah, Ebenezer, Seth, Benjamin, and daughters, Mercy, Mary, Else, and Melatiah.

The Wid. Melatiah Crocker died 2d Feb. 1714-15, aged 66 years.   In her will dated Jan. 21, 1613-14, she names her five sons; and daughters Mary, Alice, and Melatiah; also daughter Hannah (wife of her son Thomas) and her grand-daughter Tabitha.

*Children born in Barnstable.*

31.  I.   A son, born 20th Aug. 1669, died Sept. 1669.

32.  II.   Thomas, born 27th May 1671, married 25th March 1696, Hannah Green of Boston.   He died April 1728, aged 57 years.

33.  III.   Mercy, born 13th Feb. 1674, died in early life.

34.  IV.   Mary, born 10th Sept. 1677, married Nov. 1705, her cousin William Crocker.

35.  V.   Alice, born 25th Dec. 1679, married 14th June 1711, George Lewis.   She died 23d Feb. 1718.   Alice does not appear to have been a favorlte name with the Crockers. This is the only grand-child of the name, and she did not

give the name to either of her daughters.

36.  VI.  Melatiah, born 20th Nov. 1681, married Oct. 27, 1729, her cousin Timothy Crocker.

37.  VII.  Josiah, born 8th Feb. 1684, married April 10, 1711, Desire, daughter of Col. John Thacher.

38.  VIII.  Ebenezer, born 30th May, 1687, married 22d March, 1715, Hannah Hall of Yarmouth.

39.  IX.  Seth, born 23d Sept. 1689, died in Harwich, 1623, leaving no issue.  His brother Benjamin of Ipswich, was executor of his will.

40.  X.  Benjamin, born 26th Sept. 1692, graduate of Harvard College 1713.  He removed to Ipswich, Mass., and was many years teacher of the Grammar School in that town. He was a representative from Ipswich to the Mass. Gen. Court in 1726, '34 and '36.  He was a member of the south church in that town ; but as the individuals chosen for its Ruling Elders were not ordained, because Mr. Walley, the pastor, did not believe such officers were required by the gospel, he left, and united with the first church.  He was a deacon and occasionally preached.  He married Elizabeth, daughter of Rev. William Williams of Weston, and had Mary, who married ——— Gannison, and John, a deacon of the church and a man of note in his day.  Dea. Benjamin Crocker died in 1766, aged 75, and his wife who survived him married ——— Cogswell.†

7.  Eleazer Crocker, son of Dea. William Crocker, born in Barnstable 21st July 1650, was admitted a townsman in 1681. In 1692 he was one of the committee appointed to draw up a list of the proprietors of the common lands, and determine what was each man's just right therein.  After the death of Nathaniel Bacon in 1693, he was "chosen and empowered by the town to be a land measurer to lay out land."  He married 7th April 1682, Ruth, daughter of Elder John Chipman.  She died 8th April 1698, aged 34.  For his second wife he married Jan. 25, 1716-17, Mercy Phinney.

*Children of Eleazer Crocker.*

41.  I.  Benoni, born 13th May, 1682, died 3d Feb. 1701.

42.  II.  Bethia, born 23d Sept. 1683, married John Whiton March 13, 1710.

43.  III.  Nathan, born 27th April, 1685, married 10th March, 1708-9, Joanna, daughter of John Bursley, and the Barn-

---

† Alvah Crocker, Esq., of Fitchburg, in a letter says that "upon one of the oldest Grave Stones in St. Anns Church Yard, Newburyport, he finds this inscription, 'Capt. John Crocker born in 1692, died March 19, 1763.'"  This Capt. John Crocker was the great grandfather of Alvah Crocker, Esq., and if the inscription on his Grave Stone is accurately transcribed he was not a son of Benjamin of Ipswich.  Mr. Crocker says the tradition in his family, is that he is a descendant of Dea. William, but as at present advised I do not preceive how the tradition can be verified.

stable records say he also married Abigail Bursley March 10, 1713-14, evidently an error of the Clerk.

44.   IV.   Daniel, born 23d March, 1686-7, died without issue 1723.
45.   V.   Sarah, born 23d March, 1689, married Nov. 7, 1712, Joseph Bursley.
46.   VI.   Theophilus, born 11th March, 1691.
47.   VII.   Eleazer, born 3d Aug. 1693.
48.   VIII.   Ruth, born 3d Aug. 1693, married Samuel Fuller 1718.
49.   IX.   Abel, born 15th June, 1695, married April 16, 1818 Mary Isum.   The names of his children do not appear on the town records.   His wife joined the church Dec. 1723, when her son Daniel and daughter Rebecca were baptized, and Aug. 1725, her son Eleazer.   Soon after the latter date the family removed to Plymton, and returned 1757.
50.   X.   Rebecca, born 10th Dec. 1697, married ——— Robbins.
51.   XI.   Mercy, by his second wife, and named in his will.

8. Sergeant Joseph Crocker, youngest son of Dea. William, born in 1654, resided at West Barnstable.   He inherited the north-easterly part of his father's farm, bounded easterly by the Otis and Hinckley estates.   That portion of the ancient Crocker estate, on the north of the County road and bounded easterly by the lands of Mr. John Smith, was not included in his estate.*   His house was on the Meeting House road, if I construe the records rightly, not far from the present location of the Cape Cod Railroad Depot.   A reservation of three rods in width through his lands was made for that road.   In 1703 he was rated the highest, and probably was the most wealthy man in Barnstable.   He was admitted a townsman in 1678; but does not appear to have been often employed in town or other public business.   He was a sergeant in the militia company, than an office of some honor.   In his will dated 20th Feb. 1720-1, he gives to his wife Temperance all his personal estate, and the use and improvement of all his real estate during her natural life.   In most of the old wills the phrase used is, "while she remains my widow," on the presumption that the husband can bind the wife after his decease.

To his four daughters he devised all his lands and meadows lying by the mill river; to his son William, "all his housing and

---

*The same rule was adopted in Barnstable and Yarmouth in the division of the common lands; that is, one third to the townsmen, one third on the estates, and one third to the tenements.   In Barnstable only the gross number of shares alloted to each is recorded; in Yarmouth the several particulars are given.   Joseph Crocker had 80 shares, James Gorham 74 3-4, John Hamblin 71 3-4, James Hamblin, Sen'r, 69, &c.   It will thus be perceived why it was that our ancestors, were so cautious in admitting townsmen.   It not only conferred all the rights appertaining to a citizen; but made the party a proprietor of the common lands.   If a house stood on the common land, the owner was not entitled to a tenement right.   To confer the right, the house had to be on the land of the individual, and the title acquired by him according to the usuages of the times.

lands where he then dwelt," and all his wood lots ; and to Timothy "all his lands in the timber lands, at a place called Great Hill, all subject to the use and improvement of their mother during her natural life.    Noah is not named in the will, and was probably then dead.

Joseph Crocker married Dec. 1677, Temperance, daughter of John Bursley.    She survived her husband many years and died very aged.

### Children born in Barnstable.

52.    I.    William, born 25th Aug. 1679, married Nov. 1705, his cousin Mary Crocker.
53.    II.    Timothy, born 30th April 1681, married Oct. 27, 1709, his cousin Melatiah Crocker.*
54.    III.    Noah, born Dec. 1683, died young.
55.    IV.    Joanna, born 18th July 1687, married 9th Feb. 1708-9, Joseph Fuller, Jr., died April 13, 1766.
56.    V.    Martha, born 22d Feb. 1689.
57.    VI.    Temperance, 26th Aug. 1694.
58.    VII.    Remember, 26th Aug. 1699, married Samuel Annable, 3d, May 28, 1719.

### Third Generation.

(10) Jonathan Crocker, son of John, owned the land now known as the Bodfish Farm at West Barnstable.    He was a substantial farmer, owned a large estate ; and, as his father and grand-father had done, he conveyed by deeds a large part of it to his children, reserving only a sufficiency for his comfortable support in old age.    His residence on the Bodfish Farm, probably built by his father, was a two story single house, with a leantoo, or "salt box," as they were sometimes called, on the side.    This he sold in 1713 to his son-in-law, Benjamin Bodfish.    It was taken down in 1819, and the old Bodfish mansion house stands on the same spot.†    His will, which is in the hand writing of the Rev. Jonathan Russell, is dated June 1737, and the codicil thereto

---

*Physiologists may perhaps notice these two instances of the marriage of cousins. William and Mary had eight children.    One was still born, and one died aged 21 days. Of the other six, none were distinguished either for physical or intellectual vigor.    Timothy and Melatiah had five daughters, distinguished for their intellectual vigor, graceful accomplishments, and business capacity.    Beautiful specimens of embroidery wrought by them are preserved by their descendants.    A few years since a gentleman well versed in the genealogies of the Nantucket families, attempted to show that the marriage of cousins was not objectionable, and he made out a strong case.

---

†Since writing the above I have examined the records of the grants of land made in 1716.    There is great want of cleanness, in the descriptions.    The records says, "Set out to Jonathan Crocker, a piece of land at the head of his own, bounded westerly by the way that goeth up by his house, northerly by his own land to the dividing line between him and John Crocker."    John Crocker's land is bounded "easterly," evidently should be westerly, by Jonathan's, and easterly by the way to Nathaniel Crocker's.    Out of this grant the three acres on which the West Barnstable meeting house now stands was reserved.    The reservation was made in the grant to Thomas; but appears to have been taken from John's.    It seems by this that Jonathan Crocker's house in 1716, was on Dexter's Lane, and whether he ever resided in the house he sold to Bodfish is not clear.

June 1742, four years before his death. He provides for the support of his wife Thankful, *giving her the household goods she brought with her, and some bedding she had made since.* He gave his son Isaac £30 and his great chair, names his son James, and James' oldest son, to whom he gave his gun. To the Rev. Jonathan Russell he devised 20 shillings ; to the church 20 shillings ; and to Mercy Dexter then living with him £5. All the rest of his estate, real and personal, to the children of his three daughters, Lydia, Hannah and Reliance. In the codicil to his will he gives the estate which had fallen to him by the death of his brother Nathaniel, equally, in five shares, to his sons Isaac and James, to the children and heirs of his daughter Lydia Bodfish, deceased, to the children and heirs of his daughter Hannah Fuller, and to the children and heirs of his daughter Reliance Smith, deceased. At the time he made his will all his children, excepting Isaac and James, were dead, and they resided in Connecticut.

Jonathan Crocker married for his first wife, 20th May, 1686, Hannah, daughter of Lieut. John Howland. She was the mother of all his children. After her death he married Feb. 1710-11, Thankful, widow of Mr. John Hinckley, Jr., and daughter of Thomas Trott of Dorchester. He died Aug. 24, 1746, aged 84, and is buried in the West Barnstable grave yard. No monuments are erected to the memory of either of his wives.

*Children born in Barnstable.*

59. I. Lydia, born 26th Sept. 1686, married Benjamin Bodfish, 10th Nov. 1709.
60. II. Hannah, born 26th March 1688, married 10th 7th month, 1708, Shubael Fuller, of East Haddam, Conn., and removed thither.
61. III. Thankful, born 6th March, 1690, died young.
62. IV. Isaac, born April 4, 1692, married Dec. 13, 1718, Ann Smith, and removed to East Haddam, Conn., where she died June 1725, aged 30. Oct. 31, 1726, he married for his second wife Elizabeth Fuller of Barnstable. In 1729 he removed to Westchester, in the town of Colchester. He died Aug. 8, 1769, at 4 o'clock P. M., aged 77 years, 4 months, and 8 days.

*Children of Isaac Crocker born in East Haddam, Conn.*

1, Hannah, Sept. 22, 1719 ; 2, Ann, June 29, 1722, died unmarried, March 29, 1772, aged 49 ; 3, Joseph, Dec. 20, 1724, married Nov. 10, 1748, Sarah, daughter of Rev. Judah Lewis ; 4, Elizabeth, Aug. 26, 1727, married as second wife, May, 26, 1747, Simeon Ockley. She died at Williamston Nov. 9, 1797, aged 70 ; 5, Mary, April 30, 1729 ; 6, Martha, born at Colchester, arch 3, 1731 ; 7, Abigail, March 10, 1733 ; 8, a daughter, Sept.

62. 1736, died same day.
63. V. Reliance, born 28th June, 1694, married Joseph Smith, Jr., 5th Oct. 1712 ; died 4th May, 1704, aged 30.
64. VI. Jonathan, born 28th May, 1696, married Nov. 28, 1723, Elizabeth, daughter of the second John Bursley. He died Sept. 21, 1725, leaving a son Ephraim, who died Oct. 17, 1725, aged one year and 15 days.
65. VII. James, born 3d Sept. 1699, married Nov. 21, 1721, Alice Swift, born in Sandwich July 23, 1698 da'r of Jireh and Abigail Swift. About the year 1724 he removed to Colchester, Conn., and built a house near the Colchester and East Haddam turnpike which, till 1860, was occupied by his descendents. He and his wife were members of the church in the parish of Westchester. She died in Westchester Jan. 15, 1783, aged 84 ; and he died Nov. 7, 1785, aged 86. They lived in the marriage state over sixty-one years. Their children were : 1, Simeon, the Barnstable records say born at Barnstable, March 22, 1722, the Colchester, Sept. 19, 1722, (the latter probably accurate.) He married March 7, 1751, Dorothy Williams. He died at Westchester Feb. 13, 1778. His death was caused by a fall on the ice, while going from his house to his barn. She died Aug. 4, 1818, aged about 95. 2, Abigail,‡ born according to the the Barnstable record, Sept. 19, 1724, according to the Colchester, March 25, 1724, married Feb. 23, 1744, John Williams, and 2d, April 23, 1755, Enoch Arnold, died 1771. 3, Hannah, born at Colchester Jan. 17, 1726. 4, Levi, May 11, 1728. 5, Jonathan, March 16, 1730. 6, James, April 20, 1732. 7, Thankful, Jan. 27, 1733-4. 8, Lydia, Jan. 14, 1735-6. 9, Ephraim, Sept. 21, 1739. The last was a physician settled in Richmond, Mass.
66. VIII. Ephraim, born April 1702, died May 1, 1704.

(11) John Crocker son of John, born 7th Feb. 1663-4, was called Junior until 1711, when he was the elder of the name in Barnstable. He married 5th Nov. 1702, Mary, daughter of the second Nathaniel Bacon. She died March, 1710-11, aged 33, and he married for his second wife, Sarah, Nov. 11, 1711, probably a daughter of Ensign John Hinckley.

*Children born in Barnstable.*

67. I. Sarah, born 4th Jan. 1703-4.
68. II. Moses, born 5th April, 1705, married May 15, 1735, Mary Fish of Sandwich, and had 1, Nathaniel, May 7, 1736 ; 2, John, March 8, 1737-8, he was 4th and called Tanner. He married Jan. 8, 1761, Thankful Hallett ; 3,

‡ Abigail Crocker was the great grand-mother of my correspondent, D. William Patterson, Esq., of West Winstead, Conn., to whom I am much indebted for information respecting the early emigrants from Barnstable to Connecticut.

Sarah, Aug. 16, 1740; 4, Moody, Feb. 14, 1742; and 5, Edmund, Aug. 17, 1645, also Nathaniel not named in the record.

69.    III.    Mary, born July, 1707.  In a deed dated 37th Aug., styles herself spinster, names her uncle Nathaniel, deceased, and her two brothers, Moses and John.

70.    IV.    John, born Sept. 1709, called John Blue or Blue Stocking John.  In the latter part of his life he was the elder of the four John Crocker's and called first.  His house, bequeathed to him by his great aunt, Experience, stood on the easterly side of the road, a little distance north of the West Barnstable church, and was afterwards owned and occupied by Mr. Lemuel Nye.  He married Lydia Barker of R. I.  (Neither his marriage nor the publication thereof is on the Barnstable town records.)  His children born in Barnstable were: 1, Elizabeth, Feb. 28, 1738; 2, Stephen, Dec. 3, 1740; 3, Joseph, Feb. 6, 1842; 4, Allyn, Feb. 18, 1745; 5, Bathseba, Jan. 23, 1747, David Kelley; 6, Lydia, May 12, 1749; 7, David; 8, Hannah, March 13, 1753, Tobey; 9, John, May 12, 1755, called "Young Blue." He was a sea captain, and active and intelligent man. He bought the ancient Hinckley house in which he resided. His son John Barker Crocker is well known.  Abigail, 10th child of Blue John Crocker, was born Feb. 1758, Nath'l Jenkins.

71.    V.    Elizabeth, born March 1710-11.

(13) Capt. Joseph Crocker, son of John, born 1st March, 1667-8, married Ann, daughter of Lieut. John Howland, 18th Sept. 1691.  Capt. Crocker was an influential man, and was much employed in public business.  About the year 1700 he bought the house of Robert Claghorn, which stood at the east end of Lumbard's pond, and the lands adjoining which he afterwards sold to the Lothrops  His residence was at Cotuit, and his farm is now owned by Josiah Sampson and others.  His residence was a large old fashioned two story double house.  It was standing not long since.

*Children born in Barnstable.*

72.    I.    Deborah, last of Dec. 1691.

73.    II.    Prudence, born 26th July, 1692, married Oct. 2, 1712 John Gorham, Esq., of Barnstable.  She was the mother of 14 children, 13 of whom lived to mature age.  She died in 1778 aged 86.

74.    III.    Benjamin, born 5th April, 1696, married 17th Sept. 1719, Priscilla, daughter of Dea. Joseph Hall of Yarmouth. He resided at Cotuit, and died 1757, aged 61.  His children were 1, Deborah, born June 22, 1721, died early; 2, Desire, born Aug. 9, 1727, married Oct. 3, 1747, Cornelius Sampson of Rochester; and 3, Martha, born June 6, 1732.

(22) Samuel Crocker, son of Job, born 15th May, 1671, married Dec. 10, 1696, Sarah, daughter of Robert Parker. She was the mother of thirteen children, and died in 1718, aged 40. He married for his second wife, April 12, 1719, Judith Leavet of Rochester, by whom he had two children.  His farm was at the village now called Pondville, near the Sandwich line and was bounded by the road leading to Scorton.

*Children born in Barnstable.*

76.  I.    Samuel, born 12th Dec. 1697, married 2d March, 1723-4, Ruth, daughter of the third James Hamblin.  She was born in 1692, and was five years older than her husband. He had 1, Noah, Sept. 12, 1724 ; 2, Sarah, Jan. 5, 1726, married Shubael Hamblin, Jr., July 16, 1761 ; 3, Hannah, May 16, 1729, married Jan. 29, 1758, Abel Cushing of Hingham ; 4, Anna, May 8, 1731, married Jabez Bursley, Dec. 15, 1747 ; 5, Joanna, June 4, 1735, died Aug. 7, 1735, 6, Joanna.

77.  II.   Cornelius, born 24th Oct. 1698, died young.

78.  III.  Mary, 8th April, 1700.

79.  IV.   Patience, born 18th April, 1701.  She became, in 1727, the second wife of Shubael Davis, sixteen years her senior.

80.  V.    Elizabeth, born Feb. 1702-3, married James Childs Sept. 27, 1722.

81.  VI.   Cornelius, born 23d March, 1704.  (See account of him below.)

82.  VII.  Rowland, born 18th June, 1705.

83.  VIII. Gersham, born Dec. 1706, died Nov. 26, 1786, aged 80.

84.  IX.   Ebenezer, born 5th June, 1710, married Ann Eldredge of Falmouth, June 12, 1735, removed to East Haddam, Conn., 1751.  Children born in Barnstable, 1, Rowland, June, 8, 1736, married 24th May, 1763, Persis Brown, and had six children ; 2, Joanna, born Dec. 8, 1737 ; 3, Ezekiel, born Nov. 24, 1739, married Feb. 28, 1765, Lydia Arnold of East Haddam.  He removed to Richmond, Mass., where he had David, Samuel and Lucy baptized, Aug. 14, 1785.  He was one of the early settlers of Broome County, N. Y., a very pious man and regular at family worship.  One morning while engaged in his devotions, he saw his cows in the corn, and he broke into his prayer with, "David ! Sam ! don't you see those cursed cows in the corn ? run' boys ! quick ! !" and seeing them well started after the cows, took up his broken prayer, and leisurely finished it.  At 80 years he married a girl of 18, promising her, it is said, as her dower, her weight in silver dollars.  They lived together but a short time.  She

separated from him and married his grandson. 4, Tabitha,
born in Barnstable Feb. 20, 1741-2 ; 5, Bethia, baptized
Bethiel, born June 8, 1744 ; 6, Gershom, born Oct. 8, 1746,
married Jan. 17. 1769, Ann Fisher ; 7, Alice, baptized
March 9, 1748-9 ; 8, Ebenezer, born in East Haddam,
June 25, 1751 ; 9, Samuel, June 2, 1753.

85.    X.    Benjamin, born July, 1711, married 1738, Abigail,
daughter of John Jenkins of Falmouth.    He married in
1747, Bathsheba, daughter of Dea. Joseph Hall of Yarmouth.    He probably married for his 3d wife in 1759 Annie
Handy of Sandwich.    He had seven children born in Barnstable, all of whom, excepting Josiah, were baptized at the West
Church.    1, Joseph, April 15, 1748 ; 2, Benjamin, Sept. 17,
1749 ; 3, Timothy, Oct. 3, 1751 ; 4, Abigail, Nov. 91, 1753 ; 5,
Bathsheba, Nov. 11, 1755 ; 6, Peter, Jan. 11, 1758 ; 7,
Josiah, April 17, 1760.

86.    XI.    Rebecca, ———, married Eben Jones, March 20, 1740.

87.    XII.    Rachell, ———, married Joseph Howland, Jan. 18,
1738-9.

88.    XIII.    David, ———, called junior to distinguish him from
David Crocker, Esq., son of Job, married Dorcas Davis of
Falmouth, 1741, had 1, Anna, born Dec. 24, 1742 ; 2,
Rachel, 1744 ; 3, Samuel, Feb. 1747.

89.    XIV.    Sarah, ———, married Joshua Backhouse of Sandwich, Nov. 7, 1734.

90.    XV.    Tabitha, baptized Aug. 21, 1721, married Timothy
Davis of Falmouth, Feb. 7, 1760.

(81.    VI.)    Cornelius Crocker, son of Samuel, was bound,
when young, as an apprentice to a tailor, and afterwards had a
shop of his own, and worked at the business many years.    He
had a club-foot, was lame and unable to attend to business which
required much physical effort and active exertion.    He married,
Nov. 9, 1727, Lydia, daughter of Joseph Jenkins.    He resided
in the East Parish, built in 1741 the high single house near the
Agricultural Hall, afterwards owned by Ebenezer Taylor.    He
bought the ancient grist mill on Mill Creek, which he rebuilt.    He
afterwards owned the farm on the west of Rendevous lane, which
was originally Thomas Lothrop's home lot, and that part of
Joseph Lothrop's which was on that side of the lane, together
with the ancient gambrel roofed house which according to tradition, belonged to the Glovers.    He also owned the wharf known
as Crocker's Wharf, and a fish house near the same.    He resided
for a time in the gambrel roofed house, afterwards owned and
occupied by his son Samuel.    He also bought the estate known of
late years as "Lydia Sturgis's tavern," where he kept a public
house many years.    He owned other real estate, and was one of
the most wealthy men of his time in the East Parish.    His house

till within a few years has been a noted tavern stand, and a favorite resort for travellers. It has always been kept in good repair. It was built to accommodate those who attended the courts. The first court house in the county of Barnstable was built in the field next on the east. Its location caused, at that time, much excitement. The Gorhams who resided at the lower part of the town, were wealthy and influential, and insisted that it should be located in their neighborhood. They urged that such a location was nearer the center of the population, and that it would give better satisfaction to the people of the County. Gov. Hinckley and the Lothrops insisted on a more western location, and they prevailed. The Lothrops owned the land on which it was finally located. The Gorhams were so confident that the Court House would be located in their neighborhood that one or more buildings intended for hotels, were put up.

Cornelius Crocker, as has already been stated, kept a public house ; he was also engaged in the fisheries, gave employment to quite a number of men, and naturally exerted much influence, in his neighborhood and in the town. He belonged to that moderate class, among the tories who deemed it inexpedient for the colonies to adopt measures that would inevitably lead to a war with the mother country. Perhaps under other circumstances, he would have been more decided and out-spoken than he was. He had passed the age of man ; his political principles and his interests were antagonistical, and prudence dictated that he should commit no act that would render his large estate liable to confiscation.

At the commencement of the Revolution there were, in fact, four political parties in Barnstable, the lines between which were drawn with more or less distinctness. 1, The ardent whigs, of whom Dr. Nathaniel Freeman of Sandwich, and Joseph Otis, Esq., a brother of the patriot James, were the moving spirits and leaders. Dr. Freeman was then a young man, active, ardent and zealous ; but his zeal was not always tempered by the discretion of age. This party were nearly all young men, burning with indignation at the outrages which the mother country had inflicted on the colonies. In the East Parish the leading men were Daniel Davis, Esq., Sylvanus Gorham, Seth Lothrop, Jonathan Lumbert, John Thacher, Jethro Thacher, Nathaniel Lothrop, John Lewis, George Lewis, Timothy Phinney, and James Coleman. Brigadier Joseph Otis at first acted with them, but he and Daniel Davis, Esq., afterwards acted with the more moderate party. 2. The leaders of the more moderate party were older men, and more conservative in their views. Col. James Otis, Solomon Otis, Esq., Nymphus Marston, Esq., Lieut. Joseph Blish, Capt. Samuel Crocker, Edward Bacon, Esq., Sturgis Gorham, Esq., Isaac Hinckley, Esq., Shearjashub Bourne, Esq., Eleazer Scudder, and Dea. Joseph Hallett, were prominent men of the party. During the Revolution they were always in the majority in Barnstable, and the members of this party were the men who were relied on to furnish men and money, the sinews of war.

The tories were few in numbers in Barnstable. They were also divided into two parties, the out-spoken and decided, of whom David Parker, Esq., and Mr. Otis Loring were the leading men. The more moderate were such men as Mr. Cornelius Crocker and his son Josiah. Among the tories were men of wealth, of respectability, and influence. They were citizens, and so long as they did not give aid or comfort to the enemies of the country, and contributed their share to the public expenses, they were entitled to the protection of the laws, though their political opinions might not have been in accordance with the views of a majority of the people. Such protection the moderate among the whigs were willing to concede; but for making this concession, some of them were persecuted with more bitterness of feeling then were the open and avowed tories. Edward Bacon, Esq., who had been chosen a representative to the General Court, was denounced as a tory, and an enemy to his country. A remonstrance embodying these charges was presented to the Legislature and published in a newspaper at Watertown, July 8, 1776, and in consequence the seat of Mr. Bacon was declared vacant. He returned home. A town meeting was duly notified and held, and the town meeting resolved, with great unanimity, that the charges preferred against him were false and slanderous.

Capt. Samuel Crocker, to whom unintentional injustice was done in the notice of the cutting down of the liberty pole in Barnstable, was also persecuted with a malignity of feeling that is not creditable to those who took an active part therein. He was one of the most intelligent and active men of the whig party, conservative and tolerant in his opinions. His position was unfortunate; but it was not one of his own seeking or making, and for which he was in no way responsible. His father and brothers were classed among the loyalists, whether rightfully or wrongfully, to him belonged neither the censure or the praise. He was responsible for his own acts, not for those of others. Natural affection would dictate to him that he ought not to deal harshly with those who were bound to him by the ties of consanguinity. His position entitled him to sympathy; but there were those who irreverantly said that he should forsake "father and mother and wife and children," for the cause of his country. His brother, Cornelius, was not a decided politician, though he generally acted with the whig party, and therefore could not be classed among the tories. He did not possess the commanding talents of his brother Samuel, or the learning of his brother Josiah, but in his own way, he denounced, with perhaps too much severity, the excesses of the day. Such a course exposes a man to the censure of both parties.

In times when the political elements are moved to their very foundations, men cannot be neutral, they must belong to the one party or the other. To some extent Cornelius Crocker, Jr., professed to be neutral in politics, and he was therefore denounced by both parties. In front of his house stood the Liberty Pole, the emblem of progress, around which the whigs were wont to assemble ; and near by, in loving proximity, the stocks and the whipping post, lingering emblems of a barbarous code, and of a more barbarous age.

The inhabitants in town meeting, by their repeated votes, manifested their confidence in the political integrity of Capt. Samuel Crocker, against whom the shafts of malevolence seem to have been as violently hurled as against his father and brothers. Its bitterness may be judged by the 'fact that a century has now nearly elapsed, yet the feelings of animosity which it engendered have not yet subsided.

Another unhappy dissension between individuals also divided public sentiment. An unfriendly feeling which existed between Brigadier Joseph Otis and Edward Bacon, Esq., led to unpleasant political action. Mr. Otis, however, soon became satisfied that the charges against Mr. Bacon were false and malicious, and thereafter cordially co-operated with him and the conservative portion of the whig party. Mr. Bacon was a deacon of the East Church, and the matter became a subject of church discipline. The church wisely decided that "a church being an ecclesiastical body, have no right to call its members to an account for actions of a civil and public nature ; that in signing petitions against Dea. Bacon, they exercised their just right as men, and subjects of a free state ; and that in their apprehension, when they entered into a church state, they did not give up any of their civil rights ; that they did not charge the Deacon with any immorality ; but that his religious character stood as fair in their minds when they signed the petitions as before ; that if they were chargeable with any overt acts of wickedness, or breach of their covenant engagements, they were willing to answer it to the church, and to make christian satisfaction ; but that as to political controversies, they begged leave to refer them to a civil tribunal."

This extract is from the reply to the complaint of Dea. Bacon. The vote of the church assumes the same ground, but all the particulars are not recapitulated. This vote was passed June 22d, 1780, three years later than the action of the town, and after the passions engendered at the moment had had time to subside. This is contemporaneous authority and therefore valuable. Dea. Bacon had, for some time, withdrawn himself from the communion of the church, and a second vote was unanimously passed desiring and requesting him "to return to his privilege and duty and the discharge of his office in the church." On the 2d of August following a committee was appointed to confer with him, and on the 30th they reported at an adjourned meeting, "that the affair between Dea. Bacon and the Brethren, styled petitioners, was happily accommodated." Dea. Bacon returned to the discharge of his office, and harmony once more apparently prevailed in the councils of the church.

In the language of the town records, "the dissentions which divided our once happy town" were so intimately blended that it is difficult now to draw the distinguishing lines between them. "The Crocker quarrels" were two in number, one between Col. Nathaniel Freeman and others, and the family of Cornelius Crocker, and the other between Abigail Freeman* and Samuel Crocker and others. It was the latter that the town refused to take action on, on the ground that it was a private matter, and that the settlement of the questions involved, belonged to the Courts and not to the town.

As references will be made to localities in vicinity of the Court House, a brief description will not be out of place. The second Court House has been remodeled and is now known as the Baptist Meeting House. It was built about the year 1774, and stands on the north side of the road. At that time there was on the east, where Judge Day's house now stands, an ancient two story house, probably built by one of the Lothrops of the first settlers, and then occupied by the widow Abigail Freeman as a dwelling house and grocery store. The house on the east, between the Court House and Rendezvous Lane, said to have been built of the timber of the old meeting-house, is yet standing, and is occupied by the Baptist Society for a parsonage. On the west side of the lane, there was an ancient two story house, probably built by Thomas Lothrop, a brother of Joseph. This house was then owned by Cornelius Crocker, Jr., and occupied as a public house. In front of these buildings, excepting that occupied by the widow Freeman, there was a narrow green, on which the militia company often paraded during the Revolutionary struggle. In front of the Court House, and on the south side of the street, stood the public house of Mr. Otis Loring. Between the Court House and Loring's tavern was his blacksmith shop,

---

*Some of the essential features of this transaction have been the subject of controversy between the writer of these sketches and the author of the "Hist. of Cape Cod." The latter, writing with much apparent feeling, and in a tone of bitter denunciation, (See Hist. C. C., Vol. II, pp. 305–306,) controverts the assumption of Mr. Otis, that this outrage was committed by Whig sympathizers, upon a Tory lady, but charges its commission upon the Tories and their loyalist associates, against one who sympathized with the Whigs. The fact that the outrage was committed upon Mrs. Freeman is not disputed. In support of his views, Mr. Freeman quotes Dr. James Thacher, a native of the town and a contemporary of the events in controversy. It seems very singular that two such well-informed writers as Mr. Otis and Mr. Freeman should have taken such entirely opposite views of a transaction of which it would seem that the truth could easily have been arrived at by men of their opportunities of judging; and it has been the purpose of the writer of this note, to investigate the subject, with a view of endeavoring to set the transaction right; but documentary evidence in the case has not been available to him. He deems it proper, however, to here remark upon this strange contradiction, with an expression of the hope that future investigation may place the matter in controversy in its true light. [See pp. 233-4.]                                                         S.

not in the direct line between, but a little eastward.   The Sturgis tavern, which has been described, is about three hundred yards eastward from the Court House, and on the south side of the road. There has been only one change in the location of the buildings in this vicinity since 1775—the Loring tavern has been taken down. In 1774 Loring made an addition to his house, in order to induce the justices of the courts to stop with him.   During the Revolution his house was the head-quarters of the tories, and the Sturgis house of the whigs.

The exciting incidents which occurred in that vicinity, are popularly known as the "Crocker quarrels," though others beside the Crockers took part in them.   The scene of the Indian Dream was laid in that vicinity ; the Liberty pole, cut down by sacrilegious hands, stood at the west end of the Green ; the widow Freeman was tarred and feathered thereon, the difficulties between Cols. Freeman and Otis, and the Crockers, occurred there, and in the house of Cornelius Crocker, Jr., fronting thereon, and the defiant passage at arms, between Otis Loring and the Vigilance Committee, in the Blacksmith's shop.   The bitter feelings of personal hostility which these incidents engendered, has no parallel on Cape Cod, if the case between the Clarks and the Winslows of Harwich, be excepted.   Even now, individuals may be found who are ready "to shoulder their crutches, and show how the battles" were fought.

*The Indian Dreame.*   On a fine morning, just before the Declaration of Independence, the villagers found under the latchets of their doors, a small pamphlet entitled "An Indian Dream, drempt on Cape Cod, intended as a satire upon the leading men of the County, particularly on the justices of the Court of Common Sessions.   It was written with much ability, and its witty allusions commended it to the young and the old, and to men of all parties.

The Indian said, "I dreamed that I was in the spirit world, that I saw a long bench, with twelve antient men sitting thereon. (The twelve justices of the Court.)   I inquired who they were, and was informed that they had just arrived from the lower world, and that Satan (a nickname of Otis Loring) had added an apartment to his domain for their special accommodation.   I asked, who is that venerable man sitting at the head of the bench. (Col. James Otis.)   I was told that he was their Chief in the nether world, that in early life he was a painter and glazier by trade,* that he afterwards peddled goods to customers, and law to clients, that his tribe had made him a chief sachem ; but of late he thought himself to be the best paddler in canoe of State."

---

* This fact I have never seen stated in any biography of Col. James Otis.   It was during the time he travelled from house to house painting and repairing the ancient diamond glass windows, that he laid the foundation of his influence and usefulness.

In this manner the Indian described, in his dream, the twelve justices. He called no one by name; but described some peculiar trait in the character of each, so that the individual intended was known.†

The pamphlet caused much excitement at the time, and was considered a tory document. The secret of the authorship was well kept; no legal proof could be obtained respecting the author or the printer. It was a caustic satire on many who were afterwards leading whigs, and they never forgot it, or forgave the Crockers who were the reputed authors. Why this was so, it seems difficult to determine, for tories came in for their full share of the satire. If that pamphlet had emanated from a different source, I am inclined to the opinion that it would have been differently received. It was the allusions therein to the private characters of the individuals that gave offence. "The Body of the People" prevented the same justices from holding, by virtue of authority emanating from the King, their court in Barnstable.‡ The Committee arrested, or attempted to arrest, others who were satirized in the pamphlet. Private considerations probably had an influence in giving to Mr. Otis Loring so prominent a position in the Dream. He kept an opposition tavern, and had then recently enlarged his house, and was endeavoring to induce the Court to stop with him.

Mr. Loring was an outspoken and decided tory. He made no attempt to conceal his opinions. When the Vigilance Committee, of whom Col. Freeman was the Chairman, came to arrest him, he went into his blacksmith's shop and laid a long bar of iron across the fire, and heated the central portion to a read heat. His friends had given him notice of the approach of the Committee, and when they arrived he was prepared for them. He stood before his shop door holding the bar by either end. Without burning their fingers, it would have been difficult for them to have made an immediate arrest. He politely said, "gentlemen, I am ready for you, come on." Finding him determined to resist, they went away, without making an arrest. At another time, Mr. Loring was concealed in a chamber of his house for several days, to avoid arrest.

It does not appear that Mr. Loring or the Crockers had committed any overt or open act of treason. They had freely

---

† I read this pamphlet when a school boy fifty years ago, and I cannot vouch for the verbal accuracy of the words placed in quotation marks. Henry Crocker, Esq., now of Boston, sat on the same bench with me, had the pamphlet, and I read it in the school room and have not since seen it. About the year 1824, I had a conversation with Sarah Lawrence respecting it. She said, "the people said that my brother Josiah wrote it, that it was printed in Boston, brought from there in the packet, and the night following a copy was laid at the door of each man in the village." Her manner induced me to believe at the time, that there was truth in the common report, though she did not so state.

---

‡The original papers on this subject have been preserved, and I intended to have printed them, with fac similes of the signatures; but the publication must be deferred.

expressed their own opinions, usually in their own houses, and however obnoxious such opinions may have been to others, a sound policy did not demand the arrest or imprisonment of such men.   Treason should be nipped in its bud ; but perfect freedom to debate on matters of policy is the unailenable right of a free people.

<hr>

### THE "CROCKER QUARRELS."

Almost every evening, in these exciting times, the whigs met at their headquarters in the Sturgis tavern, to hear the news, and discuss current political events, and words often ran high.   One evening a large company had assembled, Capt. Samuel Crocker, and his brothers Cornelius and Josiah were present, Col. Nathaniel Freeman of Sandwich, the late Capt. Samuel Taylor of Yarmouth, and others were present.   The subject of the conversation was politics.   The principal speakers were Col. Freeman and Capt. Samuel Crocker.   The latter was a whig, and one of the most efficient of the party in Barnstable, being frequently on Committees, and was a very able and intelligent man.   He opposed the system of espionage which had been established, not only as useless, but as calculated to do injury to the cause of the country.   Inquiring of the aged whether they had tea concealed in their houses, and of young ladies whether they were whig or tory, he said was a duty not required of the patriot or the statesman.

Others of the company opposed both Capt. Crocker and Col. Freeman.   Words ran high.   The Colonel was ardent and zealous—of a nervous temperament and opposition kindled his ire.   Capt. Crocker, when excited, was earnest and irascible, and would not submit to be told that the moderate measures that he advocated was toryism in disguise.   Crimination lead to re-crimination, and re-crimination to personal violence.   Some of the company vented their spleen against the Crockers by breaking down the fence in front of the house.

Opprobious epithets never make proselytes ; like the overcharged gun, they are apt to recoil.   The violent political discussions of those days, prove no more this, that the convictions of the people were deep—that they were in earnest and that in their earnestness they sometimes over-stepped the bounds of prudence.

If the difficulties between the Crockers and the Freemans had ended as they begun, only in the use of intemperate language, the remembrance of their dissentions would have long since been buried in oblivion.

Not long afterwards the militia company paraded on the Court House Green.   Cols. Nathaniel Freeman and Joseph Otis were both present.   They were both unpopular with the soldiers, for what reason I am unable to say, probably on account of the differences in political sentiments which then prevailed, already explained in the account of parties in Barnstable. According to military usuages, when they passed through the lines, the soldiers should have presented arms. Instead of extending to them this token of respect, due to them as superior officers, every soldier, at a given signal, clubbed his musket.‖ This was received, as it was intended, as a token of disrespect, as an insult from the officers and soldiers of the Company to their superiors. Col. Otis turned to Capt. Samuel Crocker, and said in a defiant tone, "The Crockers are at the bottom of this." "You lie, sir," was the response. Col. Otis immediately raised his cane and struck Capt. Crocker a severe blow, which he returned. The spectators interfered, but before they were parted several blows were interchanged. Simultaneously, Col. Freeman made the same charge against Cornelius Crocker, Jr., who had gone or was going into his house. Col. Freeman followed him into the west room and made three passes at him with his cutlass. Fortunately neither of them took effect; but some one called out that Col. Freeman had cut down Nell Crocker, at which Elijah Crocker rushed from the ranks into the house, and, with fixed bayonet, swore he would revenge the blood of his uncle. Dr. Samuel Savage was standing in the doorway, and grasping the bayonet, turned it on one side, and with the assistance of others in the house, prevented young Crocker from executing his threat.

One or more of the blows aimed by Col. Freeman at Cornelius Crocker, Jr., took effect on the "summer-beam" of the house, and the deep incision made therein showed the force with which the blows were struck. These marks remained till the house was taken down, about fifty years ago, and were often examined by visitors.

The difficulty between Col. Otis and Capt. Crocker was satisfactorily adjusted and settled. That between Col. Freeman and the Crockers never. The only palliation for the offence is, it was done hastily and in a moment of uncontrolable excitement, caused by a palpable insult to him as a man and an officer. There is no other excuse—it cannot be justified—a man's house is his castle, his sanctuary, and he that invades it, without legal authority, commits an outrage on the rights of others. The tory proclivities of Cornelius Crocker, Jr., did not warrant Col. Freeman in

‖ Clubbing Arms. I am profoundly ignorant of military terms, and cannot say whether this is a technical or cant phrase. I am told that it is the reverse of shoulder arms,—that the breach is elevated across the shoulder, and the muzzle grasped as a club is held.

Note.—Attention has been called to the statement found on page 224 which says of Benjamin Crocker, "He probably married for his third wife in 1759, Annie Handy of Sandwich." This is rendered inprobable, by the fact that the inscription upon their gravestones in the burying-ground at Marston's Mills represent him as dying in 1785, and his wife, Bathsheba, in 1808, surviving him twenty-three years.                          S.

drawing his sword on an unarmed man, nor did the act of Col. Freeman warrant the act of Elijah Crocker in rushing upon him with fixed bayonet.

I have repeatedly heard aged men, who took an active part in the stirring events of those times, not only justify the act, but refer to it as an evidence of the patriotic zeal of Col. Freeman.* He had numerous adherents, more zealous than himself, who counselled no concession.   The Crockers had also many friends. The wound might at first have been healed; but frequent irritations caused it to fester, and its virus spread through the village, parish, and town, causing divisions in families, and alienation of old friends.   The children and friends of the parties ever entertained a bitter hostility towards each other, and their grandchildren, the men of the present generation, are sensitive on the subject, and refer to it with painful interest.

*Tar and feathering.*   Abigail Freeman, baptized in the East Church Sept. 21, 1729, was a daughter of Thomas Davis of Barnstable.   The few among the aged who remember her, call her the Widow Nabby Freeman.   April 8, 1753, at the tender age of fifteen, she married David Freeman of Fairfield, Conn.   His mother, who was a Sturgis, had married for her second husband, Job Gorham, and it appears that some of her children came with her to Barnstable.   Abigail had a son born March 25, 1757, named Thomas Davis Freeman, and she became a widow soon after that date.   She united with the East Church March 26, 1758, and continued to be a member, of good standing, till the close of her life in November, 1788.

She resided in the ancient dwelling house probably built by Joseph Lothrop, Esq., that stood next east of the new Court House, where Judge Day now resides.   Early in life she became a widow and had to rely on her own unaided exertions to procure the means of subsistence.   She kept a small grocery store, and being an outspoken tory, refused to surrender her small stock of tea, to be destroyed by the Vigilance Committee.   She was talkative, a fault not exclusively confined to her sex, was a frequent visitor at the house of Otis Loring, made no attempt to conceal her tory principles, and was sometimes severe in her denunciation of the acts of leading whigs.   Her course was not patriotic and not to be commended.   Even at the present day (1863) there are persons who condemn, with more severity, the acts of our government and the leading politicians, than did Abigail Freeman during the Revolutionary struggle; yet no sane man would consider it wise or expedient to enact laws, restraining the freedom of speech in regard to the policy of measures, or the motives of individuals.

---

*I must confess that I have myself used this argument.  I had not then investigated the facts and circumstances of the case.  In truth, there is only one essential fact, and that is, the assault.  No one denies it, and the question turns on this point; did the circumstances justify the act?  I once thought they did.  I now think otherwise.

Some of our Revolutionary fathers in Barnstable, thought differently and acted differently.    Abigail Freeman was an eye sore to them.    She kept a little grocery store, saw many persons, and would keep her tongue in motion whenever and wherever she could find a listener.    Doctors Freeman and Smith, for whom she had a strong antipathy, some of the Crockers with whom she had a private quarrel, and some of the radical whigs, resolved that a bridle should be put upon her tongue.    Ducking stools, for the cure of scolds and unquiet women, had then gone out of use, and the then modern invention of tarring and feathering, and riding on a rail, were in vogue.    Perhaps it is well that the names of the individuals who took part in this courteous ceremony were not recorded.    They were all young men, and acting in the shade of night, perhaps were not recognized in the disguises which they assumed.

When they came to the house of Mrs. Freeman she had retired for the night.    They obtained an entrance, took her from her bed to the Green, besmeared her with tar and covered her with feathers.    A rail was procured from a fence in the vicinity, across which she was set astride, and either end thereof was placed on the shoulder of a stout youth.    She was held in her position by a man who walked at her side, holding her by the hand.    When they were tired of the sport, and after they had exacted from her a promise that she would no more meddle in politics, they released her, and the gallant band soon after sneaked homeward.

Though some who took an active part in this demonstration—this visible argument for personal liberty and the freedom of speech—disliked to be known as participators; yet a strong party in Sandwich and Barnstable justified the act.

No apologist for this can now be found; but before condemning the participators, we must take into consideration the mitigating circumstances.    Its respectability and influence, if not actual participators, countenanced and supported those that were. Allowance must also be made for the excitement of the times, and that men acting under the influence of such excitement, often do things which they afterwards regret.    The Widow Freeman was a thorn in their sides—she could out-talk any of them, was fascinating in her manners, and had an influence which she exerted, openly and defiantly, against the patriotic men who were then hazzarding their fortunes and their lives in the struggle for American independence.    Sitting quietly at our firesides we may condemn such acts, and, as moralists say, the end does not justify the means.    Perhaps if we were placed in the same circumstance that our fathers were, we should do as they did.    These considerations are not presented as a justification of the gross and shameless violation of the personal rights of Widow Abigail

Freeman, but as mitigating circumstances which should temper the verdict of public opinion.

Col. James Otis attempted to heal the difficulties in town and reconcile the parties, and he partially succeeded. Deacon Bacon and Col. Freeman were his kinsmen, and his age and the eminent services which he had rendered to the town and County, entitled his opinions to high consideration. At a town meeting held May 21, 1776, he made, what the records call, an "apology!" and the town voted to hear a part of it, but not "that part relating to Abigail Freeman and the Crocker's quarrel." The reason for making this distinction is apparent, Dea. Bacon was the representative elect of the town. Joseph Otis, and others, had petitioned the General Court that he be ejected from his seat, and therefore any matter relative to Deacon Bacon's qualifications or to the petition, was pertinent; but neither Abigail nor the Crockers stood in the same relation to the town, and therefore the inhabitants, as a town, had nothing to do with their quarrels. These votes show that the men of those days thought and acted independently, and that they could not be persuaded to act in opposition to what they believed to be the right course of action, even by cne who had been President of the first continental Congress at Watertown.

Mr. Cornelius Crocker died Dec. 12, 1784, aged 80. His wife, Mrs. Lydia Crocker, died Aug. 5, 1773, aged 68. His will is dated April 5, 1782, and the codicil thereto Feb. 10, 1784. His sons Elijah and Elisha were then dead, and are not named. To Samuel he gave "all his land lying westward and northward of the way that leads from the County road, near his son Cornelius's dwelling house, to Rendevous Creek, with the dwelling house in which he now lives, and all other buildings standing on the premises," with one half of the fish house and the land on which it stood, one half of his wharf, and one half of the way to the same. His son Joseph was dead. To his widow, Elizabeth, he gave a right in the house he devised to the sons of his son Josiah, and to his grand-daughter Mary £30 in silver money. To his daughter, Widow Lydia Sturgis, he gave the westerly part of the dwelling house where he then lived, and one half of the furniture. To Cornelius he gave one half of his fish house, half of his wharf, £15 in silver money, and all the debts he then owed him. In consideration of the larger proportion of the estate given to Samuel, the latter was to make no demand on Cornelius, Jr., for debts due. His son Josiah was then dead. To his grand-sons, Robert, Uriel, and Josiah, the house in which their father Josiah had lived, with one and one half acres of land, being the east part of his homestead next the lane, and £6 each when 21; to his two grand-daughters, Deborah and Mehitable, children of his son Josiah, £6 each in silver money.

To his daughter, Widow Sarah Lawrence £30 in silver, his desk, one half of his furniture, and one quarter of his pew in the East Meeting House.

He made Samuel, Cornelius, and Lydia, his residuary legatees, giving them his grist mill, the easterly part of his dwelling house, wood-lots and meadows and all his other real and personal estate not otherwise specifically devised. His will was witnessed by Edward Bacon and his wife Rachael, and Mercy Crocker.

The sons and daughters of Cornelius Crocker were all persons of more than ordinary intellectual vigor. Josiah received a public education, and all of the family were well educated for the times. They were close observers of passing events, and were all distinguished for their conversational powers, and their ready command of language. The children of Cornelius Crocker, born in Barnstable, were: 1, Elijah, born April 12, 1729; 2, Elisha, born Sept. 14, 1730. Both died in early life, and are not named in the will of their father. 3, Samuel, born July 29, 1732; 4, Joseph, born April 12, 1734; 5, Lydia, April 14, 1739; 6, Cornelius, born Aug. 21, 1740; 7, Josiah, born Dec. 20, 1744, and 8, Sarah, whose name is not on the town records, born in the year 1749.

Capt. Samuel Crocker, son of Cornelius, a man of note during the Revolutionary struggle, married April 8, 1753, by David Gorham, Esq., Elizabeth, daughter of Capt. Samuel Lumbert. She died of consumption June 13, 1757, aged 27. He married, for his second wife, her sister Anna, May 29, 1760. His children were: 1, Abigail, July 1, 1753; 2, Elijah, Oct. 27, 1755; 3, Elizabeth, Feb. 24, 1767; 4, Anna, April 7, 1766; 5, Elisha, Aug. 30, 1767; 6, Ezekiel, Jan. 20, 1770; and 7, Susanna, July 7, 1773. Elijah, I think, died early in life. Elizabeth lived to be aged, and died unmarried. Anna married Isaac Bacon, Jr., July 1, 1793, died early leaving a large family. Elisha was a sea captain, had a family, and resided in the ancient gambrel roofed house on Rendevous Lane. He died May 15, 1817. Ezekiel, the last survivor of the family, married Temperance Phinney Dec. 28, 1794; kept a public house where Judge Day now resides. Susannah, married July 14, 1796, John Bursley, father of the present David Bursley, Esq., and was the mother of a numerous family.

Joseph Crocker, son of Cornelius, married Jan. 12, 1758, Elizabeth Davis. He had Joseph Nov. 15, 1760, who died young, and Mary born Dec. 28, 1763. He died early. His widow died Feb. 7, 1811, aged 75, and her daughter Mary or Polly married Isaac Lothrop Oct. 1796.

Lydia, daughter of Cornelius, married April 3, 1760, Capt. Samuel Sturgis, 3d. He was a captain of a Company at Cape Breton, and died Aug. 9, 1762, aged 25. She died April 9, 1825, aged 86, having lived a widow 62 years and 8 months. She was born in the house which has been named, near the Agricultural Hall ; but resided nearly all her life in the house where she died, and widely known as "Aunt Lydia's tavern." She had an only child, Sally, who married Daniel Crocker. He died April 22, 1811, aged 49. She died Oct. 3, 1837, aged 77, leaving many descendents. A grandson, Barnabas Davis, Esq., of Boston, now owns the ancient tavern.

Cornelius Crocker, Jr., married Abiah Hinckley. He had two sons ; Naler, born in 1773, many years one of the selectmen and town clerk of Barnstable. He died March 28, 1829, he had a son Henry, now living, and a daughter Abiah, first wife of Enoch T. Cobb. Cornelius also had a son Asa, born in 1776. He taught a school in Barnstable several years and died unmarried April 17, 1822, aged 46. Cornelius Crocker, Jr., died early, and his widow Abiah survived him many years, dying June 7, 1823, aged 77. For many years she kept a tavern in the dwelling house now owned by Dr. Allen, and in the more ancient house that stood on the same spot. She was a strong-minded, intelligent woman, and of good business capacity. One anecdote respecting her illustrates her character for firmness. After the death of her husband Col. Freeman called at her house on a court week, and asked to have lodgings. Her reply was, "my house is full, sir." "But," said the Col. "my friends put up here, and I would like to be with them." Her reply was, "my house is full, sir." Col. F., a little excited, said, "madam, you are licensed to keep a public house, and are bound to accommodate travellers and persons attending the Courts." "Yes," said she, "but, if my house was not full, (pointing to the marks on the summer beam) there would be no room for Col. Freeman." To this he responded, "It is time to forget those old matters and bury the hatchet." "Yes," said Mrs. Crocker, "but the aggressor should dig the grave.

Joseph Crocker, son of Cornelius, graduated at Harvard College in 1765. He did not take the degree of Master of Arts. He resided in the two story single house east of his sister Lydia's tavern, and afterwards owned by Freeman Hinckley. He taught a school some little time in Barnstable ; but on account of his feeble health and tory proclivities, was not much, if any, in public life. He married Oct. 6, 1765, immediately after leaving college, Deborah, daughter of Hon. Daniel Davis, and had five children, Robert, Uriel, Josiah, Deborah, and Mehitable. He died of consumption May 4, 1780, in the 36th year of his age, and is buried in the new grave yard on Cobb's Hill. His widow married Benjamin Gorham, Jr., and had by him Abigail, who married Aug. 4, 1803, Capt. Henry Bacon. Uriel Crocker settled in Boston, and has a son of the same name now living. Deborah married John Lothrop; Mehitable, Joseph Parker. The Wid. Deborah Gorham died in 1818, aged 72.

Sally or Sarah, daughter of Cornelius, married Capt. David Lawrence, after a very brief courtship. He was a sea captain, and was the first who displayed the Stars and Stripes in the port of Bristol, England. Dea. Joseph Hawes of Yarmouth, was his mate. Capt. Lawrence was consumptive and was unable to perform his duties during the voyage, and died soon after his return, on the 3d of October, 1783, aged 35 years. She survived till Feb. 21, 1825, when she died, aged 76. Mrs. Lawrence was distinguished for her conversational power. She had read all the current literature of the day. Her friends were among the leading men of the times, and she was well versed in local history, and in all the leading topics of conversation in her day. Her wit was keen and cut without seeming to give offence. She was not fastidious, and the point of her wit was never blunted in order to avoid an allusion which prudery might condemn. She was open, candid, and decided in all her opinions, and in the expression of them, her wit often sparkled with a brilliancy that silenced opposition. Her instantaneous reply to Col. Freeman and other members of the Whig Vigilance Committee, when they inquired of her whether she was whig or tory, was of this character, and will be long remembered. She belonged to the same school of politics with her brother Samuel, and held that the asking of young ladies such questions was not only uncalled for; but impertinent. Her most cutting rebuke consisted of only four words; and that committee never forgot them, and ever after treated her with the most marked respect. I have often heard her relate the story, but the reply she made was always pronounced in a suppressed tone of voice.

She lived a widow over forty-one years, and her house was the resort of numerous friends who appreciated her talents and listened with delight to her conversation. Intellectually she never grew old. She could, without seeming effort, adapt herself to the old and the young, the gay and the religious. She could discuss the merits of the last novel, or the doctrines of the last sermon. Her friends and relatives always treated her with marked respect, and the survivors still fondly cherish her memory.

She had a son William, who was a hatter, and died early; and Lucy, who married Holmes Allen, Esq. He built the house now owned by Mr. Frederick Cobb. He was a lawyer, a man esteemed for his talents and legal knowledge; but unfortunately became intemperate, and died in early life, leaving an only child, Henry Holmes Allen, born Aug. 14, 1801. He was three days my senior. We were school-mates and play-fellows in early life, and associates in manhood. He was honest and honorable; kind, generous, sympathetic—a man who never had an enemy. He married

Abigail T. Gorham, daughter of Edward. She died early, and he soon after died in foreign lands; but his body lies entombed beside that of his wife. He left no issue, and having no near relatives, he devised his estate to the Fraternal Lodge, of which he was an active member.

(23) Thomas Crocker, son of Dea. Job Crocker, born 19th Jan. 1674, married 23d Dec. 1701, Elizabeth Lothrop, widow of "John Lothrop, son of Barnabas Lothrop, Esq." She was the eldest child of James, son of James Green of Charlestown, and was born Nov. 14, 1662, and was twelve years older than her second husband, and five older than her first. She died in Hingham Aug. 1, 1752, aged 89. By her first husband she had a son and a daughter. The latter died early, and the son at 20. Mr. Thomas Crocker resided in the East Parish, and is styled in the records "a dealer." He died in 1718, insolvent. His indebtedness was large, and his creditors received from his estate 2 shillings in the pound, per cent. His children born in Barnstable were:

91. I. Walley, 30th July, 1703, died 2d Oct. 1703.
92. II. Thomas, 26th Aug. 1704.
93. III. Walley, 26th June 1706.

His son Thomas married 1, Mehitable, daughter of Joseph Dimmock, 1727. She died March 13, 1728-9, and he married 2d, Oct. 20, 1730, Rebecca, daughter of Benjamin Hamblin. Mr. Thomas Crocker died Dec. 5, 1756, aged 51, and his wife May 9, 1756, aged 46. He resided in the easterly part of the West Parish. His children were: 1, Walley, born Feb. 28, 1727-8 died Aug. 23, following; 2, Elizabeth, born 5th Dec. 1731; 3, Sarah, born 26th Feb. 1733-4; 4, Rebecca, 30th Nov. 1735; 5, Hope, March 1738; 6, Thomas, 23d Jan. 1740; 7, Esther, 28th Aug. 1743; 8, Barnabas, 26th Oct. 1746; 9, Huckins, 15th March, 1748; 10, Mary, 31st Aug. 1753. Elizabeth of this family married, in 1757, George Conant, and died Sept. 17, 1759; Sarah, married, May 19, 1757, Joseph Blish, Jr.; Rebecca married Oct. 25, 1757, Lemuel Nye, Jr., of Sandwich; Barnabas married at 19, March 24, 1765, Ann Smith; Mary died unmarried.

Walley Crocker, son of Thomas, married, Oct. 22, 1730, Abigail, daughter of John Annable. He had born in Barnstable: 1, Abigail, Nov. 2, 1731; 2, Temperance, Dec. 18, 1733; 3, Walley, April 18, 1737. Temperance married April 5, 1759, Daniel Carpenter.

(25) Dea. John Crocker, son of Dea. Job, born 24, 1683, married 11th Nov. 1704, Hannah. She died 10th Oct. 1720, and he married 2d, 22d June, 1721, Mary Hinckley, living in 1731. It appears that he married a third wife Nancy, her grave stones record her death July 27, 1744, aged 56. Dea. John Crocker died Feb. 7, 1773, aged 89 years and 11 months, (grave stones).

He resided on the westerly part of his father's farm, and was many years a deacon of the West Church. His children born in Barnstable were :

94.  I.   Abigail, born 5th Oct. 1705, married Oct. 28, 1731, George Howland. She joined the West Church in 1728, and after marrige was dismissed to Deerfield.

95.  II.   Zaccheus, Aug. 1, 1707, married 1734, Elizabeth Beals of Hingham. His children were, Joshua, born Aug. 6, 1735 ; Zaccheus Dec. 1737 ; Sylvanus, baptized Feb. 19, 1739, and Hannah born June 21, 1743.

96.  III.   John, 27 July 1710, died 30th May, 1711.

97.  IV.   Ebenezer, Nov. 1, 1713, married July 26, 1739, Elizabeth Lovell, Jr., and had James Feb. 19, 1739-40 ; 2, Mary, Nov. 7, 1744. He married in 1746, Zerviah, daughter of Kenelm Winslow, Esq., of Harwich, and had 3, Alvan Friday, 6th Nov. 1747 ; 4, Ashsah Monday, 24th July, 1749 ; 5, Ebenezer Thursday, 26th July, 1753, died Feb. 17, 1817 ; 6, Zerviah Wednesday, 17th July 1751 ; 7, Joshua Friday, 4th July 1755 ; 8, Kenelm Sunday, 14th Aug. 1757 ; 9, George Monday 18th Feb. 1760 ; 10, Zenas Friday, 25th Dec. 1761 ; 11, Heman, April 14, 1764.

There were four Ebenezer Crockers. The 1st son of Josiah died in 1723 ; 2d, a son of Saumel, born 1719, removed to East Haddam 1751 ; 3, a son of Dea. John, born in 1713 ; 4, a son of Ebenezer, born 1723. Ebenezer, son of John, resided at Cotuit, and the house which he built there is still owned by his descendants.

John, baptized Oct. 16, 1715.

98.  V.   Elizabeth, baptized Aug. 10, 1718.

99.  VI.   Jabez, 16th June, 1720, died 11th Dec. 1720.

100. VII.   John, 1st April, 1722.

101. VIII.   Job, 29th March, 1724.

102. IX.   Daniel, 1st March, 1725-6, married three wives, 1, Elizabeth Childs, May 19, 1748 ; 2, Phebe Winslow of Harwich, 1755 ; and 3, Bathsheba Jenkins. His children were, 1, Job, born May 6, 1749, removed to Western New York, and has descendants ; 2, Winslow, Dec. 31, 1755, resided at West Barnstable, married ―――― Blush, had a family. Edward W. Crocker of Yarmouth, is of this family ; 3, Elizabeth, March 14, 1770, she married, 1, Heman Crocker. Her son, Oliver Crocker, Esq., of New Bedford is now living, and 2, Elisha Ruggles, of Rochester ; 4, Daniel, March 8, 1762, married Sally Sturgis, and had a family ; 5, Mary, July 11, 1767, married James Davis ; 6, Abigail, Nov. 6, 1769, married Ebenezer Bacon, Esq. ; 7, Joseph, Jan. 27, 1771, married Joanna Bacon, and had Walter, James, and others now living ; 8, Prince, Sept. 6, 1772,

married Martha Nye, and has descendants living. Joseph and Prince owned and occupied the ancient Crocker house, and both lived to extreme old age. 9, Temperance, born July 28, 1776, married Ezra Crocker; 10, David, Feb. 21, 1779, married Rachell Bacon, and his sons Eben, Frederick and Henry, and daughter Caroline, are now living; 11, Josiah, Aug. 24, 1781, died unmarried at New Orleans.

103. X. Timothy, Aug. 23, 1728.
104. XI. Jonathan, born Nov. 22, 1731, married May 2, 1754, Sarah Childs. He died of the small pox Dec. 4, 1796, and his wife Sarah of the same disease Dec. 16, 1796. He was the first buried in the Crocker burying ground. He has descendants living.

(30) David Crocker, Esq., youngest son of Dea. Job Crocker, born 5th Nov. 1697, graduate of Harvard College 1716, resided on the John Crocker farm at West Barnstable. He was many years town Clerk, transcribed the ancient town records, now lost. The records of the births of the Crockers he arranged genealogically. He was many years one of the board of selectmen, and in 1742 a justice of the Court of Common Pleas. He died in 1764, aged 67 years. He married 12th Nov. 1724, Abigail, daughter of Mr. David Loring, and Jan. 27, 1757, Mrs. Mary Stuart. His children were:

105. I. A son, born Jan. 9, 1725, died Feb. 19, 1725.
106. II. David, April 14, 1726, died June 28, 1734.
107. III. Abigail, May 20, 1728, married Jan. 10, 1754, Seth Blossom.
108. IV. William, Dec. 8, 1730 (called Jr.) He resided in the house which was his father's. He belonged to the East Parish, and was a member of the East Church. He married twice, 1st in 1753 Lydia Knowles of Eastham. She died April 16, 1764, and he married 2d, Sept. 30, 1764, Mary Cobb, Jr. He died May 3, 1819, in his 89th year, and she died May 20, 1817, aged 85. His children born in Barnstable were: 1, Abigail, March 15, 1754; 2, David, Aug. 23, 1755; 3, Temperance, Jan. 2, 1763; 4, Sarah, June 26, 1765; 5, Mary, Nov. 2, 1766; 6, William, Nov. 19, 1768: 7, Matthias, July 26, 1770; 8, Ebenezer, baptized July 26, 1772; 9, Loring, born March 18, 1774. Of this family, William resided in his father's estate, and died June 24, 1844, and his brother, Dea. Ebenezer, a tanner, did also in the first part of his life. He removed to the West, where he died a few years since. Matthias was a hatter and resided in Boston. Loring was largely engaged in the salt manufacture at the common field, and died March 21, 1841. His son Loring now owns his manufactories.

109. V. Alice, born April 18, 1757, baptized July 30th, 1758,

and in the church records called the daughter of "Squire David and Mary Crocker."

110. VI. Hannah, Sept. 24, Wednesday [1759.]
111. VII. Sarah, Oct. 24, Tuesday, [1761.]
112. VIII. Lydia, Feb. 28, [1762] died Sept. 24, 1763.

(32) Thomas Crocker, son of Josiah, born 28th May, 1671, married 25th March, 1696, Hannah, [Green] of Boston. He died April, 1728, in the 57th year of his age, and is buried at West Barnstable. He resided in the ancient stone house, as before stated. In his will he makes provision for the education of his son Joseph at College. His wife, Hannah Crocker, died Jan. 23d, 1728-9 in the 53d year of her age. Their children born in Barnstable were:

113. I. Tabitha, Dec. 20th, 1698.
114. II. Josiah, 21st, April 1701, died Feb. 23d, 1728-9.
115. III. Seth, 13th June, 1708. He resided at West Barnstable on the estate which was his father's. He married three wives, 1, Joanna Leavet, April, 16th, 1730. She died Aug. 4th, 1732, aged 20. 2d, Temperance Thacher of Yarmouth, June 1st, 1734. She died July 11th, 1736, aged 24. 3d, Abigail, daughter of Joseph Blush, 1742. He died March 25th, 1770, in the 62d year of his age, and is buried with his wives in the West Barnstable grave yard. By his first wife he had a daughter Hannah, born July 18th, 1732, baptized July 23d, 1732. This child was of feeble mind. By his second wife he had Thomas, born June 8th, 1735. He married in 1756, Mercy Hamblen, and about the year 1781 removed to Lee, Mass. He had a large estate, and has numerous descendants. There have been some remarkable instances of longevity in this family.
116. IV. Hannah, born 8th May, 1711, married July 25th, 1744, Jabez Robinson of Falmouth?
117. V. Thankful.
118. VI, Joseph, born 1715, graduated at Harvard College, 1734. He was ordained Sept. 12, 1739, pastor of the church and society in South Eastham, now Orleans. He died March 2d, 1772. He married twice, had Josiah, a graduate of Harvard College, 1760; Lucia, who married Rev. Simeon William of Weymouth; and Ann, who married Rev. Wm. Shaw of Marshfield. Of the family of Rev. Josiah Crocker, the Orleans records furnish little information. His wife, Reliance, died in 1759, aged 44. He had six children who died in infancy between 1741 and 1757. His son Josiah was born in Orleans in 1740, graduated at Harvard College in 1760, and died in Orleans Jan. 20, 1764, aged 24. He had received a call to become pastor of the second Church in Yarmouth, (now Dennis) but his sick

ness and death prevented his ordination. His father caused a glowing eulogium to be inscribed on the monument to his memory in Orleans.

The Rev. Joseph Crocker was a Calvinist, a hard student, and a well read theologian. Wanting the graces of the orator, he never was a popular preacher.

(38) Capt. Josiah Crocker, son of Josiah, born 8th Feb, 1684, married Desire, daughter of Col. John Thacher of Yarmouth, April 10, 1718. He was a sea captain, and while on a voyage to Nova Scotia, was betrayed out of his course by an Irishman who pretended to be a pilot. He and all his crew were sick at the time. He died on board his own vessel in St. Mary's harbor, Annapolis Rial, Oct. 10, 1721, and was buried at Port Royal, Oct. 14, 1721, aged 37. His widow, Mrs. Desire Crocker, died in Yarmouth, on the morning of the Sabbath, May 6, 1722, and is buried in the ancient burying ground in Yarmouth.

He had two children born in Yarmouth.

119. I. Josiah, born 30th Oct. 1719, graduate of Harvard College, 1738, and ordained May 19, 1742, pastor of the church in Taunton. He entered College at the early age of 15, and was ordained at 23. He was of an ardent temperament, zealous, earnest, yet tender and persuasive in his manner. Like other zealous men, he was not always cautious in his expressions. He had many warm friends, and some enemies. His call to the Taunton church was not unanimous, and there were always some who opposed him. He was dismissed from his pastoral charge Dec. 1, 1765, but continued to reside in Taunton till his death. He was the friend of Whitefield, and possessed some of the characteristics of that eminent divine. His earnest, persuasive manner, drew together a large audience when it was known that he was to preach. It is said that a women travelled from Plymouth on foot, carrying a child in her arms the whole distance. When the load seemed heavy, or the way long, she would comfort herself by crying out at the top of her voice, "Crocker's ahead, Crocker's ahead," [See Ministers of Taunton.] He married twice. His first wife was Rebecca, daughter of James Allyn of Barnstable, whom he married July 28, 1742. She died Sept. 28, 1759. He married Nov. 5, 1761, Hannah, daughter of Col. Thos. Cobb of Attieborough. His children were : Josiah, Benjamin, Allyn, Joseph, William, Ebenezer, Rebecca, Leonard, born Oct. 2, 1762, and Hannah, Oct. 18, 1765. He died Aug. 28, 1774, in the 55th, and not the 53d year of his age, as inscribed on his tombstone. A similar mistake of two years occurs on the monument to the memory of his first wife. The Rev. Josiah Crocker has many descendants in Taunton and other

places. His grand-daughter, Hannah M. Crocker, was the author of "The Rights of Women," published in 1818.

120. II.   Desire, born 17th Dec. 1721.

(39) Ebenezer, son of Josiah, born May 30, 1687, married May 22, 1715, Hannah Hall of Yarmouth. He died 18th March, 1722-3, in the 36th year of his age. His children born in Barnstable were:

121. I.   Mehitable, Sept. 16, 1716, married Nathan Crocker, Jr., Dec. 27, 1739.

122. II.   Hannah, Oct. 10, 1718, married Eben Childs, Jr., Jan. 15, 1747, died Feb. 23, 1755.

123. III.   Susannah, Oct. 20, 1720, married George Conant, Jan 30, 1755.

124. IV.   Ebenezer, March 2, 1722-3.

(43) Nathan, son of Eleazer, born 27th April, 1685, married, 10th March, 1708-9, Joannah Bursley. He was a farmer, and resided in the old stone fort. His children were:

125. I.   Jabez, born 20th June, 1709. He married, July 6, 1732, Deliverance Jones; Feb. 9, 1737-8, Mary Baker; and afterwards Remember Fuller, and had six children: 1, Anna, March 6, 173–, married Benj. Howland March 15, 1763; 2, Deliverance, May 7, 1740; 3, Asa, Sept. 4, 1741, 4, Ruth, Aug. 25, 1743; 5, Lot, baptized March 31, 1745; 6, Mary, baptized June 21, 1747. Feb. 1750, Jabez Crocker sold his house and the lot containing two acres on which it stood, to his brother John Crocker, who was then called third. Charles Gray now owns the land. It was then bounded, northerly by the high way, westerly by Dexter's lane, southerly by land of Cornelius Dexter, and easterly by land of Col Otis. In a mortgage deed, dated 10th May, 1746, he names his brothers, Benoni, Nathan and John, and his cousin, John Crocker, Jr.

126. II.   Benoni, born 24th Feb. 1711-12, married, Feb. 19, 1736, Abigail, daughter of John Bursley. He inherited the old stone fort in which he resided, and to which he made an addition. His childred were: 1, Lemuel, born March 1, 1737, married Sarah Backus of Sandwich, 1763; 2, Barnabas. (There is a blank in the record which I fill with the name of Barnabas. Benoni had a son of that name for whom he made the addition to his house.) 3, Abigail, born May 22d, 1745; 4, Abner, Aug. 18th, 1747.

127. III.   Nathan, born 7th March 1713-14, married Mehitable, daughter of Ebenezer Crocker, Dec. 27th, 1739, and had ten children: 1, Enoch, June 1st, 1741; 2, Susannah, April 9th, 1743; 3, Deborah, March 30th, 1745; 4, Arubah, Aug. 14th 1747; 5, Elijah, Feb. 11th, 1749; 6, Nathan, Aug. 10th 1753; 7, Jonathan, March 23d, 1756;

8, Mehitable, June 8, 1758 ; 9, David, March 15th, 1761.

128. IV. Isaac, born 6th May, 1719, married, March 22d, 1738-9, Elizabeth Fuller, and had 1, Ansel, Aug. 27th, 1739 ; 2, Rebecca, March 24th, 1740 ; 3, Thomas, Sept. 19th, 1743 ; 4, Josiah, Oct. 14th, 1762 ; 5, Ansel, Jan. 22d, 1767. The names of the two last are added by a late town clerk.

129. V. John, 11th Jan. 1721-2. His father, in a deed to him, dated Oct. 12th, 1744, calls him 3d. He was in the expedition to Cape Breton, and to distinguish him from the others of the same name, was called Cape Breton John.

130. VI. Temperance, born Oct. 3d, 1724, married Joseph Annable, Dec. 31st, 1744.

(52) William Crocker, son of Joseph, born 25th Aug. 1679, married, by Justice Skiff of Sandwich, Nov. 1705, his cousin, Mary Crocker, daughter of Josiah. He died in 1741, in the 62d year of his age, his mother, Temperance, a daughter of the first John Bursley, was then living. In his will dated Feb. 10th, 1740-1, proved July 8th, 1741, names his wife Mary his sons William and Joseph, to whom he gives his West Barnstable estate ; and Benjamin, to whom he devises his lands in Saṅdwich, and meadows at Scorton. He also named his daughters, Mercy Blush and Mary Beals, and his "Hon'd mother Temperance Crocker," who then retained the improvement of his estate. He had children born in Barnstable, namely :

131. I. Mercy, 22d Sept. 1706, married Joseph Blush Oct. 28th, 1730.

132. II. A son, born 20th June, 1708, died July 4, 1708.

133. III. A daughter, still born, Aug. 3, 1709.

134. IV. William, born 9th Sept. 1710. He resided at West Barnstable, and married, in 1743, Hannah Baker, and had twelve children. He is called Mr. in the town records, then a token of respect, and his wife Mrs. Only four are named on the town records ; but the names of all are on the church records. 1, Mary (called Mercy on the church records) born March 25, 1745 ; 2, William, Feb. 6, 1744, died young ; 3, Martha, Nov. 28, 1748 ; 4, Temperance, Jan. 22, 1749 ; 5, Hannah, baptized April 22, 1751 ; 6, Josiah, July 5, 1752 ; 7, William again, Oct. 1753 ; 8, Alice, July 27, 1755 ; 9, Mercy, Jan. 1, 1758 ; 10, Josiah, June 8, 1760 ; 11, Ephraim, July, 26, 1761 ; 12, Calvin, May 1764. The latter was the late Capt. Calvin Crocker, who has descendants in Barnstable.

135. V. Alice, born Sept. 1712, married Stephen Beals of Hingham, Sept. 16, 1736. (In the abstract of his father's will I have the name Mary, probably an error, should be Alice.)

136.  VI.   Mary, born Aug. 12, 1714.
137.  VII.   Joseph, born Dec. 1718.
138.  VIII.   Benjamin, March 20, 1720, married Bathsheba Hall
of Yarmouth, April 1747.   See 85.*

(53) Timothy, son of Joseph Crocker, born 30th April,
1681, resided at West Barnstable.   He was a merchant, an ensign
in the militia, as his grave stone informs us, and a justice of the
peace.   He was married 27th Oct. 1709, by Rev. Jonathan
Russell, to Mrs. Melatiah, daughter of his uncle Josiah Crocker.
His children were:

139.  I.   Jerusha, born 12th Dec. 1711.   She married, May 19,
1741, Mr. Elijah Deane of Raynham.
140.  II.   Melatiah, born 19th March 1714, married, March 21,
1734, John Sturgis, Esq., of Barnstable.   Her children
were, Josiah, born Oct. 17, 1737, Melatiah, Oct. 11, 1739;
Timothy Crocker, March 30, 1742; Lucretia, Oct. 14, 1743.
The latter did not marry.   She was a well educated and
accomplished lady, resided in her grand-father Crocker's
house, and taught a school many years.   A large proportion
of the aged at West Barnstable, are indebted to her for
their early education.
141.  III.   Bathsheba, born 2d April, 1717, married Sept. 6,
1738, Rev. Samuel Tobey of Berkley.   He was born in
Sandwich in 1715, a graduate of Harvard College, 1733,
ordained Nov. 23, 1737.   He had twelve children.
142.  IV.   Abigail, born April 2, 1721, married Sept. 2, 1740,
Rev. Rowland Thacher, pastor of the church at Wareham.
He graduated at Harvard College in 1733.
143.  V.   Martha, born 26th Dec. 1724, married, Feb. 2, 1744-5,
Capt. William Davis, of Barnstable.   She died Jan. 5,
1773, aged 48.   Mrs. Andrews Hallett of Yarmouth, has
some fine specimens of worsted work embroidered by her
grand-mother Davis.

The dwelling house of Timothy Crocker, Esq., stood near
where Seth Parker's store now stands.   It was large, two stories
high, and most substantially built.   The style was that of the
wealthy among the first settlers.   It fronted to the east, the gable
being towards the road, and was probably built as early as 1660.
Who was the first owner I have been unable to ascertain.   In
1686, when the road was laid out, it appears to have been owned
and occupied by Increase Clap; but I doubt whether he was the
first owner.   In 1649 Mr. Thomas Daxter resided in that neigh-

---

*In 1747 there were four Benjamin Crockers, 1, Benjamin, son of Josiah, born in 1692,
removed to Ipswich; 2, Benjamin, son of Joseph born in 1696; 3, Benjamin, son of Samuel,
born 1711; 4, Benjamin, son of William, born 1720.   The Benjamin, who married in 1747,
Bethsheba Hall, is called Jr., and I inferred from the fact, that there was then an older
man of the same name in town, that the one numbered 85, X, was the person intended.   I
am now inclined to think that 138, III, was the person intended.   An investigation of the
wills, which I have not the time to do, will settle the question.

borhood, and owned the land bordering on Dexter's Lane ; but whether his land extended so far east, I have no means of ascertaining. The Rowley's who removed to Falmouth about the year 1661, owned land in the vicinity. Dea. William Crocker owned the land on the east at the settlement of the town, and it was afterwards owned by his son John. The exact bounds of this land it would perhaps be now difficult to ascertain.

This ancient mansion, while owned by Timothy Crocker, Esq., was kept in good repair, and elegantly furnished. His family ranked among the aristocracy of those days. His daughters were well educated and accomplished ladies, and his house was the resort of the learned and the fashionable. The husbands of all the daughters, excepting Martha, were men who had been liberally educated. Martha had many suitors, and some of the tea-table talk of those days is reported by her grandchildren. She might have married one who was afterwards one of the most distinguished and influential citizens of Barnstable.

Timothy Crocker, Esq., died Jan. 31, 1737, in the 57th year of his age, and is buried in the West Barnstable grave yard. I do not find the record of the death of his wife. She died a short time previous to her husband. His will was made four days previous to his decease. He gave £10 to Rev. Jonathan Russell, £10 to Mr. Joseph Crocker, Jr., and the same sum to the poor of the town. He divides his estate equally among his daughters, excepting to Jerusha, to whom he gave £10 over and above her share. Mr. John Bursley was executor.

His estate was apprised at £6 607,7,2 in old tenor currency, equal to about $3,000 in silver money. The merchandise in his· warehouse was apprised at £1,483,10 ; his homestead, including all his buildings and lands, at £1,020, equal to only $450 in silver. After the payment of his debts, there was only the real estate and £1,949,14 2 of the personal estate remaining, equal to about $300 in silver to each of the heirs.†

In later times the north part of the house was owned by his grand-daughter, Lucretia Sturgis, the school mistress, a maiden lady who is kindly remembered by the aged at West Barnstable ; and the south part by Nathan Foster.

*Conclusion.*—Here I rest ; not because my materials are exhausted, but because I am. Respecting the early families I have studied to be accurate, to the later families I have not given so much attention. Respecting the "Crocker Quarreis," as they are called on the records, I have endeavored to be impartial, and have softened many harsh expressions that I found in my notes, and have omitted some circumstances which perhaps others may think

---

† The very low prices at which the real estate and the furniture was apprised, indicates that a portion of the apprisal was in lawful money—that is, that the pound was equal to $3,33 in silver. His plate and silver was apprised at £73,10, his looking glass and p tures at £5,5, and his Indian girl at £5, about two dollars. If she was worth anything, it was a very low price to apprise her at.

important.  If I have fallen into errors, I shall be happy to make the corrections.  The part which the Crockers played in the Revolution, was one not to be omitted.  It could not be examined without noticing the parts which others acted in the drama.  I do not justify the Crockers, yet I do not believe them to be the worst of men, neither do I believe that Col. Nathaniel Freeman was a man without fault.  The facts will not justify either conclusion. Why, then, the attempt to shield their acts from criticism.  When such attempts are made, most men think there is something wrong at the bottom.  I may attempt, by and by, to do justice to the character of Col. Freeman as a man and patriot; but not by drawing a veil over his faults.  A very few among the Crockers and the Freemans object to certain portions of my article.  I was aware when writing those portions, that I was treading on the scoria of a yet smouldering volcano, which a breath would fan into activity.  I hear the distant rumblings of the approaching earthquake; but do not yet fear that I shall be engulfed thereby.

# CLAP.

Extensive genealogies of the Claps have been printed. Many of this name came over and settled in Dorchester and vicinity. Two of the name were early in Barnstable; but no descendants remain. Eleazer, a son of Dea. Thomas, of Weymouth and Scituate, was a soldier in King Phillip's war, and was slain at Rehobeth March 26, 1675. He had no family in Barnstable.

Increase, resided at West Barnstable, married, Oct. 1675 Elizabeth, Widow of Nathaniel Goodspeed, and daughter of John Bursley. His children born in Barnstable were: 1, John, Oct. 1676; 2, Charity, March, 1677; 3, Thomas, Jan. 1681, died Jan. 1683; 4, Thomas, Dec. 1684.

Increase Clap's house was on the south side of the road a little east of Dexter's lane. He purchased his estate probably of the Rowleys. when they removed to Falmouth, who were early settlers in that neighborhood, and was a proprietor of the common lands "in Rowley's right." He was living in 1697. Several of the Clap family of Scituate intermarried with the Bournes and Gorhams, of Barnstable.

# CAMMET.

I do not find this name in the works of Savage, Bond, Mitchell, or Hinman. Peter Cammet was the first of the name in Barnstable. He married, May 4, 1741, Thankful Bodfish, and had Hannah 26, 1742, and David Sept. 25, 1744. Hannah married, in 1765, John Bates, and those of the name in Barnstable are, I think, descendants of David.

# COTELLE.

___

Peter Cotelle was a Frenchman. He resided in the easterly part of the West Parish, in a small gambrel-roofed house, embowered in trees and shrubbery—an exquisite little place which he took pleasure in adorning. He was a tinker, shrewd in making a trade, and it is said that he would take advantage of his presumed imperfect knowledge of English, to drive a hard bargain. He also kept a small grocery store. He has descendants.

# CANNON.

___

This is not a common name in Barnstable, or in any part of New England. John Cannon came over in the Fortune in 1621. He was not of Plymouth in 1627. Whither he removed or went hence is unknown. There was a Robert Cannon of New London, in 1678, and one of the same name in Essex County in 1680, whose wife's name was Sarah. Mr. Savage states that there was one of the name in Sandwich as early as 1650. Capt. John Cannon was of Norwalk, Conn., 1750.

The earliest record of the name in Barnstable is April 12, 1691, where Joanna Cannon joined the church. On the following Sabbath her children, John, Philip, Timothy, Nathan, and Elizabeth, were baptized. Of these, Timothy is again named on the records. He married, Nov. 9, 1711, Elizabeth, widow of Isaac

Hamblen.   The names of his children are not on the Barnstable records.   Ebenezer was probably his son, and Joanna, who married, July 7, 1735, Benjamin Bursley, was probably a daughter.

Ebenezer ·Cannon married, in 1735, Mercy Blossom ; July 30, 1753, Patience Goodspeed.   His children born in Barnstable were :

I.     Ebenezer, March 19, 1736-7, married, in 1761, Experience Tupper of Dartmouth.*
II.    Ruth, Jan. 18, 1738-9.
III.   Nathan, April 10, 1741, married, March 23, 1763, Thankful Bassett.
IV.    Joanna, Sept. 4, 1743, married, Nov. 28, 1760, Bezalee Waste, of Dartmouth.
V.     Joseph, Dec. 14, 1745.
VI.    Timothy, baptized June 17, 1750.
VII.   Mercy, baptized June 30, 1754.
VIII   Ebenezer, baptized Jan. 30, 1756.*
IX.    Ira, baptized Oct. 12, 1740.
X.     Ziba, baptized Aug. 1762.

---

* The Ebenezer who was published to Deliverance Tupper in 1761, is called Jr.; the Ebenezer baptized June 30, 1756, is called son of Ebenezer and Patience. It is probable that there was yet another Ebenezer.

# CUDWORTH.

---

### GEN. JAMES CUDWORTH.

Little is known of the early history of this most excellent man. It is probable that he came to Boston in 1632, with his friend, Mr. Hatherly, in the ship Charles, from London. In September 1634, he was a householder in Scituate, and a freeman of the colony of New Plymouth. His house was one of the nine first built in that town, and is described as a "small, plaine, palizadoe house." This he sold to Goodman Ensign, and in 1636 built on his lot near the bridge at the harbor.

Mr. Cudworth and his wife joined Mr. Lothrop's church Jan. 18, 1634-5, and till the meeting-house was completed, in November 1636, the congregation frequently met on the Sabbath, and on other special occasions, to worship in his "small, plaine, palizadoe house."

In 1636 he was a member of the Committee appointed by the Court, to revise the Colonial laws; in 1637 he was constable of Scituate; and Jan. 22, 1638-9, one of the grantees of the lands in Sippican, where Mr. Lothrop and a portion of his church then proposed to remove. In 1640 * he removed to Barnstable, and was elected that year a deputy to the Colony Court. In the list of Deputies at the June term his name is underscored, and that of Mr. Thomas Dimmock written against it. In a subsequent entry in the same record it is stated that Mr. Cudworth was then an inhabitant of Scituate, and if so, was not eligible as a member from Barnstable, and therefore Mr. Dimmock was elected in his place. It is probable that Mr. Cudworth came to Barnstable in the Spring of 1640; but did not become a permanent resident

---

*Mr. Freeman says he came to Barnstable in 1639; Mr. Deane says in 1642. The latter is certainly wrong, and after a careful examination of the records, I find no positive evidence that Mr. Freeman is in the right. He certainly did not come in May, 1639, with Messrs. Hull and Dimmock, and I find no evidence that he came in the following October with Mr. Lothrop. Some differences, about this time, had arisen between him and his friend Hatherly, and in the entry on the court orders, June 2, 1640, it is distinctly stated that he was then of Scituate, therefore could not have been of Barnstable at that date, though he was considered one of the proprietors.

till the autumn of that year.

Mr. Cudworth's name appears only once on the records of the town of Barnstable now preserved. It occurs on the list of townsmen and proprietors dated Jan. 1643-4, and its position thereon, indicates that he resided in the vicinity of Coggin's Pond. In the church records he is named as of Barnstable April 18, 1641, March 28, 1642, and June 24, 1644. He conveyed, by deed, his second house and lot in Scituate, to Thomas Ensign, June 8, 1642. In that deed he is styled "gentleman of Barnstable," Jan. 4, 1641-2, he is called an inhabitant of Barnstable, though at that date he was absent from town. In 1642, Mr. Cudworth was again elected a deputy to the June court from Barnstable, and his name was again underscored, and Mr. Thomas Dimmock's written against it. The fact that Barnstable was entitled to only two deputies at the June terms in 1640 and in 1642, and that Anthony Annable and Mr. Dimmock served at those terms, seems to make it certain that Mr. Cudworth was sick, or absent from the town at the terms named. In Aug. 1643, a return was made of all in the colony "able to bear arms." Mr. Cudworth's name appears on the return from Barnstable, and on that from Scituate. On the former it is crossed out, and retained on the latter.

These few isolated facts are all that the records furnish relative to Mr Cudworth's residence in Barnstable. The records of the laying out of the lands at the time of the settlement, being lost, nothing is known respecting his lands in Barnstable. By a municipal regulation, an inhabitant removing from town, was obliged to offer his lands to the other inhabitants, before he could legally sell to a stranger. In such cases a memorandum of the transfer was made on the proprietor's records now lost.†

Mr. Hathway, in his deed to the Conihasset Partners, Dec. 1, 1646, styles him a "salter," that is, one who makes or sells salt, and this fact, perhaps, explains the uncertainty of his place of residence from 1639 to 1646. He had a salt work at Scituate, which it does not appear that he sold on his removal to Barnstable. This required his attention at certain seasons of the year, and explains why he was so often absent from Barnstable. A salt work was erected in Barnstable very early, on the point of land on the west of the entrance of Rendevous Creek, still known

---

† Thomas Bird, Byrd, or Bourd, was at this time a resident in Barnstable, and a servant of Mr. Cudworth. His father, also named Thomas, was one of the earliest settlers in Scituate, and a freeman in 1633. There was a man of the same name at Hartford, and another at Dorchester, one of whom was perhaps the same who was at Barnstable. As Thomas Bird resided only a short time in Barnstable, I have not taken the trouble to investigate his history. In a notice of the criminal calendar of Barnstable, under the title of Casely, I perhaps ought to have mentioned the crime of Bird. In Jan. 1641-2, for running away from his master and breaking into one or more houses in Barnstable, and stealing therefrom "apparel and victuals," he was sentenced to be whipt, once in Barnstable and once in Plymouth. His father settled with Mr Cudworth for the time Thomas had to serve, and the young man was released from the messenger's hands, though not absolved from the punishment of his crimes. He afterwards resided in Scituate.

as Saltern point. This word, Saltern, has now become nearly obsolete. It means a salt work, a building in which salt is made by boiling or solar evaporation. On some ancient records that point is called "salt-pond" point. Who owned or who established this ancient saltern I have been unable to ascertain. It was situated on the Lothrop land, on a parcel that from the situation, I should judge was owned by the Rev. John, and afterwards by his widow Ann. Neither in the wills nor in the settlement of the estates of the Lothrops is any reference had to the salt-work, and I am of the opinion, if the facts in relation to the matter are ever ascertained, they will prove that Gen. James Cudworth was the first who manufactured salt in Barnstable.‡

Before 1646 he returned to Scituate, and became, Dec. 1, 1646, one of the Conihasset Partners. At that time he resided on the South East of Coleman's hills, in a house which he sold to Thomas Robinson before 1650. After this, he resided, during life, on his farm near the little Musquashcut pond in Scituate.

In 1652 he was appointed captain of the militia company in Scituate; in 1649-'50-'51-'52-'53-'54-'55 and '56, a representative to the Court; June 3, 1656, he was chosen an assistant of the Governor, and re-elected in 1657 and 1658. In 1653 he was chosen one of the council of war; March 2, 1657-8 he was discharged, with his own consent, from his office as Captain of the militia company, and in 1659, for the same reason, he was not approved of by the Court as a deputy from Scituate, to which office he had been elected by the people. June 6, 1660, he was required to give bonds, with sufficient surities, for £500 for his appearance at the next October Court, and so from one General Court to another, till the next June, "in reference unto a seditious letter sent for England, the coppy whereof is come over in print." This letter was dated at Scituate in 1658, and was addressed by him to Mr. John Brown, then in England. It has been justly admired for its liberal and Catholic sentiments, clearly and boldly expressed.

---

‡ In 1624 a man was sent over to establish salt works in Plymouth. Gov. Bradford says he was ignorant of the business, vain and self-willed. The facts indicate that the Governor was severe in his judgement. It was evident that, in the variable climate of New England, that salt could not be manufactured by solar evaporation, in the mode common in the south of Spain, or in the West India Islands. On the other hand, the small proportion of salt contained in sea water would render the English process, by boiling in pans, be too tedious and too expensive. His plan seems to have been to reduce the sea water by solar evaporation in ponds and finish the process by boiling in pans. In selecting the sites for his ponds he was unfortunate, whether, as Governor Bradford says, from a lack of good judgment, or for other reasons, does not appear. The ponds did not prove to be tight, and to correct the fault of the bottom and make it more retentive, he covered it with a coating of clay. Similar ponds are constructed by the salt makers at the present day, and errors in the selection of sites are not always to be avoided by men of good judgement. Before this man (his name is not given) had a fair opportunity to test the value of his works, his buildings and most of his pans there, were unfortunately destroyed by fire. The little information preserved respecting the salt work in Barnstable, shows that the method was similar to that adopted by the Plymouth manufacturer. A pond was dug on the high meadow, and a dyke thrown up around it to retain the water, and prevent the ingress of more than was wanted. When the water was reduced to a weak brine by solar evaporation, it was conveyed to pans and the process completed by boiling. There was a similar establishment at Pine Hill, Sandwich.

For the expressions in another letter, addressed by him to the Governor and assistants, he was sentenced at the same court to be disfranchised.

At the Court held Oct. 2, 1660, the printed letter of Mr. Cudworth was read, and Mr. John Brown, who was present, testified that he did receive a letter subscribed by James Cudworth, of Scituate, and that, according to his best recollection, it was substantially the same as the one then read. The bonds for £500, of Mr. Cudworth, were cancelled, and the Court ordered that a civil action should be commenced against him at the next following March term of the Court. When the day came, no action was brought. The absurdity of men sitting as judges, in a case where they themselves were the plaintiffs, was too glaring, and they wisely determined to drop the action.

The firmness displayed by Gen. Cudworth, in these trying times, will ever be a monument to his memory, more endearing than brass or granite. Rather than violate his convictions of right and of duty, he submitted to disfranchisement, ejection from office, and to be placed under a bond for a larger sum than the whole colony could have paid in coin. He did not come over in the Mayflower; but he had adopted as his own, the principles of those who did, and no earthly power could make him swerve from them. Some speak lightly of those principles; but it is ignorance of their character which makes them do so.

The Pilgrims came over with their bibles in their hands, and in their hearts; that holy book was the only creed, to which members of their church were required to give their assent. They held that Christ was the only bishop to whom they owned allegiance, and that the gorgeous vestments of the priests of the Catholic and English churches, and the ceremonial observances required, were anti-Christian, and not in conformity with the usages of the Apostolic age. They came here that they might have liberty to worship God according to the dictates of their own consciences, to establish a pure and simple form of worship for themselves and their posterity. They held that the conscience was free, that man was not responsible to his fellow man for his faith, but to God alone.

These principles lie at the bottom of all that is tolerant in religion, liberal in politics, or worth contending for. The Pilgrims took another step in advance of the prevalent opinions of their time. When about to embark from Leyden, their reverend pastor, in his farewell address, says: "I charge you before God and his blessed angels, that you follow me no further than you have seen me follow the Lord Jesus Christ. The Lord has more truth yet to break forth out of his holy word. I cannot sufficiently bewail the condition of the reformed churches, who are come to a period in religion, and will go at present no further than the instruments of their reformation. Luther and Calvin were

great and shining lights in their times, yet they penetrated not
into the whole counsel of God.   I beseech you, remember it, 'tis
an article of your church covenant, that you be ready to receive
whatever truth shall be made known to you from the written word
of God."

This was not spoken for rhetorical effect, it was a sober truth,
a solemn injunction, not to forget, or transgress a prime article in
their church covenant.   The covenant of the Puritan Church
established in London in 1616, of which Mr. Lothrop was afterwards pastor, was the same in form.   The members of that
church, with joined hands, "solemnly covenanted with each other,
in the presence of Almighty God, to walk together in all Gods
ways and ordinances, according as he had always revealed, or
should further make known to them."   This covenant Mr. Lothrop
brought over with him, and on the 8th day of Jan. 1634, O. S.
(Jan. 18, 1635, N. S.) at Scituate, after spending the day in
fasting, humiliation and prayer, at evening, there was re-union of
those who had been in covenant before.   Mr. Cudworth united
with the church ten days after, and from the expression used in
the record, I infer that he had not been a member of Mr. Lothrop's church in London.

Till 1657, the Plymouth Colony had maintained the principles
of its founders ; but during the preceding twenty-six years, causes
had been in operation which had gradually disturbed the harmony
of sentiment which had at first prevailed.   Rhode Island, influenced by the liberal and intelligent counsels of Roger Williams,
had become the impregnable citadel of toleration in New England.
Massachusetts and Connecticut were founded by men who brought
over with them the same spirit of intolerance, which then prevailed in the mother country.   They enacted severe laws against
the Anna baptists, and more severe against the quakers.
Through the commissioners of the United Colonies, they urged
the magistrates of Plymouth to pass similar laws.

The "first comers" had, among their number, a large proportion of educated men.   There were very few who had not received
the elements of a good education.   They were men of large
experience, intelligent, tolerant in religion, and liberal in their
politics.   These men were the advocates of a learned ministry,
and desirous of establishing schools and seminaries of learning.
In 1657, many of these men had passed away.   Brewster and
Lothrop, the calm yet firm advocates of toleration and liberty,
were dead.   A new race had succeeded—men who had enjoyed
few educational advantages, and who, in their ignorance of better
things, had imbibed intolerant, and illiberal principles.

During this period many new men had been introduced into
the colony, some from Massachusetts, but mostly from the eastern
country.   Among these were many who had no sympathy for the

institutions established by the Puritans.   There was also another class—disappointed politicians—like George Barlow of Sandwich, of which I have had occasion to speak in no complimentary terms.

The effect on the churches was disastrous.   The Barnstable Church was rent in twain, and the difficulties did not end till the settlement of Mr. Walley in 1662.   There were divisions in the old Plymouth Church, in fact in almost every church in the colony.

A large majority of those known as first comers, then surviving, sympathized with Mr. Cudworth.   Scituate was very nearly unanimous in his support, so were a large majority in Sandwich and in Barnstable.   Of the state of feeling in other towns at that period, I have no means of correctly ascertaining.

Such was the state of public feeling in the colony in the summer of 1657; yet such was the reverence of the people for the institutions first established, that the magistrates and representatives hesitated in passing the laws recommended by the commissioners.   They simply ordained, says Mr. Cudworth, that the word "and" in an old law, should be changed to "or."   This apparently small and unimportant alteration changed, as will be seen, a salutary or harmless law, into an instrument of tyranny.

This change would have been inoperative if there had not been men in the colony in whom the spirit of persecution only slumbered, who were ready to catch at every straw and urge the people on to acts of madness.   Of this class was George Barlow of Sandwich, and as he was the type of the class, some account of him will not be out of place, in order to show what kind of men Cudworth, Hatherly and Robinson, had to contend with.

The four years from 1657 to 1661, have been called the dark ages of the colony.   It is unpleasant to recount the events of those years—to be forced to admit that such excellent men as Thomas Hinckley, Josiah Winslow, Thomas Prence, John Alden, and others, adjured, for the time being, the liberal principles of civil polity which the fathers professed, and were led astray by a senseless clamour from without, and by factious and ambitious men within.   That they unwillingly consented to enact laws restraining political and religious freedom is evident, from the statements in the letter of Mr. Cudworth to Mr. Brown ; and that they lived to regret their hasty and inconsiderate action, is verified by their subsequent acts ; but that unwillingness, and that regret does not blot from the memory, or from the statute book, the unjust laws which they sanctioned and enforced.   The precedents established in Massachusetts and Connecticut are no excuse, they and their associates were the rulers of a free and independent colony and were amenable at the bar of public opinion for their acts.*

The Puritans have suffered more from over zealous friends, than from open and avowed enemies. A community is an aggregation of individuals—one rule of act applies to both, and he that attempts to conceal or paliate wrong, does an injury to him whom he thus essays to defend. The Plymouth Colony existed seventy-one years. During sixty-seven, with the exception of a short period during the usurpation of Andros, the people enjoyed a mild, a liberal, and a paternal government. Shall we cease to honor the institutions they established because, during four years, a bigoted majority were false to the principles of the fathers?

George Barlow was the type of a class who, in 1657, inaugurated a system of terrorism in the Old Colony, and it may be truthfully said that he made more converts to the doctrines of the Quakers than all their preachers. The spirit of persecution which he was largely instrumental in introducing, raised up opponents who at first sympathized with the sufferers then with their doctrines which they at last embraced. In the towns where the Quaker preachers were not opposed and persecuted, they made no proselytes, but where they were persecuted, there they made many converts.

In a former article I have spoken of George Barlow, not in terms of commendation. The Puritans and Quakers, though opposed to each other, agreed in this, that George Barlow was a bad man. No one speaks well of him. Of his early history I know nothing. He was of Boston or vicinity in 1637, perhaps earlier. In the records of the Quarter Court held at Boston and Newtown 19th Sept. 1637, is the following entry: "George Barlow, for idleness, is censured to be whipped." From Boston he went to the eastern country, and was at Exeter in 1639, and at Saco in 1652. At these places and elsewhere, says Mr. Savage, he exercised his gifts as a preacher. On the 5th of July, 1653, at a court held at Wells, by Richard Bellingham and others, commissioners of the Massachusetts Colony, George Barlow and fifteen others, inhabitants of Saco, acknowledged themselves to be subject to the government of that Colony, and took the freemans'

---

* He that supposes that Gov. Hinckley, and those who acted with him, had neither law nor reason on their side, is mistaken. They had both. The lands in the several towns were granted on the express condition that an Orthodox church should be gathered, of at least forty families, and that a learned minister should be supported out of the products of those lands. These were legal conditions, and the grantees were bound by them. Gov. Hinckley was the best read lawyer in the Colony, and he examined the question only in its legal aspect. On that ground he was right. Whether his course was judicious is another and entirely different question. The Puritans were equally severe against men who attempted to disregard the conditions on which the lands were granted. Rev. Joseph Hull, whose learning and Orthodoxy, for making such an attempt, was excommunicated and forbidden to preach. Mr. Cudworth considered the rights of conscience as paramount to the legal obligation. Gov. Hinckley thought otherwise, and that was the point at issue between them.

oath in open court. In the record of the proceedings of the same court the following passage occurs :

"Several of the inhabitants complained that George Barlow is a disturbance to the place, the commissioners thought meet to forbid the said George Barlow any more publickly to preach or prophesy, under the penalty of ten pounds for every offence."

Soon after the last date he removed to Newbury. Of his character while an inhabitant of that town, Mr. Thomas Clark affirmed in open court, at Plymouth, on the 13th of June 1660, "that he is such an one that he is a shame and reproach to all his masters ; and that he, the said Barlow, stands convicted and recorded of a lye att Newbury."

In 1657 he was of Sandwich, and June 1, 1658, he was appointed by the Plymouth Colony Court, marshal of Sandwich, Barnstable and Yarmouth, with "full power to act as constable in all things in the town of Sandwich." Oct. 2, he was commissioned to apprehend Quakers coming to Manomett, or places adjacent, in boats. June 7, 1659, he was allowed to be a towsman of Sandwich, and June 5, 1661, his authority, as marshal, was extended to all places in the Colony.

March 5, 1660-1. The court ordered George Barlow "to pay a fine of twenty shillings to Benjamin Allen, for causing him to sit in the stocks at Sandwich the greater part of a night, without cause, and for other wrongs done by him unto the said Allen." Barlow was also ordered to return unto Ralph Allen a shirt and some other small linen, which he took from him, in the pursuit of Wenlock."

March 4, 1661-2. "George Barlow and his wife were both severely reproved for their most ungodly living in contention, one with the other, and admonished to live otherwise." (See Colony Records, Vol. 4, pages 7 and 10.) In May, 1665, he was put under bonds for his good behavior, and in the following March he was fined 10 shillings for being drunk a second time.

The foregoing extracts are from the records of the friends of Barlow, and it is safe to infer that they did not admit that which was not true. This evidence establishes the following points : That he was an idle fellow, a disturber of the public peace ; that he was a shame and reproach to all his masters ; that he was not truthful ; that he was tyrannical, that he was quarrelsome, and that he was a drunkard. In addition to the testimony of Gov. Thomas Prence may be added, it is reported that he made this remark respecting Barlow, "That an honest man would not have, or hardly would take his place." (Bishop, page 388.)

The following testimony is extracted from the writings of the Quakers. I quote from Bishop's New England Judged, (London Edition) because he is more accurate in his statement of facts than many of the early writers among the friends. In the fea-

tures of these men the poet Whittier says you could read:
> "My life is hunted—evil men
> Are following in my track;
> The traces of the torturer's whip
> Are on my aged back."

Naturally, however meek a man may be, it is hardly to be expected that a man having the traces of the whip on his own person, can describe so calmly as one who had not suffered. Bishop, Vol. 1, page 389, says: "As for this Barlow, his natural inclination is to be lazy, filthy and base to all. In his former years, he was one of the Protectors Preachers at Exeter, in New England and elsewhere; of which being weary, or having worn that trade out, or it having worn out him, he turned lawyer and so came into Plymouth Patent, where he became a notorious spoiler of the goods of the innocent by being a marshal."

June 23, 1658, Marshal Barlow arrested Christopher Holder and John Copeland,* two Quaker preachers, while on their way to a meeting in Sandwich. They had been banished from the Colony on the 2d of the preceding February, and had been whipt at Plymouth on the 8th of that month for not complying with the order of the Courts. Barlow carried them before the selectmen of Sandwich, who had been appointed by the Court, in the absence of a magistrate, to witness the execution of the law. They "entertaining no desire to sanction measures so severe towards those who differed from them in religion, declined to act in the case." Barlow, disappointed at the refusal, took the prisoners to his house, where he kept them six days, and then on 29th of June, carried them before Mr. Thomas Hinckley of Barnstable, who had that month been elected one of the magistrates and an assistant of Gov. Prence. Bishop, page 184, thus describes the scene at the execution: "They, (Christopher Holden and John Copeland) being tied to an old post, had thirty-three cruel stripes laid upon them with a new tormenting whip, with three cords, and knots at the ends, made by the Marshal, and brought with him. At the sight of which cruel and bloody execution, one of the spectators (for there were many who witnessed against it) cried out in the grief and anguish of her spirit, saying: "How long, Lord, shall it be ere thou avenge the blood of thine elect?" And afterwards bewailing herself, and lamenting her loss, said: "Did I forsake father and mother, and all my dear

---

* Before 1654 Christopher Holder resided at Winterbourne, in Gloucestershire, England. He is represented to be a well educated man and of good estate. He came to New England in 1656 and again in 1657, and spent the winter of that year in the West Indies. He returned to England in 1660 and there married Mary, daughter of Richard and Katherine Scott, of Providence, R. I. He repeatedly visited America and other countries, and suffered much in his native country and in foreign Lands. He died July 13, 1688, aged about 60. John Copeland was from Yorkshire and had also been well educated. He came to America in 1657. In 1661 he was in London, and in 1687 he was in Virginia. He married thrice, and died at North Cave, County of York, March 9, 1718, very aged. Among the first settlers it is probable they found many whom they had known in England

relations, to come to New England for this? Did I ever think New England would come to this? Who could have thought it?" And this Thomas Hinckley saw done, to whom the Marshal repaired for that purpose.†

"The Friends of Sandwich, aware of the hatred which the Barnstable magistrate had to Quakerism, with a view to cheer their brethren in bonds, accompanied them thither. These were new proceedings at Barnstable, and caused no little sensation among the quiet settlers of the district. They felt that however erroneous Quakerism might be, such conduct on the part of their rulers did not consist with the religion of Jesus." (Bowden.)

Bishop (pages 188 and 189) says that when Barlow went, in 1659, to arrest Edward Perry, "he was so drunk that he could hardly forbear vomiting in the bosom of him whom he pretended to press" as his aid. A friend of Perry who was present said to him, "Yea, George, thou mayst wash thy hands, but thou canst not wash thy heart." He answered, still laughing and jeering, and said, "Yes, one dram of the bottle will do it," and clapped his hand on his bosom. Unto which kind of washing, it seems, he is used to much, viz : To be drunk, and then to be mad, and to beat his wife and children like a mad man ; and to throw the things of the house from one place to another."

Many passages from the early writers to the same effect might be quoted. That he was honest there is much reason to doubt. Thomas Ewer charged him in open court with having on a garment made from cloth stolen from him. Barlow also encouraged and justified his children in stripping the fruits from the orchard of his neighbor Thomas Johnson. An Indian took a knife from an Englishman's house, and being told he should not steal, he answered, "I thought so, but Barlow steals from the Quakers, and why may not I do the same?"

It has already been stated that a majority of the Plymouth Colony Court had pronounced the letter of Mr. Cudworth to Mr. Brown to be *seditious*. The foregoing extracts clearly establish one point, and that is, his denunciations of Barlow are not *seditious*, without it can be proved that telling the truth is *sedition*. The other statements in his letter will also be verified by extracts from the records and contemporaneous authorities.

George Barlow does not appear to have had a family when he

---

† Mr. John Whitney in Truth and Innocency defended. London edition, 1702, page 26, describes the scene at Barnstable substantially as above; but his language is wanting in clearness. Bowden does not refer to Whitney; but he was probably misled by the ambiguous language of that author. He represents that the residence of the magistrate was "about two miles distant." It should be twelve miles. This is probably a mistake of the printer. He adds, (page 116, London edition.) "This functionary, after a frivolous examination of the prisoners, ordered them to be tied to the post of an out-house; and then, turning executioner, he gave each of them thirity-three lashes." I should not notice this gross scandal if it had not been copied by other historians without comment. (See annals of Sandwich, pages 60 and 61.) No trustworthy authority can be quoted in its support—its falsity is apparent. Bowden is usually very cautious in his statements. He refers to Norton's Ensign as his authority; but he evidently relied on and was misled by the ambiguous language of Whiting.

came to Sandwich. He married Jane, widow of the lamented Anthony Besse. She had then a son Nehemiah, ancestor of the Besses of Sandwich, Wareham, and other towns, and three daughters. By her second husband she had a son John, ancestor of some of the Barlows in Sandwich, &c.

Details of his brutality as the master of a family, have already been given. From Mr. Besse's once "sweet home," peace, comfort, and happiness, were banished. Morning and evening prayer and praise had ascended from the family altar, now desecrated by impiety and drunken revelries. The little ones who had been brought up to be kind and affectionate, one towards the other, were now rude and disobedient, and taught that it was no sin to steal from those who were not members of their church.

Barlow made high pretension to piety, and became a member of the Sandwich church. He also claimed to have studied the law, and essayed to be a lawyer. By his pretended piety, and by his plausible address, he at first deceived the unsuspecting Puritans, and they appointed him to a responsible office. This they did ignorantly, and no blame can attach to the court; but he was continued in office, and his authority enlarged, after his true character was known. For this, it is difficult to frame a sufficient excuse.

The worst of men usually have some redeeming traits of Character. Contemporaneous authorities say nothing in his favor. He was hated by every member of his family, wife, sons, daughter, and daughters-in-law; despised and avoided by his neighbors —a blot on the annals of the Old Colony which time will never wipe out.

Barlow, in the latter part of his life, was never sober of his own free choice—as an officer he was unfeeling and tyrannical, and seemed to take pleasure in wringing the last penny from the hard hand of industry—in dragging men and women to the prison and the whipping post. His career was short. An outraged people hurled him from office, and in his old age he craved charity from those for whom he had shown no piety in the day of his power.

The early writers furnish many details of his cruel acts. I shall relate one, and prefer giving it as it has been preserved by tradition.‡

---

‡ Among the first settlers in Sandwich was George Allen, a man of good standing among the Puritans, notwithstanding he was an Ana baptist. The house which he built at Spring Hill in 1646, is now owned by Mrs. Eliza C. Wing, is in good repair, and will probably last another century. He died in 1648, leaving nine children mentioned in his will, four of whom are named, Matthew, Henry, Samuel and William, the other five least children not named. Brown says that six brothers and sisters of this family were among the earliest who embraced the principles of the Friends. He says that Ralph Allen was his son, and George, Jr., was probably another. The two last named must have been men grown when they came to this country, for George had taken the oath of fidelity in England. The Allens settled at Spring Hill, and two or more of their houses yet remain, and are probably as old as any in Massachusetts. The one in which the early quakers met for many successive years, is still standing, and remained in the family till 1862, when it was sold to Frank Kerns, the present owner.

The traveller from Sandwich to Barnstable has, perhaps, noticed the ancient and substantial dwelling houses near Spring Hill.  Some of these have stood two centuries, and were the residences of the early Quakers.  In 1659 William Allen was the occupant of one of them.  He was a young man, married, March 21, 1649-50, Priscilla Brown.  His fines amounted to £86,17, and were imposed for the following offences :  £40 for twenty meetings at his house ;  £4 for attending meetings at other places ;  £5 for entertaining Quakers ;  £25 for refusing to take the oath of fidelity ;  £1 for not removing his hat in court, and the balance for expenses, &c.

In payment for these fines there was taken from him at different times :

| | |
|---|---:|
| 18 head of cattle, apprised at | £64,10 |
| 1 mare and a horse of which he was half owner ; but | |
| according to the Treasurer's accounts mare and 2 colts, | 19,10 |
| 8 bushels of corn and a hogshead, | 1,07 |
| Corn at another time, | 1,10 |
| | £86,17 |

In addition, a brass kettle was taken in payment of a fine of £1, imposed in 1660 for wearing his hat in court.  These distraints were made by Barlow at different times, and some particulars may be found in Bishop.  In the winter of 1660-61 William Allen was in Sandwich.  In June, 1661, he and 27 others were released from prison in Boston, the authorities having received intelligence that King Charles would order all Quakers imprisoned to be sent over to England for trial.  The mandamus or letter of the King was received in November, 1661, and in the Plymouth Colony persecutions and the exacting of fines ceased ; but in Massachusetts the magistrates found means to evade the royal authority, and persecutions did not entirely cease for several years.

Sandwich suffered more than all the other towns in the Plymouth Colony—in fact, only a few and unimportant cases occurred out of that town.  Many of those who were imprisoned in Boston were Sandwich men who went there on business.  Though two centuries have passed, it is not surprising that many particulars respecting the persecutions in Sandwich have been preserved.

Accounts of the sufferings endured by the Quakers in Boston, Sandwich, and other places, immediately after the events occured, were published in London, and were read by all classes.  Such events are not soon forgotten, and it takes many generations to eradicate the memory thereof from the minds of the descendants of the sufferers.  In Sandwich the principle facts have been preserved by tradition, even the localities where the events occurred are pointed out.  The preservation of so many of the houses of the first Quakers, the ownership whereof for successive generations, can be ascertained by deeds, wills, and other legal instruments, has aided in keeping in memory locations which would otherwise have been forgotten. The following incidents, said to have occurred when Barlow made his last distraint on the goods of William Allen, are yet related, and the exact location where they occurred pointed out. This story of wrong is in some particulars differently related by different persons; but the leading facts are confirmed by the records.

On the south side of Spring Hill, in Sandwich, in one of those cosey nooks, which the first comers selected for their house lots, sheltered by hills from the bleak north and west winds, the traveller on the Cape Cod Railroad has perhaps noticed an ancient dwelling which the renovating hand of modern improvement has allowed to remain as it was one hundred and fifty years ago. In 1658 it was owned by William Allen.* He and his wife Priscilla

---

\* William Allen's House. Mr. Newell Hoxie who has made the study of the antiquities of Spring Hill a speciality, is of the opinion that William Allen, in 1658, resided in a house nearer the grave yard than the Alden Allen house. The history of the latter can be traced by records from the year 1672. It was then the residence of William Allen, and continued to be till his death in 1705, when he bequeathed it to Daniel, son of his brother George, reserving the use of the south end for the meetings of the Quakers in the winter as had been customary. Daniel bequeathed it to his son Cornelius, Cornelius to his son George, George to his son William, and William to his son Alden who died Jan. 8, 1858, aged 80.

To determine the question of the age of this house I have spent some time. Outwardly the style indicates about the year 1680 as the date of its erection; but on comparing the description of the appearance of the framing and interior arrangements furnished me by Mr. Hoxie, with the description thereof given in 1705, by the apprisers of the estate of William Allen, I am satisfied that it has been enlarged three, if not four times since originally built. The original house was 18 feet by 23, two stories high  In the life time of William Allen a leanto was added on the west for a kitchen, and an addition made on the south one story high, with a leanto roof, in the style popularly known as a "salt box." Under the salt box there was a cellar. This corresponds with the description of the building in 1705 on the Probate Records. Soon after this date the "salt box" was removed or enlarged, and an addition made corresponding in size and appearance with the ancient part, making the main building 18 by 40 feet, two stories high, not including the leanto on the west, and precisely in the form it now remains. The objection to this view is, the framing of the north and south ends are precisely alike, the posts on the south not having been spliced, making it probable that both ends were built at the same time, but if so the description of the apprisers of Allen's estate is incorrect. The position of the cellar and chimney indicates that both ends were not built at the same time, and the plates are spliced precisely at the place where the addition was probably made. It may have been John Newland's house, which William Allen bought about the year 1680, but the location of Newland's house is said to have been on the south of the swamp, the cellar whereof yet remains.

All the old houses at Spring Hill have undergone similar transformations since they were built. The Wing house, probably the oldest house in Massachusetts, built before 1643 as a fortification, has been altered so often that little of the original remains. The George Allen built, according to a mark thereon in 1646, is in good preservation.

The conclusion to which I have arrived is this, that it is not perfectly certain that William Allen resided in the Alden Allen house in 1660. It is difficult to prove such a question. He may have lived in a house nearer the "grave yard," as tradition says. Portions of the tradition to which I refer are proved erroneous, namely, that William Allen married two wives, the records show that his first wife Priscilla survived him; that having no issue he devised his estate to Gideon Allen, the records show that he bequeathed it to his nephew Daniel. Both houses were near the "grave yard," and nothing is proved by that expression, and if the tradition is erroneous, as above shown, in important particulars, it creates a doubt at least, whether or not it is accurate in regard to the exact location of William Allen's house in the year 1660.

William Allen died in the Alden Allen house Oct. 1, 1705, aged about 80 years, having lived in the marriage relation fifty-five years with his wife Priscilla, who survived him, certainly thirty-three years in the house in which he died, probably the whole period. His house, during the latter part of his life, and when owned by his successors Daniel, Cornelius, George, and William, was the resort of numerous Friends at their quarterly, monthly, and weekly meeetings. The occupants were hospitable and provided liberally for all who came. It should be regarded by the Friends as their "Mecca" and be preserved as a monument of the "olden time." The associations connected with that old "south end" would be pleasant.

were among the first in Sandwich who embraced the principles of the Quakers.  His father was an Ana Baptist, a sect that held to some of the peculiar doctrines of the Quakers.  His six sons and others in Sandwich belonged to the same sect, or sympathized in the views of the elder Allen, and readily received the doctrines of the Quakers.  The father had, ten years before the time of Barlow, "laid down his life in peace."  His sons were industrious and prudent.  William had accumlated a good estate for those times, was hospitable, and his house was the resort of the early Friends. The distraints which the Marshal had made in 1658 and 9, in payment of the fines which had been imposed on him, had strip't him of nearly all his goods.  His house, his lands, a cow, left "out of pity," a little corn, and a few articles of household furniture, were all that remained, and he was living on bread and water, a prisoner in the common jail in Boston.  These things did not move him, he held fast to his faith.

Such was the condition of the family, when the Marshal appeared with a warrant to collect additional fines.  The sanctimonious Barlow was drunk.  The distress of the wife did not move him.  He took the cow which had been left "out of pity," the little corn remaining, and a bag of meal which a kind neighbor had just brought from the mill.  This was insufficient.  He seized a copper kettle, (two iron pots according to one tradition) the only one remaining, and then mockingly addressing Mrs. Allen, said : "Now Priscilla, how will thee cook for thy family and friends, thee has no kettle."  Mrs. Allen meekly replied : "George, that God who hears the young ravens when they cry, will provide for them.  I trust in that God, and I verily believe the time will come when thy necessity will be greater than mine." George carried away the goods, but he remembered the "testimony" and lived to see it verified.

Friends, and among them were many who had no sympathy for the doctrines of the Quakers, immediately provided for all Mrs. Allen's wants, and soon after the trembling Magistrates of Massachusetts, fearing that the royal displeasure would be visited on their own heads, opened their prison doors, and ordered all who were in bonds, for conscience sake, to depart.

The letter of King Charles was dated Sept. 9, 1661, and was addressed to all the Governors, Magistrates, &c., in his colonies in New England, ordering them "to forbear to proceed any further" against the Quakers, and to send such as were imprisoned to England for trial.  The bearer of this dispatch was Samuel Shattuck, a Quaker, who had been banished from Massachusetts on pain of death.  He delivered the King's letter to Gov. Endicot. It must have been exceedingly mortifying to the Magistrates, to

The men, whose names now belong to history, met there, they took sweet counsel together, and there would some of their descendants delight to assemble and recall the memories of the past.

have been obliged to give audience to, and receive the King's letter from the hands of one whom they had banished.

The news of the King's letter fell like a thunderbolt on Barlow. He had grown rich "on the spoils of the innocent," but in after times he was very poor, and often wished for the return of "the good times," as he called the four years from 1657 to 1661. In his old age he often craved Priscilla's charity. She always administered to his wants, and though he never went from her door empty handed, yet he was never grateful; and was always sighing for the return of the "good old times."

Barlow died as he lived, a poor miserable drunkard. No loving hand smoothed his brow in death, and no stone tells where he lies.

It is not surprising that the persecutions of the Quakers at Sandwich should have aroused the indignation of such men as Cudworth, Hatherly, and Robinson—it is surprising that the acts of Barlow should have found an apologist in the Old Colony. William Allen was not the greatest sufferer. Edward Perry, who resided at East Sandwich, was wealthy, a man who had been well educated, he suffered more. Robert Harper had his house and lands and all that he had taken, and suffered many cruel imprisonments and punishments. Thomas Johnson, the poor weaver, to whom Mr. Cudworth refers, was strip't of all he had. Not only were their goods taken from them, and cruel punishments inflicted; but they were disfranchised, even those who were of the first settlers and had lived in Sandwich twenty years. Oct. 2, 1658, nine were disfranchised by the Colony Court, for being, or sympathizing with the Quakers, and it was farther ordered, that no man should thereafter be admitted an inhabitant of Sandwich, or enjoy the privileges thereof without the approbation of the church, Gov. Prence, or one of the assistants.

During the Protectorates in England a similar feeling existed there, and the injudicious legislation of New England was only the echo of the Puritan opinion in the mother country. Mr. Palfrey in his excellent history of New England, remarks on this subject: "The Puritan's mistake at a later period was: that he undertook by public regulation what public regulation can never achieve, and by aiming to form a nation of saints, introduced hypocrites among them to defeat their objects and bring scandal on their cause, while the saints were made no more numerous and no better."

The following letter of Mr. Cudworth to Mr. John Brown was written in December 1658, and printed the next year in England, and probably had an influence in determining King Charles to issue his letter or mandamus. Mr. Deane, in his history of Scituate, publishes the letter substantially, omitting many passages and modernizing the language in some instances.   I prefer to give the letter as written by Mr. Cudworth:

## LETTER OF JAMES CUDWORTH.

SCITUATE, 10th mo. 1658.

As for the State and condition of Things amongst us, it is Sad, and like so to continue; the Antichristian Persecuting Spirit is very active, and that in the Powers of this World: He that will not whip and Lash, Persecute and Punish Men that Differ in Matters of Religion, must not sit on the Bench, nor sustain any Office in the Common-wealth.   Last election, Mr. Hatherly, and my Self, left off the Bench, and my self Discharged of my Captainship, because I had Entertained some of the Quakers at my House (thereby that I might be the better acquainted with their Principles) I thought it better fo to do, than with the blind World, to Censure, Condemn, Rail at, and Revile them, when they neither faw their Persons, nor knew any of their Principles: But the Quakers and my felf cannot close in divers Things; and fo I signified to the Court, I was no Quaker, but must bear my Testimony against sundry Things that they held, as I had Occasion and Opportunity: But withal, I told them, That as I was no Quaker, fo I would be no Persecutor.   This Spirit did Work those two Years that I was of the Magistracy; during which time I was on sundry Occasions forced to declare my Dissent, in sundry Actings of that Nature; which, altho' done with all Moderation of Expression, together with due respect unto the Rest, yet it wrought great Disaffection and Prejudice in them, against me; so that if I should say, some of themselves set others on Work to frame a Petition against me, that so they might have a seeming Ground from others (tho' first moved and acted by themselves, to lay what they could under Reproach) I should do no wrong.   The Petition was with Nineteen Hands; it will be too long to make Rehearsal: It wrought such a disturbance in our Town, and in our Military Company, that when the Act of Court was read in the Head of the Company, had I not been present, and made a Speech to them, I fear there had been such Actings as would have been of a sad Consequence.   The Court was again followed with another Petition of Fifty Four Hands, and the Court returned the Petitioners an Answer with such plausibleness of Speech, carrying with it great shew of Respect to them, readily acknowledging, with the Petitioners, my Parts and Gifts, and how useful I had been in my Place; Professing, they had nothing at all against me, only in that thing of giving Entertainment to Quakers; whereas, I broke no Law in giving them a Night's Lodging or two, and some Victuals: For, our Law then was,—If any Entertain a Quaker, and keep him after he is warned by a Magistrate to Depart, the Party so Entertaining, shall pay Twenty Shillings a Week, for Entertaining them.—Since hath been made a Law,—

If any Entertain a Quaker, if but a quarter of an Hour, he is to forfeit Five Pounds.—Another,—That if any see a Quaker, he is bound, if he live Six Miles or more from the Constable, yet he must presently go and give Notice to the Constable, or else is subject to the Censure of the Court (which may be hanging)—Another,—That if the Constable know, or hear of any Quaker in his Precincts, he is presently to Apprehend him, and if he will not presently Depart the Town, the Constable is to whip him, and send him away. The divers have been Whipped with us in our Patent; and truly to tell you plainly, that the Whipping of them with that Cruelty, as some have been Whipp'd, and their Patience under it, has sometimes been the Occasion of gaining more Adherence to them, than if they had suffered them openly to have preached a Sermon.

—Also another Law,—That if there be a Quakers Meeting any where in the Colony, the Party in whose House or on whose Ground it is, is to pay Forty Shillings; The Preaching-Quaker Forty Shillings; every Hearer Forty Shillings: Yea, and if they have Meetings, thou' nothing be spoken, when they so meet, which they say, so it falls out sometimes——Our last Law,——That now they are to be Apprehended, and carried before a Magistrate, and by him committed to be kept close Prisoners, until they will promise to depart, and never come again; and will also pay their Fees—(which I preceive they will do neither the one nor the other) and they must be kept only with the Counties Allowance, which is but small (namely Course Bread and Water) No Friend may bring them any thing; none may be permitted to speak with them; Nay, if they have money of their own, they may not make use of that to relieve themselves.——

In the Massachusetts (namely, Boston-Colony) after they have Whipp'd them, they Cut their Ears, they have now, at last, gone the furthest step they can, They Banish them upon pain of Death, if they ever come there again. We expect that we must do the like; we must Dance After their Pipe: Now Plimouth-Saddle is on the Bay-Horse (viz. Boston) we shall follow them on the Career: For, it is well if in some there be not a Desire to be their Apes and Imitators in all their Proceedings in things of this Nature.

All these Carnel and Antichristian Ways being not of God's Appointment, effect nothing as to the Obstructing or Hindring of them in their way or Course. It is only the Word or Spirit of the Lord that is able to Convince Gainsayers: They are the Mighty Weapons of a Christian's Warfare, by which Great and Mighty Things are done and accomplished.

They have many Meetings, and many Adherents, almost the whole Town of Sandwich is adhering towards them; and give me leave a little to acquaint you with their Sufferings, which is Grievous unto, and Saddens the Heart of most of the Precious Saints of God ; It lies down and rises up with them, and they cannot put it put of their minds, to see and hear of poor Families deprived of their Comforts, and brought into Penury and Want (you may say. By what Means? And, to what .End?) As far as I am able to judge of the End, It is to force them from their Homes and lawful Habitations, and to drive them out of their Coasts. The Massachusetts have Banish'd Six of their Inhabitants, to be gone upon pain of Death ; and I wish that Blood be not shed : But our poor People are pillaged and plundered of their Goods ; and haply, when they have no more to satisfy their unsatiable Desire, at last may be forced to flee, and glad they have their Lives for a Prey.

As for the Means by which they are impoverished ; These in the first place were Scrupulous of an Oath ; why then we must put in Force an old Law,—That all must take the Oath of Fidelity. This being tendered, they will not take it ; and then we must add more Force to the Law ; and that is,—If any Man refuse, or neglect to take it by such a time, he shall pay Five Pounds, or depart the Colony.—When the time is come, they are the same as they were ; Then goes out the Marshal, and fetcheth away their Cows and other Cattle. Well, another Court comes, They are required to take the Oath again, — They cannot—Then Five Pounds more : On this Account Thirty Five Head of Cattle, as I have been credibly informed, hath been by the Authority of our Court taken from them the latter part of this Summer ; and these people say,——If they have more right to them, than themselves, Let them take them.——Some that had a Cow only, some Two Cows, some Three Cows, and many small Children in their Families, to whom, in Summer time, a Cow or Two was the greatest Outward Comfort they had for their Subsistence. A poor Weaver that had Seven or Eight small children ( I know not which) he himself Lame in his Body, had but Two Cows, and both taken from him. The Marshal asked him, What he would do? He must have his Cows. The Man said,——That God that gave him them, he doubted not, but would still provide for him.——

To fill up the measure yet more full, tho' to the further emptying of Sandwich-Men of their outward Comforts. The last Court of Assistants, the first Tuesday of this Instant, the Court was pleased to determine Fines on Sandwich-Men for Meetings, sometimes on First Days of the Week, sometimes on other Days, as they say : They meet ordinarily twice in a Week, besides the Lord's Day, One Hundred and Fifty Pounds, whereof W. Newland is Twenty Four Pounds, for himself and his Wife, at Ten Shillings a Meeting. W. Allen Forty Six Pounds, some affirm it Forty Nine Pounds. The poor Weaver afore spoken of, Twenty Pounds, Brother Cook told me, one of the Brethen at Barnstable

certified him, That he was in the Weaver's House, when cruel
Barloe (Sandwich Marshal) came to demand the Sum, and said,
he was fully informed of all the poor Man had, and thought, if all
lay together, it was not worth Ten Pounds. What will be the
end of such Courses and Practices, the Lord only knows. I
heartily and earnestly pray, that these, and such like Courses,
neither raise up among us, or bring in upon us, either the Sword, or
any devouring Calamity, as a just Avenger of the Lord's Quarrel,
for Acts of Injustice and Oppression ; and that we may every one
find out the Plague of his own Heart ; and putting away the Evils
of his own Doings, and meet the Lord by Entreaties of Peace,
before it be too late, and there be no Remedy.

Our Civil Powers are so exercised in Things appertaining to
the Kingdom of Christ, in Matters of Religion and Conscience,
that we have no time to effect any thing that tends to the Promo-
tion of the Civil Weal, or the prosperity of the Place ; but now we
must have a State-Religion, such as the Powers of the World will
allow, and no other : A State-Ministry, and a State way of
Maintenance : And we must Worship and Serve the Lord Jesus
as the World shall appoint us : We must all go to the publick
Place of Meeting, in the Parish where he dwells, or be prevented ;
I am Informed of Three or Fourscore, last Court presented, for
not coming to publick Meetings ; and let me tell you how they
brought this about : You may remember a Law once made, call'd
Thomas Hinckley's Law,—That if any neglected the Worship of
God, in the Place where he lives, and sets up a Worship contrary
to God, and the Allowance of this Government, to the public
Prophanation of God's Holy Day and Ordinance, shall pay Ten
Shillings.—This Law would not reach what then was aimed at :
Because he must do so and so ; that is, all things therein expressed, or else break not the Law.  In March last a Court of
Deputies was called, and some Acts touching Quakers were made ;
and then they contrived to make this Law serviceable to them ;
and that was by putting out the word [and] and putting in the
word [or] which is a Disjunctive, and makes every Branch to
become a Law.  So now, if any do neglect, or will not come to
the publick Meetings, Ten Shillings for every Defect.  Certainly
we either have less Wit, or more Money, than the Massachusetts :
For, for Five Shilling a Day, a man may stay away, till it come to
Twelve or Thirteen Pounds, if he had it but to pay them : And
these Men altering this Law now in March, yet left it Dated,
June 6, 1651, and so it stands as the Act of a General Court ;
they to be the Authors of it Seven Years before it was in being ;
and so you your selves have your part and share in it, if the
Recorder lye not.  But what may be the Reason that they should
not by another Law, made and dated by that Court, as well effect
what was intended, as by altering a Word, and so the whole sense

of the Law ; and leave this their Act by the Date of it charged on another Court's Account? Surely the chief Instruments in the Business, being privy to an Act of Parliament for Liberty, should too openly have acted repugnant to a Law of England ; but if they can do the Thing, and leave it on a Court, as making it Six Years before the Act of Parliament, there can be no danger in this.    And that they were privy to the Act of Parliament for Liberty, to be then in being, is evident, That the Deputies might be free so act it.    They told us, That now the Protector stood not engaged to the Articles for Liberty, for the Parliament had now taken the Power into their own Hands, and had given the Protector a new Oath, Only in General, to maintain the Protestant Religion ; and so produced the Oath in a Paper, in Writing ; whereas, the Act of Parliament, and the Oath, are both in one Book, in Print : So that they who were privy to the one, could not be Ignorant of the other.    But still all is well, if we can keep the People Ignorant of their Liberties and Priviledges, that we have Liberty to Act in our own Wills what we please.

We are wrapped up in a Labyrinth of Confused Laws, that the Freemen's Power is quite gone ; and it was said, last June-Court, by one,—That they knew nothing the Freemen had there to do.—Sandwich-Men may go to the Bay, lest they be taken up for Quakers : W. Newland was there about his Occasions, some Ten Days since, and they put him in Prison Twenty Four Hours, and sent for divers to Witness against him ; but they had not Proof enough to make him a Quaker, which if they had, he should have been Whipp'd : Nay, they may not go about their Occasions in other Towns in our Colony, but Warrants lie in Ambush to Apprehend and bring them before a Magistrate, to give an Account of their Business.    Some of the Quakers in Rhode Island came to bring Goods, to Trade with them, and that for far Reasonabler Terms, than the Professing and Oppressing Merchants of the Country ; but that will not be suffered : So that unless the Lord step in, to their Help and Assistance, in some way beyond Man's Conceiving, their Case is sad, and to be pitied ; and truly it moves Bowels of Compassion in all sorts, except those in place, who carry it with a high Hand towards them.    Through Mercy we have yet among us worthy Mr. Dunster, whom the Lord hath made boldly to bear Testimony against the Spirit of Persecution.

Our Bench now is, Tho. Prence, Governour ; Mr. Collier, Capt. Willet, Capt. Winslow, Mr. Alden, Lieut. Southworth, W. Bradford, Tho. Hinckley.    Mr. Collier left June would not sit on the Bench, if I sate there ; and now will not sit the next Year, unless he may have Thirty Pounds sit by him.    Our Court and Deputies last June made Capt. Winslow a Major.    Surely we are Mercenary Soldiers, that must have a Major imposed upon us.

Doubtless next Court they may choose us a Governour, and Assistants also. A Freeman shall need to do nothing but bear such Burdens as are laid upon him. Mr. Alden has deceived the Expectations of many, and indeed lost the Affection of such, as I judge were his Cordial Christian Friends; who is very active in such Ways, as I pray God may not be charged on him, to be Oppression of a High Nature. JAMES CUDWORTH.

A tabular statement of the amount of the fines, &c., of the Sandwich Quakers in the years 1658, 1659 and 1660:

| | Cattle taken. | Remarks. | £ | Shs. |
|---|---|---|---|---|
| Ralph Allen, Sen'r, | 8 | 3 horses, &c. | 68 | |
| Ralph " Jr., | 4 | | 18 | |
| Joseph " | | 2 pr. Wheels and a Cloak | 5 | 12 |
| George " | 8 | | 25 | 15 |
| William " | 18 | 1 horse, 2 colts, 15 bush. corn, &c. | 86 | 17 |
| Matthew, " | 16 | 8 bush. corn, | 48 | 16 |
| John " | | | 5 | |
| Thomas Greenfield, | 1 | all his corn, | 4 | |
| Robert Harper, | 9 | house & land, | 44 | |
| William Gifford, | 15 | 1-2 house, 1-2 pig, | 57 | 19 |
| Peter Grant, | 10 | 1 horse, corn, and wheat, | 43 | 14 |
| Ralph Jones, | 4 | | 1 | |
| Thomas Johnson, | | house & land, | 10 | |
| John Jenkins, | 3 | money £8, | 19 | 10 |
| Thomas Ewer, | | money, chest, clothing, axe, | 25 | 08 |
| Rich, Kerby, Sr., & Jr., | 15 | 3 bush. corn, | 57 | 12 |
| Wm. Newland, | 2 | 2 horses, | 36 | |
| John Newland, | | 1 horse, | 2 | 06 |
| Edward Perry, | 17 | tar, feathers, &c., | 89 | 18 |
| Michael Turner, | | 9 sheep, | 13 | 10 |
| Daniel Wing, | | | 12 | |

Cattle taken, 129, 3 horses, 9 sheep, £679,02.

To the above lists may be added the names of Stephen Wing, Henry Saunders, Samuel Kerley and others. Ralf Jones' house was in Barnstable, but close to the Sandwich bound. He belonged to the Sandwich Meeting. He does not appear to have been fined only £1 for not attending meetings. Keith's wonderful story about his cows, wants confirmation.

From 1660 to 1673, Capt. Cudworth resided at Scituate. During this period he was often employed in settling differences between his neighbors, &c., but sustained no office. In 1666 he was nominated by the military company of Scituate to the office of Captain, against the advice of the Court, and his appointment was not confirmed. This vote shows that he was held in high estimation by his townsmen. June 3, 1773, Major Josiah Winslow succeeded Mr. Thomas Prence as Governor, and made honorable amends for the abuse and neglect which Capt. Cudworth had received from his predecessor. He was, at the July Court re-established into the right and privilege of a citizen, and authorized to solemize marriages, grant subpoenas for witness, and to administer oaths. Dec. 17, 1673, he was unanimously appointed Captain of the Plymouth forces in the proposed expedition against the Dutch at New York. The following quotations from his letter to Gov. Winslow, declining the appointment, I find in Deane's History of Scituate:

"Sir, I do unfeignedly and most ingenuously receive the Court's valuation and estimation of me, in preferring me to such a place. It is not below me or beneath me, (as some deem theirs to be), but is above me, and far beyond any desert of mine; and had the Court been well acquainted with my insufficiency for such an undertaking, doubtless I should not have been in nomination; neither would it have been their wisdom to hazard the cause and the lives of their men upon an instrument so unaccomplished for the well management of so great a concern. So being persuaded to myself of my own insufficiency it appears clearly and undoubtedley unto me, that I have no call of God thereunto: for *vox populi*, is not always *vox Dei*. Beside, it is evident unto me, upon other considerations, I am not called of God unto this work at this time. The estate and condition of my family is such as will not admit of such a thing, being such as can hardly be paralleled; which was well know unto some: but it was not well or friendly done as to me, nor faithfully as to the country, if they did not lay my condition before the Court. My wife, as so well known unto the whole town, is not only a weak woman, but has so been all along; and now by reason of age, being sixty-seven years and upwards, and nature decaying, so her illness grows strongly upon her.

"Sir, I can truly say that I do not in the least waive the business out of any discontent in my spirit arising from any former difference: for the thought of all which is and shall be forever buried, so as not to come in remembrance: neither out of any effeminate or dastardly spirit; but I am as freely willing to serve my King and my Country as any man, in what I am capable and fitted for: but I do not understand that a man is called to serve. his country with the inevitable ruin and destruction of his own family.

"These things being premised, I know your Honor's wisdom and prudence to be such, that you will, upon serious consideration thereof, conclude that I am not called of God to embrace the call of the General Court. Sir, when I consider the Court's act in pitching their thoughts upon me, I have many musings what should be the reason moving them thereunto; I conceive it cannot be, that I should be thought to have more experience and better abilities than others, for you, with many others, do well known, that when I entered upon military employ, I was very raw in the theoretic part of war, and less acquainted with the practical part: and it was not long that I sustained my place in which I had occasion to bend my mind and thoughts that way; but was discharged thereof, and of other publick concerns: and therein I took *vox populi* to be *vox Dei*, and that God did thereby call and design me to sit still and be sequestered from all publick transactions, which condition suits me so well that I have received more satisfaction and contentment therein, than ever I did in sustaining any publick place."

Capt. Cudworth was chosen, in 1674, an assistant, and annually thereafter till 1680. In 1674, though over 70 years of age, was re-established Captain of the Military Company in Scituate. Oct. 4, 1675, "Major James Cudworth was unanimously chosen and re-established in the office of a General or Commander-in-chief, to take the charge of our forces that are or may be sent forth in the behalf of the Colony against the enemy, as occasion may require."

In 1678 he was on the committee to revise the laws, and again appointed in 1681. June 7, 1681, he was chosen a Commissioner of the United Colonies, and Duputy Governer. In Sept. 1681, he went over to England as the Agent of the Colony, and died of the small pox in London in the spring of the following year.

Thus ended the life of one who, take him all in all, had no superior in the Old Colony. As a christian, he was meek, humble, and tolerant; as a neighbor, he was mild, humane, and useful; as a man, he was magnanimous in all his acts, and as a commander he was brave and able, and had the entire confidence of his soldiers. When disfranchised and thrust out of office, he did not murmur, he regretted that some of his ancient friends, particularly John Alden, should be led astray, and though he condemned their acts, yet he never allowed a difference of opinion to break the ties of friendship. He retired to his farm, and for thirteen years was constantly engaged in rural occupations. Referring to this period he says, they were the happiest years of his life.

. It is no credit to the memory of Gov. Thomas Prence that he had not the magnanimity to do justice to the merits of Gen. Cudworth. He had many excellent qualities, but toleration in matters of faith was not one of them, and therefore his hostility. Gov. Hinckley was a zealous Puritan; but he was more tolerant and more liberal in his views. He never joined in the crusade against the Anna Baptists, and in respect to the Quakers, many things have been laid to his charge of which he was not guilty. Whatever may have been his opinion in 1658 and 1674, he and all the assistants and deputies unanimously co-operated with Gov. Winslow in awarding justice to Gen. Cudworth. Such conduct disarms criticism. Gen. Cudworth lived down all opposition, and in his old age the highest honors in the gift of the people were freely bestowed on him.

Of the family of Gen. Cudworth, no record has been preserved. His wife was living in 1674, but had deceased at the date of his will, Sept. 15, 1681. He names therein his sons James, Israel, and Jonathan and daughter Mary's four children, and Hannah Jones.

His children were : James, baptized in Scituate 3d May, 1635 ; Mary, baptized in Scituate 23d July, 1637 ; Jonathan, baptized in Scituate 16th Sept. 1638, died here ; Israel, baptized in Barnstable 18th April, 1641 ; Jonna, baptized in Barnstable 24th March, 1643.

Besides these he had a son buried in Barnstable 24th June, 1644, who died young—a daughter Hannah, and another son named Jonathan.

James and Jonathan resided in Scituate and had families. Israel removed to Freetown.

# DAVIS.

Some of the descendents of Robert Davis* have supposed
that he was the first who settled in that part of Barnstable known
from early times as Oldtown. But this is a mistake. He was not
the first nor the second. Rev. Stephen Bachiller and his company,
settled there in the winter of 1637-8. William Chase owned a
farm there very early, probably in 1639, certainly June 8, 1642,
when he mortgaged a part of it to Stephen Hopkins. He sold out
before 1648. In the division of the fences that year, it appears
that the fence on the south boundary of his land extended seventy
rods. In 1648, the Oldtown lands were owned by the following
persons, in the following order, beginning on the east at Stony
Cove, as the mill-pond was then called: 1st, Mr. Thomas Allyn
25 acres, Mr. Andrew Hallett 8, Goodman Isaac Wells 9,
Goodman James Hamblin 9, Mr. John Mayo 7, Thomas Huckins
1, Goodman Rogers Goodspeed 2, Mr. Henry Coggin 4, Samuel
House (or Howes) 4, the Sachem Nepoyetam 30, and the Sachem
Cacomicus 10. The quantities here given included only the
cleared lands fit for planting. Forest, swamps, and meadows,
were not probably included in the measurement.

In January, 1648-9, the grist mill now known as Hallett's
water-mill, had been built and the division of the fences commenced at the mill. Mr. Allyn had purchased largely, and
Samuel Hinckley seven acres. Mr. Hallett, Mr. Coggin, and
Cacomicus, had sold out. After this date, the records furnish no
means of tracing the ownership of these lands.

Robert Davis' name appears on the list of those who were
able to bear arms in Yarmouth in August, 1643. He married, in
1646, and his daughters Deborah and Mary were born in Yarmouth the latter April 28, 1648. The birth of his son Andrew

---

* Two of the name of Robert Davis came over. Robert of Sudbury, born in 1609, came
(with Margaret Davis, perhaps his sister, aged 26) in 1638, in the confidence of Southampton
as servant of Peter Noyes, and died 19th July, 1755, aged 47. He had a wife Bridget who
survived him, and daughters Rebecca and Sarah; the latter born 10th April, 1646.

in May, 1650, is on the Barnstable, and not on the Yarmouth return, which fixes the date of his removal with sufficient exactness.

Excepting of the births of his children, the earliest entry I find of his name on the records, is 12th May, 1657, when a grant of "a parcel of common land" in the New Common Field was made to him, lying between the lands of Goodman Cobb and Goodman Gorham.   He was admitted a freeman of the Colony in 1659.

Robert Davis was not a man of wealth, was not distinguished in political life, nor was he ever entitled to the then honorable appellation of "Mister;" he was

------"An honest good man,
And got his living by his labor,
And Goodman Shelly* was his neighbor."

His character for honesty and industry he transmitted to his posterity.‡

His lands were not recorded in 1654.   His farm in 1639, was included within the bounds of Yarmouth, and with the exception of a small lot owned by Robert Shelly, was bounded on the west by Indian Lane—the original boundary between the towns—on the east, his farm was bounded by the lands of Joseph Hallett, and on the south by Dead Swamp, including the narrow strip between the present road and that swamp.   The easterly part of his farm was a part of the William Chase farm.   The westerly part he bought of the town, of the Indians, and of James Gorham, and the south was a part of the great lot of Thomas Lumbert.§   His house, in 1686, was not on the present County road, but on the higher ground north of the swamp where the first road probably passed.   In 1686, the house of Robert Shelly was the next west of that of Robert Davis, and both appear to have been on the north of the swamp.   In that year the town granted Good-

---

*Goodman Shelly was a very worthy, unambitious man, "a rolling stone that gathers no moss"—in other words, he was often removed from place to place, and was always poor. His wife, Goody Shelly, was a Bay lady, and a cobbler would say of her, was "high in the instep."   If Mrs. Lothrop or Mrs. Dimmock had a party, if she was not an invited guest, she took great offence, and her seat at church on the following Sabbath would be vacant. Rev. Mr. Lothrop complains bitterly of this trait in her character.

---

‡ All the descendants of Robert Davis for eight successive generations, have been noted for their honest dealings and industrious habits.   Of the whole number, I find only one whose character for integrity was doubted by his neighbors.   Cornelius Davis, I presume, was a descendant of Robert, though the evidence is not satisfactory.   He was not reported honest.   Perhaps his habit of carrying an Indian basket on his back was no credit to him.   It, however, is said that other peoples' goods got into that basket.   Whether or not these reports were slanderous I cannot say; but this much is certain, he did not enjoy an unspotted reputation for honesty and integrity in his dealings.   There is something in race; for even now, the character of the ancestor can be traced in the child of the ninth generation.

---

§ Thomas Lumbert's great lot was all finally owned by the descendants of Robert Davis.   In 1664, the western part was owned by Samuel Hinckley, and the eastern part by the widow of Nicholas Davis.   Robert Davis appears to have owned the north-easterly part of the Lumbert lot.

man Shelly a part of the swamp, and Robert Davis sold him "a small gore of land," so that Shelly's lands was afterwards bounded south by the present highway. This addition was made where the late Capt. John Easterbrooks' old house now stands. Fifty years ago John, Abner, and Elisha T. Davis, sons of Joseph, owned all Robert Davis' lands on the north of the highway.

Robert Davis died in 1693. His will is dated April 14, 1688, and proved June 29, 1693. He names his wife Ann. To his son Joseph he devises the land in the New Common Field, which he bought of the Indians ;‖ and to Josiah he devises the two acres of land in the Common Field, which the town granted to him in 1657. He also names Josiah's house lot, now owned by Lot Easterbrooks. He also names his son Andrew, to whom he gave five shillings, and his son Robert; also his daughters Deborah Geere, Sarah, Mercy, Mary Dexter, and Hannah Dexter. His estate was apprised at £75,13, a small sum ; but it must be remembered that money had not then been depreciated, and that land at that time was not valuable.

His widow, Ann Davis, died in 1701. Her will is dated May 5, 1699, and was proved April 1, 1701. She named Robert Davis, my son Joseph's son, daughter Hannah Dexter, grandchild Sarah Dexter, son Josiah's wife, and daughters Sarah Young and Mercy Young. The fact that she names only the younger children, indicates that she was the second wife of Robert Davis.

1.  Robert Davis of Yarmouth, in 1643, of Barnstable in 1650 where he died in 1693, probably married twice. His last wife, whom he probably married in 1657, was named A nn.

*Children born in Yarmouth.*

2.  I.  Deborah, Jan. 1645.
3.  II.  Mary, April 28, 1648.

*Born in Barnstable.*

4.  III.  Andrew, May, 1650.
5.  IV.  John, March 1, 1652.
6.  V.  Robert, Aug. 1654.
7.  VI.  Josiah, Sept. 1656.
8.  VII.  Hannah, Sept. 1658.
9.  VIII.  Sarah, Oct. 1660.
10.  IX.  Joseph.
11.  X.  Mercy.

1.  Deborah Davis married Thos. Geere of Enfield, Conn., had Shubael who has descendants, and Elizabeth born May 4, 1685, who died under three years of age. Thomas, the father,

---

‖ This fact is probably the foundation of the family tradition, that Robert Davis bought his farm of the Indians for a brass kettle. The recent discovery of the grave of Iyanough has revived the old story, which has no foundation in truth.

died 14th Jan. 1722, aged 99 years, and his wife Deborah in 1736, aged 91.

2.    Mary, married a Dexter, whose Christian name I cannot find.

3.    Andrew, to whom his father gave five shillings in his will, removed from Barnstable, perhaps to New London, Conn.

4.    John Davis is not named in his father's will and probably died young.

5.    Robert Davis, 2d, removed from Barnstable.    Mr. Deane, in his history of Scituate, says that "Tristram Davis, son of Robert of Yarmouth, born in 1654, was in Scituate in 1695. He married Sarah Archer of Braintree 1694." Mr. Savage copies the mistake of Deane.    Robert Davis, Senior, had no son Tristram. It was probably Robert that Deane intended to name.

6.    Josiah Davis' house is named in the laying out of the County road, in 1686, as next east of Samuel Cobb's, on the north side of the way.    It stood a few feet east of the present dwelling house of Lot Easterbrooks, and was taken down not many years ago.    In his will, dated 21st April, 1709, and proved the 5th of October following, he names his nine children, all of whom were then living.    To his sons John, Josiah, and Seth, he gave his dwelling house, the land he bought of James Gorham, the Common Field land, given him by his father, and one-half of the orchard lying before his door, on the south side of the road.    To his sons Jonathan and Stephen, the other half of the orchard, &c.    He names his daughters Hannah Cobb, and Ruth, Sarah and Anna unmarried.    The legacies to his daughters he ordered to be paid out of the £53 he ventured in trading at sea, £30 in the hands of his son John, and £23 in the hands of Gersham Cobb. His estate was apprised at over £500, corn being then worth 10 shillings a bushel, showing that there had been some depreciation in the currency since the death of his father.    In the division of the common he was entitled to 43 1-2 shares, a number above the average.    He was a soldier in Capt. John Gorham's company in King Phillip's war in 1675, and one of the proprietors of Gorham-town.

7.    Hannah Davis married a Dexter whose Christian name does not appear on the record.    She had a daughter Sarah.

8.    Sarah Davis married, 28th Oct. 1679, Joseph Young of Eastham, son of the first John and had a family.

9.    Joseph Davis resided in Barnstable.    His family was one of the most respectable in town.    He died, say the Church Records, Aug. 10, 1735, aged about 70 years, and his widow Hannah May 2, 1739, aged 68.

10.    Mercy Davis married first Nathaniel Young, brother of

Joseph above named, and 10th June, 1708, Nathaniel Mayo, of Eastham.

(7-6) Josiah Davis, son of Robert, born Sept. 1656, married Ann, daughter of Richard Taylor, (tailor) of Yarmouth, June 25, 1679, and had

12.    I.    John, 2d Sept. 1681, married M. Dimmock Aug. 13, 1705.
13.    II.    Hannah, April, 1683, married Gersham Cobb Feb. 24, 1702-3.
14.    III.    Josiah, Aug. 1687, married M. Taylor July 10, 1712.
15.    IV.    Seth, Oct. 1692, married Lydia Davis Aug. 6, 1727.
16.    V.    Ruth, Feb. 1694, married John Scudder, 19th May, 1715.
17.    VI.    Sarah, Feb. 1696, married Elisha Taylor 24th Oct. 1718.
18.    VII.    Jonathan, 1698, married Susan Allyn April 24, 1735.
19.    VIII.    Stephen, 12th Dec. 1700, married Rebecca ——.
20.    IX.    Anna, 5th April 1702, married Theophilus Witherell, 1724.

(10-9)  Joseph  Davis,  son  of  Robert,  married,  by  Mr. Thatcher, March 1695, to Hannah, daughter of James Cobb.

*Children born in Barnstable.*

21.    I.    Robert, 7th March 1696-7 married Jane Annable, Oct. 8, 1719.
22.    II.    Joseph, 23d March, 1698-9.
23.    III.    James, 30th July, 1700, married Thankful Hinckley Jan. 4, 1727-8.
24.    IV.    Gersham, 5th Sept. 1702, married three wives.
25.    V.    Hannah, 5th March, 1705, married Samuel Dimmock 1724.
26.    VI.    Mary, 5th June 1707, married Matthias Gorham March 1, 1730.
27.    VII.    Lydia, 12th Feb. 1709, died unmarried Dec. 30, 1763.
28.    VIII.    Daniel, 28th Sept. 1713, married twice.

(12-1) John Davis, Esq., son of Josiah, born in Barnstable 2d Sept. 1681, married, Aug. 13, 1705, Mehitable, daughter of Shubael Dimmock. Her father resided for a time in Yarmouth, and she was a member of the Yarmouth Church, and was dismissed to the East Church in Barnstable Feb. 12, 1725-6. She died May 1775, aged 89. She was blind several years previous to her death. John Davis, Esq., was a captain, a justice of the peace, &c., and was a man of note in his day. He died 29 ——, 1736, aged 58, leaving a good estate. He bought a part of the great lot of Mr. Thomas Lumbard, and the house which he built thereon is now standing, and is now owned by the successors of the late Eleazer Cobb, Sen'r, and George L. Gorham.

*His Children born in Barnstable, were:*

29. I. Thomas, Oct. 1, 1706, married Susan Sturgess Nov. 17, 1726.
30. II. John, Sept. 8, 1708, married twice.
31. III. Solomon, April 5, 1711, died July 18, 1712.
32. IV. William, April 10, 1713, died July 4, 1713.
33. V. Solomon, June 24, 1715, married twice.
34. VI. Mehitable, Aug. 10, 1717, married four times.
35. VII. William, Aug. 24, 1719, married Martha Crocker Feb. 2, 1745.
36. VIII. Josiah, Feb. 17, 1722.
37. IX. Isaac, ⎫   died Oct. 28, 1724.
        ⎬ twins, Aug. 3, 1724.
38. X. Jesse, ⎭   died Aug. 13, 1724.
39. XI. Isaac, March 1, 1727, died Nov. 2, 1727.

(14-3) Josiah Davis, son of Josiah, married, July 10, 1712, Mehitable, daughter of Edward Taylor of West Barnstable.

*Children born in Barnstable.*

40. I. Edward, 19th June, 1713.
41. II. Mary, 8th Aug. 1714.
42. III. Josiah, 2d Aug. 1718.

A Josiah Davis resided in the high single house next west of Capt. Jonathan Davis' afterwards bought by James Davis, and now owned by his descendants.

(15-4) Seth Davis, son of Josiah, was of Barnstable in 1728. Aug. 6, 1727, Lydia Davis was admitted to the East Church. Aug. 4, 1728, Lucy, daughter of Seth and Lydia Davis, was baptized. The name then disappears on the Church records. Sept. 29, 1755, a Seth Davis married Sarah Sturgis. I think Cornelius Davis was his son. He owned Josiah Davis' house, who was probably his grandfather.

(18-7) Capt. Jonathan Davis, son of Josiah, resided in Barnstable. He was a sea captain. His first wife was Elizabeth ————. She died Sept. 14, 1733, aged 32. He married, April 24, 1735, Susannah Allyn. She died Aug. 14, 1751, aged 36. According to the Church records he died Dec. 2, 1782, aged 83. His grave stones in the burying ground near the Unitarian Meeting House, say Jan. 4, 1784, in the 82d year of his age. His will was proved Jan. 1788. He names Wm. Belford and daughter Ann, to whom he gives all his estate, and his daughter Elizabeth. Neither correspond with the record of his birth. His house stood on the north side of the road, between the houses of Samuel Cobb and Josiah Davis. His daughters Ann and Elizabeth were his only children living at the time of his death. Ann taught a school several years. She married John Belford, one of the Scotch Irish, (see Delap) and had Susy Davis baptized Oct. 11, 1772; Edward, baptized Jan. 1, 1770, died young; Edward again, baptized Oct. 1778; and Davis, June 18, 1781. The descendants write their name Ford.

His children born in Barnstable, and baptized at the East Church, were:

43.   I.   Elizabeth, baptized Nov. 9, 1729, died young.
44.   II.   Elizabeth, baptized Oct. 24, 1736, died young.
45.   III.   Susannah, born July 29, 1738.
46.   IV.   Elizabeth, baptized Oct. 4, 1741, married ———— Hamlin.
47.   V.   Anna, baptized May 1, 1743, married Wm. Belford.
48.   VI.   Jonathan, baptized June 14, 1747, died young.

(19-8) Stephen Davis, called Stephen Jr., to distinguish him from Stephen, son of Dolar, who was ten years his senior, was son of Josiah, born in Barnstable Dec. 12, 1700. He bought the ancient John Scudder house of his brother-in-law, John Scudder, Jr., and six acres of land, a part of Rev. Mr. Lothrop's great lot. The old house was taken down in 1803, by his son Jonathan, and the dwelling house of the late George Davis stands on the same spot. He married, in 1723, Rebecca ————, and had a large family, the record of which on the town books is imperfect, and the deficiencies are supplied from the Church records. He joined the East Church, and was baptized March 21, 1773, at the age of 72. He died Jan. 4, 1782, aged 81, and his wife Rebecca Nov. 28, 1769, aged 60. Both have monuments in the grave yard near the Unitarian Meeting House.

*Children born in Barnstable.*

49.   I.   Prince, Nov. 17, 1724, married Sarah Coleman, Feb. 15, 1750.
50.   II.   Ann, Dec. 13, 1726, married Benjamin Cobb, May 17, 1749.
51.   III.   Isaac, Sept. 14, 1729, married Hannah Davis, Jan. 16, 1752.
52.   IV.   Rebecca, Feb. 26, 1731, married Benjamin Childs, Jr., Nov. 6, 1751.
53.   V.   Susannah, May 14, 1734, married Solomon Otis, Jr.
54.   VI.   Sarah, Jan. 20, 1737, married Jonathan Bacon, Jr., May 13, 1755.
55.   VII.   Stephen, baptized Aug. 17, 1740.
56.   VIII.   Abigail, baptized May 15, 1743.
57.   IX.   Thankful, baptized Oct. 26, 1746, married Samuel Smith.
58.   X.   Jonathan, baptized Oct. 1, 1749, married Susannah Lewis.

(21-1) Dea. Robert Davis, son of Joseph, resided in Barnstable, and lived where the late Nath'l Holmes's house now stands. He had a Cooper's Shop, and was a part of his life captain of the Barnstable and 'Boston packet. He was much employed in town affairs and was often one of the selectmen. He was a man of sound judgment, and held in esteem by all who knew him. He married, Oct. 8, 1719, Jane Annable. He has no children recorded on the town or church records. He died June 1, 1765, aged 69, and his wife Jane Nov. 27, 1766, aged 66. In his will he devises his estate to James, son of his brother Gersham Davis.

(22-2) Joseph Davis, son of Josiah, I persume, died young —I find no notice of him on the records.

(23-3) James Davis, son of Joseph, married, Jan. 4, 1727-8, Thankful, daughter of Joseph Hinckley of West Barnstable. She died Aug. 20, 1745, aged 38, and her husband about the same time, leaving a family of seven children, who were brought up by their grandfather Hinckley.

*Children born in Barnstable.*

59   I.   Hannah, baptized July 4, 1729, died young.
60.   II.   Hannah, May 31, 1731, married twice.
61.   III.   Joseph, Aug. 15, 1733, married twice.
62.   IV.   Benjamin, June 27, 1635, married Patience Bacon, May 19, 1757.
63.   V.   Eunice, Aug. 8, 1737, married ——— Jones of Hingham.
64.   VI.   Thankful, Nov. 7, 1739, married Joseph Palmer of Falmouth, Dec. 6, 1765.
65.   VII.   James, March 6, 1741, married Reliance Cobb.
66.   VIII.   David, Jan. 4, 1743.
67.   IX.   Barnabas, died young.

(24-4) Dea. Gersham Davis, son of Joseph, born in Barnstable 5th Sept. 1702, was a farmer, and was a man of good standing. His house stood where Capt. Pierce's house now stands, at the north-west corner of the great lot laid out to Thomas Lumbard. He married thrice. First, Feb. 24, 1725-6, Elizabeth Sturgis, daughter of Samuel, she died June 6, 1727, aged 21. He married 2d Mary, daughter of Joseph Hinckley of West Barnstable, Sept. 23, 1731. He married for his third wife, in 1757, Thankful Skiff of Sandwich. He died May 6, 1790, in the 88th year of his age.

*Children born in Barnstable.*

68.   I.   James, June 2, 1727, married Jean Bacon, Oct. 3, 1745.
69.   II.   Robert, July 12, 1732, and died soon.
70.   III.   Samuel, Sept. 13, 1734, married Mary Gorham, Jr., Dec. 22, 1757.

71.   IV.   Elizabeth, Aug. 12, 1736, married Joseph Crocker, Jr., Jan. 12, 1758.
72.   V.   Mary, Dec. 5, 1740.
73.   VI.   Abigail, July 12, 1744, died young.
74.   VII.   Abigail, July 12, 1746.
75.   VIII.   Mercy, Feb. 4, 1748, died young.

(28-8) Hon Daniel Davis, son of Joseph, born in Barnstable 28th Sept. 1713, was Judge of Probate, and held other offices of trust and responsibility.   He resided in the house afterwards occupied by his son Dr. John Davis and now owned by Daniel Cobb, a descendant in the female line.   He was an active man, and an ardent patriot during the Revolution.   He often represented the town in the General Court, was on committees, and performed much labor.   As I have had occasion to remark in a former article, at the commencement of the Revolutionary struggle, he was inclined to take sides with the radical portion of the whigs; but was afterwards more conservative in his views.   Barnstable had not a more devoted patriot than Daniel Davis.   He married Mehitable, daughter of Thomas Lothrop.   The land on which Daniel Davis built his house, was a part of the original allotment to Joseph Lothrop, the father of Thomas.   He married for his second wife, July 7, Mehitable Sturgis, noticed below.   Hon. Daniel Davis died 22d April, 1799, aged 85 years, 6 months, and 13 days.

*Children born in Barnstable.*
76.   I.   Mary, April 29, 1740.
77.   II.   Daniel, Oct. 10, 1741.
78.   III.   Robert, March 27, 1743.
79.   IV.   John, Oct. 7, 1744.
80.   V.   Deborah, Aug. 13, 1746, married, Oct. 6, 1765, Josiah Crocker.
81.   VI.   Thomas, Aug. 24, 1748.
82.   VII.   Desire, March 27, 1750, married Freeman Parker.
83.   VIII.   Ansel, March 13, 1752.
84.   IX.   Experience, July 11, 1754, married Joseph Annable.
85.   X.   Mehitable, July 11, 1756.
86.   XI.   Lothrop, lost at sea, no issue.
87.   XII.   Daniel, May 8, 1762.

(29-1) Thomas Davis, son of Capt. John, born Oct. 1, 1706, married Nov. 17, 1726, Susannah Sturgis, daughter of Edward. He had a daughter Susy baptized in the East Church April 17, 1737.   He died April 9, 1738, and his widow married, Aug. 12, 1739, Mr. Elisha Gray of Harwich.

(30-2) John Davis, son of Capt. John, born Sept. 8, 1708, married, Feb. 5, 1720-30, Abigail Otis, and second Anna Allen, March 23, 1736.   He had sons Josiah and John, and daughter Martha, baptized in the East Church April 25, 1742.

(33-5) Solomon, son of Capt. John, born June 24, 1715, was a merchant and resided in Boston. During the siege he removed his family to Barnstable. He was an intimate friend of Gov. Hancock. In 1791 he was dining with his Excellency in company with some of the rare wits of the day, John Rowe, Joseph Balch, and others, Mr. Davis made some witty remark, which induced Mr. Balch to say to him, "Well, Davis, you had better go home now and die, for you will never say as good a thing as that again." On his way home he was taken suddenly ill, and sat down on the steps of King's Chapel, from whence he was removed to his house in the vicinity, where he shortly after died.

Solomon Davis married Jan. 29, 1750, Elizabeth Wendell of Portsmouth, N. H. She died at Plymouth Feb. 20, 1777, aged about 47. She was the mother of all his children. He married, Nov. 18, 1777, her sister Catharine Wendell, who died April 7, 1808, aged 66. He died June 6, 1791, aged 76.

His children were : 1, John, born May 19, 1753 ; 2, Solomon, Sept. 25, 1754, died at sea Sept. 1789 ; 3, Edward, Dec. 18, 1765, died at sea Nov. 11, 1708 ; 4, Thomas, July 26, 1757, died at Falmouth, Eng., Oct. 10, 1775 ; 5, Elizabeth, Oct. 14, 1758, died Aug. 14, 1833. (She married Dr. David Townsend May 24, 1785, and was the mother of Dr. Solomon Davis Townsend of Boston.) 6, Mehitable, July 14, 1760, died Oct. 28, 1761 ; 7, Henry, Oct. 8, 1761, died March 15, 1762 ; 8, Josiah, Sept. 24, 1763, died June 29, 1777, buried at Barnstable ; 9, Isaac, April 2, 1765, married Elizabeth Fellows, died Dec. 5, 1800, at Hartford, Conn. ; 10, William, April 26, 1768, married Martha Harris, he died Sept. 14, 1804, at Dorchester. Solomon Davis has descendants living in Boston, and other places, Gustavus F. Davis president of the City Bank, Hartford, Conn., is a descendant of Isaac Davis of Boston and many others of note.

Dr Solomon Davis Townsend of Boston, son of Elizabeth Davis, born March 1, 1793, married his cousin, a daughter of Edward Davis, and is now three score years and ten. He was consulting surgeon to the Massachusetts General Hospital from 1835 to 1839, and Acting Surgeon from 1839 to 1863, when he tendered his resignation of the place he had so long and honorably filled. In the resolutions adopted by the Trustees of the Hospital, they expressed their high appreciation of his long, faithful and valuable services, of his generous devotion to the interest of that institution, of his professional skill, of his ability, sound judgment, assiduity and kindness, and his consistent and gentlemanly conduct.

(34-6) Mehitable Davis, daughter of Capt. John, born in Barnstable Aug. 10, 1717, was a remarkable woman, and deserving of especial note. She married four husbands, all men of character, influence and respectability, namely :

At 23 she married, April 9, 1741, Dr. James Hersey, a native of Hingham, a man of learning and skillful in his profession. By him she had a son Ezekiel, born Jan. 14, 1741-2. He died July 22, 1741, aged 26. His first wife was Lydia Gorham, whom he married July 27, 1737. She had a son James, born Nov. 9, 1738, and she died Nov. 9, 1740. Dr. James Hersey owned that portion of the Dimmock farm on which the fortification house stood, and whether he resided in that, or in a house that formerly stood a little west of the present residence of Asa Young, Esq., I cannot say. Dr. James was succeeded in his practice by his brother, Dr. Abner Hersey, a curious compound of good sense and eccentricity.

2d, at 26, she married, Oct. 21, 1744, John Russell, son of Dr. John of Barnstable. By him she had one son John, whose birth is not recorded. The father died Aug. 1, 1748, aged 24. The son was baptized Sept. 4, 1748, on the day his widowed mother was admitted to the East Church. He was captain of the marines on board the ill fated private armed ship Gen. Arnold, Capt. James Magee, lost in Plymouth Harbor Dec. 26, 1778, when nearly all on board perished. Though a strong, robust man, he was one of the first who perished. On his monument in Plymouth church yard it is stated that he was then 31, if so, he was born in 1747.

3d, at 37, on the 9th of May, 1754, she became the second wife of John Sturgis, Esq., of Barnstable. By him she had Sarah, whose birth is recorded with sufficient particularity, namely: at "3 1-2 o'clock A. M., Thursday, April 17, 1755, and baptized on the Sunday following;" and John baptized March 19, 1758. John Sturgis, Esq., died Aug. 10, 1759, aged 56.

4th, at 44, she married, July 7, 1761, her relative, Hon. Daniel Davis, and again assumed her maiden name. By him she had one son, Daniel, born May 8, 1762.

Her daughter Sarah married the late Mr. Isaiah Parker of West Barnstable, had a family and lived to be aged. John was a graduate of Harvard College, and died early. Her son Daniel was Soliciter General, and a distinguished man. She survived all her husbands, but at last "the woman died also," namely: on the ———— aged 87 years.

Her son, Hon. Daniel Davis, married Lois Freeman, daughter of Constant Freeman, and sister of the Rev. James Freeman of the Stone Chapel, Boston, and had a large family. Louisa, the eldest daughter, married William Minot, Esq., of Boston. Rear Admiral Charles Henry Davis, of the U. S. Navy, is his youngest son.

(35-7) Capt. William Davis owned the house and estate which was his father's. He was a sea captain, and died in 1759, aged forty years.

He married Feb. 2, 1745, Martha, daughter of Timothy Crocker, Esq., of Barnstable. She died Dec. 2, 1772, aged 67.

*Children born in Barnstable.*

1, Mehitable, March 4, 1746, married Benjamin Gorham, Jr., (called Young Fiddler) a man of more wit than sound judgment; 2, William, born Jan. 18, 1748, was clerk in the store of his uncle Solomon in Boston, and died unmarried at the age of 24, of yellow fever; 3, Catharine, born April 29, 1751, married Stephen Hall of Sandwich; 4, Elizabeth, born April 13, 1755, married Eleazer Cobb, Sen'r, and inherited half of her father's house where she resided; 5, Martha, born Aug. 19, 1758, (she was always called Patty) married John Cobb, who bought the Nathaniel Bacon, Jr., house, and had a family. Mrs. Hetty Davis Hallett, widow of Andrews, is her daughter; 6, Ruth, born Jan. 24, 1763, married Capt. Thomas Gray of Yarmouth; 7, Jesse, who died aged 2 years.

(36-8) Josiah Davis, son of Capt. John, born Feb. 19, 1722. Of this Josiah Davis I have no certain information.

(40-1) Ebenezer, son of the 2d Josiah, born 19th June, 1713. Of Ebenezer I have no certain intelligence. I think he removed to Maine.

(42-3) Josiah Davis, son of 2d Josiah, born Aug. 2, 1718, married, in 1745, Thankful Matthews; and May 3, 1760, Thankful Gorham. He resided in the house which was his father's, and sold the same, on his removal to Gorham, to the late Mr. James Davis. He had Josiah and Thankful baptized June 6, 1756; Mary, Sept. 3, 1759; Josiah, Oct. 11, 1761, and three children born in Gorham, in 1773, 1776 and 1780.

(49-1) Prince Davis, son of Stephen, Jr., born Nov. 17, 1724, was a house carpenter. He resided in Barnstable till 1760, when he removed to Gorham, Maine, of which town he was a proprietor in the right of his grandfather Josiah, who was a soldier in the Company of Capt. John Gorham in King Phillip's war in 1675. Mr. Prince Davis early joined the East Church in Barnstable, and continued to be a church member after his removal east. At Gorham his name appears as one of the selectmen, and in church affairs he was a prominent man. He was married by Rev. Mr. Green, Feb. 17, 1749-50, to Sarah Coleman, daughter of James, of Barnstable. The births of his children are not on the town records. He died in Gorham in 1809, aged 85 years, and his wife in 1804. He had five children born in Barnstable, four baptized Oct. 9, 1757, namely, Elijah, Edward, Prudence and Alice, and Temperance baptized Nov. 18, 1759; and five born in Gorham, namely, Isaac, March 27, 1762; David, Oct. 20, 1764; Rebecca, July 15, 1766; Thomas, May 14, 1768; and Jonathan July 10, 1770.

Elijah married Phebe Hopkins April 8, 1780; Prudence married Josiah Jenkins June 15, 1776, and died 1836; Alice married Enoch Frost April 22, 1779, and died 1802; Temperance married David Harding, June 23, 1781, and died 1810; Isaac did not marry, died in 1738; David married Martha Watson March 17, 1788; Rebecca married Geo. Knight March 14, 1789, died June 18, 1836; Thomas did not marry; Jonathan married Mary April 10, 1796.*

(51-3) Isaac Davis, son of Stephen, Jr., born Sept. 14, 1729, married Hannah Davis, daughter of James. His house was on the north-easterly part of Thomas Lumbert's great lot, on the south side of the road, opposite his grand-father's house. He had a son, and a daughter Rebecca baptized Aug. 3, 1755, and another daughter of the same name baptized Jan. 15, 1768, and a son Isaac born Dec. 3, 1764. The latter married Abigail Gorham, and had Stephen G., Cashier of the Shawmut Bank, Boston, Frederick of Falmouth, and others. The widow Hannah, of the first Isaac, married, June 17, 1783, Col. David Gorham, she died Oct. 3, 1810, aged 79 yrs. and 3 mos.

(58-10) Jonathan Davis, son of Stephen, Jr., born in Barnstable, baptized Oct. 1, 1749, married Susannah Lewis, born the same day, Sept. 27, 1749, or rather within a few hours of each other. He went to sea in early life, and was in after life a farmer. He had sons Stephen, Solomon, and George, and a daughter Susannah yet living. Stephen was a carpenter, removed to Falmouth, and lived to be aged, and has descendants there. Solomon was a carpenter, died a young man, and has descendants in Dennis. George was a shoemaker, and resided on the paternal estate, and died Nov. 6, 1847, aged 68, leaving one son, the present Mr. Isaac Davis. He being now the sole representative on the voting list of Barnstable, of the many Davis families of that town. Mr. Jonathan Davis died Sept. 22, 1840, aged 90. She died Sept. 25, 1841, aged 91 years.

(61-3) Joseph Davis, son of James, born Aug. 15, 1733, was a tanner and currier and resided in a house that stood near where the first Robert's stood. He married first Lucretia Thatcher Nov. 17, 1763, and had Phebe, Rebecca, who married Job Gorham, Elisha Thatcher, Mary, Lucretia, Joseph and Benjamin. By his second wife, Mary Bacon, John, Lucretia and Abner.

John, (father of Joseph and Barnabas of Boston) built a house near where the first Josiah Davis house stood. Abner (father of Adolphus and James W., of Boston,) inherited the paternal mansion. He was a lawyer, and Clerk of the Courts. Elisha Thacher was a tanner and shoe maker, died a young man,

---

* Manuscript letter of Josiah Pierce, Esq., author of her history, of Gorham, Maine. The climate of Maine seems to agree with the Davis family. Prince has more descendants than his nine brothers and sisters.

leaving a large family of young children. His widow lived to great age.

(62-4) Benjamin Davis, son of James, married, May 19, 1754, Patience Bacon.

(65-7) James Davis, son of James, married Reliance Cobb. He had James, David, and others. James removed to Boston, was a brass founder, acquired a large estate, and died very suddenly in 1862, aged 84.

(68-1) James Davis, son of Dea. Gersham, married, Oct. 3, 1745, Jean Bacon. His uncle, Dea. Robert Davis, made him his heir. His children were: 1, Elizabeth, July 2, 1746; 2, Elizabeth again, March 25, 1748; 3, Jean, April 24, 1750; 4, Patience, June 13, 1752; 5, Desire, Oct. 22, 1754; 6, Joseph, Sept. 19, 1757; 7, Robert, June 30, 1760; 8, Hannah, Dec. 19, 1762; 9, James, Jan. 19, 1767; baptized May 5, 1765; and Desire baptized Sept. 20, 1772.

(70-3) Samuel Davis, son of Dea. Gersham, married, Dec. 23, 1759, Mary Gorham, Jr., and had Ebenezer baptized July 6, 1760; Samuel, July 4, 1762; Mary, Sept. 25, 1763; Ebenezer, Feb. 17, 1765; Prince, May 17, 1767; William, June 9, 1771. This family removed to Gorham, where they had Elizabeth April 14, 1777.

(79-4) Hon. John Davis, son of Daniel, born Oct. 7, 1744. He practiced medicine many years, was Judge of Probate, and held many responsible offices. He was a mild, pleasant man, not inheriting the energy of character for which his father was distinguished. He resided in the early part of his life in the house now standing that was Col. Davis Gorham's. After the decease of his father he removed to the paternal mansion, where he continued to reside till his death. He was afflicted with cancer on the nose which nearly destroyed that organ. He had a large family. The late Hon. Job C. Davis was his son, who married Desire Loring daughter of Otis Loring—had 12 children.

———

In 1643, five of the name of Davis were "able to bear arms" in Barnstable, viz: Dolar or Dollard and his sons John, Nicholas, Simon, and Samuel; and in Yarmouth, Robert Davis, afterwards of Barnstable. Dr. Palfrey informed Mr. Savage that the graves of the ancestors of Dolar Davis were at Bennefield, Northamptonshire, and that was probably his native town. He married as early as 1618, Margery. daughter of Richard Willard, of Horsmonden, in the County of Kent, where all his sons were born, and perhaps his daughter Mary. He came over in 1634, in company with his brother-in-law, Major Simon Willard, a man of note in the history of the Massachusetts Colony. He stopped first at Cambridge, and in 1635 was one of the first settlers, and had a house lot on Water street. He sold his lands in Cambridge in 1636, and removed. He was also one of the proprietors of the lands in Concord.  In 1638 he was of Duxbury.  April 6, 1640, lands and meadows were granted to him and others, at North Hill, in that town, and on the 31st of August following, he had granted to him fifty acres of upland, and a proportion of meadows on the Namassacuset river.  May, 1641, he was bondsman for George Willard of Scituate, and is called of that town.

August, 1643, he and his sons were included among those able to bear arms in Barnstable.  He probably came to Barnstable in 1639 with the first settlers, though he did not make it the place of his permanent residence until 1642 or 3.   He was a carpenter, and a master builder; his son John was also a carpenter, and his sons Nicholas, Simon, and Samuel, probably assisted their father.   This fact furnishes an explanation of his frequent removals from place to place.  In the new settlements he found more employment than in the older.  It did not, however, require much time to construct the rude dwellings of our ancestors.  In 1643 William Chase built the house of Andrew Hallett, Jr., finding all the materials, and delivered it "latched, thatched and daubed" for the sum of £5.  Some of the first settlers put up substantial frame houses, like that of Nathaniel Bacon, which has been described; but generally they were as rudely and as cheaply constructed as Andrew Hallett, Jr's.  The chimneys were of rough stone, and above the mantel piece, which was always of wood, they were often only *cob-walls*, that is built with small sticks and clay.  The roofs were thatched, and oiled paper was often a substitute for glass.  They were not plastered—the cracks were "daubed," that is filled up with clay or mortar.  The hardware and nails required, were furnished by the blacksmith.  Saw mills had been built at Scituate, and the lumber for the best houses came from that town; but at first the boards required were sawed by hand, or hewn from split logs.

Houses of this description, having only one large room on the lower floor, whether one or one-half stories high, were quickly and cheaply built.

Neither Dolar Davis or his sons were ambitious of political distinction.  In 1642 he was on the jury of trials, in 1645 a grand juror; but was excused from serving on account of sickness, in 1652 surveyor of highways, and in 1654 constable.

In 1655 he removed to Concord, Massachusetts.  He was one of the original proprietors of Groton, and he and Mr. Thomas Hinckley of Barnstable, were of the first Board of Selectmen appointed by the Legislature May 23, 1655, and to hold office two years.  The Selectmen managed the prudential affairs of the town, laid out the lands into lots, and disposed of them to the first settlers.

In 1656, Dolar Davis was a resident at Concord, and in receipt dated April 9, of that year, calls himself of that town.  In a deed executed in that town July 17, 1658, describes himself as a house carpenter late of Barnstable.  Feb. 16, 1667-8, he ·had returned to Barnstable, where he died June 1673, aged about 80 years.

Dolar Davis' house lot was the most northerly on the east side of the ancient Mill Way, discontinued in 1669.  In his deed to Abraham Blush, dated July 17, 1658, he says, "all my house lott of lands lying by a place commonly called *Old Mill Creek*," containing two acres, and was bounded northerly by his own meadow in the Mill Pond, easterly partly upon Mr. Dimmock marsh, and partly upon his own land ; southerly, partly on the common, and partly by Goodman Huckins, and westerly, partly on Goodman Huckins and partly by Nicholas Davis.  His house stood not far from the water mill built by the first settlers on the spot where the present mill stands.

He also owned three lots of land at Stony Cove, containing twelve acres, ten acres of meadow on the north of his house lot, and on the opposite side of Mill Creek, twelve acres in the old common-field, and a lot of four acres adjoining his houselot on the south-east, bounded westerly partly upon the common, and partly by his own land, easterly by Nicholas Davis, northerly by Mr. Dimmock's marsh, and southerly by Goodman Foxwell's land.

The above described lands and meadow he sold to Abraham Blush, by deed dated 17th July, 1658.  The common land named in the above description, consisted of two acres of swamp, a little distance north-west of the Agricultural Hall, afterwards granted to John Davis, and by him sold to Abraham Blush.

Dolar Davis' great lot of sixty acres, "butted easterly upon the Indian Pond, westerly into the commons, bounded southerly by John Crocker, northerly by Henry Brown."  This he sold to Mr. Thomas Allen, who re-sold the same 22d Feb. 1665, to Roger Goodspeed.

The causeway across Mill Creek to the Common Field, which was then, and now is, the mill dam.  Mill Creek is frequently named in the description of the lands and meadows in the vicinity ; but the owners of the Mill are not named in the earliest records now extant.  Nicholas Davis owned the land adjoining the spot on which the Mill stood.  No description of his lands except the grant made to him by the Indian Sachem at Hyannis, is found on the town records.  After his death his lands were set off to his creditors, and no particular description is given.  John Bacon, Esq., was an early owner in the mill, and was part owner of the landing or dock on the west side of the mill formerly owned by Nicholas Davis, and yet the property of the Bacons.  Dolar Davis sold his farm, including his dwelling-house and meadows, for £75.  Nicholas Davis' real estate, not including the twelve acres sold to John Bacon, or the Caleb Lumbert farm which was set off to his widow as her portion, was apprised at £180.  He did not own so many acres as his father, and it is evident that the superior value of his property consisted in the buildings and improvements thereon. He had a warehouse at Hyannis, the first building erected by the English at South Sea, and a warehouse on his lot at Mill Creek. The latter contained not more than two acres, and on this there was, sixty years ago, a large and valuable frame dwelling-house, built in the style of the first comers. In absence of all evidence to the contrary, the presumption is that this ancient house and the Mill, were originally the property of Nicholas Davis.

Perhaps among all the families which came to New England, not one can be selected more deserving of our esteem and unqualified approbation than that of Dolar Davis. As a man, he was honest, industrious, and prudent; as a Christian, tolerant and exact in the performance of his religious duties; as a neighbor, kind, obliging, and ever ready to help those who needed his assistance, and as a father and the head of his family, he was constantly solictious for the welfare of all its members, cultivating those kindly feelings and amenities of life, which render home delightful. His sons and his grand-sons followed in his footsteps. They were men whose characters stand unblemished. It is pleasant to read their wills on record, and note the affection with which they speak of the members of their families, and their desire to provide not only for their immediate wants, but for the future prospective misfortunes or necessities of any of their kindred. The latter remark, however, will apply more particularly to Samuel, of whom a more particular account will be given.

The family of Dolar Davis is for convenience of reference arranged in a regular genealogical series, in order to distinguish between members of this family, and that of Robert of the same Christian name. I call Nicholas a son of Dolar. If I am asked to point to the record of the fact I cannot. Many circumstances show that they were near relatives. The fact that Nicholas was a favorite name among the descendants of Dolar who joined the Quakers, that the house lots of Dolar and Nicholas were parts of the same original lot, and other circumstances, have induced me to call Nicholas the son of Dolar.

1.    I. Dolar Davis, carpenter, married first Margery Willard, daughter of Richard Willard of Horsmonden, County of Kent, in England. He came over in 1634. His first wife probably died in Concord. He married for his second wife Joanna, widow of John Bursley, and daughter of Rev. Joseph Hall. He died in 1673, and names in his will dated Sept. 12, 1672, his children, then living. Nicholas was then dead, and left no children.

2.    I. John, born in England, married Hannah Linnell 15th March, 1648.

3.    II. Nicholas, born in England, married Mary or Sarah.

4.    III. Simon, born in England, married Mary Blood, 12th

Dec. 1660.

5.   IV.   Samuel, born in England, married Mary Meads 11th Jan. 1665.

6.   V.   Mary, born in England, married Thomas Lewis, June 15, 1653.

7.   VI.   Ruth, born in Barnstable, baptized 24th March, 1644, married, Dec. 3, 1663, Stepen Hall, son of widow Mary of Concord. He afterwards removed to Stowe, was representative in 1689.

John Davis was a house carpenter and was one of the three last survivors of the first settlers. His houselot, containing eight acres, was the first on the west of Baker's Lane, now called Hyannis road. The lot was originally laid out to Edward Fitzrandolph, who sold the same in 1649 to John Chipman; but the deed was not executed till Aug. 13, 1669, and was never recorded.* John Davis' deed of the same lot recorded in the Barnstable town records is dated Oct. 15, 1649, and signed by John Scudder.

Jan. 14, 1658, he sold six acres of his houselot to Samuel Normon, bounded northerly by his little fenced field, easterly by the Hyannis road, southerly by the woods, and westerly by the land of Mr. Wm. Sergeant. On the 26th of February, 1665, Norman re-conveyed this land, with his dwelling house thereon, to John Davis; but the land yet retains the name of Norman's Hill. He also owned thirteen acres on the east side of the Hyannis road, bounded northerly "upon Mrs. Hallet's set of," easterly by Mrs. Hallett, westerly by the Hyannis road; and an addition of five acres on the south, extending on both sides of the Hyannis road. He also owned three acres in the old, and two acres in the new common-field, half an acre on the north side of the County road, opposite his house, improved as an orchard and garden, and a quarter of an acre bought of Henry Cobb near where David Bursley's house now stands, four acres of meadow at Sandy Neck, and two acres within the present dyke, bounded westerly by Rendevous Creek.

In his will, dated May 10, 1701, proved April 9, 1703, he bequeaths to his "eldest son John all that parcel of upland and swamp that he now possesses and dwells on contained within his fence on the eastward side of the highway that leads up into the woods, estimated to be about fourteen acres, upon condition that he shall pay £30 in money to my executors as shall be hereafter ordered. And what he hath already paid to be deducted out of ye said £30.

* I refer here to an original deed which I have in my possession. Another deed of the same property dated June 1, 1649, to John Chipman was recorded that year. Why two were given of the same property is not easily explained. They are not exact copies. Perhaps the one I have, was given to correct some error in the first.

Itt—I give and bequeath to my daughter Mercy for her tender care and labor past done for me and her mother, £20 in money, and £5 a year so long as she continues to attend me and her mother, or the longest liver—her diet, washing, and lodging, in the family with her brother Benjamin, 1 cow and heifer, 2 sheep, 2 swine, and at her mother's decease, 1-2 the household stuff and bedding forever, and the southward end of the house so long as she shall live a single life.

Names son Samuel, to whom he gives 1 yoke of Oxen and a great chain.   Son Benjamin, to whom he gives nearly all his estate in consideration of his taking care of him and his mother during life.

Names sons Dollar, Timothy, Jabez, daughters Ruth Linnell, Hannah Jones' 5 children, son John's four eldest sons, granddaughter Mary Goodspeed, grand-son Joseph Davis, Daughter Mary Hinckley.          BENJAMIN DAVIS, Executor.

Signed with his mark, J. D.

Witness—Joseph Lothrop, James Cobb, Samuel S. Sergeant, (his · mark).

Appraisers—James Lewis, Jeremiah Bacon, Edward Lewis.

Am't of Inventory 268,12,4.

Nicholas Davis came to Barnstable with his father, and was able to bear arms in 1643.   Judge Sewall says he favored the Quakers at their first coming, though he did not embrace their principles till after 1657, when he took the oath of fidelity.   He was a trader, built a warehouse at South Sea, the first building erected by the English in that part of the town.   His accounts show that he dealt more with the Indians than was for his profit, and that the gift of land to him by the Sachem Hianna, was not in the end a good bargain.

June 1656, he was in the court at Plymouth when the Sandwich men were convicted and fined for refusing to take the oath of fidelity, and was a witness of the unjust usages to which they had been subjected by the cruelty of the under Marshal Barlow. He was indignant and attempted to speak, saying "That he was a witness for the Lord against their oppression," and was about to say wherein, when he was put down, and committed to prison; but was soon released.

In the same month he went to Boston to settle with those with whom he had traded, and pay some debts.   He was there arrested, sent to prison to remain till the sitting of the court of Assistants.   His fellow prisoners were William Robinson, a merchant of London, and Marmaduke Stevenson of Yorkshire, Quaker preachers, and Patience Scott of Providence, a little girl eleven years old.   He was kept in prison till Sept. 12, 1659, when he was liberated on the consideration if found within the colony of Massachusetts after the 14th of that month he should suffer death. The two Quaker preachers who were confined did not leave the Colony within the time prescribed, were again arrested, and afterwards hung on Boston Common.

On the 6th of October following the Plymouth Colony Court ordered the notorious Marshal Barlow "to repair to the house of William Newland and Ralph Allen of Sandwich, and Nicholas Davis of Barnstable, to make search in any part of their houses, or in any of the chests or trunks of the above said, or elsewhere, for papers or writings that were false, scandalous, and pernicious to the government, and return such as they may find to the court." As no return appears to have been made, it is presumed no such papers were found.

Nicholas Davis continued his business in Barnstable till 1670. In the spring of 1672 he was a resident of Newport, where he traded, but it does not appear that he had permanently removed from Barnstable. He was drowned before 9th Aug. 1672. His wife Sarah administered on his estate at Newport. Maj. John Walley administered on his estate in Massachusetts.

It does not appear that Nicholas Davis was a member of the Society of Friends. His name does not appear on the records of the Sandwich Monthly Meeting, yet he probably was a member at the time of his removal to Rhode Island, otherwise Roger Williams in his big book against the Quakers, would not have boasted, that in his public conference, with the friends of George Fox, that he made good use of the event that Nicholas Davis, one of their leading men, was drowned.

Nicholas Davis owned a large real estate in Barnstable. Hianna, the Sachem, gave him a tract of land on the inlet now called Lewis' Bay. The boundaries are indefinite; it included the land where Timothy Baker's store now stands, and on which he erected a warehouse.† He traded at New York, Connecticut, and Rhode Island, and his goods were landed at Hyannis and

† To all persons to whom these presents shall come, know yee that I, Yanno Sachem of a certaine tract of lands lying and being att the South See, in the presincts of Barnstable, in the Government of New Plymouth, in New England, in America, have for divers good reasons mee moving freely and absolutely given, granted, enfeofed, and confirmed, and by these presents do giye, graunt, enfeof, and confirm unto Nicholas Davis, of Barnstable, aforesaid merchant a certaine p̄ sell of the said lands lying att the South Sea aforesaid, commonly called by the name of Sam's Neck, bounded northerly by the lands of Barnstable bought of mee, the said Yanno, at the head of the river where the said Nicholas Davis hath now erected a warehouse, and from thence extending to the head of the river, westerly where the Indians were wont to dwell in winter, extending southerly over the mouth of the said river to the sea, and bounded westerly partly by the said river and partly by the lands of Barnstable, and bounded easterly by the harbor, commonly called Yanno's harbor.

The mark (⋈) of Yanno.

And a [seale].

Yanno Sachem above said, personally appeared before mee and acknowledged this to be his acte and deed.

Atttest, THOMAS HINCKLEY, Assistant.

Wattanwassan, the eldest son of the said Yanno, appeared before mee and acknowledged his free consent to this above said deed of gift.

THOMAS HINCKLEY, Assistant.

The above deed is dated October 26th, 1666, and recorded in Plymouth Colony Records Book of Deeds Vol. 3, Page 61.

WM. S. RUSSELL, keeper of said record.

transported across the Cape. Oysters were at that time very abundant and Davis bought them, put up in barrels, of the Indians and others, and shipped them from Hyannis. In early times the "making of Oysters," as the packing of them is called in the will of Benjamin Bearse, was a considerable business. Many of the Oysters packed were probably brought from the vicinity of Oyster Island.

He also owned two acres of land on the west of his father's land, where the late Dea. Joseph Chipman lived, including the landing and the land around the water mill, which was then probably his property. On his land he had a dwelling house which stood where Mr. Maraspin's now does, corresponding in size and appearance to that built by Nathaniel Bacon which has been described. He also had a warehouse on this lot. He had twelve acres of land on the south-east of his father's, sold to John Bacon, Esq., and already described. He also bought of Caleb Lumbard the easterly part of the great lot of Thomas Lumbard, with the house thereon. This was set off to his widow as her dower, and was afterwards owned by the descendants of Robert Davis.

(2-1) John Davis, son of Dolar Davis, married by Mr. Prince, at Eastham, March 15, 1648, to Hannah, daughter of Mr. Robert Linnell of Barnstable. He died 1703.

*Children born in Barnstable.*

8.   I.   John, born 15th Jan. 1649-50, married three wives.
9.   II.   Samuel, born 15th Dec. 1651, died unmarried 1711.
10.   III.   Hannah, married Jedediah Jones.
11.   IV.   Mary, born 3d Jan. 1753-4, married 1st, B. Goodspeed, 1676, 2d, John Hinckley, Nov. 24, 1697.
12.   V.   Joseph, born June 1656, married Mary Claghorn, March 28, 1682.
13.   VI.   Benjamin, born June, 1656, died unmarried 1718.
14.   VII.   Simon, born 15th July, 1658, died young, no issue probably.
15.   VIII.   Dolar, born 1st Oct. 1660, married 3d Aug. 1681, Hannah Linnell.
16.   IX.   Jabez, married Experience Linnell, 20th Aug. 1689.
17.   X.   Mercy, unmarried 1718.
18.   XI.   Timothy, married Sarah Perry 1690.
19.   XII.   Ruth, born 1674, married John Linnell 1695.

(3-2) Nicholas Davis of Barnstable, probably son of Dolar Davis, married, June 1661, Mary or Sarah. There is no record of his family on the Barnstable town records. He was drowned at Newport before Aug. 9, 1672.

*Children born in Barnstable.*

20.   I.   A child Feb. 1651-2.
21.   II.   Simon, 1656, drowned Feb. 13, 1657-8.

(4-3) Simon Davis of Concord, son of Dolar Davis, married 12th Dec. 1660, Mary, daughter of James Blood.

22.   I.    Simon, born 12th Oct. 1661.
23.   II.   Mary, born 3d Oct. 1663.
24.   III.   Sarah, born 15th March, 1666.
25.   IV.   James, born 19th June, 1668.
26.   V.    Ellen, born 22d Oct. 1672.
27.   VI.   Ebenezer, 1676.
28.   VII.  Hannah, born 1st April 1679.

(5-4) Samuel Davis of Concord, son of Dolar Davis, married, 11th Jan. 1665, Mary Meads (or Meddows.)

29.   I.    Mary, born Sept. 27, 1666.
30.   II.   Samuel, born 21st June 1669.
31.   III.   Daniel, born 16th March 1673.
32.   IV.   Eliza.
33.   V.    Stephen.
34.   VI.   Simon, born 9th Aug. 1683.

(6-5) Thomas Lewis, son of George, married Mary Davis 15th June 1653, and had James March 1654 ; Thomas, 15th July 1656 ; Mary, 2d Nov. 1659 ; Samuel, 14th May 1662. Thomas Lewis was probably the first town clerk of Falmouth, but I am not certain.

(3-1) John Davis, Jr., son of John, and grandson of Dolar, married Ruth Goodspeed 2d Feb. 1674. She died ——. 2d, married Mary Hamlin 22d Feb. 1692, she died Nov. 1698. 3d, married Widow Hannah Bacon 1699, widow of Nathaniel.

35.   I.    John, last of Nov. 1675, died middle August 1681.
36.   II.   Benjamin, 8th Sept. 1679.
37.   III.   John, 17th March 1684.
38.   IV.   Nathaniel, 17th July 1686.
39.   V.    Jabez, baptized 10th May 1691, married Patience Crocker, 1727.
40.   VI.   Shobal, born 10th July 1694.
41.   VII.  James, 24th March 1696.
42.   VIII.  Ebenezer, 13th May 1697.
43.   IX.   Nicholas, 12th March 1699.
44.   X.    Jedediah, 5th June 1700.
45.   XI.   Desire, born May 1705.
46.   XII.  Noah, 7th Sept. 1707.

John Davis, Jr., was a house carpenter. Feb. 21, 1677-8, the town granted to him "liberty to set up a shop on a knowl of ground over against his house adjoining to his father's fence on the other side of the highway." In August, 1683, the neighbors wanted a watering place in the swamp on the south side of his house, and the town agreed to give him five acres of land at the head of Samuel Sergeant and Isaac Chapman's lots. That now within fence, was afterwards re-sold by the town to Ebenezer Lewis.

His father gave him the fourteen acres of land he owned on the east of the Hyannis road on which he built a house. He removed to Falmouth about the year 1710, and died in 1729, aged 80, leaving an estate appraised at £1,810. He names his ten sons and two daughters, and his wife's daughter, Elizabeth Bacon, in his will, which is similar to that of his brother Samuel's. He orders a fund of £500 to pay legacies, &c.

(9-2) Samuel Davis, son of John Davis, resided in Barnstable. He did not marry. He died in 1711, leaving a large estate for those times. He owned all the land on the south side of the road, between the lot which was his father's, and the lane next west of the Barnstable R. R. Depot. Dec. 21, 1696, he sold lands in Rochester, to Samuel Chipman, for £35. His will on record is dated 25th June, 1711, and was proved on the 4th of January following. It is one of those wills that please genealogists. He says : "I freely give unto my brother Benjamin Davis, during his natural life, the use and improvement of all the uplands and meadows I bought of Isaac Chapman and Samuel Sargeant here lying together—butting against the land of Ebenezer Lewis on Potter's Neck, and so up into the woods to the head thereof and also, in like manner, to have my woodlot lying above the head thereof, and at the decease of my brother Benjamin, then my will is that Samuel Davis, son of my brother Jabez Davis, deceased, shall have all the forementioned lands, meadows, and woodlot, to him, his heirs and assigns, forever, he or they paying three hundred pounds for the same, (excepting five pounds of said sum to himself) and to have seven years time to pay out the same, after said lands come into his hands."

He further provides, that if Samuel should die or refuse to take the same, then Simon, son of his brother Joseph, to take the same, on the same conditions, and if he refuse, then the next in kin of the "Davises" to have the same offer, and the £295 to be divided as follows :

| | |
|---|---:|
| To my sister Mary Davis, | £40 |
| " Solomon, son of Jabez Davis, | 5 |
| " Brother Jabez Davis' 3 daughters, | 3 |
| " Sister Ruth Linnell, | 5 |
| "     "     "     " children, | 7 |
| " Br. Joseph Davis' 3 sons 5 each, | 15 |
| "    "    "    " daughter Mary, | 5 |
| " " Dolar Davis' son Shubael, | 5 |
| "    "    "    " daughter Hannah, | 5 |
| "    "    "    " Thankful and Mary, | 2 |
| " Sister Mary Hinckley, | 10 |
| "    "    "    " daughter Mary, | 1 |
| "    " Hannah Jones' children £1 each, | 7 |
| " Br. John Davis' 10 sons £4 each, | 40 |

| | | | | | |
|---|---|---|---|---|---|
| To Br. John Davis' 2 daughters, £1, | | | | | £ 2 |
| "  " Timothy Davis, | | | | | 20 |
| "  "    "    " son Nicholas, | | | | | 5 |
| "  "    "    " daughter, | | | | | 5 |

£182

To his brother Benjamin Davis he gave ten acres of land in the common field bought of Samuel Sargent, and other property, and to his sister Mercy Davis nearly all his moveable estate.

He also ordered a part of the income of his estate to be kept in bank, and to be distributed to such of his relations of the Davis' as may fall under decay, and be in want either by sickness or lameness or other accident—proportioned according to their several necessities—until all is distributed.

He appointed Benjamin Davis his executor. He died in 1718 and Samuel assumed the trust, and though the estate was appraised at £481,17,10, it proved insufficient to pay the legacies in full. Samuel, before making a final settlement, removed to to Connecticut. Some of the receipts call him of Groton, others of New London, and others of Coventry.

(10-3) Hannah, daughter of John Davis, married Jedediah Jones 18th March, 1681, and resided at Scorton, just within the bounds of Barnstable. In the town records only Shubael, Simon, Isaac, Timothy and Hannah, are named born previous to 1695.

(11-4) Mary, daughter of John Davis, married in 1677, Benjamin Goodspeed, and had Mary Jan 10, 1677-8, who married Ichabod Hinckley, and receipted for his wife's legacy. Nov. 24, 1697, she married Ensign John Hinckley of West Barnstable. By her last husband she had no children.

(12-5) Joseph, son of John Davis, married, March 28, 1682, Mary Claghorn, daughter of James. He resided at Chequaquet, and died about 1690. She died 1706.

*Children born in Barnstable.*

47.  I.    Simeon 19th Jan. 1683.
48.  II.   Mary, 19th June 1685.
49.  III.  Joseph, April, 1687.
50.  IV.   Robert, 13th June 1689.
James Cahoon, illegitimate son born Oct. 25, 1696.

(13-6) Benjamin, son of John Davis, died unmarried in 1718, and his estate was divided among his brothers and sisters and their representatives then living: 1, to John Davis, (Samuel died in 1711) ; 2, to heirs of Hannah Jones, deceased ; 3, to heirs of Mary Hinckley, deceased ; 4, to heirs of Joseph Davis, deceased, (Benjamin and Simon deceased) ; 5, to heirs of Dolar Davis ; 6, to heirs of Jabez Davis ; 7, to Mary Davis ; 8, to Timothy Davis ; and 9, to Ruth Linnell. Of the family of John Davis four were living in 1718, three had died leaving no issue, and five who had families. He had lands at Catacheset, Oyster Island, Cotuit, Cooper's Pond, and at the Common Field. He owned the dwelling-house which was his father's.

(14-7) Dolar, son of John Davis, removed early to South Sea. His farm was at Skonconet. He married, 3d Aug. 1681, Hannah, daughter of David Linnell. He was a house carpenter and joiner. He died in 1710, and names in his will, sons Shubael, Stephen, Daniel, Job, and Noah, and daughters Hannah, Thankful, Remember Mercy. He gave one half of his joiners tools to Stephen, and the other half and all his carpenters tools, to Job. He had two swords, which indicates that he had seen service as a soldier. The best he gave to Job, and the other to Noah. His wife is not named, and was probably dead.

*Children born in Barnstable.*

51.  I.    Shubael, 23d April, 1685, married twice.
52.  II.   Thomas, Aug. 1686 died young.
53.  III.  Hannah, Dec. 1689.
54.  IV.   Stephen, Sept. 1690.
55.  V.    Thankful, March 1696.
56.  VI.   Daniel, July 1698.
57.  VII.  Job, July 1700.
58.  VIII. Noah, Sept. 1702.
59.  IX.   Remember Mercy, 15th Oct. 1704.

(16-9) Jabez, son of John Davis, was a carpenter, and resided in Barnstable. In his will dated 29th Sept. 1710, he named all his children excepting Reuben and Ebenezer, who probably died young. He orders his sons Isaac and Jacob to be put to some trades as soon as they are capable. Inventory £538,16,08.

Jabez Davis married, 20th Aug. 1689, Experience, daughter of David Linnel, of Barnstable. He died 1710, and his widow married, Feb. 13, 1711-12, Benjamin Hatch, of Falmouth. She died a widow Dec 1736.

*Children born in Barnstable.*

60.  I.    Nathan, 2d March 1690, (town and church records.)
61.  II.   Reuben, (church records.)
62.  III.  Samuel, 25th Sept. 1692.  Removed to Connecticut.
63.  IV.   Bathsheba, 16th Jan. 1694.
64.  V.    Isaac, 23d April, 1696, died in 1718.
65.  VI.   Abigail, 26th April, 1698, married Sept. 1718, Joseph Hamblin.
66.  VII.  Jacob, Oct. 1699.
67.  VIII  Mercy, 6th Feb. 1701.
68.  IX.   Ebenezer, bap 23d June, 1706.
69.  X.    Solomon, 4th Sept. 1706.

(17-10) Mercy, daughter of John Davis, was an old maid, gentle, kind, affectionate, nurse and physician to her father and mother, her brothers and sisters, and the host who called her aunt. She died in 1733, aged about 70, and bequeathed her whole estate to her sister Ruth Linnell, to children of her brother John, and to her nephew Simon Davis.

(18-11) Timothy, son of John Davis, joined the society of Friends and removed to Rochester, and is the ancestor of the Davis's in New Bedford and Rochester. Until the discovery of Samuel Davis' Will they were unable to trace their descent from Dolar. They knew they were distantly related to the Davis's in Falmouth, descendants of John Jr., and that Nicholas, the early Quaker, was a connection, but the degree of consanguinity was unknown.

Timothy Davis married 7th of 1st month, 1690, Sarah, daughter of Edward Perry, of Sandwich. His oldest son was born in Sandwich, his other children probably in Rochester.

70.   I.   Nicholas, Oct. 28, 1690.
71.   II.   Hannah, Sept. 17, 1692.
72.   III.   Sarah, March 18, 1693-6.
73.   IV.   Rest, Sept. 17, 1700.
74.   V.   Peace, April 14, 1702.
75.   VI.   Dorcas, Sept. 10, 1704.

These dates are from the records of the Sandwich monthly meeting, and first month was then March.

(19-12) Ruth, daughter of John Davis, married, in 1695, John Linnel, one of the first who removed to South Sea. His house was at Hyannis Port, and was taken down a few years ago. She had seven children; making the whole number of the grand children of John Davis, Senior, 56. She died May 8, 1748, in the 75th year of her age, and is buried in the ancient grave yard at Barnstable.

[The Concord and Falmouth branches are here dropt.]

(47-1) Capt. Simon Davis, son of Joseph, born 19th Jan. 1683-4, was an officer in the militia, and a man of some note. At 41 he married, May 12, 1725, Elizabeth Lumbert, who died leaving no issue. At 56 he married Priscilla Hamblin, (June 5, 1740.) By her he had Mary, Feb. 28, 1741-2 ; Content, March 23, 1743-4 ; Priscilla, Feb. 17, 1745-6, and Joseph baptized July 17, 1748. She died April 1751, aged 41.

(50-4) Robert, son of Joseph Davis, probably removed to Rochester, where he had by Mary, Joseph, April 8, 1727; Benjamin, Feb. 22, 1728-9 ; Benajah, June 27, 1734.

(51-1) Shubael Davis, son of Dolar, married, Sept. 15, 1720, Hopestill Lumbert, and 2nd, Patience Crocker 1727.

(54-4) Stephen Davis, son of Dolar, married Desire Lewis March 12, 1730. He died very suddenly Dec. 7, 1756. He had Mary and Martha, twins, born April 23, 1732 ; Jonathan baptized

June 8, 1740; and Stephen born July 6, 1746. Mary married Benjamin Lumbert, Jr., May 23, 1751; Martha, Joseph Lewis, Esq.

(56-6) Daniel Davis, son of Dolar, married Mary Lothrop. Children born in Barnstable : Daniel, April 1, 1724 ; Samuel, May 8, 1727; Joseph, May 28, 1729, died June 30, same year; Jonathan, Sept. 21, 1733. Mrs. Mary Davis was dismissed Sept. 26, 1742, from the Barnstable church to the church in Lebanon, Conn.

(57-7) Job Davis, son of Dolar, married, Dec. 22, 1724, Mary Phinney. He inherited the estate of his ancestor John. He died April 4, 1751, aged 50, and his widow died at the great age of 98 years. Their children were : 1, Mary, June 21, 1725, died young ; 2, Thomas, Oct. 16, 1726, deaf and dumb, was a weaver, died unmarried; 3, Shubael, March 19, 1729, married Thankful Lewis, Jr., April 30, 1852 ; 4, Mary, July 18, 1731, married Thomas Young Feb. 1759-60 : 5, Mehitabel, March 9, 1733-4, married 1st Gershom Cobb Feb. 6, 1761-2, and 2d, Nathaniel Lothrop, 1776 ; 6, Seth, Dec. 27, 1736 ; 7, Hannah, Sept. 6, 1739, married David Childs April 4, 1758, and through her the ancient Davis estate passed into the Child family ; 8, Ebenezer, Dec. 17, 1742, deaf and dumb, a shoe maker. He removed to Maine.

(58-8) Noah Davis, son of Dolar, married, May 7, 1724, Hannah Fuller, and had Lewis, Aug. 26, 1724 ; Thankful, March 9, 1728 ; Eunice, April 20, 1734 ; John, baptized July 4, 1742 ; Joseph, Oct. 21, 1746. Eunice married Jabez Claghorn Nov. 21, 1759.

(60-1) Nathan Davis, son of Jabez, was a wheelwright, he married, 24th Nov. 1714, Elizabeth Phinney, and had Jabez 7th Oct. 1715 ; Sarah, 12th Aug. 1717 ; Elizabeth, 15th Sept. 1718 ; Isaac, 9th June 1720. He administered on his brother Isaac's estate in 1710.

Solomon, son of Jabez Davis, married Mehitabel Stertevat of Sandwich, and removed to that town.

(70-1) Nicholas Davis, son of Timothy, belonged to the Society of Friends and resided at Rochester. He was a Quaker preacher, and spent most of his time in Rochester and Dartmouth. He however travelled extensively, visiting North Carolina, Virginia, New Jersey, Maryland, Pennsylvania and New York. On his return from a journey from New York he was taken sick of a fever and died at the house of William Russell in Oblong, 10th month, 7th Oct. 1775, (after 1752 January was the first month) in the 65th year of his age. He married thrice. 1st, Mary, 2d, Hannah, and 3d Ruth. By his first wife he had Nathan born 11th month, (Jan.) 28, 1715-16; Elizabeth, 11 month, 20, 1718-19. By his second wife he had no children. By his third wife, Timothy, born 2d month (April) 9, 1730 ; Nicholas,

3 month, (May) 10, 1732 ; Abram, 12th month (Feb.) 20, 1735-6 ; (Rochester records Feb. 1, 1736) Mary, 5th month (July) 3, 1742 ; James, 3d month (May) 1743. The latter was grandfather to Wm. P. Davis of Yarmouth. Timothy of this family was a Quaker preacher. During the Revolution he was an ardent whig, and wrote a pamphlet in favor of prosecuting the war. For this, he was disowned by his brethren. [It is said, on what authority I am unable to say, that Jefferson Davis is a descendant of Timothy.]

In early times the descendants of Dolar Davis were very numerous in Barnstable ; now not one remains who is a legal voter. Many families of the name removed ; but not so many as of some other names. Many of the families have dwindled and died out.

The Davis families in Truro are descendants of Benjamin Davis, born about the year 1730. He married Betsey Webb. He had Benjamin who removed first to Chatham and thence to Reed-field, Maine ; James W. ; Ebenezer L. ; and Betsey who married Solomon Mirick, of Brewster. His son Ebenezer L. married Azubah Hinckley, and had Dianah, Solomon, Ebenezer, Betsey, Benjamin, Azubah, and Joshua H., most of whom are now living. James W. has also descendants now living.

# DELAP.

In 1688, when William and Mary ascended the throne of England, manufacturing industry had given wealth and prosperity to Ireland. In the first year of their reign the royal assent was given to laws passed by both Houses of Parliament, to discourage the manufactures of Ireland which competed with those of England. Lord Fitzwilliam says that by this invidious policy 100,000 operatives were driven out of Ireland. Many of the Protestants to Germany, some of the Catholics to Spain, and multitudes of all classes to America. Dobbe, on Irish trade, printed in Dublin in 1729, estimated that 3000 males left Ulster yearly for the colonies.

The tolerant policy of William Penn, induced many to settle in Pennsylvania. The arrivals at the port of Philadelphia, of Irish emigrants, for the year ending December 1729, was 5,655. The satiriol Dean Swift reproached the aristocracy for their suicidal impolicy "in cultivating cattle and banishing men."

The Irish emigrants who came over at the close of the 17th and the beginning of the 18th centuries, were a very different class from those who now throng to our shores. Very few could claim a purely Celtic ancestry. Those from the north of Ireland were descendants of Scots who had settled there and were known as Scotch Irish. Many were descendants of English parents, and of the Huguenots who found an asylum in Ireland after the Revocation of the Edict of Nantz. A large proportion of them were tradesmen, artisans, and manufacturers. Many settled in the Southern States. Londonderry, in New Hampshire, was settled by the Scotch Irish, and several towns in Maine. Many settled in various towns in New England, and not a few of the most noted men in our country trace their descent from these Irish refugees. Among these are some families of the name of Allison, Butler, Cathern, Carroll, Clinton, Fulton, Jackson, Knox, McDonouah, Ramesy, Read, Sullivan, Walsh, Wayne, and many others distinguished in the annals of our country. Of the fifty-six who signed the Declaration of  Independence, nine were Irish, or of Irish origin.

The influence of  this class of  imigrants has not been sufficiently appreciated.   The acts of  the British Parliament which brought ruin to Ireland, gave prosperity to America.   Wherever the Irish refugees settled, there mechanical and manufacturing industry was developed, giving a diversity of employment to the people, adding to their wealth, and making them prosperous and less dependent on the mother country.   The introduction of steam power, the construction of canals and many great public enterprises, originated with, or were promoted, and brought to a successful issue, by the descendants of  these settlers.   In the Revolutionary army many of  the most efficient officers were Irish, or sons of Irishmen.   In civil life many were eminent.   Gov. James Sullivan of  Mass., was the son of  a Limerick school master, who with other Irish families settled in Belfast, Maine, in 1723.   Gen. Andrew Jackson, President of  the United States, was the son of an Irish refugee.

Among them were  men  distinguished in literature, George Berkluy, Dean of Derry, came in 1729.   His "Theory of Vision" has made his name familiar in Europe.   His object was to establish a college for the conversion of  the red race.   He settled at Newport where he had a farm of  ninety acres.   Failing in his purposes in 1732, he gave his farm and the finest collection of books which had then come over at one time, to Yale College.   In Newport his "Minute Phylosopher" was composed, and the following beautiful lines so poetical in conception, and known to every school boy to this day :

> "Westward the Star of Empire takes its way,
>   The three first acts already past;
> The fourth shall close it with the closing day,
>   Earth's noblest Empire is the last."

Among the first settlers in this County several Irish names occur.   Higgins is a Longford name.   The Kelley's descended from the O'Kelley's, a noted clan resident near Dublin.   In latter times, several of  the Scotch-Irish settled in Barnstable, namely : William Belford, James Delap, John Cullio, John Easterbrooks, and Matthew Wood.

Charles Clinton, the  ancestor of the Clintons in New York, was born in Longford, Ireland, in the year 1690.   His grandfather William was an adherent of Charles I, and took refuge in the north of Ireland.   His father James married Elizabeth Smith, a daughter of one of the Captains in Cromwell's army.   He was a man of wealth and influence, and induced many of  his friends and neighbors to emigrate with him to America.   He chartered the ship George and Ann, Capt. Rymer, to transport them and their effects from Dublin to Philadelphia.   The whole number of passengers, including men, women, and children, was one hundred and fourteen. Among the papers of Mr. Charles Clinton is a document showing that he paid the passage money for ninety-four.

Mr. Clinton was unfortunate in his selection of a ship; but more unfortunate in his selection of a captain. Rymer was a cold blooded tyrant, of whom his officers and sailors were in constant fear, and as base a villian as ever trod the deck of a slave-ship. The George and Ann sailed on the 20th of May, 1729, from the port of Dublin for Philadelphia, poorly supplied with stores for a voyage of the ordinary length, but protracted by the infamy of the master to one hundred and thirty-five days. The passengers were not isolated individuals who had casually met on ship-board, they consisted of families who had converted their estates, excepting such portion as they could conveniently take with them, into gold, to purchase lands in Pennsylvania, and build a town where they could enjoy the civil and religious privileges denied to them in their native land. They had selected the mild season of the year for their passage, and expected to arrive in Philadelphia in July, in season to select their place of residence, and put up dwellings before winter. Such were their anticipations. They did not dream that half of their number would find watery graves before reaching the shores of America.

Among the passengers in this ill-fated ship were the father and mother of James Delap, and his sisters Rose, Jean, and Sarah. Tradition says there was another child whose name is not preserved. The Delap family were from Cavan, a county adjoining Longford, the former home of nearly all the other passengers. There were two on board whom Capt. Delap in his narrative, calls "Methodists."*

Several besides Mr. Clinton had considerable sums in gold and silver coins. This was known to the captain, and excited his cupidity, and he resolved to prolong the voyage, and to keep his ship at sea until his provisions were exhausted, and his passengers had died of famine and disease, and then seize and appropriate their goods to his own use. Such was the diabolical plan of Capt. Rymer.

The ship had not long been at sea before the passengers began to mistrust that the captain had evil designs. He was tyrannical in the exercise of his authority, and his officers and men were in constant fear of him. The ship was making slow progress towards her port of destination, the passengers had been put on short allowance, and some had already died of disease engendered by the small quantity and bad quality of the provisions

---

*No Methodist preachers came over as early as 1729. "Methodist" was a nick-name then applied to men who were very exact in the performance of their religious duties, whether Catholic or Protestant. The converts of the Wesley's were called "Methodist," and they adopted the name, as the converts of Fox did that of Quaker.

served out.   Starvation and death seemed inevitable if  no change could be effected, and the  passengers, after consultation, resolved to assume the command if  a change could not otherwise be made. The two called "Methodists," having  some knowledge of  the theory and practice of  invigation, were appointed to watch night and day all the movements of  Capt. Rymer.   One night soon afterwards, they discovered that though the wind was  fair, the ship was sailing in an opposite direction from her true course. They inquired of  the helmsman why he so steered ;  his reply was, "that is the captain's order."

This fact was communicated to the other passengers.   Several had then died of  starvation, and many  had become so weak and emaciated by want of  food and nourishment that they could scarcely stand.   Though weak and feeble they resolved to make an effort to compel the captain to keep his ship on her true course, both by night as well as by day.   One of  the passengers had a brace of  pistols.   These were loaded and put into the hands of the "Methodists," and  all the passengers who had sufficient strength remaining followed them to the quarter deck.†   With the loaded pistols in  their hands they charged the captain with treachery, with protracting the voyage, with the design of  keeping the ship at sea till all the passengers had  perished of disease or famine, and then seize on their goods.   He said in reply that the voyage had been prolonged by head winds, and not by any fault or connivance of  himself or his offcers.   They then charged him with having kept his ship off  her course in the night, thus deceiving the passengers, who were mostly 'landsmen, and unable in dark weather to judge  whether or not the  ship was on her true course ;  with issuing fuller  rations to his crew than to the passeners that he might be able to navigate his ship.   Seeing the resolute and determined manner of  the passengers, he made fair promises ; but he made them only that he might break them.‡

The Capes of Virginia was the first land made, but no date is given, from whence, according to the  pretence of  the captain, he was driven by stress of  weather to Cape Cod, making the land on the 4th of  October 1729.

This was only pretence, and though his  surviving passengers earnestly persuaded  him to land them, according to contract, at Philadelphia, or at New  York, or at any  port he could make, he refused to accede to their requests, and  obstinately kept his vessel at sea, though his passengers were daily perishing for want of

---

† Another account says this occurred in the cabin of the ship.  Prudence required that it should not occur in presence of the crew, and I am inclined to the opinion that the tradition in our family is at fault in this particular.

---

‡ Whether this uprising among the passengers was before or after land had been discovered is not named in the  narrative of  Capt. Delap.  It probably occurred before.  It is referred to in several notices of the voyage that I have seen ; but the date of its occurrence is not given, nor the  date of the first sight of land.

food. Every sailor knows that the gale which would drive a vessel from the Capes of Virginia to Cape Cod, would enable a captain of very moderate attainments to have made a harbor either in the Chespeake or in Delaware Bay, or to have reached the port of New York. Like many other villains, he did not see the goal to which his base conduct inevitably led. When off the Capes of Virginia he had wit enough to perceive the difficulty in which he was involved. If he listened to his passengers, and made for the port of Philadelphia, he would have been immediately arrested on his arrival, and his only alternative was to keep his ship at sea, avoid speaking any vessel, and persist in his diabolical purpose.

The New England Weekly Journal, printed at Boston Nov. 10, 1729, contains the following notice of the arrival of the George and Ann :

"We hear from Martha's Vineyard that some time last month Capt. Lothrop, in his passage from this place (Boston) to that island, off of Monomoy espied a vessel which put out a signal of distress to them. He making up to her went aboard ; found her to be a vessel from Ireland, bound for Philadelphia, (as they said) who had been from thence 20 weeks and brought out 190 passengers, 30 of whom were children, being destitute of provision, (having then but 15 biscuit on board) 100 of them were starved to death, among which were all the children except one, and the remainder of the passengers looked very ghastfully. They craved hard for water, of which one drank to that degree that he soon after died ; and two more died while Capt. Lothrop was aboard. Only three of the sailors were alive (besides the master and mate) and they sick. They entreated him to pilot them into the first harbor they could get into, but the master was for bringing them to Boston. They told him if he would not let the pilot carry them into what place he should think fit, they would throw him overboard ; upon which Capt. Lothrop having brought the vessel off of Sandy Point, told them there was but one house near, and spoke of going somewhere else, but they were all urgent to put them ashore anywhere, if it were but land. Accordingly he carried them in and left them there, with provisions ; 'tis thought many are since dead. Notwithstanding their extremity, and the sad spectacles of death before their eyes, and a near prospect of their own, 'twas astonishing to behold their impenitence, and to hear their profane speeches."

The renowned Capt. John Smith, and other early navigators, speak of Isle Nauset, which in ancient times extended from the entrance to Nauset harbor, south about four miles. Deep navigable waters now occupy its location. The loose sands of which it was composed have been carried southward by the currents, or blown inward, covering up the meadows, which for many years have been seen croping out on the eastern side of the beach, which has passed entirely over them, and united with Pochet islands. The harbor between the latter and Nauset Isle is now entirely filled up. Since 1729 Monomoy Point, in Chatham, has extended south several miles. The point which Capt. Lothrop calls Sandy, was then about four miles north of Monomoy Point. A vessel then entering Chatham harbor could sail eight miles in a northerly direction within the islands up to the present town of Eastham. It is certain that Capt. Rymer landed his passengers at Nauset, and in that part of the territory, now called Orleans.

When Captain Lothrop boarded the George and Ann, Monomoy Point was the nearest land ; a barren, desolate region, where neither shelter nor provisions could be procured. The point which he called Sandy point was on the north of the entrance to Chatham, probably then separated by a channel from Isle Nauset. This was also a barren, desolate region, with only one house. The settlement at Chatham was the nearest, but at that time there were only a few inhabitants scattered over a large territory. Capt. Lothrop judged it better to proceed further up the harbor to Nauset, or Eastham, an older settlement, where an abundance of supplies could be procured. The passengers were probably landed near the head of Potamomacut harbor, in the easterly part of the present town of Orleans. Tradition says they were landed on Nauset Beach ; but it was equally as convenient to set them ashore on the main land, and not on a desert island.‡

Capt. Lothrop belonged to Barnstable, and was a very reliable and accurate man. He states that the number of passengers was 190, instead of 114. I give both statements, not knowing which is the most accurate.

Of the one hundred and fourteen (or 190 as stated by Lothrop) who embarked at Dublin, less than one-half were then living —all the rest had been committed to the watery deep. Of the Delap family the father, Rose, Jane, Sarah, and another, had been buried in the ocean. The mother was living when Capt. Lothrop came on board—emaciated and very weak, in consequence of long abstinence. When food was distributed she took a biscuit, and in attempting·to swallow it a piece lodged in her throat, and before relief could be obtained, expired. Her body was taken on shore, and buried at Nauset. James, when taken from the boat, was so weak that he could not stand, and crawled from the boat to the beach. After landing the surviving passengers and some of their goods, Capt. Rymer proceeded on his voyage to Phila-

‡June 25, 1863. Not being able to clearly understand the statement of Capt. Lothrop, which I received this week, I went yesterday to Nauset beach, and examined the localities, and I feel certain that the comments made thereon are reliable and accurate. Monomoy is now called also Sandy Point, which creates confusion. By Sandy Point Capt. Lothrop meant the point at the north entrance of Chatham harbor, possibly he may have meant the point at the entrance of Potamomacut harbor; but be that as it may it does not affect the result. Now if a vessel should arrive off Chatham in such condition the news would be transmitted to Boston in an hour, then it was thirty-five days before the intelligence reached Boston.

delphia.   After his arrival the sailors, relieved from the terror in which they had been held, entered a complaint against their Captain.   He was arrested, a preliminary examination was had, and he was sent in irons to England for trial.   The charges of cruelty to his passengers and crew, of extortion, and of an attempt to embezzle the goods of the passengers, were proved, and he was condemned to be hung and quartered, and this just sentence was duly executed in Dublin.*

Such is the short and sad narrative of the passage of James Delap to this country.   No details of individual suffering are given.   The fact that more than one-half of all on board perished of starvation, is a suggestive one.   He was then fourteen years of age ; young, but the incidents of such a passage would make a deep impression, not soon to be forgotten.   So far as known, he was the sole survivor of the family—an orphan boy, weak and emaciated—a stranger in a strange land, without money, without any friend or protector but "the father of the fatherless."

Little is known of his orphanage.   From Eastham he came to Barnstable, and Nov. 5, 1729, he chose John Bacon, Jr., saddler, for his guardian, with whom he resided during his minority, as an apprentice to learn the trade of a blacksmith.†

He had a guardian appointed early that he might, as stated in the record, have an agent who had legal authority to secure the small "estate of his Honored father, deceased."   A small portion was recovered, and on the 26th of the following January apprised at £16,4s by Geo. Lewis, James Cobb, and John Scudder, Jr. The "Goods and Chattles" saved consisted of articles of men and women's apparel, bedding, table linen, woolen yarns, and a gun.

Capt. Delap always spoke kindly of his "Master Bacon." He was treated as a member of the family.   The children regarded him as a brother, and for three successive generations the relation between the families was most intimate.

* Respecting the voyage and its termination, there are some discrepencies.  Hoosack, in his life of Clinton, says the ship sailed from Dublin in May, 1729, and after a voyage of 21 weeks and 3 days arrived at Cape Cod, in the fall, where Mr. Clinton and his surviving friends remained till the following spring, when they took passage for New Winsor, Orange Co., New York.  As the ship had been insured in Dublin the captain contrived to let her slip her moorings on a stormy night, in which she was lost.  The account in Hoosack says that the captain kept his passengers at sea until he extorted a sum of money from them to land them; that Clinton wanted the officers ot the ship to seize the Captain and ship but they refused.

Eager, in his history of Orange County, N. Y., says the Captain was seized, put in irons by the passengers, and the command given to the mate, who brought the vessel in, in a few days.

Among the passengers were three of the name of Armstrong, all of whom died on the passage, Charles Clinton and wife, Alexander Dennison, and John Young, who survived. [For the information in this note, I am indebted to E. B. O'Callagan, Esq., of Albany.  I am also indebted to Hon. John G. Palfrey, and Rev. Henry M. Dexter, of Boston, and J. R. Bordhead, Esq., author of the history of New York, for assistance in compiling this article.]

† John Bacon, Jr., was the father of the late Capt. Isaac Bacon, Sen'r, and owned the house in which the latter lived, a large two story gambrel roofed house, that stood next east of the ancient Bacon mansion.  John Bacon, Jr., is called a saddler, he was also a blacksmith and a sailor.  His blacksmith's shop stood on the west of his house, near the row of ancient cherry trees, and there James learned his trade.

After completing the term of his apprenticeship, he bought the estate of Jeremiah Bacon, Jr., bounded south by the county road, the present lane to the Common Field is on the west of his land, north by Mill Creek, and east by a small run of water, containing three and one-half acres, with the two story single house thereon. His shop stood on the road, east of the run of water. The hill on the east of his shop is yet known as Delap's Hill.

In the summer season he sailed in the Barnstable and Boston packet, at first, with Capt. Solomon Otis, and afterwards as master. In the. winter he was employed in his blacksmith's shop.

June 22, 1738, he was married by Rev. Mr. Green, to Mary, daughter of Benjamin O'Kelley, of Yarmouth. She was born April 8, 1720, O. S., and at the time of her marriage had been residing in the family of Deacon Isaac Hamblin of Yarmouth. Though only 18, she was a member of the Church in Yarmouth, and was all her life a woman of exemplary piety. Her mother, Mary, was a daughter of Benjamin and Sarah (Walker) Lumbert, born in Barnstable 17th June, 1688. She was a widow many years, and resided with her daughter, was a mid-wife, a vocation which a century ago was a very common and very useful employment for females. She was experienced, and stood high in her profession. When more than four score years, when on her way to visit a patient, her horse stumbled, and she fell and broke her leg; but after being confined to her room some months she recovered, and resumed her useful labors for a short time. She died, according to the church records, May 1, 1772, aged 82 years —nearly 84 years of age, if her birth is accurately recorded.

Capt. James Delap removed from Barnstable to Granville, Nova Scotia, in the spring of the year 1775, and resided on a farm which he inherited from his son Thomas, who died young. All his family removed with him excepting his daughters Rose and Catherine. His health began to fail before he removed from Barnstable, and he died in Granville in 1789, of apoplexy, aged about 74.

He is spoken of as a "very friendly, civil man, hospitable to strangers, kind to all, and very liberal in his efforts to educate his children." His letters to his children indicate that he was a very affectionate parent, and took a lively interest in their welfare. "In person he was short, thick set, stout built, with a short neck, a form which physiologists say predisposes to apoplexy of which he had three shocks, two before he removed from Barnstable. In politics, he was a staunch loyalist, a fact that seems inconsistent with the history of his family. Though his widow was sixty-nine years of age at his death, she married John Hall, Esq., of Granville, whom she survived. She died June 4, 1804, aged 84 years. She was an exemplary and consistent Christian; an active energetic woman; and an excellent wife and mother.

Capt. James Delap had ten children all born in Barnstable, all lived to mature age, and all excepting Thomas married and had families.   The eight daughters of James Delap were all robust and healthy ; women of good sense, sound judgement, and good business capacity, most of them lived more than seventy years and had numerous descendants.

*Children of James and Mary Delap born in Barnstable.*

I.    Rose, born Feb. 25, 1739, O. S., married Ebenezer Scudder, of Barnstable, Jan, 11, 1759, and had ten children : 1, Ebenezer, Aug. 13, 1761 ; 2, James, March 14, 1764, died young ; 3, Thomas, Sept. 10, 1766, died young ; 4, Isaiah, Jan. 8, 1768 ; 5, Asa, July 25, 1771 ; 6, Elizabeth, Oct. 12, 1773, married Morton Crocker ; 7, Josiah, Nov. 30, 1775 ; 8, James D., Oct. 27, 1779 ; 9, Thomas D., Jan. 25, 1782 ; 10, Rose, April 24, 1784, died young. Mrs. Rose Scudder died April 17, 1812, aged 72 years. Mr. Ebenezer Scudder died June 8, 1818, aged 85 years. He was a man of mild, pleasant disposition, a quiet, good neighbor.   Mrs. Rose Scudder was a woman of great firmness and decision of character, and of untiring industry. She resided at Chequaquet, near Phinney's Mill, seven miles from the meeting house in the east parish, yet she often, on the Sabbath, walked to meeting, attended the morning and afternoon service, dined and took tea with her sister Catherine, and walked home in the evening, the whole distance by unfrequented roads, and more than one-half the distance through forests.   She often traveled four miles to spend an evening, and at 9 o'clock walked home alone, nearly the whole distance through a dense forest. She spun much street yarn ; but she spun it for some purpose.   She carried her knitting work with her, and knit as she walked on.   She said her work was good company on a dark night.   Her sons Ebenezer, Isaiah, Asa, Josiah and James, inherited the character of their mother, and were active business men, and successful in life.   Thomas and Elizabeth, like their father, were mild and pleasant ; but wanting in energy of character.

II.   Abigail, born Nov. 6, 1741, O. S., married, Feb. 9, 1764, John Coleman, of Granville, Nova Scotia.   He was a son of James Coleman of Barnstable.   She had several children.   Her sons James and Thomas were lost at sea.   She died in 1825, aged 84.

III.  Catherine, born Sept. 3, 1743, married Amos Otis, (my grandfather) and always resided in Barnstable.   She had two children, Amos and Solomon.   She died Feb. 28, 1819, aged 75, having lived a widow 47 years.

IV.    Thomas, born April 14, 1745, did not marry. He was master of a vessel, in the King's service, Dec. 6, 1771, while on a voyage from Philadelphia to Halifax, during a violent gale and snow storm was cast ashore on Great Point, Nantucket. All on board succeeded in getting to the shore. It was a thick snow storm and very cold. Capt. Delap perished in one of the hollows or gorges on that point. Mr. Amos Otis in another. Two of the sailors went on to Cortue Point, heading towards the town, and both froze to death on that point. Two other sailors and a boy, John Weiderhold, succeeded in getting off Great Point, and reached a barn at Squam. They covered themselves up in the hay, placing the lad between them, so that the warmth of their bodies kept him from freezing.

     The next day the vessel was discovered by people from the town, high and dry on the beach, and if the captain and crew had remained on board none would have been lost. Capt. Delap, Mr. Otis, and most of the crew, had been exposed to the storm about twelve hours when the vessel was cast on shore, and were wet, benumbed with cold, and almost exhausted, when they got to the land. The boy was the only one who had not been exposed, and who had dry clothing. Capt. Delap is buried at Nantucket, and the manner of his death is recorded on a monument to his memory. His age was 26 years, 7 months, and 11 days.

     The boy, Weiderhold, from that time made Nantucket his home. He died about thirty years ago. He was a member of the Masonic Fraternity, and a very worthy man. He often related the sad story of the shipwreck, and pointed out the spots where each perished.

V.     Mary, born Nov. 3, 1747, O. S., married Seth Backus of Barnstable, had a family of six children, Walley, Betsey, Mary, Seth, James, Thomas, and removed to Lee, Mass., where she died at an advanced age. Her son Walley was an influential man.

VI.    Sarah, born April 11, 1750, O. S., married Capt. James Farnsworth, of Groton, and removed to Machias, where she died in 1785, aged 35 years. She had a son who died in childhood, and three daughters. One married Simeon Foster, and resided at Cooper, Maine. Her grandson, Benjamin F. Foster, was a popular writing master, and author of a system of penmanship. Another daughter, Sarah, married George S. Smith, Esq., of Machias.

VII.   Jane or Jean, born Aug. 13, 1752, O. S., married, in 1772, Jonas Farnsworth, (a cousin of the Capt. Jonas who married Sarah.) Their oldest daughter, Nancy, (my mother) was born at Machias, in 1773. Having obtained of the

British authorities a permit to remove, and a protection against capture, the family embarked for Boston. On their passage the vessel was taken by the British ship of war Viper, and sent to Halifax. They afterwards took passage in another vessel, were again captured, and were finally landed at Newburyport, from whence they proceeded to his native town, Groton, Mass. When captured, several shots were fired, and at the suggestion of the Captain, Mrs. F. and her infant daughter laid on the cabin floor, which was below the water line and comparatively safe.* Mr. Jonas Farnsworth died suddenly of apoplexy, July 16, 1805, aged 57 years. She died May 1826, aged 73. They had ten children, and have numerous descendants. Their youngest son, Rev. James Delap, was a graduate of Harvard College, and collected materials for genealogies of the Farnsworth and Delap families, which remain unpublished.

VIII.    Hannah, born July 14, 1755, N. S., married Samuel Street, Esq., a Captain in the British Navy, and died soon after, leaving no children.

IX.    Temperance, born in 1757, baptized at the East Church Jan. 15, 1758, married Dea. Thaddeus Harris,† of Cornwallis, Nova Scotia, and died Nov. 9, 1732, aged 75, leaving a numerous family of children and grand-children. One of her sons was for many years a member of the Queen's Council. A grandson for several years was a minister at Hyannis.

X.    James, born March, baptized Nov. 18, 1759, married at 20, Sarah Walker, of Granville, and had twelve children. He married for his second wife Mrs. Pengree, of Cornwallis, N. S., and removed to that town. He was for many years a deacon of the Baptist Church in Granville. He lived to be an old man.

It is surprising that no contemporaneous account of the voyage of the George and Ann to this country can be quoted—a voyage unparelled in atrocity in the annals of immigration. Most that is known is traditionary. Records must somewhere exist. The newspapers of the day probably contain some information. The records of the court in Dublin, where Rymer had his trial, if copies could be obtained, would furnish authentic information.

---

* In a letter of my great grandfather, James Delap, to his daughter Jane, dated Granville, July 15, 1780, but not forwarded till Oct. 1, he says: "We want to see you very much; but as the times are, cannot. Pray write at every opportunity, for we long to hear from you and little Nancy. We heard you had a tedious time home, and were taken again. We hope all these things will work together for your good. We are old, and the times are such, we never expect to see you again. Let us endeavor to become the true children of God, so as to meet in the Heavenly Kingdom, and never more be separated."

---

† Dea. Harris was living in 1834, aged 86.

# DEXTER.

Of the early life of Mr. Dexter, little is known. He came over, either with Mr. Endicott in 1629, or, in the fleet, with Gov. Winthrop, the following year, bringing with him his wife, and children, and several servants. He had received a good education, and wrote a beautiful court-hand; was a man of great energy of character, public spirited, and ever ready to contribute of his means, and use his influence in promoting any enterprise which he judged to be for the interest of the infant colony. He did his own thinking, and was independent and fearless in the expression of his opinions. Such were the leading traits in the character of Mr. Dexter; but it must be admitted that his energy of character bordered on stubbornness, and his independence of thought, on indiscretion and self-will.

In the year 1630, in the prime of life, and with ample means, he settled on a farm of eight hundred acres, in the town of Lynn. In the cultivation of his lands he employed many servants, and was called, by way of eminence, Farmer Dexter. His house was on the west side of Saugus river, above where the iron works were afterward built. In 1633, he built a weir across the Saugus river, for the purpose of taking bass and alewives, of which many were dried and smoked for shipment. He also built a mill, and bridge across the Saugus. In these enterprises he was the manager, and principal owner.

Mr. Dexter was admitted to be a freeman of the Massachusetts Colony May 18, 1631; but disfranchised March 4, 1633, therefore his name does not appear on the printed list. He had many quarrels, and many vexatious law-suits. If the controversies respecting the iron works, in which he was a large owner,

---

* One of Mr. Dexter's descendants writes that the absence of all reference to any wife in numerous deeds, dating back to 1639, seems to make it certain that he was a widower when he came over, or lost his wife early in his residence here. The fact that his youngest daughter was marriagable in 1639, would seem also necessarily to throw back his birth date to 1590-1595; which would make him 81 to 86 when he died.

are included in the records and documents, which have been preserved, in which he had an interest, they would fill a moderate
sized volumn.   The reader of these records should remember that
they were made by the personal enemies of Mr. Dexter, and though
the facts may be accurately stated, yet some allowance is to be
made for the hostile feeling which existed in the minds of the
writers.

In March, 1631, he had a quarrel with Gov. Endicott, in which
the Salem Magistrate struck Mr. Dexter, who complained to the
Court at Boston.   Mr. Endicott in his defence, says, "I hear I
am much complained of by goodman Dexter for striking him;
understanding since it is not lawful for a justice of the peace to
strike.   But if you had seen the manner of his carriage, with such
daring of me, with his arms akimbo, it would have provoked a
very patient man.   He has given out, if I had a purse he would
make me empty it, and if he cannot have justice here, he will do
wonders in England; and if he cannot prevail there, he will try it
out with me here at blows.   If it were lawful for me to try it at
blows, and he a fit man for me to deal with, you would not hear
me complain."   The jury to whom the case was referred, gave on
the 3d of May, 1631, a verdict for Mr. Dexter, assessing the
damage at £10 sterling ($44.44.)

In March, 1633, the court ordered that Mr. Dexter "be set in
the bilbows, disfranchised, and fined £10 sterling, for speaking
reproachful and seditious words against the government here
established."   The bilbows were a kind of stocks set up near the
meeting-house in Lynn, in which the hands and feet of the culprit
were confined

> "A Bastile, made to imprison hands,
> By strange enchantment made to fetter,
> The lesser parts, and free the greater."

Mr. Dexter, having been insulted by Samuel Hutchinson, he
met him one day on the road, "and jumping from his horse, he
bestowed about twenty blows on his head and shoulders, to the no
small danger and deray of his senses, as well as sensibilities."

These facts show that Mr. Dexter was not a meek man.   He had
many difficulties with his neighbors, and one of the vexatious law-
suits in which he was engaged, he left as a heritage to his children
and to his grand-children.   Whether justice was or was not on his
side in all these cases, the troubles that environed him at Lynn,
induced him to seek a quieter home.   In 1637, he and nine of his
neighbors obtained from the Plymouth Colony Court a grant of
the township of Sandwich.   He went there that year, and with
the commendable public spirit for which he had ever been distinguished built the first grist mill erected in that town.   He did not
remain long, for in 1638, the next year, he had 350 acres of land
assigned him as one of the inhabitants of Lynn, and he

remained there certainly till 1646, when he was indicted by the Court of Quarter Sessions as a common sleeper at meetings. It is probable that he left his son Thomas, not then of age, at Sandwich, to take the care of his property in that town, and that he returned to Lynn. At Sandwich he had lands assigned to him in the first division. At the division of the meadows April 16, 1640, he had six acres assigned to him for his mill, and "twenty-six acres if he come here to live." This record is conclusive evidence that he was not of Sandwich in 1640. Mr. Freeman, in his annals of that town, is mistaken in his statement that "he was one of those able to bear arms in Sandwich in 1643." His name is not on the list; neither is that of his son Thomas who does not appear to have been of Sandwich that year. From the year 1640 to March 1646, neither the father or the son are named in the Colony Records as residents in Sandwich, though the father continued to own the mill, and was one of the proprietors of the lands.

March 3, 1645-6, Thomas Dexter, of Sandwich, was presented by the grand jury, for conveying away a horse that had been pressed for the country use. Whether this was the father or son, does not appear, nor is it material, for both were residents in Sandwich that year. The father did not remain long in Sandwich. Mr. Freeman says he left in 1648, he was certainly of Barnstable in 1651, and was an inhabitant of that town till 1670, probably till 1675.

About the year 1646 he purchased two farms in Barnstable. One to which reference has been frequently had in these articles, situate on the south-east of the Blossom farm, and adjoining to the mill stream,* and afterwards owned and occupied by William Dexter, probably his son, and the other on the north-eastern declivity of Scorton Hill. His dwelling house was situate on the north side of the old county road, and commanded an extensive prospect of the country for miles around.

He led a quiet life in Barnstable, his name occasionally appears as a juryman, and as a surety for the persecuted Quakers, showing that he did not sympathize with the Barlow party. He could not, however, entirely refrain from engaging in law suits. At the March term of the Court in 1648-9, he had eight cases, principally for the collection of debts, and he recovered in seven. In 1653, he had a controversy with his neighbors respecting the

---

* In my investigations, I have been unable to ascertain who built the first mill on the stream now known as Jones's mill stream at West Barnstable. Mr. Dexter's lands were partly bounded by that stream, and I should not be surprised if some future investigator should ascertain that he built the first mill at West Barnstable, also the Old Stone Fort, to which frequent reference is made in the Crocker article.

On Wednesday last I was at Sandwich, and for the first time examined the records of that town for information respecting the Dexter family. I found much that I regret that I had not known before writing this article. The records, in almost every instance, and I am not certain but in every instance, refer to the second Thomas Dexter. A deed of his to the town of Sandwich, is an exceedingly interesting document.

boundaries of his lands, and at his request two men were appointed by the Colony Court, "to set at rights the lines or ranges," provided the parties cannot agree among themselves. It was afterwards referred to Barnard Lumbard.

He had, soon after his settlement in Barnstable, a controversey with the inhabitants, which remained unsettled for many years. As the case has a historical interest and illustrates the leading trait in his character, I shall give some details. Some years prior to 1652, he built a causeway across his own meadow, and a bridge across Scorton Creek, and extended the causeway to the upland on Scorton Neck, at the place where the new County road now passes over. A bridge and causeway to Scorton Neck had previously been built by Sandwich men, about half a mile farther west, which had been used in common by them and the inhabitants of Barnstable. Mr. Dexter's bridge shortened the distance which the latter had to travel to their meadows on Scorton Neck, and they claimed a right to pass over the new bridge without having assisted in the building, and without paying toll; because in the year 1652, according to the Barnstable town records, "It was agreed upon by the Jury for the highways, Anthony Annable being the foreman thereof, that a Highway two rod broad go from the point of upland of Samuel Fuller's through the marsh of Thomas Dexter's to the main creek, and so cross the marshes as far as the marsh of Samuel Hinckley's. Also, it is agreed by the said Jury that a foot way go from Lieutenant Fuller's house across the creek, where Mr. Dexter's bridge was, and so straight along to Mr. Bursley's bridge, leaving Mr. Dexter's orchard on the right hand, and Goodman Fitzrandles house on the left hand."

The highway laid out passed on the west side of Dexter's farm, southerly to the old County road. The foot way corresponds in locations with the new County road, till it joins the old, and thence by the latter to Bursley's bridge.

The matter was a cause of difficulty, and remained unsettled till Obtober 5, 1656, when the Plymouth Colony Court appointed and requested M. Prence, and Capt. Cudworth, to view the place in controversy, and if they they can, put an end to it, and if they cannot, to make report unto the Court of the state of the matter.

On the 10th of the same month the parties interested, namely, Thomas Dexter, Senior, of the one part, and of the other, Samuel Hinckley, William Crocker, Samuel Fuller, Peter Blossom, Thomas Hinckley, Robert Parker, John Chipman, and Robert Linnell, appeared on the premises before Mr. Thomas Prence and Capt. James Cudworth, and the case that had caused so much trouble, was "issued" to the satisfaction of all the parties. 1, It was agreed, "that all that are interested in any marsh above the aforesaid marsh, that needs the privilege of the said way, shall pay unto the said Thomas Dexter six pence per acre, in lieu and full recompense for the said marsh wayed, forever, himself and such others as make use thereof, to make and repair the said way, proportionable to the use made of it—the gates or bars to be shut after any one's use thereof by them, to prevent damage."

Right in this case, is apparent.  If Thomas Dexter built, as he did, a causeway and bridge on his own meadow, no one had a legal right to use the same without his consent.  The owners of the meadows on Scorton Neck had a right of way to the same, and the town had a legal right to lay out such way ; and if they laid it out over Thomas Dexter's private way, he had a legal right to claim compensation.  This he claimed, and the parties interested refused to pay.  The referees decided the case in his favor, giving him six pence an acre, or about six dollars in all, not enough to pay the law expenses he probably incurred.  He had legal right on his side ; but there were other considerations which should have deterred him from exacting "the pound of flesh."  It was the only convenient place to build a bridge, it was the natural outlet of the meadows above, and before the bridge was built the owners had sometimes crossed over at that place.  It was not an act of good neighborhood on the part of Mr. Dexter to maintain a quarrel more than five years, that he might have his own way.

In the following year, 1657, he commenced his lawsuit against the inhabitants of the town of Lynn for the possession of Nahant, which he claimed as his private property by virtue of purchase made about the year 1637, of the Indian Sachem, Poquanum, or Black Will, for a suit of clothes.  This was a mercantile speculation, and the law suits which it produced were very expensive. In February 1657, the inhabitants of Lynn voted to divide Nahant among the householders, to each an equal share, and Mr. Dexter thereupon brought an action against the town for taking possession and occupying his property.  He had, up to that time, manufactured tar from the pine trees ; and the town had also exercised some rights of ownership.  This unusual mode of division made every householder an interested party against Mr. Dexter, who was then a non-resident.  The court decided in favor of the defendants, and Mr. Dexter appealed to the Assistants, who confirmed the judgment of the lower court.  Whatever might have been the justice of his claim, it would have been difficult for him to have obtained a verdict where nearly all the witnesses in the case had an adverse interest.*

After his death his administrators, Capt. James Oliver, his son-in-law, an eminent merchant of Boston, and his grandson,

---

* The law forbidding purchases of land from the Indians except by public permission, had not been passed when Mr. Dexter bought Nahant; so that it would seem that he had a legal right to make the purchase.                                                          S.

Thomas, of Sandwich, were not satisfied with the decisions of the courts, and in 1678, brought another action, and in 1695, after the death of Thomas Dexter, 3d, another was brought all with like results.   These suits continued at intervals through a series of thirty-eight years, were very expensive, and the Dexters being the losing party, their costs must have amounted to a large sum.   It was the settled policy of the first settlers, that all purchases of lands from the Indians, should be by virtue of public authority. Mr. Dexter was not so authorized, and therefore had no legal right to make the purchase.

In 1657, Mr. Dexter took the oath of fidelity, and was admitted a freeman of the Plymouth Colony June 1, 1658.   For the succeeding eighteen years he appears to have lived a quiet, retired life, on his farm at Scorton Hill.   He had passed that period in life when men usually take an active and leading part in business or in politics.   Notwithstanding his expensive law suits, he had ample means remaining.   During his life, he appears to have conveyed his mill and his large real estate in Sandwich to his son Thomas, and his West Barnstable farm to William, retaining his Scorton Hill farm and his personal estate for his own use. The latter farm he sold about the year 1675 to William Troop and removed to Boston that he might spend his last days in the family of a married daughter, where he died in 1677 at an advanced age. No attempt has been made to veil his faults—he did not bury his talent in a napkin—and in estimating his character, we must inquire what he did, not what he might have done.   Who did more than Thomas Dexter to promote the interests of the infant settlement at Lynn?  who more at Sandwich?   Others, perhaps, did as much, none more.   He knew this, and his self esteem and love of approbation, prompted him to resist those who sought to appropriate to themselves without compensation, the benefits of the improvements which he had been the principal party to introduce.   When at Lynn, he built a weir across the Saugus river, for the benefit of the fisheries, a grist mill, a bridge across the Saugus, and was foremost in establishing the iron works in 1643 ; and at Sandwich he built a grist mill, and at Barnstable a causeway and bridge across Scorton Creek and marshes; all improvements in which the public took a deep interest.   For these acts, he is deserving of credit and they will forever embalm his memory. His harsh and censorious spirit created enemies, where a more conciliatory course would have made friends.   Vinegar was an element of his character, and no alchymist could have transmitted it into oil.   He was a member of the Puritan Church ; yet tolerant and liberal in his views.   No immorality was ever laid to his charge, and judging him by the rule laid down by the Great Teacher in the parable of the ten talents, we must decide that he was a usefnl man in his day and therefore entitled to the respect of posterity.

Of the family of Mr. Thomas Dexter, Senior, very little is certainly known. Mr. Lewis, the historian of Lynn, was unable to furnish anything that was certain and reliable, and the undefatigable Mr. Savage gives but a meagre account of his family. Mr. Freeman repeats the statements of his predecessors, adding very little to the information furnished by them. It is surprising that so little should be known of the family of so noted a man as Mr. Dexter.

It is certain that he had

I. Thomas, born in England, settled in Sandwich.

II. Mary, who married Oct. 1639, Mr. John Frend, who died young. Before Aug. 1655, as is show by a deed in Suffolk Registry, she had married Capt. James Oliver. They left no children.

And he probably had

III. William, who settled in Barnstable.

IV. Francis, who married Richard Wooddy. They had eight children. They lived some years in Roxbury. In 1695, Mary and Frances, who were then widows, brought the fourth suit in behalf of their father's claim upon Nahant, against the town of Lynn, once more in vain.

In regard to the two last named, I say probably, yet I have no reason to doubt the statement that William was the son of Thomas. Messrs. Lewis, Savage, and Freeman, say he was his son; but, after the most careful research, I cannot find positive evidence that such was the fact.

Mr. Drake, the able historian of Boston, has forwarded to me the following abstracts, from the records in the Probate Office of the County of Suffolk, which furnish additional information to what was before known:

"Feb. 9, 1676-7. Power of administration to the estate of Thomas Dexter, Senior, late of Boston, deceased, is granted to Capt. James Oliver, his son-in-law, and Thomas Dexter, Jr., his grandson."

"Nov. 1678, Ensgne Richard Woodde was joined with Capt. Oliver in this administration in room of Thomas Dexter, Jr., deceased."

The Rev. Henry M. Dexter of Boston, a descendant, furnishes the following abstract of the inventory of the estate dated April 25, 1677. It includes merely "so much as is due by bill from William Troop of Barnstable, as follows:

| | | | | | | |
|---|---|---|---|---|---|---|
| Payable before or in Nov. 1677, | | | | | | £20 |
| " | " | " | " | " | 1678, | 20 |
| " | " | " | " | " | 1679, | 20 |
| " | " | " | " | " | 1680, | 10 |

£70

It is added, "this is inventory and all of the estate that is known belonging to the deceased party aforsaid, only a claim of some lands which ly within the bounds of Lynn ; the value whereof we cannot determine at present until further insight into and known."

The "claim of some lands" was for Nahant, which was worthless and to which reference has already been had.

These two extracts prove that Thomas Dexter, Senior, was a resident in Boston at the time of his death, that he died the latter part of 1676 or early in 1677, that he had a son Thomas and a grand-son Thomas, and a daughter who married Capt. James Oliver, an eminent merchant of Boston.

These facts enable us to trace one branch of his family with certainty—that of his son Thomas—who was an early settler in Sandwich, and died there Dec. 30, 1686. He died intestate, and his estate was apprised on the 12th of the following January by John Chipman, Stephen Skiff, and William Bassett at £491,5, a very large estate in those times. He owned 240 acres of land at the Plains, valued in the inventory at only £12, or one shilling an acre. He owned four valuable tracts of meadow, one on the north of Town Neck, valued at £30 ; one at the Islands near James Allen's, £90 ; one below Mr. John Chipman's new house, £4 ; and one at Pine islands, £40. He owned two dwelling-houses. That in which he resided (situated about half a mile southerly from the Glass Factory village) was a large two story building, apprised at £40 ; his barn, corn-house, &c., £10 ; his home lot 10 acres, £30 ; and a tract of 20 acres adjoining, at £30. His other dwelling was occupied by his son John, and the farm on which it was situated is described as consisting of about 28 acres of "meane land," and "two parcels of meadow that belongs to that Seate," estimated at 8 acres, all apprised at £80. The mill, now known as the town mill, with "all her appertenances," at £50. As this appriment was carefully made, and was the basis of the division of the estate, it shows the relative value of different article at that time. A pair of oxen was valued at £5, and a negro slave at four times that sum, £20, 7 cows and one steer, £12 ; 28 sheep, £5 ; 1 mare, £2 ; 1 colt, 10 shillings ; his silver ware at £5, 5 shs. ; and his household furniture, clothing, tools, &c., £25 10 shs.

The estate was settled by an agreement of the heirs in writing, dated Feb. 16, 1686-7, and is signed by the widow Elizabeth Dexter, Senior, John Dexter, son of Thomas Dexter, late of Sandwich, gentleman deceased in his own rights, Elizabeth Dexter, Jr., in her right, Daniel Allen of Swansea, in the right of Mary, his wife, and by Jonathan Hallett, in the right of Abigail, his wife. This agreement shows that Thomas Dexter, the third of the name, was then dead, and had no lineal heir surviving.

June 1647, Thomas Dexter, Jr., or the second of the name, was chosen Constable of the town of Sandwich, a fact which shows that he was not then less than twenty-four years of age, and that he was born before his father came to this country. The exact date when he became a permanent resident, and an inhabitant of the town of Sandwich, I am unable to fix with certainty. He was not of Sandwich in 1643, but probably was as early as March 1645. The Thomas Dexter named as one of the inhabitants of Sandwich March 3, 1645-6, was probably the young man, because his father was about that date an inhabitant of Lynn. In 1648, he kept the mill built by his father before the year 1640. In 1647, he was constable of the town of Sandwich. In 1655, he was commissioned by the Court, at the request of the inhabitants of Sandwich, Ensign of the company of militia. He held the office many years, and was known as Ensign Dexter, and by this title was distinguished from his father, and his son of the same name. He was often on the grand and petty juries, was surveyor of highways, and held other municipal offices. In 1680, he was licenced to keep an ordinary or public house for the entertainment of strangers.

He did not inherit the litigious spirit of his father, though he did inherit some of his quarrels respecting lands where "no fences, parted fields, nor marks, nor bounds, distinguished acres of litigious grounds." These, however, were amicably adjusted by referees, not by expensive law suits. After 1655, he was, according to the usages of the time, entitled to the honor of being styled Mister, and in the latter part of his life, being a large land-holder, was styled gentleman. From what is left on record respecting him, he appears to have been a worthy man ; enterprising, useful, a good neighbor, and a good citizen.

Ensign Thomas Dexter married, Nov. 8, 1648, Mary or Elizabeth Vincent. The record of the marriage is mutilated, but this seems to be its true reading. (In early times Mary and Elizabeth were considered synonymous or interchangeable. I have found several similar cases ; but am unabled to give reason.)

The children of Ensign Thomas Dexter, born in Sandwich, were :

I.  Mary, born Aug. 11, 1649. She married Daniel Allen of Sandwich and removed to Swansey, where she had Elizabeth 28th Sept. 1673, and Christian 26th Jan. 1674-5, and probably others. After the close of the Indian war she returned to Swansey. Mr. Savage and Mr. Freeman both err in saying that Mary was a daughter of Thomas Dexter, Senior, and that she was born in Barnstable. The record is perfectly clear and distinct.

II.  Elizabeth, born Sept. 21, 1651, and died young. (Mr. Freeman says, "said to have been a maiden in 1767.")

III. Thomas.   His birth does not appear on the record, probably in 1653.   He died, without issue, in 1679.   He was appointed, Feb. 9, 1676-7, joint administrator with Capt. James Oliver of Boston, on his grandfather's estate.

IV. John, born about the year 1656, resided in Sandwich.   He married, Nov. 1682, Mehitabel, daughter of the second Andrew Hallett of Yarmouth, and had Elizabeth Nov. 2, 1683; Thomas, Aug. 26, 1686; Abigail, May 26, 1689; John, Sept. 11, 1692.   From Sandwich he removed to Portsmouth, R. I., and was there living 24th June 1717 (Savage.)   Mr. Freeman makes a singular mistake in regard to Thomas of this family.   He says, page 79, "Thomas, born Aug. 26, 1686, who is afterwards called Jr., whilst his uncle Thomas is called Senior."   When this Thomas was born, his uncle Thomas had been dead seven years, and his grandfather Thomas died before the child was six months old, and the necessity for the use of the terms in not seen.

V. Elizabeth, born 7th April 1660.   She does not appear to have married.   She was single at the time of the settlement of her father's estate, Feb. 16, 1686-7.   Her mother, who died March 19, 1713-14, bequeaths to Elizabeth in her will dated Aug. 29, 1689, her whole estate.   This will was proved April 8, 1714, and the daughter seems to have then been living, and unmarried.

VI. Abigail, June 12, 1663, married, Jan. 30, 1684-5, Jonathan Hallett of Yarmouth, had eight children, and died Sept. 2, 1715, aged 52, and is buried in the old grave yard in Yarmouth..

William Dexter was in Barnstable in 1657.   He probably was a son of Thomas Dexter, Senior, and came with his father to Barnstable about the year 1650.   His farm was originally owned by his father.   He removed to Rochester about the year 1690, where he died in 1694 intestate, and his estate was settled by mutual agreement between the widow Sarah and her children, Stephen, Phillip, James, Thomas, John, and Benjamin Dexter, and her daughter Mary, wife of Moses Barlow.   James, Thomas and John, had the Rochester lands, and Stephen, Phillip and Benjamin, the Barnstable estate.   In the division of the meadows in 1694 William had 3 acres assigned him by the committee of the town, which was reduced to two by the arbitrators in 1697.   Stephen and Phillip, the only children of William of sufficient age, were assigned 2 acres each.   In 1703 Phillip had removed to Falmouth, and Stephen was the only one of the name who remained in town.   He had 48 shares alloted to him in the division of the common lands, considerably more than the average, showing him to be a man of good estate.   He married Sarah Vincent July 1653, and his children born in Barnstable were:

I. Mary, Jan. 1654, married Moses Barlow and removed to Rochester.
II. Stephen, May 1657, married Ann Saunders.
III. Phillip, Sept. 1659, removed to Falmouth.
IV. James, May 1662, married Elizabeth Tobey, died 1697.
V. Thomas, July 1665, married Sarah C., March 1702-3. Died July 31, 1744. Left no issue.
VI. John, Aug. 1668.
VII. Benjamin, Feb. 1670, removed to Rochester, married Mary Miller of Rochester July 17, 1695. His son, Dea. Seth, was the great grandfather of Rev. Henry M. Dexter of Boston.

Stephen Dexter, son of William, born in Barnstable May 1657, married, 27th April, 1696, Anna Saunders. He resided on the farm of his grandfather Thomas at Dexter's Lane, West Barnstable, and had,

I. Mary, 24th Aug. 1696, married March 5, 1717-18, Samuel Chard.
II. A son, 22d Dec. 1698, died January following.
III. Abigail, 13th May, 1699.
IV. Content, 5th Feb. 1701, married Eben Landers of Rochester, 1725.
V. Anna, 9th March 1702-3, married John Williams 1725.
VI. Sarah, 1st June, 1705.
VII. Stephen, 26th July 1707, married Abigail Collier 1736.
VIII. Mercy, 5th July 1709. June 1737, she was living with Jonathan Crocker, Senior, who gave her £5 in his will.
IX. Miriam, 8th March, 1712.
X. Cornelius, 21st March, 1713-14. He did not marry. With his sister Molly, he lived in a two-story single house on the east side of Dexter's Lane, opposite the Mill Pond.

Stephen Dexter, in his will dated March 17, 1729-30, names his wife Ann, his son Stephen, to whom he gave his homestead, son Cornelius, and daughters Abigail, Content, Sarah, Mercy and Miriam. Also grand-daughter Ann Williams and grand-children David and Elizabeth Cheard.

Philip Dexter removed to Falmouth, and in his will, proved June 10, 1741, names his wife Alice, sons Joseph and Phillip, and son Jabez of Rochester, and five other children. Also a son John who died 1723. He owned a mill.

James Dexter married Elizabeth Tobey and removed to Rochester. He died in 1697, leaving a daughter Elizabeth and a posthumous child. His widow married Nathan Hamond.

Mr. John Dexter was the last of the name in Barnstable. (See Childs.)

A John Dexter of Rochester, a blacksmith, settled in Yarmouth. He owned the brick house near the Congregational meeting house. He married 1st, Bethia Vincent in 1748, and 2d, Phillippe Vincent in 1758. He had Hannah Sept. 7, 1749; Isaac Oct. 7, 1751; and John June 4, 1759. He has descendants in Nova Scotia.

# DEAN.

Rev. Mr. Dean in his history of Scituate, states that Jonas Deane was in that town in 1690, that he was called Taunton Dean, and that he came from Taunton, in England. He died in 1697, leaving a widow Eunice, who married in 1701, Dea. James Torrey, Town Clerk. His children were Thomas, born Oct. 29, 1691, and Ephraim, born May 22, 1695. Ephraim married Ann and settled in Provincetown, and had Eunice Nov. 10, 1725 ; Thankful Feb. 8, 1727-8 ; Ann March 4, 1730-31, and perhaps others.

Thomas settled in Barnstable, and was admitted, May 23, 1731, a member of the East Church. He probably resided at South Sea. He married Lydia, and his children born in Barnstable were :

I.  Lydia, born July 7, 1728, married Joseph Bearse Oct. 12, 1749.
II. Thomas, April 19, 1730, married Abigail Horton.
III. Jonas, Oct. 27, 1732.
IV. Ephraim, Oct. 17, 1734.
V.  William, May 27, 1736.
VI. Eunice, Nov. 4, 1737.
    All baptized at the East Church.

Thomas Dean, son of Thomas, married Abigail Horton, (published Feb. 29, 1752,) and had

I.  Hannah, born Jan. 20, 1753.
II. Archelaus, June 26, 1755

After the latter date the name disappears on the Barnstable records. There are numerous descendants of Thomas Dean of Barnstable ; but they are widely scattered. Archelaus Dean Atwood, Esq., of Orrington, Maine, is a descendant.

# DIMMOCK.

----

Elder Thomas Dimmock and Rev. Joseph Hull, are the parties named in the grant made in 1639, of the lands in the town of Barnstable. A previous grant has been made to Mr. Richard Collicut of Dorchester, by the Plymouth Colony Court, and subsequent events make it probable, if not certain, that Messrs. Dimmock and Hull were his associates. The date of the first grant is not given ; but it was made either in the latter part of 1637, or the beginning of 1638. Soon after the first grant was made Mr. Collicut and some of his associates came to Mattakeese, surveyed certain lands, and appropriated some of them to his own particular use ; but he never became an inhabitant of the town, and failing to perform his part of the contract, the grant to him was rescinded and made void ; but individual rights acquired by virtue of the grant to him, were not revoked.

In the winter of 1637-8 the Rev. Stephen Batchiler of Lynn, and a small company, consisting mostly of his sons, and his sons-in-law, and their families, attempted to make a settlement in the north-easterly part of the town, at a place yet known as Oldtown ; but they remained only a few months. (See Batchiler.)

Some of those who came with Mr. Collicut in 1638, remained and became permanent residents, for in March 1639, Mr. Dimmock was appointed by the Colony Court to exercise the Barnstable men in their arms, proving that there were English residents in the town at that time.

April 1, 1639, the Court ordered that only such persons as were then at Mattakeset should remain, and make use of some land, but shall not divide any either to themselves or others, nor receive into the plantation any other persons, excepting those to whom the original grant was made, without the special license and approval of the government.

This order implies, that the English who were in Barnstable April 1, 1639, were associates of Mr. Collicut and restricts them from receiving any who were not of that company.

May 6, 1639. "It is ordered by the Court, that if Mr. Collicut do come in his own person to inhabit at Mattakeeset before the General Court in June next ensuing ; that then the grant shall remain firm unto them ; but, if he fail to come within the time prefixed, that then their grant be made void, and the lands be otherwise disposed of."

The language of this order cannot be misunderstood. The Court had granted the lands at Mattakeeset to Mr. Collicut and his associates on the usual conditions, namely, that they should "see to the receiving in of such persons as may be fit to live together there in the fear of God, and obedience to our sovereigne lord the King, in peace and love, as becometh Christian people ;" that they should "faithfully dispose of such equal and fit portions of lands unto them and every of them, as the several estates, ranks and qualities of such persons as the Almighty in his providence shall send in amongst them, shall require ; to reserve, for the disposal of the Court, at least——acres of good land, with meadow competent, in place convenient, and to make returns to the Court of their doings." These conditions had not been complied with—a month's notice was given—Mr. Collicut did not come in person—and the Court on the 4th of June, 1639, made void the grant to him ; but not to his associates who had then settled in Barnstable.*

As Mr. Dimmock was of Dorchester he was probably one of the original associates of Mr. Collicut. Mr. Hull and Mr. Bursley of Weymouth, and the other inhabitants of Barnstable, prior to Oct. 21, 1639, with a few exceptions hereinafter named, belonged to the same company.

Mattakeeset was incorporated and became a town called Barnstable, on the 4th of June 1639, old stile, or June 14th new stile. I am aware that the Rev. John Mellen, Jr., in his Topographical description of Barnstable, published in 1794 in the third volume of the Massachusetts Historical Society's collections, says : "There is no account to be found of the first settlement made in this town. Probably there was none made much before its incorporation which was Sept. 3, 1639, O. S. As Mr. Mellen says, there was no record of the act of incorporation made. As early as 1685 when many of the first settlers were living, Gov. Hinckley was appointed a committee of the town, to examine the records and

---

*Mr. Collicut was admitted a freeman of the Massachusetts Colony March 4, 1632-3. He was a deputy to the General Court from Dorchester in 1636, '37 and '55. Selectman in 1636. His business arrangements probably prevented him from coming to Barnstable, as he had intended. May 17, 1637, about the time he and his associates intended to remove, he was appointed Commissary, to make provisions for the troops employed in the expedition against the Pequot Indians. In 1638 he was appointed by the Court to rectify the bounds between Dedham and Dorchester, and in 1641 to run the south line of the State adjoining Connecticut. He was one of the company authorized to trade with the Indians, and was much employed in public business. He removed to Boston before 1656. In 1669 he was of Falmouth, now Portland, and in 1672 of Saco, from both of which places he was a representative to the General Court in the years named, He finally returned to Boston, where he died July 7, 1685, aged 83, and was buried on Copp's Hill.

ascertain the conditions on which the grant to Messrs. Hull and
Dimmock was made. The result of his investigation he placed
on record. He found no record of the grant or of the act of incorporation, but he ascertained that both were made in the year
1639.

Notwithstanding there is no record of the day on which Barnstable was incorporated as one of the towns of Plymouth Colony,
the date can be fixed with certainty by other evidence. It clearly
appears by the records that Barnstable was not an incorporated
town June 3, 1639, O. S. As has been already stated, a certain
conditional grant of the lands had been made to Mr. Collicut and
his associates, preliminary to the organization of a town government; and under the authority of that grant, about fifteen families had settled within the limits of the township. Mr. Dimmock
was authorized, March 1639, to exercise the men in the use of
arms, because, in a remote settlement, surrounded by bands of
Indians, in whose friendship reliance could not be placed, à military organization was of prime importance.

The terms of the Court order of May 6, imply that some of
Mr. Collicut's associates had then settled at Mattakeeset, but he
himself, it is emphatically stated, had not, and he was allowed till
the 3d of June, 1639, to remove, and if on that day he had not
removed, the grant made to him was to be null and void. He did
not remove, and on the 4th day of June the grant to Mr. Collicut
was declared null and void, and the grant transferred to Rev.
Joseph Hull and Elder Thomas Dimmock. Perhaps the reason
for not making a record was this; the grant was a simple transfer from Mr. Collicut as principal to Messrs. Dimmock and Hull
two of his associates. As no change had been made in the
conditions, no record was deemed necessary.

Beside the above, others had settled within the present territory
of the town of Barnstable prior to Jan. 1644, but had removed at
that date. Rev. Mr. Bachiler and his company, as above stated,
on lands, that prior to 1642, were included within the bounds of
Yarmouth. William Chase afterwards owned a portion of those
lands occupied by Mr. Bachiler, and as he had a garden and an
orchard thereon, it is probable that he resided some little time in
Barnstable prior to 1644.

President Ezra Stiles presumes that George Kendrick, Thomas
Lapham, John Stockbridge, and Simeon Hoit or Hoyte, removed
with Mr. Lothrop   There is some evidence that George Kendrick
was one of the first who came to Barnstable. Mr. Deane says he
left Scituate in 1638. He is named as of Barnstable in 1640, but
there are reasons for doubting the accuracy of the date. If of
Barnstable he removed to Boston in 1640 or soon after. Mr.
Deane's notice of Thomas Lapham is imperfect. He was one of
the first settlers in Scituate, certainly there April 24, 1636, and

died in that town in 1648. I find no evidence that he was ever of Barnstable. Hoit joined Mr. Lothrop's church in Scituate April 19, 1635, sold his house there in 1636 or soon after. About the year 1639 he removed to Winsor, Conn. If of Barnstable he was here very early. John Stockbridge was a wheel and millwright, and may have resided in Barnstable as a workman. I find no trace of evidence that he was ever an inhabitant. He afterwards was of Boston.

In addition to the foregoing, a few other names may be added, servants of the first settlers, who did not remain long and were never legal inhabitants.

Of the forty-five heads of families who were inhabitants of Barnstable in Jan. 1643-4, there came from

| | | |
|---|---|---|
| Scituate, | 26 | 23 |
| Duxbury, | 2 | |
| Hingham, | 2 | 2 |
| Yarmouth, | 1 | |
| Boston, | 3 | 3 |
| Weymouth, | 1 | 1 |
| Charlestown, | 1 | |
| England, | 9 | 9 |
| | 45 | 38 |

Those noted as from England had probably resided in Boston or Dorchester a short time previously to coming to Barnstable.

In the second column is placed the number of the families who were inhabitants Oct. 21, 1639.

Thus far the proof respecting the date of the incorporation of Barnstable has consisted of negations. June 4, 1639, O. S., the General Court met and entered on its records that Barnstable was one of the towns within the Colony of New Plymouth, and appointed William Casely the first constable, and he was then sworn into office.

These quotations from the records show conclusively that the Rev. Mellen was mistaken in his date, and equally as conclusively that the town of Barnstable was incorporated, according to the usages of the times, on the fourteenth day of June 1639, new style.*

That Mr. Dimmock was appointed in March, 1639, "to exercise Barnstable men in their arms," does not prove that the town had then been incorporated for, at the same court, a similar appoint-

---

*The conclusion of Mr. Otis that the incorporation of Barnstable should date from June 4, O. S., (June 14, N. S.,) seems untenable from his own reasoning. The fact that a constable was appointed, at the session of the court of June 4, is not sufficient; this officer was often appointed for places that were not at the time recognized as towns. A place not entitled to be represented in the court called not be considered as fully incorporated, and Barnstable was not so represented until the ensuing December term. The record of the "Committees or Deputies for each town" in the colony, has the following: "For Barnstable, Mr. Joseph Hull, Mr. Thomas Dimmock, made in December Court, 1639." This would seem to be conclusive that the incorporation of the town should date from Dec. 3, 1639, when the court met. **S.**

ment was made for Marshfield, but that town was not incorporated till September 1640, and then as Rexame.

No formal acts of incorporation were passed in regard to any of the towns, so that Barnstable is not an exception. A general law was passed from which I have made some extracts. The Secretary usually noted the time when acts of incorporation were passed, but the instrument itself was not recorded.

The history of Mr. Dimmock is identified with the early history of the town and cannot be separated. He was the leading man and was in some way connected with all the acts of the first settlers. On the 5th of January, 1643-4, Thomas Hinckley, Henry Cobb, Isaac Robinson, and Thomas Lothrop, drew up a list of those who were then inhabitants of Barnstable, and I infer from the order annexed to the same, that the forty-five named were also house-holders. In making this list, they commenced at the west end of the plantation, at Anthony Annable's, now Nathan Jenkins', and proceeded eastward, recording the names of the inhabitants in the order in which they resided to Mr. Thomas Dimmock, whose house stood a little distance east of where Isaac Davis' now stands.

Townsmen of Barnstable Jan. 1643-4.

1. Anthony Annable, from Scituate, 1640.
2. Abraham Blush, Duxbury, 1640.
3. Thomas Shaw, Hingham, 1639.
4. John Crocker, Scituate, 1639.
5. Dollar Davis, Duxbury, 1641-2.
6. Henry Ewell,* Scituate, 1639.
7. William Betts, Scituate, 1639.
   William Pearse of Yarmouth, 1643.
8. Robert Shelley, Scituate, 1639.
9. Thomas Hatch, Yarmouth, 1642.
10. John Cooper, Scituate, 1639.
11. Austin Bearse, came over 1638, of B. 1639.
12. William Crocker, Scituate, 1639.
13. Henry Bourne, Scituate, 1639.
14. Henry Coggin, Boston, Spring 1639.
15. Lawrence Litchfield of B., Spring 1639.
16. James Hamblin, London, of B., Spring of 1639.
17. James Cudworth, Scituate, 1640.
18. Thomas Hinckley, Scituate, 1639.
19. Samuel Hinckley,† Scituate, 8th July, 1640.
    William Tilly, Spring 1639, removed to Boston 1643.
20. Isaac Robinson, Scituate, 1639.

---

*The town record is Henry Coxwell, an error of the clerk who transcribed the list. It should be Henry Ewell.

---

†Samuel Hinckley's name is the 45th on the record. It should be the 18th. His houselot adjoined his son Thomas Hinckley's houselot. In 1640 he built a house on the east side of Coggins' Pond, in which he resided until his removal to West Barnstable.

21. Samuel Jackson, Scituate, 1639.
22. Thomas Allyn, ——— Spring of 1639.
    Mr. Joseph Hull, Weymouth, May 1639.
23. Mr. John Bursley, Weymouth, May 1639.
24. Mr. John Mayo, came over 1638, of Barnstable 1639.
25. John Casley, Scituate, Spring of 1639.
26. William Caseley, Scituate, of B. Spring of 1639.
27. Robert Linnett, Scituate, 1639.
28. Thomas Lothrop, Scituate, 1639.
29. Thomas Lumbard, Scituate, 1639.
30. Mr. John Lothrop, Scituate, Oct. 20, 1639.
31. John Hall, Charlestown, 1641.
32. Henry Rowley, Scituate, 1639.
33. Isaac Wells, Scituate, 1639.
34. John Smith, of Barnstable, 1639.
35. George Lewis, Scituate, 1639.
36. Edward Fitzrandolphe, Scituate, 1639.
37. Bernard Lumbard, Scituate, 1639.
38. Roger Goodspeed, of Barnstable, 1639.
39. Henry Cobb, Scituate, Oct. 21, 1639.
40. Thomas Huckins, Boston, 1639.
41. John Scudder, Boston, 1639.
42. Samuel Mayo, of Barnstable, 1639.
43. Nathaniel Bacon, of Barnstable, 1639.
44. Richard Foxwell, from Scituate, 1639.
45. Thomas Dimmock, Hingham, Spring 1639.

The following were or had been residents, but were not townsmen in Jan. 1643-4.

Samuel House returned to Scituate. He was of Barnstable in 1641 and 1644.

John Oates, buried May 8, 1641.

Samuel Fuller, from Scituate, had resided temporarily in Barnstable; but he did not become a townsman till after Jan. 1643-4. His cousin, Capt. Matthew Fuller, did not settle in Barnstable till 1652.

Capt. Nicholas Simpkins was returned as able to bear arms in Aug. 1643. He was one of the first settlers in Yarmouth. He did not remain long in Barnstable. John Bryant and Daniel Pryor are named as residents in 1641. Neither were then of legal age. In 1643, Bryant had removed to Scituate, and Pryer to Duxbury. John Blower and Francis Crocker were residents in 1643. Perhaps not of legal age. A John Russell was also of Barnstable in that year.

The following also returned in Aug. 1643, as able to bear arms, were not of legal age in January 1643-4 : Thomas Bourman, John Foxwell, son of Richard, Thomas Blossom, Nicholas and

John Davis, sons of Dolar, Samuel, Joseph, and Benjamin
Lothrop, sons of John, David Linnett, son of Robert, Nathaniel
Mayo, son of John, and Richard Berry.

Of the 26 from Scituate, two, at least, were of Barnstable in
the Spring of 1639, and three delayed removing till 1640. Mr.
Lothrop and a majority of his church did not resolve to remove
till June, and on the 26th of that month a fast was held
"For the presence of God in mercy to goe with us to Mattakeese."
There is no record of the names of those who came in June.
Those who came, probably left their families at Scituate, and
came by land, bringing with them their horses, cattle, farming and
other utensils, in order to provide hay for their cattle, and shelter
for their families before winter.

A majority of the earlier settlers did not come from Scituate.
The fourteen last named on the list were in Barnstable very early,
and settled near the Unitarian Meeting-House, in the easterly part
of the plantation. These lands are those named in the record as
run out by authority of Mr. Collicot. Mr. Dimmock's Lot was
the most easterly, and in 1654 is thus described on the town
record: "Imp. a grant of a great lot to Mr. Dimmock, with
meadow adjoining, at a Little Running Brook at ye East End of
the plantation, toward Yarmouth, which Lands is in the present
possession of George Lewis, Sen'r, let and farmed out to him for
some certain years by the said Mr. Dimmock."*

This description is indefinite, yet important facts are stated.
It was triangular in form and contained, including upland and
meadows, about seventy-five acres. The east corner bound stood
a little distance east of the present dwelling-house of William W.
Sturgis, and was bounded southerly by the county road, 115 rods
to the range of fence between the houses of Solomon Hinckley
and Charles Sturgis, thence northerly across mill creek to the old
common field, and thence south-easterly to the first mentioned
bound, and included a narrow strip of upland on the north side of
the mill creek meadows. The soil of the upland was fertile, and
the meadows easy of access, and productive. It was the best
grazing farm in the East Parish, and although lands and meadows
then bore only a nominal price, it is not surprising that Mr. Dimmock was enabled to rent his.

---

* This is called Mr. Dimmock's "great lot" yet. I think it was not what was generally
understood by the term "great lot" among the first settlers. In subsequent records the
tracts of land situate between Mr. Lothrop's great lot on the west, and Barnard Lumbert's
on the east, (now Dimmock's Lane) and bounded north by the County road, is called "Mr.
Dimmock's Great Lot," and is now owned by Joshua Thayer, Capt. Pierce, Wm. W. Sturgis, Mr. Whittemore, Capt. Swinerton, and the Heirs of Capt. Franklin Percival. This land,
in 1689, was owned by his son Ensign Shubael, and the record may refer to him, though he
would not have been entitled to a "great lot" only as the representative of his father, not in
his own right. Besides the above, Elder Thomas, as one of the proprietors, was entitled to
commonage, to which his son Shubael succeeded. (Commonage. This word is used by
Dr. Bond and others, to express in one word all the right which the first settlers of towns
had in the common lands and meadows, whether by virtue of their rights as proprietors, or
as townsmen.)

In the sketch of the Bacon Family, the laying out of lots on the west of the Dimmock farm is described. The lots first laid out generally extended in length from east to west, while those afterwards laid out were longer on their north and south lines.

The Rev. John Lothrop's first house stood near the Eldridge hotel. On the east of this lot seven Scituate men settled, namely, Henry Rowley, on the same lot, Isaac Wells near the Court House, George Lewis, Sen'r near the Ainsworth house, Edward Fitzrandolph on the corner lot adjoining the Hyannis road, Henry Cobb a little north from the Unitarian Meeting House, Richard Foxwell near the Agricultural Hall, and Bernard Lumbard near the mill where Dolar Davis afterwards resided.† The three last named came early, probably all of the seven.

The other Scituate men who came with Mr. Lothrop numbered from 12 to 32, settled between the Court House and the present westerly bounds of the East Parish. Those who came later, farther west. This is a general statement; there are exceptions, which will be noted hereafter.

A settlement was also made very early on the borders of Coggin's Pond. Here we find the same peculiarity in the shape of the original lots, their longer lines extended from east to west; while in all other parts of the town except in these two particular localities the longer lines are north and south. The early settlers in that neighborhood were Henry Bourne and Thomas Hinckley, from Scituate, and Henry Coggin, Lawrence Litchfield, James Hamblin, and William Tilly, probably associates of Mr. Collicut.

In an inquiry of this kind, entire accuracy is not to be expected, but these three points in regard to the settlement of Barnstable are clearly established.

1st.   In the winter of 1637-8, Rev. Stephen Bachiler, with a company consisting of himself, his sons, his sons-in-law, and his grand-sons, in all making five or six families, settled at the northeast part of the town. They remained till the Spring of 1638, when they abandoned the attempt to form a permanent settlement, and all removed.

2d.   In 1638, or on the year previous, the lands at Mattakeese were granted to Mr. Richard Collicut of Dorchester, and his associates. Under the authority of this grant, two settlements were made, the larger near the Unitarian Meeting House, and the other near Coggin's Pond. In March, 1639, there were about fifteen families in the two neighborhoods. June 14, 1639, new style, when the grant to Mr. Collicut was revoked, about twenty.

---

† I do not state this with perfect confidence of its accuracy. Respecting the Collicut lots; there are two, one laid to Barnard Lumbert, and one to Samuel Mayo. The one near the mill, afterwards Dolar Davis', I suppose to be Lumbard's, the other including Major Phinney's house lot, and the house lot of Timothy Reed, deceased, I judge was Samuel Mayo's. Both were sold early, the latter was owned in 1654 by the Widow Mary Hallett, probably widow of Mr. Andrew Hallett, the schoolmaster.

3d. June 14, 1639, N. S., Barnstable was incorporated as a town, and the lands therein granted to Rev. Joseph Hull and Mr. Thomas Dimmock, as a committee of the townsmen, and of such as should thereafter be regularly admitted. In that month Rev. Mr. Lothrop and a majority of his church resolved to remove to Barnstable, and some then came; but a great majority came by water Oct. 21, 1639, N. S., making the whole number of families then in Barnstable forty-one, the full number required.

If the names already given, John Chipman, John Phinney, John Otis, John Howland, Thomas Ewer, William Sergeant, and Edward Coleman, who came to Barnstable a few years later, are added, the list will include the emigrant ancestors of nineteen twentieths of the present inhabitants of the town of Barnstable. Capt. John Dickenson and Jas. Nabor were also early inhabitants. Nearly all the offices were conferred upon Messrs. Hull and Dimmock. They were the land committee, an office involving arduous and responsible duties, and the exercise of a sound judgment and discretion. That they performed their duties well, the fact that no appeal from their decisions was ever made to the Colony Court, affords sufficient evidence. They were the duputies to the Colony Court, and seemed to possess the entire confidence of the people.‡

Mr. Dimmock was also a deputy to the Plymouth Colony Court in 1640, '41, '42, '48, '49, and '50. He was admitted a freeman of the Colony Dec. 3, 1639. June 2, 1640, Mr. Thomas Dimmock of Barnstable, Mr. John Crow of Yarmouth, were appointed to "join with Mr. Edmond Freeman of Sandwich, to hear and determine all causes and controversies within the three townships not exceeding twenty shillings, according to the former order of the Court." This was the first Court established in the County of Barnstable. Mr. Freeman had been elected an assistant in the preceeding March, and by virtue of that office was a magistrate or judge; but he was not qualified till June 2, 1640, but Mr. Dimmock and Mr. Crow were qualified. Cases involving larger sums were tried before the Governor and assistants. The first court of assistants, or Supreme Court, convened in this County, was held in Yarmouth June 17, 1641. June 5, 1644, Mr. Dimmock and Mr. Crow were re-appointed magistrates

---

‡Mr. Hull's popularity in Barnstable soon waned. In 1640 he does not appear to have held any office. May 1, 1641, he was excommunicated from the Barnstable Church, for joining a company in Yarmouth as their pastor. He was however received again into fellowship Aug. 10, 1643. From Barnstable he removed to Oyster River, Maine, and from thence in 1662 to the Isle of Shoals where he died 19th Nov. 1665. Simple justice has never been done to the memory of Rev. Joseph Hull. He came over in 1835, probably from Barnstaple in Devonshire. He welcomed Mr. Lothrop and his church to Barnstable,—he then opened the doors of his house, one of the largest and best in the plantation, for their meetings,—he feasted them on thanksgiving days, and was untiring in his efforts for their temporal prosperity. He is not charged with any immorality, or with holding any heretical opinions; yet he was driven from the town, that probably received its name, as a mark of respect to him. His history is worthy to be preserved, and at the proper time I shall endeavor to do justice to his memory.

or assistants of Mr. Freeman, who was the chief justice of the inferior court, and assistant, or associate justice of the higher court.

Sept. 22, 1642, Mr. Dimmock was appointed by the Colony Court to be one of the council of war. On the 10th of Oct. 1642, he was elected lieutenant§ of the company of militia in Barnstable, and the Court approved§ of the choice March 3, 1645-6, the grand jury presented him "for neglecting to exercise Barnstable men in arms;" but the Court, after hearing the evidence, discharged the complaint. In July, 1646, Mr. Dimmock was again re-elected lieutenant, and the choice was approved.

In 1650, he was one of the commissioners of the Plymouth Colony, to confer with a similar commission of the Massachusetts Colony, and decide respecting the title of the lands at Shawwamet and Patuxet.

On the 7th of August, 1650, he was ordained Elder of the Church of Barnstable, of which he had been a member from its organization.

These extracts require no comment. They prove that Mr. Dimmock was held by the colony, the town, and the church, to be a man of integrity and ability. He lived at a time when the faults of every man holding a prominent position in society were recorded. One complaint only was ever made against him, and that was "discharged" as unfounded and frivolous.

After 1650 he does not appear to have held any public offices, and in 1654 he had leased his farm, though he continued to reside in Barnstable. He died in 1658 or 1659, and in his nuncopative will, attested to by Anthony Annable and John Smith, they state that "when he was sick last summer, [1658] he said, what little he had he would give to his wife, for the children were hers as well as his."

Few of the first settlers lived a purer life than Elder Thomas Dimmock. He came over, not to amass wealth, or acquire honor; but that he might worship his God according to the dictates of his own conscience; and that he and his posterity might here enjoy the blessings of civil and religious liberty. His duties to his God, to his country, and to his neighbor, he never forgot, never knowingly violated. In the tolerant views of his beloved pastor, the Rev. John Lothrop, he entirely coincided. If his neighbor was an Ana-Baptist or a Quaker, he did not judge him, because he held, that to be a perogative of Deity, which man had no right to assume.

A man who holds to such principles, whose first and only inquiry is what does duty demand, and performs it, will rarely stray far from the Christian fold. His posterity will never ask to

---

§Lieutenant was then the highest rank in the local militia.

what sect he belonged, they will call him blessed, and only regret that their lives are not like his.

In the latter part of his life Mr. Dimmock appears to have been of feeble health, and unable to perform any act that required labor or care. It appears also, that he was obliged to sell a portion of his ample real estate, to provide means for the support of himself and family, and at his death he gave the remainder to his wife, in a "will" full of meaning and characteristic of the man.

Dimmock is an old name in England, and there are many families who bear it. It has various spellings, and probably was originally the same as that of Dymocke, the hereditary champion of England, an office now abolished, who at coronations owed the service of Challenge to all competitors for the crown. In this country I find the name written Dymocke, Dimmock, Dimack, Dimuck, Dimicku. In the commission of Edward Dimmock engrossed on parchment, three different spellings of the name occur. The family usually write the name Dimmock, but many Dimick, which is more nearly in accordance with the pronunciation than any other spelling. It is probably a Welch or a West of England name, and some facts stated by Burke in his genealogy of the family favor the family tradition, that Elder Thomas Dimmock's father was Edward, and that he came from Barnstaple or that vicinity.

I.    Elder Thomas Dimmock married Ann [Hammond?] *
before his removal to Barnstable.   His children were :

2.    I.    Timothy, baptized by Mr. Lothrop Jan. 12, 1639-40, and was the first of the English who died in Barnstable, and was buried June 17, 1640, "in the lower syde of the Calves Pasture."

3.    II.    Mehitable, baptized April 18, 1642. She married Richard Child of Watertown, March 30, 1662, where she appears to have been a resident at the time. She died Aug. 18, 1676, aged 34. She had 1, Richard, March 30, 1663; 2, Ephraim, Oct. 9, 1664; 3, Shubael, Dec. 19, 1665, he married, was afterwards insane, and froze to death in the County prison; 4, Mehitable; 5, Experience, born Feb. 26, 1669-70; 6, Abigail, born June 16, 1672, married Joseph Lothrop, Esq., of Barnstable; 7, Ebenezer, born Nov. 10, 1674; 8, Hannah, twin, born Nov. 10, 1674, married Joseph Blush of Barnstable.

4.    III.    Shubael, baptized Sept. 15, 1644, married Joanna, daughter of John Bursley, April 1663.

---

*To attempt to glean in a field which has been surveyed by so thorough a genealogist as Dr. Bond, may seem presumptuous. Samuel House, Robert Linnett, and Thomas Dimmock it appears by the records of Mr. Lothrop, were his brothers-in-law. Rev. Mr. Lothrop married for his second wife, Anne, daughter of William Hammond of Watertown; Samuel House married her sister Elizabeth; Mr. Lothrop's son Thomas married Sarah, daughter of Robert Linnell; William Hammond had two daughters of the name Anne, and this would not be a case without a parallel, if both were living at the same time, and that one married Mr. Lothrop and the other Mr. Dimmock.

The children of Elder Dimmock are not recorded on the Barnstable town, or on the Plymouth Colony records. The above are from the church records, which are more reliable than either of the others. He may have had children before he came to Barnstable ; but it is not probable. The widow Ann Dimmock was living in Oct. 1683. The date of her decease is not on the town or church records. She probably died before 1686.

4. Ensign Shubael Dimmock, only son of Elder Thomas, who lived to mature age, sustained the character and reputation of his father. In 1669 he was a resident in Yarmouth ; but did not remain long. In Barnstable he was much employed in town business. He was one of the selectmen in 1685 and 6, a deputy to the Colony Court in the same years, and again in 1689 after the expulsion of Sir Edmond Andros. He was Ensign of the militia company, and was called in the records Ensign Shubael Dimmock. About the year 1693 he removed to Mansfield, Conn., where he was known as Dea. Dimmock. He died in that town Sunday, Oct. 29, 1732, at 9 o'clock, in the 91st year of his age, and his wife Joanna May 8, 1727, aged 83 years.

He inherited the real estate of his father, to which he made large additions. Of his place of residence and business in Yarmouth, I find no trace in the records. In 1686 he resided in the fortification house which was his father's. The house which his son Capt. Thomas afterwards resided in, was built and owned by him. It was built 176 years ago, and as it has always been kept in good repair, few would mistrust from its appearance that it was so ancient. It remained in the family till about 1812, when it was sold to the father of Mr. Selleck Hedge, the present owner. This house, and the houses built by Ensign Dimmock's sons, all belong to the class of buildings known as high single houses. They were of wood, and somewhat larger, but the style was the same as that of Elder Thomas'. They contained the same number of rooms, fronted either due north or due south, and on clear days the shadows of the house were a sun dial to the inmates, the only time piece which they could consult.

Ensign Dimmock, at the time of his marriage, April 1663, was only eighteen years and seven months old, and his wife Joanna seventeen years and one month. At her death, they had lived in the marriage state 64 years. His children born in Barnstable were :

5.  I.    Thomas, born April 1664.
6.  II.   John, Jan. 1666.
7.  III.  Timothy, March 1668.
8.  IV.   Shubael, Feb. 1673.
9.  V.    Joseph, Sept. 1675.
10. VI.   Mehitabel, 1677.
11. VII.  Benjamin, March 1680.

12.   VIII.   Joanna, March 1682.
13.   IX.   Thankful, Nov. 1684.

    5.   Capt. Thomas Dimmock, or Dimmack, as he wrote his
name, son of Ensign Shubael, was in the military service in the
eastern country, and was kllled in battle at Canso, on the 9th of
Sept. 1697.   He was a gallant officer, and in the battle in which he
lost his life he would not conceal himself in the thicket or shelter
himself behind a tree, as the other officers and soldiers under his
command did, but stood out in the open field, a conspicuous mark
for the deadly aim of the French, and of the Indian warriors.†
    Capt. Dimmock resided in the East Parish, and about the
year 1690 bought the dwelling-house of Henry Taylor, which
stood on the east of the common field road, where Mr. Nathaniel
Gorham now resides.   This he sold to Nathaniel Orris in 1694.
He afterwards owned and occupied his father's house, above
described.   Though only thirty-three at his death, he had acquired
a large estate.   The real estate which was his father's was apprised
at £110 ; the farm at West Barnstable bought of Jonathan Hatch,
at £72 ; land bought of Thomas Lumbert, Sen'r, Henry Taylor,
and Sergeant Cobb, £20 ; meadow in partnership with John Bacon
and Samuel Cobb, £16 ; and meadow at Rowley's Spring, formerly
his father's, £12.   He had a large personal estate, including one-
sixth of a sloop, shares in whale boats, &c.
    Capt. Thomas Dimmock married Desire Sturgis.   He died
Sept. 9, 1697, and she married 2d, Col. John Thacher, 2d of that
name, Nov. 10, 1698, by whom she had six children.   She died
29th March, 1749, in the 84th year of her age.   Her husband
wrote some highly eulogistic poetry on her death.‡
    His children born in Barnstable were :
14.   I.   Mehitabel, born Oct. 1686.   She married Capt. John
        Davis Aug. 13, 1705, and died May 1775, aged 88.   (For
        a notice of her see Davis.)
15.   II.   Temperance, June 1689, married June 2, 1709, Benja-
        min Freeman of Harwich, and has numerous descendants.
16.   III.   Edward, born 5th July 1692.   (See account of his
        family below.)
17.   IV.   Thomas, born 25th Dec. 1694.   Of this son I have
        no information.
18.   V.   Desire, born Feb. 1696, married Job Gorham Dec. 4,
        1719, died Jan. 28, 1732-3.

---

†This is the tradition which has been preserved in the neighborhood; but I find no mention of his death in the histories of the times which I have consulted.   It was the last year
of King Williams' war, and great alarm prevailed throughout New England that the
country would be invaded by the French.   Capt. Dimmock was engaged in the whale
fishery, and he may have been on a whaling voyage at the time ; but the statement in the
text is probably accurate.

---

‡I have the original in the hand-writing of Col. Thatcher.   I preserve it not for the
poetry; but because it is written on the back of a valuable historical document.

6. John Dimmock, or Dimuck, as he wrote his name, son of Ensign Shubael, was a farmer and resided in Barnstable till October 1709, when he exchanged his farm in Barnstable containing forty acres of upland and thirty of meadow, his houselot and commonage, with Samuel Sturgis of Barnstable, for a farm on Monosmenekecon Neck, in Falmouth, containing 150 acres and other lands in the vicinity of said Neck, and removed to that town, where he has descendants. His house in Barnstable is now owned by Mr. Wm. W. Sturgis. He married, Nov. 1689, Elizabeth Lumbert, and had nine children born in Barnstable, viz :

19. I.    Sarah, born Dec. 1690.
20. II.   Anna, or Hannah, last of July 1692.
21. III.  Mary, June 1695.
22. IV.   Theophilus, Sept. 1696, married Sarah, daughter of Benjamin Hinckley, Oct. 1, 1722.
23. V.    Timothy, July 1698.
24. VI.   Ebenezer, Feb. 1700.
25. VII.  Thankful, 5th April, 1702.
26. VIII. Elizabeth, 20th April, 1704, married John Lovell 1750.
27. IX.   David, baptized 19th May, 1706.

7. Timothy Dimmock, son of Ensign Shubael, removed to Mansfield, Conn., and from thence to Ashford where he died about the year 1733. His wife was named Abigail. She had six children born in Mansfield. Timothy, born June 5, 1703, is the first named on the record. He had also Israel and Ebenezer, the latter born 22d Nov. 1715, and was the grandfather of Col. J. Dimick of Fort Warren, Boston harbor. He has many descendants in Connecticut.

8. Shubael Dimock, son of Ensign Shubael, resided in Barnstable. He married Tabitha Lothrop May 4, 1699. She died July 24, 1727, aged 56 years; he died Dec. 16, 1728, aged 55 years. Both are buried in the ancient grave yard on the Old Meeting House Hill. His father, on his removal to Mansfield, gave him a share of his estate. His children, born in Barnstable, were—

28. I. Samuel, born 7th May, 1702, married Hannah Davis 1724. June 1, 1740, she was dismissed to the church in Tolland, Conn. She died in Barnstable, a widow, Oct. 13, 1755; but the family probably remained in Connecticut. They had seven children born in Barnstable : 1, Mehitable, April 25, 1722, Sabbath ; 2, Samuel, Oct. 17, 1726, Monday ; 3, Hannah, Nov. 26, 1728, Tuesday ; 4, Shubael, 31st January, 1731, Sabbath ; 5, Joseph, Feb. 19, 1733, Monday ; 6, Mehitabel, 29th Sept. 1735, Monday ; 7, Daniel, May 28, 1738, Sabbath ; 8, David, 1745. (Born in Connecticut.)
Samuel Dimmock has numerous descendants. He resided

several years in Saybrook, Conn.  His widow, as above stated, died in Barnstable, and it is said that he also died in his native town.  His son Samuel died at Albany in 1755; Shubael went to Mansfield, and it is said removed to Nova Scotia, before the Revolution; Joseph lived many years in Wethersfield, Conn., and died in 1825 at one of his daughter's in Greenville, N. Y., aged 92. Several of his descendants were sea captains and lost at sea. Joseph J. Dimock, late Assistant Secretary of State, Hartford, is a great grandson of Joseph.  Daniel, son of Samuel, lived in the eastern part of Connecticut.  David Dimock, a son of Samuel, born after his removal from Barnstable, removed from Wethersfield to Montrose, Penn., and died there in 1832, aged 87. Davis, a son of David, was a Baptist preacher of some note—a man all work—baptized 2,000 persons—preached 8,000 sermons— a practicing physician—acting county judge, &c.  The descendants of David at Montrose are among the most worthy and influential in that region.  Milo M., a son, was a member of Congress in 1852, Associate Judge, &c.

29.   II.   David, baptized 11th June, 1704   Married Thankful
         Cobb, October 14, 1746.  (Doubtful.)
30.   III.   Joanna, born 24th Dec. 1708; died January, 1709.
31.   IV.   Mehitable, born 26th June, 1711.
32.   V.   Shubael, baptized April, 1706.

9.   Joseph Dimmock, son of  Ensign Shubael, married, 12th May, 1699, Lydia, daughter of Doct. John Fuller.  She learned the trade of tailoress, and after the death of her father, Stephen Skiff, Esq., of Sandwich, was her guardian.  Her mother-in-law administered on the estate, and May 9, 1700 she acknowledges the receipt of £75. from her said mother, then wife of Capt. John Lothrop, in full for her right in her father's estate.  Several members of this family removed to Connecticut.  She died there November 6, 1755, aged 80.  Children born in Barnstable:

33.   I.   Thomas, born 26th January, 1699-1700.
34.   II.   Bethiah, 3d Febuary, 1702.  Married, 1726, Samuel
         Annable.  Oct. 22, 1751, dismissed from the Barnstable
         Church to the church in Scotland, Conn.
35.   III.   Mehitable, 22d Nov., 1707, married Thomas Crocker,
         1727, died 1729.
36.   IV.   Ensign, (?) born 8th Nov., 1709, married Abigail
         Tobey, of  Sandwich, Oct. 19, 1731, and had—1, Thomas,
         29th Oct. 1732; 2, Mehitable, 12th April 1735; 3, Joseph,
         12th July, 1740.

Joseph Dimmock resided in the east parish.  His house stood on the spot where Asa Young, Esq., now resides.  It was a two story single house like his brother's, father's and grandfather's. On his removal to Connecticut it was sold to the Sturgis's, and passed from them into the possession of Bangs Young and his son

Asa. It was taken down about 30 years ago. "Shuball Dimmack" of Mansfield, on the 6th of March, 1705-6, "for the natural affection he bears to his son Joseph Dimmock," conveyed to him eight acres of land on the west side of his great lot (now Joshua Thayer's home lot) with one acre more on the north side of the road (now the house lot of Asa Young, Esq.) This land, at the time, was under lease to Shubael Dimmock, Jr. The conditions of the deed were as follows : "That the said Joseph Dimmock shall not make sale, or give conveyance of the said given and granted nine acres of land from his heirs to any stranger or person whatever, except it bee to some or one of his brothers John or Shubael Dimmock, or their heirs of the race of the Dimmocks, unless they or either of them, or theirs, shall refuse upon tender of sale of the premises to give the true and just value thereof for the time being, that any other will give in reality, *bone fide*, without deceit, or what it may be valued at by two indifferent or uninterested persons." Similar provisions I presume were incorporated in the deeds to his other sons. Excepting one small house lot, all the lands of Ensign Dimmock passed out of the possession of the Dimmocks fifty years ago, and all the lands of the elder a century ago. As numerous as this family was at the beginning of the eighteenth century, there is now only one, a maiden lady, who bears the name in the town of Barnstable.

37.   V.   Ishabod, born 8th March, 1711.

38.   VI.   Abigail, born 31st June, 1714, married Thomas Annable April 1, 1768, his third wife and was the mother of Abigail and Joseph, the latter yet remembered by the aged.

39.   VII.   Pharoh, 2d Sept. 1717.

40.   VIII.   David, 22d Dec., 1721. (I think this David married Thankful Cobb.) David, the son of Shubael, is named in the church, but not in the town records, indicating that he died early.

11.   Benjamin Dimmock, son of Ensign Shubael, removed with his father to Mansfield, Conn. Also his sisters Joanna and Thankful ; but my correspondent, Wm. L. Weaver, Esq., to whom I am largely indebted for information respecting this and other Connecticut families, gives me no particulars respecting them.

16.   Edward Dimmock, son of Capt. Thomas, resided on the paternal estate. He was a lieutenant in the militia and his commission, engrossed on parchment, is preserved by his descendants. He was captain of the 1st Company, 7th Mass. Regiment, in the expedition against Louisburg, his commission bearing date Feb. 15, 1744, O. S. He married in 1720 Hannah ———, and had—

41.   I.   Anna, 23d Nov. 1721. Married Thomas Agrey or Egred March 7, 1749. He is said to have been the first in Barnstable who made ship-building a business. Many who afterwards built vessels in Barnstable served their appren-

ticeship with him.  He had a son John born in Barnstable Jan. 2, 1752.  He removed to Maine where he has descendants.

42.  II.  Thomas, baptized July 25, 1725, died young.
43.  III.  Edward, baptized March 17, 1726, died young.
44.  IV.  Thomas, born 16th March, 1727, married Elizabeth Bacon Oct. 7, 1755, and had Charles 10th Dec. 1756, a master ship carpenter, the father of the late John L. Dimmock of Boston, and Col. Charles Dimmock of Richmond, Va., and others; 2, Hannah, 21st July, 1758.  In her old age she became the fourth wife of Capt. Job Chase of Harwich; 3, John, 16th June, 1764.

Children of Timothy Dimmock and his wife Abigail, born in Mansfield, Conn. :
I.    Timothy, June 2, 1703.
II.   John, Jan. 3, 1704-5, settled in Ashford.
III.  Shubael, May 27, 1707.
IV.   Daniel, Jan. 28, 1709-10.
V.    Israel, Dec. 22, 1710.
VI.   Ebenezer, Nov. 22, 1715.

11.  VII.  Benj. Dimmock, son of Ensign Shubael, by his wife Mary, had the following children born in Mansfield, Conn. :
I.    Perez, June 14, 1704, married Mary Bayley Nov. 5, 1725, and had a family.
II.   Mehitabel, June 8, 1706, died Dec. 1713.
III.  Peter, June 5, 1708, died Aug. 1714.
IV.   Mary, Sept. 14, 1710.
V.    Joanna, June 22, 1713.
VI.   Shubael, June 22, 1715.
VII.  Mehitabel, Aug. 6, 1719.

12.  VIII.  Joannah Dimmock, daughter of Ensign Shubael, married, Oct. 6, 1709, at Windham, Josiah Conant, son of Excise, and grandson of Roger, a man of note in early times.  She had only one child, Shubael, born July 15, 1711.  Shubael Conant was a very prominent man in Mansfield.  He was a judge of the court, held various town, county, and state offices, and was one of the Governor's Council of safety at the commencement of the Revolutionary War.

13.  IX.  Thankful Dimmock, youngest daughter of Ensign Shubael, married, June 28, 1706, Dec. Edward Waldo, of Windham.  She had ten children, and died Dec. 13, 1757, aged 71 years.  Among her living descendants are Rev. Daniel Waldo, a grandson, of Syracuse, N. Y., aged *one hundred years* Sept. 10, 1862 ; and Judge Loren P. Waldo, late Judge of the Superior Court of Connecticut.

17.  IV.  Thomas Dimmock, son of Capt. Thomas, removed to Mansfield, Conn.  He was an Ensign in the King's service, and

died at Cuba in 1741.    He married, Nov. 9, 1720, Anna, daughter of Hezekiah Mason, a grandson of Major John Mason, of Norwich, Conn.    His children born in Mansfield were :

I.      Silas, born —————, died Dec. 31, 1721.
II.     A Son, Oct. 3, 1722, died 6th of said month.
III.    Thomas, Oct. 25, 1723, died Nov. 25, 1726.
IV.     Jesse, Feb. 6, 1725-6, married Rachel Kidder, of Dudley, and had a family.
V.      Anna, Feb. 22, 1727-8.
VI.     Desire, Jan. 23, 1732-3, married Timothy Dimmock, of Coventry, and had a family.
VII.    Lott, Feb. 14, 1733-4, married Hannah Gusley and had issue.
VIII.   Seth, June 5, 1736, died July 14, 1736.
IX.     Hezekiah, Dec. 3, 1739, married Alice Ripley and had issue.

23.  V.  Timothy Dimmock, a son of John, of Falmouth, removed to Mansfield, and married Ann, daughter of Mr. Joseph Bradford, Aug. 15, 1723, and had a family at Mansfield.

These additions make the Dimmock genealogy almost perfect down to the fifth generation.  Very few of the descendants of Elder Dimmock remain in Massachusetts.  John, a grandson, has a few descendants in Falmouth.  None in the male line remain in Barnstable.  In Boston there are a few.  Nearly all are in Connecticut, or trace their descent from Connecticut families.

The Great Lot of Elder Dimmock—Thomas Lothrop, aged 80 years on the 4th of April, 1701, testified and said that he and Barnard Lumbard were appointed land measurers of the town of Barnstable—that "we did lay out the Great Lots twelve score pole long from the foot to the head; the lots that were so laid out were Mr. Dimmock's and my father Lothrop's."

# DIER, OR DYER.

———

Of this family I can furnish little information. The family removed from Barnstable early. William, the only one of the name on the town records, married Mary, daughter of Henry Taylor, Dec. 1686, and had eight children born in Barnstable :
I.     Lydia, 30th March, 1688.
II.    William, 30th Oct. 1690.
III.   Jonathan, Feb. 1692.
IV.    Henry, 11th April, 1693.
V.     Isabel, July 1695.
VI.    Ebenezer, 3d April, 1697.
VII.   Samuel, 30th Oct. 1698.
VIII.  Judah, April, 1701.

# DUNHAM.

———

John Dunham of Barnstable, born in 1648, probably eldest son of John, Jr., of Plymouth, resided at the Indian Ponds, or Hamblin's Plain, as the neighborhood is now generally called. He died January 2, 1696-7, and in his noncupative will devises his estate, apprized at £223,13, to his wife Mary to pay his debts and bring up their children. He married, 1, March, 1679-80, Mary, daughter of Rev. John Smith, and had,

I.      Thomas, born 25th Dec. 1680.
II.     John, 18th May 1682.
III.    Ebenezer, 17th April, 1684.
IV.     Desire, 10th Dec. 1685 ;   married, March 11, 1712-13, Samuel Stetson, of Scituate.
V.      Elisha, 1st Sept. 1687 ; married Temperance Stewart, and was of Mansfield, Conn., 1729.
VI.     Mercy, 10th June, 1689 ;   married Samuel Stetson, Dec. 17, 1724.
VII.    Benjamin, 20th June, 1691.

John Dunham was a member of the Plymouth Church, and afterwards of the Barnstable.  He was not an original proprietor.  He bought of Thomas Bowman, Jr., who removed to Falmouth, Feb. 18, 1685, three acres of  land at  the Herring Brook was laid out to him, bounded east by Goodspeed's old cart way that goeth from Ebenezer Goodspeed's house to the place where the old house of the said Goodspeed was by the salt marsh ; south and west by the cove and river, and north by the commons.  On the 10th of April, 1689, 30 acres which had been granted to him several years previous was laid out to him at Oysterhead river, 65 rods square, bounded westerly by Herring River, southerly by John Leede, Senr's, marsh, easterly by John Goodspeed's cart way, and north by the commons.

# DICKENSON.

Capt. John Dickenson married, 10th  July, 1651, Elizabeth, daughter of  Mr.  John Howland of  Plymouth, and  widow of Ephraim Hicks.  She married Hicks 13th Sept. 1649, and he died three months after.  He bought the lot which I presume was originally Rev. John Smith's, containing 8 acres, bounded west by the lot of Isaac Wells, and easterly by George Lewis.  The new Court House stands near the western boundary of his lot.  In 1654, he had sold this lot to Isaac Wells, and had removed from Barnstable.

In 1653, he was master of  the Desire, of  Barnstable, owned by Capt. Samuel Mayo, Capt. Wm. Paddy, and John Barnes, and was employed to transport the goods of Rev. Wm. Leverich, of Sandwich, to Oyster Bay, Long Island. In Hempsted harbor his vessel was seized by Capt. Thomas Baxter, who had received a commission from the Assembly of Providence plantation. The matter was immediately investigated by the commissioners of the United Colonies. The Assembly of Providence disapproved of the act of Baxter, stating that he had no authority to seize the Desire, and that his commission authorized him to seize Dutch, and not vessels belonging to citizens of the United Colonies.

# DUN, OR DUNN.

John Dun came to Barnstable about the year 1720. His house stood on the hill at head, or south end of Straight Way, and his farm is yet known as Dun's field. He died July 21, 1755, aged 70, and his wife Experience Aug. 17, 1746, aged 50. He was a member of the East Church, and his children, Dorothy, Mary, and Elizabeth, were baptized April 17, 1726; John and Martha, April 24, 1726; Thomas, Oct. 15, 1727, and another Thomas Sept. 29, 1734.

Dorothy married in 1743, Josiah Smith, then a resident in Plymouth; Elizabeth was published in 1745, to Thomas Thomas, of Cambridge; but July 26, 1748, married Benjamin Casely.

He has no male descendants in Barnstable, and I have no information relative to his early history.

# DOWNS.

Respecting this family I have little information. In 1725 there were three of the name in Yarmouth, William, Edward and Samuel, and they married a trio of sisters named Baxter, daughters of Temperance, the wife of Hon. Shubael Baxter. Of the paternity of Mrs. Baxter, and how it happened that she had three daughters of the name of Baxter, before her last marriage, I am unable to explain.

William Downs, of Yarmouth, married, June, 1726, Elizabeth Baxter, and had Elizabeth Aug. 1, 1727; Desire, Dec. 10, 1728; Barnabas, Aug. 8, 1730; Thankful, Sept. 22, 1732; Mary, April 12, 1734; Jabez, March 23, 1735-6; A daughter, Oct. 29, 1737, died 7 days after; Sarah, Dec. 15, 1738; William, Dec. 5, 1740; Isaac, April 5, 1742·; Lydia, Jan. 20, 1743-4; and Benjamin, Nov. 20, 1749.

Edward Downs, of Yarmouth, married in 1728, Mary Baxter, and had Jerusha, 4th Aug. 1729; Bethia, 8th June, 1734; Thomas, 27th Oct. 1735; Robert, 6th March, 1736-7; Betty, 3d Nov. 1739.

Samuel Downs married, Feb. 25, 1730-1, Temperance Baxter. He removed to Barnstable owned and kept the public house known in subsequent times as Lydia Sturgis' tavern.* He died in 1748, and his wife Temperance administered on his estate July 6, 1748,

---

* In the notice of Cornelius Crocker, Senr, I state that the Sturgis Tavern was built by Samuel Downs in 1686. [This statement was omitted by the Editor in this reprint, it being obviously incorrect.] This information I obtained from the late Cornelius Crocker, who said he had deeds and papers to substantiate his statement. These papers cannot now be found. He was mistaken. If the house was built in 1686, it was not built by Samuel Downs, because he had not then seen his first birthday. If built by him, it was probably built in 1731. Its architecture does not indicate that it was built so early as 1684. The tradition is, that it was built the same year that the Court House was. The first County Court in Barnstable was held on the third Tuesday of June, 1686. It was a meeting to organize—no actions were tried. Neither the Court House nor the Sturgis tavern had been constructed April 1686. The Court House was probably built in the latter part of the year 1686.

In the same article I give a wrong location of Otis Loring's blacksmith's shop. It stood on the south side of the road, about half way from the Sturgis to the Loring tavern, on the spot where the shop recently occupied by Isaac Chipman now stands. The blacksmith's shop opposite the Loring tavern, was built by Isaac Lothrop about the year 1788.

which was apprized at £650. The description of the house at that time shows that the only alteration since made is the "L" on the east end. Soon after this date, she married Nathaniel Howes, of Harwich, who resided near the Herring River, and was an "inn holder."

The children of Samuel Downs were Nathaniel, Shubael, Baxter, Jonathan, Hannah, who married a Gage, Temperance, who married a Kelley, and Jane who married a Hall; all living Feb. 24, 1773.

Barnabas Downs, son of William, born in Yarmouth, Aug. 8, 1730, resided in Barnstable. His farm was on the east side of Dimmock's lane. It was on the south of the great lot of Barnabas Lumbert. His house, a small one story building, stood near the woodland. His farm contained about thirty acres of cleared land and would not now sell for more than $100, yet he kept thereon a large stock of cattle, one or more horses, and a large flock of sheep, and raised an abundance of grain and vegetables for the supply of his large family. His sheep and young cattle ran at large in the summer, and his hay he procured from the salt meadows at Sandy Neck. He was one of that class of small farmers which at that time comprised more than half of the rural population of Barnstable—hard working, industrious men, who lived comfortable, and brought up their families respectably, on means which would now be considered totally inadequate. Barnabas Downs lived on the produce of his own lands. His clothing was manufactured in his own house. With the blacksmith, the shoemaker, and the carpenter, he exchanged labor for labor. The few groceries he wanted, he obtained by exchanging his surplus produce with the trader, or by the sale of onions in Boston. He had very little money, and he needed but little. He was the most independent of men. Six days he labored and did all his work, and the seventh was a day of rest.

He became a member of the East Church in Barnstable, July 4, 1779, and regularly attended all its meetings and ordinances. As certain as the Sabbath came, Mr. Downs would be seen riding on horseback to meeting, with his wife seated on a pillion behind him. Everybody then attended meeting on the Sabbath, and if they were no better men and women in consequence, they certainly were no worse.

He married four wives; 1st, Mercy Lumbert, Sept. 20, 1753, by whom he had three children; 2d, Mary Cobb, Sept. 23, 1759, by whom he had eight children, she died April 1780; 3d, Elizabeth Sturgis, who died Feb. 1772; 4th, widow Sarah Spencer, Oct. 7, 1792. She was a daughter of Ebenezer Case, and taught a small school while a widow at her home. Whitney had not then invented the cotton gin, and cotton was then sold with the seeds, which had to be picked out by hand. Mrs. Spencer, to keep her pupils quiet, gave each a small bunch of cotton to pick during school hours. He died April 18, 1620, in the 90th year of his age.†

His children born in Barnstable were:

I.    James, born May 12, 1754, married Joanna Bacon, resided in Barnstable and had a family. He was more distinguished for his wit than sound judgment. Many anecdotes of him are related. One day when at work for Col. James Otis, the men sent him at eleven o'clock for their usual mug of beer. James was sent to the cellar; but a barrel of rum standing near, he filled the tankard with the stronger liquor. On his return, he saw Col. Otis with the workmen, and to avoid detection, he contrived to stumble down and spill the liquor. Col. Otis, who had watched his motions, called to him and said, "Jim, bring me that tankard." He obeyed. Col. Otis, smelling the vessel, discovered the trick. Instead of reproving him, he ordered him to go and fill the tankard again from the same barrel, and be more careful in returning. James did not stumble on his return.

Shubael Gorham and his wife Desire, were his neighbors, and he delighted in cracking his jokes at their expense.

II.   Barnabas, born Oct. 2, 1756. He served three campaigns in the Revolutionary War. Afterwards he shipped on board the private armed schooner Bunker Hill, Capt. Isaac Cobb. Six days after leaving port, the schooner was taken by the English brig Hope, Capt. Brown, and carried to Halifax. After his return he shipped in Boston, on board the private armed brig Gen. Arnold, Capt. James Magee, wrecked in Plymouth harbor, Dec. 27, 1778. He published an auto-biography—a pamphlet of about a dozen pages—printed by John B. Downs, a son of Prince. Many copies were sold; it is now extremely rare—only one copy was found after much inquiry. If none had been found, little information would have been lost. He furnishes few facts, and his narrative of the shipwreck is meagre and unsatisfactory.

I have often heard Mr. Downs relate the particulars of the shipwreck in plain and simple words; but with a pathos and feeling that would draw tears from the eyes of the most obdurate. Nearly half a century has passed since he told his simple story of the horrid sufferings endured by that ill-fated crew, yet few of the circumstances have faded from memory. It is from my recollection of his conversations, from the published statements of Capt. Magee, and the narrative of Cornelius Merchant, Esq., that I

† He was carried as was the uniform custom at that time, on a bier from his house to the grave, a distance of nearly two miles. I was one of the six carriers. He weighed over 200 pounds when he died, and I shall never forget his funeral, for my bones ache, even now, when I think of that long tramp with at least 75 pounds on one shoulder. In those days, it would have been deemed a sacrilege to have carried a corpse to the grave in a hearse.

have compiled the following account of the shipwreck; not from "The Life of Barnabas Downs, Jr." :

The Gen. Arnold was a new vessel, mounted 20 guns, with a crew of 105 men and boys. Of these twelve were from Barnstable, namely, Mr. John Russell, captain of the marines, Barnabas Lothrop, Jr., Daniel Hall, Thomas Casely, Ebenezer Bacon, Jesse Garrett, John Berry, Barnabas Howes, Stephen Bacon, Jonathan Lothrop, Barnabas Downs, Jr., and Boston Crocker, a negro servant of Joseph Crocker. In the Boston Gazette of Jan. 4, 1779, Barnabas Lothrop, Jr., is included in the list of survivors. It appears that he was alive when taken from the wreck, but died on his way or soon after reaching the shore. Barnabas Downs, Jr., was the sole survivor of the twelve from the East Parish in Barnstable

The Gen. Arnold, Capt. James Magee, sailed from Nantasket Roads, Boston, on Thursday, Dec. 24, 1778, in company with the privateer sloop Revenge, Capt. Barrow, mounting ten guns. In the Bay they encountered a violent north-east storm. Its severity is perhaps unparalled in the annals of New England. This is the unanimous verdict of those who lived at that time, and even to this day the aged remark respecting a very violent storm, "it is almost as severe as the Magee storm." The Revenge being in good sailing trim weathered Cape Cod, and afterwards arrived at the West Indies.

Capt. Magee was unable to weather the Race. On Friday, Dec. 25, the gale having subsided, at 5 o'clock in the afternoon, he anchored off Plymouth. Having no pilot, he did not judge it prudent to run into the harbor.

In the course of the night the gale increased in violence, and on the morning of Saturday, Dec. 26, Capt. Magee says, it was "the severest of all storms,"—a strong expression, yet the testimony of many witnesses justifies its use.

Capt. Magee was a good sailor. In the hour of difficulty and danger he was calm, hopeful, self-reliant. Without these qualities, the most experience and energetic often fail. The sixteen main deck guns were lowered into the hold, the topmasts were struck, the sails snugly furled, long scopes given to the cables, and all those other little precautions which will suggest themselves to the mind of a sailor, were taken to prevent the brig from dragging her anchors. All these precautions did not prevent her from dragging. She drove towards the shore and struck on White Flat, a shoal in Plymouth harbor.

While preparing to cut away the masts to prevent rolling and bilging, a disturbance occurred among some of the sailors who had become intoxicated. By the prudent management of the officers, order was again re-established.

The brig rolled and thumped violently on the flat, and in the course of Saturday afternoon bilged and filled with water. Up to this time the officers and crew had found shelter in the cabin and forecastle, and none had then perished. The water was nearly on a level with the main deck, the tide was rising, and no shelter could be obtained below. The high quarter deck was the only place that afforded the least prospect of safety. A sail was extended from the topsail boom on the larbord side, to the starbord quarter rail, and a partial protection from the storm was obtained. More crowded under the sail than could stand without jostling against each other, and many were thrown on the deck.

It was now Saturday afternoon. The storm raged with fearful intensity, the snow fell thick and fast, smothering the men, darkening the air, and rendering objects at a little distance invisible. The waves dashed furiously against the vessel and fell in frozen spray on the ill-fated mariners. The brig rolled and thumped so violently that none could stand without support.

The authority of the officers had ceased—each one sought, as best he could, his own safety. Some of the sailors had not only drank to excess, but to keep their feet from freezing, had filled their boots with rum, and they were among the first to yield to despair.

Capt. John Russell, of Barnstable, was the first who perished. He was large, stout, courageous, and capable of much physical endurance. He was thirty-one years of age, in the prime of life, and while exhorting the men not to despair, telling them the vessel was new and strong, and would hold together, he slipped, fell heavily to the deck, sinking to rise no more.

"Thinking o'er all the bitterness of death,
Mix'd with the tender anguish nature shoots
Through the wrung bosom of the dying man,
His wife, his children, and his friends unseen."

Mr. William Russell, the first lieutenant, had carefully watched the flow of the tide, about sunset announced the welcome intelligence that the tide was on the ebb. This gave courage to the survivors, for their only hope of relief depended on the fall of the tide. The water was then ankle deep on the main deck, and if it had continued to rise the vessel would have broken up, and all would have been lost.

At nine o'clock on Saturday evening the tide had receded, the wreck lay motionless on the flat, and no frozen spray fell on the deck.

Towards Sunday morning, Dec. 27, the wind veered to the northwest, and the cold increased. The morning sun rose in a clear sky, the wind had abated; but the cold was intense. At this time thirty had perished; some had been smothered by the snow, others were frozen, and a few had been washed off the deck and drowned.

Early on Sunday forenoon three men, Abel Willis, of Rock Island, David Dunham, of Falmouth, and John Robinson, an

Irish sailor, neither much frozen, volunteered to attempt to obtain assistance.  They took the yawl, which had caught under the larbord gang-board, and proceeded to the ice, which commenced about ten rods from the brig, and thence travelled to a small schooner, laying in the ice about half a mile to the southward, belonging to Duxbury, and then recently from Boston, with three or four men and a lady on board.  When these men reached the schooner, the living on board the wreck were elated with the prospect of immediate relief.  The men did not return.

Before leaving the wreck these men had made a solemn promise that if they reached the schooner they would procure assistance and return.  They did neither.  The survivors watched with eager eyes—they saw no movement on board the schooner—their boat was gone, and no one could now reach the ice.

Every effort was now made to convince the inhabitants on shore that some were yet alive on the wreck.  Capt. Magee tied a handkerchief to a staff, which he waived, and at the same time all the survivors simultaneously made a loud wail, hoping that the sound might reach the shore.

The people of Plymouth for some hours previously, had been aware of their situation, and made every exertion in their power, but in vain, to reach the wreck, and afford relief.  The harbor was filled with loose cakes of ice, over and through which they found it impossible to force a boat.

With the setting sun on Sunday night, the last ray of hope of relief faded away and perished—some yielding to despair, and laid down to rise no more—stout youths who had been playmates in their native village, embraced and clasped in each other's arms, quietly yielded up their spirits to God—middle aged men carried in their arms boys placed in their care, till death relieved them of the burden.  To the few yet remaining who did not yield to despair, another long and dreadful night was approaching, with no hope of relief till after the rising of Monday morning's sun.  Wet, faint with hunger, benumbed with cold, and frost bitten—the thermometer at zero — a tattered sail, and the bleached, stiffened corpses of half their late companions piled around, was their only protection from the piercing wind and cutting frost.

Under such circumstances, the stoutest heart might quail.  Capt. Magee was heard to lisp only one word of complaint — he never despaired —he cheered and encouraged his men to persevere.  Sunday night was clear, and he knew that with the thermometer at zero none could survive if they sat still on the deck.

A piercing northwest wind rendered their sufferings intense, and to pass away that long and dreadful night, various expedients were resorted to.  Unable to stand and keep in motion all the time, they sat down in circles, and with their legs crossed over one another, by constant friction, strove to keep their feet from freezing. None would have survived if our master spirit had not been there to cheer them by his words, and encourage them by his example.

Monday morning at last dawned on the sufferers — it was serene and beautiful — but its light revealed to the survivors the sad havoc which death had made on that dreary night. The quarter-deck was covered with the dead and the dying—blanched and frozen bodies were lying in every position—some as they had expired—others piled in heaps to give more room for the living, or a breast-work to protect them from the piercing wind that was seizing on their vitals.

Late on Monday forenoon, Dec. 28, relief came. Early in the morning the shore was thronged with people — some were collecting materials, and others were building a causeway, from one cake of ice to another, and thus a pathway was made to the wreck.

To relieve the living was their first care, and to distinguish between some of them and the dead, was not easy. Barnabas Downs, Jr., lay on the deck motionless and apparently dead—yet living and perfectly conscious. He heard the conversation — they had passed by him as dead. He exerted all his remaining strength to move, and exhibit some sign of vitality. He moved his eyelids, which fortunately was noticed, and he was carried to the shore — revived and soon after was able to speak.

Of the 105 who sailed from Boston on the Thursday preceeding, only 33 were then living. Of these, nine died before the end of nine days ; eight were invalids ever after, and sixteen entirely recovered. Capt. Magee and Mr. William Russell lived twenty years, Barnabas Downs, Jr., thirty-nine years, and Cornelius Marchant, Esq., the last survivor, died Oct. 1, 1838, aged 75 years. He was only 15 when he shipped, and during the storm of Saturday and Saturday night he stood at the tafel rail, with nothing to protect him from its violence.

The people of Plymouth, remarks Capt. Magee, with "that tenderness and social sympathy which does honor to human nature," then opened their houses, received the survivors as they would a brother or a father, watched over them, and administered to their wants everything which necessity demanded or kindness could suggest.

The seventy-two dead, frozen in every variety of form, were laid in Mill river to thaw before the rights of sepulchre were performed. The bodies were afterwards put into coffins, and removed to the Court House where funeral services were performed.

So solemn and affecting a spectacle is rarely witnessed. Around that ancient hall seventy-two dead were arranged. Their friends were far away ; yet real mourners were there, the people of old Plymouth attended in mass. The profound solemnity of the scene choked the utterance of the officiating clergyman — the congregation sympathized with him in feeling—the deep silence which pervaded the hall was only broken by the half suppressed sobs of the audience.    Silence is more eloquent than words — it drew tears from every eye, and its teachings were not soon forgotten.

Capt. John Russell and Mr. Daniel Hall, of Barnstable, and perhaps one or two others were interred in separate graves. About seventy were committed to one common grave, and no stone marked the place of their sepulchre till 1862, when a generous son of old Plymouth erected at his own expense, a beautiful granite monument to their memory.

The deep snow had blocked the roads rendering them impassable, and it was several days before the intelligence of the disaster reached Barnstable.    Mr. Barnabas Downs, Mr. Oris Bacon and others, who had friends on board the Gen. Arnold, immediately proceeded to Plymouth.    Of the twelve who went from Barnstable they found only Barnabas Downs, Jr., living.    Barnabas Lothrop was living when the Plymotheans reached the wreck; but he soon died.

Mr. John Thacher brought Mr. Downs from Plymouth.    No carriage* set on springs was then owned in Barnstable, and if there had been one, the deep snow with which the roads between Sandwich and Plymouth were blocked, would have prevented its use.    Mr. Thacher constructed an ambulance which at this day would excite much curiosity.    He took two long slender poles; at one end a horse was harnessed as into the shafts of a carriage, and at the other, another horse was harnessed, only in the reverse of the usual position, both heading the same way, with a space of about ten feet between them.    That space was covered with a netting, which hung down like a hammock between the poles.    On this a feather-bed and bedding were laid, and in which Mr. Downs was placed.    Mr. Thacher rode on the head horse, and thus brought the patient to his father's house.

On the sea coast, in all parts of the world, there are "moon cursers," that is men who hold that it is no sin to steal from a shipwrecked mariner.    To the everlasting honor of the Plymoutheans, they had not forgotten the rigid morality taught by their Pilgrim fathers — there were no "moon cursers" there.    Capt. Magee, the friends of the deceased who went from Barnstable, and the Vineyard, bear one testimony — every article recovered from the wreck was carefully preserved, and returned to its rightful owner or to his heirs.

The history of Plymouth will be studied as long as man exists, and the two facts we have named will ever be bright jewels

---

*Dr. Bourne had a chaise at that time, the only one then owned in Barnstable, and said to have been the first in town.   Doct. Hersey had a chair, or sulkey, whether as early as this date, I am unable to say.

in her diadem, namely, the noble, generous hospitality which her sons and daughters extended to the shipwrecked mariners of the Gen. Arnold, and second, the scrupulous honesty they displayed in restoring every article found, however small in value, to its rightful owner.

Soon after Mr. Downs was taken on shore sensation and speech were restored. While lying on the deck he could see and hear—was perfectly conscious of his situation—suffered no pain—but could not move a limb—and if left, would have died without a struggle. With the return of feeling, his pains became most excruciating. He always said that he suffered far more during the time in which he partook of the hospitality of Plymouth friends, than he did while on the wreck.

Mr. Downs lost his feet. The toes and heel of each were frozen, and the flesh sloughed off leaving stumps which did not heal over till a few months before his death. He used crutches, and ever after walked on his knees.

He married, Nov. 23, 1784, Sarah Hamblin, and had a family, several of whom yet survive. He died in the summer of 1817. That year a young physician had opened an office in Barnstable, and desirous of performing some cure that would give him a name and reputation, said to Mr. Downs, "I can cure your feet." He did so. Mr. Downs immediately after became very fleshy, and at sunset on the day of his death remarked to a neighbor that he never felt so well in his life, and exhibited his arms and legs to show how fleshy and strong he was. Two hours after he died. Dissolution commenced immediately, and he had to be buried the next forenoon.

Barnabas Downs, Jr., resided in the ancient Lumbert house, on the high ground south of Lumbert's pond. He was honest and industrious, and though he went about on his knees, he worked in his garden in pleasant weather, cut up his wood, and did many jobs about his house. In the winter, and during unpleasant weather he coopered for his neighbors. He also cast spoons, ink stands, and other small articles, in pewter or lead, a business in which he exhibited some skill.

He rode to meeting on the Sabbath on horseback, and few can now be found who can mount or dismount quicker than he did. He and his wife were admitted to the East Church Oct. 10, 1804, and his children, James Magee, Timothy, Catherine, Temperance, and Ruth Hamblin, were then baptized.

He was a pious man, and being considered a worthy object of charity, a collection was annually taken up for his benefit by the church. The benevolent often remembered him, and though he had but few of this world's goods, he lived comfortably and respectably. His wife was a pattern of neatness. Neither a paint-brush nor a carpet was ever seen in her house, yet frequent

washings had polished the walls, and the floors were as white as
sand scouring could make them.

The other children of Barnabas Downs, Sen'r, were: 3,
Prince, born Dec. 5, 1758, married ——— Bacon; 4, Mercy,
born Oct. 8, 1765, lived to old age unmarried; 5, Rachell, Sept.
7, 1766, married Shubael Hamblin, Jr., 25th Nov. 1787; 6,
Mary, born April 11, 1767, married Henry Cobb; 7, Elizabeth,
July 25, 1768, married Stephen Bearse Nov. 29, 1790; 8, David,
born Dec. 20, 1769, married Rebecca Hallett, died at sea; 9,
Samuel, June 7, 1771, married Lucy Childs May 2, 1797; 10,
Edward, Sept. 13, 1773; 11, Abigail, Oct. 7, 1778, married
Lewis Cobb, Aug. 30, 1804. He is living—she died recently.

NOTE.—The date of the death of Barnabas Downs, printed near the top of page 351,
as the reader has doubtless concluded, should read 1820 instead of 1620.

# EASTERBROOKS.

The Easterbrooks families of Barnstable are descendants of
Capt. John Easterbrooks, a native of Ireland, probably one of
the Scotch Irish. The progenitors of the families of this name at
Concord and Swanzey, came from Enfield, in Middlesex County,
England, about the year 1660.

Capt. Easterbrooks married Aug. 23, 1749, Abigail Gorham.
He was a sea-captain—a man of good sense, and sound judgment. He resided on the estate which was the homestead of his
father-in-law, bounded on the west by the eastern lane to the Indian lands. His wife died in 1794, aged 65, and he July 2, 1802,
aged 75. His children born in Barnstable were:

I.      Rachell, Aug. 10, 1750.
II.     Gorham, July 7, 1756.
III.    Elizabeth, July 2, 1759.
IV.     Samuel, Jan. 28, 1765.
V.      John. (His birth is not on the town, nor is his baptism on
        the church records.

VI.   Joseph, baptized March 27, 1768.

Capt. John Easterbrooks, Jr., was for many years captain of the Liberty, a packet from Barnstable to Boston.

# EWELL.

———

Henry Ewell was from Sandwich, in the County of Kent. He was a shoemaker, came over in the ship Hercules, Capt. John Witherley, in March 1634-5.  He settled in Scituate, and was a member of Mr. Lothrop's church.  In 1637 he volunteered and was a soldier in the Pequod war.  He was a freeman in 1638, and in 1639 removed to Barnstable, and about 1646 returned to Scituate, where he died in 1681.  He married, Nov. 23, 1638, Sarah Annable, daughter of Anthony Annable.  His children were :   John, born in Barnstable 1639-40 ; Ebenezer, 1643, and Sarah 1645 ;  and Hannah, born in Scituate 1649 ; Gersham, 1650 ;  Bethia, 1653 ;  Ichabod,  1659 ; Deborah, 1663, and Eunice.  Sarah Ewell, widow of Henry, died 1687.

Henry Ewell's house and barn, in Scituate, valued at £10, was burnt by the Indians in 1676.  His eldest son John, lived in Boston, and died at Newbury 1686.  Ichabod lived on the paternal estate, and Gershom at "Cold Spring," Scituate.  None of the name of Ewell now reside in Barnstable.

He resided at West Barnstable, near Mr. Annable's.  On the town records his name is recorded as Henry Coxswell—a blunder of the town clerk.

# EWER.

This name on the early Barnstable records is written Eure, on the Colony records it is written Ure, Eue, Ewe, and Ewer. A Henry Eue was one of the first settlers in Sandwich. Dec. 4, 1638, a warrant was directed to James Skiff, ordering him to recarry Henry Eue and his wife and their goods, to the place where he brought them. This warrant does not appear to have been executed, for in 1640 he was an inhabitant of Sandwich and had a share assigned to him in the division of the common meadows. Mr. Freeman's statement that he was the ancestor of the Ewer family of Sandwich, requires confirmation; because after 1640 his name disappears on the records.

In 1643, there was a John Eue at Hartford; but it does not appear that he was connected with the Ewers of Massachusetts and Plymouth.

"Thomas Ewer, aged 40, a tailor, embarked aboard the ship James, Jo. May, at London, June 19, 1635, for New England, with his wife Sarah, aged 28, and two children, Elizabeth, aged 4 years, and Thomas, aged 1 1-2 years. He had at least two older children, not named in the Custom House records, who came over subsequently, perhaps with their grandfather in 1638.

1.    Thomas Ewer married Sarah, daughter of Mr. Robert Linnell,* probably in London where he resided. It does not appear that he had any children born in this country. His children were:

2.    I.   Sarah, born April 1627, married, June 18, 1645, Thomas Blossom, of Barnstable.

3.    II.   Henry, born April 1629, married Mary ——, he died in 1652, and it is not known that he left issue. His widow became the second wife of John Jenkins 2d Feb. 1652-3.

4.    III.   Elizabeth, born 1631, died in Barnstable, and was buried 9th April 1641.

5.    IV.   Thomas, born 1633, married Hannah, ——, and died in Barnstable in 1667, aged 34.

Thomas Ewer settled in Charlestown, where he acquired some notoriety as a politician. In 1637 Lord Ley brought a

---

*Mr. Savage and others say William Larned, Linnett or Linnell, I find written Larnett, easily transformed into Larned. William and Robert are unlike, yet I feel confident that I am right.

charge against him for using language disrespectful to the King, and afterwards he was prosecuted as one of the friends and supporters of Wheelwright; but he recanted his opinions, proving himself not to be so firm a man as his son Thomas.

He died in Charleston in 1638, and his widow Sarah married, Dec. 11, 1639, Thomas Lothrop. Her family removed with her to Barnstable.

5. Respecting the family of Thomas Ewer, 2d, little is known. He removed to Sandwich early. In 1659 he had a family and resided near Spring Hill. He was a Quaker, and for refusing to take the oath of fidelity, and for attending Quaker meetings, was fined £20,10, which with expenses amounted to £25,8. In payment the Marshall seized a debt due him from Richard Chadwell for labor, £7,13

In money taken out of his house, 6,17

Clothing, new cloth, with other goods particularly named, 10,18

£25,8

From the new cloth taken (four yards of Kersey) George Barlow, the Marshall, had a coat made, and which he wore at Court. Ewer, seeing him have it on, asked the Magistrates, "*Whether they owned George Barlow in wearing his cloth.*" To this question Gov. Prence replied: "That if he could prove that George Barlow had wronged him, he might seek his satisfaction." For this question he was sentenced "to be laid neck and heels together." Which, says Bishop, was the injustice he received at their hands.

The Court records give a different reason of the matter. He was sentenced to lye neck and heels together during the pleasure of the Court, "for his tumultuous and seditious carriages and speeches in Court." The Magistrates being informed that he was an infirm man, and was troubled with a rupture, the sentence was not executed.

Bishop is usually accurate, but in this case he omits a material fact and leaves a wrong impression on the mind of his reader. He adds that Ewer's axe, with which he wrought, worth three shillings, was taken for a tax of ten pence to the country, and that at another time, half a bushel of grain, out of his bag at the mill, for a similar tax, for the same amount.

These were assessments legally made to pay the current expenses of the Colony. Ewer was abundantly able to pay, he resisted the execution of a law, to which no constitutional objection was made, and if his axe or his grain was taken to pay, neither he nor his apologist, Mr. Bishop, had a right to complain.

The Quakers had right and justice on their side, when they refused to pay fines imposed for not taking the oath of fidelity, or for attending meetings of their own society; but when they refused to pay their proportion of the public expenses, they were clearly in the wrong, and those of their number who resisted, were not only guilty of doing wrong to their country, but to their religious associates; because by thus resisting they prejudiced their claim for sympathy as sufferers for conscience sake.

In 1658 Thomas Ewer and most of the leading members of the Society of Friends in Sandwich were disfranchised and ordered to leave the town.  Ewer continued to reside there till 1660.  In 1661 he is spoken of as of Barnstable.  In that year he bought a part of the farm and meadows on the west of the Crocker land, then owned by .Mr. Dimmock, originally laid out, I think, to Thomas Hatch.  This small farm his descendants have continued to own till recently.

The goods seized by the Marshall were such as a tailor usually keeps, and I infer from this that he learned the trade of his father.  He died in 1667, aged 34, leaving a widow Hannah and a family of children.  I find no record of their names. Thomas Lothrop, the father-in-law of the deceased, and Shubael Linnell, his uncle, were appointed guardians of the children.

Thomas Ewer, 3d, afterwards owned the Ewer farm, and the facts and circumstances above stated make it probable, if not certain, that he was the son of Thomas Ewer, 2d, and his wife Hannah.

6.   Thomas Ewer, 3d, probably son of Thomas, 2d, married three wives.  He married his first wife about the year 1682; she died in a few years, and he married, in 1689, Elizabeth, daughter of the first John Lovell, and  for his third wife he  married, Sept. 18, 1712, Wid. Sarah Warren.

*Children born in Barnstable.*

7.       I.   Thomas, Dec. 1683, (?) died young.
8.      II.   Thomas, Jan. 1686.
9.     III.   Shubael, 1690.
10.     IV.   John, Feb. 1692.
         V.   Mehitabel, Oct. 1694, (?) died same year.
11.     VI.   Nathaniel, Nov. 1695, (?) baptized Dec. 9, 1694.
12.    VII.   Jonathan, July 1696.
13.   VIII.   Hezekiah, Sept. 1697.
14.     IX.   Mehetabel, baptized Dec. 11, 1698.
15.      X.   Thankful, Nov. 1701.
16.     XI.   Abigail, baptized April 7, 1706.

Thomas Ewer, 3d, died  June 1722, leaving  a widow Sarah, and  three sons, Thomas, John, and Nathaniel, whom  he exhorts in his will, "to live in the fear of God, and love one another, and cary dutifully to their Honored Mother."  Only three of his eleven children appear to have been then living.  His real estate was apprized at £74, and his personal estate at £83.  In 1684 his

dwelling house was on the north side of the road. In the appriz-
al of his estate his home lot is described as four acres of upland
on the south of the road. He owned the meadow which his
father bought in 1661.

    8. Thomas Ewer, 4th, born Jan. 1686. He is called a "cord-
wainer" or shoemaker, and died insolvent in 1761. He married,
June 10, 1718, Reliance Tobey, of Sandwich, and had,

17.    I.    John, born April 28, 1719, "a cordwainer" or shoemaker. He died 1782. He had 1, Ebenezer, 20th Dec.
1741, died young ; 2, John, 25th Dec. 1744, died young ;
3, David, 15th April, 1747 ; 4, Jonathan, 7th June, 1754 ;
5, Reliance, 16th June, 1756 ; 6, Ebenezer, 31st Dec.
1758 ; and 7, John, 31st Oct. 1763.

18.    II.    Mary, born Oct. 7, 1721, married Lazarous Lovell
May 29, 1760, died April 5, 1813, aged 91.

19.    III.    Sarah, March 1, 1723-4, died young.

20.    IV.    Thomas, Oct. 3, 1726, married, in 1749, Lydia Har-
low of Plymouth, where he removed and had, 1, Thomas,
Feb. 22, 1750 ; 2, Eleazer, Aug. 26, 1752 ; (he married
Abigail Lothrop and had Isaac, Barnabas, Ansel, and
Abigail. He bought the estate of schoolmaster Joseph
Lewis, in the East Parish—he was a tanner and shoe-
maker, and died young.) After his return to Barnstable
Thomas had 3, Ansel, Sept. 9, 1753, died young, 4, Seth,
July 5, 1755 ; 5, Lydia, Sept. 16, 1758 ; and 6, Ansel
again, Sept. 21, 1760.

21.    V.    Seth, born March 14, 1729, married, 1782, Elizabeth
Rich, of Truro.

22.    VI.    Sarah, born Feb. 23, 1732, married Elisha Holmes
of Plymouth, 1749.

23.    VII.    Sylvanus, born March 18, 1741-2.

    9. Shubael Ewer, son of Thomas and Elizabeth Ewer, bap-
tized Sept. 21, 1690, resided at West Barnstable. He married
June 14, 1714 Rebecca Conant of Bridgewater. He died Aug. 6,
1715, leaving an estate apprized at £152, a widow Rebecca, and
one daughter.

24.    I.    Rebecca, born 27th April, 1755. She married, June
27, 1734, Thomas Winslow of Rochester.

    10. John Ewer, son of Thomas, 3d, married July 5, 1716,
Elizabeth Lumbard. He died in 1723, leaving sons Shubael,
Joseph, (*non compos mentis*, whose estate in 1744 was apprized at
£262,15,) Benjamin, and daughter Elizabeth, all minors. He inherited the old homestead, and built a house on the land on the
south of the road. He gave to his widow all the eight acres of
land on the south of the road. His children born in Barnstable
were :

25.    I.    Shubael, (father of Lazarus, and grandfather of

Joseph Ewer, of East Sandwich.)
26.    II.  Joseph, (*non compos mentis.*)
27.    III.  Benjamin, born 1721, married Hannah Lawrence of
Hog Pond village, in Sandwich, and removed to that town.
His children were Mary, who married —— Jenny; Peleg,
(father of Benjamin, East Sandwich,) ; Nancy, who married Peter Smith, of Newbern, recently deceased ; Hannah
married —— Jones ;  and Elizabeth married ——
Lawrence.
28.    IV.  Elizabeth.
    11.  Nathaniel Ewer, son of Thomas, 3d, born, the record
says, 1695 ; but having been baptized Dec. 9, 1694, he was probably born that year.   He married, Nov. 8, 1723, Mary Stewart of
Sandwich.

*Children born in Barnstable.*

29.    I.  Silas, 27th Nov. 1724, married Lydia Garrett of Sandwich, 1746, and had Mehitabel May 1, 1747; Abigail,
March 2, 1748 ; Susannah, Dec. 5, 1750 ; Silas, Aug. 10,
1752 ; Elizabeth, Dec. 14, 1754 ; and Prince Feb. 5,
1757.
30.    II.  Nathaniel, 17th April, 1726, married Drusilla Co-
bell of Chatham, and resided, as I am informed, at Nantucket some part of his life.  Isaac Ewer, who recently
died at Osterville, nearly a hundred years of age, was his
son.
31.    III.  Desire, born 26th Nov. 1727.
32.    IV.  Gamaliel, 19th June, 1733, married Martha Fuller
1753.
33.    V.  Mary, 7th Aug. 1737, married, Oct. 26, 1757,
Thomas Churchill of Plymouth.

# FOXWELL.

Two men of the name of Richard Foxwell, of about the same age, came to New England about the year 1630. Mr. Deane was perhaps not aware there were two of the name, and it is not surprising that he has confounded them, because he supposed both Richards were the same person.

Richard, who settled in that part of Maine then known as Georgiance, was born in 1604 and was probably the younger man. He came over as early as 1631, went *home*, as our ancestors called England for many years, in 1632, and returned in 1633. He was of Scarborough in 1636, where he married, in 1636, Sarah, daughter of Capt. Richard Bonython, one of the patentees of Georgiance. His sons were Richard, John and Philip, and he had five daughters. He died in 1677, aged 73. [Folsom.]

The other Richard Foxwell probably came over in the fleet with Gov. Winthrop. He was admitted a freeman of the Massachusetts Colony Oct. 19, 1630, and was sworn on the 8th of May following. On his removal to the Plymouth Colony his name was entered on the list of those who had taken the oath of fidelity; but in 1657 he was required to take that oath, though he had previously taken the freeman's oath in Massachusetts.

Mr. Deane says he came from the County of Kent, in England. There is some evidence that he was a resident in the city of London at the time he embarked for New England. His son John was born as early as 1627, a fact which proves that he married in England. Whether his wife died before he left, or came over with him, is not known.

From 1631 to 1634 he is not named in the records. Mr. Savage intimates that during this period he may have gone home and returned; if so, it affords another curious parallism in the history of the two Richard Foxwells. He probably removed from

Boston, in 1631, to Scituate, where there was a small settlement
of men whom he had known in his native land.   In 1634 he was
of Scituate.   His house, in the spring of 1635, is described as
being on Kent street, the fourth on the south of Meeting House
lane, and as the eleventh built in that town.   This house he sold
to Henry Bourne, and in 1637 built on his houselot, numbered 50
on Mr. Lothrop's list.

In the spring of 1639 he removed to Barnstable, and built a
house on his lot near where the Hall of the Agricultural Society
now stands.   No record was made of his lands till 1662, when he
owned only eight acres, four on each side of the road.   His lot
was one of those laid by the authority of Mr. Collicut, and originally probably included the twelve acres owned by Nicholas Davis.   This would make his lot correspond in shape with the other
lots laid out at the same time.   If I am right in this, his homelot
contained sixteen acres, and was bounded west by the homelot of
Nathaniel Bacon, north partly by the swamp (then town's commons) and the lands of Dolar Davis, east by the Dimmock farm,
and south by the highway.   His lot on the south side of the road
contained four acres, and was bounded north by the highway.
east by Elder Cobb's great lot, south by the commons, and west
by Nathaniel Bacon's land.

He set out an orchard, as all the first settlers did.   A seedling raised by him, and known as the Foxwell apple, is yet cultivated.

I have seen it stated that he was a trader.   Whatever may
have been his employment, it is certain that he was very poor at
his death in 1668, for his sons-in-law refused to act as executors
to his will.

He is not named as the holder of any office ; but as private
citizen he was a good neighbor, an honest man, and and exemplary member of the christian church.

He was one of the original members of Mr. Lothrop's Church
having joined at its organization at Scituate on the 8th of January, 1634-5.   The expression used in regard to the first members,
"so many of us as had been in covenant before," evidently implies
that they had been members of his church in London.   After his
removal to Barnstable he continued to be a member in good standing till his death.

He married, as already stated, his first wife in England, and his
son John probably came over with him.   In 1634 he married Ann
Shelly, who came over that year.   His children so far as known
were :

I.   John, born in England as early as 1627.   He is named in
     1640 in connection with John Makefield, and as having two
     lambs in his possession.   In Aug. 1643, his name is on the
     list of those able to bear arms, and in Oct. 1645, was one of

the soldiers from Barnstable in the Narraganset expedition. In subsequent records, the land where James Otis now resides is called John Foxwell's house lot, from which it may be inferred that he owned a house. It does not appear that he married and had a family. He died in Barnstable, and was buried Sept. 21, 1646.

II. Mary, born in Scituate 17th Aug. 1635, married, Jan. 8, 1654, Hugh Cole, Sen'r, of Plymouth, and was afterwards of Swansea. His children were James, born 3 or (8) Nov. 1655; Hugh, 8 or (15) March 1658; John, 15 or (16) May 1660; Martha, 14 or (16) April 1662; Anna, 14th Oct. 1664; Ruth, 8 or (17) Jan. 1666; and Joseph, 15th May 1668.

III. Martha, born in Scituate 24th March, 1638, married Samuel Bacon 9th May 1669, and had Samuel 9th March 1659-60, and Martha Jan. 6, 1661.

IV. Ruth, born in Barnstable 25th March 1641.

If the Barnstable and Colony Records are reliable, Mary and Martha Foxwell were born in Barnstable, showing that the town was settled in 1635. Both records are erroneous. I have followed the church records. In the Barnstable records there is an error of ten years in the marriage and births of the children of Samuel Bacon.

# FITZRANDOLPHE.

---

## EDWARD FITZRANDOLPHE.

Mr. Lothrop says, "the young Master Fitzrandolphe" built in 1636, the 38th house constructed in Scituate. Having provided himself with a home he married, May 10, 1637, Elizabeth,* daughter of Dea. Thomas Blossom of the Leyden and Plymouth churches. He joined Mr. Lothrop's church in Scituate May 14, 1637, and his wife joined at Barnstable Aug. 27, 1643.

He sold his house in that town to Dea. Richard Sealis, and removed in the spring of 1639 to Barnstable, and built a house on his lot containing eight acres, bounded east by the road to Hyannis, which separated it from the homelot of Roger Goodspeed, and land probably then afterwards town commons, and on the west by the homelot of George Lewis. This land is now owned by the heirs of Anna Childs, Dea. John Munroe and others. He also owned a garden spot and two acres of meadow on the north of the County road, now owned by Capt. Foster, Ebenezer Bacon, Esq., and others, two lots in the Old Common Field, one of two, and the other of three acres, and ninety-two rods in the Calves Pasture. This property he sold June 2, 1649, to Elder John Chipman, by a deed witnessed by William Casely, Henry Cobb and Richard Church.† This deed is recorded in the Colony records, and is printed in the 12th volume of the records, pages 180 and 181. I have in my possession another deed of the same

---

*In my notice of the Blossom family I inadvertantly omitted to name this daughter of Dea. Thomas Blossom.

†Richard Church, born in 1608, was a carpenter, and only a temporary resident in Barnstable. He probably came to Massachusetts in the fleet with Gov. Winthrop in 1630. He removed from Weymouth to Plymouth, and was admitted a freeman 4th Oct. 1632. He sold his estate in Plymouth in 1649, stopped in Barnstable some little time, was at Charlestown in 1643, and finally set down at Hingham, and died at Dedham in 1648. He married Elizabeth, daughter of Richard Warren, and had Joseph; Benjamin 1639, (the renowned soldier) Richard, Caleb, Nathaniel, Hunah 1646, Abigail, Charles, Deborah 1657, and perhaps Mary, The dwelling house of Gen. Benjamin Church was at Fall River, and was taken down not many years since. It stood near the present dwelling house of Col. Richard Borden.

property, in the hand writing of Gov. Hinckley, acknowledged before him Aug. 13, 1669, and witnessed by his wife Mary Hinckley and Peter Blossom. In this deed it is stated that the property was sold to John Chipman in 1649. Why two deeds of the same property were given, I am unable to explain.

Soon after 1649, John Chipman sold this lot to John Davis, and Jan. 14, 1658, the latter sold six acres thereof to Samuel Norman, reserving two acres at the north end on which his house then stood. Feb. 26, 1665, Norman reconveyed this land to Davis, with his house thereon. The portion owned by Norman, is now known as Norman's Hill.

In 1649, Edward Fitzrandolphe removed to his farm in West Barnstable, "a double great lot," containing 120 acres of upland, bounded north by the meadows, east by the Bursley farm, south by the commons, and west by the lands of Mr. Thomas Dexter. On the north he had twenty-three acres of salt meadow, bound west by the lands of Mr. Thomas Dexter, on the north bounded partly by the marsh of William Dexter, partly by the common meadows, and partly by the "Committees Creek, so called," east by the upland of Mr. John Bursley, and south by his own land. This tract is now known as the Bodfish and Smith farms. In 1669 he and several families from the Cape removed to New Jersey. In Oct. 1683 his widow was living at New Piscataqua, New Jersey.

He is called in deeds a yeoman, or farmer, and does not appear to have been employed in any official station. He had received a good education for those times, and as Mr. Lothrop styles him "Master" he probably belonged to a good family. He came probably from the west of England.

His farm at West Barnstable he sold partly to John Crocker, Sen'r, partly to Abraham Blush, who afterwards sold to Crocker, and the eastern portion to Rev. John Smith, whose descendants still enjoy it.

His children born in Barnstable were :

I.  Nathaniel, baptized Aug. 9, 1640, buried at Barnstable Dec. 10, 1640.

II. Nathaniel, baptized May 15, 1642, married Nov. 1662, Mary, daughter of Joseph Holway, or Holloway, of Sandwich, and had 1, John, 1st Feb. 1662-3 ; and 2, Isaac, 7th Dec. 1664. No other children recorded. He probably removed with his father in 1669.

III. Mary, baptized Oct. 6, 1644, died young.

IV. Hannah, baptized April 23, 1648. The town record says, "born April 1949," an error. She married 6th Nov. 1668, Jasper Taylor.

V.  Mary, baptized June 2, 1650, (town record, "last of May

1651," an error,) married, 15th Jan. 1668-9, Samuel Hinckley.
VI.    John, Jan. 2, 1652.   (If not the same as the following he died young.)
VII.   John, born 7th Oct. 1653, (town records.)
VIII.  Joseph, born 1st March 1656, (town records.)
IX.    Thomas, born 16th Aug. 1654, (town records.)
X.     Hope, born 2d April, 1661, (town records.)

# FULLER.

Samuel Fuller, son of Edward and Ann Fuller, came over in the Mayflower, in 1620. His parents died soon after they came came on shore,* and he resided at Plymouth with his uncle Samuel, the first physician who came to settle in our country. He had three shares at the division of lands in 1624, Mr. Savage presumes out of respect to his father and mother. He was executor of his uncle's will in 1633, and was a freeman of the Colony in 1634. From Plymouth he removed to Scituate, where he married, April 8, 1635, Jane, daughter of Rev. John Lothrop. Nov. 7, 1636, he joined the church at Scituate, having a letter of dismission from the Plymouth church, of which he had been a member. He built, in 1636, the fifteenth house in Scituate, on Greenfield, the first lot abuting on Kent street. He had twenty acres of land on the east of Bellhouse Neck, in that town. Mr. Deane calls him "a man of Kent," from which country many of the first settlers in Barnstable came.

Samuel Fuller, as appears by the church records, was in Barnstable as early as 1641, but it does not appear that he was inhabitant of the town till after the 1st of January 1644. His brother, Capt. Matthew, the earliest regular physician in Barnstable, came a few years later. They bought of Secunke, Indian, Scorton or Sandy Neck, that is, so much of it as lies within the boundaries of the town of Barnstable. The arable land in the purchase was set off to the Fullers, the remainder, including the meadows, was reserved as town's commons and afterwards divided.

Samuel Fuller also bought meadow of his brother Matthew that was Major John Freeman's, and meadow of Samuel House, and owned land on Scorton Hill. He had a good estate for those

*This is the expression used by Gov. Bradford, who knew the parties. Mr. Z. Eddy says the Wid. Ann Fuller died in Barnstable in 1663, aged 79 years. I find no corroboration of the latter statement.

days.    His personal estate is apprized in his inventory at
£116,5,09.

He lived in the north-west angle of the town, in a secluded
spot, where travellers or others had seldom occasion to pass.    He
was very little engaged in public business.    He was constable at
Scituate in 1641, and his name occasionally appears as a juryman, and on committees to settle difficulties that arose with the
Indians, and was one of the 58 purchasers, as that company was
called.

Samuel and Matthew Fuller, though brothers, and living near
each other in a retired spot, and owning property together, were
as unlike as two men can well be.    Samuel was eminently pious,
and retired in his habits; Matthew, though nominally a Puritan,
was not a religious man; but was ambitious, and courted official
distinction.    In one instance he recanted an opinion deliberately
expressed, in order to secure the patronage of the majority.
Samuel committed no acts that he had to recant—he was an honest
man, a good neighbor, and a christian, and his posterity will ever
honor him.

He died in Barnstable Oct. 31, 1683.    He was the only one
of the passengers in the Mayflower who settled permanently in
Barnstable.    Of the 102 who arrived in that ship at Provincetown in 1620, 51 died, or just one half. in a few months.    Of the
remaining 51, or Old Stock, as Gov. Bradford calls the first company, 31 were living in 1650; 12 in 1679, of whom Samuel Fuller was one; three in 1690, namely, Resolved White, Mary Cushman, daughter of Mr. Allerton, and John Cook, son of Francis
Cook, and in 1698, seventy-eight years after the arrival of the
Mayflower, two passengers who came over in her were living,
namely, Mary Cushman and John Cook.†

1.    Samuel Fuller, son of Edward, married at Mr. Cudworth's, in Scituate, by Capt. Miles Standish, April 8, 1635,
Jane, daughter of Rev. John Lothrop.

*Children born in Scituate.*

2.    I.    Hannah, married Nicholas Bonham Jan. 1, 1658-9,
        (see Bonham.)
3.    II.    Samuel, baptized Feb. 11, 1637-8, married Anna,
        daughter of Capt. Matthew Fuller, (see account below.)
4.    III.    Elizabeth, married ——— Taylor.
5.    IV.    Sarah, baptized in Barnstable Aug. 1, 1641, died
        young.

*Children born in Barnstable.*

6.    V.    Mary, baptized June 16, 1644, married Nov. 18, 1674,

---

†Before writing the genealogies of the Fullers, I intended to have examined the Sandwich records and the Probate records with more care than I have.    I delayed writing till
the printer's boy was at my elbow, asking for copy, and the result is I have very little beside that which I furnished Mr. Savage for his Genealogical Dictionary.    Some facts that I
have, I omit, not knowing the right places in the series.

Joseph Williams, son of John of Haverhill.   He was born April 18, 1647, had Sarah 17th Nov. 1675 ; Mary, 29th Nov. 1677; John, 17th Feb. 1680 ; Hannah, 30th Sept. 1683.

7.    VI.   Thomas born, says the town record, May 18, 1650, probably on the day of his baptism, May 18, 1651.   He is not named in his father's will, and perhaps died young.

8.    VII.   Sarah, born Dec. 14, 1654, married —— Crow.

9.    VIII.   John, called Little John, or John, Jr., to distinguish him from John, son of Capt. Matthew.

10.    IX.   A child, Feb. 8, 1658, died 15 days after.

Gov. Bradford in his history states that in 1650 Samuel Fuller had four or more children.   He had Hannah, Samuel, Elizabeth, and Mary, four ; if Thomas was born in 1660, five.   In his will dated 29th Oct. 1683, he names oldest son Samuel, son John, daughters Elizabeth Taylor, Hannah Bonham, Mary Williams, and Sarah Crow, two sons and four daughters then living.   He died Oct. 31, 1683, and was one of the last survivors of those who came over in the Mayflower.   His wife not being named in his will had probably died previously.

3.    Samuel Fuller, son of Samuel, born Feb. 1637-8, married Anna, daughter of Capt. Matthew Fuller.   There is no record of his family on the Barnstable records.   An inventory of his estate was taken at his house in Barnstable Dec. 29, 1691.   It appears that he had then been dead some little time, and that his widow had then recently deceased, and her estate was settled by mutual agreement on the 30th of the same month.   All the heirs sign with their mark, showing that they had received no benefit from the schools established in the distant parts of the town.   It is presumed that they were then all of legal age.   The names occur in the following order on the agreement.

11.    I.    Matthew, married Patience Young 25th Feb. 1692-3.

12.    II.    Barnabas, married Elizabeth Young 25th Feb. 1680-1.

13.    III.    Joseph, married Thankful Blossom.

14.    IV.    Benjamin.

15.    V.    Desire.

16.    VI.    Sarah.

9.    John Fuller, born about the year 1655, was the youngest son of Samuel, Sen'r.   He resided on the paternal estate at Scorton till 1689, when he removed, with several other families from that vicinity, to East Haddam, Conn.   On the 30th of October, 1688, "Mehitabel, the wife of Little John Fuller," was admitted to the Barnstable Church, and her sons Samuel, Thomas and Shubael, were baptized, and on the 19th of May, 1689, her daughter Thankful was baptized.   Here occurs a gap in the fam-

ERRATA. In Ewer family. The late Isaac Ewer, of Osterville, was son of Seth. Richard Church at Charlestown 1653, died 1668.

ily register, for her next son John is recorded as born Nov. 10. 1697, at East Haddam. During the interval he probably had Deborah and others.

Children of Little John Fuller and his wife born in Barnstable :

17.    I.    Samuel, baptized Oct. 1688.
18.    II.    Thomas.
19.    III.    Shubael.
20.    IV.    Thankful, baptized May 19, 1689.

At East Hadam, Conn.

21.    V.    John, Nov. 10, 1697.
22.    VI.    Joseph, March 1, 1699-1700.
25.    VII.    Benjamin, Oct. 20, 1701.
26.    VIII.    Mehitabel, April 16, 1706.

Thomas Fuller of this family had by his wife Elizabeth, born at East Haddam. Ebenezer, 1715 ; Thomas, 1717 ; Nathan, 1719 ; Hannah, 1720 ; Jabez, 1722 ; Jonathan, 1725. John Fuller, Jr., married May 10, 1721, Mary Rowley alias Mary Cornwell, and had at East Haddam, Mary, 1722 ; Esther, 1724 ; John, 1727 ; William, 1730 ; Mehitabel, 1732 ; Andrew, 1734 ; Sarah, 1737. Shubael Fuller married 10th 7th mo. 1708, Hannah Crocker, of Barnstable, and had at East Haddam, Lydia, 1709 ; Ephraim, 1711 ; Thankful, 1713 ; Zerviah, 1716 ; Hannah, 1718 ; Shubael, 1721 ; Jonathan, 1724 ; and Rachell, 1727.

11.    Matthew Fuller, son of Samuel, and grandson of Samuel, Sen'r, married 25th Feb. 1692-3, Patience Young, probably daughter of George of Scituate, and had children born in Barnstable, namely :

23.    I.    Anna, Nov. 1693, married Reuben Blush, Oct. 1717.
24.    II.    Jonathan, Oct. 1696, married Rebecca Perry, of Sandwich, March 3, 1718.
25.    III.    Content, 19th Feb. 1698-9.
26.    IV.    Jean, 1704, died 1708.
27.    V.    David, Feb. 1706-7.
28.    VI.    Young, 1708.
29.    VII.    Cornelius, 1710.

This family probably removed soon after 1710.

12.    Barnabas Fuller, brother of the preceding, married 25th Feb. 1680-1, Elizabeth Young.

*Children born in Barnstable.*

30.    I.    Samuel, Nov. 1681, married twice.
31.    II.    Isaac, Aug. 1684, married Jerusha Lovell.
32.    III.    Hannah, Sept. 1688.
33.    IV.    Ebenezer, April 1699, married Martha Jones.
34.    V.    Josiah, Feb. 1709 married Ann Rowley, of Falmouth.

13.  Joseph Fuller, brother of the preceding, married Thankful Blossom, and had,

35.     I.    Remember, 26th May, 1701, married Jabez Crocker, May 27, 1755.

36.     II.   Seth, 5th Sept. 1705, died Jan. 7, 1732-3.

37.     III.  Thankful, 4th Aug. 1708, died July 3, 1728.

14.  Benjamin Fuller, brother of the preceding, married and had,

38.     I.    Temperance, 7th March, 1702.

39.     II.   Hannah, 20th May, 1704.  I think she married Rev. Joseph Bourne July 25, 1743.

40.     III.  John, 25th Dec. 1706, married Mariah Nye, March 7, 1728-9.

41.     IV.   James, 1st May, 1711, married Temperance Phinney.

30.  Samuel Fuller, son of Barnabas, married first Ruth Crocker, and Dec. 20th 1727, Lydia Lovell, probably widow of Andrew.

*Children born in Barnstable.*

42.     I.    Sarah, April 16, 1719.

43.     II.   Barnabas, April 1, 1721.

44.     III.  Eleazer, Feb. 9, 1722-3, married Elizabeth Hatch 1756.

*By his second wife.*

45.     IV.   Joshua, Oct. 3, 1727.

46.     V.    Elizabeth, Jan. 24, 1728-9, married Nathaniel Goodspeed and removed to Vasselboro', Maine.

47.     VI.   Rebekah, April 3, 1731.

48.     VII.  Lot, Sept. 18, 1733.

This family removed to Rochester.

31.  Isaac Fuller, brother of the preceding, married July 9, 1719, Jerusha Lovell.

*Children born in Barnstable.*

49.     I.    Eli, April 11, 1720, married 1746, Mercy Rogers, of Harwich, and had, 1, Martha, Nov. 17, 1747; 2, Jedediah, March 28, 1749; 3, David, June 21, 1751; 4, William, Sept. 28, 1753; and 5, Jerusha, May 2, 1756.

50.     II.   Mehitabel, March 10, 1722-3, married Thomas Ames Oct. 30, 1740.

51.     III.  Jerusha, Jan. 19, 1725-6, married John Green, of Falmouth.

52.     IV.   Zaccheus, Oct. 16, 1727, married Sarah Jones, Feb. 22, 1752.

53.     V.    Charity, Dec. 11, 1729, married Silas Lovell Aug. 7, 1760.

54.     VI.   Isaac, Sept. 9, 1731, married Susan Wardsworth, of Pembroke.

55.    VII.   Seth, May 29, 1734.
56.    VIII.  Hannah, April 9, 1736.

33. Ebenezer Fuller, brother of the preceding, married Martha Jones, and had,

57.    I.    David, born Feb. 6, 1725.
58.    II.   Jonathan, April 9, 1729.
59.    III.  Daniel, Sept. 16, 1731, married Martha Phinney Nov. 1, 1753.
60.    IV.   John, June 3, 1734.
61.    V.    William, Sept. 27, 1737.
62.    VI.   Jean, Jan. 12, 1739.

Matthew Fuller was one of the prominent men of the Old Colony—and his name is inseparably connected with her annals. I have neither the time nor the ability to write his biography—to recount in detail the various services which he rendered to the country. He was an able man; but he had his faults, which I shall not, in this sketch, attempt to palliate or conceal.

He was the son of Edward and Anne, and brother of Samuel, who came over in 1620, in the Mayflower. His parents died soon after their arrival at Plymouth. Samuel went to reside with his uncle, and Matthew remained with his friends in England till about the year 1640, when he came over. Though he was then nearly thirty years of age, probably a married man and a parent, yet he was accounted to be "one of the first born of the Colony," and had lands assigned in virtue of his right of primo-geniture. Edward and Anne Fuller had no child born in this country to claim the lands granted to "the first born;" and in all such cases the right was transferred to the eldest child of the same parents, though born in the mother country.

Little is known of his early history. This is to be regretted; because we delight to trace the successive steps by which an orphan boy became eminent. It is not known whether he studied medicine before or after he came over, or whether he was then a married man and a parent. The best authorities give the year 1640, as the date of his coming to Plymouth. The earliest date I find is April 5, 1642; but it is evident that he had been in the country some little time, probably two years. If he did not come before 1640, he was certainly a married man and a parent, because his daughter Mary was born as early as 1635.

In 1642 he had ten acres of land assigned to him near Thurston Clark's, in Plymouth, and as this is the first grant made to him the presumption is that he had not then been long in the country. The same year he was a juryman, and propounded to be a freeman of the Colony; but was not sworn and admitted till June 7, 1653.

In 1643 a "military discipline" was established by the Colony Court, embracing the towns of Plymouth, Duxbury and Marshfield.   Miles Standish was chosen Captain ;  Nathaniel Thomas, Lieutenant ;  Nathaniel Souther, Clerk ;  and Matthew  Fuller and Samuel Nash, Sergeants.

To be a sergeant in a militia was then an office of  honor, and conferred distinction on the holder.

When the company met, the exercises were always begun and ended with prayer, and  at the annual election of  officers, on the first of  September, an occasional sermon was preached.   None but freeman of  honest and good report, approved by the officers, and  by  a majority of  the company, were admitted.   Servants were not admitted, neither were freeman who were not of  honest and good report.   No conversation was allowed while the company was  on parade and the most exact discipline was exacted. For absence, without a sufficient excuse, a fine of  two shillings was imposed, and if  not paid in a month, the delinquent party was  summoned to appear before  the company, the fine  was exacted, and his name was stricken from the roll of  the company.

For  each defect in  arms or  equipments a fine of  six pence was imposed, and if  any one was defective for six consecutive months, his name was also stricken from the roll of  the company.

The arms and equipments required of  each was a  musket or piece approved ;  a sword ;  a rest ;  and a bandilier.   Only 16 pikes were required, namely, 8 for Plymouth, 6 for Duxbury, and 2 for Marshfield.

All the officers of  the company were forever after to  be known by their titles ;  each member paid six pence a quarter for the use of  the company ;  and at the decease of  a member, the company  assembled with  their arms,  and  he  was  buried as a soldier.

No person propounded for a member could be received on the day he was nominated ;  and before admission, he was required to take the oath of fidelity.   The fifteenth rule of  the company required "That all postures of  pike and muskett, motions, ranks, and  files, &c., messengers, skirmishes, seiges, batteries, watches, sentinels, &c., be always performed to true military discipline."

This company was established on the same principle as the ancient and honorable artillery company of  Boston, which has maintained its organization to the present time.

The freemen of  Sandwich, Barnstable, and Yarmouth, "provided they be men of  honest and good report," were granted by the Court liberty to  form a similar company ;  but I do not learn that they accepted the privilege.   In each town there was a military company, which included all between the ages of  16 and 60, "able to bear arms."   The "military  discipline" was not intended to supercede the ordinary trainings.   It was  intended as an honorable association of  the freemen, for instruction in the art of  war.

The date of his removal to Barnstable is uncertain. Sept. 3, 1652, the Court approved his election as Lieutenant of the militia company in Barnstable. In 1653 he was deputy from Barnstable to the Colony Court, and it is probable that he had been a resident for three or four years.

June 20, 1654, he was appointed Lieutenant under Capt. Miles Standish of the company of fifty men, the quota of the Plymouth Colony, in the proposed expedition against the Dutch Colony at Manhattoes, now New York. The men were ordered to rendezvous at Sandwich June 29, and to embark from Manomett in the bark Adventer, belonging to Capt. Samuel Mayo, of Barnstable, and join the force of the other colonies at the place appointed. On the 23d of June, the news of the conclusion of peace between England and Holland was received, and the preparations for the expedition ceased. Peace had long been desired by the colonies; they were opposed to the war, but were most loyal subjects. The order to raise the men, furnish ammunition, stores and transportation was received June 6, and all the preparations had to be made before the 30th. When the news of peace was received, all the preparations had been made, and if the war had continued, the Plymouth Colony troops would have embarked from Manomett on the day appointed.

Oct. 2, 1658, he was elected one of the council of war, and in 1671 its chairman, and one of the magistrates of the Colony, and the same year, Lieutenant of the forces to be sent against the Saconet Indians. Dec. 17, 1673, he was appointed Surgeon General of the colony troops, and also of the Massachusetts, if that Colony approved. In 1675, he was allowed 4 shillings a day for his services as Surgeon General, and for "other good services performed in behalf of the country." In addition to his duties as Surgeon General, he served as a captain of the Plymouth forces during King Phillip's war. To trace his history during this interesting period belongs to the writers of general history.

In the Quaker controversy, Capt. Fuller took a noble stand in favor of religious toleration; but he was independent, and said many things that he had better have left unsaid. Acting under strong feelings of excitement, and indignant at the course pursued by a majority of the Court, he made statements that a discreet man would not have made, thus doing injury to the cause he would aid.

At the October Court, in 1658, he was presented by the grand inquest of the Colony for saying, "The law enacted about minister's maintenance, was a wicked and devilish law, and that the devil sat at the stone when it was enacted." That he had uttered these words he admitted, and he submitted himself, without trial, to the judgment of the magistrates, who fined him 50 shillings. He charged Gov. Hinckley with having officially certified that a matter was true which he knew to be false.  Gov. Hinckley commenced an action against him for defamation.  Capt. Fuller made a public acknowledgment of  his fault and Gov. Hinckley discontinued the action.

Though Capt. Fuller was undoubtedly right, in regard to the abstract questions, underlying  the  Quaker controversy, yet the bitter language in which he expressed his opinions was wholly unjustifiable, more especially when the circumstances under which they were uttered are taken into consideration.  Capt. Fuller held a high social position in the Colony.  So did the members of the Court, whose motives he so bitterly impugned.  To the honor of the latter, it will ever be remembered, that at the same term where the grand jury indicted Capt. Fuller for speaking reproachfully of the members of the Court, those slandered members, disregarding their private grievances, and looking only to the interests of  the country, did, at the very same term of  the Court, elect Capt. Fuller one of the Council of  War ;  and, notwithstanding he continued to utter vituperative language against individual members of  the government, the Court continued to confer on him offices of honor and trust—returning good for evil.  Men do not always thus heap coals of  fire on their enemy's heads.  The members of the Court knew Capt. Fuller to be a honorable man, and that however indiscreet he might be in words, he would perform his whole duty to his country.

In private life, and in his business relations, he exhibited a litigious spirit which is not commendable.  He was often involved in law-suits with his neighbors which a more discreet man would have settled without an appeal to the courts.

These details, however, enable us to form a just estimate of his character.  That he was a man of  sound judgement, of good understanding, and faithful in the performance of all his duties, there is no reason to doubt.  In politics he was liberal, and in his religious opinions tolerant ;  but unfortunately for his reputation, he was very indiscreet.  This weakness in his character seems to have been so manifest, so well known to all, that his injudicious speeches were disregarded, and he was duly honored for the many good services which he rendered to his country.

Capt. Fuller was the first regular physician who settled in Barnstable.*  That he was a man of  some skill and ability in his profession is evident from the fact that he was appointed Surgeon General of the forces of Plymouth and of Massachusetts in 1673.  His official duties required that he should be often absent from home, therefore his practice in Barnstable and Sandwich was necessarily interrupted, and not of  that  continuous character

---

*The early ministers were usually practicing physicians, and Rev. Mr. Lothrop, Mr. John Smith, and Mr. William Scargant, of Barnstable, were not, I presume, exceptions to the general rule.

necessary for the success of a local physician. His son John and one or more of his grand-sons were physicians.

The farms of Capt. Fuller and his brother Samuel were on Scorton Neck, at the north-west angle of the town. Soon after the settlement, the town bought of Secunke Indian, Scorton Neck. The arable land at the west end thereof was assigned to the Fullers. The town of Sandwich bought the west end of the neck, so that the western boundary of the Fullers' land was the line between the two towns. Some difficulty arose respecting this boundary which was not finally settled till 1680, after the death of Capt. Fuller. The difficulty originated in an order of the Colony Court, dated Oct. 30, 1672, fixing the boundary line farther west than the Committee of Sandwich was willing to concede, thus giving a considerable tract of good land to the Fullers. Suits were brought by each party, which were finally withdrawn, and on the 30th of June, 1680, the matter was settled by agreement, the Fullers relinquished the lands they had obtained by authority of the Court Order of Oct. 30, 1672, and the town of Sandwich conceeded to the Fullers certain rights of way and the privilege of cutting fencing stuff within the bounds of Sandwich.

Capt. Fuller, by virtue of his right as one "of the first born of the Colony," and for the eminent services which he had rendered the country, had lands granted him at Suckinesset, now Falmouth, and in "the Major's purchase" at Middleboro.

Capt. Fuller died in Barnstable in 1678. His will is dated July 20, 1678, and was proved Oct. 30th following. He names his wife Frances; his grand-son Shubael, son of Ralph Jones; his son John, to whom he bequeathed one-half of his real estate; his grand-children Thomas, Jabez, Timothy, Matthias and Samuel, children of his eldest son Samuel Fuller, deceased, to whom he bequeathed the other half of his estate; and Bethia wife of John Fuller. To daughter Mary, wife of Ralph Jones, he gave £10; to daughter Anne Fuller, "now wife of Samuel Fuller," £10; to daughter Elizabeth, wife of Moses Rowley, £10; he also names Sarah Rowley, daughter of Elizabeth Rowley; Jedediah Jones, son of Ralph; Mary Fuller, late wife of his son Samuel; also Robert Marshall, the Scotchman; and Jasper Taylor. He appointed his wife Francis executrix. Witnesses of his will: Lieut. Joseph Lothrop and John Hawes. His estate was apprised at £667,04,06, a very large estate in those times. Among the items in the inventory is the following: "Pearls, precious stones, and Diamonds, at a guess, £200." †

---

†In connection with this box of jewels a marvellous story is told. Soon after Capt. Fuller's death it was missing. Robert, the Scotch servant, was charged with having stolen it. There was no proof against him—he was simply suspected. This charge so affected him, that he took no food, and finally died of grief and starvation. He was buried in a grove of wood, on the north-eastern declivity of Scorton Hill. He died in the winter when a deep snow laid on the ground. The neighbors carried his body to this place—the deep

All that is known respecting the relationship of the two Fuller families is this : in the settlement of the disputed boundary line, with the town of Sandwich, Dr. John Fuller, son of Matthew, calls Samuel Fuller, Sen'r, his uncle, consequently Matthew and Samuel, Sen'r, were brothers, and sons of Edward, and nephews of Dr. Samuel, of Plymouth. Matthew must have been born in England as early as 1610, and his older children were probably born there. No record exists of their births or baptisms in this country. This fact, though not conclusive, indicates that they were born in England. All that is known of his family is obtained from his will, of which an abstract has been given. His wife, at the time of his death, was Frances, whether first or second is not known, and whether he had other children than those named in his will is also not known. He calls Samuel his eldest son, and the order of the births of his children evidently is not that given in his will.

#### Children of Capt. Matthew Fuller.

2.   I.   Mary, married Ralph Jones April 17, 1655, and has many descendants.
3.   II.   Elizabeth, married Moses Rowley, April 22, 1652, and has many descendants.
4.   III.   Samuel, (see account of his family below.)
5.   IV.   John, (see account of his family below.)
6.   V.   Anne, married Samuel, son of Samuel Fuller, Sen'r.

    4. Samuel Fuller, son of Capt. Matthew, was a lieutenant in the Plymouth Colony forces in King Phillip's war, and was killed at Rehobeth, March 25, 1676. In 1670 he was a member of the Colony Committee appointed to view the injury done to the Indians, by the cattle of the English, and assess damages. His name also occurs as a town officer. His wife was Mary. I find no record of the births or baptisms of his children. In his will he names all his children excepting Samuel, who was born after the death of the father.

#### Children of Samuel Fuller, son of Matthew.

7.   I.   Thomas, (see account below.)
8.   II.   Jabez, (see account below.)
9.   III.   Timothy. Removed to East Haddam.
10.   IV.   Matthew, died unmarried 1697. In his will dated Boston, Aug. 7, 1696, proved May 22, 1697, he gives to his brother Timothy, of Haddam, his half of the land and

---

snow preventing them from proceeding farther, and there he was buried. Capt. Oliver Chase has recently placed two stones, one at the head and the other at the foot of poor Richard's grave. For nearly two centuries the plow has not desecrated his grave, and we hope no sacreligious hands will hereafter remove the simple monuments now erected to his memory. To this day his grave is pointed out, and some timourous people dare not pass it after nightfall. Many fearful stories are told of the appearance of the Scotchman's ghost; and for years many a wayward child was frightened into obedience by threatening to call the Scotchman's ghost, to aid the authority of the weak mother.

meadow in Middleborough, given him by his grandfather Matthew Fuller. All the rest of his estate, both real and personal, he bequeathed to his honored mother, to be disposed of for her comfortable subsistence during her natural life, and whatsoever she shall die possessed of, without any alienation shall be disposed equally amongst the rest of my brothers and sisters.

11.   V.   Anne, born 1679, married Joseph Smith 29th April, 1689.
12.   VI.   Abigail.
13.   VII.   Samuel, born 1676 (post humeus.)

5.   Dr. John Fuller, son of Matthew, resided on the paternal estate at Scorton Neck. He was a physician of some note in his day. He died in 1691. He married two wives: 1st, Bethia ———, and second, Hannah ———, of Boston, who survived him and married, Dec. 9, 1695, Capt. John Lothrop, of Barnstable.

*Children born in Barnstable.*

14.   I.   Lydia, born 1675, married 12th May 1699, Joseph Dimmock. She died in Connecticut Nov. 6, 1755, aged 80.
15.   II.   Bethia, Dec. 1687, married Feb. 20, 1706, Barnabas Lothrop.
16.   III.   John, Oct. 1689, (see account below.)
17.   IV.   Reliance, 8th Sept. 1691, married John Prince ( ?).

7.   Capt. Thomas Fuller, son of Samuel, married 29th Dec. 1680, Elizabeth, daughter of Capt. Joseph Lothrop.

*Children born in Barnstable.*

18.   I.   Hannah, 17th Nov. 1681.
19.   II.   Joseph, 12th July 1683, married Feb. 9, 1708-9, Joanna Crocker, (see account below.)
20.   III.   Mary, born Aug. 1685, married Wm. Green Sept. 1, 1731.
21.   IV.   Benjamin, born Aug. 1690. He was Lieutenant, and called junior. He married 25th March 1714, Rebecca Bodfish. She died 10th March 1727-8, and he married Feb. 20, 1729-30, Mary Fuller. His children born in Barnstable were: 1, Mary, July 15, 1714; 2, Lydia, March 23, 1716, married Dec. 2, 1742, John Percival; 3, Thomas, June 18, 1718, (see account below) ; 4, Elizabeth, Sept. 30, 1720; 5, Benjamin, Oct. 28, 1723; 6, Abigail, Nov. 29, 1725, died 1726; 7, Joseph, Oct. 18, 1730, died 1732; 8, Thankful, April 26, 1733, married April 23, 1757, Samuel Gilbert, of Conn.; 9, Rebecca, June 1, 1735, Timothy Jones paid attention to her twenty years, but did not marry. She removed with her brother Seth to Kennebec; 10, Seth,

March 14, 1736-7, married Deliverance Jones Oct. 15, 1757.
22.   V.   Elizabeth, 3d Sept. 1692, married Oct. 31, 1726, Isaac
Crocker, of East Haddam.
23.   VI.   Samuel, 12th April 1694, married Malatiah Bodfish
June 20, 1725-6, and had : 1, Abijah, Dec. 29, 1726, married Hester Anold Aug. 7, 1746, and had a family ; 2, still
born child Dec. 7, 1728 ; 3 and 4, a son who died aged 4
weeks, and Abigail June 26, 1730.
24.   VII.   Abigail, 9th Jan. 1695-6, married Oct. 25, 1721,
Jacob Chipman.
25.   VIII.   John, baptized April 19, 1696.
      8.   Jabez Fuller, son of Samuel, and grandson of Matthew,
resided in Barnstable.   Children :
26.   I.   Samuel, 23d Feb. 1687.
27.   II.   Jonathan, 10th March 1692.
28.   III.   Mercy, 1st April, 1696, married March 17, 1719-20,
James Bearse ( ?).
29.   IV.   Lois, 23d Sept. 1704, married Thomas Foster Nov.
25, 1725.
30.   V.   Ebenezer, 20 Feb. 1708.
31.   VI.   Mary.
      9.   Timothy Fuller, son of Samuel, removed to East Haddam
and by wife Sarah had :
32.   I.   Timothy, Aug. 29, 1695.
33.   II.   Mary, Dec. 19, 1697.
34.   III.   Matthias, March 24, 1700.
35.   IV.   Sarah, Aug. 7, 1702.
36.   V.   Abigail, July 5, 1704.
      16.   Lieut. John Fuller married 16th June 1710, Thankful
Gorham.   He died July 20, 1732, aged 42.   He is buried at West
Barnstable, and on his grave-stone it is recorded, "He was son of
Doct. John Fuller."

*Children born in Barnstable.*

37.   I.   Hannah, 1st April 1711, married Mr. Matthias Smith
Sept. 3, 1730.
38.   II.   John, 3d Aug. 1714, married Temperance Gorham
Oct. 29, 1741, and had : 1, Desire, Aug. 1, 1742 ; 2, John,
June 23, 1744 ; 3, Edward, Dec. 28, 1746 ; 4, Francis,
March 10, 1749 ; 5, Job, Nov. 25, 1751.
39.   III.   Mary, 1st Sept. 1715, married Seth Lothrop Aug. 11,
1733.
40.   IV.   Bethia, 1st Sept. 1715, married Joseph Bursley Dec.
20, 1739.
41.   V.   Nathaniel, 10th Dec. 1716, married Abigail Hinckley
Feb. 22, 1739.   Capt. Nathaniel Fuller, first of Sandwich,
afterwards of Barnstable, was in the French war.   He

brought home the Small Pox, and his wife and daughters
Thankful and Abigail died of that disease, and are buried
on Scorton Neck. He had a daughter Hannah who recovered, and afterwards married Matthias Smith; and
Lydia, who married Lazarus Ewer. He also had a son
Lieut. Joseph, born 1758, died Aug. 16, 1805, who married
Tabitha, daughter of Josiah Jones; he was an officer in the
Revolutionary war; and Nathaniel, who married Ruhama,
daughter of Samuel Jones. Capt. Nathaniel married a
second wife. I find no record of his family. Capt.
Nathaniel Fuller owned the west part of the farm now
owned by Mr. B. Blossom on Scorton Neck, containing
about 35 acres. His house stood on the south side of the
old way leading to Sandy Neck, and nearly opposite Ben
Blossom's house. In 1783 he sold his farm on Scorton
Neck to Edward Wing, and removed to a house just within
the boundaries of Barnstable, on the east of the causeway
leading to the Neck. It was taken down about 53 years
ago. The new road passes over the spot on which it stood.
After the death of his second wife he resided with his
daughter Hannah Smith, and died at her house. "Capt.
Nat," as he was familiarly called, was stern in his manner,
and very decided in the expression of his opinions. He was
not an industrious man, and therefore not prosperous in
business.

42.    VI.   Thankful, 19 Sept. 1718, called junior, married
Oct. 25, 1739, Nathan Russel, Jr., of Middleboro'.

19.   Joseph Fuller, Jr., son of Thomas, married 9th Feb.
1708-9, Joanna Crocker.  She died April 13, 1766, aged 76.

*Children born in Barnstable.*

42.    I.   Rebekah, 29th Dec. 1709, died July 30 1732.
43.    II.   Bethia, 2d March 1712, died July 1, 1737.
44.    III.   Temperance, 24th April 1717, married Joseph Blossom, Jr. March 30, 1737.
45.    IV.   Timothy, 3d April 1719.
46.    V.   Matthias, 6th Sept. 1723.  He married in 1755 Lydia
Blossom, and resided in a very ancient house situated on the
east side of Scorton Hill.
47.    VI.   Batheheba, 10th Aug. 1726.
48.    VII.   Lemuel, 10th Feb. 1732, married Abigail Jones, and
resided at Marston's Mills, and had, 1, Joseph, Jan. 30,
1761; 2, Benjamin, Sept. 18, 1763; 3, Samuel, Nov. 27,
1765, also Timothy and Hannah.

Thomas Fuller, son of Benjamin, Jr., and grandson of Capt.
Thomas, married Elizabeth ———.  Children: 1, Elizabeth, Jan,
21, 1743; 2, Thomas, Aug. 14, 1745; 3, Jacob, March 6, 1746;
and 4, Hannah, April 2, 1749.

# FREEMAN.

---

This is not a Barnstable name.  It is a common name in the County, and several families of the name were early of Barnstable.  Two of the name came to this County.  Edmund of Lynn, who was one of the first settlers in Sandwich, and Samuel of Watertown, who settled in Eastham.

Edmund was a prominent man of good business habits, liberal in politics, and tolerant in his religious opinions.  He was a member of the Sandwich church—the most bigoted and intolerant in the Colony—yet he did not imbibe the persecuting spirit which has condemned to everlasting infamy many of his brethen.

In his intercourse with his neighbors and associates, he was affable and obliging, and to his kindred and intimate friends, he was ever kind and affectionate.  He rested from his labors at Sandwich in 1682, at the ripe old age of 92 years.  His wife died Feb. 14, 1676, aged 76.  She was buried on a rising ground on his own farm.  He was then 86, and had lived 59 years in the married state.  Some little time after her decease he summoned together his sons and his grandsons, they placed a large flat rock resembling a pillion, over the grave of the wife.  He then placed another, resembling in shape a saddle, beside it ; and addressing his sons, he said : "when I die, place my body under that stone, your mother and I have travelled many long years together in this world, and I desire that our bodies rest here till the resurrection, and I charge you to keep this spot sacred, and that you enjoin it upon your children and your children's children, that they never desecrate this spot."

A substantial wall was built around these simple but suggestive monuments, and his descendants to this day with pious hands protect them from desecration.  Many of them regard this spot as their Mecca, which it is their duty to visit at least once in their lives.

*Children of Edmund and Elizabeth Freeman.*

For the reason stated in a note, I have not carefully examined

the records of this family.   The entries at the London Custom
are not entirely reliable.   In one place it is stated that he was
34 in 1635, and in another 45 years of age.   I have assumed the
latter to be accurate, because it is not probable that he married at
16.   His son John was born in 1622.   The Custom House records
say in 1626, also in 1627.   The family came over in 1635 in the
ship Abigail, Capt. Hackwell.

*Born in England.*

I.      Alice, 1618, married 24th Nov. 1639, Dea. Wm. Paddy.
II.     Edmund, 1620, married and had a family.
III.    John, 1622.
IV.     Elizabeth, 1623, married John Ellis.
V.      Cycellia, 1631, probably his daughter, died young.
VI.     Mary, probably born in this County, married Edward Perry.

Major John Freeman, a son of Edmund, born in England in
1622, was a more distinguished man than his father.   He removed
to Eastham, and married 13th Feb. 1650, Mercy, daughter of
Gov. Thomas Prence.   He lived to a venerable old age, and in
the ancient graveyard in that town are monuments wrought in the
mother country to his, and his wife's memory.   His wife died first,
and on her curiously wrought gravestone a heart is depicted within
which her epitaph is engraved in small capital letters.

HERE LYES
BURIED YE BODY
OF MARCY FREEMAN
WIFE TO MAJOR
FREEMAN AGED
80 YEARS DEC'D
SEPT. 28TH
1711.

HERE   LYES   THE
BODY   OF   MAJOR
JOHN   FREEMAN
DEC'D OCTOBER YE
28TH   1719
IN YE 98TH YEAR
OF HIS AGE

Samuel Freeman, of Watertown, settled in Eastham, and has
many descendants.   His mother married Gov. Prence, and there
is no known connection between the families of Edmund and
Samuel.

The earliest family in Barnstable was that of Nathaniel, who
married Oct. 1723, Mercy, daughter of Mr. James Paine, and a
grand-daughter of Col. John Thacher, of Yarmouth.   He died
Dec. 2, 1727.   His children born in Barnstable were: 1, Bethia,
July 4, 1725; 2, James, Oct. 11, 1726; and 3, Nathaniel, March

30th, 1728, died 17th April, 1728.

Stephen Freeman married, Oct. 22, 1736, Hannah Jenkins, and had a daughter Zerviah born Sept. 24, 1737.

David Freeman, from Connecticut, married in 1756, Abigail Davis, and had a son Thomas Davis born March 25, 1757. He died soon after his marriage, and his wife was the Widow Freeman who figured so conspicuously in the "Crocker Quarrels." *

Dr. Nathaniel Freeman, better known as Col. Freeman, was some time a resident in Barnstable. During the Revolutionary period, he was one of the most active among the patriots of his time. In character he was the counterpart of his ancestor, a man of talent, very decided in his opinions, and impetuous in action. Like all men of such a temperament, he made many enemies. The tories denounced him, in the bitterest of bitter terms. These denunciations never affected his reputation as a man or a patriot, but other causes did. He was not a meek man—he would not tolerate the least opposition, consequently made many personal enemies—and among the aged who knew him, few speak in his praise.

He held many offices—he was a busy man—some of his duties he had not time to perform † well—this his personal enemies noted ; but with all his faults, he was a useful man and the services he did his country are appreciated.

---

*As a full genealogy of the family is in print, it will be unnecessary for me to repeat it.

---

†See Probate Records. The poorest writing and worse spelling therein, occurs during the time he was Register.

# FOSTER.

For many of the facts contained in this article, I am indebted to Lucius R. Paige, Esq., of Cambridge. Foster is not a Barnstable name, though there were a few here early.

1. Thomas Foster, of Weymouth, had three sons:
1. Thomas, born 18th Aug. 1640, whom I suppose to have been the Dr. Thomas Foster who died in Cambridge 28th Oct. 1679, aged 39 years.
2. John, born 7th Oct. 1642, whom I suppose to have been the Dea. John Foster named below; but of this I have no absolute proof.
3. Increase.

2. Dea. John Foster settled early in Marshfield, and married Mary, daughter of Thomas and Joanna Chillingsworth, by whom he had ten children. His wife Mary died 25th Sept. 1702. He then married Sarah Thomas, who died 26th May, 1731, aged 85. Dea. Foster died 13th June 1732, aged 90, according to the record make by his son Thomas, (who was Town Clerk,) or 91, according to the inscription on his head stone, standing in the Winslow burying-ground. But if he was son of Thomas of Weymouth, he lacked a few months of 90 years.

The children of Dea. John and Mary Foster were:
1. Elizabeth, born 24th Sept. 1664, married William Carver (the centenarian) 18th Jan. 1682-3, and died in June 1715.
2. John, born 12th Oct. 1666, married Hannah Stetson of Scituate, resided in Plymouth, was deacon, and died 24th Dec. 1741.
3. Josiah, born 7th June 1669, resided in Pembroke.
4. Mary, born 13th Sept. 1671, married John Hatch, died in Marshfield 3d April 1750.
5. Joseph, born about 1674, resided in Barnstable and Sandwich, (see below.)
6. Sarah, born about 1677, died unmarried 7th April 1702.

7. Chillingsworth, born 11th June 1680, resided in Harwich, (see below.)
8. James, born 22d May, 1683, died 21st July, 1683.
9. Thomas, born 1686, resided in Marshfield, Deacon, Town Clerk, &c., died 6th Feb. 1758, aged 72, married Lois Fuller Nov. 25, 1725, had Gersham at B. Sept. 23, 1733.
10. Deborah, born 1691, died unmarried 4th Nov. 1732, aged 41.

Chillingsworth Foster, son of Dea. John and Mary, resided in Harwich, of which town he was many years Representative in the General Court. His first wife was Mercy, (I have not been able to ascertain her family name) by whom he had seven children. She died 7th July 1720, and he married 2d, Widow Susanna Sears Aug. 10, 1721, who died Dec. 7, 1730, by whom he had four children. He died about 1764, but the precise date I have not learned.

The children of Chillingsworth Foster were:
1. James, born Monday, Jan. 21, 1704-5, resided in Rochester, married Lydia, daughter of Edward Winslow, Esq., 10th July 1729. He was deacon &c. In very advanced age (over 70) he went to reside with a son at Athol, where he died.
2. Chillingsworth, born Thursday, 25th Dec. 1707, resided at Harwich, many years Representative. He married Mercy, daughter of Edward Winslow, Esq., of Rochester, 10th Oct. 1730. She died, and he married 2d Ruth Sears of Harwich, 7th Dec. 1731. His children were 1, Thankful, born in Harwich June 14, 1733; 2, Mercy, born in Barnstable May 2, 1735; 3, Chillingsworth, born in Barnstable July 17, 1737; 4, Mehitabel, born in Harwich April 18, 1746; 5, Sarah, born in H. Nov. 25, 1747.
3. Mary, born Thursday, 5th Jan. 1709-10, married David Paddock of Yarmouth, 12th Oct. 1727.
4. Thomas, born Saturday, 15th March, 1711-12, married Mary Hopkins, of Harwich, 11th July 1734, and had 1, Joseph, March 27, 1735; 2, Thomas, June 22, 1736; 3, James, Feb. 18, 1737-8; 4, Mary, July 18, 1740.
5. Nathan, born Friday, 10th June, 1715, married Sarah Lincoln, of Harwich, 14th June 1739.
6. Isaac, born Tuesday, 17th June, 1718, married Hannah Sears, of Harwich, 2d Nov. 1738, and had, 1, Isaac, May 29, 1739; 2, Samuel, May, 31, 1741; 3, David, March 24, 1742-3; 4, Lemuel, Feb. 24, 1724; 5, Seth, March 1747; 6, Hannah, March 4, 1749; 7, Nathaniel, April 8, 1751.
7. Mercy, born Wednesday, 30th March 1720, and died 28th Aug. 1720.
8. Mercy, born Sunday, 29th July 1722.

9.  Nathaniel, born Saturday, 17th April 1725.
10. Jerusha, born Saturday, 9th Dec. 1727.
11. A son, still born, March 1729-30.

Joseph Foster, son of John, married Rachell Bassett, of Sandwich.  Children born in Barnstable and Sandwich.

1.  Mary, 1st Sept. 1697, at S., married Moses Swift, of S., Dec. 24, 1719.
2.  Joseph, 19th Sept. 1698, at B.
3.  Benjamin, 16th Nov. 1699, at B., married Dec. 31, 1724, Maria Tobey, at Sandwich.
4.  William, 31st March 1702.
5.  Thankful, 3d Nov. 1703, married Sept. 25, 1725, Nathan Tobey.
6.  John, 12th April 1705.
7.  Nathan, 3d Jan. 1707-8.
8.  Abigail, 27th Feb. 1708-9, married May 15, 1735, Zaccheus Swift.
9.  Deborah, 18th Jan. 1710-11, married May 10, 1733, Isaac Freeman.
10. Ebenezer, 10th May, 1713.
11. Solomon, 4th Sept. 1714.
12. Rachell, 30th Oct. 1716, married Dec. 10, 1743, Jonathan Churchill.
13. Sarah, 23d Sept. 1721, married Nov. 11, 1742, Nathan Nye.
14. Solomon.

Nathan Foster resided in the Timothy Crocker house at West Barnstable.  He was a hair dresser and wig maker by trade, and died aged.  He married, 1st, Mary Lothrop May 21, 1753 ; 2d, Mercy Smith 1766.  Children born in Barnstable :

1.  Abigail, Sept. 24, 1756.
2.  John Bursley, June 11, 1758.
3.  Mary, Oct. 4, 1765. ( ?)
4.  James, Feb. 8, 1767.
5.  Mary, March 7, 1768.
6.  Thomas, March 4, 1771.
7.  Nathan, March 19, 1773.
8.  Abigail, Jan. 4, 1775.
9.  Joseph, July 16, 1776.
10. John, July 15, 1778.
11. Abigail, May 6, 1780.
12. Elizabeth, Feb. 16, 1783.

# GOODSPEED.

Roger Goodspeed, the ancestor of all of the name in this County, came to Barnstable in the spring of 1639. His houselot has been a fruitful theme for controversy, from the first settlement to the present day, and I shall, therefore, state with some particularity, the facts that I have collected in regard to it.

Mr. Collicut's records, as stated in a previous article, were accidentally lost at a fire in Plymouth. All that is known respecting the lands laid out under his authority, is obtained from a few ancient deeds, and the boundaries of a portion of the original lots, placed on record by the owners thereof in 1654. Goodspeed, at that date, had sold and relinquished his title, it therefore does not appear on the town records. From the boundaries of the adjoining lots, it appears that it was bounded north by Elder Henry Cobb's lot, east partly by Nathaniel Bacon's lot, and partly by John Scudder's, south by the land of John Davis', originally Samuel Lothrop's lot; west by the lot of Edward Fitzrandolphe, from which it was separated by the Hyannis road, and a line nearly corresponding with the new Mill Way laid out in 1665, and contained about eight acres, not including the swamp. It was divided into nearly two equal portions by a deep gully, through which the County road now passes. At that time this gully was narrow, with steep, precipitous banks, and impassible for teams. Within the memory of persons now living it was so narrow in some places that two teams could not pass.*

On the north of this gully, the land was rocky and uneven, and of little value for cultivation, and in 1653, had been surrendered to the town as common lands. On the south of the gully the land was better. On the south and west, that is, on that portion now inclosed by the Hyannis road and Bow Lane, there

---

*Mrs. Susannah Cobb, who, when young, lived in the neighborhood, stated that on a Sabbath, during the services, she saw a deer leap across this gully, at a point a little west of where the Custom House now stands.

was a dense swamp, (called Lewis' Swamp) † which remained more than a century in its natural state. This swamp, in 1653, had been surrendered as town's commons. On the east, including a strip on the north, by the edge of the gully, there were about two acres of good land, which was the only part cultivated by Goodspeed. On the south of Lewis' swamp there was a strip of land laid out corresponding in location with the southern part of Bow lane, called in the records "Goodspeed's Out-Let," and subsequently "the Widow Hallett's Set-Off." This name seems to indicate that at the time Goodspeed resided on this lot, he had no "Out-Let" on the north. "Goodspeed's Out-Let" extended further east than at the present time, certainly to Josiah Hallett's house, and probably to Taylor's Lane.

Meeting House Hill was called by the first settlers Goodspeed's Hill; from 1660 to 1725 Cobb's Hill, and since by its present name. A stream of water from Lewis' swamp ran across the County or King's road, and down the "New Mill Way" between the hill, and the lot now owned by Ebenezer Bacon, Esq., and emptied into a swamp in front of the dwelling-house of David Bursley, Esq., and which was in 1683, purchased by the town for a common watering place. At the foot of the hill, in front of Odd Fellows' Hall, there was a foot bridge across the stream, constructed of a single log 20 feet long, and two feet in diameter, hewn flat on the upper side.

In 1650, the traveller with a team coming from the west could not turn down either of the roads now leading to the dwelling-house of David Bursley, Esq., because there was a pond and a swamp that extended across both ways to the margin of the hill. He could not drive up the precipitous sides of Goodspeed's Hill, nor through the jagged gully where the road now passes, nor through the north end of Bow Lane, because there was no roadway there. He had to pass up the Hyannis road to the present residence of Mr. James S. Lothrop, thence through Goodspeed's Out-Let to the lot of John Scudder, and up the hill to the spot where the Patriot Office now stands, thence continue easterly across Scudder's and Lewis' lots to Taylor's Lane. *

The inhabitants residing west of the Hill were subject to the

---

† At a Town meeting held in Barnstable Oct. 26, 1769,
"Voted, That Messrs. John Lewis and Geo. Lewis (sons of Lieut. James) be allowed to fence a piece of swamp that belonged to the town, said swamp being adjoined to their swamp by their malt house, and they and their assigns to improve it forever, provided that they do not encroach upon the King's road, nor the lane leading into the woods, and make a sufficient drain to carry off the water."—[Town Records Book 3, page 34.

The bushes in this swamp were very thick. Mr. George Lewis lost a fat hog therein, which he had stuck and left for dead. It ran into the swamp and there died, and though careful search was made, it could not be found. When first ploughed, a large deposit of arrow heads were turned up. They were all made of white quartz, and were afterwards sent by Mr. Mullen as a present to some of his friends, connected with Cambridge College.

---

*This paper, it will be recollected, was written in 1862, and applied to the localities as then occupied.

same inconvenience.  In going to the mill or to their planting grounds in the Common Field, they went by the circuitous route I have described.  Lieut. James Lewis' house, which is now standing, was built about two centuries ago.  About the time that that house was built, the road on the north of Lewis' Swamp was cleared, and thus the distance was shortened.

I have heretofore supposed that there were three original allotments between Goodspeed's lot and Taylor's Lane, though I was unable to give the names of the owners of only two.  On a more careful examination of deeds and the records, I think it is evident there were only two original allotments, yet three house lots, John Scudder's being divided into two by the road called Goodspeed's Out-Let.

The following diagram exhibits the relative position of the lots.  The situations of buildings to which reference is made, are indicated by figures :

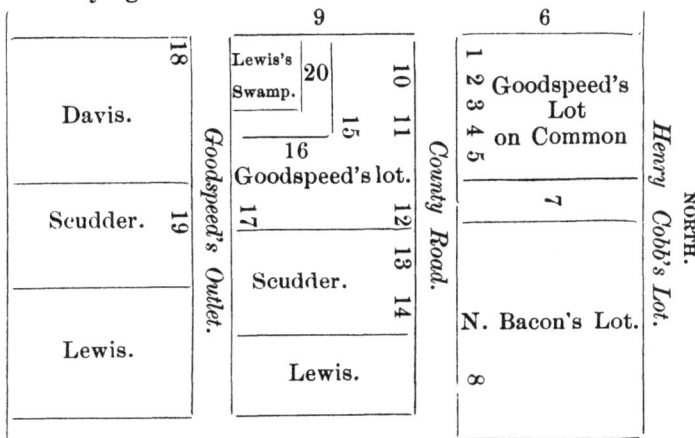

1.  Odd Fellows' Hall.
2.  School House.
3.  Meeting House.
4.  Pound.
5.  Old Parsonage.
6.  New Mill Way.
7.  Old Mill Way.
8.  Bacon House.
9.  Hyannis Road.
10.  Old Malt House.
11.  Custom House.
12.  Patriot Office.
13.  Major Phinney's house.

14.  Timothy Reed, deceased, house.
15.  Ancient Lewis house.
16.  Eben Bacon's house.
17.  Goodspeed House Lot.
18.  James S. Lothrop's house.
19.  Hallett House.
20.  Bow Lane.

In 1654 the Widow Mary Hallett owned the Scudder and Goodspeed lots.  March 31, 1659, she conveyed by a deed of gift to her son-in-law, John Haddeway, her dwelling house and the north part of the Scudder lot, and that part of the Goodspeed lot on the north of Goodspeed's Out-Let.  Dec. 14, 1661, Josiah Hallett, a son of the Widow Mary, sold to John Haddeway for £10 sterling the southerly part of the Scudder lot containing eight acres, bounded westerly by the lands of John Davis, south by John Haddeway, east by James Lewis, and south by the wood lots, with his dwelling-house standing thereon.

These boundaries are definite and clear, but the boundaries in Mrs. Hallett's deed are unintelligible to the modern reader.  She conveys the land known as Goodspeed's Hill ; but what portion of it does not clearly appear, probably that part where the Custom House now stands.

In the year 1664 the legal title to Meeting House Hill, containing about five acres, and to Lewis' Swamp was held by the town of Barnstable.  It is probable that prior to 1654 Roger Goodspeed had surrendered his title, or to use the form of expression adopted by our ancestors, had "laid down to commons" Meeting House Hill and Lewis' Swamp, and had received in exchange other lands—a common mode of doing business in early times.  A certificate of the boundaries of the land "taken up," signed by the land committee, was held to be a sufficient title.  No circumlocution was used, no good paper and ink wasted.

One acre of this land was granted to Henry Cobb in 1665— the deep bottom on the north of the Meeting House.  This grant is in the usual form, short and comprehensive ; and it would not be amiss for some modern conveyancers to study it.

"22 May, 1665, Granted that Henry Cobb shall have an acre of ground, adjoining to his land above the gate, between that and the pond, in lieu of some damage that he hath or shall receive by the highway running over or between his land from the gate to Thomas Huckins."          [Records, vol. 1, page 46.

Aug. 15, 1683, the town purchased of John Davis about half an acre of swampy land on the west side of Cobb's Hill, for a public watering place.  In a short time a large quantity of sand, brought down by the rains from the roads and hill sides, filled up the watering place, and it was sold to Ebenezer Lewis, and is now owned by Ebenezer Bacon. The deed is from the land committee in the usual form, as follows:

"November the 13, 1717. Bargained with and laid out to Lieut. Ebenezer Lewis a small gore of land by the highways, and is bounded by the ways, viz: on the south by the highway, or County Road; easterly by the way that goeth down by the brook; on the west by the way that goeth by Benjamin Davis' land or fence, down to Lieut. Nathaniel Bacon's, until it meeteth with the other way, last before mention—not to infringe on any former grant, for which he remits two shares and a half—two of them in the right of Jedediah Jones, and half a share in the right of Thomas Blossom. * DANIEL PARKER,
JOSEPH LOTHROP.

Lieut. Lewis being one of the committee, did not sign the grant made to himself.

In 1717 the new Meeting House was built on Cobb's Hill, by proprietors who purchased the land. The conditions of the sale are recorded as follows: There is no date. The authority to lay out land for public uses and setting Meeting Houses were vested in the land committee by a vote of the proprietors, dated April 15, 1715. The following was laid out in 1717:

"Bargained with and set out to Mr. John Bacon, Lieut. John Thacher, Lieut. Ebenezer Lewis, Samuel Cob, Joseph Davis, James Gorham, Thomas Lothrop, George Lewis, Lieut. Nathaniel Bacon, Samuel Lewis, Samuel Sturgis, and Nathaniel Lumbert, Jabez and Sylvanus Gorham, a piece of land lying on Cob's Hill, bounded northerly by said Nathaniel Bacon's land and partly by Samuel Bacon's land, to a stake by the fence; thence set to a Rock and soe to another Rock at the S. W. corner; and from thence sets easterly to Samuel Bacon's land, soe as to include the land on which the pound stands, not to remove said pound unless all parties concerned doe agree to it, for which they remitt fifty shares and a quarter in this division, that is to say,

| John Bacon, four and a quarter, | 4 1-4 |
| Thomas Lothrop, | 5 |
| Joseph Davis, | 5 |
| Samuel Cob, | 4 |
| George Lewis, | 3 |
| James Gorham, | 3 |
| Lieut. Jonathan Thacher, | 3 |
| Lieut. Ebenezer Lewis, | 3 |
| Samuel Sturgis, | 5 |

---

* In the third or last division, the common lands were divided into 6000 shares—28 shares made a 40 acre lot—but some of the lots were smaller, and some much larger. In the first division, 6000 shares, 43 made a lot, in the second 6000 shares, 42,—and in the Sandy Neck lots 100 shares made a lot. The lots were all apprized at the same sum, and presumed to be of equal value. If the land was poor, more acres were put into a lot—if valuable, a less number. These shares were an article of trafic, and transferred from one to another.

| | |
|---|---|
| Nathaniel Lumbert, | 3 |
| Samuel Lewis, | 3 |
| Lieut. Nathaniel Bacon, | 5 |
| Jabez Gorham, | 2 |
| Sylvanus Gorham, | 2 |

The boundaries given in this grant are indefinite; but are well known. They included all the land on the north of the carriage way that runs east and west immediately in front of the Meeting House. The East Parish still owns this land, excepting the part east of the pound, where the parsonage house stood, that has been sold. The Parish owns the land where the pound stands; but it cannot be removed without the consent of the town, and of the parties who are bound to maintain it.

The Meeting House was built by twenty-four proprietors in 1717-18, and sold Jan. 25, 1718-19, to the East Precinct in the town of Barnstable, for the sum of £450 in money. In the deed of conveyance, no land is named, but the parish immediately took possession, and have improved the land to this day, which is a sufficient title.

After the above grant was made by the committee of the proprietors of the town, the remainder of the land on Cobb's Hill was reserved for public use, and recorded as follows:

"A piece of land of about three acres lying on Cobb's Hill, laid out for public uses pursuant to the vote of the proprietors; bounded as followeth: southerly by the highway; westerly by the brook and way round to Lieut. Nathaniel Bacon's, thence by his land to the piece laid out to John Bacon and others, to Samuel Bacon's, and easterly by it to the highway."

These boundaries are not clearly stated but are well known. The three acres includes all the land bounded southerly by the present County road; westerly by the branch of Mill Way that passes on the east of the store of Ebenezer Bacon, till it joins the western branch of that way, thence by that branch till it joins the eastern branch, thence south-easterly by that way to the top of Meeting House Hill, and thence east by the carriage way in front of the Meeting House, to the County road, at a point in front of Major Phinney's barn. To a small portion of this land the town has partially alienated its title. About the year 1800 the town granted to Fraternal Lodge a small lot of land on the east of the school house in the third district, for the purpose of erecting a hall thereon.*

---

*I have been perhaps unnecessarily particular and tedious in my description and history of Roger Goodspeed's original house lots. I have done so, in order that I might be instrumental in settling the questions that have arisen relative to the maintainance of the pound, and the improvement of the pound meadows. They can be settled equitably without an appeal to the Courts. These points I think are clearly established.

The East Parish though the owner of the soil on which the pound stands, has no right to remove it without the consent of the town, and of the present holders of the pound meadows.

Before the year 1653, Roger Goodspeed removed from Goodspeed's Hill to the Indian village of Mistick or Misteake, now known by the more modern and perhaps more euphoneous name of Marston's Mills. I think he was the first of the whites who settled in that part of the town.

His six acre houselot then was bounded southerly by the land of the Indian Sachem Paup-mun-nucks, † and westerly by Oyster River. On the north of this lot he owned a neck of land containing sixteen acres. In 1665 he bought forty acres of land adjoining the Oyster River and the Indian pond of Thomas Allyn. In 1667 the town granted him sixteen acres adjoining his houselot. He also owned meadows in that vicinity. In 1659 he purchased a tract of land of Dea. John Cooper at the east of Cooper's Pond.

April 6, 1678, he conveyed all his lands and meadows at South Sea to his sons John and Ebenezer, excepting six acres, on the condition that they support him and his wife Alice during their natural lives. This instrument is on record, and is very carefully drawn. It is signed with his mark.

He joined the church in Barnstable July 28, 1644, his wife Alice having joined on 31 of the preceding December. He was admitted a freeman of the Colony June 5, 1651, and was on the grand jury that year. He was a farmer or planter, and had enjoyed no advantages for obtaining an education. He appears to have been an exemplary member of the Christian church, and to have lived, except on one occasion, a quiet and inoffensive life. In 1672, at the Meeting House in Barnstable, he charged John Jenkins with having stolen his kid and lying ; but like an honest

---

The town of Barnstable has no right to remove the pound, without the assent of the holders of said meadow. If the town should order its removal without such assent the latter would be relieved from all obligation to maintain a pound in another place, and could not be dispossessed of said meadows.

June 1, 1688. The grass that grows on the Pound Meadows was granted to James Lewis and Nathaniel Bacon, for so long a time as they shall maintain a pound for the town's use and no longer. The meadows were not granted, only the right to cut the "common thatch, goose grass or sedge that grows upon them." This is a nice distinction but the language used shows the intention of the parties. Lewis and Bacon admitted four others as partners and the meadows were divided into six lots, and the maintenance of certain portions of the pound fence was assigned to each lot. In 1778 some of the partners neglected to put up their particular portion of the fence and the town was indicted. That matter was settled, the partners found that they were obliged to put up the fence, and did so. Recently they have again neglected to keep the fence in repair and the town has taken possession of the meadows. This the town had an undoubted right to do; but a question arises whether or not those partners who have maintained their particular portions of the fence can be deprived of the use of the meadows. On the other hand, it is said that the grant was made as a whole, that the division was a subsequent arrangement not binding on the town.

The latter is the common sense view of the question. A quadrangular piece of land fenced on three sides is not a "pound for the town's use." Either of the partners had the same right that the town had. He could have put up the fence and claimed the delinquent's share of the meadow.

---

† Paup-mun-nucks was the Sachem of Masapee, now called Marshpee, the easterly part of Sandwich and the westerly and central parts of Barnstable. He ever lived on friendly terms with the whites. For several years this ancient and once powerful sagamore resided in the immediate vicinity of Roger Goodspeed.

man, after due consideration, he acknowledged that he "had no just cause, soe to say, and was sorry for soe saying, and desired Mr. Jenkins to pass it by."

He died in 1685, and his wife Alice in 1689. In her will dated Jan. 10, 1688, and proved Sept. 4, 1689, she names her son John whom she cuts off with a shilling; her daughter Ruth Davis, to whom she gives 40 shillings, a brass kettle, and half her wearing apparel; to her daughter Elizabeth, then unmarried, £20, and the other half of her wearing apparel; to her daughter-in-law Lydia, wife of her son Ebenezer, one colt and one gown; to her grandson Benjamin, son of Ebenezer, 1 colt; and to her son Ebenezer, her dwelling-house, and all her other estate.

Roger Goodspeed left no will. He divided his large landed estate to his children by deeds, and the agreement above referred to executed during his lifetime. He married Alice Layton Dec. 1, 1641. Children born in Barnstable:

2.    I.   Nathaniel, 6th October, 1642, (see below.)
3.    II.   John, June 1645, (see below.)
4.    III.   Mary, July 1647, married, 14th Dec. 1664, Samuel Hinckley.
5.    IV.   Benjamin, 6th May, 1649, (see below.)
6.    V.   Ruth, 10th April, 1652, married, 2d Feb. 1674-5, John Davis, Jr.
7.    VI.   Ebenezer, Dec. 1655, (see below.)
8.    VII.   Elizabeth, 1st May, 1658, (unmarried 1688.)

1. Nathaniel Goodspeed, son of Roger, married Nov. 1666, Elizabeth, daughter of Mr. John Bursley. He died June, 1670, and his widow married Oct. 1675, Increase Clap. He had two children born in Barnstable, namely:

9.    I.   Mary, born 18th Feb. 1667-8.
10.    II.   Nathaniel, probably. Another child beside Mary is mentioned in the settlement of the father's estate. Nathaniel Goodspeed is also named several times on the town records. After 1703 his name disappears, and a Nathaniel Goodspeed, who married Sarah, appears at Rochester, and had a family born from 1706 to 1713.

2. John Goodspeed, son of Roger, resided at Mistick. He died in 1719, aged 74, and names in his will his wife Experience, sons John and Benjamin; daughters Mary, Rose and Bathsheba, grand-daughter Ruth, daughter of his son Samuel, deceased. He left a large estate. He married 9th Jan. 1668, Experience Holway, and had:

11.    I.   Mary or Mercy, 18 Feb. 1669.
12.    II.   Samuel, 23d June, 1670, died before his father. He married, and had a daughter Ruth living in 1719.
13.    III.   John, 1st June, 1673, (see below.)
14.    IV.   Experience, 14th Sept. 1676, not living in 1718.

15.    V.    Benjamin, 31st March, 1679, (see below.)
16.    VI.    Rose, 20th Feb. 1680-1, married, July 10, 1700, Isaac Jennings, of Sandwich.    Died Dec. 21, 1721.
17.    VII.    Bathsheba, 17th Feb. 1683.
    5.    Benjamin Goodspeed, son of Roger, married Mary, daughter of John Davis, and had,
18.    I.    Mary, 10th Jan. 1677, married 7th Jan. 1702, Ichabod Hinckley.    She died Oct. 1, 1719.    Benjamin Goodspeed died early and his widow married Ensign John Hinckley Nov. 24, 1697.
    7.    Ebenezer Goodspeed, son of Roger, lived to a great age. He resided at Mistick, and owned a large real estate.    Jan. 23, 1740, he conveyed one-half of his real estate to his son Roger. Dec. 30, 1746, being then 91 years of age, he conveyed to his son Moses the other half of his real estate, in consideration of an obligation from his son to maintain him ten years, or till 101 years of age.    His signature to this deed is a very good one, written thus, "Eben—Good—speed."    In a deed dated Feb. 22, 1725-6, he names his sons Moses, Benjamin and Roger.
    He was the youngest son, and appears to have been, contrary to the usuages of those days, the favorite son.    He was better educated than any of the family.    Though his father, in 1678, conveyed the bulk of his estate in equal proportions to John and Ebenezer, something appears to have occurred that alienated the affections of the parents from John.    The latter accumulated a large estate, and was probably an avaricious man—and having his father's estate legally secured to him he forgot, as is too often the case in such circumstances, the duties he owed in love, in honor and in common justice, to his confiding parents.    Such instances are not rare, and they teach a lesson that parents should never forget.
    Ebenezer left no will.    Not profiting by the example of his brother John, he conveyed all his estate to his children in his lifetime, including the ancient homestead of his father at Mistick, bequeathed to him in his mother's will.
    Ebenezer Goodspeed married Feb. 15, 1677, Lydia Crowell of Yarmouth.    According to the records she was his only wife. May, 1694, Lydia, wife of Ebenezer Goodspeed, was a member of the Barnstable Church, and her daughter Patience was baptized, and subsequently in regular course her other children. When she was admitted to the church does not appear, and the fact that there is no record of the baptisms of the older children indicates that Lydia, the mother of Patience, and the subsequent children was not the first wife.    His children born in Barnstable, were :
19.    I.    Benjamin, 31st Oct. 1678, (see below.)
20.    II.    Son, 21st Jan 1679-80, died Dec. 20, 1689.

21.    III.   Mehitabel, 4th Sept. 1681, married Samuel Howes
18th Dec. 1705.
22.    IV.   Alice, 30th June, 1683, married Benjamin Shelly
8th Aug. 1705.
23.    V.   Ebenezer, 10th Sept. 1685, (see below.)
24.    VI.   Mary, 2d Aug. 1687.
25.    VII.   Susannah, 7th Nov. 1689, married Samuel White
May 14, 1719.
26.    VIII.   Patience, 1st June, 1692, married Joseph Hatch
or Hallett of Dighton, May 12, 1718.
27.    IX.   Ruth, 12th July, 1694.
28.    X.   Lydia, 14th Oct. 1696, married Benjamin Marston
April 26, 1716.
29.    XI.   Roger, 14th Oct. 1698, (see below.)
30.    XII.   Reliance, 18th Sept. 1701, married Thomas Phinney, Jr., March 18, 1726.
31.    XIII.   Moses, 24th Nov. 1704, (see below.)

12.  Samuel Goodspeed, son of John, married ————,
died before the year 1718, leaving one child.
32.    I.   Ruth.

13.  John Goodspeed, son of John, born in Barnstable June
1, 1673, died in 1721.  He inherited the homestead of his father,
whom he survived only two years.  He bought of John Green, of
Boston, attorney of his brother Samuel Green, the dwelling-house
and lands of the latter.  They were sons of James Green, of
Barnstable, and the estate was probably that of his father's.  The
real estate of John Goodspeed was apprized at £709, and his
personal estate at £640,79, a large estate in those times.  In his
inventory his carpenter's tools are apprized, and I infer from that
entry that he was a mechanic.  He also owned a "whale-boat and
tacklin," indicating that he was interested in the shore whale
fishery, a business in which many of the people of Barnstable at
that time were engaged.  He had also four hives of bees, which
were kept by many of our ancestors.

His house was well furnished, and among other articles of
elegance and luxury, a looking-glass is named, a very rare article
of household furniture at that date.

His will was drawn up by Dr. John Russell and is without a
date, and the names of his children are not mentioned.  To his
sons, (*Samuel*, *Cornelius* and *John*) he bequeathed all his landed
estate and houses, to be equally divided among them.  To each
of his daughters (probably *Elizabeth*, *Temperance* and *Experience*) he devised £60 in money, "a good feather-bed and furniture."  By "furniture" is meant the bedstead, bolsters, pillows,
quilts, &c., not what is now understood by the term.  To his
wife's daughter Ann he gave £5, and to her daughter Content £5,
and a good feather-bed and furniture.  If his personal estate was

insufficient to pay the legacies, he ordered the Green estate to be sold to make up the deficiency.  He gave the improvement of all his estate, during her widowhood, to his wife Remember, who, with his brother Benjamin, were appointed joint executors.

"John Goodspeed, ye son of John Goodspeed, and Remember Buck, were married the 16th of Feb. 1697-8." She was of Sandwich, a widow of a grandson of Cornet John Buck, of Hingham and Scituate, who in his will dated that year gives legacies "to all my grand-children living at Yarmouth and Sandwich." She had two daughters, Ann and Content, by her first husband.

### Children born in Barnstable.

33.   I.   Elizabeth, 10th Dec. 1698, married Edward Dillingham, Jr., of Sandwich, Oct. 10, 1723.

34.   II.   Temperance, 17th Feb. 1699-1700, married John Trowbridge July 27, 1717.

35.   III.   Samuel, 17th March, 1701, married Rebecca ——— ———, and had nine children born in Barnstable, namely : 1, Temperance, May 20, 1725 ; 2, John, Aug. 31, 1728 ; 3, Eunice, April 6, 1731 ; 4, Ann, 24th April, 1734 ; 5, Abigail, July 11, 1736 ; 6, Remember, May 18, 1739 ; 7, Samuel, March 1, 1741 ; 8, Abner, June 17, 1743 ; 9, Anthony, April 18, 1746.

36.   IV.   Cornelius, 2d Feb. 1703-4, married Mary Lovell, Jr., Feb. 19, 1745, and had Cornelius 1747.

37.   V.   John,* 16th Nov. 1708, married June 15, 1732, Rebecca Goodspeed ; children : 1, Susannah, April 22, 1736, married Nathan Thomas 1757 ; 2, Lydia, Jan. 21, 1738 ; 3, Philemon, April 25, 1742 ; 4, John, Nov. 15, 1745.

38.   VI.   Experience, 24th June, 1710, married Cornelius Annable 1729.

39.   VII.   A daughter, 4th April 1712.

15.   Benjamin Goodspeed, son of John, born 31st March, 1679, was one year younger than Benjamin, son of Ebenezer, and is called junior on the records.  He died in 1733, and in his will gives all his estate to his wife Susannah during her widowhood ; to his son Joseph, after the termination of said widowhood, his homestead, woodlot, &c.  To his son John his landing place and marsh north of Tracy's brook ; and to his son Timothy a lot of land called Barley Hill, meadow east of Tracy's brook, &c. ; all his right to Sandy Neck to his three sons equally ; to daughter Mary £60 and a good feather bed and furniture ; and to

---

* He resided near Shubael's Pond, Hamblin's Plains, and was called "Pewter John" to distinguish him from another John Goodspeed, called "Silver John."  His father and grandfather were men of wealth.  The children and the grandchildren of the avaricious are generally wanting in energy of character and therefore thriftless.  If the children are born before the parent accumulates his wealth, they usually acquire habits of industry and frugality in early life, which they retain, and therefore do not waste the wealth which they inherit.  It is very rare that grandchildren are benefited by the wealth of the grandparent, without it is secured to them by deeds of trust.

his daughter Mercy a like amount. The amount of his inventory was £1,170, and the provisions of his will are similar to those of his brother John's. He signed his name to his will with a mark, not certain evidence that he could not write when younger. He married Susannah Allen, March 1710.

*His children born in Barnstable were:*

40.  I.  Joseph, Jan. 1, 1711, married June 28, 1739, Abigail Smith, and had: 1, Benjamin, Feb. 8, 1739, married Susannah Smith 1766; 2, William, July 17, 1741, married Mary Meigs of Sandwich, March 25, 1762; 3, Josiah, April 24, 1744, married Jemima Blossom. April 20, 1762; 4, Abigail, Dec. 16, 1746; 5, Timothy, April 22, 1749; 6, Ann, 1752; and 7, Joseph, Feb. 26, 1756.

41.  II.  Mary, Oct. 12, 1713, married Benjamin Bursley, Feb. 2, 1744.

42.  III.  Marcy, Sept. 26, 1715, married Isaac Jones Jr., 1751.

43.  IV.  Timothy, married Ann Smith 1747.

44.  V.  John.  His birth is not recorded on the town records. He resided at Mystic during his minority, where he learned the trade of a carpenter. He sought in marriage the hand of Miss Mercy Bursley of West Barnstable, who, in addition to her personal charms, had, like "Mistress Mary Ford, large expectancies." In 1754 she consented to marry, and the bans were published according to the customs of the times. A difficulty arose. John insisted that their residence should be at Mystic, Mercy that it should be on her farm at Great Marshes. After four years spent in diplomacy, the difficulty was happily terminated, by an agreement that their home should be at Great Marshes, and they were accordingly married on the 29th of May, 1757.

He resided in the large mansion house since known as the residence of Dr. Whitman. In the French war next preceeding the Revolution, he shipped as carpenter on board of a privateer. A Spanish vessel was taken and brought into port, having a large amount in silver dollars and silver bullion in bars on board. The Captain and owners of the privateer succeeded in having the vessel and cargo condemned as French property, and it has always been currently reported that the Captain offered to each sailor, for his share of the prize money, as much silver as he could carry from the end of Long Wharf to the head of King, now State street, Boston, on the condition, that if he stopped to rest by the way he forfeited the whole. Goodspeed, as carpenter, had two shares. The exact amount which he received is not known, probably not over $5000. At the sale of the prize, and her effects, he bought a boat. His connections reported that he found a large sum in silver hid under the ceiling. This story is doubtful. Why should money be concealed in a boat, where the chances for loss were greater than in the vessel.

Five thousand dollars in specie was a large sum for a Barnstable man to hold in those days, and it is not surprising that the amount should be reported to be much larger. Excepting Goodspeed, and one other, all the rest soon spent their shares in riotous living. Goodspeed was frugal in his expenses, and cautious in business. A portion of his silver he loaned at high rates, interest and principal payable in Spanish milled dollars; the remainder he carefully hoarded, and much of it was inherited by his daughter, whose children spent it, having no reverence for antiquity, or love of hoarding.

Of the many stories told of "Silver John Goodspeed" it is difficult to separate the true from the false or highly exaggerated. His biography would be interesting, and teach some useful lessons. His early life of trial, his eccentric courtship, and his adventures as a privateersman or buccaneer, have a romantic interest. In after life, he devoted all his energies to the accumulation of wealth.

He had an only child, Mercy, baptized Aug. 7, 1763. She inherited all her father's and her mother's wealth, and from early childhood was educated in the belief that "man's chief end is to gather up riches." She married Dr. Jonas Whitman, a man not unlike in character to "Silver John." She had two daughters and several sons, among whom Silver John's great wealth was divided; but it soon took to itself wings and flew away,—and is now enjoyed by the children and grand-children of his poor neighbors. "Silver John's" wealth was a curse to his posterity.

19.   Benjamin Goodspeed, son of Ebenezer, born 31st Oct. 1678, resided in Barnstable, where he died in 1750, aged 72. In his will, which he signs with his mark, he devises half the improvement of his estate to his wife Hope; to son Jabez, 10 shillings Old Tenor (22 1-2 cents); to son Jonathan, 10 shillings Old Tenor; to his daughter Patience, one-half his indoor moveables; and to his son James, all his real estate, wearing apparel, cattle, &c., &c.

He married in 1707 Hope, daughter of Benjamin Lumbart, and had seven children born in Barnstable, namely:

45.   I.   Jabez, 26th Jan. 1707-8, married Reliance Tobey, of Sandwich, 1733, and had: 1, Jabez, July 31, 1737, married Margaret Bassett Aug. 6, 1761; 2, Jane, March 21, 1739; 3, Heman, Sept. 4, 1743; 4, Benjamin, May 26, 1745; by his 2d wife, Elizabeth Adams, 5, Elisha, baptized Jan. 31,

1753 ; 6, Sarah, baptized April 2, 1755 ; 7, Solomon, baptized April 25, 1762.

46.   II.   Jane, 7th Sept. 1709, probably died young.
47.   III.   James, June 1711, married Elizabeth Fuller Nov. 13, 1739, and had 1, Martha, July 31, 1741, married Samuel Winslow of Hardwick, June 12, 1760 ; 2, Mary, June 14, 1743, married Timothy Hinckley 1766 ; 3, David, Aug. 20, 1745 ; 4, Hannah, March 14, 1757 ; 5, Desire, baptized July 21, 1751 ; 6, Abner, baptized July 7, 1754 ; (Church records say daughter of Reuben, probably a mistake) 7, Temperance, Sept. 5, 1756 ; and 8, Temperance, July 19, 1759.
48.   IV.   David, 13th Nov. 1713.
49.   V.   Nathan, 7th Oct. 1715, died April 29, 1723.
50.   VI.   Patience, 25th March 1718, married Eben. Cannon July 30, 1752.
51.   VII.   Jonathan, 23d April 1720.

23.   Ebenezer Goodspeed, son of Ebenezer, born Sept. 10, 1685, married Nov. 7, 1711, Mary Stacy. He was called junior, and his son Ebenezer third. His children born in Barnstable were :

52.   I.   Rebecca, Oct. 28, 1714, married John Goodspeed June 18, 1732.
53.   II.,   Ebenezer, Feb. 7, 1715-16, married Sept. 29, 1736, Rebecca Bodfish, and had eight children born in Barnstable : 1, Thankful, March 10, 1736-7, married Oct. 20, 1757, Joseph Nye, Jr., of Sandwich ; 2, Martha, Feb. 7, 1738-9 ; 3, Edward, June 5, 1741 ; 4, Joseph, Oct. 15, 1743, married Hannah Bodfish 1766 ; 5, Rufus, Jan. 15, 1749-50 ; 6, Silas, Jan. 27, 1751-2 ; 7, Hannah, Aug. 9, 1755 ; 8, Elizabeth, Feb. 7, 1757 ; and 9, Mary, May 29, 1759.
54.   III.   Mary, Aug. 2, 1721, married John Blush, Nov. 17, 1739.

29.   Roger Goodspeed, son of Ebenezer, married Hannah Phinney Oct. 6, 1720. His father, Jan. 23, 1740, conveyed to him by deed one-half of his real estate in Barnstable. It afterwards was the property of the heirs of his brother Moses.

Children of Roger Goodspeed born in Barnstable :

55.   I.   Thomas, Oct. 27, 1721. (A Thomas Goodspeed, whose wife was Puella, resided at Hyannis.)
56.   II.   Isaac, Sept. 23, 1723, married Ann Jenkins Oct. 17, 1754, and had : 1, Sarah, Oct. 25, 1755 ; 2, Isaac, April 29, 1758 ; 3, Hannah, May 17, 1760 ; 4, Luther, Nov. 1, 1762 ; 5 and 6, Elijah and Daniel, twins, Jan. 17, 1765 ; 7, Heman, Feb. 14, 1767 ; and 8, Charles, July 20, 1769.
57.   111.   Ruth, baptised 1725 ; she probably died young.
58.   IV.   Sarah, born Dec. 5, 1827, married George Conant,

June 20, 1753, died March 14, 1754, aged 27.

59. V. Abigail, baptized July 26, 1730, probably died young.

60. VI. Elizabeth, born Nov. 14, 1731, married Jedediah Winslow of Rochester, Nov. 7, 1751.

61. VII. Joseph, Sept. 17, 1736, married Sarah Adams, Jr., June 29, 1756.

62. VIII. Hannah, baptized July 25, 1742.

31. Moses Goodspeed, thirteenth child of Ebenezer, and grandson of Roger, inherited the homestead of his ancestor, and by purchases made by him and his son Seth, the latter became the owner of all the lands that were his ancestors, and it is now the property of Henry Goodspeed, a son of Seth, and now a volunteer in the army of the United States. Moses Goodspeed married March 30, 1726, Hannah Allen. His children born in Barnstable are all named in his will dated March 1, 1774, and were :

63. I. Nathaniel, March 18, 1727, married Elizabeth Fuller of Rochester, in 1755. He sold to his brother Seth, his share in his father's estate and removed to Vassalboro', Maine.

64. II. Seth, Feb. 2, 1728-9, married March 15, 1753, Abigail Linnel. He resided on the ancient Goodspeed farm which became his by inheritance or purchase. He devised the farm to his son Allen, and the latter to the present owner, Henry Goodspeed. Seth Goodspeed died March 26, 1810, aged 82, and his wife July 7, 1805, aged 75. His children were : 1, Anna, born Sept. 29, 1753, who died unmarried Feb. 15, 1821 ; 2, Temperance, Nov. 7, 1755, married ——— Davis ; 3, Patience, Oct. 10, 1755, married Benjamin Lumbard ; 4, Abigail, April 4, 1760, married Solomon Bodfish ; 5, Hannah, Sept. 19, 1762, married Peter Blossom ; 6, Eunice, Oct. 5. 1764, married Prince Hinckley ; 7, Olive, Sept. 21, 1766, married John Marston, died Nov. 21, 1814 ; 8, Allen, Jan. 5, 1769, married and had a family, died Jan. 7, 1831 ; 9, Sophia, June 13, 1771, married Lot Scudder ; and 10, Temperance, Jan. 14, 1774, married James Crosby.

# GILPIN.

---

## ANTHONY GILPIN.

Anthony Gilpin's name occasionally appears as a land holder in Barnstable. He died in March 1655, at the house of George Lewis, and it does not appear that he left a family. His will was proved June 5, 1655. He gave all his estate in trust to Nathaniel Bacon, for the benefit of his kinsman, William Hodges of Darnton, in Yorkshire, England, and his five sisters. There are several papers on the record, filed by Mr. Bacon, respecting the estate; but I have mislaid my abstract of them.

# GILBERT.

---

## SAMUEL GILBERT.

Samuel Gilbert from Connecticut, married April 23, 1758, Thankful Fuller and had :

I.   Seth, born Feb. 4, 1759.
II.  Abigail, Jan. 1762.
III. Benjamin, June 21, 1764.

Respecting this family I have no additional information. In 1778 a Samuel Gilbert, Jr., a physician and surgeon, died in Barnstable. At the time of his death, he had some mercantile business with parties in the West Indies. He left a small estate apprized at £32,16 shs. lawful money. £137,19 in currency.

# GORHAM.

Capt. John Gorham is the ancestor of the numerous families of the name of Gorham in New England, in the British Provinces, in Rhode Island, New York, and other states in the Union. His descent is traced from the DeGorran of La Tanniere, near Gorram, in Maine, on the borders of Brittany. Several of the family removed to England in the eleventh century, during the reign of William the Conquerer. In England many of the name were men of learning, wealth and influence. The immediate ancestors of Capt. John were not men of note. His father Ralph and his grandfather James resided at Benefield in Northamptonshire, where John was baptized January 28, 1620-1. James Gorham of Benefield, was born in 1550, married in 1572, Agnes Bernington, and died 1576. Ralph, born in 1575, came with his family to New England, and was in Plymouth in 1637. On the 2d of October in that year, "Lands to erect a house upon are granted to Ralph Goarame, of some part of the waste grounds about Edmund Bumpas or Philip Delanoys house."

Of Ralph Gorham or his family little is known. Only the birth of his son John is recorded either at Benefield or at Plymouth. He probably had other children, evidently a son Ralph, born in England, for he is called, March 4, 1638-9, "the elder," showing that there were then two persons of that name in Plymouth.* He is named in the Plymouth Colony Records June 4, 1639, and April 5, 1642, and thereafter his name disappears. At the latter date he was sixty-seven years of age, and, if he was living in 1643, his name would not be enrolled on the list taken in August that year, of all between 16 and 60 that were able to bear arms in the Colony. Ralph, the younger's name, is not on that list.

It is probable that Ralph Gorham died about the year 1643, leaving no widow, and an only child John who inherited his property. This is inferred from the fact that no settlement of his es-

---

*20th June, 1635, Thomas Gorham, aged 19, and John Gorham, aged 18 years, were passengers in the Phillip, Richard Morgan master, from ———— bound to Virginia. New England was sometimes called North Virginia. A Mrs. Kathrine Gorham presented a petition to the Assembly of Rhode Island 1680.

tate appears on the records—none was required if he had only one heir, and he of legal age. During the seventeenth century, besides John and his descendants, no other person of the name of Gorham is mentioned as a resident in the Colony.

Of the early life of John, little is known. He had a good common school education, was brought up in the Puritan faith, and during life was a consistent and exemplary Christian.† He probably served an apprenticeship with a tanner and currier of leather, working at that business in the winter, and pursuing some other calling in the summer. At the first settlement of the country very few mechanics were employed at their trades during the year. All had lands assigned to them, and in the summer season labored more or less on their farms. Even the governors and their assistants had farms, which they tilled with their own hands.

At an early age he had to rely on himself,—a young man, in a strange land, with no family connections to sustain him, and little wealth to aid him in the pursuit of the business of life. However, he was an honest boy, and he grew up an honest man, and his descendants have inherited, not only his good name, but generally this trait of his character. ‡

In 1643, he being then twenty-two years of age, married Desire Howland, one of the first born at Plymouth, a young woman who had also been educated in the Puritan faith, and who, during her long life was a pattern of good works, a kind hearted woman, and a Christian in name and spirit. § She was a daughter of John, and a grand-daughter of John Tilley, both of whom came over in the Mayflower.

In 1646 he removed from Plymouth to Marshfield, and in 1648 was chosen constable of that town. In the same year he was propounded to become a freeman of the Colony, and June 4, 1650, was admitted. In 1651 he was a member of the Grand Inquest of the Colony.

In 1652 he removed to Yarmouth, and purchased the house-lot on the north County road, adjoining to the bounds of Barn-

† March 5, 1655, John Gorham was presented for "unseamly carriage toward Blanch Hull at unseasonable time being in the night." She was then the wife of Trustrum Hull of Barnstable, and afterwards the second wife of Capt. Wm. Hedge of Yarmouth. She was a bad woman, being frequently envolved in broils and difficulties. Capt. Hedge, in his will, cut her off with "a shilling," and gives as a reason that "she had proved false to him." John Gorham was fined 40 shillings, Blanch 50 shillings—a poor speculation for Mrs. Hull.

‡ In examining the history of hundreds of his descendants, I have not yet found one of the name who was convicted of crime. A few families of the name have run out, the children partaking largely of the character of their mother's families.

§ Sometimes a trifling incident affords an excellent and suggestive illustration of character. A beautiful tribute to the memory of Mrs. Gorham is found in the will of her old servant Totoo. His dying request was, "Bury me as near as you can to the feet of my mistress." There is true poetic feeling in the simple words of the dying servant. They are suggestive of a thousand acts of kindness that had lived in his memory during the eight years that his mistress had been dead,—and he craved no higher felicity in the spirit world than to be allowed to dwell near her whom he served on earth.

stable. About the same time he purchased a part of the Hallett Farm, containing 100 acres of planting land, adjoining his house-lot, and situate mostly within the then boundaries of the town of Barnstable. [Thomas Starr owned the northwest houselot in Yarmouth. This he sold to Andrew Hallett, Senior, in 1639. This house was afterwards John Gorham's.] This farm was granted to Mr. Andrew Hallett in the spring of 1639, and the boundaries of the same entered on the Plymouth Colony Records Sept. 3, 1639, as follows :

"It is granted by the Court, that Mr. Andrew Hallett shall have his greate lott of two hundred acres at Yarmouth, 80 pole in breadth, at the first beginning at the head of the cove [Stony Cove] from the marked tree, and to bear up that breadth fourty pole in length, and afterwards to be enlarged in breadth in the ranging of yt towards the other end wch was afterwards layed forth in form following, viz : from the sd tree on the east sid upon a southerly lin 40 pole [following the bounds between Yarmouth and Barnstable to the County road] and then enlarged in breadth towards the east 20 pole, and extending in length 60 pole [to the stable on the west of the Yarmouth R. R. Depot] and from thence in breadth 38 pole, [to the new Hyannis Road] and from thence extends still in length 100 pole beyond a great pond [Long Pond] to the end thereof ; [the S. E. corner is a rock marked F, called the Farm Rock in the town records] and on the north and north-west side from the said tre, 80 pole in breadth, [to the Mill Road] and in length, first 40 pole, [to the County road] and then en-larged to the westward 50 pole in breadth [by the County road to Thomas Lumbart's great lot] and thence extending itself 160 pole, and the south side thereof upon a straight line 188 pole."

The distance between the ancient monuments yet remaining is greater than given in the record. It was customary to allow for ponds and swamps and not include them in the admeasure-ment. He also owned the land on the north of the Hallett Farm, between Stoney Cove and the Mill Road, and the seventeen acres of meadow on the south-west side of the Cove, (more or less) and ten acres at Stony Cove Neck laid out to Mr. Hallett.

His farm contained very little waste land. That on the north side of the County road, excepting a few gravelly hills, near the bounds of Yarmouth, is a strong loam soil and good grass land ; and that on the south is a sandy loam, of easy cultivation and adapted to corn and rye. Taken as a whole, this farm is not so fertile as it was formerly. The light soils on the south have been exhausted by repeated crops, without returning sufficient manure ; but the loam and clay soils on the north, yet retain their ancient fertility. There were few better farms in the Colony than Capt. Gorham's—it was well watered, convenient to the meadows, and contained soils adapted to the cultivation of a great variety of crops.

He also owned the Grist Mill known as Hallett's Mill, and the landing place, or wharf, near the same. The grist mill named in the early town records (1647) was situate farther south than the present mill. The ancient dam, built by the first settlers, only enclosed the southern part of the present mill pond, then appropriately named Stone Cove. The northern portion of the mill pond was then a tract of salt meadow which has gradually worn away, since the erection of the present dam.

The tannery of Capt. Gorham was a short distance southerly from the present mill, on the west of the pond, and northerly from the site of the ancient grist mill.

He was deputy from Yarmouth to the Plymouth Colony Court at the special session April 6, 1653, and the following year he was chosen surveyor of highways in the town of Yarmouth.

At the Court held June 1, 1663, "Liberty was graunted unto John Gorham to looke out some land for accomodation, and to make report thereof to the Court, that soe a competency may be granted to him." He selected a tract of one hundred acres at Papasquash Neck, in Swansea, which was granted to him in July, 1669, and in July, 1672, Mr. Constant Southworth, Mr. James Brown, and Mr. John Gorham, were appointed a committee to purchase the same of the Indians. July 13, 1677, in consideration of the good service that Capt. Gorham had performed for the country in the war in which he lost his life, the Court confirmed to his heirs and successors forever the 100 acres of land at Papasquash Neck.

In 1673 and 1674, he was a member of the board of Selectmen of the town of Barnstable, and in the former year received the appointment of lieutenant of the Plymouth forces in the Dutch war.

June 17, 1675, Gen. Benjamin Church arrived at Plymouth, and confirmed former reports of the conduct of King Philip. The next Sunday, June 20, Philip's men made an attack on Swanzey, and rifled a few houses. Forthwith a post was sent to Plymouth for aid, who arrived at break of day June 21. Information was sent to Boston, and aid solicited; orders were issued to all the Captains of all the companies in the Colony to march without delay. Thursday, June 24, was a day of fasting and prayer, by appointment, throughout the Colony. The names of the soldiers who went from Barnstable are not recorded. Mr. John Gorham, it appears by the Yarmouth records, was captain of the militia company and a resident in that town. June 24, 1675, Capt. Gorham and twenty-nine from Yarmouth, whose names appear on record, "took their first march" for Mount Hope. These were mounted men. It is not so stated in the records; but such clearly appears: £9 were paid for nine horses lost, £10 for the hire of horses, and £11,15 10 for the loss of saddles and bridles.

Barnstable and the other towns in the County also furnished

their quotas. This appears in the division of the lands, in Gorham, Maine, granted to those soldiers or their heirs, in consideration of their service in King Philip's War. The Plymouth forces were commanded by Major Cudworth, and were at Swanzey June 28, and were joined by the troops of Massachusetts.

In the latter part of August the theatre of the war was transferred to the banks of the Connecticut. Capt. Gorham and his company marched into Massachusetts. He arrived after the total defeat of Capt. Lothrop at Sugar Loaf Hill, in which Capt. L. lost the greater part of his force, consisting of eighty picked men, "the flower of Essex." The following letter written by Capt. Gorham, is copied from the original in the Secretary of State's office in Boston. It has never been published and will be interesting to his descendants :

[*From the original in the Secretary's office.*]

MENDUM, OCTOBER th 1 : 1675

MUCH HONORED : My service with all due respects humbly presented to yourself and unto the rest of the Council hoping of your healths. I have made bold to trouble you with these few lines to give your honors an account of our progress in your jurisdiction. According unto your honors order and determination I arrived at Mendum with fifty men, and the next day Lieutenant Upham arrived with thirty-eight men, and the day following we joined our forces together and marched in pursuit to find our enemy, but God hath been pleased to deny us any opportunity therein ;—though with much labor and travel we had endeavored to find them out, which Lieut. Upham hath given you a more particular account. Our soldiers being much worn but having been in the field this fourteen weeks' and little hopes of finding the enemy, we are this day returning toward our General, but as for my own part, I shall be ready to serve God and the country in this just war, so long as I have life and health, not else to trouble you, I rest yours to serve in what I am able.

JOHN GORRUN.

Oct. 4, 1675, he was appointed by the Court, captain of the second company of the Plymouth forces in King Philip's war. Mr. Jonathan Sparrow, of Eastham, was lieutenant. Capts. Bradford and Gorham were ordered by the council of war, to rendezvous their men at Plymouth Dec. 7, Taunton Dec. 8, Rehoboth Dec. 9, and at Providence Dec. 10.

Capt. Gorham and his company were in the sanguinary battle at the Swamp Fort, in the Narraganset country, fought Dec. 19, 1675. That battle was decisive in its results, it not only crushed the power of the Narragansetts ; but it destroyed the hope of King Philip and his alies, of exterminating the white race in New England. The forces of the United Colonies had assembled on the 18th within fifteen miles of the Swamp Fort. The weather was cold and severe, the forces had to remain in an open

field, "with no other covering than a cold and moist fleece of
snow." At the dawn of day the next morning they started on
their weary march, sinking ancle deep at every step in the snow.
At one o'clock they arrived at the Fort. It was built on an island, containing five or six acres, in the swamp, surrounded with
a thick hedge and strengthened with palisades. There were two
entrances, one "over a long tree upon a place of water ; the other
at an angle of the fort, over a huge tree, which rested on its
branches, just as it had fallen, the trunk being raised five or six
feet from the ground. The latter was judged to be the only accessible entrance. Opposite the fallen tree there was an open
space within the Fort, defended in front by a log house, and flank-
ers on each side. In these the Indian sharpshooters were posted,
and to attempt to cross over on the fallen tree was almost certain
death. A part of the Massachusetts troops made the first attempt. Capt. Johnson was killed on the tree, Capt. Davenport,
who followed, met with the same fate after entering the Fort, and
a large number of soldiers were wounded or slain by the galling
shots of the Indians. A soldier named John Raymond, of Middleboro', was the first to enter the Fort.

After three or four hours of hard fighting, the English succeeded in taking the Fort. Hubbard estimates that the Indians
"lost seven hundred fighting men, besides three hundred that died
of their wounds. The number of old men, women and children,
that perished either by fire or were starved with hunger and cold,
none of them could tell." There were about eighty of the English slain, and a hundred and fifty wounded that recovered after.
Sergeant Nathaniel Hall, of the Yarmouth troops, and John Barker of the Barnstable, were wounded. I believe none from either
town were killed. Capt. Gorham never recovered from the cold
and fatigue to which he was exposed in this expedition. He was
seized with a fever and died at Swansea where he was buried Feb.
5, 1675-6. Mr. Thomas Hinckley was commissary general of the
forces, and his daughter Reliance, born Dec. 15, was so named
because the mother *relied* that God would protect the father in the
perils to which he was exposed.

In the second expedition to Narraganset, Yarmouth furnished
fourteen men under Capt. Gorham. The proportion furnished by
Barnstable was probably about the same number. No record of
their names has been preserved. The third expedition was com-
manded by Capt. Howes of Yarmouth, and the fourth by Capt.
Pierce of Scituate. The latter were in the bloody battle at Reho-
beth, March 26, 1776. Of the nine who went from Yarmouth,
five were killed: John Matthews, John Gage, William Gage,
Henry Gage and Henry Gold. Five from Sandwich were slain:
Benjamin Nye, Daniel Bessey, Caleb Blake, Job Gibbs and
Stephen Wing. Barnstable six: Lieut. Samuel Fuller, John
Lewis, Eleazer Clapp, Samuel Linnell, Samuel Childs and Samuel

Bourman.    Eastham four: Joseph Nessfield, John Walker, John M. [torn off] [Newman's Letter.]

Capt. Gorham was fifty-four years of age at his death.   On the 7th of March following, letters of administration were granted by the Court to his widow, Mrs. Desire Gorham, and to his sons James and John to settle his estate.   At the same Court Mr. Hinckley, Mr. Chipman, and Mr. Huckens, were appointed guardians of the children then not of age.

Mrs. Gorham died Oct. 13, 1683.   Capt. Gorham, it appears, was an inhabitant of Yarmouth at the time of his death, and his widow continued to reside there, though she died at her son's house in Barnstable.   Her estate was settled on the 5th of March following.   All her children were then living except Elizabeth.

[The Gorham Genealogy I wrote several years since in the form recommended in the Genealogical Register.   The columns of a newspaper are too narrow to set it economically in that form, and I have therefore been under the necessity of transcribing it. The personal notices are in the form of notes.   That peculiarity I retain.]

Capt. John Gorham, the ancestor of the family, was born at Benefield, in Northamptonshire, England, and was baptized January 28, 1620-1.   In the Benefield churchyard, no monuments of the Gorham family are found, which indicates that the family had not long resided at Benefield.   Monuments to the memory of the ancestors of the Freeman and other families who came to New England are there found.   The names of his father Ralph and his grandfather James appear in the parish register, showing that the family for one or two generations had been residents at Benefield. Capt. Gorham married in 1643, Desire, daughter of Mr. John Howland of Plymouth.   He died as above stated, in the service of his country, and was buried at Swansey Feb. 5, 1675-6.   His widow survived him and died in Barnstable Oct. 13, 1683.

Children of Capt. John Gorham and his wife Desire (Howland) Gorham.

2.   I.    Desire, born in Plymouth April 2, 1644.
3.   II.   Temperance, born in Marshfield May 5, 1646.
4.   III.  Elizabeth, born in Marshfield April 2, 1648.
5.   IV.   James, born in Marshfield April 28, 1650.
6.   V.    John, born in Marshfield, Feb. 20, 1651-2.
7.   VI.   Joseph, born in Yarmouth Feb. 16, 1653-4.
8.   VII.  Jabez, born in Barnstable Aug. 3, 1656.
9.   VIII. Mercey, born in Barnstable Jan. 20, 1658.
10.  IX.   Lydia, born in Barnstable Nov. 16, 1661.
11.  X.    Hannah, born in Barnstable Nov. 28, 1663.
12.  XI.   Shubael, born in Barnstable Oct. 21, 1667.

2.  Desire Gorham daughter of Capt. John Gorham, * married Oct. 7, 1661, Capt. John Hawes of Yarmouth. He was a son of Mr. Edmond Hawes, called a cutler, who came from London in 1635. She resided in Yarmouth, and died in that town June 30, 1700, aged 56 years. She has a numerous posterity. All of the name of Hawes in this County are her descendants.

3.  Temperance Gorham married for her first husband Edward Sturgis of Yarmouth, by whom she had Joseph, Samuel, James, Desire and Edward. He died Dec. 8, 1678, and she married Jan. 16, 1679-10, Mr. Thomas Baxter, by whom she had John, Thomas and Shubael. Edward Sturgis resided near the first meeting-house in Yarmouth. He left a large estate, which was divided among his children when they became of legal age. Mr. Thomas Baxter is called in the records "a bricklayer." He was a soldier in Capt. Gorham's company in the first expedition, where he lost the use of one of his hands by a wound. He resided after his marriage at South Sea, now West Yarmouth, and then recently settled. Unable to work at his trade, he devoted himself to study, and was much employed in public business. In partnership with his brother-in-law Shubael, and his sons, he built the fulling mill on the western Swan Pond river, and the grist mill known as Baxter's Mill, though some poetical genius of the day, gave the whole credit to his sons.

> "The Baxter boys, they built a mill,
> Sometimes it went, sometimes stood still;
> And when it went, it made no noise,
> Because 'twas built by Baxter's boys."

She died March 12, 1714-15, in the 67th year of her age. Her descendants are numerous, and among them a.e many men of literary and political distinction. All of the name of Baxter in this County are her descendants.

4.  Elizabeth Gorham married and had a family. At the settlement of her mother's estate in 1684 she was a widow.

5.  James Gorham, eldest son of Capt. John Gorham, was a farmer, and often employed in public business. In the division of his father's homestead, he had the north westerly and central portions, on which he built a large and elegant mansion house. It stood on the spot where Mr. Warren Marston's house now stands and was taken down about twenty years since. It appears by the schedule of the division of the common lands made in 1703, that he was then the richest man in the town of Barnstable. He married Hannah, daughter of Mr. Thomas Huckins, of Barnstable. He died in 1707, aged 57, and his widow 13th Feb. 1727, aged 74 years

---

*Freeman, page 273, says she married Samuel Hinckley. He is mistaken. The Barnstable and the Yarmouth records give the facts as I have stated them. Samuel Hinckley, the second of the name, married 14 Dec. 1664, Mary Goodspeed, she died 20 Dec. 1666, and he married 15 Jan. 1668-9, Mary Fitzrandolphe. He also says that Mercy Gorham "married 2d, Geo. Dennison." I find no authority for this statement. If Geo. Dennison was her second husband, her first marriage must have been consummated in very early life.

6.   Lieut. Col. John Gorham was brought up and worked at the trade of his father.   His tannery was a short distance southwesterly from Hallett's Grist Mill, then owned by the Gorhams. He was a man of wealth, ranking next to his brother James in the town of Barnstable.   He inherited the northeasterly portion of his father's homestead, with his father's dwelling-house thereon.   In 1686 it is represented as being the most easterly in the town of Barnstable.   It stood where Miss Abigail T. Gorham's house now stands, and was enlarged over a century ago.   He was a man of influence, much respected, and in the latter part of his life almost constantly employed in the public service.   He was with his father in King Philip's war.   June 5, 1690, he was appointed a captain in the unfortunate Canada expedition, and subsequently Lieut. Col. of the militia.   He was a man of sound judgment and of good business capacity.   He was much employed as conveyancer, in writing wills and in drawing up public documents.   He married Feb. 16, 1674, Mary, daughter of Mr. John Otis.   He died Dec. 9, 1716, in the 65th year of his age. His tomb is at the north-east corner of the Unitarian Meeting House in Barnstable.   It is covered with a slab of gray sand stone, and the inscription is now hardly legible.

7.   Ensign Joseph Gorham, son of Capt. John Gorham, was a shoe maker, and not much engaged in public business.   In the division of his father's estate he had the south-west forty acres of the old Hallett Farm.   It was bounded easterly by the land of his brother James, southerly by the commons, westerly by the land of Caleb Lumbard, and northerly by the highway.   This tract of land, with five acres of meadow at Stony Cove, he exchanged March 18, 1680-1, with Joseph Benjamin, of Yarmouth, for 19 1-2 acres of upland and six acres of meadow and appurtenances at Clark's Neck,* and removed to Yarmouth.   In 1683 he was exempted by the Colony Court from serving as a common soldier in the militia, because he had formerly served in the office of ensign at Barnstable.   He died July 9, 1726, aged 72, and was buried in the old burying ground in Yarmouth.

8.   Jabez Gorham, son of Capt. John Gorham, is the ancestor of the Gorham families in Rhode Island.   From an entry in Colony records, I infer that he went to Rhode Island when a lad, and was there in the time of King Philip's war.   May 5, 1677, the following record was made by the Plymouth Colony Court: "In reference unto the cure of Jabez Gorham who was wounded in the late wars, the Court doth apprehend, that in case it be not paid by some of Rhode Island concerned in it, that they judge the charge of said cure should be defrayed out of the general estate of Captaine John Gorham, deceased, both lands and moveables." After his recovery he returned to Yarmouth, and it appears

---

*Clark's Neck is in the  northerly part of Yarmouth, west of the Alms House.  It was successively called Gorham's, Matthews' and Hawes' neck.

probable that he resided with his mother, in the house which Capt.
Gorham bought when he first came to Yarmouth. His name appears on the list of the townsmen of Yarmouth 1679. In 1680
he was constable, was on the grand inquest of the Colony in
1683, and that year took the freeman's oath. His oldest child,
Hannah, was born in Yarmouth 23d Dec. 1677, and probably his
sons Samuel and Jabez were also born in that town. He was at
Plymouth at the settlement of his mother's estate in March,
1683-4. These disconnected facts show that he resided in Yarmouth till after the decease of his mother, and that soon after
that event he removed to Bristol, R. I. Mr. John Gorham, of
Providence, a descendant, has carefully collected a genealogy of
this branch of the family, which he intends to publish.

9. Lydia Gorham married Col. John Thacher of Yarmouth,
Jan. 1, 1683-4. (Freeman says Jan. 2, 1633-4—28 years before
her birth.) An amusing story is told respecting his courtship and
marriage. The first wife of Col. Thacher was Rebecca, daughter
of Josiah Winslow of Marshfield, and niece of Gov. Edward.
He was married Nov. 6, 1661, and some little time after his return to Yarmouth he and the bride called at Capt. Gorham's.
Lydia was then an infant only a few months old. Col. Thacher
taking the babe in his hands, presented it to his wife, and said in
a sportive manner, "allow me to introduce you to my second
wife." Mrs. Thacher took the babe and kissed it. July 15,
1683, Mrs. Rebecca Thacher, wife of Col. Thacher, died, and
"many lamentable verses" he wrote on the occasion. Before the
ink was dry with which he penned the elegies, he thought of Miss
Lydia who was then twenty-two and unmarried. Common decency required that he should wait three months before proposing
to marry her; but passing the house of the widow Gorham one
evening, he saw his son Peter's horse hitched at the door. Mis-
trusting that Miss Lydia was the object of his visit, Col. Thacher
on the morrow privately asked his son if he thought of marrying
Miss Lydia. The young man blushed, and frankly admitted that
to be the object of his visit. "Now," said the Colonel, "if you
will agree to discontinue your visits, I will give you my black
oxen." Peter accepted the oxen, and the Colonel married Miss
Lydia 5 months and 16 days after the death of his first wife,
whom he had so deeply lamented, and in most dolorous rhymes.
Mrs. Lydia Thacher survived her husband. She died Aug. 2,
1744, aged 82 years.

11. Hannah Gorham was living March 5, 1683-4; but I find
no subsequent information respecting her.

12. Shubael Gorham, youngest son of Capt. John Gorham,
was intended for one of the learned professions, but he fell short,
and instead of spending his minority at College, served an apprenticeship with a carpenter. After the death of his mother his
brother James was appointed his guardian. In 1696 he married

Puella Hussey, of Nantucket, and removed to South Sea. His house built that year, † near the landing at Hyannis Port, is a large two story building, kept by him as a tavern, and subsequently by Eleazer Scudder and Benjamin Haddaway. June 8, 1706, he entered into an agreement with his brother-in-law, Mr. Thomas Baxter, and his nephew, John Baxter, "whaler," to build a fulling-mill on the Western Swan Pond River, in Yarmouth, which they afterwards owned in partnership. The stream on which the mill is built is now called Parker's river, and the old dam is about a mile north of the bridge over that stream, on the County road through West Yarmouth. Nov. 7, 1710, John Baxter, "whaler," sold for £31, lawful money, to his "unkell Shubael Gorham of ye town of Barnstable, carpenter," his quarter part of said mill. ‡ He had previously, May 22, 1708, sold to his uncle Shubael for £21, in silver money, another quarter of the mill.

April 17, 1749, Shubael Gorham deeded to the town of Barnstable a road through his land from the old landing place, "beginning at the shore against a noted § great rock," thence northerly to the land of Mr. John Bearse, and the road leading to the School Lot. It passed on the west side of a swamp, or pond, and on the east side of land leased to his son-in-law, James Lovell, Jr.

Shubael Gorham did not possess the commanding talents, and energy of character, which distinguished his elder brothers; yet he was a man of good business capacity, honest, industrious and frugal. He died in 1750, in the 83d year of his age.

5. IV. James Gorham, son of Capt. John Gorham, born in Marshfield April 28, 1650, married Feb. 24, 1673-4, Hannah, daughter of Mr. Thomas Huckins, of Barnstable. He died in 1707, aged 57, and his widow Feb. 13, 1727-8, aged 74 years.

*Children born in Barnstable.*

13. I. Desire, 9th Feb. 1674-5.
14. II. James, 6th March, 1676-7.
15. III. Experience, 23d July, 1678.
16. IV. John, 2d Aug. 1680.
17. V. Mehetabel, 28th April, 1683.
18. VI. Thomas, 16th Dec. 1684.
19. VII. Mercy, 22d Nov. 1686, died June 12, 1689.
20. VIII. Joseph, 25th March, 1689.
21. IX. Jabez, 6th March, 1690-1.

---

† In 1696 leave was granted to "Mr. Shubael Gorham to cut and carry out of town's commons pine timber to build his house."—[Yarmouth Records.

---

‡ The contract for building the fulling-mill is in the handwriting of Col. John Thacher, and the deed from which the extract is made, is in the handwriting of Lient. Col. John Gorham. These papers have an historical interest, showing when, where, and by whom the first fulling mill was built in Yarmouth. They also show the relationship between the Gorhams and the Baxters, which otherwise it would be exceedingly difficult to trace.

---

§ This "Great Rock" was removed, and used in the construction of the Breakwater, and I would suggest to the town authorities that a monument be put up at the termination of the road on the shore.

22.  X.  Sylvanus, 13th Oct. 1693.

23.  XI.  Ebenezer, 14th Feb. 1695-6.

Mr. James Gorham in his will dated Nov. 4, 1707, proved Jan. 7, 1707-8 names his seven sons who were all then living, and his three daughters Desire Sturges, Experience Lothrop, and Mehetabel Gorham.

13.  Desire Gorham married one of the Sturgis family. I have not investigated her history.

14.  James Gorham resided in Barnstable.  He married Mary Joyce of Yarmouth, (See Chipman) and died Sept. 10, 1718, aged 41.  A widow Mary Gorham died in Barnstable, June 28, 1778, aged 92, according to the church records.  If Mary, widow of James, she was 98,—if Mary, widow of Col. Shubael, 90.

15.  Experience Gorham married 23d April, 1697, Thomas Lothrop, son of Capt. Joseph, and grandson of Rev. John.  She was the mother of fourteen children, and died in Barnstable Dec. 23, 1733.

16.  John Gorham married Ann Brown, 24th Feb. 1705-6. He resided at West Yarmouth, where he died in 1729, aged 49 years.

17.  Mehetabel Gorham, "daughter of James Gorham, deceased," was admitted to the Barnstable Church Jan. 15, 1714-5. She married May 12, 1715, John Oldham, and was dismissed to the Church at Scituate.

18.  Thomas Gorham was a blacksmith and resided in Barnstable.  In early times there was a blacksmith's shop on the west side of Marston's Lane, nearly opposite his father's house. There was also an ancient house on the old road near the present railroad crossing.  As both were on the land of his father, the presumption is that these were the house and shop of Thomas Gorham.  He died insolvent in 1771, at the advanced age of 87.

20.  Joseph Gorham, the records inform us, was "non compos mentis" during a considerable portion of his life.  From the facts stated I should infer that he was temporarily insane, not a person of weak mind.  His brother Ebenezer was his guardian for 27 years previous to 1760.  In 1747 he made a will giving all his property, including his share in his brother Sylvanus' estate, to his brother Ebenezer.  He died in 1762, and this will was presented for probate Jan. 4, 1763, and was objected to by Seth Lothrop and the other heirs-at-law.  The will was finally established in the Supreme Court to which it was removed by appeal, and Ebenezer inherited his estate.

21  Jabez Gorham, it appears, lived unmarried till 58, and Nov. 15, 1749, married Mary Burbank of Plymouth.  I do not find that he had any children.

22.  Sylvanus Gorham died before 1747, leaving no issue. His estate was divided among his brothers and sisters.

23. Ebenezer Gorham, the youngest son of James, resided when a young man at Scituate. Nov. 1, 1725, he was dismissed from the south church in that town, to the east church in Barnstable. Sept. 22, 1727, he married Temperance Hawes, daughter of Dea. Joseph of Yarmouth. He was a farmer, and his house stood where Sylvanus Gorham's now stands. It was a large, two story building, very ancient and may have been Joseph Hallett's, who had a house very early on the same land. She died Feb. 21, 1767, in the 62d year of her age. He died Nov. 16, 1776, in the 83d year of his age. Both have monuments in the old graveyard near the Unitarian Meeting House.

James Gorham was the richest man in Barnstable. His children inherited that wealth; but they did not inherit the art of keeping it. Excepting Ebenezer, who appears to have been brought up under different influences, they all died poor, some of them insolvent. The poor boy who saves his little earnings forms a habit of frugality, which he carries with him through life; the child of the wealthy does not feel the necessity of saving, and he spends the little sums which his friends give him in toys, or in vain amusements, and thus forms a habit which in its ultimate, leads to poverty. In a free country, where the institution of slavery is not tolerated, and where the estates of deceased intestate persons are divided equally to all the children, these causes are in constant operation, changing the relative position of families every two or three generations. I have had in these articles, frequent occasion to say that "the wealth of the parent was a curse to his posterity." Physiological reasons afford a sufficient explanation. The boy who is brought up in ease and affluence, whose every want is provided for, when he becomes a man is often lacking in energy of character,—he has not been taught to be self-reliant, the great secret of success in life, in consequence, the son of his poor neighbor, who has been taught to be frugal and industrious, and above all, to believe that he must rely on himself, outstrips the other in the race of life, and in old age, they find that their relative positions in society have been reversed. This is generally, not universally true; for some wealthy parents teach their children to be frugal, industrious and self-reliant, and they thereby escape the perils to which they would otherwise be exposed. Such boys make distinguished men—they start from a higher stand-point—have the advantage of a good education—and of friends who are able to assist them.

Lieut. Col. John Gorham, the brother of James, was his neighbor. As has been stated, he ranked next to his brother in point of wealth, both had large families, and both had the same facilities to educate their children; but no two families in Barnstable were more unlike. John was a mechanic and a military man, he had traveled more and had seen more of the world than James. The old school philosophers tell us the difference is to be attributed to innate ideas in his mind, and modern phrenologists say the same in a different form, that is, that the character depends entirely on the size and form of the brain.   Locke, in his essay on the human understanding, demonstrates that there are no innate ideas in the mind, and his followers usually maintain that,

"'Tis education forms the common mind,
Just as the twig is bent, the tree's inclined."

This couplet inculcates a sound philosophy, because in comparing the human mind to the vegetable growth, it admits innate differences, and that education does not eradiate or destroy them, only modifies them.   Franklin, in one of his poetical essays, compares the infant mind to white paper, on which you may write any character you may desire, but in this case the paper may be of different qualities, and though the same things be written, the results will be widely different.   It is also a common saying, that "he that is born to be drowned, will never be hung."   The doctrine here inculcated, savors too strongly of the fatalism taught by Mahomet, and of the predestination creed of some of the most ultra advocates of election and reprobation, to be generally assented to.   It is also said "that the poet is born, not made." This remark, if applied to Shakespeare and Burns, would require some modification; and would perhaps have to be reversed if applied to Pope or Bryant.

However men may differ on these points, the science of genealogy teaches these truths, that home influences affect the character of the child more than all that is taught by the church or in the schools; and that as a person advances in age, he becomes less and less qualified to have the management of children. It is a notorious fact that the grandmother always spoils her pet child, and that children brought up by maiden aunts, rarely prosper in life.

Mr. Deane, in his history of Scituate, justly remarks, that "nature is wonderfully impartial in the distribution of intellectual talents; and it seems to be the fixed order of Providence, that families, in this respect, should flourish and decline; nay, often, that an individual, should spring forth into eminence, whose origin was as obscure as that of the spark which, by the collision of steel and adamant, is struck out of darkness."

6.   Lieut. Col. John Gorham married Feb. 24,   1674-5, Mercy, daughter of Mr. John Otis.

*Children born in Barnstable.*

24.   I.   John, 18th Jan. 1675-6, died April 1, 1679.
25.   II. Temperance, 2d Aug. 1678.
26.   III.   Mary, 18th Sept. 1680.
27.   IV.   Stephen, 23d June, 1683.
28.   V.   Shubael, 2d Sept. 1686.

29.  VI.  John, 28th Sept. 1688.  Some of these dates are not correct.

30.  VII.  Thankful, 15th Feb. 1690-1.

31.  VIII.  Job, 30th Aug. 1692.

32.  IX.  Mercy, Dec. 1695.

Lieut. Col. Gorham died Dec. 9, 1716, if I rightly decypher the inscription on his tomb.  His will is dated Nov. 18, 1716, and was proved on the 7th of January following.  To John he gave the farm he bought of James Hamblin; to Shubael, lands at Stony Cove, and land where his house then stood, to Stephen lands adjoining Shubael's, and to Job the home farm.  His wife and sons Stephen and Shubael executors.  His personal estate was apprized at £322, and his real estate at £2000 lawful money.

His widow died April 1, 1733, and in her will, dated Nov. 7, 1727, proved April 20, 1733, she names her sons Stephen, John Job and Shubael, and her daughters Temperance Clap, Mary Hinckley, Thankful Fuller, and Mercy Bourne, and John, son of her son John.

During the French and Indian wars, from 1689 to 1704, five expeditions were fitted out to operate against the enemy in the eastern country, under the command of the renowned Col. Benjamin Church.  Connected with these expeditions, there was a "whale-boat fleet," manned by whalemen, sailors and friendly Indians.  In most, if not all these expeditions, the "whale-boat fleet" was under the direction and command of Mr. John Gorham, who, in the fourth and fifth expeditions, was commissioned a Lieut. Col., was second in command, and in case of accident was named as Col. Church's successor.  Without this fleet, all the expeditions would have proved abortive.  The French and Indians, excepting at a few prominent points, had established their headquarters at places where the transports could not approach sufficiently near to be of service, and to have marched the troops to the attack through the wilderness, would have exposed them to almost certain destruction.

Col. Church in his letter to Governor Dudley, dated Feb. 5, 1703-4, advises the Governor to provide for the expedition, "Four and forty or fifty good whaleboats, well fitted with five good oars and twelve or fifteen good paddles to every boat.  And upon the wale of each boat, five pieces of strong leather be fastened on each side to slip five small ash bars through: that so, whenever they land the men may step overboard, and slip in said bars across, and take up said boat that she may not be hurt against the rocks."

In such a fleet four or five hundred men could be transported up the shallow bays and rivers, with their guns and ammunition, and provision, for several days consumption.  At night, or in stormy weather, the boats were taken on shore, turned over, and served as tents for the soldiers.  In each boat two brass kettles, and other conveniences for cooking and rendering the men comfortable, were carried.

Lieut. Col. Gorham ranked as a Captain in the Canada Expedition under Major Walley, in 1690. In that expedition he had the command of the "whaleboat fleet" without which it would have proved still more disastrous. In the second and third expeditions of Col. Church he is not named in the authorities I have consulted; yet from an expression in one of his letters I infer that he was. In the fourth and fifth he was second in command, and performed most efficient and valuable services for his country. Col. Gorham's biography would be a work of brilliant interest; but I have not space to devote to the details.

The details of these expeditions are exceedingly interesting. Many men from the Cape were engaged in them. In the winter of 1703-4 Col. Church visited every town in the County, and enlisted a large number for his fifth expedition. Many of the officers were Cape men. In 1689 Col. William Bassett of Sandwich, and Nathaniel Hall, son of John, of Barnstable, served as Captains in the eastern country. In 1690 Major John Walley, son of Mr. Walley of Barnstable, was commander of the Canada expedition. Sept. 9, 1697, the gallant Capt. Thomas Dimmock of Barnstable, was slain at the head of his company, in a severe engagement with the French and Indians; and in the last expedition Caleb Williamson, of Barnstable, was Captain of the Plymouth forces. Other Barnstable men bore less conspicuous; but not less honorable parts in these contests. For years after these old sailors and soldiers, seated in their round-about-chairs, within their capacious chimney-corners, would relate to the young the story of their adventures in the "Old French Wars," and some of their descendants yet preserve them in remembrance.

25. Temperance Gorham married Dec. 24, 1696, Dea. Stephen Clap, of Scituate. a nephew of Eleazer of Barnstable.

Thomas, son of Dea. Stephen and Temperance, born in 1703, graduated at Harvard College 1722, was one of the distinguished men of his time. He was ordained at Windham, Conn., 1726. President of Yale College from 1740 to 1764, when he resigned and died on the following year while on a visit to Scituate. President Stiles, his successor, says, "he studied the higher branches of Mathematics, was one of the first philosophers America has produced, and equalled by no man, excepting the most learned Professor Winthrop." President Clap was also the most powerful opponent that Whitefield found in New England. (See Dean's Scituate, page 235.)

26. Mary Gorham married Sept. 21, 1699, Joseph Hinckley, of West Barnstable, and had ten children. Her youngest son Isaac was a distinguished man and an ardent patriot during the Revolution. He died Dec. 1802, aged 83. Joseph Hinckley inherited the mansion-house of his ancestor Samuel, which is yet

standing, though it is not probable that much of the original structure now remains.

27.  Stephen Gorham, born June 23, 1683, was a man of some note; but I am unable to trace his history.  He married Dec. 25, 1703, Elizabeth Gardner, of Nantucket.  Her mother was Mary Starbuck, the first white child born on Nantucket.  He had twelve children, all born in Barnstable, but the record of their children born previous to 1715 I do not find.  He removed to Nantucket, and perhaps resided some time in Charlestown.  His son Nathaniel's family, of Charlestown, was one of the most distinguished in the State.

28.  Col. Shubael Gorham was a man of enterprise—a man who persevered in whatever he undertook, till he failed or succeeded.  His name frequently occurs on the parish, town and state records, showing that he was a man that was esteemed by those who knew him.  The great act of his life, that for which he will ever be remembered, is the active and efficient part which he took in obtaining the grants made by the legislature of Massachusetts, to the officers and soldiers of the Narraganset or King Phillip's War, or to their lawful representatives.

The earliest grant made to the Narraganset soldiers is dated May 27, 1685, of a township eight miles square in the Nipmay country.  This grant was made to persons resident in Lynn, Reading, Beverly and Hingham.  This, Mr. Pierce, * the historian of Gorham, thinks was never located.

Dec. 14, 1727, two tracts of land six miles square were granted, and April 26, 1733, this grant was enlarged, giving a township equal to six miles square to each 120 persons whose claims should be established within four months.  It was found that the whole number was 840.  Seven townships were granted in the province of Maine called Narraganset No. 1, 2, 3, 4, 5, 6 and 7.  The latter was assigned to the officers and soldiers who served with Capt. John Gorham, and a few others, and was afterwards incorporated as the town of "Gorham," but was generally known as "Gorhamtown."

By an order "In Council," dated Feb. 2, 1736, Shubael Gorham, Esq., was empowered to assemble the grantees of the township.  In this order a curious mistake occurs.  It is stated that the grant was made "to the soldiers under the command of Capt. John Gorham, in the Canada expedition in 1690."  Capt. John Gorham of the Canada expedition was the father of Col. Shubael; the grant was made to the officers and soldiers who served under his grandfather in the Narraganset war.  By an order dated July 5, 1736, this mistake was corrected.  Col. Gorham was the chairman of the committee for Narraganset No. 7, and the effici-

---

*I am much indebted to Josiah Pierce, Esq., for much valuable information respecting the emigrants from Barnstable to Gorham.  I regret that I did not send him copies of papers in my possession, that would have been useful to him.

ent man in promoting in its settlement, and Capt. John Phinney, of Barnstable, was the father of the colonists.

Col. Gorham spent much time and money in promoting the settlement of Gorhamtown. He bought the shares of many who did not desire to emigrate, and his speculations in wild lands proved unfortunate. Buying such lands, is like buying lottery tickets, a few get prizes. Col. Gorham was not one of the lucky ones. He died insolvent in 1746, his own children being his principal creditors. *

29. John Gorham, Esq., 3d of the name, was an active, intelligent man. His father bought for him the estate of James Hamblin, on the east of Coggin's Pond, and adjoining to the estate of Gov. Hinckley, on which he built a large and elegant mansion house, which was taken down about forty years since. He was a merchant and was engaged in the cod and whale fisheries, in the coasting trade, and in the West Indian trade. He built the wharf at Calves Pasture point, known as Gorham's wharf, and now owned by N. & D. Scudder. This is one of the most eligible places for business in Barnstable, and for many years was the center of trade. During nearly half a century he was the most active and successful business man in Barnstable, and to give details would be to write the commercial history of the town during that period.

He married Oct. 21, 1712, Prudence, daughter of Joseph Crocker, of West Barnstable, and had fourteen children. He died in 1770, aged 82, and his widow in 1778, aged 86.

30. Thankful Gorham married June 16, 1710, Lieut. John Fuller, a son of Dr. John, and a grandson of Capt. Matthew. She resided on Scorton Neck.

31. Job Gorham inherited the dwelling-house built by his grandfather, and the lands in the immediate vicinity, and the same are yet owned by his descendants. Job Gorham about the year 1745, took down the old mansion and built the one now standing on the same spot. A part of the materials of the old house were used in the construction of the present. He married Dec. 4, 1719, Desire Dimmock, and second, Widow Bethia Freeman, of Fairfield, Conn. He died in 1762.

32. Mercy Gorham, the youngest daughter, was a woman of rare accomplishments. She married Hon. Sylvanus Bourne, and a notice of her has already been published. (See Bourne.)

7-6. Joseph Gorham, only son of Capt. John, recorded as born in Yarmouth, married Sarah ———— in 1678. His children are all recorded as born in Yarmouth; but as he resided in Barnstable till 1681, it is probable that his oldest child was born in

---

*Shubael Gorham was Col. of the 7th Mass. Regiment in the Louisburg Expedition; commission dated Feb. 2, 1744. He was also Captain of the First company. John Gorham Lieut. Col. and Captain of the Second company; com. dated Feb. 20, 1744.   S.

that town.

*Children.*

33.  I.    Sarah, 16th Jan. 1678-9.
34.  II.   Joseph, 15th April, 1681.
35.  III.  Samuel, Oct. 1682.
36.  IV.   John, 28th Feb. 1683-4.
37.  V.    Desire, April 1685.
38.  VI.   Isaac, Oct. 1687.
39.  VII.  Hezekiah, Aug. 1689.
40.  VIII. Josiah, 7th Sept. 1692.

Joseph Gorham, in his will dated July 27, 1723, proved 20th July, 1726, names his wife Sarah, sons Joseph and Josiah, daughter Desire Baxter, grand-daughter Sarah Sears, daughter of my daughter Sarah Howes, deceased ; also grand-children Thomas, Eben, and Elizabeth Howes.

The Widow Sarah Gorham, in her will dated 1st May, 1728, proved 3d Feb. 1738-9, names sons Joseph and Josiah, daughter Desire Baxter, and grand-children Rebecca, (Josiah's daughter by his first wife) Thomas and Eben. Howes, Sarah Sears and Elizabeth Crosby.

His sons Samuel, John, Isaac and Hezekiah, died young, leaving no issue.   Isaac and Hezekiah in 1714, and their father administered on their estates.

33.  Sarah Gorham married April 24, 1699, Eben. Howes, son of Jeremiah, and grandson of Thomas, by whom she had Thomas and Sarah, twins, Jan. 22, 1699-10, Elizabeth Sept. 28, 1701, a son July 5, 1704, died in infancy, and Ebenezer Sept. 8, 1705, and the mother died the day following.

34.  Respecting Joseph Gorham, the younger, I have little information.   He married Sarah ————, and had children Mary and George in Yarmouth.

40.  Josiah Gorham had three wives : 1st, Sarah ————, whom he probably married in Rhode Island ; 2, Priscilla Sears, March 11, 1721-2, and 3, Mary ————.   He died April 3, 1775, aged 82 years.

8-7.  Jabez Gorham married twice : 1st, Hannah ————, the mother of his ten children.   Hannah and Samuel, and perhaps Jabez, were born in Yarmouth, the others in Bristol, R. I. He was 88 years of age when he married his second wife Mary Maxwell, if the date of the marriage which I have is reliable. Its accuracy may well be doubted.   Respecting the descendants of Jabez, and they are a host, I do not propose to inquire.   His children were :

41.  I.    Hannah, 23d Dec. 1677, drowned in a tub of water 1682.
42.  II.   Samuel, 1682, died 1735.
43.  III.  Jabez, 1684, died 1734.

44.  IV.   Shubael, 1686, died 1734, no issue.
45.  V.   Isaac, 1689.
46.  VI.   John, 1690, died 1717, no issue.
47.  VII.   Joseph, 1692, died without issue.
48.  VIII.   Hannah, 1694.
49.  IX.   Benjamin, 1695.
50.  X.   Thomas, 1701.

12-11.   Shubael Gorham, youngest son of Capt. John Gorham, married in 1696, Puella, daughter of Stephen Hussey, of Nantucket.

*Children born in Barnstable.*

51.  I.   George, 29th Jan. 1696-7.
52.  II.   Abigail, 31st March, 1699.
53.  III.   Lydia, 14th May, 1701.
54.  IV.   Hannah, 28th July, 1703.
55.  V.   Theodale, 18th July, 1705.
56.  VI.   Daniel, 24th Sept. 1708.
57.  VII.   Desire, 26th Sept. 1710.
58.  VIII.   Ruth, 7th May, 1713.
59.  IX.   Deborah.

Shubael Gorham in his will dated 23d Sept. 1748, proved Aug. 7, 1750, says he is "advanced in years," and gives all his real estate to his son George and allows him to retain whatever he owes him or his wife.  He gives his personal estate to his seven daughters, to be equally divided to them.  His personal estate was apprized at £99,10 8; his real at £266,13 4.

51.   Respecting George Gorham I find nothing on the records.

52.   Abigail Gorham married Oct. 25, 1716, James Lovell, Jr.  She resided at Hyannis Port, and died June 28, 1778, aged 79 years.

53.   Lydia Gorham married Sept. 8, 1720, Joseph Worth, of Nantucket. *   The records say they were then both of Nantucket. They had eight sons and four daughters, who lived and married. They have many descendants at Nantucket, in New York, Indiana, and other states.  She died March 1, 1763, aged 62 years. Her son Daniel, with six in his family, removed to North Carolina in 1771.

54.   Hannah Gorham married Oct. 24, 1726, William Manning, and Dec. 21, 1732, Wm. Stubbs, of Nantucket.  She died 16th 8 no., 1751, at Nantucket.

55.   Theodate married 2d Nov. 1729, Francis Coffin, and second, Reuben Gardner.  She died 6th April, 1787, aged 81 years, leaving numerous descendants.

56.   Daniel Gorham belonged to the society of friends, and

---

*I am indebted to William C. Folger, Esq., for information respecting the Gorhams who removed to Nantucket.

in 1734 his tax for the support of the ministry in the East Parish was remitted for that reason.   He was a mariner and died in 1745 of the small-pox in London.   His will is dated Jan. 24, 1740, and was proved Jan. 19, 1746.   He appoints his "affianced brother" James Lovell, Jr., executor, and divides his estate into eleven shares, giving his brother George, 1, his sister Abigail, 1, Lydia 2, Hannah 1, Theodate 1, Desire 3, Ruth 1, and Deborah 1.   He owned four rights in Gorham-town.   Amount of estate £2,960,16,1, old tenor.

ERRATUM.—In last No. John Hale should be John Hall.

57.   Desire Gorham married   Sept. 2, 1728, Zachariah Gardner, (or Bunker) of Nantucket, and had seven sons and two daughters.   She died at Nantucket 5th 11 month, 1801, aged 91 years.

58.   Ruth Gorham married Jan. 12, 1731-2, by Shubael Baxter, Esq., to Dr. Cornelius Bennet from Middleboro'.   Her son Cornelius was born in Barnstable Sept. 30, 1732.   Her other children were Theodate who married ———— Miller ; Christina, who married Samuel Russell ; William ; Thomas ; and perhaps others.

59.   Deborah Gorham married Dec. 11, 1735, Beriah Fitch of Nantucket, and had four sons and five daughters.   Their son Jonathan Gorham Fitch, born Sept. 13, 1740, is said to have been the first child on Nantucket having a double, or two christian names.   Beriah and Jonathan were worthy men.   Some of their descendants reside in Baltimore.

As nearly all the daughters of Shubael Gorham married at Nantucket, it is probable that during some portion of his life he resided there.   However, his wife had many relatives at Nantucket and his daughters probably visited there, and as he kept the public house where travellers from that island stopped, he perhaps did not remove from Hyannis Port.

Third Generation.

It would require a volume to give as many particulars, as I have thus far, relative to each member of the succeeding generations of the Gorhams, and I am therefore under the necessity of condensing my materials into the smallest space, and give little beside names and dates.

14-2.   James Gorham, Jr., son of James, married Sept. 29, 1707, Mary, daughter of Heosea Joyce, of Yarmouth.   He died Sept. 10, 1718, aged 41.   His widow survived him.   A widow Mary Gorham died in Barnstable June 28, 1778.

*Children born in Barnstable.*

60.   I.   Thankful, 25th May, 1711.
61.   II.   Isaac, baptized April 17, 1715.
62.   III.   Hezekiah, baptized April 17, 1715.
63.   IV.   James, baptized May 12, 1717.

64. V. Mary, baptized July 19, 1719.

The will of James Gorham, Jr., is dated Sept. 10, 1717, proved Nov. 5, 1718. He names his wife Mary and sons Isaac, Hezekiah and James, and daughter Thankful. His daughter Mary was born after his death, therefore not named. He describes land in the Common Field, bounded by the land of his uncle Shubael. Executors, his wife Mary, her brother Thomas Joyce, and Joseph Davis. All the land on the north of the road, in the north-easterly part of the town, was then called the "Common Field." His uncle Shubael's house is yet standing, and was owned by the late Job C. Davis. James Gorham, Jr.'s land, I presume, was on the west.

60. Thankful Gorham married May 16, 1701, Thomas Hawes, of Yarmouth. She had four children and died in that town.

61. Capt. Isaac Gorham married Jan. 24, 1738, Hannah Hallett, of Yarmouth. She died Aug. 19, 1741, aged 24, and he married Sept. 2, 1742, Mary Cobb, daughter of Gershom. He died in Scotland Jan. 1753, and his widow married James Church-ill Feb. 3, 1756-7. His children by his first wife were Mary, who married Feb. 8, 1759, Elisha Hedge of Yarmouth, and Thankful who married John Hall of Yarmouth. By his second wife he had 1, Edward, baptized Sept. 11, 1743, who probably died young, not being named in his father's will; 2, James, baptized Aug. 4, 1745, married Widow Mary Baker, had no issue; 3, Sarah, baptized June 19, 1748, and 4, Hannah, baptized June 17, 1750. He was also the reputed father of Isaac Gorham, son of Remember Backhouse, born Aug. 19, 1746.

62. Capt. Hezekiah Gorham, twin brother of Isaac, was a sea captain. He married Widow Anna Davis May 12, 1746. In her will dated March 2, 1702, she names her sons James and Jonathan and her son Josiah Davis of Gorham, in the County of Cumberland, daughters Anna, wife of Sylvanus Gorham, and Susan, wife of Gorham Easterbrooks. Also her dwelling-house and her part of the Grist Mill, which as before mentioned origi-nally belonged to the Gorhams. I infer from her will that she was the widow of John Davis, Jr., whom she married March 25, 1736, and had Josiah, John and Martha, baptized in the East Church April 25, 1742. She was a daughter of Mr. James Allen, and was connected by marriage with some of the most influential and respectable families in the Colony. Capt. Hezekiah Gorham died Oct. 2, 1778, aged "about 60 years." His children born in Barnstable, 1, James, baptized Feb. 22, 1746-7; 2, Anna, July 17, 1748; 3, Lemuel, May 5, 1751, died young; 4, Jonathan, Feb. 4, 1753; 5, Susan, April 21, 1754; and Isaac April 13, 1760.

James of this family married Rachel Easterbrooks; Anna married Sylvanus Gorham and had a large family; Susan married

Gorham Easterbrooks July 18, 1782 ; and Isaac died at sea, leaving no issue. Jonathan married Mary Davis. He resided at first on the Mill Road, in the house now owned by the heirs of Ezekiel Hall, afterwards in a house in the fields, on the south of the County road. He was a soldier in the Revolutionary army, and after his death his family removed to Nantucket. The children of Jonathan Gorham were, 1, Susan, born Sept. 1786 ; 2, Davis, 12th Sept. 1790 ; 3 and 4, Polly and Josiah, twins, Jan. 1793 ; 5, Edward, 24th Aug. 1795 ; and 6, Isaiah, 1802. The children of this family married at Nantucket, excepting the youngest, who died unmarried. Josiah was a wealthy manufacturer of oil at Edgartown, and now resides at N. Jonathan has many descendants at N. and in California.

63.   James Gorham, son of James Gorham, Jr., baptized May 12, 1717, was a mariner, died in 1742, leaving no issue. He was published Nov. 11, 1738, to Mary Hallett, Jr., of Yarmouth ; but I find no record of his marriage. In his will dated 19th March, 1738-9, he gives all his estate, apprized at £145,14 6, to his brother Hezekiah.

64.   Mary Gorham was a singular woman. She was known as Mrs. "Slicker," and her children were called "Slickers." She was plausible in her address, and polite in her manners. Nothing seemed to vex her. She had a ready excuse for all her delinquincies, and like some lawyers, had the peculiar faculty of making the worst appear as the better reason. She was no advocate for celibacy, and held that it was no breach of etiquette for ladies to make proposals for marriage. She married Jan. 25, 1738-9, Thomas Hedge of Yarmouth, of just her own age, 19. He was only son of Thomas, a son of Elisha, and grandson of Capt. William Hedge, one of the first settlers in Y. Her children were : 1, Mary, born 1740, died young ; 2, Thomas, 1742, died young ; 3, Hannah, 1743, married Barnabas Hedge, of Plymouth ; 4, Mary, 1743, married Joshua Gray ; 5, Sarah, 1748, married Edward Hallett ; 6, Thankful, 1751, married William Thacher ; 7, Thomas, who has descendants ; and 8, James, 1758, drowned aged three years.

Mr. Thomas Hedge died June 9, 1764, aged 45, and his widow married Mr. Thomas Hallett, of Yarmouth. His fourth and her second marriage. He died April 10, 1772, aged 81 years, leaving no issue, and his widow married for her third husband Capt. Benjamin Lothrop, of Kingston. After the death of Capt. Lothrop she returned to Y., where she died June 3, 1795, aged 75 years.

16-4.   John Gorham, born Aug. 2, 1680, a son of James, married Feb. 14, 1705-6, Ann Brown. His children born in Yarmouth were :

65.   I.   Matthew, born 18th Dec. 1706.
66.   II.   Mercy, 20th Aug. 1708.

67.  III.  Desire, 20th Aug. 1710.
68.  IV.  Rose, 19th March, 1711-12.
69.  V.  Elizabeth, 27th June, 1714.
70.  VI.  Ann, 12th Jan. 1716-17.

His will is dated 20th July, 1729, proved Nov. 3 following, showing that he died that year.  He names his wife Ann, son Matthias, and daughters Mercy, wife of Ebenezer Crowell; Desire, who married Thomas Hallett, Aug. 19, 1750; Rose, who married Ephraim Crowell; Elizabeth, and Ann who married William Taylor Sept. 17, 1741.  Matthias, his only son, married Nov. 1, 1733, Mary Davis, and had born in Yarmouth, 1, Lydia, Jan. 13, 1734-5; 2, Elizabeth, Dec. 28, 1737; 3, Mehitabel, Jan. 26, 1739-40; 4, Ann, Jan. 1, 1741-2; 5, John, March 26, 1744; 6, Mary, May 16, 1746; and 7, Matthias, Dec. 17, 1743. John and Matthias married and have descendants.

18-6.  Thomas Gorham, born 16th Dec. 1684, a son of James, resided in Barnstable.  He was a blacksmith.  He married in 1707, Rachell Trott of Nantucket, and had:

71.  I.  Benjamin, 8th Sept. 1708.
72.  II.  Reuben, 10th Dec. 1709.
73.  III.  Priscilla, 18th Dec. 1711.
74.  IV.  Samuel, 18th Dec. 1713.
75.  V.  Peter, 19th Dec. 1715.
76.  VI.  Paul, 6th Jan. 1717-18.
77.  VII.  Abraham, 10th July 1720.
78.  VIII.  James, 23d June, 1723.
79.  IX.  Gershom, 22d June, 1725.
80.  X.  Abigail, 13th May, 1729.

In his will dated in 1758, and proved Dec. 3, 1771, he names his daughter Abigail Easterbrooks, to whom he gives half his lands and his dwelling-house, and to his son Benjamin the other half.  He also names his daughter Priscilla Folger.  His children did not realize anything from his estate for he died insolvent, paying his creditors 15 sh. 6d. in the £.

As he names in 1758 only Benjamin, Priscilla and Abigail, the presumption is that his other children were then dead.  Peter is named as a whaleman in 1733.

71.  Benjamin Gorham married Sarah Cobb of Yarmouth, Oct. 23, 1739, and had Samuel born Sept. 2, 1740.  No other children are named on the Barnstable records.  He was drowned in the Mill Pond in 1771.  There were five Benjamin Gorham's in Barnstable at the same time, and all residents in the East Parish, and of necessity had to be distinguished by nicknames, namely:

1.  Benjamin, son of Thomas, born Sept. 8, 1708, died 1771, was called "Moderate Ben."
2.  Benjamin, son of John, born June 18, 1715, died in 1784, was called "Old Fiddler."
3.  Benjamin, son of Shubael, born June 4, 1726, was called

Captain.   He removed early.

4.   Benjamin, son of Benjamin, born March 26, 1746, was called "Young Fiddler."

5.   Benjamin, son of David, born Feb. 23, 1747, was called "Turkey Foot."

73.   Priscilla Gorham married Eliphar Folger of Nantucket. She died 28th of the 5th mo., 1801, aged 90 years.

80.   Abigail Gorham married Aug. 23, 1749, Capt. John Easterbrooks.   She died July 2, 1802, aged 73.

23-11.   Ebenezer Gorham, born 14th Feb. 1695-6, was the youngest son of James Gorham.   He married Temperance Hawes of Yarmouth, Sept. 22, 1727.   She died Feb. 21, 1767, in the 62d year of her age ; he died Nov. 16, 1776, in the 83d year of his age.

*Children born in Barnstable.*

81.   I.   Ebenezer, 7th Aug. 1729, baptized Aug. 24, 1729.
82.   II.   Prince, 14th March, 1730-1, baptized May 21, 1721.
83.   III.   Hannah, 16th April, 1733, baptized April 8, 1733. (?)
84.   IV.   Mary, 16th June, 1735, baptized June 19, 1735.
85.   V.   Sarah, baptized May 22, 1737.
86.   VI.   Thankful, baptized April 22, 1739.
87.   VII.   Sarah, baptized April 19, 1741.
88.   VIII.   Temperance, baptized May 20, 1744.
89.   IX.   Sylvanus, baptized July 17, 1746.

The will of Ebenezer Gorham, of Barnstable, yeoman, is dated 16th May, 1772, and the codicil thereto 26th Dec. 1775, proved 6th Dec. 1776.   He says he is "advanced in years," names his grand-daughter Desire, eldest daughter of his daughter Hannah, deceased, his daughters Mary Davis, Thankful Davis, and Temperance Sturgis ; his sons Ebenezer, Prince and Sylvanus.   He says his "son Ebenezer has been missing some considerable time," speaks of the four sons of Lot Hall, deceased, for whom his son Ebenezer was guardian, and names his grand-daughter Hannah, only daughter of his daughter-in-law Hannah. In the codicil to his will, he says, "at the time of making my will it was uncertain whether my son Ebenezer was then living." He gave half of his house * to Sylvanus, and with the exception of legacies to his other children, all the rest of his estate to his sons Prince and Sylvanus.

81.   Ebenezer Gorham, son of Ebenezer, married, and was lost at sea about the year 1772.   He built the house in Barnstable

---

*Ebenezer Gorham's house stood near the location of Joseph Hallett's, and I have supposed they were the same; but on further investigation I have come to the conclusion that it was built by one of the Gorhams about the year 1686, at the time the Gorhams' made strenuous efforts to have the Court House located on their land.   The architecture was not ancient.   It had four rooms on the lower floor, and four chambers, and was built for a public house.   It had two chambers, the more ancient had only one in the center.   I am inclined to the opinion that it was built by James Gorham, Sen'r.

now owned by Mr. Ezekiel Thacher.   He married Dec. 21, 1752,
Mary Thacher ; in 1764, Hope Carver of Plymouth, and July 16,
1767, Hannah, widow of Lot Hall, of Yarmouth.   He was guardian to Daniel, † Lot, Urian and William Hall, minor children of
Lot Hall, deceased.   His widow Hannah administered on his estate in 1773, which was rendered insolvent.   Dividend 5 sh. 2d.
in the £.   It does not appear that he had more than one child,
Hannah, and that by his third wife.

82.   Capt. Prince Gorham was a sea captain, and in the latter part of his life was insane.   He built on the Gorham farm the
house now owned by the heirs of Ansel Hallett, deceased, standing on the County road near the lane to the mill.   He married
April 22, 1756, Abigail Gorham, who died Aug. 3, 1765, aged
aged 34 ; and second, Nov. 15, 1767, Desire Clap of Barnstable.
She died Aug. 20, 1813, aged 72 years.   His children were : 1,
Sarah, born June 27, 1762, married Nov. 15, 1778, Wm. H. Jackson, of Plymouth ; 2, Abigail, born May 15, 1669, married May
18, 1790, Isaac Davis, and second, Samuel Holmes of Plymouth.
After the death of her second husband she resided in Boston,
where she kept a store.   3, Prince, born Sept. 8, 1775, died, leaving no issue, at his sister Abigail's house in Boston ; 4, Eunice,
born Aug. 25, 1777, married a Capt. Shaw, of Providence, R. I.,
went on a voyage to Maderia with him, and on her return died at
her sister's house in Boston ; 5, Stephen, born July 28, 1779, was
lost at sea.   He left no family.

83.   Hannah Gorham married Thomas Gorham May 16,
1764, and had seven children.   She died April 5, 1765, aged 32.

84.   Mary Gorham married Dec. 22, 1757, Samuel Davis.

85.    Sarah Gorham, both daughters of this name died
young.

86.   Thankful Gorham married May 3, 1759, Josiah Davis,
son of John, Jr., and removed to Gorham, Me.

88.   Temperance Gorham married Feb. 7, 1765, Jonathan
Sturgis, a brother or Eben of Barnstable, and removed to Gorham.

---

† Daniel Hall married Oct. 31, 1776, Mehitabel, daughter of John Gorham, Esq.  He
was a lieut. with Capt. Magee, and was one of those who perished Dec. 27, 1778, and was
buried in Plymouth.

Lot removed to West Minister, in Vermont.  He married Mary Homer, of Boston, a
daughter of Benjamin, Jr., of Yarmouth.  He was an associate-justice of the Supreme
Court of Vermont.  His son Lot was a distinguished lawyer at Troy, N. Y., and his grandson Edward H. graduated at Harvard College in 1851.

Of Urian I have no information.  William is deserving of note for his eccentricities.
About the year 1798, he established himself in Boston as grocer and ship chandler.  He
did a large business, lived fast, and about 1806 failed for a large amount.  Afterwards he
entertained the visionary project of connecting Nobscusset Pond, by a ship canal with the
deep water of the Bay.  North Dennis was to be a city, and the rival of Boston in trade,
He planned the streets of the new city, and selected a site for the Custom House on the
northern declivity of Scargo Hill.  To obtain an appropriation for the purpose he for several years was a loby member of the Massachusetts Legislature, and continually harrased
the members to obtain a legislative report in favor of his project, and failing in his efforts,
he visited Washington several times, and it is hardly necessary to add that he was unsuc-
cessful.  He died in the Alms House, in Boston, in which city he had obtained a legal residence.

89. Sylvanus Gorham, born in 1746, was the youngest son of Ebenezer, who was the youngest son of James, son of John, the emigrant ancestor of this family. The children of Sylvanus are of the fifth generation, and three of them are now (1864) living, namely, Sylvanus, aged nearly 83, John, 75, and Hannah, wife of Nathaniel Gorham, 70. In my researches I have found no parallel case, and doubt whether there is another in New England.

Sylvanus Gorham owned a large real estate, and was a hard working farmer. He resided in the ancient house that was his father's, described in a note. He married in 1764, Anna Gorham. He died in 1805, aged 58, and his widow in 1811, aged 73. His children born in Barnstable, were: 1, Solomon, 29th Sept. 1769, died at sea, leaving a widow in Boston, no children; 2, Allyn, 19th May, 1771, married Nabby Baxter, he was connected with the Navy Yard, New Orleans, several years, died in New York, has a daughter living; 3, Ebenezer, 10th May, 1773; 4, Isaiah, 13th April, 1775; he and Eben. lost at sea—neither married; 5, Clarrisa, 12th May, 1777, married Isaiah Matthews Dec. 1, 1796; 6, Tempe, 29th March, 1779, married July 21, 1805, Samuel Gray; 7, Sylvanus, born 4th April, 1781, now living, married Lydia Hallett; 8, Betsey, 12th March, 1783, died 1800; 9, Sally, 17th March, 1785, married Josiah Lewis; 10, Isaac, 3d April, 1787, married, died away from home, his wife and child died nearly at the same time; 11, John, 28th March, 1789, now living, married Lydia Cobb April 12, 1804; 12, Ezekiel, 16th June, 1791, married during the last war, sailed from Hyannis with Chas. Easterbrooks, and was not afterwards heard from; and 13, Hannah, 26th Nov. 1793, now living.

(27-4). Stephen Gorham, born 23d June, 1683, son of John and grandson of Capt. John, married Dec. 25, 1703, Elizabeth Gardner, of Nantucket. She was a daughter of James Gardner, son of Richard, Sen'r. Her mother was Mary Starbuck, born March 30, 1663, being the first white child born on Nantucket.

Respecting Mr. Stephen Gorham, I have very little information. He owned a part of the old Gorham farm and probably resided thereon in the early part of his life. His twelve children were all born in Barnstable. The record of the births of his children born previous to 1715 I do not find, though the record is referred to in a subsequent volume. His wife died July 22, 1763. From Barnstable I think he removed to Nantucket, and from thence to Charlestown, Mass.; but am not entirely certain. Children:

90. I. Mary.
91. II. Susannah.
92. III. Sarah.
93. IV. Nathaniel, 1709.
94. V. Lydia.

95.  VI.   Barnabas, 20th March, 1715.
96.  VII.  Zaccheus, 20th April, 1717.
97.  VIII. Elizabeth, 6th July, 1718.
98.  IX.   Eunice, 20th March, 1720.
99.  X.    Stephen, 20th Feb. 1722.
100. XI.   Josiah, 2d June, 1723.
101. XII.  Lois, 5th Nov. 1727.

90.  Mary Gorham married Andrew Gardner of Nantucket, and had eleven children, nine of whom lived to be married.

91.  Susannah Gorham married 1st, Daniel Paddock, who was lost at sea in 1743; 2d, Jonathan Folger, his third wife. She died July 12, 1777.  When very aged she taught, at Nantucket, a school for young children.

92.  Sarah Gorham married Daniel Hussey of Nantucket, and had seven children.  He died in England 1st 6 mo. 1750. She died at N. 18 7 mo., 1748.

93.  Capt. Nathaniel Gorham, born in 1709, resided in Charlestown.  He died early, but his widow (Mary Soley) was living in Boston in 1796.  His children were: Nathaniel, born 27th May, 1738; John, Harvard College 1759, died early; Stephen, and probably others.  Nathaniel, the son, was a distinguished man.  He died June 11, 1796.  After being fitted for admission to the University, he went an apprentice to Mr. Nathaniel Coffin of New London, Conn.  He finally settled in Charlestown, and in 1763 married Rebecca, oldest daughter of Caleb Call, Esq.  He was a representative from Charlestown when the Revolutionary troubles began, and he took a decided stand among the Patriots and was forced effectually to seek an asylum in the town of Lunenburg, with his wife and seven small children, and stripped of all his property.  In 1778 he was representative from that town, a member of the Board of War, and was constantly employed in the most important trusts.  In 1785 he was chosen speaker of the House of Representatives, and a delegate to the Continental Congress, and in 1787 was a member of the Constitutional Convention.

His son, Hon. Benjamin Gorham, member of Congress, &c., &c., died Sept. 27, 1855, aged 80.

Stephen Gorham, son of the first Nathaniel, married Mary White.  His son John, born in Boston 24th Feb. 1783, Harvard College 1801, studied medicine with Dr. John Warren.  He continued his studies in London, Edinburg and Paris.  In 1809 he was appointed to the professorship of Chemistry in Harvard College, and in 1816 was Erving Professor.  He published a work on Chemistry in two volumes octavo.  He died 27th March. 1829, aged 46.  (For additional information respecting this branch of the family, see General Register 1853, 1854, and 1856.)

94.  Lydia Gorham was the first wife of William Swain, Jr., of Nantucket.  She died May 1765.

97.    Elizabeth Gorham married David Bunker of Nantucket, who was lost at sea in 1755.

98.    Eunice Gorham died 13th July, 1790, aged 70.

100.    Josiah Gorham lived at Nantucket several years, and was a captain in the whaling business.  In 1756 he was in a whaling sloop, and with five other vessels, was taken by the French and carried to France.  After his release he removed to Eastern, Washington Co., N. Y.  He owned a good farm in that town, and died in 1803, aged 90.  His wife Deborah was received 29th 7 mo. 1765, a member of the Friends Meeting at Nantucket, and renewed her connection 27th 8 mo. 1773.  He obtained the good will of the Indians resident in Washington County, and they did no injury to him or his family during the Revolution.  Several battles during that war was fought near his residence.

101.    Lois Gorham married Jonathan Macy of Nantucket.  She was a very worthy woman, and her descendants are numerous at Nantucket, in New York State, Virginia and California.  Josiah Macy of New York, is her grandson and has been a very active and enterprising sea captain and merchant.

(28-6.)    Col. Shubael Gorham, son of Lieut. Col. John, born Sept. 1686, married his cousin Mary, daughter of Col. John Thacher of Yarmouth.  He died in 1746, and his widow Mary was probably the Widow Mary Gorham who died June 28, 1778, aged 89.

*Children born in Barnstable.*

102.    I.    John, 12th Dec. 1709.
103.    II.    David, 6th April, 1712.
104.    III.    Mary, 7th Feb. 1714.
105.    IV.    William, 6th May, 1716.
106.    V.    Lydia, 28th June, 1718.
107.    VI.    Hannah, 22d May, 1720, died young.
108.    VII.    Hannah, 1st May, 1721.
109.    VIII.    Shubael, 27th June, 1723.
110.    IX.    Joseph, 29th May, 1725.
111.    X.    Benjamin, 5th June, 1726.

Col. Shubael Gorham had no estate to dispose of by his will.  At his death he was hopelessly insolvent.  James Lovell, Jr., was appointed Aug. 16, 1746, to administer on his estate.  The inventory is dated Dec. 11, 1746, and his personal estate is apprised in Old Tenor at                                                                                                    479,18,6
and his real estate at                                                                                     2,365

————————

2,844,18,6

He had 55 oz., 17 pwt., 12 grs. of plate, valued at £99,15s.  A part of this marked with the arms of the Gorham family, has been preserved by the descendants of his son John.  Members of his own family were his principal creditors.  He lost his property in his endeavors to secure to the officers and soldiers in King

Phillip's war, or their legal representatives, their just dues.  In
his strenuous efforts to do justice to others, he was unjust to himself, and involved himself, for the benefit of others, in liabilities
which he was unable to meet.

102.  Col. John Gorham, son of Shubael, was distinguished
as an officer in the colonial forces in the latter French wars.  He
was at the taking of Louisburg, and rendered similar services to
those which his grandfather had rendered in the previous wars.
He resided in Barnstable till the year 1742, when he removed to
Falmouth, now Portland, and was sometime a resident at Gorham.
In 1749 he resided in Boston.  He built the first mills in the town
of Gorham, was a large land holder ; but did not become a permanent resident.  After the close of the French war he visited,
Europe and he and his wife were presented at the Court of St.
James, and had an audience with the King, a distinction to which
few of the subjects of royalty attain.

He married March 9, 1731-2, Elizabeth, daughter of James
Allyn, one of the most accomplished ladies of her time.  They
had fifteen children ; but I have not a complete list of them.
Those born in Barnstable were: 1, Susannah, 21st Nov. 1732,
died March 1738 ; 2, Mary, 3d Dec. 1733, died 8th Jan. 1738 ;
3, Anna, 28th July, 1735, died 18th March, 1738 ; 4, John, 26th
Dec. 1736 ; 5, Christopher, 10th Jan. 1737-8 ; 6, Elizabeth, baptized 16th Dec. 1739 ; 7, Daniel, baptized March 1, 1740-1.  The
other children were born after the removal of the family in 1742,
to Falmouth : 8, Sea Deliverance, a daughter, was baptized at the
East Church July 22, 1744, and was christened by that name because she was born at sea.  Three of the other children were
Mary, Susannah and Solomon.

Elizabeth Gorham of this family married Daniel Rogers of
Kittery, Maine, and had four children.  Mary married Eben.
Parsons, a large ship owner and merchant of Boston, well known
to all our aged sea captains.  Christopher died at sea unmarried.

103.  Col. David Gorham resided on the old homestead in
Barnstable.  His dwelling-house, yet remaining, was afterwards
the dwelling-house of Dr. John Davis and of his son Job C.
Davis, Esq.  He was with his brother John at Cape Breton and
the taking of Louisburg, * and was engaged in other military services.  During the Revolution some parties unjustly charged him
with being a tory, because he would not advocate the extreme
measures of younger men.  He was many years Register of Probate, and kept the records very carefully.  He was much in public life, was active, energetic, and capable ; but was never a popular man.  In the latter part of his life he was intemperate, and
many of his old friends lost their confidence in him as a man of

---

* Blind Abner, whom the middle aged remember, was a slave of Col. David Gorham,
and was with his master in his eastern campaigns.

integrity and honor. They had reason to, for the civil law was his standard of morality. His intemperate habits was the cause of this change, and while we can honor him in youth and middle age, impartial justice requires that no veil be drawn over his short comings in after life.

Col. David Gorham married three wives, namely : Aug. 2, 1733, Abigail Sturgis, she died Feb. 11, 1775, aged 63 ; 2, to Elizabeth Stevens, of Truro, in 1775, and 3, to Hannah Davis June 17, 1783. She died at the house of Eben. Sturgis Oct. 3, 1812, aged 79 years, 3 months. Mr. Sturgis and Eben. Bacon, Esq., took care of her property and provided for her support during the latter part of her life. He died in 1789, aged 77. His children born in Barnstable, were : 1, David, Aug. 24, 1735, died young ; 2, Elizabeth, Aug. 22, 1737, died young ; 3, Edward, April 23, 1739, living in 1756, probably died soon after ; 4, Lydia, May 30, 1741, married Jan. 26, 1764, Capt. Edward Bacon, Jr. ; 5, William, July 12, 1743 † ; 6, Shubael, born Feb. 3, 1745, died 1748 ; 7, Benjamin, ‡ 23d Feb. 1747 ; 8, Abigail, March 5, 1749, married Oct. 12, 1775, Dr. Jeremiah Barker, of Falmouth, now Portland, § Maine. He married 2d, Temperance, widow of Hon. Wm. Gorham ; 9, Shubael, Feb. 18, 1751-2, died at sea, leaving no issue ; 10, Mary, May 21, 1754. The Rev. Dr. James Freeman, of Boston, paid attention to Mary ; but she declined his offer, and afterwards married, in 1778, William Prentiss. She died in Barnstable July 8, 1784, aged 25, leaving no issue.

104. Mary Gorham married Oct. 24, 1734, Mr. Stephen Clap, of Scituate.

---

† Hon. William Gorham, when young, wrote a splendid hand, and assisted his father in the office of Register of Probate. About the year 1770 he removed to Gorham, Maine, and was a prominent man during the Revolution. He was on the committees of safety, correspondence and vigilance, and most of their patriotic and spirited papers were written by him. He held many municipal offices, was president of the convention to consider the matter of the separation of Maine from Massachusetts; Judge of Probate 1782, and of the Court of Common Pleas 1787, and held both offices till his death in 1804. He married twice. 1st, Widow Temperance White of Scituate, in 1769, and 2d, Temperance Garret. He had a son Francis born in 1775, who died young, and his only daughter Fanny Tyler, died in 1698. (See Pierce's History of Gorham.)

---

‡ Benjamin Gorham, son of Col. David, was called "Turkey Foot," to distinguish him from the other Ben. Gorhams. After his marriage, Oct. 15, 1775, to Desire Thacher, his father built a house for him on Dimmock's Lane, which in a few years was removed to a lot on the Gorham farm. He removed to Gorham, Maine, was there in 1789; but January, 1791, had returned to Barnstable, and died not long after. He is called on the records a "spendthrift." He had no business capacity—a man of weak intellect, and his wife was a yet weaker vessel, though a member of the church, an honest woman and good neighbor. Their children are not on the town records, some were probably born in Maine. 1, Edward, baptized April 28, 1776, was a respectable man, married Widow Joana Polond [Webb] and had Fanny, Rhoda, Eliza, Mary and John, born in Boston; 2, William, baptized Jan. 25, 1778, a worthy man, married Charlotte Beals, resided in Portland, and had William, Charlotte, and Joseph B.; 3, Christopher, never married, died at sea, he and Polly and Shubael stammered, and were only one remove from idiocy; 4, Polly, died unmarried, had David 1809; 5, David, baptized April 1786, a respectable and worthy man, resided in Maine; 6, Shubael, baptized July 11, 1790, died single in 1840.

---

§ Dr. Barker practiced in Barnstable several years before removing to Portland, and must be included in the list of physicians of that town.

105.  William Gorham was a mariner—he was living in 1746.

106.  Lydia Gorham married July 27, 1737, Dr. James Hersey, an elder brother of the noted Dr. Abner, and died Nov. 9, 1740, aged 22.

107.  Hannah Gorham, first of the name, died in infancy, the second daughter of the same name, married July 24, 1748, Mr. Edward Crosby.

108.  Shubael Gorham, Jr., was a mariner, and died in 1748, aged 25 years, leaving no issue.

109.  Lieut. Joseph Gorham was of Annapolis in 1750.  He married Ann Spry, an English lady, and had children: Joseph William, Amherst, James Wolf, John, Benjamin, Mary, Anna, Lydia, and Abigail.

110.  Benjamin Gorham, youngest son of Col. Shubael Gorham, was a ship-master.  He married 1st, Nancy, daughter of Eben. Hinckley, and had, 1, James, who was a merchant in Cuba, and married Charlotte Kneeland; 2, Benjamin, a shipmaster, married 1st Nancy Kneeland, 2d, Frances Harrington; 3, Samuel, settled in New York, and his second wife was Ellen Rankin; 4, John, who died young; 5, Nancy, who married 1st, Anthony Glean, of Cuba; 2d, James Macomb, of Matamoras.  See Genealogical Register, 1859.

(29-6).  John Gorham, Esq., son of Lieut. Col. John, married Oct. 2, 1712, Prudence Crocker, daughter of Joseph, of Barnstable.

*Children born in Barnstable.*

111.  I.    Joseph, 26th Aug. 1713.
112.  II.   Benjamin, 18th June 1715.
113.  III.  Ann, 13th Jan. 1716-17.
114.  IV.   Deborah, 13th Nov. 1718.
115.  V.    John, 10th Nov. 1720, died young.
116.  VI.   Thankful, 10th Feb. 1721-2.
117.  VII.  Mary, 1st Jan. 1723-4.
118.  VIII. Nathaniel, 30th Sept. 1726.
119.  IX.   Experience, 23d June, 1728, died young.
120.  X.    Mercy, 5th July, 1729.
121.  XI.   Naomi, 16th June, 1731, died young.
122.  XII.  Abigail, 1st June, 1731.
123.  XIII. Prudence, 16th Aug. 1734.
124.  XIV.  Rachel, [no record.]

John Gorham, Esq., died in 1769, aged 82, and his widow in 1778, aged 86.  In his will dated Nov. 4, 1762, proved 19th Oct. 1769, he gave to his wife Prudence, in lieu of dower, one-half of his house, and one-half of his land between the road and Coggins' Pond, one-half his orchard, and also the use of so much of all his other buildings as she shall have occasion for.  Also 2 cows, 10 sheep, all his indoor moveables and provisions, his negro girl Peg, half the services of his negro Cesar, and the use of one-third of all his other real estate. To his son Benjamin his silver hilted sword, and to his son Nathaniel the remainder of his armory, and his house and homestead, reserving to his wife the improvement as above stated. To his sons Benjamin and Nathaniel, to be divided equally, all the rest of his real estate, they paying his just debts and legacies. To Nathaniel his negro man Cesar, reserving as aforesaid, and his husbandry tools. To his four daughters, Thankful, Mary, Abigail, and Rachell, £3 apiece in addition to what he had already given them. To his daughter Prudence £33,6,8. and a right in the house so long as she remains single. He names his grand-daughter Thankful Annable, and grandson John Gorham, to whom he gives 3 shs., and all his wearing apparel, to his grandson Daniel 30 shs., and to his grandson Joseph £6 at 21, and to each of the daughters of his son Joseph, deceased, 30 shs. To his son Benjamin he gives all his live stock, my negro girl Peg, and his moneys, debts, &c., to pay his debts, legacies, funeral charges, &c., and if not sufficient, Nathaniel to pay half of the deficiency, and if there should be a surplus, Nathaniel to have half thereof. He appoints his son Benjamin executor. Witnesses, David Phinney, Thomas and James Allyn.

To his will there are three codicils annexed. In the first, dated Oct. 21, 1765, he states that his daughter Abigail having died since the execution of his will, he gives to his grand-daughter Sarah Gorham, daughter of his daughter Abigail, deceased, £3, when 18 or married. Witnesses, David Phinney, James Allen, Sarah Lumbard.

In the second codicil dated Jan. 12, 1767, he states that his daughter Prudence had married since the execution of his will and he therefore revokes the legacies given to her, and devises to her the same as given to his other daughters, £3.

In the third codicil dated 3d Nov. 1768, he states that whereas his daughter Mary Clap had died since executing the second codicil, he gives to his grand-daughter Prudence Clap, the same legacy he gave to her mother, to be paid at 18 or marriage. Witnesses, David Gorham, Edward Bacon, Enoch Hallett.

111. Joseph Gorham married Dec. 8, 1737, Abigail Lovell. He removed to Norwalk, Conn., where he died in 1760 of the small pox, and his wife, and children probably born at Norwalk, returned to Barnstable. His children were: 1, John * ; 2, Daniel ; 3, Joseph, of whom I have no information ; 4, Abigail,

---

*John Gorham was a mariner and is described as being 5 feet 6 inches in height, and of sandy complexion. After the death of his father he lived with his grandfather in Barnstable. He married April 28, 1771, Thankful Butler of Falmouth, and after residing many years in that town, removed to Nantucket, where he died 23d July, 1801. His widow Thankful died 18th June, 1840, aged 90 years and 85 days. He was a soldier in the war of the Revolution, and under the act of Congress, of July 4, 1836, his widow was entitled to a pension of $46.66 per annum from March 4, 1831; but she dying in 1840, the pension was obtained by her only surviving child, William Gorham.

who mrrried Nov. 30, 1770, Daniel Smith, Jr., of Nantucket; 5,
Deborah, who married Jan. 16, 1772, Peleg Bunker of Nantucket,
and died 25th Sept. following ; 6, Susannah, who married James
Perry, Jr., and resided many years in the State of Maine. She
died in the Alms House, Nantucket.

112.   Benjamin Gorham, called "Old Fiddler" to distinguish
him from the others of the same name, resided in the Ebenezer
Hinckley house, next east of Gov. Hinckley's new house, which
his father probably bought for him.   He married Sept. 3, 1741,
Mary Sturgis, of Yarmouth, May 8, 1722.  His children were :
1, Sturgis, born June 28, 1742 ; 2, Deborah, July 6, 1744, died
in infancy ; 3, Benjamin, March 26, 1746 ; 4, Mary, Oct. 8,
1748, married 1st Capt. John Russell, lost with Capt. Magee, 2d, Otis Loring, and died March 11, 1811 ; 5, Mehitable,
Nov. 28, 1755, married Daniel Hall Oct. 31, 1776, also lost with
Capt. Magee.  She died Sept. 22, 1784 ; 6, Olive, March 12,
1759, married Melatiah Bourne, Jr., of Boston, Sept. 24, 1778,
(see Bourne) ; 7, Edward, Feb. 15, 1762.

Sturgis Gorham, Esq., son of Benjamin, was a successful
business man.   He was a merchant, engaged in the fisheries, and
in the coasting and West India trade.   In the Revolution he was
a whig, and was on many committees, and did much good service
in the cause.   He built a large and elegant mansion house opposite his grandfather's, on the west side of Coggins' Pond.   This
house has been cut up and shorn of its fair proportions, and the
builder, if now living. would not recognize it. *   He married
Sept. 13, 1763, Phebe Taylor, who died Nov. 7, 1775, aged 31,
and July 12, 1778, to her sister Desire Taylor, who died Dec. 15,
1786, aged 30.   His children were: 1, Nancy, born Sept. 4,
1765, died in infancy ; 2, Nancy, 4th Sept. 1767, died unmarried
Dec. 27, 1791 ; 3, Debby, 12th May, 1769, married Oct. 2, 1786,
James S. Lovell, of Boston ; 4, Mary Sturgis, 26th July 1772,
married May 3, 1795, John Palfrey, Jr., Esq., of Boston, father
of the Hon. John Gorham Palfrey of Boston ; 5, Edward S.,
25th March 1774, died in infancy ; 6, William Taylor, 17th Oct.
1775, died  May 5, 1790 ; 7, Edward S., 29th Nov. 1779, died in
infancy ; 8, Phebe T., 30th Sept. 1781 ; 9, Edward S., 31st Oct.
1784, died in infancy ; 10, Charlotte, 22d June, 1786, married
1813, Thomas L. Harman, of New Orleans. She died in Bath,
Eng., in 1821, leaving three children : Thomas L., Francis S.,
and Charlotte.

Sturgis Gorham, Esq., died April 26 1795, aged 52 years.
In his will he gives one-half of the profit of his wind mill to his
sister Olive till her son Sylvanus is 21.   He gives legacies to his
grandsons James and Joseph Lovell, and the remainder of his es-

---

* The late Mr. Jabez Hinckley  said that for building the front stairway, Mr. Gorham
paid him for seventy-five  days work.   Every part of the house and  its surroundings were
finished with the same care.

tate equally to his daughters Charlotte and "Polly," (Mary Sturgis). May 5, 1795, John Palfrey, Esq., of Boston, was appointed guardian of Charlotte. His estate was settled April 13, 1802 ; after paying debts and legacies the balance was £683,13,10. His real estate was sold to Elijah Smith, of Chatham for £900.

Sturgis Gorham, Esq., for many years was *the business man* of Barnstable. On his shoulders the mantle of his grandfather fell. He did much to develop the business, and advance the prosperity of his native town. He exerted a wide influence, but it is perhaps doubtful whether that influence was always salutary. He was a slaveholder, as many at that time were ; and if common report is reliable the poor slave rarely had a harder master.

Benjamin Gorham, son of Benjamin, (called Young Fiddler) resided in the house that formerly stood where Capt. John T. Hall's now stands. He had not the business capacity of his brothers ; but was a man of wit and a boon companion. The following story is told of him, and illustrates his general character : When a boy he had a dog that was very troublesome, and annoyed his mother very much. One day he went home and with a serious air said, "Mother, I have sold my dog." "I am very glad, Benjamin, she was so troublesome—how much did you get for her?" "$500." "Did you, Benjamin !" "Yes, mother, I did, most certainly." "What did you get your pay in, Benjamin?" "Aye, that's it,—in bitch pups, at $50 apiece." This story is the origin of the common saying, applied to a man who makes a bad batter trade : "He got his pay in bitch pups." He married first, Mehitable, daughter of Capt. Wm. Davis. She died Dec. 1788, and he married 2d, Deborah, widow of Mr. Josiah Crocker, by whom he had, before marriage, one illegitimate daughter Abigail, who married Capt. Henry Bacon Aug. 4, 1803. Capt. Bacon had an only daughter Eloisa, who died single in 1835.

Edward Gorham, § son of Benjamin, married Jan. 6, 1785, Abigail, daughter of Capt. William Taylor, and resided in the easterly part of the town, on the estate which was the property of his father-in-law. His wife died Sept. 19, 1820, and he died Sept. 9, 1822, aged 60. His children were : 1, John Taylor, born Jan. 7, 1786 ; 2, Hitty, Jan. 4, 1788, married April 29, 1804, Dr. Ansel Davis ; 3, Lucy, Sept. 27, 1789, married Sept. 29, 1808, R. D. Shepherd, of New Orleans ‖ ; 4, Caroline, Aug. 26, 1791, now living unmarried ; 5, Desire T., Aug. 27, 1793, married Capt. Daniel C. Bacon ; 6, William Taylor, Sept. 19,

---

§ On one occasion he reproached David Loring for his drunkenness and improvidence. Loring replied—I admit sir, I have not Bacon provided for my dinner; neither have I a Shephard to watch over me by night.

---

‖ He paid Mr. Waterman twenty dollars for performing the marriage services—the largest fee named in the record. Mr. Chas. De Wolfe, of Bristol, R. I., who married, Oct. 24, 1801, Mrs. Nabby Green, paid a doubloon ($16) the next highest fee.

1795 ; 7, Nabby Thacher, June 8, 1798, married Henry H. Allen ; 8, Benjamin, Feb. 6, 1800, a graduate of the military academy at West Point, died unmarried ; 9, Mary Sturgis, now living, married Thomas Gray, of Boston.

118.    Nathaniel Gorham, son of John, was unlike any of the family—he was eccentric in his habits, and in his manners, and strenuously opposed any innovations of the customs of the fathers.   He drove his team with a long pole, because the first settlers did so ; and for the same reason, he would never have a tip-up-cart.   In dress, he not only adhered to the fashions of his ancestors ; but, in some particulars was an oddity.   He wore his shirt with the open part behind, and fastened at the back of the neck with a loop and a nail.   He lived on a very simple diet. Salt meat broth, bread and milk, hasty pudding, and samp, were his favorite dishes morning, noon, and night.   He had a natural aversion to spirituous liquors, and never drank any during his life. If his sons had inherited that antipathy, they would have been better men.

During the Revolution he manufactured salt at Sandy Neck by boiling sea-water, a slow and toilsome process ; but not irksome to him, because the first settlers, whom he venerated, had been engaged in the same business.   For several successive days during the winter of 1780-1, ¶ he drove a four ox sled, loaded with wood, on the ice across the harbor, from Sandy Neck to Calves Pasture Point.   Since that date the harbor has been frozen, so that persons crossed on the ice, but at no time since sufficiently to bear a team.

Notwithstanding his oddities, he was industrious, honest, and prudent, an obliging neighbor, and a good citizen.   He married Oct. 30, 1751, Anna, daughter of George Lewis, and had 1, Lewis, 11th Nov. 1753, and 2, George Lewis, 3d Oct. 1763.   His children were : 1, Anner, born 29th March, 1775, married Thos. Harris of Boston, July 12, 1798 ; 2, David, 6th Aug. 1778, married Hannah Nye ; 3, John, 16th July, 1781, married 1st, Martha Cobb April 12, 1804, 2d, Lucy Cobb May 30, 1813 ; 4, Henry, 8th Aug. 1785, married Polly Hoxie ; 5, Sarah, 12th May, 1793, married Barnabas Hinckley.

Lewis Gorham * resided in the mansion-house of his father and grandfather, at Coggins' Pond.   He was a blacksmith by trade, and for many years was a deputy sheriff.   He married April 14, 1774, Sarah, daughter of David Phinney.   She died Feb. 10, 1851, aged 97 years, 1 month, 6 days, and at her death had living 5 children, 30 grand-children, 64 great grand-children, and 4 great great grand-children.

¶ This is the tradition and it is probably accurate, for the winter of 1780 is represented as the coldest known.

*During the Revolution he took an active part in local proceedings in Barnstable, and from him I obtained some information not acceptable to Mr. Freeman.

George Lewis Gorham resided in the house which his father purchased of Capt. William Davis. He married March 25, 1784, Phebe, daughter of Joseph Davis, and for his second wife her sister Mary, then only 16. After the death of Mr. Gorham she married Dea. Joseph Hawes of Yarmouth, whom she survived. His children were: 1, Phebe, born Feb. 8, 1785, married James Childs; 2, Nathaniel, Oct. 9, 1789, married Hannah Gorham April 11, 1813; 3, Deborah, March 19, 1792; 4, Anna L. April 21, 1795, married Nymphas Davis Aug. 7, 1814; 5, Benjamin Davis, July 29, 1798; 6, Mary Davis, Dec. 1, 1808, married N. S. Hallett.

(31-8.) Job Gorham, son of Lieut. John, born Aug. 30, 1692, married Dec. 4, 1719, Desire, daughter of Thomas Dimmock. She died Jan. 28, 1732-3, and he married 2d, in 1735, Bethia, widow of Isaac Freeman of Fairfield, Conn. She was a Sturgis, born in Yarmouth. Capt. Job Gorham died in 1762, and his widow Bethia July 11, 1769, aged 73.

*Children born in Barnstable:*

124. I. Temperance, 23d July, 1721.
125. II. Thomas, 13th Aug. 1723.
126. III. Edward, 12th Sept. 1725, died young.
127. IV. Desire, 17th March, 1727-8,
128. V. Job, 6th Nov. 1730, died young.
129. VI. Sarah, baptized 15th Aug. 1736, died young.

The will of Job Gorham of Barnstable, gentleman, is dated 12th Sept. 1753, and proved Nov. 2, 1762. He names his wife Bethia Gorham, daughters Temperance Fuller and Desire Gorham, to whom he gives legacies. All the remainder of his estate he gives to his son Thomas, whom he appoints his executor.

124. Temperance Gorham married Oct. 29, 1741, her cousin John Fuller, a great grandson of Capt. Matthew Fuller.

125. Thomas Gorham, during the latter part of his life was blind. He was a man of sound judgment, and of industrious habits. After he became blind, he performed many kinds of labor which others in his situation would not have attempted. Timothy Swinerton, the ancestor of the family of that name, lived with him when a boy. Mr. Gorham, instead of having the boy to lead him, put the boy on his horse, and taking the crupper in his hand walked behind the horse. When walking alone, he kept his cane in constant motion before him.

He married 1st, Hannah Gorham, daughter of Ebenezer, May 16, 1754. She died April 5, 1765, and he married 2d, Widow Rebecca Jones of Yarmouth, in 1765. She united with the East Church Sept. 6, 1767, and on the 13th of that month, Edward, Lucy and Sarah, children by her first husband, and Mary by her last, were baptized. His children were: 1, Job, born 12th Dec. 1754, who married Sept. 2, 1786, Rebecca Davis. He was a

sea captain, inherited the ancient Gorham homestead, and was
lost at sea Feb. 1804, while on a voyage to Copenhagen, in a
vessel belonging to Stephen Gorham.   He has children surviving.
2, Isaac, 29th Ap. 1756, died in New Jersey Prison Ship; 3, Desire, 16th Oct. 1757, married 1st, ——— Richmond, 2d, ———
Hill; 4, Ezekiel, 3d Dec. 1758, removed to So. Carolina, was a
sea captain lost at sea, and left no issue; 5, John, 7th March,
1760, was a sea captain, lost at sea and left no issue; 6, Elizabeth, 10th June, 1761, married ——— Tenter; 7, Hannah, baptized 28th June, 1763, married ——— Burr; 8, Temperance,
baptized 17th Feb. 1765, married ——— Johnson; 9, Mary, 11th
Sept. 1766, married Elijah Childs, father of the late Dea. Samuel
Childs, May 10, 1785.   Mr. Thomas Gorham, in his will dated
July 28, 1795, gives to his wife Rebecca, who was a woman of a
weak intellect, a dower in his estate, (a gift he could not avoid)
to his oldest son Job all his estate excepting dower, and 20 shillings to each of his other children.   He names his youngest son
John, daughters Desire Richmond, Elizabeth Tenter, Hannah
Burr, Temperance Johnson, and youngest daughter Mary.

[By an oversight I omitted several families resident in Yarmouth.   This article is too long to make additions.]

Note.—While the Gorham genealogy was going through the
press additional information of some of the later branches of the
family was forwarded by a descendant in Gloucester.   Col. John
Gorham (102,) died of small-pox, in London, about the year
1750, while prosecuting his claim for expenses in the Louisburg
Expedition.   His son Solomon died in Gloucester, Dec. 20, 1795,
aged 47.   His daughter Elizabeth married Daniel Rogers of Gloucester (not of Kittery, Me.,) and Eben. Parsons, who married
her sister Mary, was also some time of Gloucester.   His widow,
Elizabeth (Allyn) married second Col. John Stevens of Gloucester, in 1775, and died Dec. 25, 1786, in her 73d year.   Her
grave-stone bears this inscription:

"She supported thro' Life the Christian Character and moved in the Various Circles of
Domestic Life with Honor and Dignity.
              The Affectionate Wife,
               The Tender Mother,
              The Exemplary Widow,
               The Pious Friend."

# GREEN.

In 1653 a Mr. Groom owned land adjoining Dea. Cooper's houselot. There was a Mr. John Groom in Plymouth from 1638 to 1650, when he disappears at Plymouth and appears in Barnstable. Dr. Shurtleff seems to favor the notion that John Gorham and John Groom were the same person. Land for a houselot was granted to John Groom in 1638. John Gorham was then only 17, and it is not probable that he was the person intended. Mr. Savage mentions Nicholas, Henry and Samuel Groom; but not John of Plymouth. I have thought the name on the Barnstable records was Green, and therefore refer to it in this connection. There was an Isaac Green, a surveyor, afterwards of Falmouth, who probably resided some little time in Barnstable.

James Green, who died in Barnstable in 1731, aged about 90, was a son of James of Charlestown. He married Nov. 19, 1661, Rebecca Jones of Dorchester, and had,

I. Elizabeth, Nov. 14, 1662, married 1691, John Lothrop, of Barnstable, 2d, Thomas Crocker, 23d Dec. 1701. She was four years older than her first, and twelve older than her last husband. She died in Hingham Aug. 1, 1752, aged 89.

II.   James, Dec. 15, 1665.   In 1688 and 9, master of the ship Success, of Boston.

III.   Thomas, Jan. 2, 1666.   He owned a house in Barnstable which he sold to John Goodspeed before the year 1721.

IV.   Richard, April 7, 1669.

V.   John, Feb. 24, 1771.

VI.   Esther, Sept. 27, 1675, married ———— Frothingham.

VII.   Samuel, July 20, 1680.

William Green, a descendant of James, married March 25, 1709, Desire, daughter of John Bacon, Esq. She died Dec. 29, 1730, aged 41, and he married 2d, Sept. 1, 1731, Mary Fuller. He died Jan. 28, 1756, aged above 70, (Church Records) and his widow Oct. 23, 1756.

He resided in a high single house on the lot next west of Nathaniel Bacon's, given to him by his father-in-law, (see Bacon) and afterwards owned by Lot Thacher.

*His children born in Barnstable were:*

I.   Warren, born June 9, 1712.

II.   Desire, Oct. 24, 1718.

III.   William, July 17, 1721.

IV.   Sarah, Dec. 27, 1723.

V.   Mary, baptized Sept. 5, 1725.

VI.   John, born April 12, 1726.

VII.   James, Sept. 17, 1728.

William married Mary Conant Oct. 1745. James married Feb. 14, 1755, Ruth Marshal of Freetown, and removed to East Haddam. He had five children,—was a blacksmith, and a Captain in the French War. Isaac Green, I think, belonged to this family. He removed to Falmouth, married 1st, Sarah, 2d, Judith, and died Jan. 1, 1739-40. He had by his first wife Sarah, Jonathan, Elizabeth, Sarah and Martha, after 1700, and by his 2d wife, Lemuel, April 29, 1719, and a daughter Abigail born Jan. 21, 1722. This name is sometimes written Groon.

Rev. Joseph Green, of Barnstable, belonged to another family. To him I am much indebted for the careful manner in which he kept the church records. He resided in the parsonage near the Meeting House in the East Parish. He married Nov. 18, 1725, Hannah, daughter of the Rev. Jonathan Russell, and had:

I.   Joseph, born 12th Sept. 1727.

II.   Martha, 17th Nov. 1730.

III.   Hannah, 6th June, 1745.

Mr. Green died Oct. 4, 1770, and is buried in the Old Burying Ground on Lothrop's Hill. On his tombstone the following epitaph is engraved :

> "Here lieth
> The Body of the Rev. Mr. Joseph Green
> The worthy pastor of this church
> As a Gentleman a Friend a Christian and a
> Minister
> His character was greatly distinguished
> His natural abilities were conspicuous
> And much improved by study and application
> In human and sacred Literature he greatly ex-
> celled
> His principles were evangelical and candid
> In prayer and preaching
> His Gifts were generally and justly admired
> Temperance Purity Prudence Benevolence Res-
> ignation
> Devotion and exemplary Diligence in his Mas-
> ter's Service adorned his character
> His mind was sedate his Temper placid
> His Affections and Passions regulated by Rea-
> son and Religion
> His manners courteous generous and Hospitable
> His conversation entertaining instructive and
> serious
> A dutiful Son an affectionate Husband and a
> tender Parent
> A sincere Friend and a faithful Minister
> Greatly and to the last beloved and honored by
> his People
> Born June 21 O S 1701
> Graduated at Harvard College 1720
> Ordained May 12 O S 1725
> Departed this life in assured hope of a better
> Oct 4 N S 1770 in the 70th year of his age
> And 46th of his Ministry
> Think what the Christian Preacher Friend
> should be
> You've then his character, for such was he."

Notwithstanding this fullsome panegyric which some unwise friend caused to be engraved on his tombstone, Mr. Green was an excellent man in all the relations of life. He was a moderate Calvinist, and his ministry, an account of which will hereafter be given, was most successful. As his tombstone says, he was "be-loved and honored by his people."

Till recently it had always been the custom of the parishion-ers to cut and draw the wood, and prepare the same for the minis-ter's fire on the week following the annual Thanksgiving. After his death, in 1770, the people turned out as usual. Mr. Green had always given them flip and prepared for them a good dinner, and they expected the custom would be continued. When the teamsters had unloaded they expected to be invited in ; but no one came to the door. After waiting some time, Abner, negro slave of Col. David Gorham, was sent into the house. Abner, went into the kitchen, found no preparations were making for a dinner, and that there was no flip on the side-table. He came out, and raising his hands over his head, said in a solemn sing-song tone: Mister—Green—is—dead.

Joseph, son of Rev. Joseph Green, of Barnstable, was a graduate of Harvard College in the class of 1746, and of Yale College in 1752. He was settled in the ministry at Marshfield in 1753. From that town he removed to Yarmouth, and Sept. 15, 1762, was ordained pastor of the West Church. He died Nov. 5, 1768 aged 41 years.

He married Hannah Lewis, daughter of Rev. Isaiah of Westfield, and had Isaiah L. Green born in Barnstable Dec. 28, 1761, Harvard College 1781, and a distinguished man. Was a member of Congress 1805-9 and 1811-13, collector of customs, &c., and died in 1841, leaving a large family. 2, Abigail, who married Oct. 24, 1802, Capt. Charles De Wolf, of Bristol, R. I.

Martha Green died unmarried Jan. 1791, in the 61st year of her age. Hannah, his third child, died in infancy.

Madam Hannah Green, wife of Rev. Joseph Green, Sen., died June 6, 1745, on the day of the birth of her daughter Hannah.

John Green of Barnstable belonged to another family. I have heard it said that he came from French Guiana. His house is yet standing, and is the second east of the Court House. He married in 1763 Elizabeth, widow of Shubael Baxter of Yarmouth, and had John and Elizabeth baptized in 1768, James in 1771, and Sarah in 1775. She died March 27, 1782, aged 45. Her son Shubael by her first husband, born June 14, 1758. John Green was not popular with the boys, and they troubled him in his old age. Some curious stories are told of his adventures, but they are hardly worth preserving.

# GARRETT.

Dea. Richard Garrett was the first Town Clerk of Scituate. He married Lydia, daughter of Elder Nathaniel Tilden, and had Joseph 1648, John 1651, Mary 1655, Richard 1659. Richard married 1695 Persis, daughter of Capt. Michael Pierce, and had Ann, Deborah, and John born 1706. * His second wife was Martha Tobey of Sandwich, whom he married 10th Sept. 1712. Andrew Garrett of Sandwich, probably a son of Richard, Jr., married Dec. 20, 1753, Temperance Parker, and April 17, 1760, Lucy Davis. He removed to Barnstable, and owned the estate and wharf afterwards owned by Dea Joseph Chipman. His children were: Andrew, born Feb. 25, 1755, who married, was a Lieutenant in the continental army, was taken prisoner by the Indians, with whom he resided four years, adopted their habits, and it is said took one to wife. On his return his wife, a Salem woman, believing him dead, had married and had a child. They agreed to part, and he married Miss Blish, and afterwards resided at Annable's Pond. 2, Jesse, born Feb. 20, 1761, was lost with Capt. Magee Dec. 27, 1778; 3, Isaac, born May 17, 1763; 4, Temperance, Aug. 19, 1765; 5, Susannah, Oct. 7, 1768. A widow Susannah Garrett died in Barnstable July 7, 1789, perhaps a third wife of Andrew, Senior.

---

* Deane.

# JOHN HALL.

———

The precise date when John Hall came to Barnstable, I cannot ascertain. I find no evidence that he came before 1641. As he removed to Yarmouth before the records of each man's land was made, the exact location of his houselot and of his other lands, I am unable to give. All that I can say certainly is, that his house was in the vicinity of the new Court House, that he owned a small tract of land near Cooper's Pond, and that his great lot of forty acres was at the Indian Ponds. I presume that he bought the house and lands of Gen. James Cudworth, and on his removal to Yarmouth he sold to James Naylor, who sold July 21, 1656, to Thomas Lothrop. If I am right, his eight acre houselot was bounded north by the present County road, west by Freeman Hinckley's Lane, south by the commons, and east by Isaac Wells, the boundary line being not far from the present street called Railroad Avenue. Anciently there was a highway, commencing at the County road between Eldridge's Hotel and the Savings Bank building, and running north to the landing, on the north of Potter's neck, as the land in that vicinity was called. He owned four acres of land and meadow on the east side of that ancient highway, and twenty-six of land on the west, and three acres of meadow on the north. (See Maybor.) These twenty-six acres embraced certainly two of the original allotments, probably those of Mr. Cudworth and of Henry Rowley.

About the year 1651 he removed to Yarmouth, and his farm containing 147 acres, in Conny * Furlong at Nobscusset, is described on the records. It is a short distance north-easterly from the meeting houses at North Dennis, and a part of it yet owned by his descendants. He also owned 15 acres of upland on the west of Coy's Pond, and 12 acres of meadow in that vicinity, and rights of commonage.

John Hall, Sen., was not distinguished in public life. In

---

* The lands in Yarmouth first laid out were divided into furlongs, each of which was known by a particular name. Snakes, Rabbits Ruin, Lone Tree and others, are named. The name of Mr. Hall's I cannot make out clearly, it is Conies, Canny, or Cunningham, perhaps.

1647 he was constable of the town of "Bastable," as the name of the town was sometimes written by the early inhabitants.  He was surveyor of highways in Yarmouth in 1653, and on the grand inquest in 1657 and 1664.  As a private citizen, he was eminently distinguished for his moral worth and religious character.†  A more honest and upright man in all his dealings, it would be difficult to find.  He died in 1696, at a very advanced age, and was probably buried in the Hall burying ground in Dennis.  In his will dated July 15, 1694, he names his son Samuel, whom he calls eldest, John, Joseph, William, Benjamin and Elisha, who it appears were then living in Yarmouth, and his sons Nathaniel and Gershom.  His will was proved Aug. 29, 1696.

The tradition in the family is that he came from Wales ; but nothing is certainly known on the subject ; neither is it known whether he married before or after he came over.  I infer from Richard Henchman's letter, that his nine sons were the children of one wife.‡  As these names have already been given, it is unnecessary to repeat them.

(1-2.)  Samuel Hall, his oldest son, was bound as an apprentice to Francis Baker, blacksmith ; but he was not treated well by his master, and in 1655, by the order of the Court, his indentures were made void, his father paying £8.  He afterward learned the trade of a cooper.  He married Elizabeth, daughter of Thomas Folland of Yarmouth.  He died in 1696, leaving no issue.  In his will dated Oct. 7, 1693, he names his wife Elizabeth, and all his brothers.  His widow married April 27, 1699, Jeremiah Jones, and she died in 1711.

(2-1.)  Dea. John Hall, son of John, Sen., resided on a farm at Hocanom, in Yarmouth.  I find no record of his marriage, but presume * he married Priscilla, daughter of Austin Bearse of Barnstable.  He was a deacon of the Yarmouth church, and died Oct. 24, 1710, aged 73 years.  He was buried in the old graveyard in Yarmouth, where he has a monument erected to his memory.  If he was 73 at his death in 1710, he was born in 1637, as above stated.  His widow died March 30, 1712, aged 68 years.

Children of Dea. John Hall, and Priscilla Bearse, born in Yarmouth :
10.  I.   John born 4 (gone.)

---

† See Letter of Richard Henchman Feb. 1687, published in Yarmouth Register.

---

‡ Perhaps the John Hall named by Mr. Frothingham as of Charlestown in 1632, and who was No. 19 on the records of the 1st church in Boston, was the Barnstable man.  If so, his wife Bethia and sons John and Sheban, did not die as stated by Mr. Savage.

---

* I find no record of this marriage ; but nevertheless presume it to be the fact.  Her age corresponds with that of Priscilla, daughter of Austin Bearse, and she names all her children excepting the first and last, after her brothers and sisters.  Mr. Freeman copies this without credit in his account of the Bearse family, nearly all of which is a transcript of my article, which he has appropriated to himself, p 297,

11.  II.    Joseph, 29th Sept. 1663.
12.  III.   daughter, middle Nov. 1668.
13.  IV.    Priscilla, Feb. 1671.
14.  V.     Hestar, April 1672.
15.  VI.    Mary, 1st March, 1673.
16.  VII.   Martha, 24th May, 1676.
17.  VIII.  Nathaniel, 15th Sept. 1678.

10.  John Hall, 3d, married April 30, 1694, Margaret, daughter of John Miller of Yarmouth. He died March 21, 1734-5, in the 70th year of his age. This gives the year of his birth 1666, showing that he was younger than Joseph. His wife died Jan. 13, 1723-4, in the 56th year of her age. His children born in Yarmouth were: 1, Mehetable, 17th March, 1694-5, married Shubael Taylor Sept. 6, 1716, and died young; 2, Sarah, 18th March, 1696-7, died March 28, 1732; 3, Margaret, 13th Sept. 1699; twins 7th March, 1701-2, both died young; 4, Priscilla, 13th May, 1704; 5, Bethia, 24th July, 1706, died Oct. 6, 1744; 6, John, 24th Aug. 1708, died March 1, 1745; 7, Isaac, 23d Aug. 1712, died Oct. 2, 1735.

11.  Dea. Joseph Hall grandson of John, and was a man of note in his day. He married Feb. 12, 1689-90, Hannah, daughter of John Miller. She died Aug. 23, 1710, and he married 2d, Widow Mary, relict of John Morton, and a daughter of Joseph Faunce of Plymouth, born June 2, 1681. She died in Yarmouth May 31, 1761, in the 80th year of her age. Dea. Joseph died Jan. 29, 1736-7, in the 73d year of his age. His children born in Yarmouth were: 1, Hannah, 20th Feb. 1690-1; 2, Priscilla, 28th March, 1693, married Sept. 1719, Benjamin Crocker; 3, Margery, 24th Feb. 1694-5; 4, Joseph, 6th Aug. 1697, married and had a family of 12, several of whom were distinguished; 5, Daniel, 18th July 1699, married Lydia Gray of Harwich May 18, 1721, the first couple published in Yarmouth under the then new law; he afterwards married two other wives, and was a deacon and man of note. His youngest son, Samuel, removed to Ashfield, 1777. Dea. Daniel had 15 children recorded, and 4 not recorded, two of whom were named David and Elizabeth; 6, Josiah, 12th Aug. 1701, married Rebecca Howes Oct. 15, 1730; 7, David, 6th Aug. 1704, Harvard College 1724, ordained at Sutton, Mass., 1729, a friend of that distinguished divine, Dr. Jonathan Edwards. He married, had twelve children, and died May 8, 1789, aged 86, and in the sixtieth year of his ministry. 8, Mary, 30th March, 1712, married Elkanah Howes, 1734; 9, Peter, 19th May, 1715, married Abigail Sears Dec. 21, 1738; 10, John, 3d Jan. 1716-17; 11, Barshua, 5th July, 1719.

Joseph Hall, son of Dea. Joseph of Yarmouth, married Rebecca. He died 1771-2, aged 74, and his widow died March 10,

1791, aged 91. Children born in Yarmouth: 1, Hannah, 10th Sept. 1721, died young; 2, Joseph, 7th June, 1723, married Zippera Young; 3, Edward, 22d Jan. 1725, died April 20, 1765; 4, Hannah, 18th Dec. 1726, married Nathaniel Bassett; 5, Rebecca, 16th Jan. 1731, married James Howland; 6, Nathaniel, 6th Jan. 1733; 7, Stephen, 9th Jan. 1736, married Mary Freeman; 8, Betty, 16th May, 1738, married Prince Sears; 9, Nathaniel, 1st June, 1740, married Mehetable Howes; 10, Barnabas, 20th April, 1742, married Mary Crocker; 11, Priscilla, 24th July, 1744, married Jeremiah Howes; 12, Daniel.

(1-3). Dea Joseph Hall, son of John, Sen., was an early settler in Mansfield, Conn. He was Town Clerk, and a prominent man. He died in Yarmouth May 31, 1736, aged 73 years, probably while on a voyage to his native town. He left no issue. His widow Mary died in Mansfield Feb. 3, 1717-18.* (Manuscript letter of Wm. S. Weaver, Esq.)

(1-5). Capt. Nathaniel Hall was, if we except Joseph, the most distinguished of the sons of John Hall, Sen. Richard Henchman, the school-master of Yarmouth, in a letter to Dr. Increase Mathew, dated Yarmouth, Feb. 1686-7, says: "There is in this town one Mr. Nathaniel Hall, a man descended of eminently religious parents; who were very happy in all their children, being nine sons, men whom this Nathaniel is reckoned to excel, who in the late wars received a wound (the bullet remaining in his body) that has taken away, in a great measure, the use of one of his arms" &c. Capt. Hall was a corporal, in the first expedition, in 1675, under Capt. John Gorham; a sargeant in the second, in 1676, in which expedition it is probable he received the wound for which he claimed and received a pension. The earliest record I find is dated July 7, 1681, when the Court allowed him £15 and all fines imposed on persons in Yarmouth, who were convicted of selling spirituous liquors. There had evidently been some previous action, for June 9, 1683, £8 was allowed him for his continued lameness, and it is stated in the record June 5, 1684, that $40 had been paid to him in money and a license granted to him to keep an ordinary, and all the fines imposed on parties in Yarmouth who should sell *drink* contrary to law. In final settlement of his claim, an annual pension of five pounds per annum for life, was offered him, which he accepted June 2, 1685.

Being unable to attend to any business that required physical

---

*Mr. Savage blesses Dea. Joseph, Sen., with a family. He did not follow my manuscript, yet I think I am right. Our Probate Records say he had no children at the time of his death. The Yarmouth records are silent on the subject. So are the Mansfield, of which town he was the Clerk, and he would probably have recorded the births of his own children if he had any. Mr. Weaver, who has carefully examined the records, writes to me that "he probably had no descendants." Mr. Savage confounds the two Dea. Joseph Halls. It is very curious if both should have had children of the same names and born on the same days.

strength, he devoted his leisure time to the study of surgery and
medicine, in which, aided by his father-in-law, Rev. Mr. Thornton, who was a physician as well as a minister, he acquired much
skill and performed several difficult surgical operations with success.  In 1687 he had, in a great measure, recovered from the
effects of his wound, and proposed to remove to Boston and establish himself in that town as a physician.  To accomplish this
was the object of Mr. Henchman's letter.  He removed to Hingham, where he practiced medicine  several years, and from thence
to Lewes, Sussex County, Penn.

In 1689,  it appears by Church's history, that he again was a
soldier in the French and Indian wars of that period.  He was a
Captain and fought with great bravery under Major Church in the
defence of Falmouth, now Portland, Sept. 21, 1689.  Mather in
his Magnalia, and he certainly knew, states that the Capt. Nathaniel Hall who fought so bravely at Falmouth, was the same
man who had served as an officer in King Phillip's war.

The history of his keeping an ordinary or tavern, in Yarmouth, presents many curious points.  The Court conferred on
him  the sole right of keeping an ordinary in Yarmouth, then including the present town of Dennis, and forbid all others from
selling wines or spirituous liquors  without license, and constituted
him an agent to prosecute all offenders, and gave him the fines
collected.  He had absolute power conferred on him, and the
grant was to continue during his natural life.  Excepting at his
house no traveler could procure lodging.  The consequence was,
his house was thronged with customers and was the resort of the
intemperate and the lascivious.  In two years he became dissatisfied, and his wife who was a very pious woman, was utterly disgusted with the business of keeping an ordinary.  He sought
other employment, and sold out  to Jasper Taylor Sept. 17, 1690,
"the liberty and privilege of keeping a house of public entertainment in said Yarmouth, to retail all sorts of strong drink, without further license  during the natural life of said Hall, with one-
half of all the fines taken of any English person for retailing
strong drink without license in said Yarmouth."  In the enjoy-
ment of the privileges conveyed, Taylor avers that Hall covenanted to save him harmless.  The papers are full of legal quibbles,
and it is difficult to sift out the simple truth.  The following are
some of the facts : Taylor was complained of for keeping an ordinary without license, and was amerced in £4 fines.  At the October term of the Court of Common Pleas held in Barnstable on the
first Tuesday in October, 1703, Taylor sued Hall on his covenant
and obtained a judgment, and from this judgment Hall appealed
to the  Suserior Court to be held in Plymouth.  He did not deny
in his "Reasons of Appeal" that he had made such sale, but that
the covenant was void in law, and "no covenant."  In law Mr.

Hall was probably right; but he was nevertheless morally bound to fulfil the conditions of his bargain. He would not be morally bound to do an illegal or immoral act; but he was bound in honor to restore money that he had obtained by an illegal contract, and the court rightly held that he was so responsible.

Mr. Nathaniel Hall married before 1675, Ann, daughter of Rev. Thomas Thornton of Yarmouth. There is no record of his children in Yarmouth or Hingham. In reply to my inquiries, I am informed that a family of the name settled early in Sussex, but my correspondent was unable to ascertain whether the Halls of that County were the descendants of Nathaniel.

(1-6.) Mr. Gersham Hall, son of John, Sen., was a prominent man. He resided some time in Chatham, from which town he was a deputy to the Colony Court in 1791. He resided in Harwich most of his life, and was a useful and influential man during the early settlement of that town. He built the grist mill known as Hall's Mill, and his residence was in that vicinity. He married first Bethia, daughter of Edward Bangs. She died Oct. 15, 1696, aged 54. For his second wife he married Dec. 7, 1696, Martha Bramhall of Hingham. She died July 2, 1733, aged 69 years. He died Oct. 31, 1732, aged 85 years, and was buried in the Hall burying ground in Dennis, where he and his wives have monuments. The record of his family is lost. His children were: 1, Edward, who married twice, and died in Harwich Jan. 22, 1727, and his widow Sarah married Aug. 12, 1728, Mr. Daniel Legg of Yarmouth. His children were: 1, Bethia, born Dec. 31, 1709, married Andrew Clark, Jr., Aug. 20, 1729; 2, Hannah, Feb. 1, 1711-12, married Feb. 22, 1728-9, Tully Crosby; 3, Mary, Oct. 15, 1714, married Nov. 28, 1734, Gershom Hall; 4, Edward, April 19, 1717, married, had a family, and died Feb. 1797, aged 80 years; 5, Sarah, April 27, 1720, died young; 6, Patience, July 15, 1726.

2. Jonathan Hall, son of Gersham, had by wife Hannah, Gersham, born Oct. 25, 1715, who married his cousin Mary.

3. Samuel Hall, son of Gersham, born 1669, married Patience Rider Feb. 2, 1696-7. He died in Harwich Feb. 19, 1729-30, and his widow married Thomas Clark, Esq.

4. Mercy Hall, daughter of Gersham, married John Chase.

5. Bethia Hall, daughter of Gersham, married Kenelen Winslow.

Capt. William Hall, son of John Senior, removed to Mansfield, Conn. He bought June 24, 1695, a thousand acre right of land in Windham, now Mansfield. He died June, 11, 1727, aged 76, and his wife Easter Feb. 19, 1727. His children were: 1, Isaac, who married April 24, 1700, Sarah, daughter of John Reed of Windham, and had ten children; 2, James, who married Mehitable Wood Oct. 15, 1716, and had ten children; 3, William, who married Hester ——— July 20, 1708, and had a family. He probably had other children. Mr. Weaver writes that "there was a Theophilus Hall who married Ruth Sargeant March 2, 1719-20, but whether the son of Benjamin or William I am not certain."

(1-8).  Benjamin Hall, son of Jonn Senior, removed first to Harwich and afterwards to Mansfield, Conn., when he purchased land Sept. 15, 1708, and was then called of M. He married Feb. 7, 1677, Mehitabel Matthews of Yarmouth. He died in Mansfield Aug. 7, 1737, aged 93 years, and his widow Mehitabel Feb. 20, 1740-1, aged over 90. Little is certainly known respecting his family. His children were probably all born in Harwich, and the record is lost. He had a son Barnabas who married Mercy, and had a family, the oldest born May 23, 1710; also a son Shebar, who married Abigail and had a family, the oldest child born June 13, 1711. Theophilus above named was perhaps his son.

(1-9).  Elisha Hall, youngest son of John, Senior, resided in Yarmouth. He married Lydia, who died Feb. 23, 1723-4. His children were: 1, Ebenezer, born Nov. 20, 1681, married Mehitabel Eldredge Sept. 27, 1705; 2, Elisha, June 14, 1682, married Mary Howes Sept. 1709; 3, Tabitha, Dec. 18, 1683, married Wm. Cook March 18, 1707; 4, Judah, Jan. 18, 1685, married Mehitabel; 5, Phebe, March 23, 1689, married Jacob Cobb April 3, 1716; 6, Job, Sept. 14, 1691; 7, Sylvanus, May 17, 1693.

Elisha Hall, son of Elisha, and grandson of the first John, married Mary Howes Sept. 1709, and had 1, Elisha, 26th Aug. 1710; 2, Mary, 27th July 1712; 3, Thankful, 31st Jan. 1715; 4, Joshua, 18th April 1717, he removed to Connecticut, thence to Ploughed Neck, Sandwich, where he has descendants; 5, Stephen, 16th July, 1719; 6, Bethia, 17th March, 1722; 7, Elizabeth, 14th Dec. 1724; 8, Phebe, 20th Jan. 1630; 9, Lydia, 16th Jan. 1733.

Judah Hall, son of Elisha, married Mehitabel, and had 1, Judah, born in Plymouth 1st June, 1714; 2, Abner, born in Yarmouth 21st Feb. 1719; 3, James, 23d Aug. 1719; 4, Giles, 14th July 1721; 5, Thomas, 26th April 1724; 6, Enoch, 27th Dec. 1725; 7, Sylvanus, 15th June, 1727.

(I have generally and that is my intention to trace the families one generation farther; but the Halls can hardly be called a Barnstable family, and as Mr. Weaver of Williamantic, and Mr. Paine of Harwich, are interested, I resign the labor to them.)

# HATHAWAY.

In early times this name was written as it is usually pronounced, Hadaway. Four of the name came over. Arthur, who settled in Marshfield, and afterward removed to Dartmouth; John and Joseph of Taunton, and John of Barnstable.

John Hadaway of Barnstable, was born in the year 1617, as appears by the Custom House record, and by his deposition dated March 1, 1658-9. He came over in 1635, in the ship Blessing from London. July 1, 1656, he married Hannah, daughter of Mary Hallett, presumed to be the widow of the school-master, Mr. Andrew Hallett, the elder. She died early, and he married May 1, 1672, Elizabeth, daughter of Edward Coleman of Yarmouth. She was born in Boston 28th Feb. 1651-2, and was thirty-five years younger than her husband.

About this time he removed to Yarmouth, not to Taunton as stated by Mr. Savage, and built a house on a clearing in the woods, about a quarter of a mile west of the spot where the Town House in Yarmouth now stands, and known as Thompson's fields, because a man of that name subsequently owned the lot. The late Mr. Paul Rider afterwards owned the old Hadaway house and estate. He was taxed in Yarmouth in 1675 and 1676, showing that he removed as above stated. His rate was eight pence in 1675, evidence that he was at that time a man of small estate.

His estate in Barnstable was equal to an average of the estates of the first settlers, yet it soon passed into the hands of others. March 31, 1659, by a deed of gift, his mother-in-law conveyed to him the land now owned by Major Phinney on the north of the railroad, and the land where the Custom House now stands, with the dwelling-house thereon. Dec. 14, 1661, he bought the house and lands of his brother-in-law, Josiah Hallett, situate on the south of the railroad, for £10 sterling. In this purchase was included three acres of meadow at Blushes point, bounded north by the beach, east by the meadow of Abraham Blush, and south and west by "Old Mill Creek." As rights of commonage pertained to these lands and dwelling-houses, Hadda-way at that time was not a poor man.

John Hathaway of Taunton, was a very respectable man, owned a large landed estate, and was often employed in the business of the Colony. Our John was a different man. During a portion of his life he was intemperate in his habits, improvident, and wasted his own and his wife's estate. He belonged to the class of persons that I have described under the name of Caseley, and to which I shall have occasion hereafter to refer.

He died in Yarmouth in the year 1697, aged 80 years. In his will dated Aug. 3, 1689, proved Feb. 20, 1696-7, he names his wife Elizabeth, and his sons Thomas, John, Gideon, and Edward. He refers to daughters by a former wife, but does not name them, and to two daughters by his wife Elizabeth. His widow is named in the settlement of her brother Edward's estate in 1714. At the division of the common lands in 1710, Thomas is the only one of the name mentioned in Yarmouth, and there were none at that time of the name in Barnstable.

The record of the births of the children of John Hadaway is imperfect. On the Barnstable records four are named, namely:

I.    John, born Oct. 1675, died same year.
II.   John, Aug. 16, 1658.
III.  Hannah, May 1662.
IV.   Edward, 10th Feb. 1663-4.

Named in his will.

V.    Thomas.
VI.   Gideon.

He left Sarah, and probably two other daughters.

As this family is nearly extinct, I have not devoted much time to tracing its genealogy. The ancestor was an eccentric man, and many individuals among his descendants had their peculiarities. The children for several generations were brought up in secluded spots, at a distance from neighbors, and this fact probably had an influence on their characters.

John and Edward Hadaway, sons of John, died or removed from Yarmouth before 1710. Gideon married Jan. 21, 1697, Patience Beaumond of Dorchester, and perhaps removed to that town. Of Hannah I find no account. A Sarah Hadaway, probably a daughter of the first John, married Oct. 11, 1710, John Page, of whose history I know nothing.

Thomas remained in Yarmouth till about the year 1715, when he removed to Barnstable. He married Dec. 15, 1698, Sarah Baker of Yarmouth. I find no record of his children by this marriage. James, afterwards of Barnstable, and Hannah who married Feb. 15, 1728, John Lothrop, were probably his children. For his second wife he married May 19, 1714, Sarah Marchant of Yarmouth, and removed to Barnstable, where he had:

I.    Lot, born May 6, 1717.

II. Sarah, June 24, 1718.
III. Temperance, May 23, 1720.
IV. Patience, Feb. 27, 1724-5.
V. Susannah, Sept. 3, 1726.
VI. Thomas, Dec. 3, 1730.

James Hadaway, probably son of Thomas by his first wife, married Oct. 9, 1730, Bethia, daughter of Barnard Lumbard, and had :

I. Lois, born 17th April 1732.
II. James, 13th Nov. 1733.

He died in 1733, leaving Widow Bethia and one small child. At the time of his death he was in the whaling business.

James, the second of the name, had a farm* at Rowley's pond, afterwards called Lewis', and of late years Hadaway's pond. His house, built perhaps by one of the Lewis family, stood on the south side of the pond. He was a very odd man, a firm believer in withcraft, and other strange fantasies. He lived to the ripe age of 95, a healthy old man, and to the last capable of great physical endurance. He married Dec. 9, 1756, Mary Lumbard, and had Benjamin, Lewis, John, and Hannah, whom I remember—perhaps others. For his second wife he married Mary, or Molly, as she was usually called, widow of Eli Phinney, one of the most efficient men in Barnstable during the Revolutionary period. She was a daughter of Jabez Phinney, and was born 3d Dec. 1735, and was perhaps one of the smallest specimens of humanity. She was the mother of nine children by her first husband, six of whom were living at the time she married Hadaway. She died Jan. 12, 1821, aged 85 years.

Of James' children John did not marry, and his father called him his boy more than 60 years. Benjamin has descendants. His house was destroyed by fire Feb. 1799.† His two sons were sleeping in a chamber at the time, and could not be approached by the stairway which was in flames. The eldest perished in his bed, the second was rescued by the father only to survive and suffer a few hours. Both are buried in one grave in the west burying-ground near the East Church. In attempting to rescue his children the father was badly burned, and for some time it was feared that he would lose his eyesight.

Thomas Hadaway youngest son of Thomas, married Dec. 18, 1757, Huldah Smith, daughter of Matthias of West Barnsta-

---

*George Lewis' great lot was at Rowley's pond. Jan. 12, 1662-3, George Lewis, Sen., and his son George, Jr., conveyed the same to Edward and John, sons of George, Sen., namely : 27 1-2 acres on the northerly side to Edward, and 27 1-2 on the southerly to John. The latter was killed in the Rehobeth battle March 26, 1676, and his lands passed out of the family and for many years have been known as the Hadaway farm.

---

†The house which he built on the same spot with funds contributed to him, was also destroyed by fire the present year.

ble.  He had several children, among whom were Frederick, Benjamin and Hannah.  Benjamin was called carpenter Ben. to distinguish him from the son of James.  He was a deputy sheriff, a captain of a militia company, and jail keeper for a time.  He was a very strong man,  and among other feats he took up a barrel of rum and drank from the bung.  He bought of Mr. Eleazer Scudder the ancient Gorham mansion house at Hyannis Port, where he resided and  kept a  public house.  He  married his  cousin Hannah,  daughter  of  James Hadaway,  and  had  a large  family  of daughters.  He was as eccentric as any of the name, and his history is an  illustration of  the saying, "Truth is stronger than fiction."

His sister Hannah sued him for money that she said she had deposited with him, taking no security therefor.  He denied having received it.  A few days before the case was to be tried, he remarked to his wife that he would go on board a vessel in the harbor, and purchase a barrel of flour.  He did not return. Search was made for him.  His hat was found in the surf on the shore, his boat was adrift, and the oar which he used in sculling was also found near by.  These circumstances seemed to prove beyond controversy, that in attempting to board the vessel in the harbor he was accidentally drowned.  Guns were fired, sweeps were dragged, oil was poured on the waters, and every effort was made to recover his body without success.  No one had seen him go away, and his family and neighbors believed he was dead, and an administrator was appointed on his estate.

Soon after he left, there was a report that he had been seen at his brother Frederick's in Vermont, but nothing reliable could be obtained, though it was reported that letters had been received from him.  Twenty-one years after he left he as unexpectedly returned to his house.  No one knew  where he came from, or how he came, and it was  some time before the members of his family could realize that he was among the living.  Capt. Hadaway in his dealings with strangers was considered an honorable man ; but with members of his family or his relatives, he was the most eccentric of  men.

Frederick married a Marchant, and  removed  to  Vermont. He was as eccentric as any of  the family.

Hannah married Capt. Thomas Appleton.  She resided in Boston, Gloucester, and Barnstable.  She was a woman of good understanding, well informed, and was distinguished for her colloquial powers and her ready wit.  For  fifteen years after her marriage she  lived in good style, and associated with the intelligent, the gay and the fashionable.  Notwithstanding, she was a Hadaway all  her days—odd, eccentric, a firm believer in witches and witchcraft.  Surprising stories she would tell of  witches she had seen and known, of their strange transformations, and of the strange influence that they exerted over others. Those stories she dressed up in all the charms of eloquence, and would half persuade her hearers that they were true. She was the great-grand-daughter of the first John, inherited his peculiarities, and education, extensive reading, and association with the intelligent, failed to root out the seeds of fanaticism which in early life had been so deeply implanted in her mind, that they had become a part of her very being.

# THOMAS HATCH.

Many of the name Hatch came over early. Elder William of Scituate, who came from Sandwich in England in 1635, with wife Jane and five children, was a noted man in the early history of the Colony. Two of the name of Thomas came over, and settled in Massachusetts, and afterwards removed to the Plymouth Colony. One of them was made a freeman of Massachusetts May 14, 1634, the same day that three others were, who were afterwards among the first settlers of Yarmouth. Thomas whom Mr. Deane calls an elder brother of William, settled in Scituate, and died there about the year 1646, leaving a family. Mr. Savage calls this man the freeman; but circumstances incline me to the opinion that it was the other Thomas who was made free May 14, 1634.

Thomas Hatch, the ancestor of the family in this country, was one of the nine who proposed, Jan. 7, 1638, O. S., "to take up their freedome at Yarmouth." On the 5th of March following his name is entered on the record with those who proposed to become freemen at the next court, but there is no mark against it indicating that he then took the required oath. In 1641 he had removed to Barnstable, and at the court held the first of June that year, he with others of that town, was again "propounded to be admitted a freeman at the next court." His name does not appear on any list of freemen of the town of Barnstable. He had taken the "oath of fidelity" before his removal from Yarmouth, and in some instances this seems to have been considered as the equivalent of the freeman's oath.   In August 1643, his name appears on the roll of those "able to  bear arms in Barnstable," and in the following January on the list of approved inhabitants of Barnstable.

Very little  is certainly known respecting him.   He does not appear to have been employed at any time, in any public business.   He was not a man of wealth, and  no record of his lands has been preserved.   In 1648 Mr. Anthony Thacher claimed eight acres in the "West Field"* in Yarmouth that had been bought of Thomas Hatch.   This was the usual allotment, and the probability is that he had an equal proportion of  the lands both in Yarmouth  and in Barnstable assigned to him.   I am inclined to the opinion that his houselot in Barnstable was near the Crocker farm  at  West Barnstable.   Lands in that vicinity were afterwards owned by his son Jonathan, and  by him sold to Capt. Thomas Dimmock.

He died  in 1661, leaving a widow Grace and son Jonathan and daughter Lydia, wife of Henry Taylor.   Mr. Savage calls him "a young man."   He was a grandfather and in my judgment had ceased to be young.

A pleasant  story is told respecting his courtship.   It is said that he was son of a farmer and served his father before learning the trade of a tailor.   His wife was also a farmer's daughter, and in time of harvest assisted him  in the fields, and was very expert in the use of the sickle.   Two young  men asked her hand in marriage and  it was agreed that the one who should  reap the larger piece in a given time should win the prize.   The land was marked off and  an equal proportion assigned to Miss Grace.   She was the best reaper, and having decided that she would marry Thomas Hatch, she slyly cut over on the part set off  to him, and in consequence Thomas came out ahead, claimed and received her hand in marriage.

This story was related by a grandson of Thomas, and has been preserved  as a family tradition, and whether true or false is immaterial.   I doubt whether Grace, the widow of  Thomas Hatch, was the heroine of the story ; if so, she was different from other mothers—she must have been a second wife—for if Jonathan and Lydia had been her children, she would not have allowed them in youth to have been aliens from their father's house and exposed to all the temptations of a wicked world.   I have no other evidence that she was a second wife.   I want no other. Thomas Hatch was a church member, and a freeman, a man whose life was a living testimony of his fidelity to the principles

---

*"The West Field" was an open tract, cultivated by the Indians, bounded southerly by Dennis Pond, westerly  by the bounds of Barnstable,  northerly it extended  nearly to the present County  road, and easterly to Hawes' Lane.   The lot of Thomas  Hatch was in the immediate vicinity of the homestead of the writer.

which he professed. He was not a man of note, yet he was an honest man and a good neighbor. It is unnatural to suppose that a man who sustained the character that Thomas Hatch did, would have allowed his only son, and only daughter, to have been exposed to temptations, as they were, if there had not been some superior controling influence at home.

Of the family of Thomas Hatch little is known beside what has been already stated. His children† were both probably born in England. At his death in 1661 he was probably aged, not "a young man." Of the time of the death of his widow Grace, I find no record.

2. Jonathan, born about the year 1624.

3. Lydia, born about the year 1626, married Henry Taylor Dec. 19, 1650, and had a family.

He probably had other children, but none are named as surviving in 1661.

Jonathan Hatch was a man of indomitable energy of character—no difficulties discouraged him—no misfortunes swayed him from his onward and determined course of life. He was a pioneer in the march of civilization, and the history of his life, if faithfully written, would present many points of romantic interest. "The boy was the father of the man." At the early age of fourteen, it appears that Jonathan was bound as an apprentice to Lieut. Richard Davenport, of Salem. His father and mother and sister removed to Yarmouth, leaving him among strangers, in a strange land. Davenport was a soldier,—a man of impetuous spirit, and Jonathan, after remaining with him two years, deserted from his service and came to Boston, probably with the intention of obtaining a passage by water to Yarmouth. Sept. 2, 1640, he was arrested in Boston as a fugitive from service, and "was censured to bee severely whiped, and for the present is committed for a slave to Lieut. Davenport." [Mass. Rec.] Whether Jonathan escaped "the severe whipping," does not appear; however that may be, it is certain that twenty severe whippings would not have compelled a boy of his spirit to have returned to the servitude of Lieut. Davenport. He had legs and he made a legitimate use of them, and they brought him safely to his father's house in Yarmouth.

His troubles did not cease on his arrival at the Cape. Dec. 1, 1640, Capt. Nicholas Sympkins charged him with slandering him. The result was, the Captain had a fine of forty shillings

†The evidence that Jonathan and Lydia were children of Thomas Hatch is not entirely satisfactory. It rests on these facts: May 27, 1661, his widow Grace presented an inventory of his estate. March 3, 1662-3, Jonathan Hatch and Lydia, wife of Henry Taylor, were appointed administrators on the estate of Thomas Hatch, deceased. They are not called his children, but the presumption is that they were. It will be noticed that nearly three years elapsed after the death of Thomas, before administrators were appointed. If Thomas had been a brother of Jonathan and Lydia, they would have had a right to claim letters of administration after the death of Grace. I name this as possible, not as probable.

imposed on him, and Jonathan escaped without punishment. March 1, 1641-2, he "was taken as a vagabond, and for his misdemeanors was censured to be whipt and sent from constable to constable to Lieut. Davenport at Salem." At the Court held April 5, 1642, this sentence was re-considered. The court had no authority to order the arrest of a party as a vagabond, because he had escaped from the service of a master residing in another jurisdiction. He was "appointed to dwell with Mr. Stephen Hopkins," who was enjoyend to have a special care of him.

Mr. Hopkins died in 1644. Jonathan did not probably reside long with him, for soon afterwards he appears to have been a resident in Barnstable. Aug. 23, 1645, he was one of the four men forming the quota of the town of Barnstable in the expedition against the Narragansets and their confederates.

The foregoing records of the early life of Jonathan do not present his character in an amiable point of view. His parents appear to have taken no interest in his welfare, and this can be accounted for only on the supposition that Grace was a second wife. I am not a writer of eulogy. I must present such facts as I find on record ; and my inferences must be logical or they are worthless. The boy was exposed to temptation on every hand—he had no friends on whom he could rely—he was a bond servant—"a slave"—and that servitude his proud spirit could not brook—he resisted—he escaped from servitude ; that, in the eye of the law, was criminal—and for that he was imprisoned, and for that endured cruel stripes. Though his conduct is not legally justifiable, we cannot but admire his bold and manly resistance of the intolerant spirit of the age, and of the law which banished him from the home of his father, and which deprived him of the liberty which he claimed as a free born citizen of the British realm.

Jonathan Hatch married April 11, 1646, Sarah Rowley, daughter of Henry Rowley, by his first wife—a daughter of William Palmer, Sen. From the latter's will dated in 1637, I infer that Sarah's mother-in-law, though a church member, was not a kind-hearted woman. She was a step-mother to Sarah as I have presumed Grace had been to Jonathan. Their experience in early life coincided—they lived long in married life, and were blessed with a family of eleven children, nine of whom had families of their own.

After his marriage he probably resided several years at West Barnstable before removing to South Sea. Oct. 7, 1651, he and Samuel Hinckley were prosecuted by the grand jury for hiring land of the Indians, and March 2, 1651-2, he was again prosecuted for furnishing an Indian with a gun, powder and shot. Feb. 1652-3, he was on the jury that laid out the road from Sandwich to Plymouth, and in 1657 took the oath of fidelity.

The grant of his lands was recorded Feb. 14, 1655, but it is probable that the grant was made and that he removed to South Sea at an earlier date. His lands are thus described : ''Fifty acres more or less of upland, with a little parcel of marsh adjoining, at a place commonly called Sepnisset on ye South Sea,'' also eight acres of meadow, four at Oyster Island, which is very particularly described. One-half of this farm he subsequently sold to Thomas Shaw, and they sold the same May 27, 1661, to Mr. John Thompson, who re-sold to John Lovell about the year 1674, and the latter's descendants yet hold most of the ancient Hatch farm and meadows under the title derived from Thompson.

In the deed of Hatch and Shaw to Thompson the upland is described as being at a creek commonly called Se-paw-ess-is-set *alias* Se-pau-is-set,* and is thus described : "Fifteen acres lying on ye south side of ye said creek, bounded southerly and westerly by ye commons, easterly by a little swamp, northerly partly by ye said creek and partly by ye harbour ; and thirty acres bounded southerly by ye said creek, lying 140 rod long by ye sea side and 40 rod into ye woods."

At this time there were very few whites settled at South Sea. Roger Goodspeed who resided at Mystic, was probably his nearest neighbor for several years. At that time oysters were very abundant in the waters in the vicinity of his residence, and many barrels were annually pickled and sent to market. For many years after the settlement of the town, all the lime used for building purposes was manufactured in the vicinity of Sep-nis-set from the shells of the oysters. Dry wood cut into small pieces was procured, and a kiln built of alternate layers of shells and wood, the whole was covered with turf, excepting a small opening at the top and another at the bottom where the fire was set, and the shells converted by the heat into quick-lime, of a superior quality.

Many Indians dwelt near the residence of Goodman Hatch. The wigwam of Paup-mun-nueke, the sachem of the Massapees, was about a mile distant. He traded with them, visited them, and at times was perhaps too familiar with them. It was policy for him to be on good terms with them—they were his neighbors, and if by his conduct he had excited them to hostility, they had it in their power to do him much injury. In June, 1658, it was proved in court that an Indian named Repent had threatened to shoot Gov. Prence on his return from Plymouth. Mr. Hatch was charged with having justified Repent, but there was no proof, and

---

*This name, which occurs in the last Number, is called in the records a place and a creek. Its termination, however written, indicates that it was a place or village by the water. The Indians probably dropped the final syllable when they referred to the creek, calling it Sipanesse, which perhaps means a little stream where coarse grass grows. It appears to have been the name of the creek, or lagoon, on the south of the residence of Mr. Seth Goodspeed. After the Hatch farm came into possession of the Lovell family large additions were made.

he was by the court admonished and released.

May 27, 1661.  Goodman Hatch sold his farm at Sipnesset and removed to Saconecet, Suconnesset, or Suckinesset,* the Indian name of the town of Falmouth.  He is not named in the colony records till 1685 as one of the original proprietors, but their records and deeds and other papers preserved in the family prove that he was.  At a meeting of the proprietors held Nov. 29, 1661, it was voted,

"That Jonathan Hatch and Isaac Robinson, because they have built their houses,† shall have lots by their houses,—that is to say, Jonathan Hatch to have ten acres by his house lying against the neck, [lying by the Herring Brook.]   And Isaac Robinson to have four acres by his house, and eight acres next adjoining to Jonathan Hatch towards Pease's land.  Also because they think themselves wronged, to be put out of the Neck, we have considered that they shall have an acre and a half of meadow within the Great Neck, towards Pease's land."

Goodman Hatch's farm at Falmouth contained eighty acres, and for several years he was the agent of the proprietors, and was employed at times in running out the bounds of lots, and attending to sales and transfers of rights.  He could not give up his old habit of trading with the Indians, and June 7, 1670, was fined £3 for selling them liquor.

He bought three Indians of Capt. Church—a man and his wife and a child—June 3, 1679, the brothers of the woman appeared in court with Goodman Hatch, and it was agreed that the man and his wife should be released for £6, and that the child should remain with Goodman Hatch till 24 years of age and then be released forever.  He claimed his pound of flesh ; he forgot that when a boy he had been bound to Lieut. Davenport—that he had repudiated his service.  Had not the Indian boy the same right—or did the difference in color abrogate the right of the one, and establish that of the other.

June 24, 1690, he took the freeman's oath at the County Court in Barnstable.  He was then about sixty-four years of age.  Time had tempered the fire and impetuosity of his youth, and he had become a sober, religious man—the venerable patriarch of a

---

*This name is a compound of Sucki, black; po quauho·k, the round clam or quohog; and et or set, place; means the place where Suck-au-hock or black wampan was made. The Indians had two kinds of money, beads of wampan, the black of which three was considered equal to a penny English, and the white of half the value of the black.  The white was called wampam, [white] and the black Suck-au-hock by the Indians, but the English called it all wampam, or wampam-peage.  The white was made from the stem of the periwinckle; the black from the dark colored portion of the shell of the quohog.  Some English attempted to counterfeit it; but not finding it a paying business gave it up.  The counterfeits were readily detected by the Indians.

†This record conflicts with the family tradition that Moses, son of Jonathan, was the first white child born in Falmouth, and that he was called Moses because he was born under the shelter of a whale-boat, and on a bed of rushes.  Unfortunately for the romance of the story, Jonathan Hatch built a house in Falmouth two years before the birth of his son Moses.

large and esteemed family of children and grand-children. After that date, his name seldom appears on the public records. He had acquired a large landed estate, and was ranked among the wealthy of those times. His papers show that he continued to do business till the close of his long life. As one of the agents of the proprietors of Falmouth, he was often called upon to take the care of their interests, and they could not have been committed to a more careful hand. He died Dec. 1710, aged about 84 years. His will is dated Sept. 15, 1705, and was proved Jan. 4, 1710-11. He says he is aged, names his six sons, Thomas, Jonathan, Joseph, Benjamin, Samuel and Moses, and his daughters Mary Weeks, Sarah Wing and Mercy Rowley, and appoints the latter his sole executrix.

Children of Jonathan Hatch and Sarah Rowley, his wife. Born in Barnstable. (The discrepancies between the Barnstable and Falmouth records are noted.)

4.  I.   Mary, July 16, 1647.
5.  II.  Thomas, Jan. 1, 1649.
6.  III.  Jonathan, May 17, 1652, May 16, 1652.
7.  IV.  Joseph, May 7, 1654, June 10, 1654.
8.  V.   Benjamin, Sept. 7, 1655, June 6, 1656.
9.  VI.  Nathaniel, June 5, 1657, Sept. 3, 1658.
10.  VII.  Samuel, Oct. 11, 1659, Oct. 4, 1660.

*Born in Falmouth.*

11.  VIII.  Moses, March 4, 1662, March 4, 1663.
12.  IX.  Sarah, March 21, 1664, March 23, 1665.
13.  X.   Mercy, April 27, 1667.
14.  XI.  Lydia, May 16, 1669.

(4-1.) Mary, the eldest daughter of Jonathan Hatch, married a Mr. Weeks, as we learn from the will of the father. William Weeks of Falmouth, married March 16, 1669, Mercy, daughter of Mr. Isaac Robinson. I am inclined to the opinion that she died early and that he married for his second wife Mary Hatch. The names of the children of William Weeks were Mercy, Mehitable, Sarah, Experience, Mercy again, Jonathan, Benjamin and Lydia. These names are common in the Hatch, not in the Robinson family. In these times the mother usually adopted the names of her brothers and sisters, and I feel confident that Mary Hatch married William Weeks of Falmouth. Sarah married Nathaniel Wing, and Mercy married Nathan Rowley.

(5-2.) Thomas Hatch, named in honor of his grand-father, was a farmer and resided in Falmouth, where he died. He married Abigail Codman, Feb. 22, 1679, called of Falmouth—perhaps daughter of Robert of Edgartown.

*Children born in Falmouth.*

15.  I.  Hepsibah, 9 Jan., 1681.

16.  II.   Thomas, 25 April, 1685.
17.  III.  Sarah, 16 Sept., 1687.
18.  IV.   Stephen, 19 Jan., 1689.
19.  V.    Nathaniel, 16 March, 1693.
20.  VI.   Mary, 16 March, 1693.
21.  VII.  Aiareth, 16 Jan., 1695.
22.  VIII. Jonathan, 9 April, 1697.
23.  IX.   Peter, 25 July, 1700.

(6-3.)   Capt. Jonathan Hatch, son of Jonathan, was a farmer and resided in Falmouth, where he died. Oct. 2, 1689, he was chosen ensign of the military company. June 24, 1690, at the County Court, he took the freeman's oath. There are three entries of his marriage on the records, all probably intended for the same; but apparently not the same. I presume he married Dec. 4, 1676, Elizabeth Weeks of Falmouth, another entry may be read *Bethia Weeks* another *Elizabeth Walker.**

*Children born in Falmouth.*

24.  I.   Jonathan, 5 June, 1678.
25.  II.  Sarah, 17 Sept., 1682.
26.  III. Mehitabel, 19 March, 1684.
27.  IV.  Mary, 24 June, 1689.
28.  V.   Nathaniel, 30 July, 1693.
29.  VI.  Ebenezer, 29 Nov., 1696.

Jonathan of this family married Bethia Nye Dec. 22, 1703; and had Solomon 1704; Thankful 1706; Ebenezer 1709; Nathan 1710; Moses 1712; Benjamin 1715; Timothy 1732? Ebenezer married Oct. 25, 1720, Lydia Hatch.

(7-4.)   Capt. Joseph Hatch, perhaps excepting Moses, was the most distinguished of Jonathan's sons. He was a soldier in

---

*Mr. Freeman in his history, Vol. 2, page 474, gives a genealogy of this family full of mistakes, and full of positive assertions. He says "Thomas came from Kent 1634, born in Sandwich." This may be so, and it may be, from Wales, but there is no record. His name is not on the list of those who embarked at Sandwich in 1634-5; and the Massachusetts records prove that he came over earlier, for he was made a freeman of that Colony May 13, 1634, N. S., nearly a year prior to the embarkation from Sandwich. Mr. Savage says Jonathan was perhaps a son of Thomas, and born at Sandwich, Eng. On this slippery foundation Mr. Freeman positively asserts, that Thomas came over from Kent in 1634,

He also asserts that Thomas was a member of the church in Barnstable June 1, 1641. This may be so—it is hard to prove a negative—especially when there is a hiatus in the list of the admissions to the church from 1638 to 1643. Perhaps some clairvoiyant filled up the gap for his special accommodation.

He says Jonathan had lands in Falmouth in 1660. It is surprising that this fact is not named either in the proprietor's, the town or the Colonial records. I have yet to learn that there were any whites settled in Falmouth at that date—and if there was, Jonathan Hatch was not of the number, for he did not probably remove from Barnstable till after May 27, 1661.

He calls the 8th child of Capt. Joseph Hatch, Bethia; her name is plainly written on the town and on the church records Rebecca. He states that Benjamin, born 1655, married Mary Hamblin (so Ba rec. but F. says Lumbee) June 17, 1678." The Falmouth records say Benjamin Hatch married Mary Hamblin; the Barnstable records say George Lewis, Jr., married Mary Lumber. He says that the second wife of Benjamin was named "Alice, the record has it Ellis." The Barnstable church record has it Ellis, a contraction for Elizabeth. On the Falmouth Church record it is plainly written Elizabeth. Her maiden name was Elizabeth Eddy, born at Martha's Vineyard May 3, 1659. In his list of her children he omits her son Eddy born Aug. 2, 1700.

King Philip's war, 1675 and 6. He was lieutenant of the militia company in 1702, and afterwards captain. He inherited the homestead of his father, acquired a large estate, and exercised a wide influence. He married Dec. 7, 1683, Amy Allen of Chilmark. She joined the church in Barnstable, and was baptized Aug. 3, 1701. On the church records her name is uniformly written Amie. On the formation of the Falmouth church, Oct. 10, 1708, she with others was dismissed to that church. Capt. Joseph Hatch died Feb. 16, 1735, aged 83. (Grave Stones).

Children of Capt. Joseph Hatch born in Falmouth:
30. I.   Lydia, 13th July, 1685.
31. II.  Amy, 10th July, 1687.
32. III. Joseph, 3d Aug. 1689.
33. IV.  Ichabod, 28th Oct. 1691.
34. V.   Ruth, 9th Nov. 1693.
35. VI.  Joanna, 2d June, 1696.
36. VII. Elizabeth, 1st Nov. 1697.
37. VIII. Rebecca, 25th Jan. 1700.
38. IX.  Ebenezer, 26th March, 1702.
39. X.   Barnabas, 29th Nov. 1703.

Lydia married a Mr. Gifford, a Quaker; Amy married Jonathan Delano of Tolland, Conn.; Joseph, Jr., married in 1713, and May 1, 1735, Rebecca, a second wife. He removed to Tolland, died in Falmouth 1751; Ichabod married Abigail Weeks Dec. 2, 1714; Ruth married Dea. Solomon Swift of Tolland and Kent, Conn.; Elizabeth married Aug. 1, 1722, Stephen Skiffe of Tolland; Rebecca married a Mr. Berry, and settled in Kent about 1740; Ebenezer married in 1741, Sarah, aged 24; Barnabas married Abigail Lasrell of Duxbury, Mass., in 1728.

8-7. Benjamin Hatch was a farmer. In 1729 he removed to Mansfield, Conn., and died there or in Tolland before the year 1736. He married three wives: 1st, Mary Hamblin, Jan. 17, 1678, a daughter of James, Jr., of Barnstable. At the time of her marriage she had not completed her sixteenth year. She died early, and he married March 16, 1682, Elizabeth Eddy, who was born at Martha's Vineyard May 3, 1659. In another record her name is written Eliza. She was admitted to the Barnstable church July 14, 1710, and was dismissed to the church in Falmouth the following October, and died soon after. For his third wife he married Feb. 13, 1711-12, Experience, widow of Jabez Davis, of Barnstable. She was a daughter of David Linnell, and died a widow Dec. 1736, aged about 72.

Children of Benjamin Hatch born in Falmouth:
40. I.   Abigail, Aug. 4, 1679.

NOTE.—Mr. Freeman says Jonathan Hatch married Abigail Weeks of Barnstable, thus adding another alias to the name of his wife Elizabeth. If the readers of the records are reliable, Capt. Jonathan was a valiant man, taking to himself four wives in the month of Dec. 1678—another "Blue Beard." I do not however find that he was indicted for polygamy.

41. II. Mary, March 3, 1681.
42. III. Nathaniel, Feb. 7, 1684.
43. IV. Benjamin, Oct. 17, 1686.
44. V. John, Feb. 16, 1689.
45. VI. Elizabeth, March 25, 1692.
46. VII. Melatiah, Oct. 4, 1693.
47. VIII. Timothy, Oct. 19, 1695.
48. IX. Hannah, May 7, 1698.
49. X. Eddy, Aug. 2, 1700.
50. XI. Solomon, May 7, 1704.

Benjamin Hatch of this family removed to Brewster, then Harwich, and married Aug. 11, 1715, Mary Bangs, and had James, May 1, 1716 ; Mary, April 21, 1720 ; Benjamin, May 11, 1724 ; Ruth, June 20, 1733. He died in Brewster Feb. 14, 1769, aged 83. (Grave Stones).

Timothy Hatch had a family. His son Major Jethro, born Sept. 17, 1722, who removed to Kent, Conn., seems to have preserved all the traditions of the family. In April and May, 1816, Moses Hatch, Esq., of Danbury, Conn., a graduate of Yale College, carefully wrote down the statements of Major Hatch, then 94 years of age. He states that his ancestor was a tailor by trade, and that his wife was the daughter of a farmer born in Wales. He relates the story about the reapers which has been told. He states that his ancestor married only one wife.

Melatiah also married and had a family. J. M. Hatch, Esq., of Rochester, N. Y., is a descendant, and to him I am largely indebted for information respecting the family.

9-6. Nathaniel Hatch, son of Jonathan, born in 1657 or 1658, is not named in his father's will, and he has no family record, these facts make it probable that he died young.

10-7. Samuel Hatch was a "cordwainer," resided in Falmouth where he died in 1718. His wife Lydia was admitted to the Barnstable Church Oct. 5, 1701, and his daughters Kerziah and Lydia were baptized on the 9th of Nov. following ; Samuel, James and Zaccheus, June 7, 1702 ; Edward July 2, 1704 ; Anne, Sept. 1, 1706. His other children were probably baptized in Falmouth. The town record is imperfect. He probably resided some time at Chilmark, to which place several of his family removed. The name of his eldest child on the family record appears to be Eleazer, perhaps Ebenezer ; on the church records the name is written Kerziah.

51. I. Eleazer, (Kerziah, ch. rec.) Sept. 23, 1694.
52. II. Samuel, Feb. 28, 1694.
53. III. James, Aug. 23, 1696.
54. IV. Lydia, May 30, 1699.
55. V. Zaccheus, Feb. 10, 1701.
56. VI. Edward, bap. July 2, 1702.

57.   VII.   Anne, bap. Sept. 1, 1706.
58.   VIII.   James, and probably married Abigail Knight, of Tisbury, July 24, 1718.
59.   IX.   Martha, married David Cottle of Chilmark, Dec. 9, 1728.

Samuel Hatch, son of Samuel, married Dec. 1, 1724, Mary Clifford, of Chilmark; James married March 22, 1720, Judith Cottle, of Chilmark, second wife; Edward married Rebecca Weeks at Falmouth Aug. 17, 1727, and died at Falmouth 1750. Matthew Rowley was appointed Feb. 1750, guardian of Wait, minor son of Edward. Anne married David Butler of Chilmark, Dec. 2, 1725; Joseph married Lydia Cottle of Chilmark, Dec. 30, 1726; Lydia married Ebenezer Hatch (son of Jonathan and Elizabeth), Oct. 25, 1720.

11-8.   Dea. Moses Hatch, youngest son of Jonathan, reputed to be the first white child born in Falmouth, was a man of note in his day. He was admitted to the Barnstable church June 19, 1698, and his wife Elizabeth Aug. 2, 1702. Oct. 10, 1708, both were dismissed to the Falmouth church, of which he became a leading member and "the first deacon." He was a wealthy farmer, a man of good business capacity, and a good citizen. For one act he will ever be remembered. He gave to the town the land on which the first church was built, now a public square, ornamented with trees—a beautiful place of which the citizens are justly proud. He died "20th of May, 1747, in the 85th year of his age," and is buried in the ancient burying grounds in Falmouth.

Dea. Moses Hatch married May 9, 1686, Hepsiba Eddy of Tisbury, said to be a younger sister of Elizabeth, wife of Benjamin Hatch. For his second wife he married Elizabeth, daughter of Col. John Thacher of Yarmouth, Oct. 18, 1699. She died May 18, 1710. A Moses Hatch married about this time Hannah, widow of Joshua Bangs, and a daughter of John Scudder of Barnstable. She was baptized 5th Oct. 1651, consequently was twelve years older than Dea. Moses, and as Mr. Savage suggests, the disparity of their ages renders it doubtful whether Dea. Moses married the widow Hannah Bangs. On the Falmouth records is this entry, "Hannah, wife of Capt. Moses Hatch, died May 13, 1739." Capt. Moses was a son of the Deacon, and if he married the widow the disparity was still greater. The last wife of Dea. Moses was named Patience. The early records of Falmouth are difficult to decipher, and are not always reliable. There is no full record of the family of Dea. Moses Hatch. The following is obtained from various sources, and is an approximation to accuracy:

60.   I.   Abiah, born Feb. 1, 1686-7, died on the 13th, and was buried on the 14th of same month.

61.   II.  M * * *, a son, twin child with Abiah, died same day, buried 2d.
62.   III.  Moses, Oct. 6, 1688, died Oct. 23, 1688.
63.   IV.  Hepsiba, Feb. 16, 1690, married Benj. Nye of Falmouth, who died in 1716 insolvent.
64.   V.  Elizabeth.  She married Timothy Hallett of Yarmouth, died Oct. 24, 1744, aged 44.
65.   VI.  Rebecca, bap. June 18, 1704, married in 1733 James Lewis, of B., died July 5, 1740, aged 36.
66.   VII.  Hannah, bap. Oct. 14, 1705.
67.   VIII.  Moses, probably born before the year 1700.
68.   IX·  Sylvanus.  I have it noted that he had a son Sylvanus, but I cannot quote my authority.

Capt. Moses Hatch of Falmouth, probably a son of Dea. Moses, married April, 1724, Mary, daughter of Rev. Joseph Lord of Chatham.  Her birth is thus recorded by the father: "Mary Lord born 19-20 (2) 1701," that is, on the night of the the 19th of April, 1701, O. S.  Their children were: Sylvanus, Jan. 24, 1725; Moses, May 28, 1732, (married Prudence Gorham Sept. 1766) ; Joseph, March 8, 1735 ; Hepsibah, Feb. 12, 1737.

It is also stated that she had another child, and died during her confinement, Jan. 27, 1742-3.  The latter date is doubtful, and taking all the circumstances into consideration, I am inclined to the opinion that the Hannah, wife of Capt. Moses, recorded as having died May 13, 1739, was a blunder of the clerk.  He should have written Mary, wife of Capt. Moses Hatch, died May 13, 1739.  If I am right in this supposition, the difficulties are explained.  That this is right, his subsequent or second marriage seems to favor.  If his first wife died Jan. 27, 1743, N. S., then he married the second very soon after the death of the first, for his son Jonathan was born Dec. 17, 1743, and Benjamin Sept. 10, 1745.

The Rev. Charles Gorham Hatch, to whom I am under obligations for materials .for this article, is a descendant of Capt. Moses.

Sylvanus Hatch, probably son of Capt. Moses, had Sylvanus, who resided some time at Great Bend, Penn., and finally settled in Illinois ; Samuel, who settled in Rome, N. Y. ; John, in Pompey, Onandago Co., N. Y. ; Solomon, in Manluis, N. Y. ; Charles—Orias, who was a tory and served in the British army ; and Jethoe, who was killed at the massacre at Wyoming.

I intended to have extended this genealogy one generation further ; but on comparing my copies of records I find so many discrepancies, that it is unsafe to trust them.  Every one complains of the difficulty of deciphering the early town records of Falmouth, and I judge not without reason, for no two transcribe them alike. The proprietor's and church records were better kept.

I would like to give a particular account of the "Little Hatches" of Falmouth ; but am unable. They were children of Barnabas Hatch, who married in 1776, his relative Abigail Hatch, and had two sons and seven daughters. Six of the daughters were less than four feet in height, and could stand upright under the old fashioned "lift latch" on the front door of their father's house. Neither of the six married, but lived and died in their father's house. The other daughter, Rebecca, was of common size, and married Robert Hammond.

The two sons were Barnabas, born June 15, 1788, and Robinson, born Nov. 9, 1790. Both of these were of low stature. The one whom I knew was scarce four feet in height—a *portly* gentleman, almost as broad as he was long.

The desendants of Jonathan Hatch are very numerous. Many are in Connecticut, and in New York, and in the Western States. Among them are many distinguished men, and most of them inherit that energy of character for which their ancestor was noted. They claim to be of Welch descent, and that the "honest blood" of their maternal ancestor yet flows in their veins.

# THE HALLETT FAMILY.

Several of the name of Hallett came early to New England. William, the ancestor of the Long Island family, was born in Dorcetshire, England, in 1616, joined in the settlement of Greenwich, Conn., whence he removed to Long Island, and Dec. 1, 1652, purchased of Jacques Bentyn, one of the Directors of Van Twiller's Council, 161 acres of land at Hellgate, at a place known as Hallett's Cove. "In the fall of 1655, the Indians destroyed his house and plantation at Hallett's Cove, which induced him to take up his residence at Flushing. Here he was appointed Sheriff, in 1656, but the same year was deposed by Gov. Stuyvesant, fined and imprisoned, for entertaining the Rev. Wm. Wickenden from Rhode Island, allowing him to preach at his house, and receiving the sacrament of the Lord's Supper from his hands.   Disgusted at this treatment, Mr. Hallett, on the revolt of Long Island from the Dutch, warmly advocated the claims of Connecticut; and being sent a delegate to the general court of that colony, he was appointed a commissioner or justice of the peace for Flushing.   Afterwards he removed to Hellgate, where he lived to the age of about ninety years.   He had two sons, William and Samuel, between whom in 1688 he divided his property at Hellgate Neck.   William second, died in 1729, aged 81.   He was a justice of the peace and captain of a company of militia.   He had ten children, eight of whom married and had families.   Samuel, son of William, died Dec. 27, 1724.   He was a man of consideration in his time.   He had an only son Samuel and several daughters.*

Richard Hallett, of Boston, had a daughter Alice, who married 1st, Mordecai Nichols in 1652, and 2d, Thomas Clark, of Plymouth.   Richard does not appear to have left any male descendants.   A person named Angell Hallett is mentioned in the settlement of Capt. Bozoan Allen's estate, of Boston, 1652.   There was a George Hallett, Sen'r, of Boston, a freeman in 1690, consequently there was at the same time a George Hallett, Jr.   A Widow Lydia Hallett married at Boston 27th Nov. 1661, John Drummond.   There was a James Hallett at Windsor, Conn., in 1643, represented as a poor thievish servant.   (See Savage.)

Mr. Andrew Hallett, gentleman, was the ancestor of the Yarmouth and Barnstable families.   He came over as early as the year 1637, and was of Plymouth March 1638-9.   Respecting his family there is very little on record.   His son Andrew was one of the first settlers of Sandwich.   Another of his sons (probably Samuel) is named as being of Yarmouth in 1639.†

---

*For an interesting account of the Long Island family, see Riker's Annals of Newtown.

†In making this investigation I was assisted by the late Judge Nahum Mitchell, author of the history of Bridgewater; and by the late William S. Russell, Esq., author of Guide to Plymouth, and other historical works; both good authorities.   Since the above was written Mr. Freeman has published his history of Cape Cod.   He says "we have no authentic information in regard to Mr. Andrew Hallett, Sen'r., and must rely on the conclusions of others."   [Vol. 2, page 199.

Mr. Hallett is often named in the Plymouth Colony Records, considered "authentic" by Hutchinson, Bancroft, Baylies, Drake, Palfrey, and many others known to fame.   Mr. Freeman "relies on the conclusions of others."   He says that by his wife "Mary, in England he had Bathsheba, Andrew, Samuel, John, Hannah probably born in Barnstable, Josias and Joseph."   Where does he find this account?   Not in Deane, Savage, or Winsor.   To the latter he refers only to misquote.

Mr. Freeman positively asserts, that Mr. Hallett had the children named.   I find no record of his marriage; no record of the births or baptisms of any of his children—no record of his death or of the settlement of his estate; yet there is no good reason for doubting that the families of the name in Yarmouth and Barnstable are his descendants.   The evidence, however, is circumstantial, and does not justify positive statements.   In no family has its traditional history been better preserved, or the family papers more carefully kept, some dated in 1654; but it unfortunately happens that the tradition extends only to the second Andrew, and none of the papers of the first have been saved.   I shall endeavor carefully to discriminate between that which is certain, and that which is only probable.

Mr. Andrew Hallett, Sen., was a householder in Plymouth and in Yarmouth, and probably in Barnstable.   In those times men did not build houses to let, they built them to occupy, and in fact the legal meaning of the term householder, was a man who had a family: it was not applied to a man who owned a house, occupied by a tenant.   This view of the

The widow Mary Hallett of Barnstable, was probably his wife.  Her daughter Hannah Hallett married John Hadaway July 1656.  Josias Hallett was her son, and probably Joseph Hallett, of Barnstable.

This account is unsatisfactory ; but it is the best I have been able to obtain after much research.  Mr. Hallett's children were probably all born in England, and the parish registers in that country would probably furnish the desired information.

He was styled "gentleman," a title bestowed upon few in the Colony.  It shows that he was a man possessed of a good estate, and a man of some note in his native land.  He was among the very first who came to Mattakeset, but did not make it his place of residence till 1641.  His son Samuel was of Yarmouth in 1639, and is spoken of as a young man, for whom his father was responsible.  (Court Order, vol. 2, page 20.)

March 5, 1638-9, the Colony Court ordered the Committee of the town of Yarmouth, consisting of Mr. Anthony Thacher, Mr. Thomas Howes, Mr. John Crowe, Mr. Nicholas Sympkins, William Palmer, Philip Tabor and Joshua Barnes, to make the first division of the planting lands, to be divided equally "to each man according to his estate and quality, and according to their instructions."  Thacher, Howes and Crowe, had surveyed the lands during the previous winter, and it appears that Mr. Hallett was also in Yarmouth, and had "assumed to himself" more land than was thought equitable, and the Colony Court appointed March 5, 1638-9, Joshua Pratt, of Plymouth, and Mr. John Vincent of

matter, I think, makes it probable, if not certain, that the elder Mr. Hallett had a family.
That the widow Mary Hallett, of Barnstable, was the widow of Andrew Hallett, Sen'r., rests on this evidence : in 1654 she was a resident in Barnstable, and probably had been for several years.  She and some of her children were the owners of one of the original allotments of lands, purchased one of the first settlers, for in the list of the persons who in January, 1644, were proprietors of the common lands, there was no one of that name, Mr. Hallett being then a resident in Yarmouth.  He was living July 1646, but his residence at that time is not named; but it was probably Barnstable.  He died soon after this date, before the year 1648.  His estate was probably legally settled, and a division thereof made among his heirs; but unfortunately no record was made.
Up to July 7, 1646, the records of judicial acts are in the handwriting of Mr. Nathaniel Souther, after which there is a chasm of two years and three months, to Oct. 3, 1648.  In the Probate record, there is a similar chasm.  During that period there does not appear to have been a permanent Secretary.  The court orders during that time are in the handwriting of Gov. Bradford, Antony Thacher and others.  The first record made in the court orders by Nathaniel Morton, so many years Secretary of the Colony, is dated Dec. 7, 1647, probably written up from the minutes of others, for he did not perform all the duties till Oct. 1648.  The Judicial acts and the Probate records were not written up by him, and the papers are now lost.  Notwithstanding, the records of Barnstable and some incidental entries on the Colony records, will enable us to arrive at a conclusion which, if not entirely satisfactory, is probable.
In 1647, at the time of Mr. Hallett's death, Andrew and Samuel were of legal age.  Josias and Joseph were minors, if they were able bodied and came over with their parents, because in Aug. 1643, all males able to bear arms were enrolled, and their names not being on the list it is safe to infer that they were not 16 in 1643, or 21 in 1647.
Mr. Hallett left a good estate.  Mr. Freeman says : "Winsor gives his estate at £1180," a misquotation, for if so, he was a very wealthy man, a farm of of fifty acres and its appertenances could then be bought for £10.  In the division of his estate it appears that Andrew, Samuel, and Joseph, had the "Hallett Farm" or great lot of 200 acres, and the widow Mary, Hannah and Josiah, the estate at Goodspeed's Hill and appertenances.  Mr. Andrew Hallett, Sen., was the only man of the name in the Colony, old enough to have been the father of this family, and I think it a legitimate inference, that the Wid. Mary was his wife, and Andrew, Jr., Samuel, Hannah, Josias and Joseph, his children.

Sandwich, to view the lands, "and make report thereof unto the Court, that if these proportions which Mr. Andrew Hellott hath assumed to himself there shall be so p'judiciall to the whole, that then some just and equall order be taken therein, to prevent the evil consequences it may be to the whole plantation."

No report of the committee is on record, and it would appear from the subsequent action of the Court that Mr. Hallett had not "assumed to himself" a greater proportion of the planting lands than he had a right to claim. On the 5th of May, 1639, the Court ordered, "that the proportion of lands granted to Mr. Andrew Hellott, at Mattacheesett, shal be and remain unto him, and those that are appoynted to set forth the bounds betwixt Mattacheese and Mattacheeset shall lay forth the said proportion unto him in a convenient plase there." (Court Orders, vol. 1, page 121).

The two hundred acre lot of Mr. Hallett was laid out, approved by the Court and recorded Sept. 3, 1639. A particular description of this lot is given in the account of the Gorham family, who were afterwards the principal owners. June 17, 1641, a new boundary line was run between Barnstable and Yarmouth. This line divided the Hallett farm into two parts; the larger in Barnstable contained 150 acres, and the smaller in Yarmouth containing forty-four acres.

Oct. 7, 1639, "It was ordered by the Court that the seventeen acres of meadow lying at the Stony Cove (Mill Pond) in Yarmouth, shall be laid forth for Mr. Andrew Hellott, on the south west side of the said Cove, and if it want of that proportion, then to be made up on the other side, and ten acres more upon the Stony Cove Neck."

Mr. Hallett's name first appears on record in March 1638-9, but he had probably then been in the country several years. He was then a resident in Plymouth, where he had a dwelling-house and seven and one-half acres of land situate on the "new street." This estate he sold to Thomas Cushman, who conveyed it to Thomas Lettis March 28, 1641-2.

Nov. 25, 1639, Mr. Hallett bought for £10 sterling, of Dr. Thomas Starr, of Duxbury, seventeen acres of land in Yarmouth, in two divisions, and twelve acres of meadow "with the frame of a house to be set and made with a chimney, and to be thached, studded and latched, (daubing excepted) by William Chase, who was agreed with all and paid to the doing thereof by the said Thomas Starr, before the bargain was made with Mr. Hallett." [Deeds, page 50.] No boundaries are given in the deed. The houselot was at the north west corner of the town of Yarmouth, and adjoined his "great lot" on the west, south by the highway, east by by the lot of Robert Dennis, and north by the mill pond. It is now owned by Joshua Hallett and others. The other division of the land was in the West Field, and he soon after sold it to Robert Dennis. He was of Plymouth Sept. 1, 1640, and of Yarmouth June 17, 1641, showing that he and his son Andrew became permanent residents of Yarmouth about the same time.

Sept. 8, 1641, Mr. Hallett mortgaged to Mr. William Paddy, to secure a debt of £5, 4s, and to William Hanbury to secure a debt of 29sh, "all that his farm in Barnstable, with all and singular the appertenances thereunto belonging, and all his right, title and interest of and into the same, and every part and parcel thereof." The mortgage was for one year, and the reason he gives for making it is, "that hee is now going into England, and is not able to pay them," and therefore freely assigns the property for their security.

After his return from England he resided certainly three years in Yarmouth, and perhaps till his decease in 1647. The mortgaging of his farm for so small a sum indicates that he was not a man of wealth ; but the following generous act proves that he was a man of property, or he would not have given a cow to the poor of Yarmouth. The following is extracted from the Plymouth Colony records, vol. 2, page 70 :

March 5, 1643-4. "Whereas information is given to the Court that there is a cowe or a heiffer in calve given or disposed by Mr. Andrew Hallett, Sen., of Yarmouth, for the benefitt of the poore of the said towne of Yarmouth, which for the ordering thereof was referred to the Court by the said Mr. Hellot, by his letter under his hand, bearing date the first day of March, 1643— the Court doth therefore order that the said cowe or heiffer in calve shal be on Mayday next delivered to Thomas Payne, of Yarmouth, who shall have her three years next ensuing, and the milk and the one-half of the increase during that tyme, and after the said three years are expired, the poore of Yarmouth shall have her and the encrease, to be disposed of by the townsmen of Yarmouth from tyme to tyme to other ppr persons dwelling in the said town, as they shall think fitt, and for such town, reserving the benefitt of the said stock for the benefitt of their poore, and not to be allienated to any other use."

At the March term of the Court in 1642, Mr. William Hanbury recovered in an action of debt on a note for £6 9s, 9d, judgment against Mr. Hallett for the amount of the debt, 2 pence damage, and the cost of the suit. At the July term in 1646, Samuel Harvey, "in action of trespass upon the ease," £6 5s, debt, 15 shillings damages and costs of suit.

This is the last entry of his name on the records, in connection with any business transaction. May 14, 1648, Mr. Thomas Howes "laid down seven and one-half acres of meadow at the lower end of Rock (Lone?) Tree furlong late Mr. Hallett's."

June 7, 1648, Robert Dennis claimed seven acres of land in the West Field bought of Mr. Hallett. In a deed dated Feb. 20, 1654, the great lot of Mr. Andrew Hallett, deceased, is named.

In Lechford's Plain Dealing, he is called a schoolmaster. If so, it is surprising that his son Andrew did not learn to write till some time after he was a married man. However, there were many in those times who could read fluently; but were unable to write. That was not considered a necessary accomplishment, and it did not necessarily follow that the man who could not write was ignorant; yet we may safely presume that a teacher of youth would have instructed his own children in the elementary branches of education. His other children were better educated; but, notwithstanding, Andrew was the most respectable and succeeded best in life.

Mr. Hallett, as above stated, was called a gentleman, a word that at that time had a very different meaning attached to it, than it has at the present time. When applied to a man, it meant that he was connected with the gentry or wealthy class—that he was not a mechanic or common laborer, and that he had received a good education. Rank and title were more regarded in those days than at the present time. Of the first settlers in Barnstable, about thirty were entitled to be called "goodman," four to be called "mister," and one "gentleman." What his employment was the records do not inform us. He was engaged in too many lawsuits for a teacher, yet Lechford was probably right. He had not been officially employed in the public service, yet the Colony Court decided that he had rendered some public service and was entitled to a liberal grant, and though objection was made to the amount, yet the Court confirmed it, and the towns of Barnstable and Yarmouth acquiesced.

Too few incidents of his life are known to enable us to form a just estimate of his character. That he was a man of some note in the Colony, has already been shown. He speculated in wild lands; but in doing so he only followed the fashions of the times. Every one traded in land, from the minister in his pulpit to the cobbler on his bench. He was frequently a party in law suits. They are not always to be avoided; for the over-reaching and the dishonest ought not to be allowed to possess in peace the wealth of others. However, the man of peace, the good citizen and obliging neighbor, very rarely appeals to the law to obtain redress for every offence against his property or his good name. His experience and observation has taught him that it is not the better way. The self-willed, the wayward and the stubborn, as a class, are most frequently engaged in lawsuits. Mr. Hallett did not recover damage in any of his lawsuits, and it may thence be inferred that he was a little stiff-necked, and believed his own to be the better way, a trait of character which many of his descendants, down to the fifth generation, inherited.*

However wayward he may have been, his generous donation to the poor of Yarmouth will ever be remembered, and make us regret that we know so little of the man.   If at the present time a man should present a cow to the  poor, the act would not be heralded in the newspapers as an act of great benevolence, but in order to  form a just estimate of  the  value of the gift, it must be borne in mind that cattle were then scarce in the Colony, and that a cow was  then the equivalent of a good sized farm, or of the wages of a common laborer for a year.

There is no record of his death.   In the division of the fences in Barnstable Feb. 28, 1647, *Mr.* or *Mrs.* Hallett is named, but not in the  subsequent division in 1649.   This entry is probably in old style, and would be 1648, new.   Not much reliance, however, is to be placed in it.   He probably died in 1647, as above stated, but if the entry in the division of fences is reliable, in the spring of 1648.

Of  some of the members of the Hallett family I have spoken in a note.   John Hallett, who settled in Scituate, was one of the Conihasset planters in 1646.   Mr. Deane calls him a brother of Andrew of Sandwich.   Mr. Savage copies from Deane, and remarks that his account is "confused."   He has not made it any clearer.   Both mix up the families of Andrew, Sen., with that of Andrew, Jr., and hence the confusion.

Similarity in the family names of the Scituate and Yarmouth families probably induced Mr. Deane to call them relatives.   They probably were ; but John of Scituate was too old a man to be called a son of Andrew, Sen., without some more certain evidence than has yet been obtained.   Richard Curtis married "Lydia," daughter of John Hallett, in 1649, presuming her to be his oldest child, 1609 is as late a period as can be assigned for the birth of the father.   In some families there are as great or a greater disparity in the ages of the children, but such cases are rare, and in the absence of records it is not safe to make such presumptions.

Mr. Deane had  but little  exact  information respecting  the Hallett family.   He evidently did not know that there were two

*Few men could  tell a story more gracefully or better than the late Hon. John Reed. He frequently told the following, remarking that he was an eye-witness.   It is a good illustration of a peculiar trait of character for which many of the Hallets of other days were noted.   Perhaps  it was the manner in  which the  story was told that made it interesting. The fourth Jonathan Hallett  and Joshua Hallett were at work together shingling a building.   One proposed to put up a stage ; the other said, "We can put on two or three courses more without one."   The first said to himself, "I can  shingle as long as you  without a stage, and I will not again propose to put up a stage," and the other made the same resolution.   They continued  nailing on course  after course, both resolved not to  yield, till both were  seen  standing tiptoe  beside  the building, nailing on shingles as high above their heads as they could possibly stretch,  neither yielded till it was impossible for him  to drive another nail.   This singular contest attracted  spectators, and the merriment which it excited had, perhaps, an influence in inducing them  to take a common sense view of the matter and put up a stage.

**Andrews.** John, son of Andrew, Jr., he calls a son of John of Scituate, and the wife of Richard Curtis he calls in one place "Ann," and in another "Lydia." He informs us that John Hallett was an extensive land holder ; that his house was near the harbor at Scituate, and that Hallett's Island near the "stepping stones," still retains his name.

Bathsheba, the first wife of Mr. Richard Bourne, on the authority of Mr. Freeman, I called a daughter of Andrew, Sen. ; but the statement wants confirmation.

Family of Mr. Andrew Hallett, Sen. All his children probably born in England :

2. I. Andrew, born about 1615, married Ann Besse, died in 1684, (see below.)

3. II. Samuel, was sixteen years of age, or upwards, in 1643, consequently was born in England before the year 1627. He came to Yarmouth early, before the removal of his father from Plymouth, as the following record dated June 17, 1641, seems to prove, because Mr. Hallett had no other son to whom it could refer, Andrew being then of age and a resident in Sandwich, and neither Josias nor Joseph, if they had then came over, was over twelve in 1639.

"It is ordered by the Court, that Mr. Andrew Hallett shall pay Massatampaim† one fadome of beads [wampam] within two moones, beside the nett he alleadgeth the sd Massatampaim soold him, for the deare that Mr. Hellot's sonn bought of him about two years since."

In the division of his father's estate a part of the "Hallett Farm" situate within the boundaries of the town of Barnstable, and the homestead bought of Dr. Starr in Yarmouth, appears to have been set off to him, and was sold by his administaators, probably to Capt. John Gorham who was the owner in 1652.‡

He had no family. Neither widow nor children are named in the settlement of his estate. He was drowned at Eastham, and the particulars are thus recorded by Mr. Lothrop on the Barnstable church records : "Thomas Blossom and Samuel Hollet

---

†Mas-sa-tam-paim was the sachem of Nobscusset, or Yarmouth. He sold the lands in the north part of Yarmouth and Dennis to Mr. Bradford, and his release in the handwriting of Anthony Thacher is yet preserved. He lived to be very aged. The first syllable of his name signifies great—the whole perhaps "great sagamon," but I am not certain. It is sometimes writen "Mas-am-tam-paigne."

‡In the Gorham article I state that Capt. John purchased the whole of the "Hallett Farm" about the year 1652. A more careful examination of deeds and the other records, satisfies me that he did not at first purchase the whole. The forty-four acres of the "Farm" within the boundaries of Yarmouth, excepting some small portions, has never been sold, and the descendants of Andrew, Sen., still hold it by virtue of the original grant in 1639, also a tract of about 15 acres on the west of Long Pond ; I am also inclined to the opinion that he did not at first purchase the northwest portion of the "Farm" which appears to have been set off to Joseph, who sold to James Gorham, a son of Capt. John. My recent investigations seem to lead to this conclusion. I am perfectly certain that I was in an error when I stated that Capt. John Gorham bought the whole of the "Hallett Farm," and those who keep files of these articles are requested to make the correction by interlining before "Hallett Farm" the words "a large part of."

drowned at the Harbour of Nocett att their first Setting out from thence aboute a fishing voyage April 22, 1650."

"June 5, 1650, Letters of administration are graunted unto Mr. Tho. Howes [of Yarmouth] and Samuel Mayo§ [of Barnble] to administer upon the estate of Samuel Hollet, and to pay the debts as fare as the estate will amount unto by equall proportions."

The foregoing extracts show that Samuel Hallett came to Yarmouth with the first settlers in the winter of 1638-9, that he remained in that town till the removal of his father in 1641, engaged in the fisheries, and probably had the care of his father's estate before his brother Andrew removed from Sandwich ; that he died unmarried in 1650, and probably on account of his losses at the time of his shipwreck, he did not leave a sufficient estate to pay his debts in full.

4.    III.    Hannah, born about 1627, married July 1, 1656, John Haddaway.    (See Haddaway.)

5.    IV.    Josias was born after the year 1627.    He was a mariner, and is named as living in 1663.    From the notices of him in the records, it is inferred that he did not sustain a good character for sobriety.    In the division of his father's estate, the southerly part of the homestead was set off to him, containing eight acres.    This land is now owned by Major Sylvanus B. Phinney, and is that part of his homestead which is situate on the south of the swamp.    Anciently there was a highway between the swamp and the railroad, called Goodspeed's Outlet.    Josias Hallett's house was on that road.    Dec. 14, 1661, he sold this estate and three acres of meadow at Blush's point to John Haddeway, for £10 sterling.    In the deed he is called "sometime of Barnstable."    He had then removed, perhaps to Sandwich.    Being a householder it is probable that he had a family, though no children are named on the town or church records.    The Jonathan of Sandwich in 1684, was a son of Andrew, not of Josias.

6.    V.    Joseph, probably the youngest of the family, married in 1666, Elizabeth ————.

Of this family no record has been preserved.    It is evident from the Colony records that he had at least one child.    Lois Hallett, who married April 10, 1690, was probably his daughter. She removed to Stonington, Connecticut, in 1715.    In 1686 he had a house on the north side of the county road, between the houses of Joseph Benjamin (now Nathan Edson's) and James Gorham's (now Warren Marston's).    Whether his house stood on the Hallett Farm or not, I am unable certainly to determine.    In the Gorham article I presumed that it stood on the west of the mill road ; but having since obtained some additional informa-

§Capt. Samuel Mayo had vessels employed in the coasting and fisheries.    In 1647 the town granted him liberty to erect a fish house on the point of land below his house now called Crowell's point.

tion, I am inclined to the opinion that Joseph had the northwest part of his father's great lot or farm set off to him in the division of the estate, and that he built his house thereon, not far from the location of the dwelling-house of the heirs of Ansel Hallett, deceased.  He was a townsman in 1670, and at the division of the common meadows in 1697 had one acre allotted to him.  He is not named in the division of the common lands in 1706, and the presumption is that some time between 1697 and 1706 he removed from Barnstable.  If he had died the settlement of his estate would appear on the Probate Records.  His lands were afterwards the property of James Gorham.*

The widow Mary Hallett is described 31st March, 1659, as "now living in Barnstable," implying that Barnstable had not been her permanent place of residence.  Her lands at Goodspeed's Hill in 1654 are thus described : "Eleven acres of upland, more or less, bounded northerly by the highway, easterly by James Lewis' land, southerly by her own land, (called also Josias') westerly upon John Davis, stretching upon a sett off four rods into the swamp (Lewis' swamp) across the north end of John Davis' land."  In the Goodspeed article, No. CVII, there is a diagram of this land.  It is those portions of the Goodspeed and Scudder lots, bounded north by the County road, east by James Lewis, south by Goodspeed's outlet, which separates it from Josias Hallett's land and John Davis', and west by the Hyannis road, which separated it from John Davis' houselot ; but did not include Lewis' Swamp, now the houselot of the heirs of F. W. Crocker, Esq., deceased.  These eleven acres are now owned by the heirs of Timothy Reed, Esq., Major S. B. Phinney, Eben. Bacon, Esq., heirs of F. W. Crocker, Esq., deceased, and by the United States, (Custom House lot).

The three acres of meadow at Blush's Point, afterwards Josias', are also described as her property.

There is no record of her death, and her name does not appear after 1659.  She probably removed, perhaps with her son Josias to Sandwich.  That she was the widow of Mr. Andrew Hallett, Sen., there is very little reason to doubt.  She is called in the Barnstable records "*Mrs. Hallett.*"  Titles meant something in those days ; her husband, wherever he was, was called *Mr.* There was only only one man of the name prior to 1654, who was entitled to that distinction, and that man was Mr. Andrew Hallett, Sen., the husband of Wid. Mary Hallett.

(2-1.)  Andrew Hallett, Jr., is the common ancestor of all the families of the name in Barnstable and Yarmouth.  He was one of the first settlers of the town of Sandwich, and at the di-

---

*Mr. Hallett probably had other children than those named.  The first wife of Robert Davis was probably his daughter.  Davis resided in Yarmouth until the death of Mr. Hallett when he removed to Barnstable, building his house next west of Joseph Hallett's house lot on a tract of land probably the property of his father-in-law.

vision of the common meadows, April 16, 1640, he had seven and one-half acres assigned to him. The division of the common lands and meadows in Sandwich was made "according to each man's estate and condition," or "quality," a most aristocratic rule. In the other towns there were three elements on which the division was made: 1, personal rights; 2, to the owners of tenements or dwelling houses; and 3, the estate and quality. This was an equitable mode. One third was distributed in equal shares to the legal inhabitants, one third equally to the owners of dwelling-houses, without reference to the cost, and the other third to the inhabitants in the same proportion that taxes were levied. The proprietors of Sandwich rejected the democratic principles involved in the first and second elements, and divided by the third, literally observing the rule, "To him that has much, shall much be given."

The division was made by a committee of ten, five representing the aristocracy, and five the townsmen. The first five awarded to themselves, one hundred and fourteen acres, nearly one third of the whole. The other five were more modest in their demands, and took only forty and one-half acres,—leaving to be divided to the other 56 inhabitants named, 214 1-2 acres, less than four acres to each, 7 1-2 acres being awarded to Andrew Hallett, it shows that he had at that time a good estate and was comparatively a wealthy man.*

The farm of Andrew Hallett, in Sandwich, was that lately owned by Paul Wing, deceased, at the Tack Factory village, about in the center (from east to west) of the settlement made in 1637. This tract the Indians called Mos-keeh-tuk-gut.†

July 28, 1640, he sold his farm in Sandwich to Daniel Wing, by whose descendants it was owned till recently. No consideration is named, and the deed is a specimen of the brevity in which conveyances of real estate were often made, in early times.

"I, Andrew Hallett of Sandwich, have sold unto Daniel Wing, of same town, and to his heirs and assigns forever, my dwelling-house in Sandwich, with three acres of land joyning to it, and the corn now growing upon it, with the cow-house. It lieth between the land of George Shawson‡ and William New-

---

*This is a fair specimen of the justice displayed by a majority of the first settlers in Sandwich. By the aid of the notorious Barlow (father-in-law to the wife of Andrew Hallett, Jr.,) they maintained their ascendency twenty five years, when they were succeeded by a better class of men. Of the members of the Committee Mr. John Vincent, Richard Bourne, Geo. Allen and Robert Bodfish, should be excepted from the censure due to the recorded acts of the committee.

†Mr. Freeman says the Indian name of Sandwich was Shaume. He is mistaken, Shaume or Shawmet, as its name implies, is a neck of land now known as Town Neck. The swell of land on the south is sometimes called Shaume Hill; but there is no evidence that it was so named by the aboriginers.

The first settlement in Sandwich was made at Manomet in 1627, and the foundation of the trading house built that year can yet be traced, the spring from which they obtained water is yet to be seen, and the remains of the landing place or wharf. It is on the south side of the river, about half a mile west of Monument Depot, on the Cape Cod Railroad. A settlement was made at Mos-keeh-tuk-gut in 1637, and soon after at Scusset, Spring Hill land; and two acres of planting land at Ma-noo-nah-Skussett; and five acres of planting land lying near Spring Hill; and four acres wanting one quarter of meadow near the Pine Neck; and two acres of meadow lying [illegible] and one acre and a half lying in the Neck, being yet undivided; with all commons, and all pasture, and all profits and appertenances whatsoever, thereunto belonging.

Witness my hand this twenty-eighth day of July, one thousix hundred and forty.                    The mark of

H

Andrew Hallett.

Signed and delivered in presence of

Edward Dillingham,

John Wing.

Taken out of the original deed and entered on record by me,

Thomas Tupper,

Town Clerk.

From Sandwich Andrew Hallett removed to Yarmouth, of which town he continued to be an inhabitant till his death in 1684.   In 1642 he bought the dwelling-house of Gyles Hopkins, the first built by the English in Yarmouth, and ten acres of land. This house was probably erected by Mr. Stephen Hopkins, by virtue of a grant made by the Colony Court dated Aug. 7, 1638. It stood on land now owned by Charles Basset, a little distance northwesterly from the house of Joseph Hale.   Traces of the foundation are not yet entirely obliterated.   The ten acres of land were bounded northeasterly by the lands of Mr. Nicholas Simpkins, and southwesterly by the lands of Robert Dennis.   In 1644 he bought fifteen acres of upland of Mr. Nicholas Simpkins adjoining his own on the east and three acres of salt meadow.

In 1655 he bought the farm of Robert Dennis.   The original deed in the handwriting of Mr. Anthony Thacher, has been preserved, and the following is a copy:

"These presents bearing date the twenty-fourth day of Feb-

---

and other places.   No settlement has been made at Shawne or Town Neck to this day. The account of the division of the common meadows, I think, sustains this view beyond any controversy or doubt.   Moo-ne-noo-ne-nus-cus-set—the village   Moo-re-noo-ne-nus-caul-ton—the river or stream.   I have before remarked that Indian names are descriptive terms.   These long names have been contracted to Scusset.   The meaning of the long name applied to the river seems to be the murmuring stream, or perhaps a better translation is "the stream where murmuring sounds are heard in the evening," the name of the village implies "a landing place on that stream."   A similar name was sometimes applied to the long valley which terminated at Scusset or West Sandwich.   In all languages there is an analogy between sound and sense, and particularly in arbarous or unwritten languages.   Our English word murmur is one of this character   and the Indian Moo-ne-noo-ne is one of the same character and represents the same idea.   The Indian names of birds and beasts, were often imitations of the song or cry of each.   The crow, the black-bird, the duck, the goose, and all the birds were continually chanting to the Indian their individual names, and so did the beasts of the field and the buzzing insects.

---

‡George Shawson, Mr. Winson says, was of Duxbury in 1638, and removed to Sandwich in 1640.   He removed to Stamford, Conn., before 1644, where he died Feb. 19, 1695, leaving descendants.

ruary Ano Domini 1654, made between Robert Dennis of Yarmouth in the Colony of New Plimouth in New England, carpenter, for the one party, aud Andrew Hallett of the same towne husbandman on the other part, witnesseth that Robert Dennis, aforesaid, for and in consideration of the sum of *ninety* pounds in good merchantable pay in New England to him by the said Andrew Hallett, and before the unsealing and delivery of these *presents* well and truly satisfied and paide, the receipt whereof the said Robert Dennis doth hereby acknowledge and thereof and of every *part* and pr cll thereof doth fully acquite exonerate and discharge the said Andrew Hallett, his heirs, executors and administrators, and every of them forever by these presents have graunted, bargained, sould, enfeoffed, and confirmed, and by these presents doe graunt, bargain, sell, enfeoffe and confirm unto the said Andrew Hallett and unto his heirs, *that* messuage or dwelling-house, with the allottment of laud the said house stands in and upon, containing six acres be it more or less, lying, situate and being in Yarmouth aforesaid, neere adjoining on the easter side unto the lands and dwelling house of him the said Andrew Hallett and now in the tennor and occupation of him the said Andrew, and also forty-six acres of land be it more or less next adjoyning to the same, bounded on the wester side with the ffarme lot of lands late Mr. Andrew Hallett's, deceased, on the easter side, with an allotment of lands late Emanuel White's and now common, and a lot of land now in the tenure and possession of Mr. Antony Thacher, on the souther end with soid allotment of (obliterated, probably Antony Thacher) the ponds and parte of the above-said ffarm lott, and partly on the norther end with the lands of the said Andrew Hallett all lying and being in a field known and commonly called the west field, and also thirteen acres of land more or less lying and being in a parcell of land commonly cald stony cove, and also two acres more or les lying and being in a furlong cald Rabbett's min, between the lands of Wm. Lumpkin and Richard Pritchett at Nobscussett and three acres in a furlong there cald plain furlong next adjoyning the country farm, and also nine acres more or less of marsh meadow lands lying abutting on ye foresaid land cald Stony Cove, and the two rivers or creeks cald Stony Cove river, and a creek cald Sympkins creek and ye meadow lands of him the said Andrew Hallett; together with all and singular houses, edifices, buildings, barnes, staules, pounds, orchards, gardens, casements and fflitte commodities, emoluments, and hereditaments thereunto belonging, or in any wise appertaining, or therewith enjoyed or accepted, deemed, reputed or taken to be pte or pcell of the same or any pte or pcell of the lands above recited, and all the estate, rights, title, interest, claim demanded whatsoever of him the said Robert Dennis and Mary his wife and Thomas fflawne or any or either of them off in or to the same or any pte or pcell of the same. To have and to hold the said bargained messuage or dwelling house lands and premises, with their and every of their appertenances, unto him the said Andrew Hallett his heirs and assigns forever, to the only proper use and behoofe of him the said Andrew Hallett and of his heirs and assignes forever. In witness whereof the said Robert Dennis has hereunto set his hand and seale.

*Signed, sealed and delivered*       ROBERT DENNIS.    L. S.
        *in presence of*
    JOHN CROWE,
    The marke RICHARD HORE,
    ANTONY THACHER,
        A: U: I: C: V: G:                    [or something like it.]
This deed is recorded according to order pr me Nathaniel Morton, Clarke of the Court."

May 10, 1648, the lands of Robert Dennis,* situate in the West Field, are described in the Colony records, as 12 acres bought of Peter Warden, 10 of Mr. Edmond Hawes, 7 of Mr. Andrew Hallett, and 4 given him by the town. Thomas Flawne had 13 acres in the same field, making the 46 acres sold.

The records of the laying out of the houselots in Yarmouth are lost. They contained from five to six acres each, and no person was allowed to own two adjoining lots, without he maintained a dwelling-house on each. They were laid out on the north side of the County road, the lands on the south being reserved as planting grounds, and enclosed by a common fence. The western lot adjoining the bounds of Barnstable was Dr. Thos. Starr's, sold in 1639 to Mr. Andrew Hallett, and afterwards owned by Capt. John Gorham. Four acres of this lot are now owned by the Gorhams, and two by the Halletts. The second lot was Robert Dennis', the one conveyed in the foregoing deed, and is now owned by the Halletts, Mr. Eldredge Lovell, and Joseph Gorham. The third lot was sett off to Gyles Hopkins, and sold by him to Andrew Hallett, Jr., in 1642. This lot probably included the houselot now owned by Mr. Jarius Lincoln, Jr., certainly Capt. Charles Bassett's, Mr. Joseph Hale's, and Mr. John Bassett's, Mill Lane being then probably its northeastern boundary. The fourth lot was Capt. Nicholas Sympkins', and sold by him in 1644 to Andrew Hallett, Jr.

The Mill road was laid out by the first comers as a private way. Hopkins' and Sympkins' land extended across Mill Pond meadows, and included land in Stony Cove Neck or Sympkins' Neck, as it is sometimes called, he owning to the creek which still retains his name. This road led to the ancient landing-place or wharf on the north of the Grist Mill.

By subsequent purchases Andrew Hallett, Jr., became the largest land holder in Yarmouth, owning about three hundred acres of the best lands and meadows in the town. On the north side of the road his farm extended from the Gorham houselot to the Hawes farm, where Mr. Edward W. Crocker now resides, and included nearly all the meadows on the north. On the south side of the road, he owned from the bounds of Barnstable nearly to Hawes' Lane. From him the westerly part of the County road in Yarmouth obtained the name of Hallett street, which it has retained to this day. Beside the ample domain already described, he owned lands and meadows in Barnstable, 1000 acres in Windham, Conn., and rights to commonage in Yarmouth, equal to 500 acres more.

The mode in which he acquired this large estate I shall at-

---

*Robert Dennis was a carpenter, and had a wife Mary. He had only one child record-ed as born in Yarmouth, Mary, 19th Sept. 1649. I think he removed to Newport, and was afterwards a man of note. Thomas Flawne appears to have resided in the family of Dennis. Mr. Savage does not name him.

tempt to elucidate. Two words, industry and economy, are the keys which unlock the whole mystery. If he was the eldest son, he was entitled to a double share of his father's estate, and if so, his share was not over £20 in value. He may with propriety be called the representative man of the rude social organization of his times. The great majority of our fathers lived precisely as he lived, and practiced as he practiced, and thus laid a sure foundation for our present prosperity. The inhabitants of this County fifty years ago were, with very few exceptions, the descendants of the first settlers, and inherited from them habits of industry and economy, their respect for the laws, and the religious institutions in which they were trained up.

Andrew Hallett, Jr., did not acquire his wealth by official services. His name frequently occurs on the records, but not in connection with any office that conferred much honor or afforded him large emoluments. In 1642, '56 and '58, he was a surveyor of highways; in 1651 and 1679 constable. In 1659 he was appointed by the Court one of a committee to raise money for the support of the ministry in Yarmouth. In 1660, '67 and '75, he was on the grand jury; and Oct. 30, 1667, he was appointed by the Colony Court, at the request of the town, a member of the land committee of Yarmouth. None of those are offices of honor or profit; but they show that he was a man in whom his neighbors had confidence, that he was a man of common sense and sound judgment. When a young man he was unable to write, yet soon after he came to Yarmouth he acquired that art, for in 1659 I find his name subscribed to the verdict of a jury of inquest.

He took the oath of fidelity while a resident in Sandwich, and his name and that of his father appears on the list of those who were able to bear arms in Yarmouth in August, 1643. On the criminal calendar his name does not appear. In those times the most trifling faults were noted, and he who escaped a prosecution must necessarily have lived a blameless life. He also kept his name off of the civil docket. He had no lawsuits. This is negative testimony; but establishes all we wish, he was a quiet peaceable man, minded his own business, and did not intermeddle with that of others.

He was a member of the church in Yarmouth; but circumstances show that he did not entirely acquiese in all the crude notions promulgated by Mr. Matthews. He often attended the meetings of Mr. Lothrop, and Mr. Walley and some of the members of his family afterwards joined the Barnstable church. He was an exemplary member of the church of Christ, constant in its attendance on its ordinances, and in his family, no wordly care was ever a bar to the performance of his whole duty as a parent.

Perhaps I am unnecessarily particular, that I state facts and circumstances that are too trivial, and had better be left unsaid.

Perhaps it is true ;  but considering the second Andrew Hallett as a representative man, and that his history is the history of hundreds of others, I am induced to particularize, and perhaps repeat some things, because I happen to know more of him than I do of those equally deserving, whose biography I omit.

The house which he bought of Gyles Hopkins in 1642, was probably the same that Mr. Stephen Hopkins built in the summer of 1638, and if so, was the first house built by the English on Cape Cod below Sandwich.   It was small and poorly constructed, and was occupied as a dwelling not many years.   As the first house built by the whites, it has an historical interest.   It stood on the eastern declivity of the hill, about seventy-five yards north-westerly from the present dwelling-house of Mr. Joseph Hale.   A depression in the ground and a rock in the wall, mark the place of its location.   An excavation was made into the side of the hill to level the ground, and the stone and cob work chimney was built against the bank, and outside of the frame of the house.   It probably contained at first only one room.   The excavation into the hill, and the chimney, covered nearly the whole of the west side, and the other three sides were covered with hand-sawed or hewn planks, and the roof with thach.   The walls were not shingled on the outside, or plastered on the in.   The seams in the boarding were filled or "daubed" with clay.   Oiled paper supplied the place of glass.   The sills were hewn from large logs, and projected into the room, forming low seats on three sides. The floor was fastened to sleepers laid on the ground, and even with the lower edge of the sills.   A ladder to the chamber and a cleet door with a wooden latch and string, completed the fixtures of the house.

In this rudely built shanty, two of the children of Gyles Hopkins, who came over in the Mayflower, were born, and here resided a number of years the most opulent man of Yarmouth. Nearly all the houses of our ancestors were of this description. The memorandum of the contract for building the house of the elder Mr. Hallett, preserved in the deed of Dr. Starr, proves that his house was of the same description.   Gov. Hinckley resided in a house of similar construction many years.   De Rassier's description of Plymouth in 1627, shows that the walls of the houses in that town were covered with hewn or hand-sawed planks, and unshingled.   As late as 1717 it was not common to plaster the inside walls.   The seams between the boards on the Meeting House built that year on Cobb's Hill were filled with morter, or "daubed" precisely in the same manner as practiced by the first settlers. That boards were used in the construction of their dwellings, by the first settlers, is also shown by the agreement made  June 19, 1641, between the inhabitants of Barnstable and  the Indian chief Nepaiton, to build the latter a house.   A part of the contract was that it should be built, "with a chamber floored with boards, with a chimney and an oven therein." This contract, and the contract by Dr. Starr with William Chase in 1639, establish the fact that boards were used by our ancestors in the construction of their houses. In 1640 there was a saw mill in Scituate, but Mr. Deane says "we are without date when it was erected."

Some writers on our early history speak of the "log cabins of ancestors." I find no evidence that they built a single log-house. The timber in the vicinity of the settlements was unfit for such buildings. Before the erection of saw mills, there were sawyers in all the towns; and within the last fifty years, old houses have been taken down which were originally covered with hand-sawed planks or boards. In 1640 boards were cheap in Scituate, and for many years after the settlement, much of the lumber used in the Plymouth Colony was brought from that town.

The fortification houses of our fathers were built, the lower story of stone, where it could be conveniently procured, and the second of wood. In a part of Yarmouth (now South Dennis) where no stone could be conveniently found, a block house was built for defence. This in its construction resembled a log-house, but no one calls such a structure by that name. Many common houses like that of John Crocker were surrounded by a palisade, and were intended as places of resort, should the Indians prove unfriendly.

Major Gookin in speaking of the wigwams, of the Indians, says some of them were large and convenient, and more comfortable than many houses built by the English. Mr. Lothrop calls some of the houses of our ancestors, booths, indicating that they were most uncomfortable residences in the winter. Some he calls pailsado, meaning I presume that the walls were built of two parallel rows of poles, and the space between filled with clay or other material Others were frame houses not large or elegantly finished, but warm and comfortable. Dwellings of the latter description, only a few men who were comparatively wealthy, had the means to build.

In such rude shelters from the piercing storms of the winter of 1639-40, the great mass of our ancestors resided more happily and more contentedly than do their descendants at this day, in their well built and well furnished mansions. Mornings and evenings they thanked their Heavenly Father for the many blessings He had vouchsafed to them; that their lines had fallen in such pleasant places; that He had held them as in the hollow of His hand, protecting them from the savages among whom they dwelt, and the wiles of the more savage men, who had driven them from their native land. Such were the feelings of our ancestors, they were ever conscious of being under Divine protection, and were ever happy, contented, and thankful. It is a sufficient honor to descend from such a race of men. We need not trace our ancestry farther. The more closely we study their character, the greater will be our reverence for them. The study will make us more contented with our lot in life, happier and better men.

In the summer of 1640 they had their lands to clear, fence and plant, to build roads, and do many things that are incident to the settlement of a new country, and they found little time, if they had the means, of improving their dwellings. Many of them resided all their days in the houses they first erected. Improvements were made from time to time. The thatched roof, the paper windows, and the cob work chimney disappeared, and shingled roofs, diamond glass windows and brick chimneys and ovens were substituted. As the family increased the house was enlarged, first by adding a lean-to, and afterwards by adding another story. Some of the largest old houses now remaining, one of which will be described in this article, were built by adding one room at a time.

The second house in which Andrew Hallett, Jr., resided, in Yarmouth, stood on the west side of the mill road, a little distance north of the house now occupied by Mr. John Bassett. It has been suggested that this was the Sympkins house repaired and enlarged. The family tradition is that he built it.

He bought the Sympkins land in 1644, but did not build his house till some time afterwards, if the family tradition is reliable, that Jonathan, born in 1647, first saw light in the old house. The new house was built on a little knoll, and fronted due south, as all ancient dwellings did. By such a location, our fathers secured two objects which they considered essential: the rays of the sun at noon, or dinner-time, as they called that hour of the day, shone parallel with the side of the house, and their "great room" in which they lived, was on the sunny or warm side of the house. The chimney was uniformly built on the west side, and projected outside of the frame. The exact size of Andrew Hallett's new house cannot be stated accurately: it was about 22 feet by 26 on the ground, and was only one or one-half stories high. The arrangement of the rooms was the same as in the Dimmock house, which I have described. The "great room," about 17 feet square, occupied the southeast corner. The fireplace was eight feet wide and four deep, and the mantle, which was of wood, was laid about five feet and a half high, so that the family could pass to the oven,* which opened on the back of the fireplace near the south corner. There was a small kitchen or work room at the northwest corner; at the northeast corner a small pantry, with a trap door leading to the cellar. Between the pantry and the great room was a bed-room, the floor of which was elevated about two feet, to give greater depth to the cellar. The bed occu-

---

*The oven projected out on the west side of the house. I am not aware that there is a single specimen of these old chimneys and projecting ovens now remaining in this County. Mr. Oris Bacon's was the last I recollect in Barnstable. A man passing a house of this construction, and thinking to pass a good joke on the lady thereof, knocked at the door; on her appearance, he said: "Madam, do you know your oven has got out of doors?" She replied, "Will you have the kindness to bring it in, it is too hot for me to handle?"

pied near all the space, and it was so low in the walls that a tall person could not stand upright therein. A ladder in the front entry led to the chamber, which was occupied for weaving and lodging rooms. No part of the house was ever painted or any of the rooms papered. The windows were of small diamond shaped glass set in lead. No blinds or curtains were needed, and none were ever used.

The furniture of the house was for use, not for show. Half a dozen flag bottomed, one low and one large armed chair, a table, a large chest, and a cradle, all of domestic manufacture, was the furniture usually to be seen in the summer in the great room, and in the winter a bed occupied one corner, and the looms another. On one side of the room there were usually two large "trencher shelves,"† on which the pewter ware of the family was displayed, an iron candlestick, an hour glass, a pen and ink horn, the bible, and hymn book.

A clock or timepiece was an article not to be found in the settlement. Time was reckoned thus, "daylight, sunrise, sun an hour, two hours and three hours high, and the reverse in the afternoon. When the sun shone, they could tell the precise apparent time at noon, and they had marks by which they judged very accurately of the time from 9 A. M. till 3 P. M. Sun dials were early introduced, and many had them fastened to posts set in front of their houses.

If we lay aside one consideration, the cost of fuel, it may be safely said that for comfort, convenience and health, nothing superior to the old fashioned fireplace has yet been invented. Grates, stoves and furnaces, in comparison with them, are only contemptible contrivances for saving a little fuel, engendering gas, dust, and headache, and shortening a man's days. Talk with the aged, they will uniformly tell you that the happiest hours of their lives were spent in the corner of an old-fashioned kitchen fireplace. In the long winter evenings the younger members of the family occupied the low bench in the left chimney corner, the smaller one perhaps mounted on the dye-tub. Here they were warm and comfortable, and could read or play without molestation, or gaze up to the stars through the capacious chimney. In the other corner sat the mistress of the family in her low rocking-chair, and in front, the father in his round-about, or in an old-fashioned arm chair.

In those days there was a social equality now unknown. There were no visits of ceremony,—no calls to leave a card; but neighbor called on neighbor, without previous invitation to spend a long evening. In such cases, all the children of the neighborhood assembled at the house left vacant by the parents. They parched corn, cracked nuts, and played blind man's buff, hunt the slipper, thread the needle through the eye, hull gull, and many other plays and games, which

---

†This name seems to imply that our ancestors used trenchers, or wooden dishes on which to cut and serve their meats.

the boarding-school Miss now regards with horror, though she can witness with delight the indelicate girations of the ballet dancer, or unseemly pranks of a French waltz.

The old folks first discussed the English news, though it was four or five months old. Some one had had a letter from their relatives in the father land. This was passed around from family to family, and read and discussed by the whole vicinity. The ministry—the church—the acts of the Court—and the crops, were subjects that passed in review, and often familism, pedo-baptism, quakerism, and witchcraft, came in for a share of the conversation.

The young and the old enjoyed these social meetings, now only known in recollection. They are past—another King has arisen who knows not Joseph, and all arguments is estoped by repeating the quaint Latin dictum,

> "*Tempora mutantar,*
> *Et nos mutamur in illis.*"

That is, times change, and we must change with them, an *argument* which many call a "clincher." The Dutchman's wife expressed the same sentiment, perhaps in stronger language, when she said to her husband, "Dear Vill, I vish as you, you'd do as other people do." Thus it is the good customs of our fathers are rejected, because the vain call them old fashioned.

The fire was never suffered to go out during the cool season, and very rarely in the summer. Every morning in the winter, the coals were raked forward, and a ponderous back-log put on, with two or three smaller ones, as riders. A large fore-stick, four feet in length, was laid on the andirons, and two or three smaller ones between that and the back-log forming a bed into which the coals raked forward were shovelled. Some dry sticks were laid on these, and in a few moments a large fire was sparkling on the hearth. Wood cost nothing in those days, and our ancestors always enjoyed the luxury of a good fire in cold weather, and however cold the weather, the great room was warm and comfortable. They always provided themselves with pine knots, then abundant, and in the long winter evenings these were used instead of candles.

The kitchen or backroom was small and little used, excepting for a store room. The tubs and pails, and the spinning wheels, when not in use, were kept here, and a pile of wood for the morning's fire.

All the clothing and bedding of the family was made in the house. The flax and the wool were spun and wove by the inmates. The cloth for the thick clothing of the men was sent to the clothier to be fulled, colored and pressed.

Goodman Hallett lived on the produce of his farms. Indian corn was his principal crop, though every family had rye, and most of them raised sufficient wheat for their own consumption. They also cultivated peas, of which many were sent to Boston and other places to sell; beans, pumpkins, squashes, cucumbers, melons, turnips, beets, carrots, parsnips, and onions.    Potatoes were not raised by the first settlers, and it was many years before they were produced in large quantities.    Cattle were scarce and of high price, and few were killed for beef by the first settlers; but in time they became abundant and cheap.    Goats were kept, and their milk was used.    Horses were early introduced; but the country did not become well stocked till fifty years after the settlement of Plymouth. Pigs multiplied rapidly, and were soon abundant in all the settlements.    Poultry of all kinds was raised.    Deer and other wild animals suitable for food then roamed in the forests, and the shores, at certain seasons, were covered with flocks of geese, ducks, plover, and other birds.

Clams, quahogs and oysters, could be obtained at any season of the year, and codfish, mackerel, bass, eels, and other fish, were then more easily taken than at the present time.

None but the idle and the dissolute complained.    The first settlers, after securing their first crop in 1640, never suffered for food, —they always had an abundance of that which was wholesome and palatable.    At first they were short of clothing.    They had to patch up that which they brought out of England.    The skins of the deer and other animals, dressed by the Indians, were soft and pliable. These supplied many of their wants and furnished them with warm and comfortable, though not elegant articles of dress.

The little money they obtained by the sale of peltry, oil and fish, was carefully husbanded and used to supply their most pressing wants.    Tools, iron and some kinds of building materials, were indispensable, and it was many years before they were fully supplied.

The first settlers in Barnstable were as independent and as contented a community as ever existed.    They had food enough and to spare,—they were comfortably clad, and though their houses were open and cold, these defects were supplied by adding wood to their winter fires.    While they suffered the inconveniences incident to a new settlement, they had no cause to complain of smoke, dust or gas in their rooms.

The spring of 1641 was cold and wet.    Hooping cough prevailed to an alarming extent among the children, yet only three deaths occurred in Barnstable during the year.    The bills of mortality for the first fourteen years, exhibit an average longevity of seventy years, showing that the inconveniences to which our fathers were subjected were not prejudicial to their health.    Their diseases yielded to the simple remedies which our mothers gathered in the fields and the forests.—[Ch. Records.

Goodman Hallett is called a husbandman.    By honest industry, skilful management and economy, he accumulated a large estate. In 1676 his tax was equal to one twentieth of the whole assessment. At this time, it may seem difficult to comprehend how he accumulated so much by farming.    But let any young man, of sound health, practice in any calling  in life as Goodman Hallett practiced, and  he will always succeed.

He may also have been  engaged in the fisheries, and  probably was,  for nearly  all the first settlers were at  certain seasons of the year.    The Mayos', Allyns', Lothrops', Gorhams' and Dimmocks', accumulated good estates in the coasting and West India trade.

They were not sole  owners of their vessels.    Others who did not take an active part in these employments were interested as owners, and shared the profits.

His out of door arrangements were as  rude as those within, On the east of his house there was a fine spring of water, in  which he placed a large hollow log for a  curb.*    The supply was pure and abundant, and in times of drought was the resort of the neighborhood. His large wood-pile was in front of his house, not cut and piled , but standing on end, on each side  of a large pole  resting on  crutches, settled into the ground.    Forty cords he considered a year's  supply, and it was cut up as wanted for the fire, into pieces three and four feet long.    Some of the logs used  were large, and required the strength  of two men to roll  them in, and  adjust them in the fireplaces for backlogs.

Goodman Hallett built his cribs as all in those times did, with slender poles.    Posts were  set at each  corner having short branches left thereon, about three feet from the ground. On those branches two stout poles were laid, 12 or 15 feet  long.    Across these smaller ones, four feet in length, were closely  laid.    The sides were  constructed with long poles, and the roof  with boards overlapping  each other.    At each end there was a door or opening.    He had several, in  which he stored his large crops.    Corn was then the  measure of value.    With it a man could  pay his taxes or his debts,  buy houses and lands ; the necessaries or the luxuries of life.    To have corn in the crib, in those times, was like having  stocks and  money in the Bank  at the present time. To say of a man "he has plenty of corn in his cribs," was equivalent to saying he had money in his purse.    Goodman Hallett was not proud,  but he delighted to  exhibit to  visitors his extensive granaries, his herds  and flocks, and the breadth of his  cultivated lands.    Excepting for hominy or samp, he consumed very little of his corn till it was a year old.†

---

*Till about the year 1770 this was one of the best springs of water in Yarmouth. Though  on high  land, it afforded  an abundant supply of cool, clear, and excellent  water. About that year, during an earthquake, the spring suddenly ceased to flow.    It still affords water ; but its character is entirely changed.    A few years ago the old  hollow tree was removed, and the spring  cleared out, and a new curb put in,  yet the water is poor.    During the same earthquake several springs in various parts of the country were similarly affected. The jarring of the earth probably  changed the direction of the fountains.    The old  spring near the Gyles Hopkins house also  failed about the same time.    The fountain which formerly supplied it is now entirely dried up or turned in another direction.

†"Pointing to one crib he would say, 'there is my last year's crop,' then to another,

His barns in the field on the east of the mill road, were as rudely constructed as those now seen on the western prairies. Large stacks of salt hay stood near, surrounded by a fence. The barn, or cow-house, as it was called, was for the protection of the stock, not for the storage of fodder. No English hay was then cut. All the fresh fodder which the first settlers had, was the stalks and husks of the Indian corn, and a poor quality of fresh hay cut on the high meadows.

In the field by his house and in his barn field he set orchards. The Kentish Cherry brought over by the Pilgrims, had rapidly multiplied by suckers, and were always set on the outer edge, to protect the less hardy trees within. The apple trees were raised from seeds, brought from England, and were generally of inferior quality. The pignose, however, was very productive and a good winter apple. The Foxwell, yet cultivated, is a Fall apple of fair quality. The pears were also seedlings, and many of them worthless sorts; but the trees were hardy and long lived. A seedling planted by him is a good autumn fruit, and yet propagated by grafts from the original tree. The French sugar, a very early pear, was introduced soon after the settlement and grafted into the poorer seedlings.* The iron pear, now known as the Black Worcester, a winter fruit, was introduced early—and afterwards the Catherine from the vicinity of Boston, and the Orange, a pear of superior quality. Several of the pear trees planted by Goodman Hallett yet remain, monuments of the hardy industry of the first comers, and living mementoes of the primitive simplicity of other days.

However rude may have been his dwelling, and however inelegant may have been its surroundings, it was the home of a happy and a contented family. To live a good life was his constant endeavor. He was not ambitious, he did not seek office, or honor, or wealth. He humbly acknowledged that all he had was

---

'there is my crop of the year before,' and then to another he would say, 'in that crib are the remains of the former year's crop.'"

This passage I have extracted from an unpublished biography of "Rock" Richard Taylor, the ancestor of the Taylors resident in Yarmouth and Chatham. It was furnished by the late Mr. William Bray, who obtained it of his grandmother, Mrs. Elizabeth Bray, who lived to great age and retained her faculties to the last. When young she was a seamstress; and after finishing her days work, Rock Richard (so called to distinguish him from another Richard Taylor, who was called "tailor") invited her to walk out with him, and that conversation then occurred. Taylor was a vain man, and perhaps I do injustice to Goodman Hallett in the quotation. The latter's cribs were of the same description, and he probably had in the prime of his life many more than Taylor, whose farm at Hockanom was valued at only one-seventh of Hallett's ample domain. Mrs. Bray was seventeen when she had the conversation referred to with Richard Taylor, and she knew nearly all the first settlers. Her grandson William, when a child, delighted to hear her speak of the first settlers, and from him I obtained much that is interesting respecting the olden times.

---

*Solomon Otis, Esq., born in 1696, said the two sugar pear trees on the east of his house, were large trees when he was a boy—that they had not increased in size but little within his recollection. They were grafted when small near the root. If his statement is reliable, they were grafted as early as 1670. A sugar pear tree on the John Seudder estate was as old. None, however, of this variety are so ancient as the kinds known as full and button pears. The Ewer pear, a seedling, was esteemed by our ancestors as one of the best.

lent to him by the Lord, to enable him to do good, and to be useful, not to be wasted in luxurious living, or in vain and ostenta-
tious display.  He lived as his neighbors lived.  No room in his
house was made a sanctum sanctorum, nor had he any furniture
that was too good or too costly for his family to use.  "Nothing,"
he would say, "was valuable that was not useful."  Again.  "A
large house makes a slave of the wife, and elegant furniture
drouges of the daughters."  He had Indian servants who assisted
him in the labors of the field.  They were not fed and clothed to
do that which he could do better himself, for it was his common
remark, "He that waits on himself, is well served."  When asked
why he lived in so small a house, he replied, "Comfort lives in a
small house and needs no servants; care in a large one, and requires many."  Vanity may turn up her nose in disgust, or laugh
when these sayings are repeated; the gay and the thoughtless
may affect to despise; but he that marks well the stern realities
of life, will see truth buried, not deeply, in those simple, com-
mon-place sayings.

In his domestic arrangements, Goodman Hallett reduced his
theories to practice.  "Daylight," he would say, "was cheaper than
candle-light," and as soon as the day broke he was up and
dressed.  He kindled the fire, brought water from the spring,
went to his barn, fed his cattle, his pigs and his poultry, and
milked his cows.  On his return, he found all the members of his
household up and dressed, and breakfast prepared.  Sitting down
in their accustomed places, the older daughter read a passage from
the Bible, and a few stanzas from a favorite hymn.  Goodman
Hallett kneeling down, in a fervent prayer craved the blessing
and protection of Heaven on his country, his church, his household, and his dear friends in England.  Most earnestly did he
pray that the Great Shepherd would watch over and protect the
companion of his life, and gently lead the tender lambs of his
flock.

The labors of the morning and the religious exercises, had
prepared them to partake of their meal with thankful hearts.  No
cloth covered the well scoured table.  A large wooden bowl
graced the center, filled with savory broth, and hulled corn supplied the place of bread.  Each had a pewter spoon, and all
dipped from the same dish, as the Saviour and his disciples did on
the eve of the crucifixion.  No betrayer dipped his hand into the
dish, and while imitating the custom of the Great Master, they
never dreamed that a generation would thereafter arise who would
despise a custom which they reverenced.  After the bowl was removed, bread or samp, milk, butter and honey, a slice or two of
meat, or a plate of fish, succeeded.  Goody Hallett also had tea,
made from some favorite herb, that she had brought from the garden or fields.  During breakfast Goodman Hallett told pleasant

stories about home, as he called Old England, to which the children were never tired of listening. When the repast was ended, he returned thanks for the bountiful supply of the good things they had enjoyed, and the many blessings which had been vouchsafed to him and his family.

The school lasted only a few weeks in each year, and however deep the snow or hard the storm, the children never failed of attending. Goodman Hallett would remark, that "it was as great a sin to cheat children of their learning, as of their money." They were all provided with Indian moccasins and snow shoes, and however difficult it is to learn the art of wearing the latter, the children of those days acquired it almost as naturally as young ducks learn to swim. The school was kept by the second Mr. John Miller at his house, which stood on the spot now occupied by the high school—a good mile distant from Goodman Hallett's. If a term of the school was then in session, the children had their dinners put up, and were ready to start at half past eight. The roads were never cleared of snow in those days. Some were partially broken out with teams, but not so as to supercede the necessity of snow shoes, especially after a recent storm. It was a pretty sight, to see the little ones trailing along on their snow shoes towards the school-house; but it was a common occurrence then, and excited no curiosity.

If there was no school, and the weather was stormy, the parlor was a scene of varied industry. When the breakfast table was cleared off, and preliminary arrangements made for the dinner, the looms, which in cold weather stood in a corner of the parlor, were in motion, and the girls were merrily turning their spinning wheels. Meantime the master of the house, assisted by an Indian servant, had watered and fed his large stock, and chopped the wood for the daily fire. He was not lacking in mechanical ingenuity, and on stormy days did many little jobs which saved money. His wife frequently repeated the old adage, "A stitch in time saves nine," and Goodman Hallett acquiesced. Taking his awl, his leather, thread, wax and knife, he seated himself in the chimney corner, and successively examined the shoes of the family. If a tap or a patch was wanted, he put it on, or if there was a seam that required stitching, it was not overlooked. The andirons were of wrought iron, and had hooks on the front in which the spit rested. Wild fowl and venison were then abundant, and for the family dinner a sirloin had perhaps been spitted. Goodman Hallett turned the spit, and from time to time basted the meat from the contents of the dripping pan. The vegetables, which had been prepared in the morning, were hung over the fire, and at precisely twelve o'clock, if a bright day, the dinner was ready.

Before partaking of the meal, a blessing was craved. The meat was cut on a wooden trencher, and served on pewter plates. Vegetables and bread, samp or hulled corn, was on the table, and at every meal "spoon victuals" of some kind formed a part of the repast. Beer, which was regularly brewed every week, was used as a substitute for tea or coffee, and by the workmen, in the place of strong drink.

It was a saying of Goody Hallett, that "the girl who did not know that the dish-water should be heating during meal-time, was unfit to be married." Abigail was in her teens, and remembered this saying. When the dinner was finished the water was hot, and the table was soon cleared, the dishes washed and put in their places on the "trencher" or in the cup-board.

By three o'clock the tasks of the day were finished. Goody Hallett had woven her five yards, Abigail had spun six skeins of woolen yarn, and Dorcas four of flax. The wheels were put away, the parlor swept and dusted, and clean sand was "lumped" on the floor or the old "herren boned," an act in which the women of those days displayed their good taste. The girls had a small looking-glass, an article of luxury which few families in those days possessed, before which they arranged their toilet. The Hallett's were never extravagant; but they always dressed neatly. The petticoat was the principal article of dress, on which the most labor was expended. It was made of cloth of domestic manufacture, sometimes colored, of two thicknesses, and quilted throughout. On the lower border and on the front, there was some ornamental needle work. Over this a "loose gown" was worn. This was of also domestic manufacture, sometimes white; but usually checked or colored. It was open in front, and did not extend so low as the under garment. The sleeves extended about half way from the elbow to the wrist. They had long knit gloves or "sleeves," which they wore when they went out. The neck and breast were covered with a handkerchief ordinarily; on great occasions, with a bodice or a stomacher. White worsted stockings and Indian moccasins completed the winter apparel. This was the common dress of the woman. For the Sabbath and great occasions, the wealthy had gayer and more costly garments of foreign manufacture. These were carefully preserved, and handed down from generation to generation. Dresses are yet preserved in which mother, daughter and grand-daughter were successively married. All had checked aprons which they wore when employed in household duties, and often a clean nice starched one was put on the afternoon and evening.

When they went out they had bonnets, and cloaks of thick cloth with a hood or covering for the head attached. For many years a bright red or scarlet was the fashionable color for these garments.

The common dresses of the men were short clothes or breeches, a long vest, with lappets covering the hips, a round about coat or jacket for every day, and for the Sabbath a long coat, cut a little crossway, not "straight down" in front, with a standing collar. The wealthy indulged large in silver buttons; but for every day wear horn was used. The pilgrims all wore round hats, but in after times they adopted the cocked hat of the cavaliers. They wore long blue woolen stockings that extended above the knee, and were kept in place by a buckle and strap on the lower part of the breeches. Shoes fastened with large buckles completed their dress. Boys and men wore short clothes and long stockings. In summer stockings and shoes were dispensed with, and trowsers took the place of small clothes, the leg of which extended below the knee.

At the evening meal, in addition to "spoon victuals," they usually had "short cakes" baked before the fire on a pan or in a spider.

In the evening the women were employed in knitting or sewing, and occasionally in making a kind of bobinet lace, on board frames, a few of which have been preserved. Farmers in those days selected a small portion of their best flax ground, on which they sowed a double portion of seed, that the product might be of a fine and soft texture, fit to manufacture into lace. Goodman Hallett kept a good fire, and as his beer barrels were never empty, he rarely was without company. Capt. Gorham and Mr. Thacher often spent an evening at his house, and though the use of tobacco was prohibited by the "honorable Court," yet smoke from the pipe often curled up the chimney on the long winter evenings.

Our ancestors were systematic in their domestic arrangements. Monday was washing-day, a custom which has survived to this day. On Tuesday the clothes were ironed. Wednesday in summer was baking-day, but not in the winter. Thursday and Friday were devoted to spinning and weaving, and Saturday was baking-day the year round. For dinner on that day the Pilgrims eat fish, perhaps because the Catholics, all of whose customs they abjured, dined thereon Fridays. Baked beans, and Indian puddings were always found on their tables on the Sabbath, a custom yet continued in many families.

Saturday at 4 o'clock in the afternoon all servile labor for the week had ended. Preparations for the Sabbath had been made—the wood cut and brought in—the Sunday meal had been prepared, and preparations made to keep the day holy to the end thereof. In the evening the children were instructed in their catechisms. They retired early. The Sabbath was a day of rest—all went to church morning and evening. They never allowed the weather to interfere with their religious duties, it was never too wet, never too hot, never too cold to go to meeting.

In summer the male portion of the family were employed in out of door labors from sunrise till the shades of evening began to fall. Toil, hard and unremitting was their portion, but it was cheerfully performed. At hay time and harvest the girls assisted their fathers and brothers in the field. Their wants were few, and by industry and economy were easily supplied. Goodman Hallett acquired wealth, and every young man may do the same, if he will practice

as he practiced.   He was temperate in all things, took  care of what
he had, and every year spent less than he earned.

From year to year there was little change in  Goodman Hallett's
habits, employments and mode of living.   He added  a leanto  or
"salt-box," as they were often called, to the west side of his house,
making  two  rooms  in front and  enlarging  the kitchen.   His increased family rendered this enlargement necessary.   The west room
was sometimes called the weaving-room.   Generally the object of
building a leanto was to have a place for the looms and the spinning-
wheels—a manufactory in miniature.

Goodman Hallett died in the spring of 1684.   He was at least
seventy years of age.   His surviving children had married, and left
the paternal roof.   In early times it was customary, in making the
inventory of a man's estate, to apprise the furniture in each room of
the house by itself.   It was a good custom—it not only furnished a
description of each room, but all the articles of furniture were enumerated in detail—carrying you into the family circle—unveiling its
secrets—laying open  its  wants, its  hopes, its  pursuits, its  aspira-
tions ;—picturing  the stern realities of a social life, over which two
centuries have spread the mantle of forgetfulness.   The uncovered
ruins of Herculaneum do not portray the habits, mode of living, and
character of the  ancient  Romans, in  a stronger light,  or in  more
vivid colors, than  do these old inventories, the marked traits of the
Pilgrim  character.   In that city we see the  evidences of luxury  in
contrast with squaled  poverty, and everywhere unmistakable records, that gross licentiousness prevaded all classes of its society.   The
human heart, being  ever the same, its surroundings will impress on
its character, an ultimate form, which the man has no  power  to
shake off.

Our fathers were eminently a religious people ;—with them  the
future was ever present in thought—the Bible was their creed—their
laws were based on its precepts, and their daily intercourse was regu-
lated by some of  its familiar texts.   Their children were brought up
under these influences or  surroundings—they were taught that industry and frugality were virtues—that idleness and  wastefulness  were
sins to be repented  of, and for which they would  have to answer at
the final judgment.   These old inventories exhibit no evidence of
prodigality—no squalid  poverty—no traces of licentious life.   They
exhibit  a rude social organization,—but beneath that organization
they  portray a noble race—with  hardy virtues—of  honest lives—
content to live on the fruits of their own unremitted toil.

Andrew Hallett's, Jr.'s, estate was apprised by John Miller and
John Thacher May 19, 1684, and sworn to by his  widow Ann Hallett on the 31st of the same month.

In the "parlour" or "great room."

"His purse and apparell,"                                    £90,10,6
Books in the parlour,                                            13,6

| | |
|---|---|
| A cup-board, | £3,10,0 |
| The bed furniture—all, | 10,05,0 |
| The great table—forme and stools, | 1,14,0 |
| A chest and chairs, | 1,00,0 |
| The trundle-bed and furniture, | 3,10,0 |
| Pewter, | 2,15,9 |
| Brass mortar *bac*,* iron scummer, dripping-pan, tin pans—all, | 15,2 |
| A Tunnell, spoones, candlesticks, a warming-pan—all, | 10,10 |
| An hour-glass, a brush, fier-slice and tongs—a brass skillett, | 6,06 |
| Trammells, beer barrels, iron skillett, trays—all, | 17,00 |
| Spoones, trenchers, rowling pin, looking-glass, bottles and jugs, | 8,01 |

| | |
|---|---|
| All in the parlor, | 116,16,04 |
| Deducting purse and apparel, | 90,10,06 |

| | |
|---|---|
| The furniture including bed, | 26,05,10 |

Such was the furniture in the parlor of the most opulent man of his times. The list was taken by honest and honorable men, and sworn to by the surviving widow who certainly knew what she had in her house. The looms and the cradle had disappeared. Goody Hallett was too old to weave, and she had done all her rocking, many years before.

The "cup-board" or *beaufet* is apprised as an article of furniture. They were not then permanent fixtures. They were semicircular in form, and placed in the corner of a room or in a recess by the chimney, and could be removed from place to place. The lower part was closed by doors, and the upper open, containing several shelves, in form like a segment of a circle, and on these, the little earthen and glass ware of the family was displayed. The apprisement covers the value of the cup-board and its contents. By the word "furniture" in the inventory, is to be understood everything that belonged to the bed, including curtains and valances. The "forme" or *settle*, was a seat made of boards, with a high back—a rude sofa—and in cold weather was placed in front of the fire,—the seat and back protecting the occupants from the cold air of the room.

The chest and chairs are apprised at one pound. In the chest were deposited the most valuable articles of the family, and it was secured by iron hinges and a lock. At one end there was a *till* in which the money and valuable papers of the family were kept. It was well made, and must have been worth ten shillings, leaving the same sum as the value of all the chairs in the house. "Trammells" suspended from a cross bar in the chimney were then universally used. Cranes and hooks are modern inventions. The "beer barrels" are named as a part of the parlor furniture. As it was customary to brew every week, it is probable they were not of large size—only kegs—and being mentioned in connection with

*Bac, probably a misspelling intended for Box iron—an instrument then used for ironing clothing, as flat irons now are.

the articles about the fireplace, perhaps they had usurped the place of the dye-tub, which had disappeared.

In the chamber.

| | |
|---|---:|
| A mulett, | £0,02,0 |
| A bed and furniture—all, | 6,18,0 |
| 22 yards of wool cloth, a suit of curtains and vallens, 2 cover-lids, | 6,06,00 |
| A coverlid, a blankett, wool cloth, hops, a chest—all, | 3,10,00 |
| A chest, a box, 6 pairs of sheets, a table-cloth, pillow case—all, | 05,08,06 |
| A table-cloth, napkin, hunney bees and hives, flax—all, | 04,15,00 |
| Sadles, pillion and cloth and bridles, Indian corn, rye—all, | 3,05,00 |
| 5 cushens, linnien and wool wheels, bacon and beefe, scales and waits, | 1,19,06 |
| Siften trough, meal and corn sives, bedstead and lumber in the chamber, | 00,15,0 |
| | 32,19,00 |

From the above, it appears that his house was only of one story, and the chamber was unfinished. The bee hives are named as being in the chamber. They were made of straw, and were put under cover in the winter, but the necessity of keeping them in the chamber till the 19th of May does not appear, without there was an opening in the side of the house through which the bees could enter.*

In the leanto and kitchen. (The two first items are placed with the furniture in the chamber—probably in the kitchen.)

| | |
|---|---:|
| Winnowing sheet, horse geers, Iron pots and kettles, | £3,08,00 |
| Frying pan, bellows, pot hooks, milk pails, and straining dish, | 7,00 |
| In the leantoo, brass and iron—a hathell, a tub and churn, | 5,14,00 |
| Earthen ware, milk vessels and lumber in ye leanto, | 0,19,00 |
| A table, | 10 |
| 2 barrells, a cowle, a bagg, 2 pillow cases, | 12,06 |
| Tallow, hoggs fat, malt, linen, yarn, wool and yarne and flax, | 2,17,00 |
| Arms and ammunition, | 3,02.8 |
| (Added at the end.) | |
| A bed and bedding thereto belonging in ye kitchen, | 6,18,00 |
| 3 yards of cloth, | 15 |
| A sun dial and knife, | 2 |
| | £25,05,2 |

Though this inventory does not state with so much particularity as many do the room in which each article was kept, yet it enables us to form a correct opinion of the appearance of each room, and gives a clear insight into his mode of living and domestic arrangements. It clearly appears that the house was only one story, that the chamber or garret was not divided into different

---

*Jonathan Hallett resided in the old house till 1695, when he built his new house which was for the times an elegant two story building—the lower story being built on the same model as the old one. On the east side the upper story projected over the lower. If the chamber of the old house projected in a similar manner, shelves under the projection would be a convenient place for bee hives. I give the facts as I find them, and offer the above only as suggestive.

apartments, and was unfinished. The small bedroom on the lower floor seems to have been connected with the kitchen, not with the parlor.

His other personal property consisted of "Cartwheels, with

| | |
|---|---|
| plow and ax, tackling, howes and shovel, | £5,6,00 |
| Pitch forks, sythes, 3 augurs, and other tools, horse fetters, | 1,4,0 |
| Horses, mares, sheep and swine, | 21,02.0 |
| 2 oxen, 15 cows, and 23 young cattle—all, | 64,15,00 |
| 18 jags of hay, a grindstone a *lime*, a peck, | 4,15,00 |
| Boards and Bolts, | 00,10,00 |
| A drawing-knife, spit, and other small things, | 00,10,02 |
| Debts due the estate, | 2,10,00 |
| | 100,14 |

As boards and bolts are connected in the same line, I infer that sawing boards by hand had not been discontinued in 1684. He had little grain on hand, but a large stock of cattle, indicating that in the latter part of his life the raising of stock was his principal business. Forty head of cattle were apprised at only £64,15—$215.83, or an average of only 15,37 each, showing that during the forty-five years since the settlement of the town, cattle had depreciated about 75 per cent. in value.

| | |
|---|---|
| His personal estate amounted to | £271,13,09 |
| and his real estate, | |
| "In housing, lands and meadows," | 909,00,00 |
| Total, | £1,180,13,09 |

His will is dated two years before his death. It is signed with his mark, A. A., not conclusive evidence that he was unable to write, for many good scholars have so signed their wills, but the fact leads me to doubt the accuracy of a remark made in the former part of this article, "that he learned to write after he was a married man." The provisions of the will are very clearly expressed, and it contains much historical information, and will repay the labor of a careful perusal. "The Hallett Mill" is not named in his will or inventory, showing that if he ever was an owner in it, he was not at the time of his death.

[From Plymouth Rec. p. 194.]

## WILL OF ANDREW HALLETT.

To all Christian people to whome these presents shall come: Know yee that I, Andrew Hallett of Yarmouth, in ye Colony of New Plymouth, being weake in body by reason of sore pains and aches, yet blessed be God at this time present I have my reason and understanding fresh and timely, I doe make this my last will and testament as followeth: First, I doe bequeath my soule to God that gave it unto me, and my body to ye dust from whence it was formed by a desent and comely Buriall, and for that portion of Temporall blessings that God hath been pleased to posess me of, I do will and bequeath as followeth: First, I doe will and bequeath to my loving wife one-third part of all my whole estate of moveables both within my house and also one-third part of all my cattell that I have not disposed of for ye comfort of her life and at her dispose to whom she shall see cause to give it unto, also my will is that my said wife shall have and Injoy ye easter end of my said house I now live in during her naturall life, and ye thirds of all ye profits or Improvements of all my lands, both upland and meadow, during her naturall life, and then to returne as followeth in this my will. And to my son Jonathan Hallett I will and bequeath little calves pasture, so called, which is from my old field fence and bounds that is betwixt me and ye said Andrew Hallett and John Gorham with ye broken marsh belonging to ye said pasture butting against ye old mill pond. Also I doe give unto my said son, Jonathan Hallett, my great table and my great bedstead and ye drawne cushings and ye cubbord and ye stands in ye Easter end of my now dwelling-house after my decease and ye decease of my wife. And also I do give unto my said son Jonathan twenty pounds of my estate, and then my will is that my son Jonathan Hallett and my son John Hallett shall equally make a division of all my lands and meadows whatsoever both within fence and without with all housings whatsoever shall be standing upon my lands considering of quantity and quallity and so to make a division as you may agree yourselves, but in case you cannot agree to divide ye said and housings then to chose indifferent men between you to make a division of ye said Housing and lands and meadows and when equally divided then my son Jonathan to have ye one halfe and my son John to have ye other halfe, only my son Jonathan to have ye first choyce of ye lands and housing after devition, and my son John Hallett to have ye other halfe of ye housing and lands and meadows, only ye said John Hallett my son to pay to his brother Jonathan Hallett ye just sum of ten pounds, also what I have already given to my son John Hallett I doe now confirme to him as his owne proper right and for ye farme I bought of John Fenny,* Senr, of Barnstable, I doe confirme to my two sons Jonathan Hallett and to my son John Hallett, to them and their heirs forever to be equally divided between them two, but concerning my other lands before mentioned in this my will, that in case either of my sons Jonathan Hallett or John Hallett shall dye without I shew of their bodies lawfully begotten, then I doe give liberty to either of them to will their part of their lands and housings to whom they please, provided it be to any of their owne kindred of ye Halletts, but in case any of my said sons doe die without any issue and—without any will then my will is that my son that doth survive shall have ye one halfe of his said brothers lands that is deceased, and ye other halfe of his said lands to his three sisters and their heirs forever, but in case that both my said sons shall dye without any Issue and without will as above said then all my said lands and housing to fall to my three daughters, that is to say to Ruhamath and Abigail and Mehettabell and their heirs forever, to be equally devided between them three. And to my daughter Ruhamath Bourn I doe confirme to her what she hath already, and doe will to her ye just sum of twenty pounds more of my estate, and to my Grandchildren as Timothy Bourne I do will five pounds; and to Hanah Bourne I doe will five pounds, and to Elezer Bourne I do will five pounds, and Hezekiah Bourne I doe will five pounds of my estate. And to my daughter Abigall Alldin I dce confirme to her what I have already given to her and do will unto her my said daughter Abigall twenty pounds in money that I lent unto her husband Jonathan Alldin. And my will is that my daughter Abigall Aldin shall have six pound paid more to her by my Executor, and to my daughter Abigall's children I give twenty pounds, that is five pounds to each of them, to be paid by my Executor unto all my children above expressed either at ye

---

*Finney or Phinney.

day of their marriage or when they shall come to ye age of one and twenty years or sooner if my Executor shall see cause, and to my daughter Mehettabell I do will and bequeath unto her ye just sum of sixty pounds with what she hath had already of my estate, and to my grandchild John Bourne he shall have pounds when he shall come of age of one and twenty years, to be paid by my Executor out of their estates according to proportion of what they have of mine estate. Bee it further knowne by these presents that I doe make and appoint my loveing wife Ann, and my son Jonathan Hallett and John Hallett joynt Executors to this my last will and testament as witness my hand and seal this fourteenth day of March Ano Domi one thousand six hundred eighth one eighty and two.

The marke of A. A.
Andrew Hallett,
and a (seal.)

Signed and sealed in presence
of us, Thomas Thornton, Sen.
    John Miller.
      This will is proved at ye
      Court held at Plymouth
      ye 4 June, 1684.
    Nathaniell Morton, Secretary.

Of the family of the second Andrew Hallett no perfect record has been preserved. He married Anne or Anna Besse, daughter of Anthony of Lynn and Sandwich. Tradition says she was only fourteen at marriage, that she was a strong, healthy woman, and was the mother of twins before she completed her fifteenth year.* That she was very young when married, the known age of her mother confirms. After the death of her husband, she occupied the easterly part of his house. Her grandson John Bourne resided with her, and her son Jonathan occupied the west part of the house. She died in the spring of 1694, leaving a will dated June 23, 1684. To her grandson John Bourne, she gave her bed in the chamber with the curtains, valances, and all that belonged to it, and her great brass kettle or 22 shillings in money. To her youngest daughter, Mehitabel Dexter, her satin gown† and mohair petticoat. All the rest of her estate, apprised at £180,07,06, (£67 of which was in money) she gave equally to her three daughters, Ruhannah Bourne, Abigail Alden, and Mehitable Dexter. Her wearing apparel, consisting of articles of wool, linen, and silk; hose, shoes, hat, &c., was apprised at

---

*The tradition further relates, that on the day following the birth of her children, she requested her mother, who acted as nurse, to take care of the babes, while she went out to seek birds eggs for them. The grandmother at that time could not have been over thirty, for she had children of her own fifteen years younger than her grandchild Abigail, and if Ruhama was one of the twins, not far from twenty. Several similar instances of early marriages have occurred in the family, one during the present year 1864. [See Cudworth for account of Barlow family.]

†In the inventory it is called "Satinistow," a word not found in the dictionaries— and in another place, silk. For many years some of the articles belonging to the first comer were preserved as heir-looms, and some are now probably in existence.

£15,00,00, or 50 dollars in silver money, showing that on the Sabbath and on holidays she dressed in great style.

Children of Andrew Hallett, Jr. :

7.   I.   Ruhama, ———, married Job Bourne 14th Dec. 1664, by whom she had five children. He died in 1676, and she married ——— Hersey. She was living in 1714. (See Bourne.)

8.   II.   Abigail, born 1644, married Capt. Jonathan Alden of Duxbury, Dec. 10, 1672. He was the son of John Alden and Priscilla Mullins, born in 1627, and was seventeen years older than his wife. He inherited the homestead of his father in Duxbury, and died Feb. 1697, leaving an estate apprised at £309. She died Aug. 17, 1725, aged 81 years, and has a monument in the old graveyard in D. Her children were Andrew, Jonathan, John and Benjamin.

9.   III.   Dorcas, bap. June 1, 1646. She was not living in 1684, and probably died young.

10.   IV.   Jonathan, born Nov. 20, 1647. (See account bebelow.)

11.   V.   John, born Dec. 11, 1650. (See account below.)

12.   VI.   Mehitabel, ———, called youngest daughter. She married Nov. 10, 1682, John Dexter of Sandwich, and had Elizabeth Nov. 2, 1683; Thomas Aug. 26, 1686; Abigail May 26, 1689; John, Sept. 11, 1692; and after the latter date removed to Portsmouth, R. I. (See Dexter.)

(10-IV.)   Of the early life of Jonathan Hallett little is known. He was not taxed in Yarmouth in 1676, and does not appear to have been a resident. Jan. 30, 1683-4, he married Abigail Dexter, daughter of Ensign Thomas Dexter of Sandwich, and grand-daughter of Mr. Thomas Dexter of Lynn, In 1684 he was constable of Sandwich, and an inhabitant of that town. He was thirty-six when married, and his wife twenty-one years of age. After the death of his father he removed to Yarmouth, and resided in the west room of his father's house till 1695, the year after the death of his mother, when he built his new house, afterwards known as the Jeremiah Hallett house. As all the houses built about that time were of the same description, some account thereof may not be uninteresting. The lumber for its construction came from Scituate, the Bangor of those times. It was two stories high, and at first contained only two rooms, exclusive of the attic. It stood where Mr. Joseph Hale's house now stands, fronted due south, and was about twenty-four feet in front, by eighteen in the rear. The timber was large, and the boarding an inch and a quarter in thickness. The chimney was built within, not outside of the frame. On entering the front door you stepped over the sill, the entry floor being a foot lower than the threshold. In the entry a circular stairway led to the chamber and attic.

Passing into the great room or parlor you had to step over a cross timber. That room was seventeen feet square, and no part of it was ever plastered or finished. The chimney projected into the room, with no finishing boards put up around it. The fireplace was seven feet wide, four feet deep, and five and a half high, with an oven at the south end. The hearth was laid with flat stones, picked up in the fields. The sills, which were large sticks of timber, projected into the room and formed low seats on three sides. The windows were of small diamond shaped glass set in lead. No planed boards, no plastering, paper or paint, was used in that house from the day it was built in 1695, till it was taken down in 1819. Outwardly the house appeared very comfortable. The upper story, on the east, projected over the lower. This projection was adorned with some rude ornamental work, in the form of acorns, hanging beneath. Subsequently two additions were made. A one story leanto on the rear for a kitchen and pantry, and a leanto or "salt-box" on the west side. The inside of these additions were ruder, if possible, than the original structure. The back stairs were made of a pine log, with scores cut therein. There was no railing, and to go up or down them in the dark, was a feat that few would venture to attempt.

The furniture of the house was as mean as the interior finish. His father's house was elegantly furnished in comparison.

Jonathan Hallett, after the decease of his father, was the most wealthy man in Yarmouth, and his brother John ranked next to him; yet with all their riches, neither was contented—neither was happy. I have heard the aged remark that the men of the third generation were, as a class, an ignorant and superstitious race. The ardent piety of the first comers had degenerated into lifeless formalities; their wise economy into a desire to hoard; and their simple, unaffected manners, into coarseness—often to rudeness and incivility. The first Jonathan Hallett was a type of that class of men. Hundreds now living can testify that his house was as cold, as cheerless, and as comfortless as I have described. He had money to let to all who could give good security, and were willing to pay a liberal percentage, yet he had no money to expend in finishing or plastering his rooms, none to make his home pleasant and comfortable. His excuse was, "my father's house was never plastered." The seams of his father's house was "*daubed*," and it was warm and comfortable. Jonathan could not afford that small expense, he caulked the seams with "swingling tow" which cost nothing. This was the character of the man, he was greedy of filty lucre; denied himself the comforts and conveniences of life, lived as meanly and as sparingly as the poorest of the poor, that he might add to his already well filled coffers.

Generally the first settlers had not the means, and those that had were obliged to send out to England for the articles they

wanted, and shippers in those days charged enormous profits.
Thirty per cent. was a moderate rate.  Forty, fifty, and even one
hundred per cent. was paid.  In Jonathan's time it was not so.
Some manufactures had been established, communication with the
mother country was more frequent, there were importers who sold
goods at a moderate advance, and the Colonies were well supplied
with articles of convenience and comfort.  We cannot respect the
man who, to save a little more money, will go bare-foot in winter ;
who will run the risk of breaking his neck in clambering up a
notched log, and who lived all his days in a house that neither the
joiner, the plasterer, nor the painter ever entered.   There is a gol-
den mean in the path of life which neither the miser nor the
spendthrift ever see.  The former never perceives the deep gulph
that separates prudent management from miserly hoarding and the
latter that which divides an honorable, generous hospitality, from
wasteful extravagance.

Goodman Andrew Hallett, after providing in his will for the
comfortable support of his widow, making liberal bequests to his
daughters, and giving to his son Jonathan his little Calves Pasture, as a token of his right of primogeniture, gave all the remainder of his large estate to his two sons, enjoining on them to make
a peaceful division thereof by mutual agreement.  They quar-
relled about the boundaries of the little Calves Pasture, the birth-
right of Jonathan, and they spent two years and a half in vain attempts to divide peaceably and by mutual concession and agreement, when they put themselves under bonds of £800, each to the
other, to abide by the award of Mr. Nathaniel Bacon, of Barnstable, and Col. William Bassett, of Sandwich.  Jonathan had
the western portion of the farm, John the eastern.  The present
road to the wharf being the division line on the north side of the
County road,  That there was some unpleasant feeling between
them and their families, is indicated by the fact that Jonathan's
descendants called John's, "other side Halletts."

March 5, 1686-7,  Jonathan, Hallett, for £20 in current
money, bought of his brother-in-law, John Dexter, of Sandwich,
a negro slave called Harry, aged 29 years.  The bill of sale, yet
preserved, is drawn up with much formality—signed, sealed and
witnessed.

In 1710 he continued to rank as the most wealthy man in
Yarmouth, and his brother John next.  He was an extensive
landholder in Yarmouth and in Barnstable.  March 28, 1698-9, he
bought of Samuel Bradford, of Duxbury, for twenty pounds in
current money, a thousand acre right of land in Windham, Hartford County, Connecticut, "being the fifth lot at the crotch of the
river," and  also a houselot of twelve acres  abutting on the river,
with  rights of commonage.  It is probable  he sold his Windham
farm, for none of his family removed to that town.

His will is dated Dec. 5, 1716, and was proved Feb. 14, 1716-17. He names his five sons, Ebenezer, Thomas, Timothy, David and Jonathan, and his daughters Mehitabel Sturgis, Elizabeth Crowell, and Abigail Hallett. His real estate was apprised at £2000, and his personal estate for a large sum.

The men of the third generation had very slender means of acquiring an education, generally their piety had degenerated into lifeless, unmeaning formalities; they were church members; but not of the noble, self-sacrificing race by whom the country was settled. Jonathan Hallett loved money better than he loved the church; he was industrious, and gathered up riches which his children put to a better use than he did. He died Jan. 12, 1716-17, aged 69 years, and his wife died Sept. 2, 1715, aged 52 years. Both are buried in the old burying-ground in Yarmouth, where monuments are erected to their memories.

The record of his family is lost. The leaf of the record on which it was written is gone. His children were born, the oldest perhaps in Sandwich, the others in Yarmouth.

13.   I.   Mehitabel, married Edward Sturgis, Nov. 25, 1703.
14.   II.   Ebenezer. (See account below.)
15.   III.   Thomas, born 1691. (See account below.)
16.   IV.   Jonathan, 1694. (See account below.)
17.   V.   David. (See account below.)
18.   VI.   Abigail, married Hatsuld Freeman, of Harwich, Jan. 18, 1719. She lived to great age, about 100 years, and is buried in the old burying-ground in Brewster.
19.   VII.   Elizabeth married Paul Crowell Oct. 21, 1714.
20.   VIII.   Timothy. (See account below.)

(10-10.) Mr. John Hallett, son of Andrew, born in Yarmouth Dec. 11, 1648, was a corporal in the company of Capt. John Gorham in King Philip's war. He was not taxed in Yarmouth in 1676. I have not carefully investigated his history; but he was a man of more note than his brother Jonathan, as the Mr. affixed to his name indicates. His house, precisely of the description of his brother Jonathan's, stood a little in the rear of where Capt. John Eldridge's house now stands, and was taken down about forty years ago. Though ranking as second in point of wealth among the inhabitants of Yarmouth, his house was never finished, never plastered, papered or painted, facts that show that he had as penurious a disposition as his brother. He was constable of the town of Yarmouth in 1682, and held other offices.

He married Feb. 16, 1681-2, Mary, daughter of Mr. Joseph Howes. The Register of his family on the Yarmouth Records is lost. In his will dated May 14, 1725, he names his children then living. He died June 10, 1726, aged 78, and his widow, Mrs.

Mary Hallett, June 1732, aged 73 years.  Both are buried in the old burying-ground in Yarmouth.

Children of Mr. John Hallett born in Yarmouth:

21.  I.  Thankful, married Joseph Basset Dec. 3, 1719, his second wife died Aug. 12, 1736.
22.  II.  Andrew, born 1684.  (See account below.)
23.  III.  John, 1688.  (See account below.)
24.  IV.  Joseph.  (See account below.)
25.  V.  Samuel.  do
26.  VI.  Seth.  do
27.  VII.  Hannah, ————, married her cousin Ebenezer Hallett June 27, 1728, died April 20, 1729, at the birth of her first child.
28.  VIII.  Mary, ————, died unmarried April 22, 1751.
29.  IX.  Mercy, ————, died Nov. 13, 1747.
30.  X.  Hope, born 1705, married Joseph Griffeth of Harwich. July 24, 1729, died July 5, 1784, aged 79.

(14-11.)  Ebenezer Hallett, son of Jonathan, was a farmer and resided in Yarmouth.  His dwelling-house, which has been owned by four successive generations of Ebenezer Hallett's yet remains.  It was originally of the same description with his father's, but by several additions of one room at a time, it is now a large two story mansion house.  Though originally of the same description with his father's, it was better finished and furnished.  In his family record I find this entry, "Our house was in danger of burning August 9, 1746."  Perhaps there is no house in the County in which so much wood has been consumed as in this.  The Ebenezer Halletts, especially the second, were noted for keeping large fires.

He married Aug. 14, 1712, Rebecca Howes.  She died March 23, 1724-5.  2d, his cousin Hannah Hallett, June 27, 1728.  She died April 20, 1729.  3d, Mercy Gray, May 30, 1737, who survived him.  In his will dated 10th May, 1760, he gives to his wife Mercy one-half of the moveables in the east end of his dwelling-house, two cows, one steer, one-third part of his sheep and hogs, sundry articles of provision, one-third part of his grain in the ground, the improvement of the east end of his dwelling-house, one-quarter of his barn, and a third part of his real estate, as her right of dower or thirds during her natural life; twelve loads of pine and twelve loads of oak wood annually, cut "convenient for the chimney," and a horse to ride to meeting and elsewhere by his son Ebenezer.  She survived her husband several years; but her connection with the family was an unhappy one.

He gives legacies to his daughters Ann Crowell, Sarah Gray, and Rebecca Hallett, to his grandchildren Ebenezer, Susannah, John, Temperance, Rebecca, Mercy and Jonathan Whelden, and his son-in-law John Whelden.  To Ebenezer Whelden he made an additional bequest of "one-third part in acres of the southern end of the woodlot commonly called the "New Society" where once Simeon Porridge lived. To his grandson Ebenezer Hallett, he gave one pair of gold sleeve buttons, and his coat with silver buttons ; and to his grandson Edward Hallett one Jack-coat with silver buttons on it. He appoints his son Ebenezer executor, makes him his residuary legatee, and charges him with the payment of his debts and legacies.

(15-3.) Thomas Hallett, styled gentleman, son of Jonathan, born in Yarmouth in 1691, owned and resided in the large, ancient mansion-house now standing on the corner of Hallett St., and Wharf Lane. It was originally built on the same plan with that of his father's which has been described, but was better finished at first, and has since been kept in good repair. The Halletts', as a race, are able-bodied men, and average in stature above the common height. Thomas was an exception. He was a short, thick-set man. During the latter part of his life he was of feeble health. For many years he was afflicted with a sore leg—a disease which usually set at defiance the curative skill of the physicians of his time.

Thomas Hallett, lived in better style than many of his neighbors, and died April 10, 1772, aged 81, leaving a good estate.

He married April 9, 1719, for his first wife, Sarah, daughter of Dea. Joseph Hawes. She was born April 1, 1696, and died soon after her marriage, leaving no issue. He married Feb. 8, 1721-2, Hannah, widow of Andrew Gray of Harwich, and North Yarmouth, Maine. She died Feb. 6, 1749-50, and he married for his third wife, Aug. 19, 1750, Desire Gorham. She died Dec. 1767, aged 57. For his fourth wife he married Mary, widow of Thomas Hedge, and a daughter of James Gorham. (See Gorham genealogy No. 64.)

In his will dated 21st Feb. 1770, proved May 4, 1772, he gives to his wife Mary Hallett in lieu of thirds, the improvement of all his real estate during her natural life, one-third of his in-door moveables, and his best cow. To his nephew Thomas Hallett, son of his brother Jonathan, a piece of land on the south side of the road on which Thomas' house stood, containing two acres. To his nephews Jonathan and Jeremiah, sons of his brother Jonathan, £6 or $20 each. To his nephew Ebenezer Hallett, Jr., £6. To his nephews Jonathan and Abner, sons of his brother David, £4 each. To his nephews Moses, Joshua, and Isaac, sons of his brother Timothy, deceased, £6. All the rest of his real and personal estate he gave to his adopted son Joshua Gray, son of his second wife Hannah Gray.

(16-4.) Dea. Jonathan Hallett, owned and occupied the house which was his father's residence, and which I have described. Notwithstanding he lived in a house so meanly furnished, he had the means of living better. He was a man of sound judgment, and exercised a wide and deserved influence among his neighbors and acquaintances. There is a common saying, often repeated, and that has some truth in it—"the shoemaker's wife and the blacksmith's horse go unshod." Dea. Jonathan was a carpenter, though agriculture was his principal employment; and though he had time to finish off, and put some of his neighbor's houses in good order, he never found time to keep his own in decent repair.

He and his wife united in full communion with the Barnstable Church Sept. 8, 1728, and continued to be a member till July 1, 1744, when he was dismissed to the West Church in Yarmouth of which he was soon after elected one of its deacons, and continued to be till his death. He was many years one of the Selectmen of the town of Yarmouth, and held other municipal offices. His children were all well educated for the times. His son Jonathan was fitted for Cambridge College, and his father desired him to enter; but the son preferred rather to be a farmer than a clergyman.

He married Feb. 17, 1719-20, Desire Howes, with whom he lived in the marriage state fifty-five years, till April 3, 1775, when she died aged 78 years. He died May 24, 1783, aged 90 years, and is buried in the ancient burying-ground in Yarmouth, where monuments are erected to his and his wife's memory.

In his will dated July 17, 1779, he names his sons Jonathan, Thomas and Jeremiah, and daughters Desire Bacon and Mehitable Swift, and his four grandchildren, Elkanah, Isaiah, Mehitabel and Desire Crowell. He gave his dwelling-house to Jeremiah, hence the name by which the old house was known in modern times, and the lot of land on the south of the road on which his son Jonathan's house stood to Jonathan. This lot was bounded easterly by the land of Col. Enoch Hallett. To Thomas and Jeremiah he gave his orchard on the west of Jonathan's house.

Children of the second Jonathan Hallett born in Yarmouth:
Two daughters 20th Nov. 1720, still born.

| | | | |
|---|---|---|---|
| 40. | 1. | Desire, 18th Jan. 1721-2, married Samuel Bacon 1747. |
| 41. | II. | Jonathan, 10th Nov. 1723. (See account below.) |
| 42. | III. | Prince, 12th Sept. 1725, died July 3, 1728. |
| 43. | IV. | Abigail, 25th Aug. 1727, died June 26, 1728. |
| 44. | V. | Thomas, 7th July, 1729. (See account below.) |
| 0. | VI. | Abigail, 3d June, 1731, died June 23, 1731.* |
| 0. | VII. | Prince, 3d June, 1732, died June 23, 1732. |
| 45. | VIII. | Jeremiah, 20th Sept. 1733. (See account below.) |
| 46. | IX. | Joshua, 19th March, 1735-6, died 10th May, 1736. |
| 47. | X. | Sarah, 28th June 1737. |
| 48. | XI. | Mehitabel, 7th May, 1740. |

(17.) David Hallett, son of Jonathan, removed to Hyannis, and settled on the land which was his father's. His house was one

---

*Abigail and Prince. I find this so on the record; but it looks like a mistake of the clerk.

of the first built in that village.  He married 19th Aug. 1719, Mary, daughter of John Annable of West Barnstable.

*Children born in Barnstable.*

49.  I.   Abigail, 26th June, 1720, married Prince Howes of Yarmouth, Aug. 3, 1739.
50.  II.   Jonathan, 1st Dec. 1722, married Aug. 5, 1744, Mercy, daughter of Dea. Samuel Bacon, and had John, 4th Oct. 1745; Jonathan, 9th Dec. 1749; Nathaniel, 28th Nov. 1752; Anner, 20th March, 1755; Samuel, 26th March, 1758; Benjamin, 18th Jan. 1760; Edward, 6th April 1762; William and David.  Capt. Benjamin of this family resided at Osterville, and was the father of the late Hon. Benjamin F. Hallett.
51.  III.   David, 12th Dec. 1744, married July 18, 1753, Sarah Lewis.  2d, Sarah Butler, Feb. 12, 1756.  He died Nov. 1763.
52.  IV.   Elizabeth, 9th Jan., 1726.
53.  V.   Mehitabel, 21st Ap. 1729, married Shubael Baxter of Yarmouth, 1746-7.
54.  VI.   Remember, 12th May, 1731, married Jabez Marchant of Yarmouth, Jan. 4, 1753.
55.  VII.   Sarah, 28th May, 1733, married Jabez Parker 1751.
56.  VIII.   Annah, 14th May, 1737, married Nov. 1, 1759, Elisha Kent, of Goodfield.
57.  IX.   Mary, 11th May, 1739, married Nov. 22, 1761, Timothy Hamblin.
58.  X.   Abner, 19th May, 1741.  He married Susan ———, had a son Abner and others.

Timothy Hallett, son of Jonathan, owned and resided in the dwelling-house now occupied by Mr. Eldridge Lovell of Yarmouth. He was a farmer, and a very respectable man.  He married, first, Feb. 18, 1719-20, Thankful Sturgis, who died at the birth of her first child—still born—10th Jan. 1721, and both were buried in the same grave.  Second, to Elizabeth, daughter of Dea. Moses Hatch of Falmouth.  She died Oct. 23, 1744, aged 44 years, and he married May 23, 1745, Thankful Jones of Barnstable,‑ his third wife. He died as recorded on his grave stones, Jan. 24, 1771, in the 69th year of his age.  His grandson Benjamin made the following record in his family bible: "My grandfather Timothy Hallett died July 7, 1770, in the 66th year of his age."  "My grandmother Elizabeth Hallett died Oct. 23, 1744, aged 44 years."

Children of Timothy Hallett born in Yarmouth:

59.  I.   Timothy, 7th May, 1725, died Aug. 3, 1747.
60.  II.   Elizabeth, 12th June 1727, died June 7, 1728.
61.  III.   Moses, 20th April, 1629.  He was an ignorant, self-conceited man.

62.   IV.   Benjamin, 9th Oct. 1730, married Bethia Jones of Sandwich Ap. 26, 1759.  He was pilot of a vessel bound to Halifax, lost at sea, and all on board perished.  He left no issue
63.   V.   Elizabeth, 16th Nov. 1735, died Dec. 20, 1735.
64.   VI.   James, 12th April, 1737, died young.
   (On the family record of Benjamin Hallett, grandson of Timothy, the name of *James* is not given.  Joshua Hallett, now living,
(1858) says he does not recollect of having heard his father say he
had a brother James.  On the family register, the birth of Joshua
is recorded in the year 1737, which corresponds with the record of
his age at his death.)
65.   VII.   Joshua, 10th Jan. 1738-9.  His house, yet remaining,
is the most westerly on the north side of the County road in
Yarmouth.  He married Dorcas Eldridge.  He died Aug. 19,
1821, aged 84, and his wife April 26, 1813, aged 72 years.
His children were :
Bethia,   Feb. 5,  1763,  died aged—yrs.
Elizabeth, Oct. 31, 1764,   "    "   88  "
Lydia, Feb. 21, 1767,       "    "   82  "
Dorcas, April 20, 1770,     "    "   85  "
Mary, June 23, 1772,        "    "   86  "
Patience, April 26, 1775,   "    "   —  "
Joshua, April 12, 1778,     "    "   85  "
Omitting Patience, who died in infancy, the average of the
family, parents and children, is 83 years and some months.
   Bethia married Elkanah Crowell and resided at West Yar-
mouth.   Elizabeth or Betsey as she was called, lived unmarried and
died in her father's house.  Lydia married Obed Howes, Esq., of
Dennis.  Dorcas was marked at birth with bunches of grapes on
her face.  She married at 62 her cousin Benjamin Hallett.  Mary
married, first, Josiah Baker.  2d, Robert Dixon ; and 3d, Capt.
Eben Howes of Yarmouth.  She resided for a time in the Western
States ; but after her third marriage in Yarmouth, and died of
apoplexy in 1858.  Joshua married twice.  He was a carpenter,
and resided in a house on the opposite side of the road from his
father's.  He died in 1863.
66.   VIII.   Isaac, born 24th Aug. 1742, was the youngest child
of Timothy.  He was a deacon of the Yarmouth church, and
his family, as well as his brother Joshua's, are long lived.  He
married in 1761 Elizabeth Eldridge.  He died Oct. 5, 1814,
aged 72 years, and his widow March 1, 1831, aged 86 years.

*Children born in Yarmouth.*

Benjamin, Nov. 3, 1762, died Feb. 28, 1838, aged 76 years.
Thankful, Oct. 10, 1764, died Aug. 14, 1831, aged 68 years.
Isaac, Dec. 6, 1766, died 1857 aged 90 years.
Elizabeth, Feb. 23, 1769, now living, aged 95 years.  [Died March
   26, 1866, aged 97.]

Anna, March 26, 1771, died Sept. 24, 1823, aged 52 years.
Deborah, Aug. 3, 1773, died Sept. 24, 1857, aged 84 years.
John, Jan. 28, 1775, died 1853, aged 78 years.
Rosanna, May 1, 1778, now living. [Died June, 1867, aged 89.]
Samuel, Sept. 23, 1780, died April 23, 1829, aged 48 years.
Levina, Jan. 13, 1783.
Elisha, March 8, 1777, now living.

Benjamin of this family married for his first wife, Feb. 16, 1786, Abigail Matthews, and had Elsey Oct. 12, 1786, and Sophia May 3, 1791. Both of whom married the late Capt. Nathan Hallett. For his second wife he married, June 19, 1832, Dorcas Hallett.

Thankful married Reuben Rider Dec. 1, 1785, and lived in Yarmouth.

Isaac married Rebecca Matthews, resided in Barnstable, and had a family. In his old age he lived with his daughter Ruth Sears.

Elizabeth, who married 1st, Prince Crowell, and 2d, Isaac Gorham, is now living. Though in the ninty-sixth year of her age, she keeps house, does her own work, runs her own errands, and is as well as most persons at seventy. A day or two since, while returning with her milk, she toppled down—jumping up quickly, she exclaimed: "I have not spilled one drop of it."

Anna married Barnabas Marchant of Barnstable, and removed to Falmouth.

Deborah married Capt. Ezra Crowell, and resided in Barnstable.

John married Lydia Thacher, and resided in Barnstable. In his old age he and his wife removed to Chatham.

Rosanna married Nov. 26, 1799, Zenas Howes, who died in 1853.

Samuel married Lydia Ewer of Barnstable. He owned his grandfather Timothy's house, which he sold. In the latter part of his life he was a resident of Barnstable.

Levina married, 1st, Trustrum Nye, of Falmouth. 2d, William Cobb of Nantucket.

Elisha married, 1st, Dorcas Small of Lubec, 16th Feb. 1809. She died Jan. 27, 1848, and he married 2d, Hannah W. Davis of Lubec. He is a ship carpenter, and a part of his life has resided at Lubec. He has recently removed to that vicinity, where he has a farm, on which there is a lead mine, which has been wrought.

(22.) Andrew Hallett, son of John, born in Yarmouth in 1684, built a house of the same description with his father's on the land opposite the Barnstable Bank building. He married July 23, 1713, Mehitabel, daughter of John Annable of West Barnstable.

*Children born in Yarmouth.*

67. I. Desire, April 21, 1714, married July 20, 1732, James Hawes.
68. II. Stephen, Oct. 5, 1721, married in 1743, Mercy Joyce. She died Oct. 23, 1763, and he married 2d, Widow Thankful Taylor. His children were Mary, June 12, 1744; Anna, March 30, 1747; Joseph, Dec. 11, 1748; Mercy, Feb. 17, 1752; Stephen, Aug. 16, 1754; Mehitable, June 10, 1757; Sarah, April 12, 1760; Mary, April 10, 1767; and Levi July 16, 1769. Joseph married Ruth Taylor, and had Joseph, and David and Asa twins. He was lost at sea with Howes Taylor. His brother Levi was also lost at sea in 1789. Anna, Mercy and Mehitabel, did not marry, resided in the east part of their father's house, and died in old age. Stephen married Desire Hall and had Susan and Mercy. He drank to excess, spent the large estate devised to him by his father, and died a town-pauper

Andrew Hallett died April 26, 1751, aged 67, and his widow Mehitabel Oct. 28, 1767, aged 72. In his will dated 23d April, 1651, proved May 7, 1751, he is styled yeoman, names his wife Mehitabel, to whom he gives one-half of his dwelling-house, privilege of the well, barn room. one-half of the fruit yearly growing in his orchard, use of one-third of his other real estate, one-third of his .personal estate, and sufficient wood at the door, cut fit for the fire, to be furnished by his son Stephen. To his daughter Desire he gave a piece of land on the east of Hawes' Lane, ten acres of woodland adjoining Jonathan Hallett's, and one-half of his moveable estate. All the rest of his estate he gave to his son Stephen.

(23.) John Hallett, Esq., son of John, born in Yarmouth, was married Aug. 24, 1716, by Peter Thacher, Esq., to Thankful Thacher. He died April 8, 1765, aged 77 years, and his widow Thankful Feb. 9, 1768.

He built the large mansion-house now occupied by the widow Elizabeth Gorham and Howard Crowell. He was Sheriff, and a man of note in his day, but I have not space to trace his history. His children born in Yarmouth were:

69. I. Mary, 17th Dec. 1717, m. Jan. 24, 1727, Isaac Gorham of Barnstable, and had Mary, who married Elisha Hedge, and Thankful, who married John Hall. She died Aug. 19, 1741, and is buried near the East Church in Barnstable.
70. II. John, 9th Aug. 1719, married Feb. 12, 1747, Rebecca Hallett. He died Feb. 14, 1760. His children were: Mary, Dec 26, 1748, died young; Charles, April 4, 1751, married Lydia Thacher, and was the father of the late George Hallett, Esq., of Boston, and of the late Mr. Oliver Hallett, and others; Martha, Nov. 2, 1753, died unmarried in 1794; and John, May 4, 1756, married Hannah Hallett Apr. 10, 1781, and resided at Great Island.

81.    III.   Peter, 7th Oct. 1721, married in 1739, Eunice Allen of Harwich.   She died Aug. 26, 1752.   His second wife was Sarah ———, who died Feb. 13, 1760, and he married for his third wife Lydia Buck (or Bearse) in 1761.   He died Feb. 1794.   He was the father of nineteen children, whose fortunes in life were widely dissimilar.   His children were Rebecca, Jan. 15, 1743, married ———Bray ; John Allen Nov. 14, 1745, married ——— Mackey ; Elkanah, Sept. 16, 1749 ; Eunice, Dec. 24, 1751 ; Lot, April 12, 1754 ; Hannah, Oct. 1756, married Gersham Cobb, and has descendants ; Temperance, Sept. 1758 ; Benjamin, Aug. 13, 1762, died at sea on the coast of Africa, 1790 ; George, July 21, 1764 ; Prince, April 16, died a pauper in Y. ; Job, Feb. 26, 1767, died young ; Lydia, Feb. 23, 1769, married Zenas Hallett ; Sarah, Feb. 10, 1771, married and removed ; Peter, March 2, 1775, died at sea ; Mary, Sept. 19, 1777, married Joseph Hallett ; Job, July 28, 1779, of Boston, now living, and three others who died young, making 19.

(24.)   Joseph Hallett, son of John, built a house like his father's between his brother John's and Andrew's.   He married Abigail ——— 1722, and died Sept. 19, 1735, and his widow Abigail Sept. 18, 1768, aged 67.   His oldest child was born in Barnstable, his other children in Yarmouth.

72.    I.   Roland, 7th Aug. 1723.   (A Rowland Hallett married Jane Sears in 1772.   He resided at Hyannis, had a son Rowland and other children.

73.    II.   Joseph, 25th June, 1725, married 1745, Mary Joyce.

74.    III.   Abigail, 15th June, 1727, married Samuel Gorham April 20, 1747.

75.    IV.   Hannah, 23 Oct. 1729, married Josiah Gorham Oct. 9, 1755, and 2d, Thomas Allyn.

76.    V.   Eunice, 8th Jan. 1731-2.

77.    VI.   Elizabeth, 25th April, 1734.

(25.)   Samuel Hallett, son of John, married June 15, 1727, Susannah Clark of Harwich.   He resided in the house which was his father's.   His family register I do not find on the Yarmouth records.   His estate was settled Jan. 4, 1757, his widow Susannah being then living.   His children named in the settlement are :

78.    I.   Enoch, born in 1737, was one of the leading men during the Revolutionary period.   He was a Colonel of the militia, and afterwards Sheriff of the County.   He resided in the house which was his grandfather's, already described. Though one of the most prominent men in the County—a man of good business capacity—a man of influence and highly respected, yet he was satisfied to reside in a house that neither the joiner, the plasterer, nor the painter ever en-

tered, and in which the four winds of Heaven might contend for the mastery. His first wife was Thankful Hawes, who died Dec. 9, 1778, and he married May 25, 1780, Abigail Rider. He died March 8, 1788, aged 51 years. He had fourteen children born in Yarmouth, namely: Samuel, April 8, 1756, died Jan. 29, 1778, at Lancaster, viz: while in the public service; Barnabas, Dec. 27, 1757, married three wives, and has descendants; Enoch, Feb. 19, 1760, married Mary Sears; Heman, Jan. 27, 1762, died unmarried; Abner March 27, 1764, married Mary Hallett, and had daughter Serena, now living—he died in Aux Cays 1797; David, March 21, 1766, died at sea, had no issue; Susannah, Dec. 29, 1767, died 13th Feb. 1768; Susannah, March 7, 1769, married Heman Bangs and removed to the West; Ascha, Aug. 31, 1772, married and removed; Thankful, Sept. 3, 1774, resided with Rev. John Mellen, Jr., and died at Cambridge; Rhoda, Aug. 29, 1776, married Edward Marston; Abigail, Oct. 27, 1781, married Crocker Marston; Nancy, April 7, 1783, died young; and Samuel Clark, Feb. 13, 1785; died unmarried at sea.

79. II.   Clark, died at sea.
80. III.  Thankful, married David Taylor 1749.
81. IV.   Susannah, married ———— Bangs.
82. V.    Sarah, died unmarried. She was insane and supported by the town.

(26.) Seth Hallett, son of John, born in Yarmouth in 1699, resided at Hyannis. He married May 8, 1729, Mary Taylor. He died May 1, 1757, aged 58, and his widow Mary, Oct. 9, 1763, aged 62. Both are buried in the old graveyard at Hyannis.

*Children born in Barnstable.*

83. I.    Temperance, April 18, 1729.
84. II.   Hannah, Dec. 4, 1731.
85. III.  Deborah, April 14, 1734.
86. IV.   Joseph, Sept. 21, 1736.
87. V.    Thankful, Sept. 21, 1736, married John Crocker 4th June, 1760.
88. VI.   Abigail, Aug. 8, 1738.

And I have also noted that he had a son Rowland born in 1743, died Aug. 10, 1816, aged 73. (See Roland son of Samuel.) This Roland married Jane Sears, and among his children was the late Seth Hallett, Esq., of Hyannis.

36. Ebenezer Hallett, son of Ebenezer, born in Yarmouth Dec. 29, 1719, married Dec. 12, 1741, Elizabeth Bangs. He died March 6, 1807, aged 87 years. He was a farmer, and resided in the house which was his father's. After he was sixty years of

age he set out an orchard, and lived to gather the fruit many years. His children born in Yarmouth were :

89.   I.   Ruth, 18th Sept. 1743, married Eben Howes.
90.   II.   A son, 7th Sept. 1745, died 15th of same month.
91.   III.   Edward, 6th April, 1747, married Sarah Hedge, and had Nathan, Dec. 10, 1768 ; Ansel, Nov. 1, 1770 ; Hannah, March 16, 1773 ; Olive, April 16, 1775 ; Betty, Aug. 2, 1777, died young ; Betty, Nov. 2, 1779, married John Eldridge ; Edw. Bangs March 16, 1782 ; Sally, June 18, 1784 ; and Nancy Jan. 4, 1787. The father of this family died aged 49, but his children were all long-lived, and he has numerous descendants.
92.   IV.   Ebenezer, 22d May, 1750. He was a farmer, and was one of the first contractors to carry a weekly mail to Boston. (See Thacher.) His children were : Lot, Oct. 17, 1777 ; Catte, Feb. 4, 1780 ; Ann, April 13, 1783 ; Ebenezer, May 22, 1785 ; Matthews C., May 25, 1787 ; Elizabeth, Feb. 4, 1790 ; Lucy, March 21, 1795 ; and Randall, Jan. 24, 1799. All are now deceased excepting Elizabeth, wife of Charles Sears, Esq.
93.   IV.   Bette, 17th March, 1752.
94.   V.   Lucy, 4th July, 1754, died Sept. 6, 1765.
95.   VI.   A son, 13th Oct. 1758, died Nov. 24, 1758.
96.   VII.   A son, 23d June, 1759, died July 25, 1759.
97.   VIII.   Elizabeth, 23d March, 1764, married Eben Whelden.
98.   IX.   Lucy, 20th Jan. 1768, married John Eldridge.

41.   Jonathan Hallett, son of Dea. Jonathan, married Thankful Crowell. By mistake she took rats-bane instead of salts, and died in six hours. He died Feb. 6, 1814 ; aged 90 years. His children were : Lydia, born 11th Aug. 1745, married Josiah Miller ; Thankful, 16th Sept. 1747, married Barnabas Hedge and removed to Maine ; Howes, 21st July, 1749, married Temperance Hedge ; Jonathan, 13th June, 1751, married Sarah Hedge ; Azuba, 4th Dec. 1752, married Ansel Taylor ; Solomon, 23d Nov. 1754, married Deborah Chapman and removed to Kennebec, Maine ; Elisha, married Elizabeth Hawes Oct. 15, 1779, removed to Kennebec ; Isaiah, 10th Aug. 1762, died of small pox in Boston harbor—left no issue ; Zenas, 9th Aug. 1768, married Lydia Hallett ; and Josiah, 27th Aug. 1765, married Elizabeth Matthews.

Howes Hallett of this family was, in 1789, skipper of a new fishing vessel, owned principally by a Mr. Evans of Providence, R. I. She was lost in a gale on Nantucket Shoals, and all on board perished, namely : Howes Hallett, master, Josiah Hallett, Daniel Hallett, Edmond Hallett, Levi Hallett, Joseph Hallett, Josiah Miller and Moody Sears.

44.  Thomas Hallett, son of Jonathan, married Sarah Hamblin, and had Ezekiel, 5th April, 1757, died at sea unmarried; Desire, 15th April, 1759, married Barnabas Hallett; Judith, 31st May, 1761, died single at Sandwich; Sarah, 14th July, 1763, married Barnabas Hallett; Ruth, 21st July, 1765, died single at Sandwich; Thomas, 6th Sept. 1767; Ezra, 28th March, 1769; William, 13th March, 1775, married Abigail Thacher; Elizabeth, 12 Nov. 1778, died single at Sandwich.

47.  Jeremiah Hallett, son of Jonathan, married Hannah Griffeth.  He died Nov. 12, 1819, aged 86.  His children were: Hannah, born 18th June, 1760, married John Hallett April 10, 1781; Mary, 1st Sept. 1763, married Abner Hallett.  She lived a widow many years, and was a living chronicle of the history of the Halletts; Thankful, 6th Oct. 1764, married James Sears; Jerusha, 14th March, 1767, married Ebenezer Marston; Daniel, 20th Oct. 1769, lost at sea 1789; Rebecca, 3d Sept. 1772, married 1st, David Downs, 2d, Barnabas Bacon; Jeremiah, 28th June, 1775, committed suicide 1837; and Joseph, 2d April, 1778, married Lucretia Taylor.

Lines composed by the Rev. Timothy Alden, on the death of Mr. James Sears' wife and two infant children:

> The Sovereign Power that reigns above,
> Recalls these pledges of his love;
> The mother with the tender babes,
> Retires from light to death's cold shades.
> The infants free from human harm,
> There sleep as on the mother's arms.
> Thus to fulfil the sentence just,
> The mortal part returns to dust;
> Together lay the small and great,
> While lasts the intermediate state,
> But at the resurrection day
> The soul reanimates the clay.
> Made then immortal friends in heart;
> To Christ united ne'er shall part;
> The sure approach of that great day,
> May drive all gloomy thoughts away,
> And free the mind from sorrows past,
> With joys that shall forever last.
> God's judgments now as dark as night,
> Will then uplet as noonday light,
> Displaying wisdom Infinite,
> Why bosom friends must part so soon,
> The offspring cease in early bloom,
> Though this is far from present choice,
> Is all for good in wisdom's voice,
> That wisdom reigns, let all rejoice.
> When late retired to take my rest,
> I viewed your care as one distressed,
> These thoughts arose within my breast,
> If they a drooping heart can cheer,
> Accept them from a friend sincere.

(61.) Moses Hallett, son of Timothy, was born in Yarmouth April 20, 1729. He married four wives, namely :
1, Phebe Hamblin, in 1751, died Nov. 28, 1769.
2, Elenor Hamblin, ——— died Sept. 7, 1771, aged 38.
3, Lydia Goodspeed, 1772, died Feb. 16, 1791, aged 53.
4, Betty Crowell, a daughter of Ephraim.

He died Dec. 14, 1809, aged 80 years, and at the time of his death had only one unsound tooth. His widow survived him several years.

His children born in Yarmouth, were :

I.  James, 11th Sept. 1752, married Dec. 24, 1778, Susannah Taylor, and had a large family. Capt. Timothy Hallett was a son.

II.  Elizabeth, 21st May, 1754, married Jonathan Bassett and removed to Kennebec.

III.  Mary, 18th March, 1756, married Nov. 26, 1778, Jeremiah Crowell,

IV.  Abigail, 8th Feb. 1758, married Wm. Taylor.

V.  Timothy, 9th Jan. 1759-60, died May 5, 1776.

VI.  Phebe, 4th Aug. 1763, died single in old age.

VII.  Keziah, 26th March 1766, died unmarried Feb. 12, 1806. She was a woman feeble in mind and in body.

# THE HAMBLEN FAMILY.

As nearly all the first settlers of Barnstable came from London and the County of Kent, it is probable that James Hamblen, the ancestor, came from that city, as stated by Mr. David Hamblen in the New England Historic and Genealogical Journal. Of his early history little is known. He appears to have been an early member of Mr. Lothrop's Church, though the date is not found on the record. His son Bartholemew was baptized April 24, 1642, but the baptism of his older children, James and Hannah, do not appear on the record. It is probable that they were born in England, and that neither they nor their mother came over so early as the father. This was a common occurrence in early times. The father came over, and when he had provided a home sent for his family.

He was one of the earliest settlers, and was in Barnstable in the spring of 1639. His houselot, containing eight acres, was at Coggin's Pond, and was one of those that I presume were laid out under the authority of Mr. Collicut. It was bounded northerly by the lot of Gov. Hinckley, easterly by the Commons, (now the ancient graveyard) southerly by the Commons, and westerly by the highway, which at that time after crossing the hill on the west turned to the north on the borders of the pond to Gov. Hinckley's old house, which stood near the pond, and thence turned easterly, joining the present road at the head of Calve's Pasture Lane. In 1686 the present road was laid out through Hamblen's lot, and leaving a triangular shaped portion of it on the north of the road. Afterwards, in 1693, the location of the road having been changed, the Hamblens were allowed to enclose that part of the old road situate between their land and the pond, and adjoining to Gov. Hinckley's. The westerly portion of the road which was discontinued, opposite the south end of the pond, was reserved as a public watering-place, and is so occupied to this day.

His other lands were six shares and six acres of upland in the Calves Pasture, twenty acres of upland, and the meadow on the north, bounded easterly by the land of Henry Bourne, and westerly by the land of Dea. John Cooper. His great lot of fifty acres was bounded south-westerly by the great Indian Pond, southerly by the lot of Thomas Lothrop, and northerly by the Commons. It was the most northerly of the Indian Pond lots, and his son John built a house thereon. The Hamblens were among the first settlers in that part of the town, and that region of country is now known as Hamblen's Plain.

In 1686 James Hamblen, Senior's, house is described as standing on his twenty acre lot, on the north side of the highway, between the houses of Mr. Russell (known in modern times as Brick John Hinckley's) and Dea. John Cooper's, now owned by Mr. William Hinckley and others. In the year 1653 this land is called on the records Mr. Groom's land, but in the following year, 1654, Goodman Hamblen's.

James Hamblen, Sen'r, died in 1690. In his will dated Jan. 23, 1683-4, he names his wife Anne and all his children. To James he gave £10, to Bartholemew, £5, and to his daughter Hannah, "according to ye desire of my mother," £5. All the rest of his estate he gave to his wife during her natural life, and after her death to be divided equally among his children. He had a large real estate. His personal estate was apprised at £19,17.3.

Goodman Hamblen was not much in public life. He was an honest man, a good neighbor, and a sincere christian. He was industrious, and prudent in his habits, and brought up his children to walk in his footsteps. His descendants have, with few exceptions, inherited the good qualities of their ancestor. The Hon. Hannibal Hamlin, Vice President of the United States, is the only one among them who has been eminent in public life. To give a full genealogy of the family would require a volume. I cannot use all the material I have collected without transcending the limits of a newspaper article.

Several of this name came over early. Capt. Giles Hamlin, of Middletown, was a shipmaster, and a man of note in his time. There was a Clement Hamlin of Boston, in 1776. James, of Barnstable, is supposed to have been a brother of Giles, but I have seen no evidence that renders it probable. Capt. Giles wrote his name *Hamlin*; James, *Hamblen*. This is not conclusive evidence; but if they were brothers the probability is they would have written their names in the same manner. On the Colony Records, except in two instances, his name is written Hamlen. The exceptions are an instrument to which he affixed his own signature, and an exemption in 1657 from serving on the grand jury in consequence of sickness. His sons wrote their name *Hamblen*, Rev. Mr. Lothrop wrote the name uniformly *Hamling*; Rev. Mr. Russell *Hamblin*. In 1642

James *Hamlen* was admitted a freeman of the Colony, and in 1643 was constable of the town of Barnstable. The usual spelling is *Hamblin*, but the descendants of James are not uniform. Eleazer, the great-grandfather of Vice President *Hamlin*, dropped the *b* as a useless letter, and his descendants have continued to do so.

Family of James Hamblen.

His son James and daughter Hannah were probably born in England, his other children in Barnstable.

2.  I.   James.
3.  II.  Hannah.
4.  III. Bartholemew, 11th April, 1642, bap. April 24.
5.  IV.  John, 26th June, 1644, bap. June 30.
6.  V.   Sarah, 7th Nov. 1647, bap. same day.
7.  VI.  Eleazer, 17th March, 1649-50, bap. same day.
8.  VII. Israel, 25th June, 1652, bap. same day.

This record shows that Goodman Hamblen was very exact in the performance of what he believed to be a religious duty, that none of his children should die unbaptized.

James Hamblen, Jr., son of James, was probably born in London. He came over when a child, and resided all his life in Barnstable. At first on his father's Coggins' Pond lot; but in 1702 he had removed to Hamblen's Plain, West Barnstable, when his son Ebenezer occupied the old homestead, which he afterwards sold to Col. Gorham. He was a farmer, an exemplary member of the Church, and a good citizen. He married 20th Nov. 1662, Mary Dunham, probably a daughter of Dea. John, of Plymouth. She died April 19, 1715, aged 73, and was the mother of fourteen children born in Barnstable, namely :

9.   I.   Mary, 24th July, 1664, married Ben. Hatch June 17, 1678.
10.  II.  Elizabeth, 13th Feb. 1655-6, married John Scudder 31st July, 1689, died in Chatham Jan. 1742-3, aged 77.
11.  III. Eleazer, 12th April, 1668.
12.  IV.  Experience, 12th April, 1668.
13.  V.   James, 26th Aug. 1669.
14.  VI.  Jonathan, 6th March, 1670-1.
15.  VII. A child, 28th March, 1672, died 7th April, 1672.
16.  VIII. Ebenezer, 29th July, 1674.
17.  IX.  Elisha, 15th March, 1676-7, died 20th Dec. 1677.
18.  X.   Hope, 13th March, 1679-80, married Wm. Case May 9, 1712.
19.  XI.  Job, 15th Jan. 1681.
20.  XII. John, 12th Jan. 1683.
21.  XIII. Elkanah.
22.  XIV. Benjamin, baptized March 16, 1684-5.

4.   Bartholemew Hamblin, son of James, resided on his father's twenty acre lot, adjoining Dea. Cooper's, and Mr. Russell's

home lots.   He was a farmer, a worthy and respectable man.   His and his brother Eleazer's names appear as soldiers in the company of Capt. John Gorham in   King Philip's   war.   The Hamblens were largely interested as original proprietors of the township of Gorham, in the State of Maine.

He died April 24, 1704, aged 62 years and 14 days, leaving an estate apprised at £309, 6sh, 8d, which was divided by an agreement dated May 31, 1704, his widow receiving one-third, each daughter £15, and the balance to his sons.

He married 20th Jan. 1673, Susannah Dunham, perhaps a sister of Mary, wife of James Hamblen, Jr.

### Children born in Barnstable.

23.  I.   Samuel, 25th Dec. 1674.
24.  II.   Mercy, 1st June, 1677.   She joined the church Aug. 17, 1707, and married Edward Milton Nov. 10, 1709.
25.  III.   Patience, 15th April, 1680.
26.  IV.   Susannah, 16th March, 1682, unmarried July 13, 1718, when she was admitted to the church.
27.  V.   Experience, 13th Feb. 1684.   She was admitted to the church May 5, 1728, married Isaac Lewis 13th Sept. 1732, and died 24th July, 1749.   [Church Records.]
28.  VI.   John, 19th June 1686, died 26th April, 1705.
29.  VII.   Ebenezer, 23d March 1689.
30.  VIII.   Mary, 23d May, 1691.
31.  IX.   Bethia, 26th Nov. 1693.
32.  X.   Reliance, 30th Nov. 1696, unmarried Nov. 26, 1727, when she joined the church.

John Hamblen, son of James, resided at Hamblen's Plain, West Barnstable.   He was a farmer.   His wife Sarah Bearse was an early member of the Church, he did not join till late in life.   The will of his son   John, who died unmarried in 1734, furnishes many particulars respecting this family.

John Hamblin, son of James, married Aug. 1667, Sarah, daughter of Austin Bearse.   His children born in Barnstable, were :
33.  I.   Melatiah, 1st July, 1668.   She was living in 1734, and it appears was then unmarried.
34.  II.   Priscilla, 30th April, 1670.   She married, had deceased in 1734, but had two surviving children.
35.  III.   Sarah, 1st July, 1671.   She married, was living in 1734, when she had three children.
36.  IV.   Martha, 16th Feb. 1672-3, married 30th Dec. 1696, Samuel Doane, was living in 1734, and then had four children.
37.  V.   Experience, 16th April, 1674.   She married 20th Feb. 1695, Jabez Lewis.   Her brother John says she had five chil-

dren living in 1734, which is probably accurate, though the records name only four. She removed to West Yarmouth, and the Lewis families in that vicinity are her descendants. She died July 26, 1766, aged 92 years and three months.

38. VI. Hannah, 16th Feb. 1675-6, married Sept. 9, 1714. John King of Harwich, and her brother John says had six children in 1734. She was his fourth wife as I have it noted on the record, certainly his third. He had a numerous family.

39. VII. Esther, 17th March, 1677, married 6th March, 1705, her cousin Jonathan, and had seven children living in 1734. [See Jonathan.]

40. VIII. Thankful, Oct. 1679, died Oct. 1683.

41. IX. John, 10th March 1680-1. He died unmarried in 1734. His will dated April 10, 1734, proved July 3, is one of those from which the genealogist reaps a goodly harvest of facts. He was a wealthy man, left a large estate and much due him on land and mortgage. He gives legacies to all his brothers and sisters, and to his numerous nephews and neices, and did not forget his church and the pastor thereof. He resided in the dwelling house which was his father's at Hamblen's Plain, owned equally by himself and his brother Benjamin.

42. X. Ebenezer, 12th May, 1683. (See below.)

43. XI. Abigail, 25th April, 1685. She married 13th April, 1711, her cousin Elkanah. She died 29th May, 1733. (See Elkanah )

44. XII. Benjamin, 11th Feb. 1686. (See below.)

John Hamblin, Sen., died in 1718, aged 73 years. His wife Sarah died previously. In his will dated Jan. 3, 1714, proved March 8, 1717-18, he gives to his son John one-half of his tenement at Indian Pond, one-half of his dwelling house and barn and one-half of his lands, and to his son Benjamin the other half, and to his son Ebenezer his tenement at Cooper's Pond, and the lands adjacent. It appears that he had a large landed estate, and that he owned three houses or tenements. That at the Indian Pond he did not occupy himself. The dwelling house which he occupied was farther north on the "Plain." His personal estate was apprised at £168,0,8. He names his nine daughters and three sons. As his daughter Thankful died in 1683, it seems that he had another younger than Benjamin not named on the record.

7. Eleazer Hamblin, son of James, was a soldier in Capt. John Gorham's company in King Philip's war, and an original proprietor of the town of Gorham, in Maine. I have not carefully examined his record, and know but little of his history. His wife was an early member of the church, and he joined in 1686. I think he resided at Hamblen's Plain. The Eleazer Hamblins patronized the lawyers more than all others of the name ; but I may be

doing injustice in making the remark in connection with the elder Eleazer.

He married 15 Oct. 1675, Mehitabel, daughter of John Jenkins, and had six children born in Barnstable:
45. I. Isaac, 20th Aug., 1676.
46. II. Joseph, 20th Nov., 1680.
47. III. Mehitabel, 28th March, 1682, married Nov. 8, 1714, John Sanderson.
48. IV. Shubael, 16th Sept., 1695.
49. V. Elisha, bap. 30th July, 1685.
50. VI. Ichabod, bap. 30th May, 1687.
The two last probably died young and therefore their names do not appear on the town record.

(8.) Israel Hamblin, the son of James, was born the 25th of June, 1652. It appears by the church records that he married twice. His first wife was Abigail, who died about the year 1700, and his second wife was named Jemima. He resided in the east parish. His house stood by a pond yet known as Israel's pond on Dimmock's lane, about a mile and a half south of the County road. His nearest neighbor was more than half a mile distant. He cleared away only a small space in the forest, now again covered with trees. I am not informed respecting his occupation. He lived in a solitary spot, and farming could not have been his principal occupation. He is called Mr. on the records, which shows that he was a man of some note.

Children of Israel Hamblen by his first wife Abigail, who was perhaps a daughter of Joshua Lumbard.
51. I. A child, 1687, died 1687.
52. II. Thankful, 24th Aug., 1689, married May 11, 1710, her cousin Ebenezer Hamblin, son of John. She joined the church Oct. 1713, and was living at the death of her husband in 1736. The history of her family which will be given proves that it is not well for so near relatives to marry each other.
53. III. Prudence, 24th Aug., 1689. She married in 1727, Joseph Gates, of Preston.
54. IV. Israel, 15th March, 1694, married 29th May, 1715, Dorcas Godfrey of Yarmouth, and Jan. 17, 1738-9, Bathsheba Baker. His name appears on the Yarmouth records, and he had by wife Dorcas, Israel, born Feb. 13, 1725, and by Bathsheba, Thankful, Dec. 29, 1739, and Israel, June 4, 1741, all born in Yarmouth.
55. V. Joseph. Respecting this Joseph I have no information. He was called second to distinguish him from the other two of the same name.
56. VI. Jemima, 15th Aug., 1699.
By his second wife Jemima.

57.  VII.  Jacob, 28th May, 1702, married Content Hamblen
Aug. 18, 1731.  He and his wife were dismissed from the
East Church to the Church in Gorham, Maine, Oct. 28, 1750,
to which town they had previously removed.  He was one of
the first settlers, and he and his family were in the garrison in
1746, and remained there during the Indian war.  I do not
find a record of his family.  He had sons Joseph and Daniel,
and has descendants.

58.  VIII.  Ann, 10th April, 1706.  She was admitted to the East
Church 1728.  She married a Mr. Tilson in 1750, and removed to Middleboro.

(11.)  Eleazer Hamblen,* son of James, 2d, born April 12,
1668, removed to Harwich.  His wife was named Lydia, of Yarmouth.  I think she was a Sears.  Respecting the time of his death,
I have no certain evidence.  I am inclined to the opinion that he
died soon after the birth of his son Elisha, and that the Lydia Hamblen who married Sept. 30, 1706, Thomas Snow, was his widow.
In March, 1726, as appears by the school returns, there was no
family of the name of Hamblen in Harwich.  The Eleazer Hamblen
who married Sarah Sears in 1718 was probably another man, the
son of Isaac of Barnstable.

Children of Eleazer Hamblen born in Harwich :

59.  I.  Elisha, Jan. 26, 1697-8, married Elizabeth Mayo, of
Eastham, and had Elijah, March 22, 1722-3, and perhaps
others.

(13.)  James Hamblen, son of James, 2d, born 26th Aug.,
1669, married Oct. 8, 1690, Ruth Lewis.  He united with the
West Church March 10, 1727-8, and his wife June 23, 1729.

*Children born in Barnstable.*

60.  I.  Mary, 24th June, 1691.  Became a member of the church
Dec. 21, 1718, and was baptized same day.

61.  II.  Ruth, 25th Jan., 1692-3, married Samuel Crocker, Nov.
2, 1723.

62.  III.  James, 17th July, 1696, married ———, had Silas,
April 15, 1722 ; Caleb, Feb. 8, 1723-4 ; Deborah, Jan. 19,
1726-7 ; Benjamin, Jan. 1, 1730 ; David, Jan. 11, 1732 ;
Hannah, Aug. 30, 1735.

63.  IV.  Benjamin, Nov. 8, 1702 ; died 23d Jan. 1732-3.

64.  V.  David, June, 1708 ; died 4th Nov. 1732.

65.  VI.  Hannah, June 17, 1709.  Nov. 25, 1735, she was admitted to the West Church and baptized, being then confined

---

*Following in the track of so eminent and careful a genealogist as the late Mr. David
Hamblen, I did not expect that the labor of writing the Hamblen genealogy would be an
arduous task.  I have full abstracts from the town, church and probate records, and other
original papers, yet many questions arise which I cannot satisfactorily resolve.  There were
three Eleazers who were cotemporaries, and four Ebenezers.  To keep their families distinct, requires more labor than I have now time to devote to it.  If I find leisure for the
investigation, I will append a note at the close of this article giving the result of further
examination.  If any of the family, or others, can assist me, I will thank them to write me.

to her bed with a consumption. Her gravestones at West Barnstable give the date of her death Nov. 7, 1735, a mistake.
66.  VII.  Job, 25th June ; died 28th Sept. 1732.
67.  VIII.  Deliverance.

(14.)  Jonathan Hamblen, son of James, Jr., born March 6, 1670-1, married 6th March, 1705, by Mr. Russell, to Esther Hamblen, daughter of John. He died 22d June, 1743, aged 74, according to the record, and his wife died Sept. 1, 1746, aged 69.

*Children born in Barnstable.*

68.  I.  Solomon, 5th Dec. 1705 ; married Oct. 1735, Rebecca Taylor, of Yarmouth, and had Hannah July 31, 1737.
69.  II.  Content, 12th Dec. 1707, married Aug. 18, 1731, Jacob Hamblen.
70.  III.  Priscilla, 13th July, 1709, married Capt. Simeon Davis June 5, 1740, died April 1751, aged 41.
71.  IV.  Zaccheus, 17th June, 1711, married July 29, 1736, Mary Lumbard. There is no record of his family on the town books.
72.  V.  Jabez, probably born in 1713, baptized July 13, 1718.
73.  VI.  Jonathan, baptized July 13, 1718, married Thankful Buapas Dec. 12, 1744, and had Thankful April 18, 1747 ; Jonathan, March 22, 1749 ; Tabitha, Jan. 14, 1751, and Content, May 6, 1753, died Feb. 22, 1776.
74.  VII.  Sarah, baptized 13th July, 1718, married. There were two Sarah Hamblens of about the same age. One married David Smith April 8, 1736, and the other Ephraim Lewis Oct. 8, 1736.
75.  VIII.  Josiah, Oct. 15, 1720, died March 1, 1789.

(16.)  Dea. Ebenezer Hamblin, son of James, Jr., born 29th July, 1674, was a prominent man. He married 4th April, 1698, Sarah Lewis ; but it does not appear on the records of whom she was a daughter. George Lewis, Jr., had a daughter Sarah born in 1659, but she could not have been the mother of his children. Ebenezer, son of John, married Thankful Hamblen, who survived him. Ebenezer, son of Bartholemew, married Thankful Childs 1722.

Dea. Hamblen removed to Sharon, Conn., where he died in 1755, aged 81. His children born in Barnstable were :
76.  I.  Ebenezer, 18th March, 1698-9. An Ebenezer Hamblen, whose wife was Prudence, had John and Israel baptized Sept. 3, 1721. He afterwards married perhaps Hopestill Davis, widow of Shubael, and a daughter of Joshua Lumbard born in 1686. Judging by the age, it may have been the father who married Hopestill. An Ebenezer, perhaps this man, had Hopestill born in Rochester April 23, 1726. "Mrs. Hopestill

Hamblen died Oct. 1756, aged above 60."—[Church Records.

76.   II.   Mercy, 10th Sept. 1700.
77.   III.   Hopestill, 23d July, 1702.
78.   IV.   Cornelius, 13th June, 1705.
79.   V.   Thomas, 6th May, 1710.
80.   VI.   Isaac, 1st July, 1714.
90.   VII.   Lewis, 31st Jan. 1718-19.   Lewis was grandfather to Capt. Nathaniel Hamblen, of Boston, and Hon. Frederick Hamblin, of Elira, Ohio.   He married Experieuce Jenkins April 12, 1739, and had Sarah born in Barnstable Jan. 3, 1739-40 ; Nathaniel, born in Lebanon, Conn., Nov. 29, 1741 ; Lewis, born in Lebanon Dec. 19, 1743 ; he then returned to Barnstable and had Sarah Dec. 17, 1745 ; Mary, Dec. 16, 1747 ; Philemon, April 2, 1751 ; Mercy, March 25, 1753 ; and Perez, Sept. 26, 1755.

(21.)   Elkanah Hamblen, son of James, Jr., married April 14, 1711, Abigail, daughter of John Hamblen, she died 29th of May, 1733, and he married Aug. 11, 1734, Margaret Bates, of Plymouth, also called of Agawam, and married June 9, 1734.

*Children born in Barnstable.*

91.   I.   Sylvanus, 20th July, 1712, married April 24, 1741, Dorcas Fish, of Falmouth, and had Sylvanus baptized Oct. 11, 1741 ; Simeon, June 17, 1744 ; Patience, Oct. 25, 1745 ; Barnabas, April 26, 1747 ; Rachel, June 2, 1751.
92.   II.   Reuben, 13th March, 1714, married May 29, 1739, Hope, daughter of Benjamin Hamblen, and had Elkanah, June 1, 1740, died 19th April, 1750 ; Benjamin, May 7, 1742 ; Abigail, Feb. 23, 1743, married Lemuel Howland of Sandwich, Dec. 11, 1765 ; Lemuel, April 4, 1746 ; Thomas, Sept. 26, 1748 ; and Hannah, Aug. 4, 1753.
93.   III.   Abigail, 17th Oct. 1715.
94.   IV.   John, 2d Nov. 1717, married Jan. 23, 1740, Jerusha, daughter of Shubael Hamblen, and had John, June 16, 1743 ; Lydia, Oct. 21, 1746, and probably others.
95.   V.   Rachell, 7th Sept. 1720, died 1722.
96.   VI.   Patience, 12th June, 1721.
97.   VII.   Tabitha, 14th April, 1723.

(22.)   Benjamin Hamblen, son of James, Jr., baptized March 16, 1684-5.   Benjamin, son of John, remained in Barnstable.   Benjamin, son of James, Jr., removed to Eastham, and was engaged in the whale fishery.   His death is thus noticed in the Boston News Letter of Aug. 25, 1737 : "We hear that sometime in the beginning of July, that Capt. Atherton Hough, master of a whaling vessel, being in the streights, killed a large whale and brought her to the vessel's side as usual to cut her up, and as the hands were hoisting the blubber into the hold, the runner of the block gave way, and fell with great force on the head of a man that stood underneath, viz: Benjamin Hamblin, of Eastham, Mass., and instantly killed him."

He married Oct. 25, 1716, Anne, daughter of Samuel Mayo, of Eastham, and had :

98.   I.   Cornelius, 1719, who married Jane Young June 23, 1748, and had a family. He died Nov. 8, 1791.

99.   II.   Benjamin, married March 24, 1747-8, Lydia Young.

100.   IV.   Eleazer. (This Eleazer may have been the ancestor of Vice President Hamblen, but circumstances do not favor the supposition.)

101.   V.   Lydia, married Aug. 30, 1743, John Wilcut, of Hingham.

Of the family of Samuel Hamblen, son of Bartholemew, I find no record.

(29.) Ebenezer Hamblen, son of Bartholemew, born 23d March, 1689, married Thankful Childs 25th Oct. 1722, and had Elizabeth 1st Oct. 1723. A Thankful Childs who was admitted to the West Church in 1720, afterwards was dismissed to Middleboro'. I presume this Ebenezer removed to that town; but as there were several Ebenezers I cannot state positively.

(41.) John Hamblen, son of John, born March 10, 1680, died unmarried in 1734, leaving a large estate, which he disposed of April 10, 1734, by one of those wills which rejoice the heart of the genealogist. He remembers his nine brothers and sisters, and his numerous nephews and neices. He gave to the West Church £4, and to Rev. Mr. Russell £3. He appoints his brother Ebenezer and Dea. John Crocker his executors. His will has enabled me to trace the family of the first John Hamblen with perfect certainty.

(42.) Ebenezer Hamblen, son of John, resided on the estate which was his father's, at Great or Nine Mile Pond, called in early times, Cooper's Pond.* He died in 1736, aged 53 years. In his will dated Oct. 25, 1735, proved July 7, 1736, he names his wife Thankful, his sons Gershom, Ebenezer, Timothy, Nathan, Daniel and Samuel, and his daughters Elizabeth, Dorcas and Thankful Bangs. His widow Thankful died Jan. 15, 1768, aged 78. She joined the Church Oct. 1713, and was a member of the East Church at the time of her death.

Ebenezer Hamblen and his cousin Thankful Hamblen were

---

*Mr. Freeman in his Annals of Barnstable says, page 250: "On the records it is often called Cooper's Pond. It was known to the early settlers as the Great Indian Pond." Mr. Freeman has confounded, as he often does, two things that are entirely separate and distinct. The "Great Pond," or Nine Mile Pond, situate between the westerly part of the East Parish and Chequaquett, or Centreville was called by the early settlers Cooper's Pond, because Dea. John Cooper owned a large tract of land on its borders. It was never known as the Great Indian Pond. The Indian Ponds are between Hamblen's Plain and Marston's Mills, and their waters flow into Marston's Mill stream. If Mr. Freeman had carefully read the records, he would not have made the blunder.

married by Rev. Mr. Russell May 11, 1710.   Their children born
in Barnstable were :
102.   I.   Isaac, Feb. 1711, died aged 7 weeks.
103.   II.   Gershom, July 19, 1713, married Aug. 9, 1739, by
Mr. Green to Hannah "Almony," a name I have not met
with before, perhaps Almy.   His children born in Barnstable were Martha, May 11, 1740; Enoch, Jan 23, 1742-3;
Gershom, Sept. 16, 1745; George, Feb. 3, 1749.
104.   III.   Thankful, 6th Aug. 1715, married Joseph Bangs, of
Harwich, Sept. 18, 1735.
105.   IV.   Nathan, 29th June, 1717, deaf mute.   He was living
at the death of his father, 1736.
106.   V.   Ebenezer, 26th Nov. 1719.   He joined the East
Church when 17 years of age.   He married Joanna Hamblen Dec. 3, 1755,* and had Joanna baptized April 17,
1757, Ebenezer, Dec. 14, 1760.   He was chosen a deacon
of the East Church July 3, 1765.   His wife died May,
1790, in the 70th year of her age.
107.   VI.   A daughter, still born, Sept. 1720.
108.   VII.   Samuel, 7th Jan. 1722, deaf mute.   A Samuel Hamblen, Jr., perhaps deaf and dumb Samuel, married Nov.
16, 1749, Joanna Bumpas, and had Rebecca, Sept. 13,
1750.   This Samuel died early.   Another Samuel married
Dec. 13, 1750, Temperance Lewis.   She joined the East
Church April 4, 1756, and had Elijah baptized Nov. 28,
1756; Temperance, April 18, 1762; and Seth, March 10,
1765.   I give my minutes without spending much time to
investigate.   The records are deficient in regard to several
families of the name of Hamblin, and want of time com-
pels me to leave it to some future investigator to supply deficiences.

109.   VIII.   Dorcas, 5th June, 1727, deaf mute.
110.   IX.   Timothy, 3d Sept. 1728.
111.   X.   Elizabeth, 20th Nov. 1730.
112.   XI.   Daniel, 2d April, 1735, married Nov. 3, 1757, Deliverance Childs, and had Abigail July 2, 1761.

(44.)   Benjamin Hamblen, son of John, born 11th Feb.
1686-7, married May 29, 1709, Hope Huckins.   Both joined the
Church July 19, 1714.   He resided at West Barnstable in a two
story house with a leanto (or salt-box, as sometimes called.)   He
died in 1718, and his widow married in 1719, Ebenezer Childs.
His estate was settled April 6, 1724, and Joseph Hamblen was appointed guardian of the children.   His personal estate was apprised at £230,16,9.

*As there was no Joanna Hamblen born about the year 1720, I hazard the opinion that
her maiden name was Bumpas, and that she was the widow of Samuel Hamblen, Jr.

*Children born in Barnstable.*

113.   I.   Rebecca, 17th May, 1711, married Thomas Crocker Oct. 20, 1730, and died May 9, 1756.

114.   II.   Hannah, baptized July, 1714.

115.   III.   Benjamin, baptized 18th Nov. 1716, married 1740, Mehitabel Black, of Sandwich, and 2d, Mehitabel Childs June 1766, and had Mary, July 16, 1741 ; Benjamin, Feb. 25, 1742-3 ; Nathaniel, Feb. 21, 1744 ; Jane, March 23,· 1746 ; Ichabod, June 28, 1749. By his second wife, Mary April 12, 1767 ; Lewis, Dec. 24, 1768 ; Benjamin, Sept. 30, 1770.

116.   IV.   Hope, baptized 31st Aug. 1718, married May 28, 1739, Reuben Hamblen.

(45.)   Isaac Hamblen, son of Eleazer, born 20th Aug. 1676, married Sept. 14, 1698, Elizabeth Howland. He died in 1710, and his widow married Nov. 9, 1711, Timothy Cannon. His brother Joseph Hamblin administered on his estate, and the final settlement and distribution was made Feb. 20, 1737-8. Eleazer, of Harwich, late of Barnstable, yeoman, Joseph, of Yarmouth, blacksmith, and Elizabeth of Barnstable, acknowledged the receipt of £52,0,6, of their uncle Joseph in full for their father's estate.

Children of Isaac Hamblen born in Barnstable :

117.   I.   Eleazer, 22d Aug. 1699. An Eleazer Hamblen married 25th Feb. 1721-2, Jane Phinney. This could not have been Eleazer, son of Isaac. The latter married Sarah Sears, of Harwich, to which town he removed, and at first is called a yeoman, afterwards a trader. He had Barnabas March 30, 1719 ; Sarah, March 16, 1720-1 ; Eleazer, May 24, 1723. For his second wife he married Alice Phinney, of Barnstable, Dec. 10, 1724, by whom he had other children in Harwich of which I find no record. His name disappears in Harwich about 1740, and a family probably the same appears in Bridgewater. I have carefully investigated this matter, the proof is not conclusive, but there is little reason to doubt that the Eleazer born in Harwich May 24, 1723, was the Eleazer who resided successively in Bridgewater, Harvard, Western, and finally removed to Maine, and is the ancestor of the family of the name in that State, of whom Vice-President Hamlin is one. This Eleazer was a prominent man in his day, an officer in the Revolutionary army, and otherwise distinguished. He married first Lydia Bonney, and had a very large family. To four of his sons he gave the names of Europe, Asia, Africa and America. I have several sheets of closely written

---

NOTE.—Mr. Otis at a later date, ascertained that "Irael's Pond" was named for Israel Hamblin, Jr., and not for his father.     S.

matter in reference to this Eleazer and his descendants; but I have not time to transcribe them.

I have several specimens of the handwriting of Eleazer, son of Isaac, written at different periods of his life. This is not conclusive evidence, but it enables me to trace the wanderings of the man and his avocations. It is known by tradition that the ancestor of the Maine Hamblens was a near relative of Isaac, of Yarmouth, that he spoke frequently of the children of Isaac, calling them his relatives. There is another circumstance not of much weight, but in the connection is deserving of notice. There is a most striking family resemblance between the Hamblen's of Maine and the Yarmouth family. One who was well acquainted with the latter, though he had never seen the Vice-President, would, if he should casually meet with him, be strongly inclined to address him as Mr. Hamblen.

117.    II.    Isaac, baptized 20th July, 1701, died young.

118.    III.    Joseph, 4th June, 1702. He was a blacksmith, and resided about a mile east of the Congregational Meeting House in Yarmouth. He married Elizabeth Matthews March 3, 1726-7. He died 19th Jan. 1777, aged 75 years. His children born in Yarmouth were: Hannah, March 3, 1728-9; Phebe, April 11, 1731, married Moses Hallett; Sarah June 11, 1733, married Thomas Hallett; Isaac, March 14, 1735; Elizabeth, Feb. 4, 1737-8; Rebecca, April 4, 1740; Joseph, June 15, 1742.

119.    IV.    Elizabeth, Oct. 1705, married Deacon Barnabas Chipman of Barnstable, Feb. 20, 1727-8, and died in 1753, aged 48.

(46.)    Joseph Hamblen, son of Eleazer, born Nov. 20, 1680, resided in Barnstable. He was a prominent man, of good business capacity, and lived to great age, dying Aug. 27, 1766, aged 86 years. He was married by Mr. Russell 27th May, 1704, to Mercy Howland. His children born in Barnstable were:

120.    I.    Alice, 4th Feb. 1705, married John Howland, Jr., 1728.

121.    II.    Seth, March, 1708, married Sarah Blush Oct. 9, 1735, and had Mercy Nov. 15, 1737; Sarah, Aug. 15, 1737; Abigail, Aug. 14, 1741, married John Smith Jan. 18,1764; Seth, Aug. 20, 1744; Alice, Aug. 12, 1747.

122.    III.    Sarah, 4th April 1711, married Ephraim Lewis Oct. 7, 1736.

123.    IV.    Joseph, March 10, 1715, married Dec. 8, 1738, Hannah Lovell, and had Micah 11th Nov. 1741. Major Micah Hamblen, an officer of the Revolution, died Aug. 8, 1797. He married Abigail, daughter of Samuel Parker and had Hannah, Joseph, Micah, Temperance, Geo. W., Thomas, Abigail.

124. V. Southworth, 21st May, 1721, married Dec. 13, 1744, Martha Howland, and May 12, 1757, Tabitha Atkins, and had Bethia July 3, 1758 ; Eleazer, March 25, 1760 ; Southworth, April 12, 1762.

His wife Mercy died soon after the birth of Southworth, and he married Sept. 5, 1751, Widow Hopestill Davis, a daughter of Joshua Lumbard, born in 1686. She died Oct. 1756, aged, says the church records, above 60. She was 70 years of age at her death. As there was no other Joseph whose age corresponded with Hopestill's, I feel confident of the correctness of this statement.

(48.) Shubael Hamblen, son of Eleazer, born 16th Sept. 1695, resided at West Barnstable. He married 25th March, 1719, Eleanor Winslow, of Harwich. She was a member of the church in Harwich, and was dismissed to the Barnstable church Aug. 16, 1719.

*Children born in Barnstable.*

125. I. Jerusha, 4th May, 1722, married 24th Jan. 1740, John Hamblen, and had John June 16, 1743 ; Lydia, Oct. 21, 1745, and probably others. Jerusha Hamblen, who married Oct. 9, 1760, Benj. Hamblen, Jr., is probably of this family.

126. II. Shubael, 20th Sept. 1724, married Martha Lumbard March 7, 1751 ; 2d, Sarah Crocker, July 16, 1771, and 3d, Ruth ———, and had ten children, namely : Joshua born July 2, 1752, O. S. ; Susannah, April 15, 1754, N. S. ; Timothy, Feb. 2, 1756 ; Sarah, Feb. 1754, married B. Downs, Jr. ; by his 2d wife, Martha May 31, 1762 ; Susannah, Feb. 15, 1765 ; Shubael, July 18, 1766, married Rachel Downes ; by his 3d wife, Ruth, Nov. 21, 1768 ; Mercy, April 16, 1771, and Hope, Nov. 11, 1733. By his first marriage he came into possession of the dwelling-house and farm of Capt. Jonathan Lombard, on the east side of Dimmock's Lane. He filled up Capt. Lombard's well, and removed his house, a high single one with a leanto, to a very high hill on his farm, that he might have "a clear air and a good prospect," and all his life he and his children after him, lugged their water about half a mile up hill from Lumbard's Pond.

127. III. Eleanor, 18th Oct. 1726, baptized Oct. 23, died young.
128. IV. Joshua, 21st Aug. 1728.
129. V. Mehitabel, 4th Dec. 1730, published to Benjamin Childs 1752.
130. VI. Eleanor, 15th April, 1733, baptized April 15, 1733, joined the church Sept. 30, 1761, married Moses Hallett, of Yarmouth, 1771.
131. VII. Lydia, 15th Nov. 1735.

The genealogy of the Hamblens I wrote very rapidly often sending the manuscript to the printer without looking it over and revising it, consequently I have made mistakes which will mislead the reader. Since it was printed I have revised the article, and request those who keep files of these papers to note the following errors:

55. V. Joseph Hamblin. I say "respecting this Joseph I have no information." I had, but I wrote under the impression that the Joseph who married Sept. 1718, Abigail Davis, was Joseph, son of Eleazer.

Abigail Davis' history I omitted to give in my account of her family. She was a daughter of Jabez Davis, born 26th April, 1698. After the death of her father in 1711, she removed to Preston, and was a member of the church in that town, and dismissed to the Barnstable church July 9, 1721 and on the division of the church she joined the East. In the church records the following curious passage occurs:

"July 28, 1725. The Brethren voted that Abigail Hamblen, wife to Joseph Hamblen, shall desire the Pastor, before the congregation, to inform of her sorrow and repentance for her inconsistency in her profession in going to the assemblies of the Quakers on the Lord's Day, of choice and disputing much for them upon her return from Nantucket, before she be admitted unto the privileges of the church." It does not appear by the record that she complied with the requirement of the Brethren. The children of Joseph and Abigail Hamblin do not appear on the town record. On the church records three of their children are named: Lois, baptized May 26, 1722; Esther, April 23, 1727; Susannah, May 12, 1728. Joseph Hamblen died soon after the latter date, and his widow married —— Barlow. Her death is thus entered: "April 25, 1740, Abigail Barlow (formerly Hamblen) departed this life very aged." As she was only 42, I do not perceive the propriety of calling her "very aged."

No. 158, (11.) The first paragraph I wrote from recollection of the facts. On recurring to the Probate Records I find that Eleazer Hamblin, son of James, 2d, died in 1698, and that his widow administered and afterwards married Thos. Snow as stated.

76. I. I say perhaps Ebenezer Hamblen married Hopestill Davis. She married as afterwards stated, Joseph Hamblen.

[END OF VOLUME I.]